Dwight D. Eisenhower

Dwight D. Eisenhower

Soldier Of Democracy

Kenneth S. Davis

KONECKY&KONECKY

Konecky & Konecky
150 Fifth Avenue
New York, N.Y. 10011

This edition published by special arrangement with
John Hawkins & Associates, Inc., New York.

ISBN: 1-56852-059-X

Printed in the United States of America

For
Lydia E. Davis and Charles D. Davis
my mother and father

Author's Note

ANY WRITER undertaking the biography of a living man finds himself at once face to face with insoluble problems. He must proceed without benefit of the perspective which time alone can give. He is without access to the abundant documentary evidence which will be available to future historians. There is grave danger that the conclusions he draws from present facts will be falsified by later events. It is even possible, if unlikely, that the essential character of his subject will change as history proceeds. I am only too aware that this cannot, in the nature of things, be a definitive biography. Only that which is static can be sharply defined; no life is static until it is ended; and Dwight Eisenhower, at present writing, is intensely alive. All that I can do is draw as accurately as possible a portrait of a man in motion, the outlines of whose figure, the very shape of whose character are necessarily blurred somewhat by that motion.

Much of the material for this portrait was gathered, and some of the book itself was actually written, several months before I met General Eisenhower. I saw the man at first in somewhat the same way as a future historian might see him—"for a thousand leagues have nearly the same effect with a thousand years," as Benjamin Franklin wrote to George Washington from France on a March day in 1780. Distance, whether in space or time, serves as a filter through which come only the more salient and lasting features of a personality. Faced with this problem of distance, I necessarily began by seeking out the shadows of the man, the traces of him left on the minds of those who had known him in the past. I sought to reconstruct the living man out of a mass of details which I gathered *about* him, proceeding with that antlike industry employed by fiction writers of the "naturalist" school. I had to conceive character from the outside in, drawing on the objective rather than the subjective.

Later, when I lived for several weeks at General Eisenhower's personal headquarters, this objective conception of his character was corrected and supplemented by subjective impressions of his personality. I was enabled to observe my subject from two points of view, and in fusing the two images thus obtained I hope I have given the completed portrait a certain stereoscopical depth and solidity.

A few people who read the present work in manuscript were fearful that, in the opening sections, too much emphasis was being placed on the early history and general character of the Eisenhower family. Later, after they had read the book as a whole, they concluded that the early material was not only interesting in itself but essential to an understanding of Dwight Eisenhower's character. The family, as the book makes clear, is remarkably close-knit. Its members, however separated from one another by spatial distance, still think of themselves *as* a family, deriving much of their individual characters from their family relationship. And this is particularly true of Dwight Eisenhower, whose devotion to the family is both the cause and the explanation of much that is distinctive in him. Far more than most men, he is explicable in terms of influences which operated on him during his earliest years. Hence the history of those influences is not a prelude to his story but an integral part of it.

K. S. D.

Contents

CONTENTS

By Way of Introduction

It is June 6, 1944, a decisive day in the life of the Western world. Only a few hours ago the radio announced that "under the command of General Eisenhower, Allied naval forces supported by strong air forces began landing Allied armies this morning on the northern coast of France." Since then the radio has been blaring almost continuous reports of the progress of our troops. The man whose portrait we are to contemplate in this book has reached the supreme, the climactic moment of his career thus far.

Only a few minutes ago a radio correspondent asked this man if he were not nervous.

"Nervous?" the supreme commander is said to have replied. "I'm so nervous I'm boiling over inside."

But, the correspondent goes on to say, the commander does not reveal his nervousness. Outwardly he is perfectly calm, perfectly poised, absolutely confident. His months of intense preparatory work are done. His decision has been made. The rest, for the time being, is in the hands of God, the troops, and the tactical commanders from whom he cannot expect to receive detailed reports for many hours. He seems to feel strongly his own helplessness, and even uselessness, in this hour when active command has passed almost wholly, if temporarily, to the tactical leaders. All he can do now is wait.

No doubt he fingers those three lucky coins—a French, a British, and an American—which he always carries with him. No doubt his lips shape over and over again a silent prayer as he looks up into the sky, watching those planes which streak southward, by his order, toward France. The sunlight falls upon a face that has steady bright blue eyes spaced far apart; upon cheeks which are broad and rugged, with the jaw muscles working in them; upon a wide mouth which seems shaped for easy laughter but which is drawn now into a hard, grim line. He is experiencing again the terrible loneliness of supreme command in an hour of decisive action.

Eisenhower has experienced it many times in recent months, and he will experience it again and again in the months to come.

Once, on a July night in 1943, he experienced it most acutely as he stood on a point of Malta beach projecting out into the Mediterranean. The night (perhaps he is remembering it now) was warm, bright with the light of a high-riding moon, and noisy with wind. The island, with its bomb-ruined buildings, was all silver-gray—and across the sea was spread a broken, quaking path of silver. The wind roared through the shattered roofs on the island and whipped up foaming whitecaps on the sea. It worried him, that wind, as he stood there nervously fingering those same three lucky coins. The waves might play havoc with landing craft, heading then toward Sicily. A gale could turn paratroop landings into a catastrophe. But then, as now, there was nothing he could do but wait. Not until the next day could he know if the operation he had directed had gained an initial triumph or suffered a disastrous reverse. But in that lonely hour on the beach, as in his lonely hours today, he knew again the full weight of his responsibility. A triumph he could and would distribute among all those who helped to make it. A failure would be his alone. He braced himself against a gust of wind, holding himself erect, fingering those lucky coins.

Next day, when the reports came back from Sicily, he said over and over again to the men who were with him: "By golly, we've done it again. We surprised them. By golly, we've done it again."

The same acute pitch of loneliness was experienced before Salerno, and dozens of times during the period of preparation for the assault on western Europe, the moments when he made final decisions as to points of attack, the disposition of troops, the timetable and proportionate emphasis on tactics and strategy for the vast bombing of Europe, the tactical commanders, the million details of logistics. Gradually he has learned to live with it—not easily, perhaps, but gracefully and with a kind of pride that has no taint of arrogance.

Not many months ago he referred to it with boyish wistfulness in a cable to his friends in Abilene, Kansas.

BY WAY OF INTRODUCTION

"If the home folks try to high-hat me and call me by titles instead of Dwight, I will feel I am a stranger," he wrote. "The worst part of high military command is the loneliness which prevents comradeship." Then, with a touch of homesickness, a nostalgia for familiar ground on which he might walk in easy certainty: "I wish I could be home and gather at the old café with the gang."

ii

What is the nature of this loneliness? Chiefly it consists of this: where other men have an external human standard against which to measure their conduct he, in his hours of supreme decision, has none.

For the most part, those men who serve under him shape their decisions within a pattern already laid down; but often it is for him to determine the final shape of the pattern which guides them. To be sure his loneliness is mitigated by the distribution of authority through military organization, by his relations with his staff, with the Combined Chiefs of Staff, and with the political chiefs of the Allies. But there remains a vast area of decisive action within which he must operate unaided. He can listen to advisers; others may originate ideas and even implement them, but the final decisions are his. The final responsibility is his.

Within the area he dominates, the supreme commander must be the arbiter of right and wrong, of truth and error. In a very real sense the truth is whatever he says it is, and is made so by his saying it.

For example, there may be a dozen possibilities for an action of crucial importance, every one of which is fraught with grave risks and no one of which appears to be better than the others. The commander, testing these possibilities by the most finely graded standards, backing his decisions with three decades of study and experience, can reject most of them quite easily. But sometimes it happens that, after the most careful consideration, two or more possibilities remain. To the commander's mind they present an equality of merit, an equality of danger. How is he to choose between them? He has in such a case no external guide; he is thrown altogether upon his inner resources. It is for him a moment of pure decision, unqualified by empirical elements and unsupported by an objective logic. Yet if time is a factor he does not hesitate

] 3 [

for long. He makes his choice. Viewed objectively, it must be a blind choice, a leap in the dark—but he makes it with an appearance of calm certitude. He dare not reveal to subordinates, whose lives may depend upon his decisions, the doubts which torture him. Men lean upon him, drawing their strength from his, judging themselves through his eyes. He must give them confidence.

But from where does he derive his own?

Whatever a man really is, deep inside him, is likely to be revealed in such a moment, or in a succession of such moments. Later it may stand out for all the world to see, focused in the pitiless light of history. Structures of piety, expressing the basic life feeling of the man, are erected out of such pure acts of will. The commander has been called upon to exercise great power. Therefore, he has expressed in action a part of his idea of Power, of its nature and source and of his own relation to it. Inevitably, as his position demands of him crucial choice after crucial choice, he outlines a good portion of his innermost character, revealing the secret nature of his piety, in great actions involving perhaps millions of men. For that reason his essential self, and the forces which have shaped it, may become matters of great importance to history.

BOOK ONE

Portrait of a Family

CHAPTER I

Journey to a Far Country

As though to taunt them in farewell, Pennsylvania spread before their eyes her greatest attractions. The dawn of that mid-March day in 1878 broke chill but clear, and as the sun rose higher in the east the chill gave way to a warmth which left no doubt that spring had come. Already some of the shrubbery was actually in leaf, and the tree buds were everywhere swollen. The grass in the lawns of Elizabethville was a rich dark green. Above the gardens and over the fields and hills beyond the town the sparkling air held the tangy odors of freshly turned soil, of smoke from last summer's burning leaves, of new green life thrusting its way above the winter earth.

Already the youngest and the eldest of the Eisenhowers, climbing into the wagon which was to bear them to the railway depot, were homesick. Looking back at the old homestead and at the rolling acres surrounding it, they were aware of a tearful nostalgia, though the tears were rigidly suppressed. It was as though they saw the house, not with a present vision, but through the eyes of memory across a thousand miles of lonely American landscape. Their excitement at voyaging to a far country was shot through with the ache of a particularly final good-by.

The nine-room house was, for its time and place, quite an elaborate one, and it had served the Reverend Jacob Eisenhower in a dual capacity: as a residence and as a meeting place for religious services. Jacob had purchased the one-hundred-acre tract on which it stood, at the edge of Elizabethville, in 1854, paying for it exactly $3,698.46¾, according to records of deeds in the Dauphin County Courthouse. The house he had built of red brick, two stories high and with a good-sized attic. It stood on the highest point of his land. Behind it he had erected one of those famous Pennsylvania Dutch barns which has become a standard symbol of lush earthy richness, and various other outbuildings, all of which were separated from the house by a distance of almost two hundred yards. The family's water, all of it, had come from a never-failing spring which flowed abundantly in the back yard. From the house itself a large lawn swept downward in a gentle slope. Close by was a vineyard from which the family had sold each year great baskets of grapes. There was an orchard of mixed fruits and, as old neighbors remember, a hundred hives of bees from which great quantities of honey were sold. Beyond stretched the sloping fields which Jacob had tilled on weekdays with the industry and skill that are traditional among the Dutch. Inside the house the rooms were large and light; there were many windows. Largest of the rooms was the one on the first floor which had served as both living room and place of worship. High in the wall at one end was a small cupboard in which the *Spiritual Hymns* had been stored between one Sabbath and the next.

The house had seen much of life and death. Fourteen children, six of whom grew to maturity, had been born of the union between Jacob and his wife Rebecca. Nine had been born and six had died in the house to which the Eisenhowers now bade farewell. Four who had been born there—Hannah Amanda, David, Abraham, and Ira—were in the wagon rolling now inexorably around a bend in the road, which hid the house from view, and on through the streets of Elizabethville.

The two eldest of these four, the sixteen-year-old Amanda and the fourteen-year-old David, found the parting particularly hard. They had many friends: Milton Miller and Clem Stroup, boon companions of David's and the "stars" of the community spelling bees; Philip Eberly, with whom Amanda had hunted Easter eggs on the Eisenhower farm; the little girl who grew up to become Mrs. Kate Romberger and who, more than sixty years later, would vividly remember this sad day. It was unlikely that any of these close friendships could survive the inevitable years of separation. For both David and Amanda it was the end of a happy, intimate, profoundly satisfying world.

Partially by virtue of his position as pastor, partially by his personal qualities, Jacob had made of his home a center of community activity. In it had been held many spelling bees, singing circles, socials of all kinds, as well as the weekly church services and prayer meetings. From it had radiated those out-of-door parties which require the vital participation of those who attend them: strawberry festivals, corn-husking parties in the autumn, sleighing and skating parties in the winter. The Eisenhowers kept open house for all strangers who passed by. No vagrant in need of food or shelter was ever turned away. A small room in the attic, where Jacob had repaired shoes for the family, had in it a bed on which many a tired stranger had found rest for a night. Once each year the members of Jacob's flock had gathered at the house for a love feast, held in the large room downstairs. Some families had come as far as seventy-five miles to attend this special event. The house, large as it was, was filled to overflowing with guests, and the overflow slept in the barn. For two days there were prayer meetings and services for which the Reverend Eisenhower saved his best sermons, and a kind of open confessional during which those present related freely and frankly their religious experiences. Traditionally these feasts were in imitation of the agapae of the early Christians, during which the worshipers partook of very simple food, usually only bread and water. As kept by Jacob's flock, the feasts were much less frugal; they were not only occasions of the deepest religious communion but also social events characterized by great good-fellowship.

Now all of this was ended. The house and land had been sold a short time before to Jeremiah Speck, who paid $8,500 for it, apparently in cash. Four of the acres had been deeded earlier to David Kolva, Elizabethville blacksmith, in return for "shoeing" the Eisenhower wagon. Thus all property ties with Pennsylvania were severed, and as the Eisenhowers boarded the train they could feel the spiritual ties snapping one by one. They had barely managed to keep the tears back as they said their good-bys to the host of friends and neighbors who were gathered on the depot platform. It was with an effort that they smiled and waved now through the train windows.

As the train pulled away from Elizabethville the sixteen-year-old Amanda broke down completely. The sight of those figures on the platform dissolving into the distance, of the last houses of the village gliding by, was too much for her self-control. She sobbed aloud. David and the others stared unhappily out of the windows while a sympathetic stranger leaned across the aisle to ask what the trouble was.

"We're going to Kansas!" the girl sobbed, as though that explained everything. "To *Kansas!*"

It seemed incredibly far, as remote as another planet.

2

But if the parting was difficult for these younger Eisenhowers, it must have been even more so for the eldest, the eighty-four-year-old Frederick, father of Jacob. Looking at the drifting landscape through the train windows, he must have felt that with this departure his personal death was accomplished. The past had been more alive to him than the present for many years now, and it was to the past and its scenes that he now said good-by.

He had been born in Elizabethville in 1794. In all of his long life he had never ventured beyond the hills of Pennsylvania. Nevertheless, he had witnessed many profound changes, and they had cut him off from his youth more completely than years alone could have done. He had seen the skill of men's hands and the strength of their bodies replaced in trade after trade by the inhuman power of steam and iron. His own trade, that of weaver, had been contracted and finally crushed altogether under the impact of the industrial revolution. Through three wars and a vast surge of westward energy he had seen the scattered regionalized people of his first years conquer a wilderness and become a unified nation. He had seen the railroads come through the Pennsylvania valleys to weaken those roots which anchored a people firmly to one soil, in one landscape. Time had been sacrificed to space; traditions had given way to mobility. No doubt it was good for the young in such a land. They were given a future to shape as they would, unfettered by ancient customs and traditions. But it was hard, very hard, for the old to be deprived of their past. Frederick must have regretted deeply the lost years, peopled with the dead.

He was the living repository of the family legends. Through him the family memory extended, if vaguely, back into a distant past when ancestors of the present-day Eisenhowers were (it is said) mounted and armored warriors in a medieval German army. The name "Eisenhower" stems apparently from "Eisenhauer," which may mean "iron hewer," though it is interpreted in the family legends to mean "iron striker." From this medieval warrior tradition the family, late in the sixteenth century, had turned sharply away. From that time on the main theme of the family story had been a religious one, and the religion was strongly pacifist. From that time on the shape of the family's character and its principal geographic movements were determined by the teachings of one Menno Simons, who first proclaimed his views in Zurich in 1528.

Menno Simons claimed to have rediscovered true Christianity after centuries of organized corruption and distortion of Jesus's principles. He denied the whole sacerdotal idea, the idea of a divinely authorized priesthood. He would admit of no authority outside the Bible and the enlightened conscience of the individual. The existing church, he proclaimed, does not have a Christian character, nor is the civil authority Christian—though it is the duty of all true Christians to obey the lawful requirements of "an alien power." In other respects, the true Christian should make no compromise with the world; in so far as possible he should, with other Christians, withdraw from the world and follow the dictates of his own conscience, inspired and guided by the Word of God. . . . It was a teaching with which the pantheistic Baruch Spinoza is reported to have had "an intense fellow feeling." It was also a teaching which invited intense persecution from the State, whose claims to a genuine authority were denied, and from the Roman Catholic Church, which had a vested interest (to put it mildly) in the sacerdotal idea. The teaching, however, persisted, spreading rapidly from Switzerland to Germany, Holland, and France. Out of it arose the various Mennonite sects—the Amish, the Dunkards, the Brethren in Christ —all of whom practiced non-conformity with the world and, as a part of this, a deep opposition to militarism and war.

Among the first to embrace the new teaching were the ancestors of the present-day Eisenhowers. At that time they were living in the Palatinate of Bavaria, a Rhine province with which a great-grandson of Frederick's was to form a decidedly unpacifistic acquaintance in the autumn of 1944. Here they suffered religious persecution during that worst of all ideological wars, the thirty years which devastated Germany from 1618 to 1648 and out of which grew certain dark forces which were to culminate in Hitler. The Eisenhower forebears escaped those dark forces by fleeing to Switzerland, where they found sanctuary for a century or so, and then moving to Holland, where they lived for an indefinite but relatively short period. From Holland, early in the eighteenth century, they sailed for America.

Frederick's information was that three Eisenhower brothers, or a father and two sons, came to Pennsylvania with a colony of co-religionists in 1732. There is evidence that the date may have been somewhat later. Volume I of *Pennsylvania German Pioneers* records that among the Palatines who arrived in Philadelphia on the ship *Europa,* sailing from Rotterdam in 1741, were Hans Nicol Eisenhauer, Johan Peder Eisenhauer, and Johan (x) Eisenhauer. (Various spellings of the family name are scattered through the records, including "Isenhauer" and "Joshower.") On November 20, the very day of their arrival, they took oaths of allegiance to the government before Ralph Assheton, Esq., at the Philadelphia courthouse.

There is evidence, too, that part of the family in those first American years was not committed to the extreme pacifism of the Mennonite sect to which they belonged. Frederick was fond of recounting stories about a forebear of his who had served gallantly in the War of the Revolution. One such story concerned an Indian battle allegedly fought north of Harrisburg sometime during the war. This earlier Frederick (who spelled his last name "Eisenhauer") and two brothers were said to have encountered fourteen marauding Indians and to have killed twelve of them in a pitched battle. The Eisenhauers were feted as heroes by their neighbors, but they reportedly took small pleasure in this fact. They were disgusted, the story goes, because two of the Indians had got away. . . . In 1776, a Frederick Eisenhauer (perhaps the same one) was a private in Captain Peter Grubb Jr.'s company of Miles Regiment, which suffered such severe losses in the Battle of Long Island on August 27 that General Washington ordered its reorganization. On January 30, 1777, Frederick was listed as a "second corpral" in Captain Benjamin Weiser's company of Northumberland County Militia.

The spelling of the family name seems to have become definitely "Eisenhower" by 1790, for it is listed that way in the first United States census. By this time the Eisenhowers were an "old family," as such things went in the Pennsylvania of those years. The Frederick who was born in 1794, who journeyed now toward Kansas, could feel that his roots ran deep into the American earth and that his youthful way of life was backed by a long and honorable tradition. Whatever deviations his fathers may have made from the strict beliefs of the River Brethren, he himself was a profoundly orthodox communicant of his sect.

They were called River Brethren because the original communicants, all of German stock, lived on or near the Susquehanna. In 1862 they officially established themselves as the Church of the

Brethren in Christ. It was a religion which required far more active participation from its believers than do most Protestant sects. Its usages and customs were changed very little by the passage of the years. Non-conformity with the world continued to be a part of church practice, and non-resistance and non-violence were an important part of church doctrine. The members wore distinctively old-fashioned clothes: the men in dark plain suits with peculiar shallow-bowled black felt hats, the women in long plain dark dresses and little white bonnets (for indoors) or large dark bonnets (for outdoors). A profound conservatism, which extended itself to the very soil they farmed, characterized these people. Indeed, they tilled their hilly, erosible soil so wisely that, generations later, the United States Department of Agriculture pointed out their farms as models of soil conservation. Great emphasis was laid on the more spartan of the virtues, the virtues of self-reliance and self-denial. Intemperance of any kind, particularly in the use of alcoholic beverages, was considered an act of impiety—and any kind of vainglory or extravagance was considered a form of intemperance. On the other hand, the accumulation and retention of property was almost an act of piety; prosperity was considered a mark of God's favor. Hence the Brethren became known as "close" and "shrewd" in their business dealings, though scrupulously honest.

God, evidently, had favored Frederick the weaver, for in the old days he had certainly "prospered with his looms." He had been a skillful worker, justly proud of his handiwork. Samples of it, a century later, were scattered among descendants in Pennsylvania and Kansas: bedspreads, heavy linen tablecloths, pillow cases, heavy linen shirts in which even the buttons were made of thread tightly knotted. He had increased his prosperity by marrying a Barbara dan Miller of Millersburg, who brought to her husband a "very generous dowry." He had not traveled far to find a wife; Millersburg is a village on the Susquehanna, only ten miles west of Elizabethville. She was some five years older than he, the daughter of a John and Susanna Miller, and was reputed to be a "blood relative" of General Winfield Scott. Like Frederick, she came of German stock, and she shared his strong religious beliefs. With her dowry they built a three-story frame house on a hillside near Millersburg, devoted the lower half to a workshop for Frederick's looms, and lived themselves on the two upper floors. Here they had raised six children to maturity, three boys and three girls.

The children had been "strictly brought up." Obedience of and respect for the parents had been rigidly enforced, and any violation of their religion's code of conduct had been swiftly punished. The discipline, if stern, was just. Mistakes had been made, of course, by the parents. No doubt Frederick himself, as he rode toward Kansas, would have admitted one serious error in his treatment of John, his eldest son. John, who had died at the age of nineteen, "took after" his mother in appearance and character. He had been a sensitive, imaginative child—too imaginative. He had liked to play alone in the garret of the hillside home. One day he told the family that he had found a man in the garret with whom he played. "I have lots of fun chasing him around the chimney," he insisted. How Frederick had whipped him for lying! When the boy insisted that the story was true Frederick had whipped him again. Still the boy stuck to his story. Finally, parental anger at his stubbornness and concern for his truthfulness had given way to a reluctant admiration for his courage, an admiration which had remained in the family ever since. Everyone agreed that the boy should not have been treated so.

But whatever mistakes had been made, the children had turned out well. The girls had made good wives, and the boys, Samuel and Jacob, had become good farmers and honest, stalwart citizens. Frederick had been able to give them all an excellent start in life, and they'd made good use of their advantages.

Perhaps Jacob was the most outstanding among them. He had been born in the hillside home on September 26, 1828, and from early childhood had evinced a great interest in books. Everyone said he should be a minister, and a minister he had become. A good one, too, from all accounts. But that hadn't prevented him from "prospering with his acres," as Frederick had "prospered with his looms." He, too, had augmented his fortunes by marrying a woman who brought to her husband a generous dowry. Her name was Rebecca Matter, her childhood home was near Elizabethville, and she was a year and a half older than Jacob. The Matters, like the Eisenhowers, were River Brethren and they, too, had swerved from the pacifist line to provide soldiers for the American Army during the Revolution. One of Rebecca's great-grandfathers, a Corporal John Matter, and one of her great-uncles, a Second Class Private John Matter, had served in Captain Martin Weaver's company in 1781. Rebecca herself, however, shared her husband's strongly pacifist beliefs. She filled very capably her considerable position in Elizabethville as a minister's wife.

Later an act of charity on Jacob's part had, inadvertently one hopes, served to increase still further the sum of his property. He took into his home and cared for a maiden aunt, Elizabeth Miller. It is said that Elizabeth was a perfectly normal girl until she reached the age of twenty, but that at that age she became suddenly "simpleminded" because of some unrecorded shock or illness. She was an elderly woman with the mind of a child when Jacob made his home her own. When she died at the age of eighty Jacob quite naturally inherited her property, of which there was a good deal—enough, at least, to make the other relatives jealous. Their resentment took the usual form. Jacob was accused of taking care of Elizabeth for the sole purpose of acquiring her estate, an accusation to which Jacob, so far as is known, did not deign to reply.

With the possible exception of the Miller family—a temporary exception in any case—Jacob was universally admired and respected. People had come a good many miles to hear him preach, and they had looked up to him because he and all his family lived by his beliefs with a rigid consistency. He generally spoke in German, for that was the language of his community, basing his sermons always on the New Testament. He preached brotherly love, the forgiveness of enemies, the sinfulness of violence, the sacredness of man's word, the duty of hospitality, and the immortality of the soul. Though as a matter of principle he kept aloof from politics and politicians, he had made his position on the burning political question of his youth very clear indeed: he was profoundly and irrevocably opposed to slavery. Consequently, during the bloody years from 1860 to 1865, a kind of private spiritual civil war had raged within him, principles arrayed against principles. At such a time a man committed to both abolition and pacifism suffered inevitably great turmoil of mind.

Jacob's position in those years had not been made easier by the fact that numerous close relatives, less committed to their religion than he, were fighting in the Union armies. These included his own brother Samuel, enlisted from Lancaster County in Company F, 92nd Regiment, Ninth Cavalry. Moreover, Jacob had become a great admirer of Abraham Lincoln long before such admiration was universal. During the period when most of the "best people" looked upon Honest Abe contemptuously as an ignorant and uncouth backwoodsman, Jacob sensed in the man a sympathetic spirit, an idealized reflection of his own earthy shrewdness and strength. (When his next to the youngest son was born in 1865, three months after the President was assassinated, Jacob named the boy Abraham Lincoln.) Nevertheless, he had stuck to his pacifist principles, even during that tense summer of 1863, when Ewell's cavalry had brought the war to within twenty miles of the Eisenhower home a few days before the Battle of Gettysburg, less than three months before Jacob's son David (who was to become the father of a general) was born.

Even after the Civil War was ended, the old sense of peaceful order and stability did not return. Frederick, whose good wife Barbara had died in 1862 and who thereafter had lived in Jacob's house, regretted the restlessness which seemed to flow with the west wind across the Pennsylvania hills. Had he known the historic significance of that restlessness he could have taken no comfort in his knowledge. It meant that the era of agrarian individualism which had shaped him was dying in the East.

During the war the people of both North and South had been forced, often against their will, to think of themselves as citizens of a nation first and of a state only secondarily. Even the South of Jefferson Davis had been forced to conscript troops and otherwise conduct the war on a national basis, as the North had done—and when the war was ended and the Union had emerged as a fact beyond question, a wave of wholly new national feeling swept America. A new sense of space, of the nation as a continental power, was both expressed and symbolized in the westward thrust of the railroads. For the most part, the new mood had an economic base. The problem of demobilizing hundreds of thousands of troops, of shifting from a war to a peace economy, could be solved most easily by expanding the frontier to the West, especially in view of the swift increase in immigration from Europe. But even families and communities which did not suffer from economic insecurity were affected by the restlessness, feeling themselves to be, not pushed from the East, but drawn by the West.

The railroad companies did nothing to soothe this restlessness. They flooded Pennsylvania with propaganda extolling the virtues, economic and otherwise, of the West. Their call was answered by thousands upon thousands of families who moved to the plains states, carrying with them little or no capital, wholly unprepared for the kind of extensive farming which a secure livelihood in the West required. Wheat prices crashed after the Franco-Prussian War of 1870. In 1874 Kansas and Nebraska suffered a plague of grasshoppers which, in the areas affected, destroyed every green thing. Ruined settlers began drifting back into the East with depressing tales of heat and drought and dust storms, of loneliness and physical privation. They were vastly outnumbered by those who stayed on and by those who continued to come, driven out of the East by the financial panic of 1873 and the national depression which followed. The railroad propaganda was unabated.

Certainly it was no acute economic need which caused Jacob Eisenhower and his neighbors to turn their eyes westward. To Frederick it seemed that there was no reason whatsoever for them to leave their fat Pennsylvania farms. But the Brethren saw Opportunity shining beyond the sunset, and on Sundays, in the Eisenhower home, they began in the early 1870s to talk of moving to Kansas.

From the first, the Brethren thought in terms of a colony rather than in terms of individual and separate family migrations. They had noticed that most of the bitter failures drifting back from the frontier were men and families who had tried to "go it alone." Colonies, generally speaking, had succeeded, or at least had stayed in the new land. Then, too, the Brethren were used to thinking and acting in community terms, more so than most Americans. Centuries of persecution from alien groups had developed strong community traditions and a realization of the benefits to be derived from co-operative group endeavor. Moreover, the religion itself tended to hold the individual and the group together in a kind of dynamic tension, a tension whereby certain kinds of individualism were strongly asserted (economic self-reliance, for instance), while other kinds (individuality of dress and social custom) were as strongly denied.

In any case, the social organization and its authority were not wholly external to the individual; they were simply the outer expressions of an inner persuasion held in common by many individuals, each of whom was responsible, in the last analysis, only to God. Thus the Brethren, as individuals and as a group, were well-equipped spiritually and physically to maintain themselves as a cultural or social "island," surrounded either by a physical wilderness or by a people of alien belief. They had done so with notable success in Pennsylvania, and they could do it in Kansas. . . . The discussion had gone on sporadically for years. The decision to uproot whole families and transport them to virtually unknown lands is not one to be taken lightly. But gradually what had been a vague consideration of possibilities crystallized into a definite plan. . . .

So it was that Frederick now looked for the last time upon the country of his ancestors and of his own long life. As he gazed through the train window he could not but be acutely conscious of the chill, exhausted loneliness of the very old.

True, the trip itself was hardly a lonely one. Six Eisenhowers in addition to Frederick had left Elizabethville: Jacob, Rebecca, and the four children. At Harrisburg, where they changed trains to board the main line west, they would be joined by two more Eisenhowers: Jacob's sister Catherine, who had married Samuel Pyke and who was now moving with her husband and children, and Jacob's brother Samuel, who was also moving with his family. At least four other families would join the party at Harrisburg, among them the families of Wash Jury and Benjamin Gish.

3

The River Brethren had planned their Kansas project carefully and well. Advance agents had traveled extensively over the state, seeking a suitable spot for colonization. They had decided upon Dickinson County, an undulating prairie section lying approximately one hundred and fifty miles west of the Missouri River and about halfway between the state's north and south borders. Many decades later publicists would find a symbolic significance in the fact that here, in the most literal physical sense, is the heart of the nation. In Osborne County, some seventy miles from Abilene, is the geodetic center of the nation, from which the United States Coast and Geodetic Survey calculates latitude and longitude; on the Fort Riley Military Reservation in Geary County, some twenty miles east of Abilene, is the geographic center of the United States.

The advance agents of the Brethren would evidently have agreed with a description of the county written at about the time they first saw it and included in a *History of the State of Kansas,* published by A. T. Andreas in Chicago in 1883.

"A more beautiful prairie country would be difficult to find," asserts this unknown rhapsodist. "Streams of pure, clear water are found at intervals of a few miles along which grow ash, walnut, hackberry, elm, oak, and cottonwood. . . . Timberland embraces three and one half per cent of the county. Scattered over the face of the county are a great many artificial groves and fine orchards, which tend to break the monotony of the scene. . . . There is little wasteland, and the acres are but few which are not susceptible to cultivation. The soil is excellent and exceedingly deep, all of it alluvial, upland as well as bottomland, subsoiled with lime and clay. . . . Valleys of many of the Eastern rivers, such as the Connecticut and the Mohawk, sink into insignificance compared with those of the Smoky Hill. In many places a man can stand on his own threshold in these valleys and view tracts of land three and four miles square, the soil of which is not only unexcelled but unexcellable."

The description, taken all in all, is more accurate than one would expect. Dickinson County, today as then, is an extremely rich agricultural area, well suited to a diversified farming which has placed its special emphasis on wheat. The climate is that of a border country between North and South, mingling, according to many complaining citizens, the worst features of both; but it is invigorating and, as population statistics show, one of the most healthful in the world. The temperature range is tremendous, extending from 20 degrees Fahrenheit below zero to more than 110 above. There are long springs and falls, periods of generally pleasant weather. Hot dry winds are common in July and early August, militating against too much emphasis on corn in the cropping system, but the summer nights are generally cool because of the steady sweep of wind across the open country.

If the River Brethren were impressed by Dickinson County, the county was even more impressed by the River Brethren. The unknown writer in Andreas's afore-mentioned *History* described the colony of which the Eisenhowers were a part as "one of the most complete and perfectly organized . . . that ever entered a new country." Certainly it was far and away the best-organized colony to enter Kansas up to that time, much better equipped, for instance, than the colonies of New England Abolitionists who had come into eastern Kansas with the aid of Eli Thayer's Emigrant Aid Society in the 1850s.

The Eisenhowers and their companions constituted the advance guard, so to speak, of the colony as a whole, the bulk of which was to come out in the spring of 1879. One of the first things this advance guard did (though it is not recorded that the Eisenhowers had a hand in it) was erect a large frame building in the village of Abilene, a building eighty feet long and twenty feet wide, in which the incoming settlers could be "accommodated" until suitable buildings could be erected on their own farms. This building was ready and waiting on Friday, March 28, 1879, when thirty Brethren from Frederick County, Maryland, arrived. On the following day there was even greater excitement in Abilene, when approximately two hundred Brethren arrived from Lancaster, Cumberland, Dauphin, Lebanon, and Franklin counties, Pennsylvania. Throughout that spring other and smaller groups arrived until there were more than three hundred River Brethren in the county.

They came completely equipped to begin farming at once. More than fifteen carloads of freight accompanied them, including the huge eight-horse wagon which David Kolva had "shoed" for the Eisenhowers back in Elizabethville. Dozens of such wagons were brought in, and they made so great an impression on the earlier settlers that old-timers in Abilene still talk about them. They also talk about the amount of money the River Brethren brought with them. The Marietta *Times,* reporting the departure of the colony from Pennsylvania, said that they took with them "not less than $500,000 in money," but gossip among no doubt envious neighbors in Kansas tripled that amount. Nor had the spiritual welfare of the colonists been neglected in the well-laid plans. The Brethren brought with them at least two ministers—the Reverend Jacob Eisenhower and the Reverend Benjamin Gish—as well as a bishop, the Reverend Jesse Engle. Thus there was from the first a perfect church organization in the new land.

As a matter of fact, there were two church organizations, for the colony divided into two groups when it arrived. One group settled north of the Smoky Hill River, which bisects the county from west to east, and this group may have constituted the flock of the Reverend Mr. Gish. The other group settled on farms south of the Smoky Hill, in the vicinity of a place (not a village but simply a location) called Belle Springs, where a cemetery, a creamery, and a church building were later established, in that order. To at least a part of this latter group the Reverend Jacob Eisenhower was minister.

He settled on a one-hundred-and-sixty-acre farm seven miles south of the river, a farm with a deep, rich alluvial soil. There he erected a large house which, like the home in Elizabethville, contained one large room designed to serve both as parlor on weekdays and as meeting place for the Brethren on Sundays. It was not until 1894 that the Belle Springs church building was erected; before that time the Brethren met at various houses for Sabbath services, most of which were still conducted in the German language. Behind his house Jacob erected a huge barn in the style of the Dutch, and it, too, was reminiscent of the Eisenhower property in Pennsylvania. But the structure which aroused the most interest on the part of earlier settlers was the large all-wood Dutch windmill, with a wheel of wooden sails at the top, which Jacob built near the barn.

CHAPTER II

David Eisenhower Takes a Wife

A WIND BLEW CONSTANTLY—and fresh country eggs could be purchased for five cents a dozen! These were the most vivid impressions of Dickinson County in March 1878, to be retained in later years by David and Amanda Eisenhower. The two young people were in no mood to be receptive of favorable new impressions. They regarded the featureless landscape—the sweeps of treeless prairie leaning down toward tree-lined streams—through eyes which longed for the relatively lush green beauty of the Pennsylvania hills.

The Kansas to which they had come was just emerging from the most turbulent period of her history. When the South fired upon Fort Sumter, civil war had already raged for six years down the valley of the Kaw. It had begun with the passage of Douglas's "squatter sovereignty" bill in 1854, a bill which in effect invited North and South to fight it out for possession of the Kansas Territory. It had continued in murder and fire and pillage, in pitched border battles that recognized none of the established usages of war, until 1865. Abolitionists of Puritan stock, pouring into the eastern third of the territory before 1860, made of that section a crude pioneering version of New England, marked by the rugged if intolerant idealism of the old New England mind. Lawrence, the Free State settlement where much of the fighting centered, took on the aspect of a Massachusetts town. Strange, complex, symbolic figures came to the fore during those bloody years. John Brown, the half-mad fanatic with wild eyes and flowing beard, a Bible in one hand and a rifle in the other, murdered Pro-Slavers in the name of God and died upon the scaffold (guilty of high treason, "guilty as hell") to become a martyr to liberty. Jim Lane, a fascinating creature of light and shade, made of Abolitionist sentiment a platform from which he stepped into the Senate. There, by maneuvers of a doubtful ethical quality, he helped to sustain Lincoln during the war years and to secure the President's second nomination. A few years later, having revealed himself as the most cynical of political opportunists, he died by his own hand to round out a tragic legend. Dr. Charles Robinson, sober and responsible leader of the Abolitionists, nevertheless ordered one hundred Sharps rifles in April 1855, to arm his men, and thereafter took an active part in the battles of Bleeding Kansas. He had come as agent for the New England Emigrant Aid Society, and he remained to become, in 1861, the first governor of the new state. . . . There were other figures of almost equal symbolic stature—stormy, colorful, legendary.

Nor did the violence and the rise of violent heroes end in Kansas with the Civil War. They simply transferred their scenes westward, lost their ideological character, and provided the substance for ten thousand lurid tales of the Western frontier. Sporadic Indian wars spread themselves, in scattered vicious skirmishes, across the High Plains. As late as the early 1870s white settlers were massacred by Indians in Saline County, only a few miles west of the land Jacob Eisenhower was to settle. For four memorable years violence was centered in the very town in which the Eisenhowers were later to live, the town of Abilene.

The Kansas Pacific Railroad reached Abilene in 1867. Joseph McCoy established his famous stockyards in the little town, the only market outlet for some millions of Texas cattle. Abruptly, what had been the tiniest of villages, slow of growth and virtually unknown to the outside world, became notorious the nation over as the most lawless community in the whole Western frontier. The drive up the Jesse Chisholm trail, across a thousand miles of Texas, Oklahoma, and southern Kansas, required months of desperately hard labor on the part of cowboys. They were at best a rough and lawless group, many of them fugitives from the justice of more civilized areas. Once they had herded the longhorns into the yards beside the railroad tracks, they "let go" completely. Scores of gamblers, prostitutes, and gunmen took up residence in the town to provide the facilities for this "letting go." A district known as "McCoy's Addition" or "Hell's Half-Acre" was built a mile and a half north of town, consisting almost exclusively of saloons, gambling halls, and bawdyhouses which ran day and night. There were twenty-five to thirty one-story frame buildings, each with ten to twenty rooms. As the hundreds of cowboys poured into Abilene each season, all varieties of lawlessness flourished, and shootings became an almost daily occurrence.

It was not until Abilene was incorporated as a town in 1869 that any serious effort was made to bring law and order into the community, and this effort was at first resisted with great success by the lawless elements. All of the first town marshals were either killed or driven out of the community after brief tenures of office. Finally one Tom Smith, of Kit Carson, Colorado, applied for the job and succeeded, by virtue of his strong character as much as by his skill with fists and weapons, in enforcing for a time the ordinances against carrying firearms and for the licensing of saloons. Smith, a polite, soft-spoken, even deferential man, promptly became one of the legendary heroes of the old West. He was succeeded after a few months by an even greater legendary hero: Wild Bill (James Butler) Hickok, a Union sharpshooter in the Civil War and a notorious frontier figure who, at the time of his Abilene appointment, was reported (by himself) to have killed forty-three men, not counting those shot in the war. His skill with revolvers was fabulous. He could dent a coin tossed into the air, drawing and shooting with marvelous speed and with either hand. He could keep a tin can dancing in the dust by pumping a steady stream of bullets into it from his two revolvers. And in Abilene he succeeded in living up to the inflated reputation which he, aided and abetted by the exaggerations of frontier gossip, had made for himself. He once killed two men who were fleeing in opposite directions, and did it with such rapidity that a boy witness swore on oath that only one shot was fired. The number of men killed by him during his term as town marshal is a matter of debate, but it was great enough to make him the most awe-inspiring figure of that lawless time. By 1872, when the big terminal cattle market had moved farther west with the railroad, he was firmly established as Abilene's most famous citizen, and he would remain so all down the years to 1942, when a home-town boy assumed command of an army in England.

Thus the Kansas which the Eisenhowers came to know in 1878 had been born of struggle, baptized in blood, and confirmed (through violence) in a curiously mingled character. A sincere idealism was mixed with the most cynical pragmatism; a lurid cow-town viciousness intermingled with a persimmonish New England prudery; and a passion for economic liberty was counterbalanced by a Puritan desire to legislate the private morality of citizens. It was a state which went to extremes. In the eighties and nineties it would be a center of agrarian radicalism, a leader of the Populist revolt against the "money power" of the East. By the mid-1930s it would be a bulwark of reaction, struggling (in a kind of blind emotionalism) to maintain the political forms of an agrarian economy against the collectivizing forces of an advancing technology. It would produce Earl Browder, standard-bearer of the Communists, and Alf Landon, standard-bearer of the right-wing Republicans, in 1936. It would produce political leaders of the struggle for isolation, and journalistic leaders of the fight for intervention in the early 1940s. Through all the changes and self-contradictions of its history, only one thing would remain constant: a deep belief in democracy, a belief that the individual man *is* the center and measure of all value on earth.

With the typical Kansan, democracy would continue to be first of all a matter of instinct and personal practice, and only secondarily a matter of philosophic principle. In the latter field, the field of abstractions and laws, the state would take occasional anti-democratic turnings. One governor would make a serious effort to suppress freedom of speech and press with regard to labor troubles down in the southeast corner of the state. On another occasion the Ku Klux Klan would ride the Kansas plains in quite a fearful display of protofascism. In still later years there would be occasional expressions of a vicious anti-Semitism in Wichita. But the instinct for democracy, however frustrated by ignorance and by faulty definitions, would stay sound and true, and it would save the state from such excessive violations of the democratic spirit as have occurred in other areas. Perhaps the best explanation of this instinctive (rather than rational) democracy lies in the fact that the state has never become industrialized and as a consequence there have never developed, to the degree one finds in industrial areas, a class of employers and a class of workers, a class of rich owners and a class of poor dispossessed, with the snobberies and envies and guilt complexes which such a class structure inevitably produces. There are variations in economic status, to be sure, and there are consequent instances of what a Marxist might call a "rudimentary class consciousness." A few of them will be encountered in the story of the Eisenhowers in Abilene. But, generally speaking, a man here is judged pretty much for what he himself is. Family means little;

there are no "old families." Class means virtually nothing; the average Kansan is hardly aware that there is such a thing as a "class."

In 1878 there was already evident a sharp divergence between what William Allen White, many years later, would call the "two Kansases." The eastern section of bluestem hills and diversified farming was, as we have seen, a frontier edition of New England. The western section of short grass and wheat belonged wholly to the West. In the eastern section, Puritan Abolitionists set the dominant moral tone. In the western section, gamblers in cattle, wheat, and (later) oil set the tone. And in the portion of the state to which the Eisenhowers came the two Kansases met and mingled with each other. To the east of Dickinson County lay the hill-chopped, intensively farmed valleys of the Kaw and Neosho, and the Flint Hills on which the tall bluestem grasses seemed to flow like sea waves in the wind. To the west lay the flat, semi-arid country of wheat and buffalo grass, where only the wheat flowed with the wind; the short grass hugged the earth like a carpet. In Dickinson County both wheat and corn were raised; in the native pastures were found both bluestem and buffalo grasses; and here the traditions of Puritan discipline and Wild West lawlessness existed side by side and exerted on the very young an almost equal influence.

By virtue of his religious training and his essential nature, David Eisenhower was, even as a boy, more closely identified with the Puritan east than with the gambling west. But as he stood upon his father's land he was almost within physical sight of Jesse Chisholm's trail, and he could not escape its cultural influence. Three million Texas longhorns had come up that trail in four years. Along it, and especially at its end, men had lived and died with a magnificent violence. They had shaped a tradition of hard work, courage, endurance, and self-reliance; of contempt for too much luxury and ease of living. It was an ideal not wholly alien to David's own; it would have a tremendous effect on the character development of David's sons.

2

No longer did the vast herds come trampling up from the South, wreaking destruction on the fields of those farmers who had been so unfortunate as to have settled on or near the trail. Jacob Eisenhower could cultivate his land in peace and prosperity, and this, since he was an excellent farmer with a sufficiency of working capital, is what he very promptly did. The essential routines of his life in Kansas were much the same as they had been in Pennsylvania. On weekdays he worked hard in the fields, driving not only himself but his sons. On Sundays his neighbors gathered at his home to hear him preach. The love feasts continued, for a time, to be an annual event. With his surplus capital, as the years passed, he interested himself in a small bank in the tiny village of Hope which lay less than five miles from his farm and would, in later years, be his post office address. The children grew up in the awareness that they would inherit a very comfortable property.

Amanda adapted herself swiftly to the new country. Soon both she and David had come to love the broad sweeps of prairie, the beautiful economy of a landscape which, out of a sense of distance between man and man, brought to each individual a realization of his own lonely integrity beneath vast and indifferent skies. Jacob purchased a team of fast ponies, and these, racing over the ungraded roads and across unfenced pastures, made the weekly marketing expeditions to Abilene, twelve miles to the north, a pleasure rather than a chore. Amanda had an enormous amount of *joie de vivre*. She was small and quick, with a warm, bubbling sense of humor, and was as a consequence tremendously popular with the other boys and girls her age (there were not many) who lived near by. She liked the farm and farm life.

Her younger brother David was a different kind of personality. He was quiet, rather moody, much given to introspection. His was not a decisive mind. It was with difficulty that he made choices among various objective opportunities, but once a decision was made he clung to it with the utmost stubbornness. In his teens he found himself at odds with his environment. He was not happy in the work of the farm. The endless repetitions of the same simple tasks, year after year, outraged something within him which longed, obscurely, for scholarly pursuits. He decided early and definitely that he would not become a farmer. This may have appeared to Jacob as sacrilege, he who identified the good life with the life of the soil and who let it be known that he expected his sons to be farmers; but whatever opposition Jacob made to David's decision only served to strengthen the boy's determination.

There was only one part of the work on the farm which did appeal to David, and that was the work of repairing the mechanical equipment. Doctoring mechanical ills gave some scope for logical inquiry; it presented problems, and he liked to solve problems. He liked to tinker with the windmill, with the farm machinery, and he liked to play at inventing mechanical gadgets of his own. The neighbors began to speak of him admiringly as a "natural-born" mechanic, and as the years passed this gradually opened his eyes to a doorway through which he might escape from the farm. He decided that his best chance to get on in the world was to become an engineer, and that his only chance of becoming an engineer was to go away somewhere to school. At the back of his mind was the hope that, once he got to college, he might find other opportunities which would serve, even better than engineering, those obscure longings within him.

He discussed these matters often with Amanda, who was always sensitive to his moods and quick in her understanding. She encouraged him. The idea of his going away to college excited her, for a "college man" in those days was a rare being whose very membership in the family would boost the prestige of the Eisenhowers in the community. She helped him plead his case with Jacob, while old Frederick, nodding in a corner, brooded sadly upon the changes which time brings to families. Jacob, himself a "bookish" man, had great respect for the life of the mind, and perhaps his initial opposition to the scheme was more apparent than real. At any rate, he yielded. He agreed to finance David's entrance into a little school, which has since passed out of existence, known as Lane University.

The school was named after Jim Lane. It was operated by the United Brethren Church, and it was located in Lecompton, a village which from 1855 to 1858 had been a center of the political struggle between the Free Staters and the Pro-Slavers. For those three years Lecompton had been the territorial capital of Kansas, and Congress had been persuaded by the Pro-Slavery men to begin construction there of a large stone capital building. The building remained unfinished when, in 1865, Lane University was founded. The school proceeded to erect its first building on the old capital foundations. Here, in the autumn of 1883, David Eisenhower, whose twentieth birthday was in September of that year, was enrolled.

Before his first term was out his last living link with a distant past was snapped. After the Christmas recess old Frederick saw in his grandson's departure for school the last scene in a drama that no longer interested him. Frederick the weaver was eighty-nine years old. He was sick and unutterably weary. Too long had he outlived his world. In March of 1884 he died, and was buried in the Belle Springs Cemetery, hard by the Belle Springs Creamery which, owned and operated by the River Brethren, had already developed a large and prosperous business. . . .

Lane stressed religious education and was for the rest a kind of cross between a liberal-arts college and a vocational-training institute. In this limited curriculum David chose to pursue a "general" course. He studied Greek, certainly; the Bible he read in later years was printed in Greek. He took courses in rhetoric and penmanship, learning to write such a beautifully flowing hand that his talent was much in demand, later on, for recording important events in family albums and Bibles. He also studied mechanics. What other subjects he studied is unknown.

He came home in the summer of 1884, at the end of his first term, to provide Amanda with a living subject for quite sinful and embarrassing displays of pride. She loved to "show off" her brother whenever visitors came. She was not always tactful. On one Sunday the Pyke family (Catherine Eisenhower, Jacob's sister, had married a Pyke) came to visit the Eisenhowers, and Amanda used David as a kind of family jewel to impress her cousins.

"Dave, I want you to put on a little style," she kept saying. "Let them know you've been away to school."

At least one of the cousins, a girl who had longed to go away to school but who had been denied the opportunity, was badly hurt by this. The River Brethren were opposed to sending girls away from home to college; for them a woman's place was most emphatically in the home; and so all the Pyke girl could do, in the face of Amanda's shameless display, was withdraw into a corner of Jacob's house and brood tearfully upon the injustice of her lot.

Among those who frequented the Eisenhower home that summer was a young man named Chris Musser, who had known the Eisenhowers in Pennsylvania and who had arrived in Kansas in March, a few days after Frederick was buried. He was employed by a neighbor of the Eisenhowers, a farmer who lived near the Belle Springs Creamery. He was a member of the River Brethren and had, of course, come every Sunday to Jacob's home to hear Jacob preach.

There he had met Amanda. By the time David arrived from school Chris Musser's visits were not limited to Sundays. He squired Amanda to all the social gatherings of the community: the festivals, the picnics, the church socials; and before the summer was ended he and Amanda were engaged to be married. The wedding took place on November 30, 1884. Amanda became Mrs. C. O. Musser, the wife of a man destined to become a leading figure in the history of the Belle Springs Creamery—a history in which all the Eisenhower family would be much involved—as well as one of the most prosperous farmers in Dickinson County.

Amanda had been glowingly happy that summer, and perhaps this fact made David more than normally susceptible to romantic impulses. At any rate, in that autumn of Amanda's marriage, the autumn of his second term at Lane, he noticed in his classes a slender, graceful girl with remarkably brilliant eyes and a wide, mobile mouth; a girl who gave an impression of immense, stimulating vitality. She smiled at him—even after more than sixty years had passed her smile would be a delightful thing to see—and he was lost. He was not the only one. She was one of the most popular girls in school. Several young men competed for her favors, including one handsome young fellow whose handle-bar mustaches and dashing manner should have given him a distinct advantage over the sober-mannered and rather shy David. Nevertheless, David entered the competition. He could not help himself.

She had come to Kansas, he discovered, from Virginia. She was a year and five months older than he. Her name was Ida Elizabeth Stover.

Her early pictures reveal that she was an extremely attractive girl, and it was no doubt her physical attractiveness which first drew him toward her. But it is probable that what held him, with such compelling force that he forsook for a time his ambition to become an engineer, was his recognition in her of a strength and a living wisdom superior to his own. The two young people seemed to supplement one another. He remained at that time a quiet, imaginative, introspective personality, unsure of his place in the world, unsure even of what he wanted that place to be. She was vivacious, energetic, decisive, perhaps less imaginative than he, and certainly less given to solitary brooding. Perhaps it was his more lyrical personality which attracted her. Perhaps she sensed instinctively that he would add color and mood to what might otherwise be a rather bleak and prosaic, if thoroughly practical, life. At any rate, the attraction between them was mutual. The dashing young fellow with the handle-bar mustaches soon found himself out of the running.

Before the term was out David was convinced that marriage to this girl was more important to him than a degree from Lane could possibly be. He seems to have proposed to her, and been accepted, in the spring of 1885. They were not, however, married at once. No doubt David had to cast around for some work which would enable him to support a wife, for even at this juncture he steadfastly refused to take up farming. It would have been easy for him to have done so. Jacob's standard gift to his children, upon their marriage, was a one-hundred-and-sixty-acre farm and two thousand dollars in cash. He had made this present to Amanda upon her marriage to Chris Musser and he was prepared to make it now to David. But David decided instead to go into business. He seems to have been in sufficient doubt of his own business acumen to look around for an experienced partner. He found one in a young, newly married man named Milton D. Good, who was at that time clerking in an Abilene clothing store. With Good furnishing the business experience and David furnishing most, if not all, the capital, it was arranged that the two start a general-merchandise store in the small but at that time growing village of Hope.

Jacob made less objection to this than might have been anticipated. Young Mr. Good, it seems, had a great deal of what has since become known as a "selling" personality, and all of the Eisenhowers, including Jacob, were favorably impressed by him. He was popular in Abilene. Businessmen there spoke highly of him. And so it was that even when David mortgaged his farm for an additional two thousand dollars in order to finance the new enterprise, Jacob agreed to the arrangement, partly influenced, no doubt, by the fact that the mortgage was held by Chris Musser's father. One can imagine David's unnatural exhilaration that summer. It seemed to him that he had at last shaken himself free of his old doubt and indecision and that, with such a wife and such a business partner, his future happiness and prosperity were assured.

The wedding took place on David's twenty-second birthday. Hanging today in the front room of the Eisenhower home in Abilene is a framed marriage certificate. It records that "David Eisenhower, Hope, Kansas, and Ida Stover, Lecompton, Kansas, according to the ordinances of God and the laws of the State of Kansas, were united in marriage on the 23rd of September, 1885," with the Reverend E. B. Slade of the United Brethren Church of Lecompton officiating. The ceremony was held in the chapel of Lane University.

3

She was to become the mother of one of the great captains of history. What of her family, her background, her own early life?

The history of her family is remarkably similar to the history of the Eisenhowers. Its dominant theme, as in the case of the Eisenhowers, is a religious one, and the religious convictions of the two families were either the same or closely similar. Apparently the Stovers lived in Switzerland at the same time as the ancestral Eisenhauers, having fled there from Germany to escape religious persecutions in the seventeenth century. From Switzerland in the 1730s two Stover brothers, Christian and Jacob, emigrated to America. In the new country they separated. Christian settled in Pennsylvania, probably forming one of the colony to which the Eisenhauers belonged. Jacob, who is described (in Veach's *The American Lineages of the Veach and Stover Families*) as an "interesting character and enterprising, it seems, to a fault," pushed on into the unexplored country west of the Blue Ridge Mountains to become one of the earliest settlers in the valley of the Shenandoah in Virginia. He profited in land transactions as colonies of Germans, all of whom were members of various Mennonite sects, settled along the river from Strasburg to Staunton. He was, according to tentative genealogical data, a great-grandfather of Ida Elizabeth.

She was born in Mount Sidney, Virginia, on May 1, 1862. Her father, a farmer, was Simon P. Stover, born in Mount Sidney in 1820, and her mother was Elizabeth Link Stover, born in Mount Sidney in 1824. Thus her parents were already in middle age when she was born, and her mother died when she was very young. There were eleven children, too many apparently for a wifeless man to care for, and Ida Elizabeth was sent at the age of seven to live with a brother of her mother, her uncle Billy Link, who became her legal guardian upon the death of Simon Stover in 1874. He kept her inheritance for her until she was twenty-one. While she was still a child two of her brothers came to Kansas, and she seems to have decided then that she wanted to come to Kansas too. Her guardian, however, would not permit her to come until she was twenty-one. She came then with her cousin, Mary Ann Link, who had just married an Emanuel Beam. She arrived in Topeka in May or June of 1883.

Though the Civil War ended shortly after her third birthday, it exerted a dominant influence on her life. Her parents abhorred slavery and were as a consequence distrusted, perhaps even persecuted, by patriotic Southern neighbors. This did not spare them when Northern armies came raging down the Shenandoah Valley, laying waste the towns and farms. The Stovers, without even the moral support which belief in a cause might have given them, were caught in a nightmare of pillage and fear. Reportedly, the horror of the experience was partially responsible for the early death of Ida's mother. It left Ida herself convinced that war is the ultimate wickedness. Otherwise her childhood was a happy one. She was extremely popular in the community, a bright student in school (where she was taught by a brother, J. Worth Stover), and a devout member of the church.

She was eager for an education. Her inheritance, though a small one, gave her liberty to follow her desire despite the general disapproval with which members of her sect regarded higher education for women. She entered Lane in the fall of 1883. There she studied (among other subjects) music, history, and English. Music was one of the great loves of her life. The first major purchase made with her inheritance was a handsome ebony piano which, through much of her later life, would provide her only means of aesthetic enjoyment and self-expression.

CHAPTER III

Flight and Return

Looking back, it must have seemed bitterly ironical to David Eisenhower that the town should be named "Hope" and the business partner "Good." He started out with such high hopes and with every prospect of success. There seemed no reason, scarcely even a possibility, for failure. Yet he failed. He failed in his own handling of business detail. He failed even more disastrously in his judgments of the people with whom he had to deal. And since the failure came about despite the chances in his favor, he could not do otherwise than place the blame upon himself. It hurt him so deeply, wounding him at the very roots of his confidence, that he never completely recovered from it. Never again did he dare risk security to gain independence; never again did he dare bet heavily on his own enterprise and talents.

The town, no larger now than it was then, consists of a few blocks of scattered houses and one main street, the upper end of which is flanked by a block or so of business buildings and the lower part of which is residential. It draws its meager life exclusively from trade with a small agricultural community around it, doomed by the automobile and by the nearness of Abilene to a humble and precarious existence. The population has never been more than a few hundred. The main line of no railroad passes through it. It lies on no main highway. On all sides the land lies level and wind-swept. During the summer droughts the hot winds scurry eddies of dust along the unpaved streets; during winter blizzards the drifts of snow pile high against the few obstacles to the wind. There are more trees there now than there were in the 1880s. In those days the village must have presented to a visitor from New England, say, a dreary prospect indeed.

But in the winter of 1885–86 there was that in the village which did not entirely belie the village name. The village was growing.

There were many young people there in proportion to the total population—the youth was not then drained off to the cities as rapidly as it is today—and there was in the atmosphere of the town a certain youthful freshness and promise. Among these young people flourished an active social life.

David Eisenhower and his bride were, for a few months at least, a part of that. The general-merchandise store stood on the main street, a two-story building with the shop on the first floor and two small apartments on the second floor. The Goods lived in one apartment, the Eisenhowers in the other. Amanda and Chris Musser, watching proceedings with a no doubt critical eye because of the loan Musser's father had made, seem to have been convinced quite early that the young Eisenhowers were living "too high." Just what "high living" consisted of in the Hope of those days is difficult to ascertain. It may be that Ida Elizabeth spent money foolishly; she was never gifted with that commodity known as "money sense." Perhaps the Eisenhowers entertained too much, with the Goods, in the tiny apartments. Perhaps they ate more expensive food and dressed in more expensive clothes than their income justified. If so, it was an experience they were never to have again. On the other hand, it may be that the young couple were simply too exuberantly happy and casual in their treatment of things which seemed, to the property-conscious River Brethren, very serious and important. It would have been easy to brand oneself as flippant and lightheaded in that community of extremely conservative religious folk.

During the first two years the business seemed to go well. The volume of sales was consistently high, and the turnover rather more than satisfactory. Both David and his partner were well liked by the townspeople, and they did not hesitate to extend credit to their friends. It seems at first to have escaped David's notice that the proportion of his business done on a credit basis was dangerously high. Only gradually did he discover that extending too much credit to his customers made it necessary for him to seek credit himself, and that this process, if long continued, could lead to ruin. Apparently he paid less attention to the bookkeeping than he should have done, trusting his partner to do this chore, but he began to notice that some of his customers' bills were quite large, that they'd been running for a long time, and that they were steadily growing. In the back of his mind developed a small but constant nagging worry.

Meanwhile his personal responsibilities were becoming greater. He became a father. On November 11, 1886, Ida Elizabeth was delivered of her first child, a boy whom they named Arthur B. Sixteen months later she was again with child.

They were to have many children, and this fact made it absolutely imperative that David succeed in business. How horrible if he lost everything! He began to take a more active interest in business detail and spent many hours poring over the books with Milton Good. He turned a good deal of cash over to his partner to be used to satisfy the demands of his creditors, perhaps using for this purpose the remnants of the inheritance Ida Elizabeth had brought to him with their marriage. The books appeared to balance again, or to come close enough to balancing to enable David to breathe more freely.

Then, sometime in the autumn of 1888, the blow fell.

It is difficult at this late date to discover precisely what happened. There was no court case, and hence there are no court records. Perhaps David and his partner had an open quarrel. At any rate, Milton Good and his wife seem to have left Hope in something of a hurry, and David awoke one morning to find that the bills which he had assumed were paid had not, in fact, been paid. There were fruitless reproaches and recriminations, charges of dishonesty (which were never legally proved) and of extreme negligence (which was an obvious fact). The old nagging worry returned to assume monstrous proportions. David pored frantically over his books, sought to put off the creditors who were hounding him, and began to hound in turn those who owed him money. If every single one of the bills due him were paid he just might manage to squeeze through! It was a vain hope. He lived in a nightmare which grew steadily more horrible as the swift days passed. What excuse could there be for him who had started with everything in his favor? He saw in the eyes of his family and in those of his family's friends a cold and stony reproach. He imagined that everyone was aware of his impending disgrace.

It was his first, perhaps his greatest, test, and he did not face it well. Actually, he did not face it at all. In self-violation, in violation of the frontier tradition of courage and self-reliance which he himself accepted, he sought only to escape from the scene of his humiliation. He turned everything over to a local lawyer. Leaving behind his infant son and his wife, now heavy with child, he accepted the first job he could find—a low-paying job in the shops of the Cotton Belt Railroad at Denison, Texas. Back in Hope, the lawyer to whom he had entrusted his affairs completed his ruin. The store was sold; the mortgage on the farm, now held by C. O. Musser, who had assumed it from his father, was foreclosed; every available asset was converted into cash which was used to pay off debts, of which the lawyer's own fee turned out to be a considerable additional item.

There are extant several pictures of David Eisenhower as he appeared in those years and several pictures of him as he appeared in 1926 and after. The contrast between these two sets of pictures is striking. The earlier ones show a handsome, rather weak face, mustached heavily, with soft dreamy eyes—the face of an introvert. He faces the camera as though he is not really looking into the lens but is, instead, looking inward upon a private world of his own. The later pictures show a much more rocklike visage, the jaw set firmly, the eyes much more direct in their gaze. He seems to be watching the lens—without boldness, but also without timidity. The contrast between these two sets of pictures is a fairly accurate representation of the transformation which had been wrought in the man himself. If David Eisenhower never again dared bet on his own enterprise, neither did he ever again run away from an obligation. If he never developed that aggressiveness which might have insured the full use of his abilities, he did develop a stubbornness which enabled him to hold his own, to maintain his integrity against whatever forces might be brought against it. The crisis at Hope caught him unprepared; his defenses were down. Thereafter he was almost wholly defensive in his basic attitudes, but his defenses were high and strong.

Even greater than the contrast between these two sets of pictures is the contrast between the ways in which David and Ida Elizabeth faced the catastrophe which had come upon them. By that catastrophe David was for a time overwhelmed. By that catastrophe Ida Elizabeth was thoroughly aroused. All her latent fighting instincts, all her strength and determination began to express themselves. Milton Good may have robbed them. The lawyer might be cheating them. She got hold of some lawbooks and proceeded to study law. Left alone to weather the storm, fully as sensitive to the censure in the relatives' eyes as David had been, she was determined to salvage what she could. She lost her fight, of course. Perhaps she had no case. Certainly she had no money. The time for the birth of her second child was almost upon her. And in the end all she salvaged from the wreckage was some household furniture, including the ebony piano. But she had fought back valiantly, and as instinctively as David had run away; she had been strengthened rather than weakened by her experience.

Always afterward David Eisenhower had a horror of debt, and he never again went into debt. In later years his children were often to hear him say, apropos of the unhealed wound he had suffered at Hope: "If only they'd paid their bills I'd have been able to pay mine." Indeed the very sight of a bill seems to have been so distasteful to him that he always arranged with the firms where he had charge accounts that no bills be sent him.

"I'll keep track, and I don't want you sending me bills," he told storekeepers with emphasis. "I'll pay promptly the first of every month."

He always did. But more than two decades later one of the firms in Abilene with whom he had done business for years happened, through accident, to send him a bill at the first of a month. Apparently a new girl had been hired for the office, one who did not know of David's arrangement. He went to the store, bill in hand, and paid it on the day he had received it. Never again did he trade at that store. . . .

On January 19, 1889, in the absence of her husband, Ida Elizabeth was delivered in Hope of her second son. She named him Edgar N. She had been sure that Arthur would be a businessman, because during the time she had carried him her mind had been much occupied with the new merchandise store in Hope. She was equally sure that Edgar must become a lawyer, because her mind had been occupied with the study of law during the time she carried him.

Several weeks after Edgar's birth she traveled southward with her two sons to join her husband in Texas. Before she left Dickinson County it was arranged that a Mrs. Rugh in Abilene, a friend of hers, should keep for her the ebony piano which she prized so highly.

2

The Texas interlude was strictly that—an interlude, a period of recuperation. It was to last less than two years.

During those two years the Eisenhowers lived in a small, multi-gabled frame house which faced the railroad tracks. The house, though doubtless remodeled, still stood in 1944. Arthur, the eldest son, would remember it as supported by "stilts," and he'd remember that he used to play under it, a dark and sheltered place, a cool retreat from the summer sun, when he was four. He'd also remember how flat and dry the country was, flatter even than Dickinson County in Kansas, and how the herds of goats grazed in the fields adjoining the house. Bales of cotton were stacked high along the railroad tracks in front of the house. Near by was a tiny wood (the house stood on the very edge of town), and often in the summer Ida Elizabeth used to take her two children there—Edgar in her arms, Arthur trotting sturdily by her side—to gather ferns. Not far away, to the north, was the Red River, where silt-laden water the color of blood flowed in a tortuous stream between wide and shallow banks. The river, shallow as it was, symbolized their exile. They were cut off from the North, cut off from family and friends, facing in their solitude a future which seemed dark indeed.

One more thing Arthur would remember from those long-ago days, though very vaguely. He'd remember the gloom which seemed to settle over the house when his father and mother talked of Kansas and of the disaster they had suffered there. Those were unhappy years. The work itself on the railroad gave David some satisfaction, for he was working with machines as he had always liked to do. He worked for a time in the shops; later he worked on the road, making the run between Denison and Tyler. But the pay was hardly enough to keep his wife and children at a bare subsistence level. He was making less than forty dollars a month, and he spent many sleepless nights worrying about how he could increase his income at least enough to match the inevitable increase in his family. Certainly he could draw no self-confidence from his past. He had had two ambitions: first, to become an engineer; second, to become a successful businessman. In both ambitions he had been frustrated almost before he began. The specter of past failure haunted his days, darkening his vision when he tried to peer into the years ahead.

He turned inevitably to religion. Both he and Ida Elizabeth began a serious examination of their religious beliefs, seeking out the premises while rejecting some of the conclusions of the River Brethren orthodoxy. "God will provide," the River Brethren said, but they didn't trust God to do so independent of their own efforts. If the provision were not made they placed the blame not on God for his unkindness, but on the unfortunate individual for his improvidence. If one succeeded he might say, "God has prospered us," in tones of pious humility (an open show of pride was of course a grievous sin), but if he failed it was his own fault, a fault discovered of God, and hence in the last analysis a mark of God's disfavor. It was hardly a comforting belief for one who had just failed so disastrously in a business venture, and at that point both David and his wife needed all the comfort, all the strength they could find.

They studied the Scriptures intensively. They sought out what seemed to them signs and portents. And they started along paths which plunged them quite abruptly into a murky mysticism. For did not the Scriptures teach that God is to be apprehended, not through any process of reasoning, but directly through the mystic processes of "conversion" and "illumination"? The experience of God is the only valid source of religion, and this experience can be gained only by faith, through a process of feeling rather than a process of reasoning. Studying his Greek Bible, David concluded as Menno Simons had done that an established church is no necessary part of Christianity but an adjunct which may help in so far as it spreads Christ's teachings or hinder in so far as it distorts them. Ida Elizabeth would, in the years ahead, go even further and declare that an established church is always distortive of Christ's teachings. She would proceed into areas where religion comes dangerously close to intolerant dogma—a fact which would have its influence, real but difficult to assess, on the character development of her children.

Fortunately both of them possessed a great deal of common sense, so that they never in their mystical wanderings lost sight of hard, practical, objective realities—and it is even possible that they would have been less successful in their rearing of children (it is hard to imagine how they could have been *more* successful) had their religion been more "enlightened" and "modern." For them the virtues were matters of absolute principle rather than relative practice, matters of dogma rather than expediency, and so they impressed the virtues upon their children with greater force than might otherwise have been the case. Personal cleanliness, truthtelling, self-discipline, the necessity for earning one's privileges with hard work, the most scrupulous honesty in money matters—all of these became, for the Eisenhower children, articles of cardinal belief, instilled in them almost from birth. If the parents' religion was in its essence a quite fluid emotionalism, its outer surface was very solid, consistent, practical.

In David's case, religious mysticism was strangely alloyed with engineering logic. It was probably during the Denison period that he began working on a chart of the pyramids in Egypt. It was a huge wall chart covering twelve or sixteen square feet, and it purported to show how the lines of the three pyramids—the angles of the passageways within them, the lines of the inner rooms—prophesied biblical events which occurred after the pyramids were completed. He extended on his chart the outer dimension lines of the structures, the lines of the passageways, and so on, working out a scheme whereby the intersections of these extended lines had a symbolic meaning. The chart seems to have fascinated the elder of the Eisenhower children later on when their father explained it to them. It became one of the family treasures. In 1944 it was still to be seen in an upstairs room of the house in Abilene.

But the chief source of David's strength, in that time as in later ones, was his wife. She supplied the driving energy which he lacked. She had the kind of vivid, intense personality which radiates light and warmth, making life a full and colorful thing for those around her. She took full responsibility for managing the house and caring for the children. She maintained, at least outwardly, a bright, cheerful optimism through most of the dark hours; and (whether consciously or unconsciously it is hard to say) she managed to help her husband restore somewhat his badly damaged self-confidence. During the Denison period she became, in everything but name, the head of the family, but she did it in such a way as to stimulate rather than blight her husband's self-respect. She encouraged him to make decisions by which she must abide. She freely admitted that she didn't understand money, that he was far her superior in this respect, and that the handling of family finances was therefore his right as well as his privilege. She impressed upon her children, sometimes with the rod, that the father's word was law for them all. The father sat always at the head of the table. It was the father who said grace before meals. And so she maintained the outward forms of the old German patriarchal family which was, of course, traditional among the Pennsylvania Dutch. There is no doubt that she loved him deeply. The very qualities which may have weakened him as a businessman—his distaste for ruthless competition, his eagerness to serve others regardless of recompense, his quiet sensitivity, his extreme modesty—all of these qualities were endearing to those who were intimately associated with him.

Sometime early in the spring of 1890 Ida Elizabeth informed her husband that she was again with child. The news, coming at a time when the family fortunes were at their lowest ebb, was not an occasion for any great rejoicing. On the contrary, it was an occasion for increased anxiety. Soon there would be another mouth to feed, and from where was the food to come? The nervous tension in David must have increased a good deal as the long, hot Texas summer came on. One can imagine him staring wide-eyed into the hot darkness above his bed while his mind twisted and turned in search of a feasible plan for the future.

In late June his unhappiness was turned to active grief by news from home. On June 22 David's mother—the Rebecca Matter who had married Jacob Eisenhower in Pennsylvania so long ago—died on the farm south of Abilene. She was sixty-five years of age. Jacob was now left alone, and before long he was asking his son David to come home, come back to Kansas where he belonged. But how was David to come back, much as he wanted to? With another child coming, he could hardly be expected to throw up his job, his one certain means of livelihood, to return to a country where he had already failed once and where he could not be certain of bettering himself now. So the hot dry months dragged on in Texas, adding their unhappy weight to the burden of exile, until it was autumn again. . . .

In the mystery of Time the past is shaped continuously by the living present. Only as a moment gathers history, receding endlessly into the past, does it gather meaning. The event itself, isolated from the stream of Time, is static, weightless, meaningless—and even in Time it becomes the source and not the sum of its significance. The latter is assigned to it in endless flux and variation so long as the memory of it remains in the minds of men; so long, in other words, as it has consequences. Forgotten, consequentless, it dies. Here, then, is an event—and who shall say even now what weight shall be assigned to it? In October, when scattered trees and shrubs flamed with death across the Texas plain, Ida Elizabeth Eisenhower was delivered of her third son.

Not even symbolically within the bosom of the family was there a roll of drums, a fanfare of trumpets. The new life began obscurely in a dark hour, and even the mother had no predictions to make for it on the basis of prenatal influence, as she had done for her first two sons. She was merely thankful that the new infant was strong and healthy, for he might need all his health and strength to get through the years ahead. She named him after his father. And one evening David, the father, wrote the new name into the family Bible, wrote it in that beautifully flowing hand of his: "David Dwight Eisenhower, born October 14, 1890. Denison, Texas."

3

In the autumn of 1889 the Belle Springs Creamery—now grown into one of the largest and most prosperous enterprises in Dickinson County—built a big new plant beside the railroad at the edge of Abilene. Young C. O. Musser was appointed foreman of the plant. Among the River Brethren who owned and operated the creamery, Chris Musser was recognized as one of the promising young men, "solid," and with a "good head on his shoulders." It was to Chris Musser that old Jacob turned, after Rebecca died, for help in getting David Eisenhower back into Kansas.

Nothing loath, Musser promptly wrote to David in the closing months of 1890, offering a job as a mechanic or engineer. It may be that he felt somewhat guilty for having profited on the mortgage deal at David's expense. It is certain that he recognized David's very real mechanical ability. And David—sick of exile, encouraged by his wife to return—accepted the offer. The pay was not much higher than he was getting on the railroad, but no doubt the chances for advancement would be better, and at least he would be home again among friends and relatives.

It is possible, too, that David's sense of disgrace at the failure of his Hope venture was now somewhat mitigated by the fact that Jacob's own fortunes had declined. The small Hope bank in which Jacob had been interested had failed, taking with it a good portion of Jacob's savings. Fortunately Jacob had already divided much of his estate among his children. Each of the latter had by now received the standard gift of a one-hundred-and-sixty-acre farm and two thousand dollars in cash, and Amanda (or her husband), Abraham, and Ira had all made wise use of these gifts. Abraham was now established in Abilene in his dual capacity as veterinarian and River Brethren minister, though he planned to move soon to California. Ira was a River Brethren minister in Topeka, Kansas. Only David had lost his inheritance, and the family was by now willing to admit that the fault may not have been all David's.

One day in the spring of 1891, David, Ida Elizabeth, and the three children—the youngest in his mother's arms—boarded a passenger train in Denison and bade a final farewell to Texas. All that day and the following night they rode. Next morning, at Kansas City, they changed trains, boarding the Union Pacific for the ride west to Abilene. "Gateway to the West," that was the proud title Kansas City claimed for itself. Would it mark for this family the threshold of a happier future? David, riding up the valley of the Kaw, could believe so as the sense of home-coming swelled up in him. Beyond Junction City, beyond the Flint Hills, his avid gaze fed on familiar scenes until, as a climax to it all, the long sloping wave of land rolled up, bearing on its crest a cluster of trees and white houses and low brick buildings. Abilene. Home. When he stepped down beside his wife upon the station platform he carried in his pocket the sum total of his capital: twenty-four dollars. Behind him somewhere on the tracks was a freight car bearing all his worldly goods, save that ebony piano of his wife's which waited for them to claim it in the home of Mrs. Rugh.

A few days later they moved into a little house on South East Second Street, just south of the railroad tracks, a house with high-pitched gables whose one pretension to luxury was some fretted woodwork, in the style of the 1870s, at the angle formed by the pitch of the roof. Surrounding the house was a yard which proved at once too small to contain the play of Arthur and Edgar, a fact which Ida Elizabeth soon pointed out to her husband.

"I spend all my time trying to keep the boys quiet and out of other people's yards," she complained. "It's a terrible strain on both the boys and me."

Both Arthur (who was now five years old and would be ready for school next fall) and Edgar were extremely active children, and the youngest at the age of eight months gave every evidence of becoming fully as active as his brothers. If the family were already cramped for space, what would the situation be in another year or so? But there wasn't much that David could do about it at that point. His wage at the creamery was less than fifty dollars a month. He couldn't afford to rent a larger house; it required every cent he made to clothe and feed his family in the house they already had. So they stayed on in the little house, and before they finally moved from it three more children had been born there, and one had died.

The first was Roy J., born August 9, 1892. Like his brothers, he was strong, vigorous. But the fifth son, Paul A., born on May 12, 1894, had a different fate. He was sickly and in a few months he was dead. The sixth son—and by this time the parents were longing for a daughter—was born on February 1, 1898. They named him Earl D.

A few months later the move was made. David's brother Abraham owned a two-story white frame house at 201 South East Fourth Street, set at the west side of a three-acre tract on the southern outskirts of Abilene. When at last Abraham carried out his long-postponed migration westward, having sold his veterinarian's practice, he gave David the opportunity to rent the house with an option to buy later on. This seemed the perfect answer to Ida Elizabeth's prayer, and David accepted the offer eagerly. The terms were easy, partially because the father, Jacob, who had been making his home with Abraham, would stay on in the house with David.

CHAPTER IV

The Family: A Society in Miniature

Of a healthy society the family is not only a portrait in miniature, it is also the vessel of racial continuity through which the roots of the living culture can draw nourishment from a warmly human past. Out of it grow the human values which are the substance of social justice, the very essence of democracy: the values of tolerance, sympathetic understanding, self-discipline and self-sacrifice in the common good, love—all those values which are summarized in the Golden Rule. It is a measure of social disintegration and cultural decline when the family ceases to function as a vital unit. The family's authority is an *inner* one, a recognition within the individual man of ties of blood and tradition which are not alien to him but are, in the deepest metaphysical sense, his own. By this authority the individual integrity is not only maintained but strengthened. It is no accident that the great religious leaders extend the family metaphor to all mankind: God is the father, and all men are brothers. But when the family's authority dies it is replaced by an *external* authority whose tools and language and politics are those of an alien Power. The individual tends to lose his individuality; the People become the Masses.

In Central Europe the disintegration of families gave rise to a horde of rootless, frustrated, violent men, of whom one Adolfus Hitler, son of Alois Schicklgruber-Hitler, was to become both symbol and leader. He was born, a year and five months before David Dwight Eisenhower, in Braunau, Austria-Hungary, of a family so closely inbred as to be almost incestuous. The father, born himself out of wedlock, had been thrice married. For his third wife, Adolf's mother, he had chosen one Anna Polzl, a second cousin who was twenty-three years younger than himself. He was an embittered man. He had served as a minor Austrian civil servant, retiring at the early age of fifty-eight, convinced that his life had been frustrated, that lesser men had claimed rewards which properly belonged to him. He had wandered thereafter from farm to farm (apparently speculating in land) in the little townships around Linz. He was a family autocrat, short-tempered, already nearly sixty when Adolf was born, and he used his children harshly whenever they crossed his will. Adolf was often beaten. The son sided with the mother against the father so consistently that one suspects him of an Oedipus complex. He learned early to hate.

Thus Adolf Hitler, like the millions whose bloody death wish he was to personify, was born of a divided house in a divided country of a Europe seething with unrest, bleeding from the recurrent clashes of opposing ideologies. Ideologies, undigested by rational minds, shaped his education; they were a part of the very air he breathed. Old values had died—desiccated, it seemed, in an arid intellectualism —and there were no new ones to take their places. Queer things had happened to markets and to God and to family life under the economic impact of the industrial revolution and the cultural impact of the new rationalism. Nothing was certain any more. Science, reason, analysis—these had destroyed the old faiths, and whatever new faiths they proclaimed had, as a requirement of their establishment, a social revolution of some kind. Men of power and privilege grew afraid, and their fear took ugly shapes of hate. . . . Inevitably there was a revolt against science, reason, analysis. A new romanticism sought to turn the wind. Philosophers arose to deny that reason is a guide to truth. They proclaimed the supremacy of "feeling" over "thinking," of "racial blood" over "idea," of mystic dogmatism over scientific doubt, of physical power over all creative mental force. The gap between these extreme views of the world— the unfeelingly scientific and the irrationally romantic—grew wider, and in the middle ground the living symbols of compromise, fruitful compromise, withered and died one by one for lack of nourishment. Adolf Hitler and the rootless hordes were set free to pursue the only kind of power they could understand. Men on white horses, latterday imitation Caesars, would soon be roaming the Western world.

In mid-America the Eisenhowers of Abilene were, for all their misfortunes, a happy, stable family. On the whole, the father's business failure seems to have sweetened rather than embittered them. They faced life without flinching; they took the blame for their own failures and worked hard for their successes; they loved one another. They derived their individualities from their membership in the family, thought of themselves always *as* a family, and were so cohered by this deep family feeling, by religious traditions, and by economic necessity as to form a distinct, almost an organic, unit. It is difficult to tell the story of any one of them, until the sons grew up and left the home, without telling the story of all.

In both the literal and figurative meaning of the phrase, they lived on the wrong side of the tracks in their home town. The Union Pacific and Santa Fe tracks divided the community into two parts, the North Side and the South Side. On the North Side lived the merchants, doctors, lawyers, bankers—the men of weight and prestige in the community. On the South Side lived the wage earners: the railroad workers, the carpenters, the bricklayers, the mechanics, with here and there an elderly retired farmer. Perhaps this description of the town's organization is a trifle arbitrary—there was a considerable intermingling of "classes" in all sections of the community—but, generally speaking, it is a true one. The children of North Side families definitely looked down on children from the South Side. The latter were made to feel their inferiority, and this had its effect on the outlook of all the Eisenhowers, particularly on the four oldest sons. They lived at the southernmost edge of the South Side. Though respected by all who knew them, they had no social prestige whatever. They were common people, poor people. In the face of active or passive snobbery they developed an acute sense of their own togetherness, of their individual responsibilities to one another. They did not bewail the injustice of their lot. They were determined in spite of it, or even because of it, to succeed.

Since they were convinced that they could make their way up the ladder of success, their low social and economic status in the community developed in the sons no active sense of class and class-allegiance. They were completely isolated from the ideological storms which swept older lands where the economy had "matured." Politics did not interest them, save as an opportunity for picnics and torchlight parades. Even from the agrarian radicalism which arose in Kansas in the 1890s they were isolated. David, the father, quietly supported McKinley in 1896, disavowing the Populists and Bryan and Free Silver. Arthur, the eldest son, vividly remembered in later years how he carried a torch for McKinley through the streets of Abilene on a mild October evening. The great issue of that year meant nothing to him, nor to the others.

Their only "ideology," if it may be called that, was their religion, which was "other-worldly" in its emphasis. One night each week was devoted to Bible study. The family had three Bibles, the one in Greek which David read, a German one belonging to Jacob in which the record of births and deaths was written, and the King James version which the mother and the children read. At the weekly family Bible meeting the children took turns reading biblical passages, which were then discussed, not critically but very seriously as the unquestionable Word of God. All of the boys got to know the Bible well and memorized long passages of it, so that in later years they often surprised their associates by quoting chapter and verse to embroider an argument. On Sundays the whole family went to Sunday school in the River Brethren meeting house. Their uncle Chris Musser was Sunday-school superintendent, and Aunt Amanda sometimes taught the boys' Sunday-school class. Mrs. Ida Hoffman, however, was the regular teacher, and years later she would remember how fidgety the Eisenhower boys were and how they never seemed to pay any attention or take any interest in the lesson. After Sunday school the boys came home to do the cooking and the housework, while the parents stayed on for church services. Sunday was the parents' day off.

The rather strict religious training which the boys received did not, perhaps, produce the precise effect which the parents desired. None of the boys was converted to any strict orthodoxy. None of them became particularly "religious" in the ordinary meaning of that term. Indeed, all the boys would seem later to react against religious dogma and insist upon subjecting it to a rational examination. But whatever his personal beliefs about God and immortality, each boy was to retain all his life long a profound respect for the moral tenets which the parents derived, or thought they derived, from their religion. The boys might say that around the core of mystical nonsense was a good solid husk of common sense. They shucked off the husk and threw away the core.

Though David had been reared in a German-speaking community and could read and speak German, he refused to do so around the house. Some of the sons later studied German as a subject in school, but they were not encouraged in this by the father. He seems to have sought deliberately to cut the ties of language and, to some extent, of custom, which bound him to the Old World. He wanted his children to be, in quite an exclusive sense, American.

After the move to the house on South East Fourth Street, the economy of the family was somewhat improved, but this was due more to the fact that the new property yielded all the family's food than to any increase in the father's cash income. David's work in the creamery, though it carried the euphonious title of "engineer," continued to be in actual fact that of a mechanic. Early in the 1900s he strove once again to make himself an engineer in fact. He enrolled for engineering courses in the International Correspondence Schools, studied them assiduously, and received on December 31, 1904, a certificate of completion for the following courses: "Arithmetic, Mechanics, Steam and Steam Engines, Dynamos and Motors, and Mensuration." In 1944 the certificate, neatly framed, would still be hanging on the wall of an upstairs room in his house. He had every right to be proud of it. But one cannot say that his pay was increased much, if any, by this extra industry of his. In all his twenty years at the creamery it is doubtful that his pay was ever as high as one hundred dollars a month. Indeed, he was never to make more than two hundred dollars a month at any time in his life, and he did not make that much until the second decade of the new century was far advanced and all of his children, except the youngest, had left home.

2

The fact that on this low cash income, low even for the Abilene of those days, six healthy boys could be reared, and reared with outstanding success, is a tribute to the mother, Ida Elizabeth. She passed a minor miracle of industry and management.

One can imagine her wandering through the house before they moved into it in the last year of the nineteenth century, studying it, carefully judging its strengths and weaknesses. There would be more room here, certainly. Two stories and an attic. From the outside the house looked rather more than presentable. It was quite nice, really, all neatly painted in white, standing up on its corner lot with great stretches of space for light and air on all sides of it. The front door opened to the south. The front yard was narrow; only a few steps separated the sidewalk (which would not be paved with brick for many years) from the front porch, which ran the full width of the house; but back or north of the house was a large yard in which the children could play—and of course there was all that space to the east, almost three acres. To the west, across Chestnut Street, was

Lincoln Grade School which, with its large playground, occupied the whole of one block. The children, when not actually in the schoolroom, would be under the mother's eyes all day. She'd not have to worry about their crossing streets and getting themselves into mischief on long daily treks to a distant building. Inside the house was nice too. Perhaps the rooms were a trifle small, but there were a lot of them, and that would be an advantage for a large family. With so many children, privacy for anyone was at a premium, and the more rooms, the more privacy. Even so, they'd have to double up in the bedrooms.

One can also imagine her wandering over the land adjoining the house, viewing it through calculating eyes, estimating its various resources. Here was her kingdom. She must organize it for defense against want and, if possible, for conquest of a higher standard of living. What forces were at her command?

Well, there was the barn, for one thing. It was a huge barn, one of the largest in the community, and it stood on the north edge of the large back yard, facing Chestnut Street. There were stalls for horses, and shelter for whatever other animals they chose to raise. The barn door was large enough to permit passage of a team and wagon. There was an immense hayloft which could hold seven or eight tons of loose prairie hay, just about the amount that an acre of land east of the house would produce in a year. They'd be able to feed their livestock with the produce of their own land. . . . Of course the hayloft and those steeply sloping roofs, thirty feet off the ground at their highest point, would be a temptation for children, and she'd have to lay down some strict rules for their play there; otherwise they'd be breaking bones in long falls. At the very pinnacle of the roof, facing the street, was a large square sign which said, "Dr. A. L. Eisenhower, Veterinarian." Extending in a wing south of the main structure was the old operating theater, thirty by eighty feet in size: another play place for the children.

The family could and would have a horse. They'd need one to haul produce, as well as for drawing the buggy, though most of the plowing would be done by hired teams from near-by farms. They'd have two cows, chickens, ducks, guinea hens, pigs (they were to have five or so at a time), and Belgian hares. They'd have their own milk and eggs. They'd cure their own meat. In the back yard was a smokehouse, a little shack beneath which was a trench that extended beyond the confines of the walls. In this trench beyond the walls a smoldering fire would be built, the trench would be covered with boards, the smoke would all go into the shack where the meat was hanging. They could use ordinary kindling wood for this; it would do quite well enough.

They'd have a very large garden, of course, approximately a half acre in size, fenced in for protection against the chickens. Irrigated and intensively cultivated, it would supply all the family's vegetables, with a surplus for sale. Potatoes, cabbage, tomatoes, onions, radishes, lettuce, sweet corn, beets, peas, beans—it would be hard to name a vegetable they wouldn't raise. They were even to raise celery, carefully heaping up the earth along the stalks to blanch them. At one side of the garden they'd have a strawberry patch, twenty by thirty feet in size, which would not only give them all the strawberries they could eat, but yield a small surplus for sale. Beyond the garden fence a small orchard of fruit trees would be set out which would give them an abundance of cherries, apples, and pears. A small vineyard would yield all they needed of grapes, with a surplus for sale. The mother could be counted upon to keep the fruit jars well filled and the pie shelf in the pantry loaded with fruit pies. An acre of hay and an acre of field corn, or kaffir, would also be planted each year for stock feed, and the crops would be rotated so that soil fertility would be maintained, in the tradition of Pennsylvania Dutch husbandry. The land was completely surrounded by a row of maple trees which, later on, would be topped because they sucked so much moisture and plant food from the ground.

A lot of hard work would be needed, certainly. Everyone would have to pitch in and do his share. But if the work was well planned and properly directed it would still leave time for children's play— and in any case it wouldn't hurt the boys at all to learn early that only through hard, honest effort can any real progress be made in the world. There was, in the family as she managed it, a time for everything: a time for work and a time for play, a time for careless fun and a time for serious contemplation, a time to sleep and a time to arise. For all of them she conquered time and made it subservient to their wills.

The day began for them with the sunrise in the summer, and long before sunrise in the winter. During the winter months the boy who had the responsibility of building the fire in the stove must arise at five o'clock. This particular chore, a most unpopular one, was rotated among the boys, so that no one of them had to do it for more than a week at a time. Of all the boys, Dwight was the hardest to arouse in the mornings. During the week that he was assigned the fire-building detail everyone in the family was awakened before Dwight was cajoled or threatened out of his warm bed. Next came the milking and stock-feeding chores. Out into the iron-cold of a winter dawn trooped the mother and all the sons who were big enough to help. The mother did most of the milking. Arthur, though he tried hard enough, could never learn to draw the milk down properly—and it was not until Edgar managed to learn, later on, that the mother was sometimes relieved of this chore. After the milking she went back into the house to prepare breakfast while the boys fed and watered the horse, the cows, the pigs, the poultry. There were eggs to gather. There was kindling to be split. Sometimes the father helped, but often he had been called out to the creamery in the middle of the night to repair a machinery breakdown, so that he slept as late as possible in the morning. By the time the older boys were in from the yard and the younger ones were dressed and downstairs, a big breakfast was waiting. There were steaming cups of coffee to warm chilled bodies and great quantities of food for sharpened appetites: eggs, bacon or ham or sausages, often stacks of buckwheat cakes richly buttered and soaked in syrup.

In the summertime the garden and the fields were the centers of home work. Here again each boy had his assigned task. Edgar and Dwight did most of the planting, for they had what the mother called "planters' hands," and things grew well for them. They managed the hotbeds and from them transplanted the tomatoes and cabbage plants into the garden rows. Much of the marketing of surplus vegetables was done by house-to-house sale. The horse would be hitched to the buggy, the buggy piled high with vegetables, and two of the boys would drive up to the North Side to sell to the "rich" people across the tracks. Sometimes a coaster wagon was used for this marketing. In addition each of the boys, as soon as he was old enough, went to work in the Belle Springs Creamery, firing furnaces, making boxes, washing cream cans, pulling ice, and so on. The family badly needed the full use of each boy's earning power. Once a boy went to work in the creamery, his share of the chores was assigned, so far as possible, to a boy who still had no outside work.

They were all of the earth, earthy. Not for them the dull pain of feeling themselves cut off from the world, forever imprisoned incommunicado on an island of self. They felt themselves to be rooted, organically rooted, in the soil. They knew reality through their hands and eyes and ears, through numberless pleasant and painful contacts with it. Arthur, in later years, would offer an explanation in almost lyrical terms of the fact that he had had to visit a doctor only three times in thirty-nine years. He'd say that in his belief the goodness of the good earth on the Eisenhower acres had somehow entered his body and the bodies of all the other boys. He'd remember the sense of well-being which flooded over him when the boys rested under the hot sun in the corn rows, digging their bare feet into the loose soil—the cool, health-giving soil. He'd have a phrase which he'd repeat musingly: "With the brothers gathered round and my feet in the cool soil." They loved good food, and often at the table one of them would slip a morsel of special "goody" under the plate in order to display it later in triumph and eat it with gusto before the envious eyes of the brothers who had finished eating. The favorite food for all of them was "pudding meat," a Pennsylvania Dutch dish consisting of all the last scraps from a freshly butchered hog, preserved in lard and melted out on cold winter days to be eaten, preferably, with fried mush. In later years all of the boys would agree with Aunt Amanda that very few people know how to make good "pudding." ("It's the liver that gives the flavor," she says emphatically. "Lots of people don't put in the liver, and it's flat without it.") They'd pay extremely fancy prices for jars of the "real thing," Arthur going as high on one occasion as a dollar a pound. . . .

The family discipline was rigid. If a boy failed to do a good job of, say, hoeing the corn, he was at once sent back to do it over, even though it was late in the evening. Any attempt to play hooky from an assigned chore brought swift and generally corporeal punishment. One knew, therefore, that during worktime he must give all of himself to work. But one also knew that during playtime he could give all of himself to play. The time for play was an earned right, and the energy for play was not qualified or diffused by the nagging conviction, deep down, that one really should be doing something else: hoeing, or choring, or studying. Thus one educative function of the mother's management, imposed by necessity but carried through with a profound living wisdom, was to develop in each boy a resilient, decisive, truly integrated personality. The capacity for productive work, for getting things *done,* which the boys were to display in later years, would frequently amaze their associates.

It would not be because they had a great deal more energy than most men, but because they knew how to use the energy they had. They would not be attenuated by an excess of self-doubt, nor divided by an incapacity to choose among a multitude of possibilities. They'd forget themselves in their work. They'd think habitually in terms of program. They would be, in the literal meaning of the phrase, self-controlled.

3

Fortunately the mother was able to plan her work efficiently, to work very hard, and then to relax completely and let her strength be renewed. If she had not been able to do so she must have broken under the burdens she had to bear. There was nothing soft or easy about her life. There was so much to think about, so much which, in a less remarkable woman, might have dissipated vital energy in a futile and all-pervasive anxiety. Economic pressures, the necessity to bolster her husband's morale, the often serious injuries which the boys suffered in accidents—always there was some matter of vital importance which required, on her part, quick, sure decisions and a wide variety of skills. She became a skillful practical nurse, for one thing, and in this capacity she served not only her own family but the neighborhood as well. From among the myriad crucial scenes in which she played the leading role, here are two which give insight into the character of the family at the turn of the century:

One day when Earl was three or four he was playing in the tool shed while Dwight was busy at the workbench making a toy. Dwight had been using a butcher knife and had carefully laid it on a window sill so that the inquisitive Earl couldn't reach it. But while Dwight's attention was occupied Earl managed to drag a chair below the sill, climb up on it, and reach for the knife. He couldn't quite grasp the handle, but he dragged the knife to the edge of the sill with his finger tips until it fell, blade down, striking him in the left eye.

He screamed. Dwight, terror-stricken, swept him up in his arms and ran with him to the house. There the mother soothed both of them, bathed the injured eye, and sent Dwight running for the doctor. But there wasn't much that a doctor could do. The sight in that eye was seriously impaired. Dwight was heartbroken. Several years later Earl and a brother were playing with a crokinole board in the music room, next to the ebony piano. In the roughness of their play a crokinole peg struck Earl directly in the already injured eye. The pain was horrible, and the sight in that eye was completely and permanently extinguished.

But the significant fact is that these injuries to Earl were never spoken of in the family. The mother would not have her children going through life reproaching themselves, or each other, for accidents of childhood. These things happen, she might have said. They are no one's fault. Any life truly lived is a risky business, and if one puts up too many fences against the risks one ends by shutting out life itself. You should avoid the bad things as much as possible, of course, but when they come you must take them without flinching, without useless recriminations, and certainly without a self-destroying bitterness. . . .

The second scene involves her youngest son, Milton Stover.

He was born on September 15, 1899, only a few months after the family had moved. The parents had prayed for a girl, and it is reported that the birth of still another son so disappointed the father that he walked for miles through the town before he could bring his unhappiness under control. Perhaps it was the parents' disappointment which caused them to let Milton's hair grow long, like a girl's; it curled around a sensitive face which, so framed, looked girlish. The parents gave him more attention than they had the elder sons. Otherwise the baby boy was like the others, sturdy and strong, and he early learned to regard his long curls as a crown of thorns. It was in his fourth year that he awoke one morning to find his throat aching, his eyes burning, his face flushed with fever. He whimpered, and the six-year-old Earl, who shared his bedroom, carried the report to the mother.

The family doctor, Dr. Conklin, Sr., was summoned and, after an examination, named the disease. Scarlet fever! Horror swept the family. Scarlet fever was an even more dreadful disease in those days than it is now, and the proportion of fatalities was high. Those who survived always suffered, it seemed, some terrible aftereffect. Moreover, the disease was highly contagious. The whole family was threatened! There would have to be a quarantine, six long weeks of it. Six weeks. If the entire family were imprisoned for that long, if David could not go to his work in the creamery, nor Arthur and Dwight and Edgar go to school and do their outside work to pad the income, the family would suffer economic catastrophe. They'd have to go deeply into debt. How would they ever pay for the doctor and the medicine?

The doctor listened sympathetically while David and Ida Elizabeth presented their case. There'd have to be a strict quarantine, of course. The health of the community demanded it. But had anyone except the mother and Earl been in close contact with Milton since the latter became ill? No. And Milton had developed his symptoms only in the last few hours? Yes. Well, then, perhaps something could be worked out. Perhaps it would not be necessary to quarantine the whole family and the whole house. Perhaps the room in which Milton lay, and the room next to it, could be sealed off from the rest of the house and the mother, with Milton and Earl, kept there. Of course it would be a terrible ordeal for the mother and Earl. The two rooms were very small, and six weeks is a long, long time—especially for an active six-year-old boy. But if this were done the father could continue his work and the other children could go to school. Moreover, these others would be protected against contagion. The mother did not hesitate. She agreed at once to the arrangement.

Earl would remember those six weeks as the most horrible experience of his life. There was barely enough space in the two rooms for him to move around in. He couldn't even make a normal amount of noise because Milton was so terribly ill. The disease hung over him, too, as a constant threat, and the determined mother dosed him constantly with sulphur and molasses, a nauseating concoction. The only person he saw from outside was the doctor. Food, cooked by Dwight or Edgar or the father, was slipped through the doorway, which was kept open just long enough to receive it. Only through closed doors could the imprisoned ones communicate with the rest of the family.

Milton's illness was, in itself, a thing of almost Dostoevskian horror. For a week the fever raged so high that the four-year-old boy lay alternating between a raving madness and total unconsciousness. The mother fought desperately for his life, using cold packs, bathing his face, soothing him when feverish nightmares terrified him. The doctor, looking down at the tortured figure on the bed, shook his head gravely. Death seemed almost certain. Even if the boy survived, there would be incalculable and permanent consequences. So high a fever might impair the brain tissues, might leave the boy blind or deaf, might in short leave him worse than dead. But the fever departed at last, and the boy lay white and weak—so weak that he could scarcely move. He was only barely alive—but he lived. And even then the horror was not ended. Earl would remember all too vividly the pustule which formed on Milton's neck, a huge, ugly thing. It was as though all the disease-wasted tissues in the sick boy's body were gathering there, putrefying. When it broke a full cup of black, thick ooze came out, a syrupy mass of blood and pus.

They waited then through the long weeks of convalescence to see what the aftereffects would be. The doctor tried to prepare them for the worst. They watched, too, for symptoms of the disease in Earl. Both watches ended more happily than had been anticipated. Milton was left terribly weak, and many years passed before his physical strength matched that of his brothers, but the only permanent injury which the disease gave him was a weakening of the eyes. This was a handicap, certainly, for one whose career was to lead through journalism to government administration and, in the 1940s, to the presidency of a college; but it was not so serious as to lessen perceptibly the effectiveness of the man. His eyes in later years would have a tendency to dance and dart, focusing for only a second or so on any one object, but this disability would be so minor as to go unnoticed until attention was called to it. Earl, who had suffered so many dosings with sulphur and molasses, who had been soaped and scrubbed repeatedly and had had his hair washed in formaldehyde, never caught scarlet fever at all—nor did anyone else in the family.

4

This family, a self-contained economic and cultural unit, a self-contained society in miniature with relatively few necessary links to the larger society surrounding it, came to the end of an era in 1905. On March 4 of that year Arthur, the eldest son, left home to make his way in the world. His was, in a way, a pioneering task. He was to prove in the larger world the efficacy of the family's values. His success or failure would provide a measure of self-confidence for the younger brothers when they, too, at last left home.

He was eighteen years old. Among his assets were a strong body, a quick intelligence, an unshakable personal honesty, a habit of hard work, and a dogged but not overly confident ambition for a business success. He had little else. When he boarded the Union Pacific for Kansas City he carried with him a green valise, bound with straps, which contained all his clothes save those he wore. In his pockets were a few dollars, barely enough to feed and shelter him while he searched for a job, and a letter of introduction to the Lombards, whose financial interests in the Kansas City of those days included the Cornbelt Bank and the Lombard Investment Company. Unlike the brothers who were to follow him, he had no tradition of fraternal success to sustain or inspire him. It was he who must initiate that tradition.

Before the train pulled out from the station he was homesick. It was with an almost tearful emotion, a sense of helpless loneliness, that he looked out upon the station platform. His mother was not standing there. She had not accompanied him to the station. She disliked public farewells, as she disliked any public display of emotion, and so she always said her good-bys on the little side porch of the Eisenhower home looking across the street toward the school. She smiled as she said them to Arthur, while Dwight and the others looked on, and she gave him cheerful, voluble advice. Not until many years later did her children discover that, when Arthur was gone and she was in her bedroom, she wept bitterly. She could feel her children growing away from her, straining against the ties of the family, and breaking them at last, one by one, until she was alone.

The Union Pacific station in Kansas City stood, in those days, in "The Bottoms," near where the Kansas and Missouri rivers flow together. Arthur, stepping off the train, could see from the station platform the house on the river bluff which had been carefully described to him, the house where he was to rent a room. It seemed a long way off, and the valise was heavy. Assuming a casual self-confidence he was far from feeling, he went up to the first of a series of horse-drawn hacks which were tied up at the station rail.

"Yes *sir*," said the driver, reaching for the valise.

But Arthur drew back.

"How much?" he asked.

"How much to where?"

"To that house up there."

The driver looked in the direction indicated and said, as he again reached for the valise, "Fifty cents."

Arthur backed away, disconcerted. Then he turned and almost fled down the platform. To a boy who had been working in the Belle Springs Creamery for eleven dollars a month, fifty cents represented an enormous expenditure of effort, far more than would be required to carry the heavy valise up to that house on the bluff. No doubt dismay was evident in his facial expression, for as he went up the platform he was accosted by a man in an official-looking cap who addressed him as "sonny" and asked what the trouble was. The man, evidently an official of the road or of an express company, seemed sympathetic. Arthur explained his trouble, leaving out the fact that the fifty-cent fare had frightened him.

"I can drive you up," the man said in a kindly tone. He gestured toward a spring wagon tied up at the rail. "Hop in."

Arthur gratefully mounted the wagon, and in a minute or two he was joined by the driver, who gossiped cheerfully as they rode through the dirty streets of "The Bottoms" and up the winding drive which climbed the bluff. In front of the boardinghouse he stopped. Arthur climbed down, tugging the valise. He thanked the driver profusely.

"Glad to help you out," the driver said. "That'll be fifty cents, please."

Arthur's jaw dropped. He reddened under the driver's quizzical gaze. Then in black despair he pulled out his pocketbook, took from it a fifty-cent piece, and deposited the coin in the driver's outstretched hand.

"Thanks, sonny," the driver said cheerfully. "And good luck to you."

It was hardly an auspicious opening for a financial career, and if there were elements of humor in the boy's discomfiture they escaped him at the time. Alone in his room, he was overcome by dark forebodings. He pulled out his letter of introduction to the Lombards and read it through. He knew now that he'd never have the courage to present it; the Lombards were too big, too important, to be approached by a green, gawky country kid. That evening he noticed in the Kansas City *Star* an advertisement for office help, inserted by a firm of hay dealers. He applied for the job next day and was accepted.

He had studied bookkeeping, typing, and shorthand in Abilene. He used all three skills on his first job. For various reasons he was unhappy. He was homesick. He disliked his work, perhaps because he was not particularly efficient in it, and he disliked his employer because the latter outraged his country piety. The employer, it appears, was among the most profane of men, going so far as to dictate profanity into his letters. This meant that Arthur was forced to transcribe a series of oaths which, to him, seemed almost personal insults. He was getting a mere five dollars a week, barely enough to live on even in that era of expensive money, and he quickly decided that the pay was not high enough to compensate the damage done his morals. In late April he took his letter of introduction, which he had saved, and his courage, which was now somewhat restored, and went with them to the Lombards, who promptly offered him a job. The pay was considerably higher than the hay dealer's would meet and the job itself seemed, to Arthur, almost too important for one of his limited experience. It worried him. Nevertheless, he took pleasure in presenting to his employer his resignation, effective immediately.

He was not to report for work at the Lombards' for a few days, and in the interim his fear of the new job grew by leaps and bounds. He had none of that awareness of general family ability which was to help his younger brothers toward a poised self-assurance. His father had failed in business; he was desperately afraid of failure himself. He seems to have inherited much of his father's diffidence, which, combined with his later business success, gave rise to the impression among some of his cousins that he was "snooty" and "conceited." On the second day of his wait he walked past the office building where he was to work and saw, from the street, that a new office was being fitted out. The realization swept over him that this new office was to be his. His! The Lombards had told him he'd have one. He stared. Then he walked away, almost ran away. When he had recovered somewhat he walked back to the financial district and put his application in at every firm that would accept it between Wyandotte Street and Grand Avenue on Tenth Street. He never went back to the Lombards, who, since they had failed to obtain his address, had no way to reach him.

On May 1 he went to work as a messenger boy for the Commerce Trust Company, one of the firms at which he'd applied on his day of fear. The job was by no means as grand as the one at the Lombards' had promised to be, but Arthur was happy in it. Nor was he ever to regret his decision—if so instinctive a reaction may be called a decision. As Kansas City grew, the Commerce Trust Company prospered, growing with successive mergers until it became one of the largest banks in the Middle West. Within the organization Arthur climbed steadily toward the vice-president's chair he was to occupy in the 1930s and after. Soon the people of Abilene began to hear that Arthur was "doing well in the city," that he was "on his way to making a pot of money." The first of the Eisenhower "success stories" was begun.

In the following year—May 20, 1906—Jacob Eisenhower, he who had for so long preached River Brethren doctrine and who had led the family migration from Pennsylvania, died in the house on South East Fourth Street. He was in his eightieth year and had long been feeble. His death served to emphasize the era's end.

With him died from the family all living memory of that regionalized agrarian America which, after a last titanic effort of civil war, gave way to the continental, industrialized, urbanized power. However isolated the Kansas family might be, or appear to be, the sons would be swept one by one into gigantic currents of change. Arthur's career would rise with the growth of monopoly capital in the Middle West, Edgar's with the growth of West Coast corporations, Earl's with the electrification of the country, Milton's with the expansion of government bureaucracy, and Dwight's with the bloody birth of a new world organization through two global wars. Only Roy would seem to keep out of the main stream of history, and even he, as a civic leader in a small Kansas town, would play a quiet part in the great drama of transition.

BOOK TWO

Youth in Kansas

CHAPTER I

The Emerging Individual

THE MOTHER had named her third son after his father, but almost from the first she called him by his middle name, Dwight. She did so for two reasons. In the first place, it was confusing to have two Davids in the family. Whenever she called to one the other was likely to respond. And in the second place, she happened to dislike nicknames. A person ought to be called by his right name, she firmly believed, and it annoyed her that Arthur should be called "Art" and Edgar "Ed." She was determined that her third son should have a name which could not be shortened or otherwise abused. By the time this third son had graduated from high school he himself had reversed the names. When he registered at West Point he did so as Dwight David Eisenhower.

Even so the mother was foiled again. The perfect and inevitable front name for an Eisenhower is "Ike," and when Edgar and Dwight went to school that nickname was applied to both of them. Edgar became "Big Ike" and Dwight "Little Ike," and the same names were applied later on to the two youngest sons, Earl and Milton. The mother, however, steadfastly refused to recognize these nicknames. In later years, whenever anyone spoke of her most famous son as Ike she'd shake her head and frown in a puzzled way, though her eyes twinkled.

"Ike?" she'd say. "Who's Ike?"

Who was he? Only gradually did he emerge from the close-knit family character to assume an individuality, a personality of his own, and even then his personality was not a striking one. It presented few salient features on which a writer might hang the telling word, the striking phrase. Of his first seven years no significant anecdotes survive. He was one of many, neither the oldest nor the youngest, and his story was submerged in the story of the family. He was, in all respects, "normal." He had cried neither more nor less than most infants. He had learned to walk and talk at a normal age. There was nothing obviously precocious about him.

In only one respect, but an extremely important respect, was he farther advanced (as were his brothers) than most children are at the same age. Each individual begins his life with a tacit, infantile assumption that he and the world are one. Only gradually and painfully does he learn to disentangle the self from the non-self, the ego from the environment, and of course many people never learn this lesson really well but remain childishly egocentric all their lives long. In Dwight's case, however, this process of disentanglement was quite abrupt and final. In so large and hard-pressed a family he received none of that special attention to personal whim which might have tended to set him apart, in his own mind, as a being of special rights and importance, with special claims upon the world. His social attitudes were early matured. The desires of others were as important in the total scheme of things as his own desires—often in the first years they were more important—and he learned this great social lesson so soon and so thoroughly that it became an integral, instinctive part of his personality. Out of it would arise that mental quality of selflessness and objectivity which, in later years, would seem so remarkable to all who knew him well.

There is valid symbolism in the fact that the earliest authentic anecdote of Dwight, the very first clear glimpse we get of him through the memories of his older brothers, reveals him in the yard of the house on South East Second Street moodily rocking a baby buggy containing an infant brother. This was in the late spring of 1898, and the baby brother was Earl, who had been born on February 1 of that year. The seven-year-old Dwight performed his unwelcome chore in a somewhat unusual manner. He lay flat on his back on the grass beneath the buggy, grasped that annoying vehicle by its back axle, swung it forward, caught the front axle, swung it back, and so on, for all the period of his servitude. A couple of years later Dwight rocked his youngest brother Milton in precisely the same way. It was his "patented process" of baby tending.

His early pictures—formal family photographs taken when he was a junior and senior in high school, casual photographs showing him in the yard with his brothers—reveal a boy of medium height, perhaps a trifle small for his age. His light hair is neatly combed—obviously a concession to the photographer. His regularly featured and rather thin-cheeked face appears freshly scrubbed and gives an impression of eager vitality. The lips are unsmiling, but one can tell that they must smile easily, for the face as a whole appears more than commonly mobile and expressive. There is no apparent self-consciousness before the camera. His eyes look directly into the lens, and the directness and candor of that gaze are the most remarkable things about the pictures. They are the things which, forty years later, would remain unchanged.

That level-eyed gaze somehow gives the feel of reality to the only extant information about Dwight's mental traits during those first years of his life. He had, according to Arthur and Edgar, a passion to *know*. His mind was stimulated by ideas, but it derived its greatest satisfaction from facts. A casual statement of alleged fact would arouse him to investigate, to determine whether the statement was true or false. He liked to have the exact names for objective things: trees, plants of all kinds, machinery parts, the tools he used. He wanted things clear and definite. Vagueness seems to have exasperated him; it moved him only to clear away the vagueness and establish, solidly and certainly in his mind, the facts as they really are "out there."

"If I were to say those flowers out there were Dutch iris, and he thought they were Japanese iris, he'd go out and examine them," Edgar would explain in later years. "If he couldn't tell by that, he'd get out the books and look them up. His curiosity is inexhaustible. It always was."

His early life, however, was almost exclusively physical rather than mental in its interests. In grade school he and Edgar were considered average students. They were more interested in athletics than in books. Physically Dwight developed more slowly than Edgar, who in any case was the elder by almost two years, which makes a great difference in the physical size and strength of a growing boy. The fights which so frequently punctuated their relationship were always won by Edgar. The beatings which Dwight suffered at his brother's hands did not prevent the two from being great friends most of the time, and they certainly did not deter Dwight from fighting again whenever the two quarreled, but they did rankle in the younger boy's mind as the years passed. One gathers that a major ambition of Dwight's through all those years was to "lick Ed" just once and pay him back for past wrongs.

The mother's attitude toward these recurrent battles was (despite her religious "pacifism") one of *laissez faire*. One day when relatives were visiting her Dwight and Edgar began fighting in the yard. The relatives called the mother's attention to it. The mother merely smiled and shook her head.

"But aren't you going to stop it?" one of the visitors asked.

"They have to get it out of their system," the mother said composedly. "You can't keep healthy boys from scrapping. It isn't good to interfere too much."

On another occasion, a Saturday morning, the mother was doing her week-end baking over the old coal stove when a fight broke out between Dwight and Edgar, who were also in the kitchen. Earl, who had been playing with Milton in the dining room, rushed to the kitchen to see Edgar sitting astride the prostrate Dwight, giving the latter an unmerciful pounding. Edgar was shouting "Give up?" and Dwight was yelling "No!" Then Edgar grasped Dwight's hair and began to thump the younger boy's head upon the floor. Dwight began sobbing, though still stubbornly refusing to "give up." It was more than Earl could stand, and he started across the kitchen to help Dwight. The mother, without turning from the stove, said sharply to Earl, "Let them alone." Five minutes later Dwight and Edgar were friends again, playing together in the yard.

Undoubtedly this attitude of hers was born of a profound knowledge of the character of her sons. Edgar's superior size and strength gave him an unfair advantage over the younger boy when the two fought together, but on the other hand Dwight had a dangerous, ugly temper when aroused. On one occasion, when Dwight was twelve, he flared up in sudden violent anger against Arthur over some trifling incident. A brick was lying at his feet, and before he had regained control of himself he had seized that brick and flung it with all his might at the head of his oldest brother. Fortunately Arthur managed to duck in time; Dwight had fully intended to hit him. A temper like that must be curbed else it prove seriously injurious to others and, especially, to the boy himself. Perhaps the fights with Edgar which forced him to yield, at least physically, to another's will would help him to learn self-control.

However often and violently they might fight each other, they stood together against outsiders—as did all the Eisenhower boys. Time and again one of them came to the aid of another when attacks were made by boys outside the family. Earl, for instance, fought often and bitterly on behalf of Milton, whose temper exceeded his physical strength in the years following his bout with scarlet fever.

For them the world was neatly divided into Eisenhowers and non-Eisenhowers, and their allegiance to the former was absolute. Both Edgar and Dwight would, in later years, describe the family of their youth as a "closed ring."

The two were the "ornery" ones of the family. They encouraged each other to explore the outermost margins of safety, courting danger deliberately as a pleasurable element in their play. All the Eisenhower boys loved to play tag on the barn roof, and they used to dare one another to go to the very edge of that roof and lean over the sheer drop to the ground. But Dwight and Edgar were not satisfied with this amount of risk. They insisted on climbing to the very pinnacle of the roof and up onto the veterinarian's sign which Dr. Eisenhower had erected there. They'd sit astride that sign and hang down from it, thrilling to the realization that a fall from that height would almost certainly mean death. The mother whipped them repeatedly for this; she had issued flat orders prohibiting play on the roof. But not long after each punishment the boys would be up there again. No doubt their awareness that being caught would mean punishment added to the thrill of their play.

Once, while prowling through an attic room above the operating theater, they found an unopened bottle of beer. They didn't know who had left it there, nor what to do with it; they were too young to consider drinking it themselves. Finally they carried it out into the yard and, on a sudden inspiration, caught a hen. Dwight held the hen while Edgar poured the beer into her.

"From that time until her death she was the craziest thing you ever saw," Edgar recalled forty years later. "She never walked. She always ran or flew. And I can remember one time when she decided to raise a family and Mother set her on a nest somewhere near the other nests. But every time this hen came off, she came off on the fly, circled the barn once or twice, and went back to the nest. It seems to me she never stopped to eat, drink, or scratch, and she never raised any chickens."

They made games of their work, encouraged in this by the mother. Sunday, as we have seen, was the parents' day off, and the boys had all the cooking and housework to do that day. They came straight home from Sunday school to prepare the Sunday dinner while the father and mother stayed in church for the sermon. Dwight and Edgar were the official cooks. From all accounts they were quite good ones. It is doubtful, however, if the family would have enjoyed the pastries the boys concocted if they'd always known just how those pastries were prepared.

One favorite story in the family concerned an apple pie which Dwight and Edgar prepared one Sunday morning. Edgar made some slighting remark to Dwight, who promptly let fly at him with a handful of dough. Thereafter, for several minutes, the two played baseball with the dough, dropping it on the floor once or twice in the process. By the time the boys heard their parents drive up in the buggy the kitchen was a mess and the dough was several shades darker than it should have been. Hurriedly Dwight collected the grimy dough, dumped it onto the breadboard, flattened it out with a rolling pin, and shaped it into the pie tins. Meanwhile Edgar policed the kitchen. The parents noticed nothing wrong when they entered. Browning in the oven concealed the grayness of the dough, and when the parents ate the pie they pronounced it "pretty good for kid cooks," though the crust was, perhaps, a trifle heavy. Some years passed before Dwight and Edgar told the true story of that pie.

They roamed far afield—all through Abilene and out into the surrounding country—in their search for adventure. One spring, when the boys were about eight and ten respectively, a series of exceptionally heavy rains brought the Smoky Hill and its tributary creeks out of their banks around Abilene. The brown water of Mud Creek covered parts of Abilene itself. Dwight and Edgar, starting out from home shortly before noon to carry a lunch to their father in the creamery, made a wide detour to watch the flood. Up against the railroad embankment they found an old boat, a leaky affair with no oars in it; the owner, if any, was not in sight. The boys climbed in. Down through the town south of the tracks they drifted with the stream, until a man standing on a sidewalk above the flood called to them. They had found a board to use as a paddle by this time and they pulled over to where the man was standing. He wanted them to ferry him across the flooded area. He'd pay them twenty-five cents if they would. Twenty-five cents! It was a small fortune to boys who rarely had any pocket money. They accepted promptly, ferried the man across, and proudly pocketed the quarter.

They thought they had found the best of all possible ways to make money. They began to tour the flooded area in their boat, searching for other ferry fares. They found none, but they did pick up some other boys, and all of them floated down a large drainage ditch bordering Buckeye Street toward Mud Creek. Loudly they sang

"Marching through Georgia," until some big boys climbed into the boat and sank it. Dripping wet, the boys climbed up on dry land. Mr. Volkman, one of the Eisenhower neighbors, was passing by. At the sight of Dwight and Edgar he stopped abruptly.

"Your mother is looking for you," he said ominously. The boys looked guiltily at each other as the man went on, "Do you know that it is now the middle of the afternoon, and you haven't brought your father his lunch?"

They had completely forgotten not only their father's lunch but their own! On the mother's list of crimes this would rank among the highest. Slowly, reluctantly, they made their way home. They found their mother waiting for them with two large maple switches in her hand. She hustled them upstairs, forced them to strip off their wet and muddy clothes, and then gave them the worst whippings they ever received. To disobey her orders was bad enough. To flout so flagrantly the father's authority smacked of high treason against the family. She sent them, hungry as they were, to bed without supper. Never again did the boys forget the father's lunch.

They did, however, have other flood experiences. Both of them in later years would vividly remember the great flood in the spring of 1903, the greatest flood in the history of Kansas. The Smoky Hill was miles wide. Much of Abilene's South Side, and all of the fields to the east and south of the Eisenhower home, were under water. Dwight and Edgar, of course, explored the flood. This time they couldn't find a boat, but they did find a piece of boardwalk floating against a bank and they mounted it at once. They were Huckleberry Finn and Jim, the runaway slave, floating the Mississippi on a raft. No suitable board for a paddle presented itself, so they guided their craft by paddling with their hands. Slowly, and then with a gradual increase in speed, they floated down the flood toward the river. They were pleasantly aware of danger. Above the normal river channel the water ran swift and deep, twisted into dangerous eddies, bearing on its crest all manner of flood debris.

But before they reached the main channel, where they would almost certainly have drowned, a farmer standing far away on the railroad embankment called to them and kept on calling. It was difficult to paddle toward him across the stream, but they managed to do so. The farmer was quite stern with them. He gave them a lengthy lecture on the foolish risks they had been running. He mentioned the possibility of his telling their father about it. The boys went home in a chastened mood.

They had played at war, just as the country did, at the turn of the century. They "remembered the *Maine*" in a hundred games, using wooden sticks for guns. They stalked Spaniards and Moros through the jungle thickets along Mud Creek. A tiny knoll became San Juan Hill up which, as Roughriders, they gallantly charged, fighting and dying gloriously. The mother, in one of her rare moments of interference with their play, strongly disapproved. For the first time they encountered her extreme pacifism as she lectured them on the wickedness of war. Thereafter the game of war was faintly flavored for them with the spice of sin.

But the one continuous game they played, all through those years, was "Wild West." They assumed the roles of Bat Masterson, Wild Bill Hickok, Billy the Kid, Jesse James. They were gunmen, quick on the draw, shooting with deadly aim from the hip. Across the yard and around the corners of buildings they would stalk one another, their hands hovering over imaginary holsters, ready to flick out the trusty six-shooter and fire in a split second. Then they'd quarrel over which of them was "dead." With whatever pocket money they managed to earn they bought paper-backed Western novels and pulp magazines, devouring their contents with greedy eyes. They played out all the stories they read. Abilene became again the wildest of cow towns, and Wild Bill was cleaning it up again with his smoking guns. Edgar would remember one favorite story about Will Bill killing six men in a saloon brawl when he first became town marshal, and about the burial of those six men in the Abilene cemetery. The boys could never find those graves, but the story itself they accepted as "gospel truth."

One summer and fall Edgar worked at odd jobs for the county sheriff, a man named Brown who had served through the border fighting of the Civil War. Edgar picked apples for Brown in the latter's orchard and helped make cider and apple butter. The man and boy became friends. Thereafter both Edgar and Dwight used to spend hours with the sheriff, listening spellbound to stories of the old wild days, of Indian battles and rebel raids and those long rides across the parched plains, where men and horses died in an agony of thirst. One such ride lasted for days after all the canteens were empty. When at last the party came to a stream, a dirty, shallow stream with bloated mules killed in some earlier battle still lying in it, all the men flopped down in the water, buried their faces in it, drank deeply of it. Brown supplied with gusto the most gruesome details. The boys could see that wide and empty land, the lonely heroic figures of the men, and they could smell death at that stream. They longed for the old wilderness days. There were no North Side and South Side then, no sissy civilization with its unfair class distinctions. A man in those days was respected for his manhood; the rich were far away. . . .

2

The rich weren't far away from Dwight and Edgar's workaday world. They were a part of that world. They were the "snooty people" on the North Side to whom the boys must sell their garden produce. They were the children in school who made fun of the hand-me-down clothes the Eisenhowers had to wear. Both Edgar and Dwight were forced to wear their mother's old button-top shoes to school in the early grades and were deeply hurt by the laughter this aroused among sons and daughters of more prosperous homes. Derision, however, did not turn them inward, in brooding intro-spection. They fought it, and conquered it, with their fists. They felt often that the world was against them, but it never occurred to them to run away from it. The net result was a strengthening of the family solidarity. Edgar, in later years, would say: "It made us scrappers. It was always us against odds. We developed a sort of feudal feeling."

But the kind of hostility they encountered on the North Side as they marketed their vegetables from house to house could not be conquered with fists. This was the unhappiest of all their many sum-mer jobs. At grade school, with a few exceptions, they were with the children of families little higher, on the economic scale, than their own. With Bud Huffman and the Sniders and the Curry girls they were at ease. They could play together on a basis of equality. But in the summertime, dragging behind them a coaster wagon loaded with vegetables or driving a buggy piled high with produce, they must penetrate a strange and hostile country where insults could not be openly resented lest sales be reduced. Back doors opened to their knocks. Housewives stood on back porches looking *down* upon the Eisenhower boys. "They'd make us feel like beggars," the mature Edgar would say grimly, remembering.

] 73 [

The housewives would tear down the leaves of the roasting ears to see if there were worms in them, so that after the first two or three houses only ears with a worm or so in them were left. Then, since the ears had been mauled and because a worm hole was visible, these "snooty" people would insist on a lowering of the price. And how low those prices were to begin with! Tomatoes at five cents a pound, roasting ears a penny apiece, great bunches of carrots and radishes and beets at two cents apiece! The boys had worked hard raising those vegetables. The family needed every cent of money they could earn. And these "snooty" people with all their money haggled about paying a fair price for the things they bought.

The resentment went deep, very deep. It seems to have inspired not a blind hatred of the people who hurt them, but a profound contempt for the meanness which, in so hurting them, these people expressed. Dwight and Edgar would avoid that particular meanness in their own lives as if it were the blackest of plagues. Never would they employ the prestige of high position as a weapon against the self-respect of other people. Quite the contrary. . . . Decades later, Edgar as a prosperous lawyer invariably bought out completely any boy who came to his house selling vegetables. He'd buy the produce whether he needed it or not. And Dwight, after his rise to fame, would make it abundantly clear that there was nothing he disliked more intensely than snobbish pretensions. There'd be no hierarchy in his personal relationships. He'd insist that all men should look at one another through level eyes.

North Side hostility—but of a kind which could be physically resented and overcome—became more acute in its manifestations when the Eisenhowers entered the seventh and eighth grades. Lincoln School, across the street from the Eisenhower home, had only six grades. For the seventh and eighth grades every child in town attended Garfield School, and Garfield lay in the enemy's country north of the railroad tracks. Here North Side and South Side met head on, and the collision was a violent one.

It was almost traditional that there be, every year, at least one major fight between a South Side and a North Side boy. These contests were like those of Homer's heroes; they were contests of champions. Whoever fought from the South Side represented all South Side boys that year. If the South Side boy won, things were easier for all South Siders at Garfield; if he lost, things were even more difficult than they had been before. The arrangement was no doubt dictated by Abilene's cow-town tradition and by the Western pulp novels which all the boys read. It was as though a gunman representing Good ordered a gunman representing Bad to leave town by sunset. If Bad accepted the challenge, the two fought with revolvers at sunset and one or the other was killed. The code for such duels by appointment prevented any outside interference, but the outcome might greatly affect the life of the community as a whole.

Fights between Abilene boys in those days were rugged affairs which often ended with one of the opponents stretched unconscious on the ground. Arthur Eisenhower would remember all his life a fight he had with a boy who had bullied him for a long time. It was after Arthur had spent a summer working in the Belle Springs Creamery and was, as he put it, "in the pink of condition." He challenged the bully. The two went up an alley and fought there until Arthur knocked the bully down and out. On another occasion, also vividly remembered, it was Arthur who was knocked out. . . . The rules for such fights were quite definite, if never formally stated. One must fight with his fists—"rassling" and kicking were considered unfair—and with his fists one must fight "clean." Any obviously unfair tactics would turn the sympathy of the watching crowd against the boy who used them.

The Eisenhowers' formidable fighting reputation was first established at Garfield by Arthur's battles—and it was enhanced by Edgar's. Most famous of the latter was the one in which Edgar represented the South Side against a North Side boy named Davis.

Davis was a much larger boy than Edgar—so much taller, in fact, and so much longer of reach that Edgar could not at first hit his face. The circle of spectators shouted advice to Edgar. "Hit him in the stomach!" cried his partisans as his first blows missed badly. Edgar took the advice. He ducked Davis's flailing arms and came in close, pumping short, hard blows into the taller boy's body. He stayed in so close, keeping up a steady pounding of the bigger boy's mid-section, that Davis's superior reach was of no advantage to him. Gradually Davis, nauseated by the body punishment he was absorbing, began to double over, and his guard came down lower and lower to cover his abdomen. Whatever speed he had had was pounded out of him. And when his speed was gone and his face was low enough Edgar came up swiftly with lefts and rights to the jaw until Davis lay senseless on the ground.

It had been a great fight, one of the greatest of Abilene boy fights up to that time. But even this terrific battle was overshadowed the following year by a classic contest between Dwight Eisenhower and Wesley Merrifield. Abilene citizens who saw the latter—and there are many of them—would still speak of it with awe forty years later. It was, they'd insist, the "toughest kid fight" they'd ever seen.

Wesley Merrifield was the acknowledged champion of the North Side. Unlike Davis, he was short, but he was thick-bodied, heavy for his height, and long-armed. He was remarkably fast, and his strength and endurance were famous among the boys of the whole town. Altogether he was a far more formidable opponent than Davis had been—while Dwight was smaller than Edgar had been at the same age and was inferior to Edgar as an athlete. At thirteen he was relatively slender, and though everyone knew that he was game, he was notable neither for his strength nor his speed. Indeed, in the scratch football games which the boys played Dwight was generally placed in the line, despite his small size, because he was considered too slow for the backfield. There seemed to be but one possible outcome of any struggle between Dwight and Merrifield. The only question was how long Dwight would be able to stay on his feet.

It was on an October evening after school. The challenge (later no one would remember what it was) had been given and accepted earlier in the afternoon. Since then most of the school had waited breathlessly for the appointed hour. A large crowd, tense with excitement and loud in their partisan talk, accompanied the two boys to a vacant lot on Third and Broadway, across the street from the city hall. The ring was formed. In its center Dwight seemed more than ever lonely, slender, and doomed against the stocky iron-toughness of his opponent. The fight began.

In the opening stages things went in ways that had been expected. Dwight was absolutely game. He didn't shy away from Merrifield's fists, nor seek to stick it out by simply covering up. He kept boring in, hitting as hard and often as he could and taking all the punishment that Merrifield could give him. He took far more than he gave. Merrifield, with his superior strength and speed, landed innumerable solid blows on Dwight's face and body. As the minutes passed, adding up to far more than the normal time consumed in a fight, it became obvious that Dwight was beaten. His face was bruised and bleeding. Both eyes were black and swollen. He was obviously tired. He moved more slowly and his breath came in hoarse rasps through his swollen lips.

But it was here, where most fights end, that the amazing part of this fight began.

Dwight wouldn't yield. Despite his weariness and the tremendous punishment he had taken, he kept coming in—and some of his blows landed and did damage. Merrifield's face, though by no means as badly battered as Dwight's, showed marks of battle, and he, too, was slowing down. He had used up that explosive strength which must back a truly decisive blow. Somehow Dwight had managed to avoid a knockout before that extra strength of his opponent's was gone. From now on it would be a battle of attrition, a violent measuring of the limits of exhaustion. The decision would be not to the boy with the greatest strength and skill, but to the boy who could endure the longest.

Twenty minutes passed by. Half an hour. Forty-five minutes.

One of Dwight's eyes was now completely closed; both of Merrifield's eyes were blue and puffy; both faces were bleeding pulps. The show had become, in the fascinated eyes of the spectators, an epic of brutal courage. The boys could hardly lift their aching arms. Still they fought on. They'd come together. First one and then the the other would land blows which neither had the swift energy to block. Then they'd break apart and circle feebly, panting, until their strength was sufficiently renewed to enable them to come together again. Again they struck one another. Again they broke away. Again they circled.

A full hour passed by. Still the struggle continued. The crowd watched in hushed awe.

It seemed impossible. Both boys had long since fought beyond the limits of a purely physical courage and had entered the realm of moral stamina. No longer was this a simple matching of skill and physique, or of the ability to bear quick pain. When the physique is exhausted and skill no longer counts, when the sharp pain gives way to an aching ordeal which has no apparent end, one must draw his fighting stamina from the spirit. Determination, fortitude, the very essence of self-control are then measured. The contest becomes one of character; its continuance becomes a spiritual achievement.

Behind the rim of prairie far to the west the sun went down. Shadows blurred together to form an all-pervasive dusk. Neither boy had yielded. Neither had any intention of yielding. But no matter what spiritual resources they drew upon, it was no longer possible for them to continue. The muscles of their bodies refused to work, and when they came together now it was only to shove each other feebly with their fists.

They came together and broke apart for the last time. Both of them dropped their hands and braced themselves to keep their knees from buckling. They looked at each other through black, swollen lids, struggling for breath.

"Ike," Merrifield gasped at last, "I can't lick you."

It was a concession which Dwight, for his part, was still unwilling to make. His almost shapeless face twisted into a painful grimace as he tried to grin.

"Well, Wes," he jerked out, "I *haven't* licked you."

The fight had lasted more than two hours. At home Dwight barely managed to stagger upstairs to his room. When Edgar came home from his work at the creamery (he was out of school that year, helping to support the family), he found his brother collapsed upon the bed. When he saw Dwight's face his anger was murderous.

"All I want to know," Edgar said through clenched teeth, "is who did it. That's all I want to know."

Dwight, with almost his last energy, shook his head. It was Wes Merrifield, he said, and it had been a fair fight. Wes was a great fighter. . . .

Three days went by before he was able to return to school.

3

A few months later there occurred an event which not only measured to the full his fortitude but which, in retrospect, reveals the nature of his values and the strength of his commitment to them.

He was running home from school one afternoon when he slipped and fell, skinning his left knee. His trousers were not even torn; the injury to the knee was no more than a scratch. He got to his feet and ran on. By the time he reached home he had almost forgotten the incident. But two mornings later he awoke to find his left leg aching quite badly, and by that evening his foot was black and so swollen that it was with difficulty, and in great pain, that he removed his shoe and stocking. Dr. Conklin was called. He examined the leg gravely, pointing out to Dwight and the family a streak of red running from knee to foot.

"Blood poisoning," the doctor said. "It's serious."

He treated the leg and then went into another room with the father and mother to discuss the case. It might, he said, be possible to avoid amputation. They'd know tomorrow. The mother and father looked at each other, horror-struck.

Dwight spent a sleepless night in great pain. When the doctor came next morning the blackness had advanced up the leg, and the whole leg below the knee was swollen. The doctor drew a circle just above the blackness. Dwight, his teeth clenched, looked at the doctor quickly. The doctor saw that the boy understood.

"If we do it now we can save the rest of the leg," he said gently. "The longer we wait, the more we'll have to take off."

Dwight shook his head in grim finality.

"You won't take any off," he said flatly.

"But it's the only possible way of saving your life," the doctor explained. "It won't be as bad as you think. You'll——"

"No," Dwight said in a tight, strained voice. "I'd rather die."

The doctor looked at the father helplessly and then got to his feet. All of them, excepting Edgar who stayed beside Dwight's bed, left the room. The two boys could hear the murmuring voices in the hall, the dread word "amputate" repeated again and again. Dwight grasped Edgar's hand and tugged at it desperately.

"You got to promise me you won't let 'em do it," he sobbed. "You got to promise. I won't be a cripple. I'd rather die."

Solemnly, looking his younger brother straight in the eye, Edgar promised.

Then Dwight, in agony, asked for a fork to bite on, to keep from screaming, and Edgar brought it to him. Dwight lay, the fork clenched between his teeth, through endless hours of pain, while the swollen blackness climbed past the knee and his fever mounted. The world seemed to dissolve in a screaming whirlpool of pain, and he reached again for his brother's hand.

"I'm going out of my head," he gasped. "Don't let 'em do it while I'm out of my head. Ed, you got to stand guard. Promise?"

Edgar promised, and he stood guard for two days and nights while Dwight muttered and screamed through feverish nightmares and the doctor came, again and again, to match his professional arguments, his deep concern for the family, against the boy's uncompromising will. Edgar shared his brother's values, the physical values of the frontier. To be a cripple, an object of pity, to be incapable of full physical participation in life, was worse than death. For on the frontier life itself was almost wholly physical. On the frontier one could not be truly alive, truly a man, unless he were physically whole, strong, self-reliant. Edgar watched with horror as the black swelling advanced up his brother's thigh. The leg became as thick as the boy's body. But he remained unshaken in his determination to keep faith with his helpless brother, even when the doctor asserted that, once the blackness reached the pelvis, a horrible death would be only a few hours away.

"Nothing we can do will save him then," the doctor said, pleading with David, with Edgar, with the mother. "This is our last chance."

The parents could not make up their minds. They knew Dwight would hate them if they permitted the amputation. So Edgar's attitude was decisive. And Edgar's attitude was strengthened rather than weakened when the doctor, in helpless outrage, muttered the ugly word "murder." All right, then, Edgar told himself, Dwight will die. Let him die! When night came Edgar lay down on the floor, across the threshold, so that no one could enter the room without awakening him. While the doctor, grimly angry, waited for the boy to die, the parents knelt and prayed, prayed for the miracle which was all, the doctor hopelessly insisted, that could now save their son. . . .

And the miracle came! The black swelling reached the pelvis. Dwight sank into total unconsciousness. Life was flickering, flickering out in labored breaths hour after hour, until, quite suddenly it seemed, the swelling began to subside. The fever began to subside. The blackness faded. After a while Dwight awoke, white and exhausted, but breathing easily now. He was alive and whole. In the backwash of pain he grinned triumphantly. He had won! Three weeks later, though still pale and weak, he *walked* out of his room.

CHAPTER II

Widening Horizons

H<small>E</small> CROSSED THE TRACKS to enter Garfield School. It was a symbolic act. It meant a broadening of his horizons as abrupt and as permanent in its effects as an Atlantic crossing would be in later years. At Lincoln School the classroom had been less than one hundred yards from his home; the school ground was but an extension of the Eisenhower yard. Life remained narrowly focused in the white house on the corner. But at Garfield, and two years later in high school, the ties of home, though they still remained unusually strong, were attenuated. His life at once achieved a double focus: home *and* school; and around these focal points reached a world infinitely wider and richer in its possibilities than any he had known before. The possibilities, however, were not markedly different in kind from those he had heretofore perceived. They required of him no major shift of perspective. The new possibilities, like the old, were external, physical, spatial, stimulating to action rather than thought, to the practical body rather than the contemplative mind. They demanded of him an extension only, and not a revision, of his frontier values. His world, enlarged, continued indifferent if not actually hostile to inward brooding and abstract speculations. It was a world of, by, and for the extroverted.

The high school which he entered as a freshman in 1904 occupied the first floor of the city hall. The building was a monstrosity of Moorish arches and rounded turrets, in the style foisted upon municipal governments the length and breadth of the land by Richardson's passion for "modified Romanesque." Built of red brick, it was topped by a massive bell tower from which the bell rope dropped down into one of the very rooms where high school classes were held. The south portion of the building housed the equipment of the volunteer fire department, and when an alarm was given every boy in school was a "volunteer." Academic calm was shattered by the swift entrance of an excited fireman who tugged madly at the rope. Below the iron clamor of the bell the boys rushed to drag the hose cart from its shelter and down the streets of the town, followed by a sizable portion of the town's population. The leaping flames consumed, not wood alone, but whatever interest the boys may have had that day in scholarly pursuits. The interest was probably not great. It was a school which Tom Sawyer would have loved; Stephen Daedalus would have found it unbearable.

The town was as primitive as its high school. It was just beginning to impose a physical and legal organization on what had formerly been a scattered collection of houses and stores unlinked by pipes or wires, or by any but the mildest tax requirements and civic ordinances. Until barely two years before Dwight entered high school the town lacked even a water system; each family had to draw its own water from its own well or from a neighbor's. It was not until 1903 that the town had a sewer system. There would be no paved streets in Abilene until 1910. But the years of Dwight's adolescence would be years of swift growth and improvement in the town's physical plant. In 1905, while Dwight was out of school working at odd jobs in the creamery and elsewhere around the town, a suitable high school building was erected. By the time he was graduated in 1909 the town itself would seem almost new. All through those years there would be a great stir of physical energy, an active realization of purely extensive possibilities—and Little Ike would find himself, with few reticences, frankly in harmony with his environment.

The reticences themselves were significant, not of any maladjustment, but of his wholehearted acceptance of prevailing values. He was evidently at some pains to impress his associates as simply "one of the gang," a "good fellow" untainted by any intellectual brilliance. Probably it was a partial disguise assumed unconsciously; perhaps that is why the disguise itself was so successful. At any rate, in contradiction of the facts, his teachers and classmates would remember him as a "wholesome," "typical" boy, in no way outstanding or even "different," save perhaps in the obsessive interest he developed in history during his junior and senior years. Actually his scholastic record is remarkable, considering the fact that he made it while engaged in athletics and while earning all his way in long hours of out-of-school work. In his freshman year his grades, on a percentage basis, were: English, 91; English composition, 86; physical geography, 86; algebra, 86; and German, 89. When the blood-poisoning episode occurred in the spring, he was forced to leave school, having completed only seven months of the nine-month course. In the following year, while working full time, he managed to complete his freshman studies. During his sophomore year, 1906 –07, his grade average was several percentile points higher than it had been his first year. And in his junior year, though his primary interests were ostensibly football and baseball, and though he was working at nights in the creamery, his grades were among the highest in the school. By this time the school was grading numerically, with I representing an average of 94 or better, II an average of 85 to 94, and so on. Dwight made I's and I-pluses in English, English history, and geometry. His only II (and III was "average") was in Latin, a subject which, like most boys, he detested. In his senior year his associates would regard him as a "whiz" in both mathematics and history, though their over-all impression of him as merely an "average" student would remain unchanged.

The grades give evidence, not only of his capacity to learn, but of the nature of his mental interests. In algebra his record was truly average. His monthly grades in it varied from a low of 67 (three points below passing) to a single high of 95, and they fluctuated ten or twenty points from month to month. But in geometry his grades averaged close to 100, or "perfect"; for every grade period in this subject he was given a I-plus. In conjunction with other evidence, this would seem to indicate that his mind had no natural bent toward generalized speculation, where the terms are altogether abstract and symbolic, but that he dealt easily and effectively with subjects in which the terms are objective and concrete. Algebra has no obvious relation to reality "out there"—but one can easily visualize, as solid entities, the spatial figures of geometry.

His interest in history, an interest which would continue for the rest of his life, seems to have developed in the autumn of 1907. His first recorded history grade is a II. The second is a I. Thereafter he made I-pluses exclusively. His teachers began giving him extra-long assignments in the subject, to keep him from being bored in class. But here, too, he seems to have avoided all abstract generalization. His natural interests would not have led him in that direction, and he was not encouraged by either teacher or environment to shape in his mind even the most rudimentary philosophy of history.

His interests were all pragmatic and particular: a large part of his reputation for historical scholarship at that time seems to have derived from his phenomenal memory for names and dates, and it is probable that he conceived history to be simply a succession of events and personalities whose interactions made interesting stories. The books he studied presented history almost exclusively as a collection of facts uninformed by trend or process, and a disproportionate number of those facts (or so a philosopher of history might claim) dealt with wars and military leaders. The school taught a two-dimensional history, a history of surfaces, lacking depth. History was men fighting, exploiting, inventing, extending; history was *not* (with a few exceptions) men thinking, feeling, believing, shaping universal concepts, creating and destroying ideologies, expressing themselves creatively through a hundred forms of art and science. History was *what* happened (slightly falsified here and there in the interests of "patriotism"), with very little of the *how* and practically none of the *why*. . . .

He did ask "why" often enough in his physics class, as some of his classmates would remember, though the "why" in physics is always identified with the "how" (the "why" which has to do with initial forces, with first causes, belongs in the realm beyond physics, the realm of metaphysics). Like his father at the same age, physical problems intrigued him, and he enjoyed solving them. His mind was adept at analysis. He was quick to seize upon errors of fact and of reasoning. And he seems to have used his skill as much for the purpose of tormenting his teacher, a young fellow named Kessler who didn't know his subject very well, as for drawing from that teacher the last ounce of information. Poor Kessler was frequently pilloried before his class by the merciless Dwight; one pities in retrospect his stammering, red-faced confusion.

For the rest, Dwight "fitted in" willingly and completely. With Bud Huffman and Edgar, who was now a classmate of his and who overshadowed him as an athlete, he helped to shape in the school a kind of South Side ideal of physical prowess and rugged courage. To some extent he seems to have flaunted, at first, his South Side "toughness" and to have professed a contempt for refined and polished manners. He made of his *persona* an active rebuke of North Side "niceness" and was so successful in it that many North Siders looked upon him as too rough and uncouth to be included in "nice" social gatherings. He was never, for instance, accepted as a member of the Bums of Lawsy Lou, an organization which had the social prestige of a high-rating fraternity or sorority among the students—though later on, when he became a football and baseball notable, he was sometimes invited to Lawsy Lou parties and picnics. Girls who were his classmates in those first years would remember him as careless of dress, his hair almost always uncombed (he was a "terrible dancer," in contrast to Edgar, who was "swell on the dance floor"), possessed of a fiery temper which flashed dangerously now and then through his normally sunny temperament. Many of them found his lopsided grin completely charming and felt themselves challenged by his apparent indifference to them. (The indifference was only apparent; actually he was, among girls, painfully shy.)

Everyone sensed in him a stubborn integrity—he was, in body and in spiritual core, as hard as a rock, and he permitted only his friends to take liberties with him—but there was nothing dominating about his personality. Indeed, he seems to have lacked to a remarkable degree in one so energetic and capable even the desire to dominate. It seems never to have occurred to him that he might be "better than"; no one had suggested such a thing to him, and he'd have taken small pleasure in it if anyone had. There were few—and that few would probably not have included himself—who'd have predicted for him a great future. There is no evidence that he ever indulged in such dreams of purely personal power and glory as marked the youths of an Alexander or a Napoleon, or of that strange Austrian creature who even then was convincing himself that he was a "destiny." He remained one of many. He was a "regular guy," happily extroverted, owning a comfortable membership in that majority which existed outside the fences of North Side snobbery.

The mood of the majority—hostile or at least indifferent to "bookishness" and "sissy" culture—was one to which other personalities did not so easily adjust. These may have included Paul Royer, who would become a lawyer, Dickinson County's attorney in the 1940s, and who would remember Dwight as a "tough cooky" whom he disliked in school for that reason. They certainly included, ten years later, Dwight's own youngest brother Milton. The younger boy limns by contrast many features of Dwight's youthful character. It is significant of the prevailing mood that Dwight's closest friends would remember Milton as "different" (in a disparaging sense) from the other Eisenhowers, and far different from Dwight. Milton was "the kind of kid who plays in the school orchestra and likes to read all the time." Turned inward in his first years by the limitations his illness had placed on his physical strength, he had little active interest in athletics. He gravitated to the North Side as naturally as Dwight shied away from it. He cared about appearances. He felt that the life of the mind was important. He wanted to become a writer. While still in high school he would go to work for Charlie Harger as a reporter on the Abilene *Reflector,* and he would be influenced directly or indirectly by that literature of protest which sprang out of the Midwestern soil in those years: Lewis, Cather, Anderson, Dreiser; a literature which bitterly deplored the crushing of the interior life under a deliberate externalism across the prairie farms and in the prairie towns. Milton, to some extent at least, could feel that protest rising in himself as he looked at Abilene (though he loved the place). Dwight, at the same age, would not have known that the protest existed—and would have repudiated it if he had.

Externalism was the order of the day, and it suited him. If the frontier had disappeared physically in 1890, it was a continuing spiritual reality, vivid and powerful, through all of Dwight Eisenhower's formative years. He was, in his youth, an almost unmitigated "Western man," in the American rather than the Spenglerian sense. Only the physical was "really real"; the mind was but the tool of the body; ideas were valid only in so far as they were schemes for immediate practical action. An advanced European might have considered him and his associates, even then, as "primitives," anachronisms in the twentieth century, if only because they had relaxed wills and would have found absurd the concepts of "destiny" and "dialectical materialism," "superman" and "proletarian," had they so much as heard of them. The frontiersman, without thinking about it, stood for diverse multiplicity, for individual freedom, for simplicity, particularism, pragmatism. He found himself temperamentally opposed to an enforced unity, to collective authority, to complexity, to generalization, to idealism as a metaphysic. He lived for the day. An idea was true if it "worked" within the situation which called it forth. Means, within very broad limits, could be justified by ends.

It is easy to show how this frontier philosophy, unless it be tempered by an idealism which basically contradicts it, can become the enemy of the democracy it seems to express, of that very freedom it ostensibly supports. We have seen it happen in twentieth-century America. An unqualified pragmatist is likely to become a "realistic" worshiper of "Power," a "power" politician and a "power" philosopher. For if truth is merely the efficacy of an idea, then truth may be only another name for survival or persistence. An idea which survives, which "conquers," must be true for that very reason: it has "worked," it has "succeeded"; and "might," since it *makes* "right," is soon identified with it.

But in Dwight Eisenhower's case pragmatism *was* tempered by a measure of practical idealism. The latter derived from a long tradition of River Brethren piety, from the very organization of the family, and from the natural tendency of his own character. He could never subscribe wholly to the view—even in his most "practical" moments in later years—that "truth" and "justice" are merely relative terms whose meaning varies from one situation to another. He had, almost in spite of himself (for he blended a conservative respect for authority with a wild cow-town individualism), certain underlying principles of action which could be broadly grouped under the Golden Rule, which involved his profound belief in common people and his contempt for selfish egotism and for aristocratic pretensions. There was nothing coldly calculating, nothing relative in his belief in democracy; it was an absolute, instinctively held, upon which all relativities of action must rest. If, in later years, he ever supported for even a moment forces hostile to democracy, he did so in the name of an immediate expediency which (or so he told himself) would lead to an eventual democratic victory. Pragmatism for him was never an ultimate philosophy—perhaps it never is for anyone—but only a tool, a kind of loose strategy for dealing with worldly necessities.

In his case, more than in most, the child was father of the man. His career would be a flowing upward curve with no breaks in it, no sharp doublings-back and shifts of direction. Its conclusions were all inherent in its beginnings. The boy, with his eager face and sharp externalized mind, his courage and physical toughness, his charm of personality and his selflessness and his integrity, had all the essential attributes (in embryonic form) of the supreme commander.

2

Six MacDonell first saw Abilene in 1900, his eighth year, when he moved into the town with his parents and two older brothers, one ten and the other fourteen years older than he. The family was poor, and Catholic in a predominately Protestant community, and the boy's life was never easy. At first he was known by his given name, John. The story of the origin of his nickname "Six" gives a casual glimpse of the cultural life among Abilene school children at his time.

In the autumn of 1903, when John was in the sixth grade, the children of both Lincoln and Garfield schools were thrilled by the announcement that an "art exhibit" was coming to town. When the exhibit arrived—it consisted of reproductions of famous paintings, sent on tour from Topeka—the teachers led their classes to it, forsaking for a day the usual study schedule. The children looked upon it as a kind of holiday, despite the art lecture to which they were compelled to listen. Inevitably one of the pictures was Raphael's Sistine Madonna, and the speaker referred to it more often than to any of the others. None of the boys obtained any clear idea of what "Sistine" referred to, and they had scarcely clearer ideas of the meaning of "Madonna"; it sounded like "Sixteen Mac-Donell" to them, and before they had returned to the schoolroom they had applied that name to John. Later the nickname was shortened to "Six." As things turned out, it was a happy inspiration, for MacDonell was to become a baseball pitcher of considerable note in the Middle West, and his nickname became a definite asset. Was not the great Christy Mathewson himself, he whose famous "speed ball" would win 372 big-league baseball games, called the "Big Six" after the new six-cylinder motorcar which was in those days the epitome of smooth power?

The greatest influence on Six's life as a boy was exerted by a young bachelor, Joe W. Howe, who published and edited in Abilene a weekly newspaper, the *Dickinson County News*. Abilene recognized Six as among the "underprivileged" boys, his opportunities severely limited; and Joe Howe, seeing the shy, lanky youth on the streets, took a sympathetic interest in him. The boy was lonely, none too happy at home, and starved for affection. He would always remember, as a climactic point in his youth, the evening Joe Howe persuaded him to attend the organization meeting of a "new club to be known as the Knights of Honor." Six, bashful and convinced of his own inferiority, wasn't eager to go, but Joe Howe insisted, and at the meeting (wonder of wonders!) Six found himself nominated and elected president! The boy ("I was just a green dumb kid, I didn't know beans") walked home in a daze. Perhaps he'd amount to something after all! The club itself, sponsored by Howe and by a Herrington merchant named Percy Schilling, filled a place in the community similar to that now filled by the Boy Scouts. To Six it seemed a marvelous organization, with a clubroom that was open at all times and that had some sports equipment in it, with a ritual to be followed at meetings and all sorts of planned activities to engage in between meetings. Forty years later he would be able to recite, word for word, the formal pledge with which each meeting was closed: "We leave this room to go our separate ways. We pledge ourselves to act always as honorable gentlemen until we meet again." And forty years later, in Salina, Kansas, Six himself would be working with boys, sponsoring a midget baseball team, as a kind of living testimonial to Joe Howe's friendship.

A year or so after the inception of the Knights, Six's father died, leaving the family destitute. The boy, it seemed, would have to quit school and go to work full time, young as he was. But once again Joe Howe—who by now was convinced that there was "some mighty fine stuff in that lad"—came to the rescue. Joe taught Six to set type and gave him a job in the back shop of the *News,* paying him on a piece-work basis, so much per stick. Six became both fast and accurate in his work. He could earn fifty or sixty cents a night in Joe's shop. He stayed in school.

By this time his fame as a southpaw pitcher, with a speed and control far beyond his years, had spread through the boy community of the town. He had prestige and popularity. A growing self-confidence, though it stayed far this side of conceit, had given him poise. Nevertheless, he was surprised and delighted when, in the winter of his freshman year at high school, he was approached by the Eisenhower boys, Big Ike and Little Ike, and informed that he, Six Mac-Donell, was to be the pitcher for the Abilene team in the coming spring. It seems that the boy who had done the pitching in preceding seasons—a much larger and older boy than Six—had left town. The Eisenhowers didn't *ask* Six to pitch; they told him he was going to. The Eisenhowers, Edgar especially, were "big shots" in the school because of their athletic records. Ed had starred in football that fall, the fall of 1907; Dwight, though no star, had done a competent job at end—and he had long since joined the ranks of heroes as a result of his two-hour battle with Wes Merrifield. For a mere freshman to be approached by these two was an honor Six deeply appreciated.

Before long he had become Dwight's closest friend.

Dwight, two years older than Six, had not been a member of the Knights; later Six would not remember that Dwight had even attended a meeting as a guest. But on the baseball diamond the two were closely associated. Dwight, watching from his position in right field, took a sponsor's pride in the younger boy's performance in the pitcher's box. Six was nervous at first. His control, with all those people watching, was not as good as it had been in "kid games." But he won half his games that first season, a very creditable performance, considering his youth and lack of experience, and it was obvious that he would develop into an extraordinary player. Dwight liked the way the boy handled himself, liked the boy's shy grin, his modesty, his determination always to do his best. Six, for his part, would say of Dwight in those years: "He was on the right side of everything, and a regular fellow. He had all the guts in the world, and the ability to dig things out for himself in his studies." In his remaining three years of school baseball, Six won every high school game. His only loss in all those years was a game played, not with another high school team, but as a town team against the freshman team from Kansas University. In the story of this single loss Dwight figures prominently.

It was one of those games sponsored by Old Man Shearer, who ran the shoe store on the corner of Third and Broadway and who was a baseball enthusiast. Whenever a team representing another town sought a game in Abilene, Shearer would make up a team composed mostly of high school boys to meet the visitors. The gate receipts of such games were divided among the players, who sometimes made as much as $3.50 apiece—"big money," it seemed to them, for doing what they loved to do. When the announcement was made that the K.U. freshmen were coming, there was more than usual excitement in the town, for the college boys were reputed to have a better than average team, and the local people by that time were eager to match their southpaw against the best available competition. Dwight was especially eager. He was sure there'd be a college scholarship in it for his friend if Six won the game.

Six was in his best form that day. For the first few innings he pitched no-hit ball, while Abilene managed to score a run off the first-class K.U. pitcher. It looked like a shutout, and Dwight, who was playing center field that day, was "talking it up" with great enthusiasm. But in the last inning, with the score 1–0 and with a K.U. man on first base, Bill Moore, one of the university's heaviest hitters, came to bat. Perhaps Six's arm was tiring. At any rate, he pitched to Moore, and Moore connected with a hard drive straight over the pitcher's box and over second base. Dwight ran forward, then realized that he had misjudged the ball, ran back five or six steps, and sprang into the air. But he was too late. The ball was too high for him. All he could do was chase it madly while Moore rounded the bases in a home run. And that broke up the ball game. K.U. won, 2–1.

Dwight's misjudgment might have passed unnoticed if he himself, in thorough self-disgust, had not called attention to it.

"Damn it, Six, I cost you that game," he said. "If it wasn't for me I bet you'd have got a scholarship."

Six tried to soothe him. It was just a game, Six said. You win some. You lose some. He pointed out that Dwight himself, who was the leading hitter on the team that year, had won plenty of games for the pitcher. But Dwight couldn't look at it that way. For six months afterward he kept referring to his mistake and blaming himself bitterly. Later, when Six was playing pro baseball, he realized ever more strongly how rare it is for a man to assume responsibility for his own errors, especially when those errors might remain hidden—and Dwight's misjudgment, as Six kept pointing out to him, would not even have been classed as an error in the books. . . .

It was through Six that Dwight became a friend of Joe Howe's. He used to come to the *News* office with Six and watch admiringly while the latter's flying hands set type and pulled proofs. By the fall of 1908 the office was one of the hangouts of a whole gang of boys, and of that gang Dwight and Six were leaders by popular consent. Joe Howe, who had no family ties, who was a member of the school board, and was always actively interested in boys, liked to have the gang around. He fixed up a little room for them and provided boxing gloves, which they used with more enthusiasm than skill. He gave them free access to his office library, which was amply stocked with exchange papers from all over the country (it was easier for a country editor to arrange "exchanges" with city papers in those days than it is now) and with "review copies" of books from Eastern publishers, as well as with books Howe had bought. He became the umpire of their quarrels and the moderator of their discussions. He spent a great deal of time just "chinning" with them, sitting in on their "gag" sessions during which all manner of subjects—religious, political, economic, personal—were reviewed.

He seems to have found Dwight particularly attractive. He couldn't understand why all the boys called him "Little Ike" or "Ugly Ike," when "Smiling Ike" would have been both a pleasanter and a more accurate name. For though Dwight had a quick temper, he never held a grudge for long; he was grinning a wide, infectious grin most of the time. Joe Howe remarked that Dwight had self-assurance but no conceit, that he hated conceit in anyone else, and that he actually disliked to have flattery applied to himself. On the occasions when Joe Howe helped Dwight with school assignments he was not impressed by the boy's scholarship. Dwight was, Howe would remember, an "average student." But the man would also remember that Dwight "could write a good theme, properly punctuate it . . . and make it connect properly as to subjects and points he wanted to make"; that he could "make a good speech for a high school boy, memorize it easily, but if he forgot certain lines he was able to fill in and then generally pick up the lines farther on"; and that he was "especially observant—he could walk through a plant or watch someone who was adept at his work and be able to relate to you about everything he had seen." The boy didn't like to write and put off his theme work as long as possible. The writing itself was articulate rather than inspired, being characterized by economy, logical organization, and a careful regard for facts rather than by originality of idea or expression.

Through Joe Howe we catch glimpses of Dwight's rather ambiguous relation to Authority. On one occasion, in the fall of 1908, Dwight and a couple of his gang came to Howe's office in high dudgeon. The principal of the school had informed them that because they had failed to complete certain class assignments they would not be permitted to play in a football game scheduled for the coming week end—one of the most important games of the season. Dwight considered the principal's ruling arbitrary, unfair, and hostile to a proper school spirit. It was Joe Howe's duty, as a member of the school board and a loyal supporter of the team, to compel the school authorities to reverse their decision. If for nothing else, Joe should act on behalf of the injured boys because he was their friend. But Joe demurred. He argued that he was in no way responsible for the boys' failure to do their school work. Dwight agreed that the work should have been done, but he insisted that he and the others should be permitted to make it up after the game. Joe still shook his head. He didn't see, he said, where he came in; he couldn't interfere with the running of the school. Dwight's anger shot out in a searing flame of words, repudiating his friendship with Joe Howe and promising that neither he nor the others would ever come to the office again. They left, slamming the door behind them.

But the principal himself finally decided to let the boys play—and a day or so after the game Dwight and the others came back to the *News* office, grinning sheepishly. The friendship with Joe Howe was restored on the tacit assumption that Dwight had been in the wrong.

On another occasion Dwight and Six played hooky from school on a cold winter's day in order to go ice skating down Mud Creek to the Smoky Hill. The principal suspended them from school and assigned them a great deal of extra work which must be done before they could be readmitted as students in good standing. Both boys were working in their out-of-school hours, and the tasks seemed to them excessive. Again they came to Joe Howe and requested his intervention on their behalf in the name of their mutual friendship. Again Joe Howe demurred. Again he pointed out that he was in no way responsible for the boys' flouting of school requirements. Dwight regarded him with angry disgust.

"You're one hell of a friend!" he shouted, and left the office, vowing never to return.

Six's attitude, modified by his profound gratitude for all Joe Howe had done for him, was less intransigent. He told Joe that Dwight would come back when he'd thought things over. And sure enough, Dwight did, grinning and admitting his mistake.

He had a highly developed sense of justice. Joe Howe noticed that fact on dozens of occasions. After football games Dwight often took the lead in reprimanding boys who had played "dirty," and though he was a rough player himself, who always took advantage of his opponents' weaknesses, he was always "clean." His sympathy with underdogs was notable, partially because he considered himself to be one of them—and often he extended a practical helping hand to a boy who was in difficulties. One of the bonds of friendship between him and Six was the low economic and social status which they shared in the community. In the "gag" sessions he often argued in favor of a greater economic equality: he could not see why some people in the town should have to work long hours for little pay while others, who did very little work or none at all, lived in luxury on relatively high incomes. With the example of his own family constantly before him, he could never accept the argument that the North Siders lived better because they were "smarter" or had other claims to innate superiority. But his arguments in this direction never, as Joe Howe would remember, went farther than a kind of vague local protest. He certainly never generalized his arguments to favor a change of "system"—he was not inclined toward generalizations, as we have seen—and he was not personally embittered by the fact that he himself was one of the hardest-worked boys in town.

"That was the outstanding thing about his character, I think," Joe Howe would say in later years. "He would take any job he could do and he seldom complained that the work was too hard. He took hard work for granted."

It was in the *News* office that Dwight seems first to have developed a taste for serious reading. The Eisenhower home library consisted almost exclusively of the Bible, a multitude of religious tracts, publications, a few school textbooks, and some technical books on engineering. For amusement Ed and Dwight consumed paper-backed Frank Merriwell and Western novels by the score. But of reading which broadens interests, stocks the mind with information, and sharpens the critical faculties, Dwight had done very little. His interest in history was still developing when he first came to the *News* office, and it was stimulated there by (first) the exchange newspapers which Joe Howe encouraged him to read. He got into the habit of dropping in almost every day to read papers from New York, Cleveland, St. Louis, and a dozen other faraway places. He seems to have felt very strongly the lure of distances.

"I like to read what is going on outside of Kansas," he told Joe Howe. "Makes me realize that Kansas isn't all the world."

From the newspapers he turned gradually to the books, and before long he was browsing through the quite extensive collection, concentrating on history and biography. One volume which seems to have had a tremendous influence on him was a *Life of Hannibal* —author unknown—in which the campaigns of the Second Punic War were described in detail. Other boys had looked at that book and had even tried to read it, attracted by the prospect of exciting war stories, but all of them had abandoned it after a few pages, complaining that it was "too deep" for them. Dwight read it with evident pleasure, and ever afterward Hannibal—whose strategical and tactical brilliance had been so tragically frustrated by unsound logistics—was among his heroes.

But Joe Howe's office was by no means the only hangout for Dwight and his friends, nor even the chief one. The latter distinction belonged to the Tip-Top Restaurant, of which the proprietors were Otto Smith ("He had the sweetest tenor voice I ever heard," Ed would recall) and Ralph Lucier. The Tip-Top was, for the men and boys of the town, a kind of community forum, a clearing-house for news and opinions. Here Dwight was introduced at an early age to the mysteries of poker, at which he became quickly an expert, and here (as in the small room Howe had provided) the boys used to hold impromptu boxing matches in the basement. Here, too, Dwight displayed a facility in argument which some of the townspeople would remember forty years later. He seems to have been able to force an opponent's argument through a series of leading questions and then, with a triumphant swoop, reveal an error of fact or a contradiction in his opponent's reasoning. For the most part, debate was a game of skill with him: often, when he was himself cornered in an argument, he would avoid the consequences with a sudden witticism accompanied by his most engaging grin; but when he was interested in a conversation for its own sake he knew how to glean from it the information he wanted. He listened well, and he asked the proper questions at the proper time.

His physical energy, his animal spirits were too high to be exhausted even by the regimen of school, sports, and hard labor to which he submitted himself. As he did with his assigned chores at home, he strove at the creamery to break down the lines of demarcation between work and play. Once he and Edgar decided to play a practical joke on one Harry Rumbarger. It was in the freezing room, the floor of which was a checkerboard of trap doors beneath each of which was a compartment in which three-hundred-pound cakes of ice were frozen. Above them was a hand crane of steel, running on tracks of steel, operated by an iron wheel. Since the floor was always wet, Dwight, remembering his high school physics, saw that an electric current shot into the crane would give whoever touched the wheel a nasty jolt. Accordingly he and Edgar wired the crane, and when Harry Rumbarger took hold of the wheel he was knocked unconscious. The boys, certain that they had killed a man (and under the circumstances it is a miracle that they had not), were frightened almost out of their wits. They immediately detached the wire and gave first aid to Harry, who quickly recovered. Harry never knew what had hit him. The boys never told him, or anyone else, and they never again played a practical joke in which elements of danger were present.

In the winters Dwight worked on alternate evenings in the engine room, which was some forty feet in height and contained a (then) new stationary steam engine, two huge boilers, and a large coal bunker. At hourly intervals he labored terrifically, shoveling coal into the firebox. In between times he studied his lessons, in the light of a naked electric bulb hanging from a long drop cord, or played penny-ante poker with Six and Bud Huffman and other members of the gang who dropped in. During one winter Six sometimes took over the firing detail for a shift or two so that Dwight could date a girl, Esther Baumgarth, with whom he was having a minor affair.

Generally speaking, Dwight's relations to girls in those years were as ambiguous as his relations to Authority: he felt both drawn to them and repelled by them. His desire for their companionship was often frustrated by an even stronger desire to maintain an absolute independence, and by a pride which had perhaps been more highly sensitized than most by his early encounters with North Side snobbery. Dating girls, he found, left one vulnerable to the deepest kind of hurts. Bud Huffman would remember that on football trips Dwight talked one autumn, with an elaborate casualness that deceived no one, about a certain Myrtle Hoffnell, who was an attractive girl and one of the most popular in school. But for all his evident attraction to her, he dated her only twice. He had arranged a third date and had come uptown one evening to keep it, dressed in his best clothes and with his hair carefully combed for a change. But the fickle Myrtle had "stood him up." She had gone riding with Earl Briney in the Brineys' family car, one of the first Buicks in Abilene. At the same time (as Six would remember) Dwight discovered that Myrtle had been having a succession of dates in one evening, arranging for one boy to bring her home early so that she could go out with a second, and sometimes even with a third. Completely disillusioned, feeling doubly snubbed, he never asked her for a date again.

But his real "secret passion" through all of his high school years was Gladys Harding. She had blue eyes and golden hair and a "perfect complexion"; she was notably intelligent, and she had that North Side prestige which amounted to a psychological barrier between her and Dwight. It was for her sake that he wished, sometimes, he might be accepted as a member in good standing of the Bums of Lawsy Lou. Under the circumstances she seemed to him as aloof, as unapproachable, as a young goddess. He worshiped her silently, and from a distance.

3

In his senior year at high school, 1908–09, he gave his first notable evidence of his capacities as an organizer and leader. In those days school athletics were almost wholly divorced from school administration and were indeed somewhat frowned upon by most teachers as an unjustifiable interference with classroom work. The school had no hired coaches and furnished no athletic equipment. The coaching problem was relatively easy to solve. There was always some young man about town who was glad to coach, "just for the fun of it." But the problem of supplying athletic equipment —uniforms, balls, bats, masks—was a serious one which threatened at times to halt sports altogether. The South Side boys who were the mainstays of the football and baseball teams came from families too poor to buy any "extras." To solve this problem, Dwight had been one of the instigators of an Athletic Association, in his junior year, through which the boys pooled their own limited resources and solicited outside funds to purchase the equipment. But the association, that first year, had no official standing in the school. It threatened to fall apart. There could easily be some bitter discussions about who "owned" the equipment.

He took the matter up with school authorities, asked for official recognition of the organization, and obtained it. He himself told the story, in typically terse prose, in the 1909 edition of the school annual, the *Helianthus.* Under the heading "Athletics," signed by "Dwight Eisenhower," he wrote: "Early in the fall of 1908, the High School boys organized an Athletic Association for the year. After electing Dwight Eisenhower president, Harry Makins vice-president, and Herbert Sommers secretary and treasurer, we proceeded to do business. Deciding not to play any baseball that fall, we started on football at once." And so on. He "did business" so effectively that year that the association became a permanent organization. Forty years later it would still be operating.

But even with the association it was not always possible to solve in so orderly and efficient a manner the problems which arose. There was the problem of transportation for the team, when no money was available for train fare. Dwight solved this problem in typically pragmatic fashion. There were freight trains, weren't there? And didn't they run from Abilene to the town where the team was to play? And if the whole team piled onto one of those trains, the brakemen would be so outnumbered they wouldn't dare to try throwing the boys off, would they? So they "bummed" their way in boxcars to at least one of their games—and won that game.

He took part in the senior-class play that year, *The Merchant of Venice Up-to-Date.* He played "Lancelot Gobbo, a servant of Shylock." The script, aside from a stridently inaccurate imitation of Elizabethan blank verse, bore no relation to Shakespeare. The plot, says an extant program, "centers around the rivalry between Captain Antonio of the Abilene High School football team and Shylock, a former player on the Chapman team." No one had less interest in dramatics than Dwight, but since his part gave him an opportunity for a burlesque of serious acting, he played it with gusto, contributing no small part to what was, in the memory of townspeople, a hilarious evening. . . .

There were thirty-one in the graduating class that spring. The commencement address was made by Henry J. Allen, then editor of the Wichita (Kansas) *Beacon* and later governor of the state. Dwight listened with mingled emotions. He was leaving a world he knew, a world which, whatever its limitations, had a definite program and definite goals. He was entering a world which seemed to him vast and nebulous in the extreme. Of what this was to be the "commencement" he had no inkling. Beyond a desire to "continue his education," probably at Kansas University, he had no designs upon the future, and he seems to have regretted in himself a lack of "ambition." Other boys seemed so sure of what they wanted to do. . . . Perhaps the prophecy made for him in the *Helianthus* was as good as any. Edgar, according to the class prophet, would serve two terms as President of the United States. Dwight (no politician in high school) would become a professor of history at Yale.

CHAPTER III

Controlled Drift: The Strategy of the Relaxed Will

Edgar was among those in the graduating class who knew what they wanted to do. His basic attitudes toward life had always been simpler and more direct than Dwight's. They had less ambiguity than Dwight's; the frontier philosophy he espoused was less mitigated by an essentially alien "idealism." He measured success quite frankly in terms of power, power in terms of money; and if his ambition were not of the overweening sort which is wholly devoid of compassion (he'd always avoid, as we've said, the "meanness" of snobbery), it was far more personal and precise than Dwight's was ever to be. He had developed in high school a taste for public speaking and debate. To his competitive, not to say combative, nature, debate was simply verbal fighting in which one sought to overcome an opponent, using words for ammunition and ideas for weapons. Moreover, "the politics," as the afore-mentioned writer in the *Helianthus* put it, "interested him." Adding up his preferences, his choice of a profession was a simple matter. Was not the courtroom an arena for verbal battles in which the winner carried off valuable cash prizes? And did it not serve as the most convenient platform from which to launch a political career? So he announced to the family one evening that he intended to go to the University of Michigan (because a high school teacher whom he greatly admired had gone there) and enter the law school.

"I knew it!" the mother said smilingly to the father. "It's because I studied those lawbooks in Hope. I was sure he'd be a lawyer!"

But the mention of Hope reminded the father of his single disastrous experience with a lawyer. Generalizing from that experience, he seems to have concluded that the law was too often a medium for deception, fraud, trickery. What did lawyers do except complicate the obvious and then charge fat fees for simplifying it again?

And who were likely to be a lawyer's clients—who except outright criminals or businessmen who wanted to "put something over" on someone? If lawyers dealt at all with honest, God-fearing, hard-working folk, it was generally to fleece the latter.

Both parents made a kind of fetish of non-interference with their sons' vocational choices, partially from religious scruples and partially because both of them had suffered, in their youth, from the efforts of their elders to compel them into methods of livelihood. David's father had sought to make a farmer of his son, and Ida Elizabeth's guardian had prevented Ida's migration to Kansas for as long as he had legal control over her. Nevertheless, David could not avoid trying to persuade his son from a path which led so narrowly through a morass of immorality. Why didn't Edgar take up medicine instead? *There* was a respectable profession! If Edgar would enroll at the University of Kansas in a premedical course, David might manage to help the boy along financially, even though it meant skimping the rest of the family. This was only a suggestion, mind you . . .

But Edgar, as he himself explained in later years, chose to consider it a "challenge." He spurned what appeared to him to be a "bribe." He was more determined than ever to follow his chosen profession. And David, however sad his disappointment, quietly dropped the matter.

It was, thereafter, all up to Edgar, and he was by no means certain that he could solve unaided the problem of financing a college education, for all his flaunted independence. Indeed, as he viewed the problem in Abilene it appeared even more difficult than it would appear to be in Ann Arbor later on, when he was face to face with it. He discussed the matter very seriously with Dwight. And nowhere is the nature of the family solidarity more evident than in the arrangement which the two youths agreed upon that summer. According to Edgar, it was Dwight who made the original suggestion.

"We both want to go," Dwight is reported to have said, "but you know what you want to do, and I don't. Besides, you're the oldest, so you ought to go first. Why don't I stay out next year and work and send you all the extra money I make? Then the next year you stay out and work and send me the money you make. We can take college work on alternate years that way and both end up with college educations."

Edgar agreed to this arrangement with enthusiasm. He spent the summer working in the creamery, applied for entrance into the university, and was accepted. A warm September morning witnessed another farewell on the little side porch of the Eisenhower home. Again the mother gave voluble, cheerful advice. Again she retired to her room to sorrow in secret over the disintegration of the family. In only a few years now they'd all be gone, all her sons, and the white house on the corner which had been so full of life would seem by contrast so lonely, so empty. But there the similarity with Arthur's departure ends, for Edgar was much more sure of himself and of what he wanted to do than Arthur had been. He was neither shy nor diffident. His will tensed to meet the "challenge" of the world.

Viewed superficially, Dwight's life that year, the year of 1909–10, was an almost aimless drifting, and the stream on which he drifted appeared to circle in a slow eddy, moving neither forward nor backward. He himself seems to have viewed it that way. All through that year he was vaguely dissatisfied with himself, feeling that he wasn't "getting anywhere." He had been out of school for months now, and still he didn't know what he wanted to do in the world. Only in terms of physical growth did he seem to be making progress. He broadened out that year. His chest grew thick and deep, and the muscles of his sloping shoulders and of his arms and legs became as hard as iron. Tensing the muscles across his abdomen, he could take there without flinching the hardest blow that his brother Earl could deliver. He was heavier now than Edgar and increasingly sure that he could give his older brother that long-postponed "licking" when they met again. At the creamery the heaviest work gave him pleasure, for it sent surging through his body a strength and energy he had never known before.

His drifting referred only to the direction and not at all to the content of his life. His days were filled with the hardest kind of work. He pulled ice, fired furnaces, loaded wagons, and, now and then when he was "off" at the creamery, did various odd jobs around the town. Faithfully he saved his money—spending part of it for shotgun shells (his only "luxury") so that he and the gang could go hunting, sending the rest of it to Ed, who by the time his freshman year was ended had received more than two hundred dollars from Dwight. Hunting quail, rabbits, and squirrels, generally with Six MacDonell, seems to have been his chief recreation that year.

On cold winter days he sometimes forged an excuse note to Earl's schoolteacher so that Earl might come along. He heated bricks at home, wrapped them in blankets, and deposited them on the floor of the buggy to keep the boys' feet warm. Then they all drove far out into the country. There the twelve-year-old Earl would be left to watch the horse while Six and Dwight roamed across the fields. Earl was the exploited one on these expeditions. Not only must he stay in the buggy while the bricks grew cold and his feet froze; he must also promise, before Dwight permitted him to come along, that he would clean all the game the boys brought in. He was allowed to shoot only twice on each expedition, once when the boys first arrived in the field and once when Dwight and his friend returned with their bag. At home Earl sometimes had to pick and clean as many as ten quail while Dwight, with callous cheerfulness, "cleaned up" to go downtown. . . .

That was the year of his first "girl," his first "steady date," though this seems to have been more in the nature of a close friendship, a sort of highhearted comradeship, than of a serious romantic affair. She was Ruby Norman, who had red hair and violet eyes, and had achieved a considerable local fame as a violinist. Her closest girl friend was Minnie Stewart, who, though only a year or so older than Dwight, was teaching mathematics in the high school. Both of them were much taken by Dwight's casual charm, a charm enhanced by his apparent unawareness of it. They saw him almost every evening, and always he was affable, fun-loving, poised; he was, they thought, remarkably mature for his years. They used to talk together about his "wonderful personality" and his "reality"— the word "real" somehow attaches itself to all descriptions of him as he was at that time—and they admired together his "powerful physique" and (with a perception uncommon in Abilene) his "splendid intellect." Neither of them accepted the prevailing notion that Dwight was just an "ordinary" student. Minnie Stewart thought him brilliant. His fund of general information was far larger than that of most youths his age. His mind was remarkably quick and retentive. His talent for mathematics impressed her. She was sure even then that he would go far. But when she said something of the sort to Dwight he shook his head, grinned ruefully— and changed the subject. He wasn't going anywhere at the time. The months passed pleasantly enough, but they passed *him*. *He* stood still.

A lost year, Dwight seems to have thought. A wasted year. For a quarter of a century he would regret it. He'd always be several years older than his classmates and competitors. In any job where promotion depended largely upon seniority he'd be likely to lose out. . . . Yet a biographer can find in that year a pattern of great and prophetic significance. Actually Dwight was gaining in character development far more than he lost in immediate advantage—and even the loss of immediate advantage was to prove, in the end, an illusion. He gained a valuable perspective of himself and his career, a perspective he would retain all his life long, and as part and parcel of this he gained a vital strategy which would vastly increase his effectiveness. He lost only those opportunities for easy success which might have lessened the kind of strength he needed at the climax of his career.

The perspective he gained was simply an outgrowth and confirmation of social attitudes that had matured long ago in the Eisenhower home. It was the perspective of the detached observer. He got into the habit of seeing himself and his career from the outside, watching both of them with a tolerant good humor—as though he were a happy god on Olympus looking down upon a protégé. Because he was older than his competitors and because this fact seemed to him an insuperable obstacle to any spectacular advancement, he looked upon his vocation as a kind of game which one should play as well as possible but which it would be a mistake to take with tragic seriousness. Thus traits which had always been remarkably small in him—traits of egotistic desire, of purely selfish ambition, discouraged by the Eisenhower home environment—were now permanently stunted. And though he early resigned himself to a career of small glory, character traits encouraged in the Eisenhower home prevented his resignation from leading to a lazy indifference. He had a great quantity of disciplined energy; unused, it would have soured in him and made him unhappy. He had a habit of hard work; for it he could never substitute a habit of frivolous play. So he worked hard. He was determined in his good-humored way to go as far as he could. He was equally determined not to break his heart because he could go no farther.

The vital strategy which developed out of these attitudes is one which, though profoundly significant, is difficult to describe. Its very essence is its indefiniteness, its endless adaptability, its repudiation of "system." Its design is never rigid, and what shape it has is for the most part imposed by external necessities. Its inspiration is never a willful egotism—it is drawn by an objective goal rather than pushed by a purely subjective desire—and the success it achieves is likely to be measured in relatively impersonal social terms. It is the strategy of the relaxed will, of controlled drift, of creative compromise. It is a peculiarly *democratic* strategy. Perhaps the best way to explain it is to contrast it with the totalitarian strategy which was developing during those years in millions of European youths and which was epitomized (in its most extreme form) in Adolf Hitler.

Dwight Eisenhower, encountering obstacles, looked upon them as objective problems and set to work solving them, or surmounting them with whatever labor was necessary. If he failed—why, then, he failed; one could not hope to win every time. Hitler looked upon obstacles as malignant personalities to whom he often submitted without an outward struggle, though he seethed inwardly with hatred and frustration. He loafed, but not in any relaxed and restful way. He became spiritually tense and violent. Failure was something too horrible to be admitted, ever; to admit even a small failure as his own would be to admit that he was as other men, and not a superman, a great genius, after all. Dwight Eisenhower never expected or even wanted to mold the world in his own image; he regarded himself largely as an image of that world and a part of it; compromise, in his view, was a necessary arrangement between ego and non-ego, and no opprobrium should be attached to it. But to Hitler the world was either enemy or inert material to be molded on the pattern of his will. In every case it was all or nothing with him; in his view all such terms of compromise as "mercy" and "generosity" and "modesty" were admissions of a disgraceful weakness. It followed that, whereas Dwight had a remarkable capacity for making friends, Hitler and the hordes of rootless men he represented were essentially solitary, incapable of any genuine friendship, and even scornful of it.

A man like Eisenhower does not seize power and use it to implement his will. He *accepts* it with no great eagerness and exercises it in the interests of those who granted it. Never would he regard power as having its source *in* him, belonging to him personally; always he would regard it as something distinct from himself, a kind of stream to which he must submit in the very process of controlling it. And great power could be given him only by a relatively stable society which recognized creative compromise as both the foundation of stability and the means of evolution.

2

That year revealed, as clearly as any that was to follow, the fact that Dwight Eisenhower was not the conqueror type. He was not one to storm the world by frontal assault and seize from it the objects of his desire. He lacked the kind of will which can clearly define such objects. He may have lacked the kind of imagination necessary for conceiving the assault. Certainly he lacked the ruthlessness and egotism which are necessary to the assault's success. He did not so much *make* his opportunities as take advantage of them when they presented themselves to him, and in the spring and summer of 1910 they presented themselves through the person of Everett E. Hazlett, Jr.

Swede Hazlett, they called him in Abilene. He had blond hair, was more than a year younger than Dwight, and came from a prosperous North Side family. He had been "brought up astride a pony," a fact which, in conjunction with the proximity of Fort Riley ("World's Largest Cavalry School"), had determined his ambition. At the age of twelve he had entered into correspondence with his congressman, seeking an appointment to West Point; and three years in a military school in Wisconsin, where his father had hoped to "cure" him, served only to strengthen his desire for an army career. The West Point appointment, however, never materialized. In lieu of it the congressman offered, in the spring of 1910, an appointment to Annapolis. It wasn't, in Swede's view, a particularly attractive offer. The heroes he wished to emulate were the dashing cavalry officers of the Civil and Indian wars. He had, as he expressed it, "some misgivings about the sea." Nevertheless, since it seemed to be the best he could do, he accepted the appointment. In May he left school to go to Annapolis, there to "prep" for the Academy's entrance examinations which were to be held in June. He found to his dismay that he was deficient in mathematics. He would have to cover in a few weeks a year's course in algebra and geometry. He tried valiantly to do so, but in the June examinations he failed. By this time he had seen enough of Annapolis to become enthusiastic about it, and he wrote at once to his congressman asking for a reappointment. The congressman, whose

Naval Academy appointment was not much in demand among his Kansas constituency that year, was glad to oblige. . . .

Since Swede had attended the North Side grade school and had gone only one year to Abilene High School, his acquaintance with Dwight had remained casual, limited to summer vacations during Dwight's high school years. It ripened in that summer of 1910 into an intimate friendship. In June, Dwight had been appointed night foreman at the creamery, having entire charge of the plant from six o'clock each evening until six o'clock in the morning. This was considered "quite a responsible job" for a youth of nineteen, though Dwight had only two men under him, and Swede was impressed by it. He was even more impressed by Dwight himself. He liked Dwight's frankness, honesty, modesty, and he recognized as Ruby Norman and Minnie Stewart had done that Dwight's mind was superior. He became one of the gang which dropped in during the long summer evenings to play penny-ante poker with Dwight in the engine room. Before long the creamery was Swede's chief hangout during the hours he was free from the job he had taken in the office of a small manufacturing concern downtown. With Dwight he occasionally raided the creamery's refrigeration plant for ice cream, or for cold-storage eggs and chickens, which were then fried on a well-scrubbed shovel over the fire beneath the boilers. Swede's inclusion in these enterprises, which could have cost Dwight his job had they been discovered, testifies to the fact that the friendship between the two youths had become as close as that between Dwight and Six.

Swede's mind, naturally, was full of Annapolis lore. In slack periods at the office he was studying for the entrance examinations, and at the creamery at nights he talked to Dwight with enthusiasm about the Naval Academy. Dwight listened politely at first, and then with a quickening interest. Gradually it dawned upon Swede that his friend's interest was not wholly academic.

"Look, Ike," he burst out impetuously one evening, "why don't you come with me? You'd like it there and you'd make a fine naval officer. We could have a swell time together."

It was obvious that Dwight had been thinking along those lines. The idea wasn't bad, he admitted. It would give him a career, and he was tired of this aimless drifting he had been doing ever since he graduated from high school. He was sure, from what Swede had told him, that he'd like the Academy and the Navy. There was just one little difficulty.

"You," he pointed out, "have the only appointment available from this district."

"From the congressman, yes," Swede said. "But the senators have appointments, too, and maybe all of them haven't been made for next year."

"I don't have any political pull," Dwight objected. "I don't even know anyone who has."

"Well, anyway, it can't hurt to try," Swede said.

Dwight agreed that it wouldn't hurt to try. He didn't make up his mind to do so, however, until he'd thought the matter over carefully. Six MacDonell, thirty-five years later, would vividly remember sitting on a curbing of Abilene's main business district, with Dwight beside him, listening to the latter's arguments. The arguments were designed ostensibly to persuade Six that he should go with Dwight and Swede to a "service school" (Six didn't even know what a "service school" was until Dwight explained), but the younger boy suspected at the time that Dwight was mainly trying to persuade Dwight. In any case, Six already knew what he wanted to do when he graduated in 1911. He was going to play professional baseball. Already scouts for St. Louis and Kansas City teams had come to Abilene to watch his work. He'd have no trouble getting a contract in the minors.

"There's no future in it," Dwight warned.

Six thought there was. From the minor leagues he would go to the majors. He'd become famous doing what he loved to do, and before his left arm gave out he'd have earned enough money to keep him comfortably for the rest of his life. Dwight argued that the whole thing was too risky; too much depended upon the "breaks" in a sports career, no matter how good you were. Six ought to go to college. He could play baseball there, get more experience, and he'd have something to fall back on if the baseball career fell through. It was advice which Six, later on, would wish he had taken, but at the time he merely pointed out that it would be impossible for three Abilene boys to obtain Annapolis appointments in the same year. Dwight would be lucky if he got one himself. . . .

Perhaps the chief factor influencing Dwight's hesitation was his knowledge of his parents' attitude toward war and militarism. His mother's attitude was especially hostile to the profession of arms, which in her view was allied to sin, if not actually identified with it. He remembered only too well the censorious attitude she had displayed toward the war games he and Ed had played during the Spanish-American War, and he remembered the references she had made to the horror of the Shenandoah Valley raids and counter-raids during the Civil War. He must expect painful scenes at home if and when he made his ambition known there. He hated the thought of hurting his mother so deeply.

But it was his life, after all. Here, at last, was a definite program, with a definite goal. His vital strategy involved a relaxed drifting within limits, but it also involved the application of swift, decisive action when those limits were reached. He felt, deep inside him, that the limits had been reached now. He could drift no longer. So one evening soon after his conversation with Six he showed Swede the rough draft of a letter he planned to send to both Kansas senators, asking for an appointment to the Naval Academy. He wanted to know if, in Swede's opinion, the letter was worded in such a way as to get results. Swede, overjoyed, thought it was.

At this point Dwight Eisenhower's career was for the first time directly involved in the main stream of national history. Perhaps he himself has never been aware of how much he owes to the tide of political liberalism which swept the Western prairies from 1896 through 1912.

After the assassination of McKinley, Populist-Muckraking-Anti-trust sentiment achieved national power (or was dissipated, depending on your point of view) through Theodore Roosevelt's Progressive Republicanism—and one consequence was the election to the United States Senate in 1908 of Joseph L. Bristow, the first senator from Kansas to be elected under the state's new primary law. Bristow was a reformer. In the late 1880s he had begun his career as district clerk in Lawrence, Kansas. Here he made friends with a round-faced youngster named William Allen White, who at that time was a none-too-brilliant student at the University of Kansas. At about the time young Will White went to Emporia to buy the *Gazette* with borrowed money, Bristow went to Salina to buy the *Journal*. During McKinley's first term Bristow had served as fourth assistant postmaster general and had achieved a national reputation through a postal investigation personally conducted in

Cuba which resulted in the conviction of a number of men for fraud. In the meantime his editorials in the *Journal* (they were among the first in Kansas to praise LaFollette) were doing much to further Will White's political education. In 1903 White was instrumental in having Bristow appointed, by Roosevelt, to investigate the Post Office Department. Again Bristow proceeded with fearless integrity, exposing many instances of malpractice and fraud.

In 1908, when Bristow decided to run for the Senate against the incumbent, Chester I. Long, White became Bristow's unofficial manager. Writing for his *Gazette* and for Nelson's Kansas City *Star,* White attacked Long as a "reactionary," a "machine politician" who served, not the people, but "special interests." The editorials had their effect. When the primary votes were counted Bristow had won the nomination (tantamount to election) by a safe margin, and all hands agreed that White's support had been a major factor in the decision. Thus it was that when Dwight Eisenhower sought his service-school appointment he sent his application to a man who abhorred the "spoils system," who was determined to decide issues and choose men according to merit, and who therefore was holding competitive examinations for all West Point and Annapolis appointments. It was an unusual procedure in that day, when such appointments were generally used as building stones in political fences. Chester Long would probably not have followed it. Had Long continued in office, Dwight Eisenhower—with his total lack of the kind of political pull effective with the Long machine—might have had small chance of favorable consideration.

As it was, Abilene numbered among its citizens several personal friends of the new senator. Chief among them was Phil Heath, who had come to Abilene in 1900 to edit the Abilene *Chronicle,* a progressive Republican paper which was a daily rival of Charles M. Harger's conservative *Reflector.* Heath had formerly worked on a Democratic paper in Michigan, and—as a bright-eyed, humorous, pipe-smoking old man—would serve as Democratic postmaster in Abilene during Franklin Roosevelt's administration. Though he was nominally a Republican in the early 1900s, he couldn't, as he put it, "stick the stand-patters." In the split between the left and right wings of the Republican party, which even then was evident and which would culminate in the Bull Moose campaign of 1912, Heath took his stand far on the left side of the left wing. He had supported Bristow's campaign for the nomination and he supported Bristow and the other insurgent Republicans in their fight against the amended Payne-Aldrich Tariff Bill. Thus Bristow's friendship with Heath was political as well as personal, and the senator had specifically asked Heath for recommendations for service-school appointments.

Once his mind was made up Dwight proceeded with typical energy and dispatch to work toward his goal. He canvassed the town's leading professional and businessmen in search of advice and assistance. Here the respect which the Eisenhower family had earned for itself in the community paid dividends. Dwight found, to his delight, that the civic leaders were eager to help him. Whatever rancor may have remained in him from his early encounters with North Side snobbery (and it wasn't much; he didn't hold grudges) was now completely dissipated. His gratitude for the help he received would remain a vital thing all his life long. Bristow was the only senator who had appointments available, and Dwight wanted letters of recommendation to send to him. Among others, he saw Charlie Case, son of a leading merchant; Sterl, another leading merchant; and Charlie Harger. All of them promised to write. But Harger told Dwight frankly that if he sought an appointment from Bristow, Phil Heath was the man to see.

Heath would always remember that hot summer afternoon when Dwight, his lean face shining with perspiration, his hair neatly combed, came to the *Chronicle* office. The boy was a bit embarrassed. He was not accustomed to seeking favors, and the direct gaze of his blue eyes seemed to say that he was not seeking one now. All he wanted was a fair chance. He told Heath that he was seeking the appointment, that he'd seen Case and Harger and the others.

"They tell me that you're the man to see, though," he said.

Heath looked the boy up and down and smiled quizzically.

"So you want to be a sailor," he said. "Aren't you afraid you'll get seasick?"

Dwight grinned his lopsided grin.

"I guess I can stand it if I do," he said.

Heath hadn't known Dwight well. To him Dwight was just one of the boys around town, a pretty good athlete, not particularly outstanding in any way. But he liked the boy, and he admired the Eisenhower family.

"Sure," he said. "You and that Hazlett boy ought to make a

pretty good team. I happen to know Bristow and I'll be glad to recommend you."

In early September, Dwight was notified by Senator Bristow that vacancies for both service schools were available and that he, Dwight Eisenhower, was authorized to appear at the office of the state superintendent of public instruction in Topeka, October 4 and 5, to take a competitive examination prepared by the War Department. The high-ranking men in this examination would be assigned to take entrance examinations, later on, for Annapolis and West Point.

At home Dwight's newly formed ambition met, as he had anticipated, with a mixed reception. Ed, home for the summer after completing his freshman year at Michigan, was enthusiastic. (That was the summer Ed had appendicitis and rolled in agony on the floor of the Eisenhower parlor until the attack passed off. He wouldn't let any of the local doctors operate. Only a short time before one of them had operated for appendicitis on a boy actually suffering from food poisoning, with fatal consequences—or so Ed had heard. He risked peritonitis, waited until he returned to the university, and there had the father of his roommate operate on him.) The enthusiasm of Roy and Earl and Milton was tinged with awe: Annapolis was so far away, so glamorous. But the parents were opposed. . . .

Yet, strangely enough, the very theology which led the parents to oppose their son's ambition prevented their passing upon him the kind of judgment which might, in effect, have exiled him from the family. To have done so would have been to exercise the very violence they abhorred; it would have been an impious assertion, for in the last analysis no man has the right to judge another. Only God has that right. Their religious beliefs, as we have seen, were in the Puritan tradition which denies the necessity or even the efficacy of a mediator (a priesthood, or organized church) between the individual man and God, which insists that a man's salvation involves his conscious participation as an individual in the grace of God. It was a tradition which led inevitably to religious tolerance, despite the zealous excesses of New England colonists. It led now to the sad conviction that Dwight's choice of a career was, on the ethical level, a matter between himself and his Maker. True, his choice involved a compromise with the world which seemed to put him far beyond the pale of even River Brethren piety—and Ida by now had sought out an even more "primitive" and rigid Christianity—but he was a good boy. If he was sure he was right, the mother might at least hope that he was. God, she could assure herself, moves in mysterious ways.

Perhaps he would fail in his examinations. It was, she knew, a slender straw, for she had every confidence in his abilities, but she grasped at it. The time, after all, was short. He had barely four weeks in which to prepare, and he'd be competing with boys who had made up their minds long ago and had been preparing for months. Certainly failure was a possibility.

Dwight himself recognized that it was. He took steps to avoid it. Presumably the examination at Topeka would be much the same as the one for which Swede had been studying all summer. Swede had been to the "cram school" in Annapolis and knew all the short cuts. Couldn't Swede help him? Swede was eager to do what he could. He suggested that Dwight come to the manufacturing-plant office every afternoon at two o'clock so that the boys could study together, Swede acting as tutor, until five. During those three-hour sessions Swede did barely enough work for his firm to keep from being discharged. Dwight, he discovered without surprise, was a remarkably apt pupil; his mind absorbed facts and held them with seemingly little effort, and it cut with swift, keen logic through the knottiest of problems. Within two weeks, according to Swede's own account, "Ike's God-given brain had sped him along until he was 'way ahead of his self-appointed teacher." By October 4 Swede was sure that Dwight was ready for the test, that he'd pass with flying colors. Dwight, characteristically, was not so sure.

"But I'll do the best I can," he said as he boarded the train for Topeka. "I can't do more than that."

Two days later he returned to Abilene, calmly satisfied that he *had* done his best, but far from confident that his best was good enough. The algebra part of the examination, he told Swede, had been easier than he had expected, but the history and geometry parts had surprised him. They were "awfully tough." He had been so sure of his knowledge of these subjects that he hadn't bothered to "cram" on them, and now he was afraid that his failure to do so had cost him his chance for an appointment. It was an irony which did not amuse him. . . .

Thirty-five years later there was on file in the Kansas Historical Library in Topeka, among the papers of ex-Senator Bristow, a record of the grades made by the eight candidates who gathered in State Superintendent Fairchild's office on those early October days of 1910. The record sheet contains notes written in longhand by Bristow himself. "Dwight Eisenhour" (note spelling) stood second among the eight candidates, four of whom wanted *only* West Point appointments and four of whom would accept either West Point or Annapolis. "Eisenhour," evidently deciding at the last minute to give himself all possible chance of success, was listed as an "either," and he stood first among those so listed. His grade average was $87\frac{1}{2}$ out of a possible 100. The boy who beat him had scored $89\frac{2}{8}$. The nearest competitor behind him had scored $79\frac{3}{8}$. Dwight had scored 73 in United States history, 79 in general history, 90 in spelling, 77 in geometry, 94 in algebra, 99 in grammar, 90 in geography, and 96 in arithmetic.

One afternoon Dwight came to Swede's office, solemnly displaying a letter he had received from Senator Bristow. He was proud of it, but not particularly happy. He had been given an appointment, but it was to West Point instead of Annapolis. Swede, who had been looking forward so eagerly to Dwight's companionship, was bitterly disappointed. He urged Dwight to write to the senator, state his preference for the Navy, and ask for a reconsideration. Dwight muttered that it wouldn't do to "look a gift horse in the mouth." After all, he had stated his willingness at Topeka to enter either Annapolis or West Point. But he toyed with the idea until, a few days later, Swede happened to be rereading an Annapolis pamphlet and discovered that one must enter the Naval Academy *before* his twentieth birthday. Dwight and Swede had known, of course, that the age limits for entry were sixteen to twenty, but they had assumed that these limits included the twentieth year.

"Well, that settles that," Dwight said. "I was twenty on October 14."

"They wouldn't need to know," Swede argued halfheartedly. "They haven't any way of proving when you were born. You could knock off a couple of years and nobody'd be the wiser."

Dwight shook his head. It would be risky. At such a juncture one would be a fool to tempt fate with a lie. And Swede could not but agree. Anyway, they'd be together for several months more. The West Point entrance examinations would not be held until January, the Annapolis ones not until the spring, and registration would not be until June.

At home the parents reconciled themselves to Dwight's career. They knew there was no chance of his failing his entrance examinations. When Dwight had proudly announced his appointment his mother had said, without batting an eye, "That's fine, Dwight. I was sure you'd do it." Afterward she had gone upstairs to her room and wept. . . .

The parents were not the only ones who regarded Dwight's choice of a career with small favor. One or two of his high school teachers thought he was limiting needlessly his chances for advancement in the world. The orthodox River Brethren, of course, did not consider a military career wholly respectable, no matter how great its success. It is reported that Ruby Norman could not contemplate with any great enthusiasm an army career, particularly for a boy as bright as Ike, though she seems to have kept her views to herself. As for Minnie Stewart, she was frankly dismayed. She was sure he was making a great error, and she told him so. She hated the thought of his wasting a superior mind, a splendid character, in an organization where brains and character counted, she thought, for very little. In almost any other field he'd be bound to go far.

"There's just no *future* in the Army," she told him flatly. "You're just throwing yourself away."

Dwight grinned, shrugged—and changed the subject.

3

Meanwhile he had become again a student in Abilene High School. During the summer Bud Huffman and Six and Orrin Snider (a huge boy from a farm near by who had starred for three years on Abilene football teams and who in 1909 had taken Judge Parent's place as coach) had urged Dwight to come back for "graduate work." They pointed out that it wouldn't hurt him to study some advanced science courses—mathematics and chemistry and physics —if he planned to attend either of the academies. Just incidentally, he'd be able to play another season of football. . . .

The incidental fact was the decisive one. The new physical strength and energy which had surged through him all that year demanded expression. He was large enough now to be really effective on a football field. Six MacDonell was quarterback, Bud Huffman played halfback, and Dwight played tackle, next to guard Ralph Lucier, who was one of the proprietors of the Tip-Top and who, some years later, would marry Ruby Norman. Even at tackle, a normally unspectacular position, Dwight managed to star that year. He was not only heavier but faster than he had ever been before. He opened beautiful holes in the opposing lines through which Bud Huffman snaked his way for dazzling off-tackle runs, and his defensive play was equally effective. Of the six games that fall, Abilene won three, tied one, and lost two, scoring a total of 82 points for the season against 13 points for opponents. Junction City in the first game, played two days after Dwight's return from Topeka, eked out a 2–0 win, but in all the other games involving traditional school rivalries—St. John's Military Academy, Enterprise, and Salina—Abilene came out the winner.

It was in the Salina game, played in Abilene on November 11, that Dwight was most outstanding. The Salina team had been unbeaten that year. It was coached by a former Kansas University football star who was actually paid for his services, a rare thing among Kansas high schools at that time. Orrin Snider and his team were therefore particularly anxious to win this game. Rivalry between the two schools had always been intense. The Salina coach's favorite play was a hidden ball-delayed-buck sort of thing, run over the tackle position. After the ball was snapped from center it was screened while two backfield men, running interference, hit the tackle position simultaneously. The ball carrier, suddenly revealing himself a second or so after he'd been expected and charging hard, caught the opponents off balance. The combination of deception, concentrated power, and speed had proved irresistible in earlier games. It worked well the first two or three times it was run over Dwight's position. But Dwight, finding himself knocked out of the play, was not inclined to repeat his tactics. Thereafter he stopped the play cold by the simple expedient of stepping aside, letting the interference pass by, and then charging through the hole in the Salina line to stop the Salina halfback on or behind the line of scrimmage. He also contributed greatly to the success of Abilene's offense. The Abilene backfield, sparked by Six and Bud, managed to score two touchdowns.

Toward the end of the game the Salina boys grew desperate. Their play became rougher. In the last quarter, Six at quarterback called a fake play. He took the ball himself, started around right end, and then suddenly passed to Bud Huffman, who was running wide around left end. A Salina boy named Forrest Ritter came charging through. He tackled Six viciously after Six had passed the ball. Realizing his mistake, he scrambled to his feet and in doing so brought his head hard against the point of Six's jaw, knocking the latter boy unconscious. Six quickly recovered, but Dwight was furious. He was convinced that his friend had been deliberately injured by the Salina boy. For the remainder of the game there was no holding him. With savage deliberateness he "roughed" a good half of the Salina team and was restrained from inflicting further damage only by the game's end. The final score was 16–0. The Salina coach came up to Snider, grinning ruefully. He would, he said, "give anything" to have as fine a tackle as "that Ike Eisenhower of yours. . . ."

Dwight was going to school only in the mornings. He continued to work in the evenings at the creamery. He continued to study with Swede Hazlett in the afternoons. He was far happier than he had been the year before. From earliest childhood, vagueness and indecision had exasperated him, and he was glad that the vital decisions had now been made. Cheerfully he accepted a future which had a definite pattern to it, and in the glow of Swede's admiring friendship his self-confidence expanded, became firm and sure. When in January he went to St. Louis to take his West Point examinations he had no fear of the outcome. He took them easily and passed with a high grade. He was on his way.

In February, Swede Hazlett left Abilene to go to Annapolis, there to continue his studies under the guidance of the "cram" school. He was to be triple certain this time that he would pass. And he did pass. He entered the Naval Academy in June.

That year Dwight had a fox terrier named Flip who had formerly been part of a dog act in the Parker Circus, which wintered in Abilene. Either Flip did not fit into the act properly, or the act itself was broken up. At any rate, one of the circus men gave the dog to Dwight one day, and before long boy and dog were inseparable. Flip virtually ignored Earl and Roy and Milton, but for Dwight he gladly performed all his tricks. He could jump from the hayloft window, fifteen or twenty feet above the ground, and by running down the wall and then springing straight out land on all fours without injury to himself. He could stand on his hind legs, jump through hoops, and do flip-flops. As the months passed he became one more strong tie between Dwight and home, another tie which must be strained if not broken when the time for departure came.

It came inexorably. It arrived in early June, on a warm, lazy golden day. Red roses were blooming on the trellis. The earth was rich and dark between the green rows of vegetables in the garden. The deep blue of sky and the yellow radiance of sun seemed to cohere in the lush emerald substance of the lawns. Dwight's perceptions were unusually acute that day. The mood of farewell etched in sharp lines of finality everything he saw and heard and felt. From the upstairs windows he looked out across the Lincoln school ground, trampled bare by children's feet, recalling scene after vivid scene from his grade school days. A block away was the Curry house where he had so often played with the flock of Curry boys and girls. When he looked out of the south window he saw Joner Callahan's house with waves of green wheat behind it, tossing gently in the warm wind of afternoon. Beyond, hidden behind its screen of willow and cottonwood, flowed the Smoky Hill, where he had skated in the winter and swum in the summer year after year. In a wide, flat field to the east a farmer was riding his cultivator up and down the long rows of corn. Everything seemed more beautiful than it ever had before. . . .

From his pocket Dwight pulled out the heavy watch his grandfather, Jacob, had given him long ago, and it told him that the final moments had come. The train would be in soon. His ticket—how long it was!—was folded in his pocket. His heavy packed bag was on the floor beside the door, waiting for him to take it. He gave one last look around the room he was leaving. Then he seized the bag and went downstairs.

Already he had said most of his good-bys. To Ed, back again from Michigan and who was to work through the coming year at the creamery, and to his father and Earl, also working in the creamery, he had said good-by in the morning. To Roy, working in an Abilene drugstore that summer, learning to be a pharmacist, Dwight had also said good-by that morning. To Bud Huffman and the rest of the gang, to Ruby Norman and Minnie Stewart, he had said good-by the day before. Six had gone off to St. Joseph for his first season in the minor leagues. (Later on his career would be even more directly involved with Bristow than Dwight's had been, for Bristow was to give him a job, first as reporter and then as backroom man, on the Salina *Journal*.) Only Milton and his mother and Flip were waiting downstairs. Somehow that made the last scene more difficult, lonelier in its finality, than it would have been if everyone had been home.

They waited for him on the side porch. Dwight put down his bag, leaned down to pet Flip. Then he straightened up. His mother smiled at him cheerfully enough, but he could see that she did so with great effort. Her eyes were unusually bright, and her lips quivered as she spoke to him.

"You take care of yourself, Dwight," she said. "And be a good boy."

"Sure, Mother. Sure. I will."

Then suddenly, for the first time in the sight of her sons, she was crying. Dwight and Milton looked at her in embarrassed astonishment, and Dwight put an awkward arm around her, hugged her tightly.

"I'll be back before you know it, Mother," he said in a strained voice. "Please, Mother! And I'll write you often while I'm gone."

He turned to Milton and said gruffly, to hide his embarrassment: "Milton, I'm counting on you to look after Mother."

And somehow that was too much for Milton. His self-control gave way completely and he bawled out loud.

"Aw," said Dwight embarrassedly. "Aw, for goodness' sake!"

He seized his bag, gave Flip a curt order to "stay home," and hurled a last good-by over his shoulder as he almost ran into the street. Quickly, never once looking back, he walked northward toward the station. From far away, across miles of rolling prairie, came the sad, lonely whistle of the train.

BOOK THREE

West Point and the First Command

CHAPTER I

The Metal and the Mold

THE COUNTRY in all its complexity of enterprise, its spatial immensity, its loneliness of distance and of crowds, unrolled itself outside the train windows as he journeyed eastward on the steel rails, tracing in reverse the migratory trail of his forebears. It was a far different country from that which Jacob and old Frederick and the adolescent David had seen thirty-three years before. In eastern Kansas—through Manhattan, Topeka, Lawrence, through the dozen tiny villages and the valleys pent by limestone hills—the difference was not so apparent. But Kansas City was a tangible portent of that mysterious East from whose looming shadow (the factory chimneys coughing smoke into the sky) Jacob and his neighbors had sought escape. To a youth whose farthest remembered journey had been that single one to St. Louis, Kansas City was still overpowering. The East had moved into the West. The two met and bred upon the banks of the Kaw and the Missouri a giant child seething with hybrid energy. A kind of heterosis had thrust those towers of brick and concrete above the river bluffs and spilled across the bottom land this ugly waste of flat brick buildings and mean streets thick with the stench of packing houses. Here the frontier was forever lost. Here was focused a sophisticated urban culture of which he had as yet scarcely an inkling. Standing on the depot platform among the bustling multitude, Dwight Eisenhower was aware of his greenness.

Then the train for which he waited rolled up the tracks, the locomotive hissing steam as its terrific drive wheels ground reluctantly to a stop. The great cars were poised in front of him. From now on, across Missouri and beyond, it would be new country. But as he lifted his bag and climbed the iron steps he could tell himself that, after all, Arthur was getting along all right in this very city, and Ed had done all right in Michigan. What they had done he could do. There was no reason to be afraid. Seated again beside a window, he could even laugh at himself a little for being so nervous. There was nothing at all he could do about it now. He was practically in the Army already. The oath he'd take in a couple of days would simply confirm the fact. From now on it was the Army which must make the decisions, removing from him a large measure of personal responsibility, and all he had to do was relax and live for the moment. He could effortlessly watch the world, a vast new world, roll by. Kansas City's towers were lost in the distance behind him, the Missouri fields and towns gave way imperceptibly to Iowa's, and the land leaned gently down toward the Mississippi. He gazed avidly at the great sweep of muddy water below the roaring bridge. Beyond lay the flat rich fields of Illinois. Abruptly the country seemed more certainly ordered and more prosperous—the houses were larger, the trees were larger—than any he had seen before.

The outward face of history was serene as it spread endlessly across town and countryside, hill and stream, yielding only now and then to the nervous spasm of a city. Outwardly there was an enormous, timeless peace. The houses and the men who paused in their work to watch the train go by seemed as integral to the landscape, as calmly secure, as the mighty elms which thrust their roots so deeply into the American earth. He watched, not moodily, but with a quick attentiveness to individual impressions; he noted the condition of the crops, the way that house was built, the pattern of the slag heaps above the first mines he had ever seen. His mind shaped swiftly from his vision separate factual items, storing them away for future reference in his remarkably commodious memory. He could not have been aware that the peaceful scenes were but an outward seeming, that beneath them surged, through America and beyond, a long-pent violence. That peaceful world out there was poised upon a volcano which rumbled dangerously in this summer of 1911, its pressures building inexorably toward the mightiest explosion the world had ever known.

Through the remainder of June and all of July, as Dwight yielded himself good-naturedly to the West Point mold, the serene face of a world he had never thought to question seemed about to slip off, as a deceitful mask, and reveal a reality of passionate hatred, of bloody violence, and of agony whose depth and sweep would pass all human understanding. A French expedition had occupied Fez in the spring. A German firm had promptly charged that the French action threatened large interests which this firm had established on and behind the harbor of Agadir. The French denied the charge, offered to facilitate the inspection of the harbor by impartial witnesses to prove that there were no German installations of any sort around the harbor, and settled down for anticipated lengthy negotiations. Then on July 1, without warning, the Kaiser announced to a trembling Europe that he had dispatched his gunboat, the *Panther,* to Agadir. The situation was so delicate that a word, a single rash deed, could provoke the conflict. There followed weeks of secret conferences in the chancelleries of England and the Continent, a firm public speech at last (on July 21) by Lloyd George, in which he clearly implied that England would fight beside France if Germany attacked, and then a gradual withdrawal by the Germans from their precarious position. The politicians could breathe again. War would not come this year.

But in Vienna that summer there was one who must have accepted the temporary settlement, not with relief, but in a kind of despairing disgust. The twenty-two-year-old Hitler, still submerged in the tide of anonymous rootless men, was reading the newspapers with a feverish interest. Through the weeks of crisis he could see the chaos that was in him extending itself over all the world. He longed for it to happen. The Hero, the Great Man, would then have his opportunity to rise or to die in all the glory of a Wagnerian tragedy. One can imagine him in the cafés, pouring out his fanatic Teuton patriotism before all who will listen to him. For two years now he had lived in the abyss, a failure as artist and as man, barely supporting himself with wooden drawings and lifeless paintings sold, for the most part, to shopkeepers and furniture manufacturers who used them to advertise their products or to decorate them. Vienna, indeed all of Austria, was the image of his failure. Already he was toying with the idea of going to Munich. If war came he would serve with the German Army. He was aware of history flowing in mighty currents of power, and if war came he could become, first a part of that stream, and then himself a Power.

From all of this Dwight Eisenhower, whose future was so deeply involved in it, would remain for a long time curiously isolated. For him history was what *had* happened, a collection of facts; he had no conscious participation in its present making. There is a certain irony in one's picture of this mid-American youth, his mind occupied with external scenes and with the prospects for a great record on the Army's football team, riding toward his appointment with a destiny he might never wholly understand. There is a juxtaposition of incongruous elements: the naïve enmeshed in the sophisticated, the simple in the complex; with the naïvely simple maintaining its iron-hard integrity amid all the complex pressures, and winning the final victories, because Life is on its side. The play of chance within the framework of necessity, the slow freezing of the fluid possible into the solidly inevitable seem as processes so evident in this eastward train ride. Eagerly Dwight's gaze seeks the hills which for his father had meant home, the hills of Pennsylvania. Eagerly, if a trifle nervously, his mind accepts the impact of the cities—Pittsburgh, Harrisburg, Philadelphia—rising in a crescendo to the crashing climax of New York. It's a big world, all right, with a lot of people in it—bigger, and with more people, than he had imagined. Manhattan Island is an anchored ship with a thousand clustered masts, and perhaps he is glad to escape its claustrophobia as he boards the last train of his journey, the train driving up the Hudson to the Point of which he had dreamed for so long.

The frontier is dead, but he is its living heritage. . . .

2

The special, running up the West Shore Railroad, was crowded with West Point appointees. Looking at them, listening to their talk, Dwight could feel an expansion of self-confidence. If this was his competition he should not have too much trouble meeting it. Nearly all of the boys were younger than he, and not only in years. Many of them were timidly quiet. Others revealed their fearful tension through loud talk and nervous laughter. By contrast with their scared immaturity he felt more poised and mature than he ever had before. He turned to look again across the broad sweep of the Hudson and at the granite cliffs which seemed to loom precariously over the tracks at his left. Of course it wouldn't do to underrate these kids. Some of them looked smart, all right, and when their scaredness wore off a lot of them would no doubt seem suddenly mature. But the very fact that they all seemed to take it so seriously gave him an initial advantage over them. As for himself, he was determined to "fit in," have as much fun and keep out of as much trouble as possible, without ever letting the system "get" him. He understood that on the first day the new cadets were given a rough time. He was good-humoredly prepared to take it.

All the same he was aware of a sudden tightening of his abdominal muscles when, bag in hand, he stood at last with the other boys on the platform of the tiny station. He looked up apprehensively at the granite cliffs which seemed to merge, without a perceptible interruption of texture, into the granite castles at the top. This was it. Even in the boiling sunlight of one of the hottest days of the year those granite walls looked cold. One could easily imagine dark, damp dungeons beneath them. He remembered the prison walls he had seen at Joliet, far to one side of the tracks, and he remarked in these towering buildings the same grimness, the same frozen hostility to any free and easy spontaneity. Then he heard some of the other boys saying out loud the thoughts he would have kept secret, and he looked at them and relaxed again. Men had built this place, and men ran it. He was not afraid of any man. He could even enjoy the scenery, which was pretty swell after all, as he joined the ragged line for the climb up the long steep drive to the Plain.

Thereafter he was, for some hours, too busy obeying orders to do any thinking at all. First, in the Administration Building, he registered. His registration form, still on file at West Point, records in his undistinguished penmanship that he had studied "geography, arithmetic, United States history, spelling, music, and grammar" in primary school, and that in his senior year in high school he had studied "economics, physics, United States history, English, civil government." He also stated, in response to one question, that he did not use tobacco in any form, and, in response to another, that he had earned his own living "partially for six years and wholly for two years as a refrigeration engineer, also fireman." Then, in swift succession, one after another of his relationships with the outside world were broken off. He gave all his money to the treasurer and was informed that from now on all his financial transactions must be carried on by check, drawing against the account into which the treasurer would place his cadet salary. This meager salary must be his sole income. If he overdrew his account he must get along as best he could until his credit was re-established by his pay, and if at any time he was caught with cash upon his person he would be subject to immediate dismissal. He felt himself to be as naked spiritually as he was physically when he stood before the doctors for his final physical examination. The doctors found him to be in perfect condition, and his five feet ten and a half inches of height placed him automatically in the tallest cadet company, F Company, on the left flank of the parade line. His civilian clothes and his baggage were checked in at a checking room, where they would be kept, he was told, until his second-class furlough came up two years from now—unless he was dismissed before that time. A room and a temporary roommate were assigned to him.

He was now a "Beast," subjected first of all to the peremptory orders of boys who, though most of them were younger than himself, displayed a brisk, cool poise. Clad in gray jackets and white duck trousers, they snapped their orders. They were the "Beast Detail," third-class men who lined up the "Beasts" and sent them on the run to the barbershop, to the cadet store for the first issue of uniforms and bedding, and back to the barracks, trotting still despite the load they must carry. Even then there was no rest. The "Beasts" were ordered out for their first drill, and the third-class men, delighting in their first exercise of authority, "poured it on." Smiles were "wiped off," chins were drawn in, and the boys who only hours before had been lounging civilians stood stiff as ramrods, shoulders back and chests out and abdomens drawn in, along a dressed line. They were told that they were "Beasts," a disgrace to the Academy, unworthy even of the contemptuous attention of upperclassmen. Some of the faces grew white and strained as the afternoon hours, brilliant with heat, moved swiftly by. Some of the "Beasts" were too tensely eager to please. Dwight, seeing them out of the tail of his eye, could tell that they'd crack if they didn't watch out. There was no danger of his cracking. He was grinning inwardly, spiritually relaxed, aware of a certain flamboyant absurdity in what was, no doubt, a necessary initiation. Those kids out there in their immaculate uniforms, with all their high and mighty attitudes and their curt, contemptuous orders, were trying so hard to deny their immaturity, to prove that they were men.

But when five o'clock came, the absurd, if he considered it so, gave way to the sublime. As one of a group of 265 youths, the largest class ever to enter West Point up to that time, he stood in a gray line on the parade ground to watch a review of the corps. In full-dress uniform, moving as an organic unit, arms and legs coordinated in a perfect rhythm, the cadets marched by as the band played. The flags, the guns, the music, the beautiful and brave young men—this was the bright face of war as a Kansas boy might have dreamed it. It had the stylized beauty of a dance form. It gave one a sense of belonging to something very high and fine, something which extended immeasurably beyond himself, and he could not fail to be impressed. He was in the proper mood of proud yet humble dedication when he took, with the others, the oath of allegiance:

I do solemnly swear that I will support the Constitution of the United States and bear true allegiance to the National Government; that I will maintain and defend the sovereignty of the United States paramount to any and all allegiance, sovereignty, or fealty I may owe to any State, county or country whatsoever, and that I will at all times obey the legal orders of my superior officers and the rules and articles governing the Armies of the United States.

Long ago, on August 21, 1819, William Wirt, Attorney General of the United States, had ruled that "the corps at West Point form a part of the land forces of the United States, and have been constitutionally subjected by Congress to the rules and articles of war, and to trial by courts-martial." Dwight Eisenhower was in the Army. It was a new game, with new and difficult rules, and he could enjoy most of it—as a game. Some of it was absurd, of course. He had his moments of secret rebellion. But on the whole he played it cheerfully enough, and well enough, if without distinction.

The first few weeks, extending through a record-breaking spell of heat, were the most difficult. Everything was done at double time, it seemed, under a broiling sun. Nightfall found most of the plebes in the "Beast Barracks" sleeping a dreamless sleep of exhaustion. In preparation for the summer encampment at Fort Clinton, three weeks after Dwight's entry on June 14, the process of indoctrination and of physical hardening was speeded up. Quickly the new cadets discovered that the West Point mold was a rigid one, austere, puritan in its definitions of duty, honor, country, inflexible in its sharp discontinuity with all which might bend its product in fatal moments from a course of rigorous exactitude. It was designed to shape not authors but instruments of a national destiny. Those who submitted to it must forfeit a large area of vital decision which might otherwise be theirs. They were not to make the definitions; they were, themselves, to be defined by them. The first emphasis was all on obedience as the counterpart of command, and for those who would not or could not obey dismissal was both swift and inevitable.

The code indicated clearly enough that certain types of men were not wanted. When these types were encountered, when they deviated from the sharp, clear lines or declared war on the "system," they were coldly, automatically rejected. Edgar Allan Poe had declared war. "Running it" again and again to Benny Haven's tavern, there to drown his hatred of the system in Benny's whisky, he had called the Point a "God-forsaken place"; his dismissal had been particularly inglorious. James A. McNeill Whistler, though he seems not to have been unhappy there, found the Point's academic requirements rather boring and was not heartbroken when the instructors, disagreeing with his stated opinion in an examination that silicon is a gas, sent him down. Dwight Eisenhower's own first roommate was among those found wanting. He is reported to have been something of a social snob, inclined to look down upon the plebeian Eisenhower, who heartily disliked him. He wept bitter tears, literally, when his superiority went unrecognized, and when he took to fainting on the drill field, generally in the shade of a tree, he was soon sent packing.

As for Dwight, his strategy of the relaxed will called for a suspension of judgment on matters which, at their first impact, seemed hostile to his natural tendencies. He could yield outwardly with relatively few mental reservations, and those few were not of the aggressive, egotistic variety whose suppression would make for a dangerous sense of personal frustration. His physical toughness made it relatively easy for him to meet the demands of drill and march and calisthenics, which to other boys were difficult indeed. His sharp externalized mind would fit easily into a system of education which was, in the narrowest and most rigid sense, technical and "scientific." Factual subjects which, to Whistler for example, had seemed boring would, to him, seem keenly interesting. He had perhaps mental tools which men like Poe and Whistler either lack or fail to exercise, tools of self-discipline, of objective logic, of retentive memory, of penetrating analysis, and he had none of the essential egotism of the artist type. He felt no great urge toward self-expression. Ideas for him were reflections of the outer world, to be accepted, rather than creations of an inner consciousness, to be asserted. And if, with all these advantages, his scholarship at the Point was not brilliant it was only because he did not choose to make it so. The attitudes of his high school days carried over into the new environment. He had no desire to be known as a "bone file," a "bookworm," a "grind." He was far more interested in becoming a football star.

The Point, that summer, for all the depth of its tradition and the wealth of its history, had an unfinished look. Its mood was as much anticipatory as it was retrospective. It was in the midst of the greatest expansion of physical plant and was aware of swift transition at the entrance of the new century. The Officers' Mess Building had been completed in 1903. The North Barracks had been completed only a year before Dwight's entrance. An immense riding hall was, when Dwight first saw the Point, in the process of construction. The East Academic Building would not be completed until 1913. At the same time there was a rapid succession of superintendents. Colonel Albert L. Mills was succeeded in 1906 by Hugh L. Scott, and he in turn was relieved in 1910 by Thomas L. Barry. Clarence P. Townsley was to succeed Barry in 1912 and would be superintendent at the time of Dwight's graduation.

But these outer changes reflected no profound inward change. West Point as education, as an influence on national life, continued in the pattern laid down almost one hundred years before by Sylvanus Thayer, "The Father of the Academy." It was Thayer who had established the rigid discipline of the mold into which Dwight now fitted, who had abolished vacations and replaced them with infrequent furloughs, who had issued the regulation depriving cadets of outside financial assistance, who had divided classes into sections so that the brighter students need not be held back by those who could barely satisfy minimum requirements. Thayer had been the first to recognize the significance of the Point as a *national* institution, in a time when the Union was an uncertain thing. (Was not Grant's magnanimity at Appomattox due in part to the fact that he and Lee were both West Point men?) And Thayer had devised the curriculum whose essential details were to shape Dwight Eisenhower's training. As Henry Adams once said, the American Government projected through West Point "the first systematic study of science in the United States"[1]—and it was Thayer who had made that projection. Breaking completely with the tradition of a liberal or classical education, he had based his pedagogical ideas on those practiced at the Ecole Polytechnique in Paris. Science was power, and each cadet was to become a unit of disciplined force, a machine instrument in the hands of the state. Nothing which could contribute to that end would be omitted from the Academy; nothing which

[1]Quoted on page 261 of *The Story of West Point,* by Colonel R. Ernest Dupuy, published by the Infantry Journal, 1943.

failed to contribute to it would be included. The humanities gave way to physics, chemistry, engineering.

As the first pioneer among the nation's technical schools, West Point has had far more influence on American education than most people realize. The educational revolution which paralleled the industrial revolution of the nineteenth century in America was presaged by Thayer's administration and partially sustained by the products of that administration. It led through the Morrill Act of 1862 to the establishment of such land-grant schools as the Kansas State College of Agriculture and Applied Science of which, in 1943, Dwight's youngest brother Milton became president.

One can glimpse a curious significance, which can be extended to the whole of our national life, in this fraternal relation between soldier and educator within the Eisenhower family. Is the West Point idea a success as education? Are the products of the technical schools competent to deal with the manifold complexities of twentieth-century living? Perhaps part of the answer is implicit in the successes and failures of Dwight's career. Perhaps part of it is explicit in Milton's stated reactions to his own education and in the struggle he was making in the 1940s to fuse technical training and a liberal education within one institution. While Dwight fought through a catastrophe which might be described as a colossal failure of education, Milton was struggling with what he conceived to be contributing, if not primary, causes. A decade had separated the births of the two boys; it measured the difference between the frontier as reality and the frontier as fading memory. That which Dwight accepted with little question stirred in Milton a nascent rebellion. The kind of education on which Dwight (with significant reservations) throve mightily was an education which to Milton in later years seemed dangerous in the extreme. The older brother saw that technology made effective soldiers. The younger brother saw, in the tendency toward a more and more exclusive specialization, a major threat to democracy. Milton was deeply concerned with the failure of technical training, as he saw it, to develop in the individual citizen a capacity for sound value judgments.

As defined by the West Point system, judgment was as much a quantity as a quality, its weight increasing as one ascended the scale of command, and it was balanced always by an equal quantity of unquestioning obedience. The design was to train soldiers, not educate men. If education was achieved in any measure it was a by-product. But in the summer of 1911, as Dwight adjusted himself to a world as cut off from the normal one as a monastery, it was already evident that the discipline of the Point would be for him an external affair. His basic attitudes and beliefs were already set; four years on the dedicated Plain could do nothing to change them. The metal was hard enough to take a high surface polish, under extreme pressures, without cracking—and it was polish which West Point gave him, polish and the basic mental tools of his trade.

Effortlessly, through comic laughter rather than tragic rebellion, he maintained his integrity. He had his secret life. In the little time he had free he liked to wander over the Plain, climb the cliffs below and the hills above the Academy buildings. History, fused with geography, was visible here in a panorama of great beauty. From the ruined ramparts of Fort Putnam he could look far out across the Hudson and, studying the terrain, see how it was that these towering cliffs were the military key to the colonies. So long as defenders could cling to these towers they could control the river and nullify the military effectiveness of an enemy occupation of all the surrounding country. Had the British recognized early enough the strategic significance of West Point and brought their overwhelming force to bear upon it, they could have split the colonies in two. It was lucky for us that the treachery of Benedict Arnold had been frustrated, that Washington's strategic sense had been sounder than the British, that Kosciusko's fortifications had been so well designed. . . . Dwight, as he told his son John in later years, never tired of such on-the-spot speculations. As laboratory studies he considered them a major factor in his education as a cadet.

3

After the departure of the unfortunate Johnny, he who had fainted on the drill field, Dwight's roommate was a fellow Kansan, Paul Alfred Hodgson, who came from Wichita. "P.A.," they called him. He was a tall lad, tall enough to rate F Company, and he had a rather shy and serious manner which Dwight had from the first found strangely attractive. The attraction was mutual. In a curious way the two were friends before they had spoken to each other, simply through mutual observation and an occasional self-conscious smile on the parade ground. Then, at the last parade before summer encampment at Fort Clinton, at the end of three weeks of "Beast," it was announced that the men would be allowed to choose their own tent mates. Dwight and P.A. turned instinctively to each other—and the two were "wives" (West Point parlance for roommates) from that time on.

They got along amazingly well together. Their personalities supplemented each other in many ways, though their interests were similar. Both played football on the Cullum Hall (plebe) squad that fall, and both played well enough to be regarded by their seniors as future "A" men. Both were "recognized" (that is, spoken to, breaking down the rigid social barrier between a plebe and an upperclassman) by several upperclassmen during the year. Both of them delighted in after-hour bull sessions during which a lookout was stationed outside their room to warn the boys inside of the approach of any upperclassman. But P.A., though by no means a spoilsport, took Academy regulations much more seriously than Dwight was able to do. He was sometimes horror-struck by the reckless chances Dwight took. In the old South Side tradition which he and Ed had espoused in Abilene, Dwight continued to court danger deliberately as a pleasurable element in play, measuring the outermost margins of safety, until it seemed a miracle to P.A. that his friend was never involved in really serious trouble.

It is reported[2] that on one occasion Dwight and Cadet Larkin,[3] during the plebe year, were ordered by upperclassmen to appear at a certain spot after taps in their full-dress coats. P.A. was horrified as his grinning roommate completed preparations for the appointment. But to P.A.'s pleas Dwight turned a deaf ear. He and Cadet Larkin appeared at the assigned place, just as the last notes of taps were fading away, with buttons shining and crossbelts gleaming white. They stood at attention, their faces betraying no flicker of emotion while the initial astonishment of the upperclassmen gave way to outraged anger.

"What's the meaning of this?" roared the spokesman for the group, pointing at Dwight's naked legs.

"Nothing was said about trousers, sir," explained Cadet Eisenhower in accents of injured innocence.

---

[2] By Alden Hatch in his *General Ike: A Biography of Dwight D. Eisenhower*, Henry Holt and Co., Inc., 1944.

[3] Later Major General Thomas B. Larkin.

THE METAL AND THE MOLD

If his troubles were never as serious as P.A. feared they would be, they nevertheless formed a constant accompaniment to his scholastic and athletic careers. He gathered rather more than his share of demerits. The "skin sheets" (records of "delinquencies") for 1911 contain the following entries opposite his name: "Late at chapel; late to target formation 7:05; absent at 8 A.M. drill formation; room in disorder afternoon inspection; Sunday overshoes not arranged as prescribed at retreat; tarnished brasses at inspection; chair not against table at 8 A.M. inspection; late at guard mounting; shelves of clothespress dusty." In 1912 the skin sheets record of him: "Late at 9:30 gym formation; shoes under bed dirty; failed to execute 'right-into-line' properly; in room in improper uniform 1:50 P.M.; alcove not in order; late at breakfast; late to dinner; absent at retreat formation; dirty washbasin at retreat inspection," and so on. Many of his infractions were reported by himself. However casually he might seem to regard other segments of Academy life, he subscribed wholeheartedly to the honor system. And he walked off without complaint his earned "slugs"—hours of stiff marching up and down, eyes straight ahead, rifle held just so across the aching shoulder.

The fact of his membership in F Company might be taken as evidence that the things which happen to a man are "like" that man, as though the quality of a personality were what determined its accidents. F Company suited Dwight's temperament absolutely. It occupied much the same position at West Point as the South Side boys had occupied in Abilene High School. The men of that company, averaging six feet in height, were traditionally rough and tough, contemptuous of "runt" companies, scornful of serious efforts toward scholastic or corps-rank advancement, but arrogantly proud of their athletic prowess. At his second summer camp, as a yearling, Dwight was one of the leaders of F Company raids on a runt company's supply of "boodle" (West Point for forbidden food) and of the water dousings which were the fate of runt-company members who were so unwise as to stray uninvited down F Company Street. He exercised leadership without seeming to do so, partially by virtue of a quick mind and an abundant energy, mostly because he was almost universally liked. By the end of his plebe year he had a considerable prestige, born of his efforts not only in football, but in boxing, baseball, and track.

Among his friends in F Company was a fellow classmate from

Moberly, Missouri—a lad whose long sad face and heavy lower jaw quickly branded him as the "ugliest man in his class." To Dwight's intense disgust, one insensitive cadet went so far as to apply to the Missourian the nickname "Darwin" because of a fancied resemblance to an ape. But before long the Missourian had more enviable claims to distinction. His slow, humorous drawl, his complete lack of "side," and above all his athletic ability won for him many friends and admirers. On the athletic field his drawling slowness gave way to a surprising speed; on the baseball diamond he was particularly outstanding. His name was Omar Bradley.

Of Dwight's mental attainments only one anecdote survives from his plebe year. P.A., partially because he himself agonized over his writing, was awe-struck by the ease with which his roommate could toss off an English theme. Sometimes Dwight did not even begin to write until a bare half-hour before the theme was due. Yet these casual efforts of his invariably scored a higher grade than the products of P.A.'s painful hours. At the end of the plebe year Dwight's rank in English was 10 out of a class which had now shrunk to 212.

His total academic standing for the year was fifty-seventh in the class—far higher than he was ever to score again at the Point. He was content to remain at the bottom of the "engineers," the name applied to those cadets who were in the upper sections of their classes. His rank in military engineering was thirtieth in the class, and in history thirty-ninth.

CHAPTER II

Dedication: Duty, Honor, Country

Eᴀʀʟʏ ɪɴ ᴛʜᴇ ᴀᴜᴛᴜᴍɴ ᴏꜰ 1912 Swede Hazlett had an experience rare indeed among the midshipmen at Annapolis: he felt a thrill of pride in the exploits of an *Army* football player. Sports writers for Eastern newspapers, forecasting the 1912 season, predicted great things of an Army yearling, one Ike Eisenhower from Kansas. They called him a "huge Kansan," and some of them prophesied for him All-American honors. A New York paper carried a two-column picture of Eisenhower punting. Swede, risking censure as a harborer of traitorous sentiments, proudly displayed it to his friends. The picture found its way to Abilene, and there, too, it was a source of pride. Bud Huffman and Orrin Snider were surprised to find their friend described as a "plunging halfback," he who had been too slow for the backfield in high school, and they were equally surprised by his published weight of 190 pounds. Obviously Ike had reached his "full growth" since leaving town.

He was scheduled that season for the left halfback position. There he would understudy Geoffrey Keyes, a first year man (senior) and the Army's great star of the preceding season. It was a responsible spot for a yearling. But Dwight had learned a lot of football on the Cullum Hall team, and he was determined that when he went into a game as Keyes's substitute there'd be no noticeable decrease in the quality of Army play. He worked hard, much harder than he did at his studies. Marty Maher, the trainer, saw nothing casual or easygoing about Ike on the practice field. In the practice sessions Ike was the first out and the last in every evening, and though his play was clean it was, in Marty's words, "mighty rough behind the line." He tackled hard, he blocked beautifully, and he ran with terrific drive, counting more on sheer power than on shifty speed for his gains as a ball carrier. Marty had seen a lot of athletes come and go. He had noticed with regret that good athletes seldom became better at West Point. Something in the system—too much standing at stiff attention, too much tense drill, not enough relaxation—seemed to prevent the proper development of an athlete. But Dwight looked good, and he seemed to know how to relax, and Marty was confident he'd be a mainstay of the team before the season was ended.

The confidence was not misplaced. Keyes was injured in practice a few days before the first game with Stevens on October 5, and Dwight in the halfback position contributed mightily to the Army's easy 27–0 win. In the second game, too, with Rutgers on October 12, Dwight was a standout. He garnered a lot of publicity for his part in Army's 19–0 victory. "He's one of the most promising backs in Eastern football," claimed the cautious New York *Times*. But Keyes was back in shape for the game with Yale on October 19, and Dwight seems to have spent most of the time on the side lines, watching unhappily as Yale, despite a starring performance by Keyes, won 6–0 in a hard-fought contest. On the following week, in the game with Colgate, Keyes was again outstanding in an 18–7 Army victory, but the Academy yearbook, the *Howitzer,* for 1913, says of this game that "Eisenhower in the fourth quarter could not be stopped," indicating that Dwight replaced the star in the closing period. The Holy Cross game scheduled for the next week was canceled. Probably this event caused no great unhappiness at West Point. The Army team must have welcomed the chance to get into the best possible shape for the game with the Carlisle Indians on November 9. The boys had "pointed" for that game all season.

Carlisle in 1912 meant Jim Thorpe, probably the greatest all-around athlete America has produced. On the football field he had demonstrated in every game that he could "do everything"—pass, kick, run, block, tackle. "Stop Thorpe" had become a national cry among the football-conscious, as "Stop Grange" would be in the 1920s. So far no one had stopped him. He was a legendary figure. One can imagine the tense excitement which swept the Army stands when he trotted out onto the field. . . . It was soon evident that the Army team, though a strong one, was not equal to the task which had been set for it. Thorpe made football history that afternoon. Time and again he broke away for what the *Howitzer* later described as the most "wonderful and spectacular runs" ever seen on the Academy field. He swept the ends, he crashed through the center of the line, he swivel-hipped his way through the tiniest holes on off-tackle plays. Against such a player ordinary tactics could be of no avail. When Dwight replaced Keyes at left half he went out for just one purpose. He arranged with the right halfback to give "that Indian" the "high-low" the next time he came through the line. Dwight was to hit Thorpe high on one side, and the other halfback was to tackle low on the other. This procedure, if timed properly, can almost break a man in two.

Months later, in Abilene, Dwight told his round-eyed brothers, Earl and Milton, just how the procedure had worked.

"Carlisle had the ball," Dwight explained, shaking his head in awe at the very memory of it. "We knew Thorpe would take it on the next play and we knew he'd come through the line because the line had never stopped him before. Well, we timed it just right. We gave him the old high-low, the old one-two, just like that. He'd made a big gain before we stopped him, but we really stopped him. Hard. When we got up he was still lying on the ground. We were sure we'd laid him out for good. But he managed to stagger to his feet in a minute or two and take his place behind the line. Even then we weren't worried because we were sure we'd ruined him for the rest of the day. But do you know what that Indian did? On the very next play he took the ball and went right through us for ten yards!"

The game ended with the score 27–6 in favor of Carlisle—and it was Dwight who limped from the field, not Jim Thorpe. Dwight had twisted his knee, not seriously but painfully. Marty Maher worked hard on the injured knee, strapping a brace around it, and the doctor said that if Dwight were careful for a few days he'd be in shape for more football.

The Tufts game, the following week, was anti-climactic. Tufts was weak, and the Army should have won by a big score. Actually the final score was quite close, 15–6 in favor of Army. "A disappointing game," said the *Howitzer*, summing it up—and part of the disappointment was that "in this game Eisenhower was hurt and was unable to get back into shape the rest of the season."

He was seriously injured. He knew that as soon as it happened. The knee he had twisted in the Carlisle game was now broken, and he lay flat on the ground, gritting his teeth and clawing the turf in agony. But his physical pain even in that moment was overbalanced by his mental anguish. Would he be able to get back in shape for the Navy game? He'd have traded all the playing he'd done so far that season for just one quarter in the Navy game.

Dr. Charles Keller, the chief surgeon, shook his head as he examined the knee.

"Not the Navy game," he said. "Not this year. Maybe never. You'll have to spend several weeks right here in the hospital flat on your back. By the time you leave we'll be able to tell more about your future chances."

Dwight was reminded of something.

"How long did you say I'd have to stay here, sir?" he asked.

"Thirty days anyway. Maybe longer."

Dwight managed a weak grin. There was one bright spot, anyway. Only a day or so before he had received one of his heaviest "slugs"—"six demerits and twenty-two punishment tours in the area during the next thirty days." The thirty-day clause would save him from ever having to walk those tours at all. As a matter of fact, this slug, and Dwight's subsequent injury, resulted in the only known change which Dwight's presence in the Academy was ever to make in the West Point system. Thereafter the wording of slugs was changed to leave out all reference to the period during which the punishment tours must be made.

P.A., who was also earning his "A" in football that fall, came often to the hospital to visit his roommate. He brought the latest gossip. He noticed with satisfaction that Dwight was keeping up with his class assignments. He noticed, too, that Dr. Keller gave Dwight's knee the most devoted care. The doctor had great affection for the big Kansan, and he was happy to say, when Dwight at last left the hospital, that the boy had every chance for a complete recovery.

"Provided you don't do anything foolish," he said with emphasis to the departing Dwight. "That knee has been badly hurt, and joint injuries take a long time to heal. The knee's weak. It'll remain weak for months to come. Don't put any more weight on it than you have to."

At riding drill, for instance, the doctor went on, Dwight might take part in the maneuvers on horseback, but he must *not* engage in those portions of drill which required constant mounting and dismounting. Too much pressure on the bent knee might undo months of healing.

Perhaps the doctor had a premonition. At any rate, it was in riding drill, in the immense Riding Hall which had been completed only a few months before, that Dwight suffered the very disaster which the doctor had feared. The riding master was an extremely strict disciplinarian, driven by a deep fear of the cadets he must face every day. He was afraid they might take advantage of him and laugh at him behind his back. He was particularly afraid that Cadet Eisenhower, who had claimed for himself the privilege of sitting astride his horse while others mounted and dismounted, was laughing at him. Something in Dwight's poised self-assurance was particularly irritating to him; it seems to have aroused an unbearable sense of inferiority in one who was himself emotionally unbalanced. There came an afternoon when the drillmaster could contain himself no longer. Flatly, in cold, angry tones, he charged Dwight with malingering and ordered the cadet from that time forth to take part in all the movements of the drill.

Dwight, in view of the doctor's orders, could have refused. The weight of the West Point system was on his side, not the drillmaster's. But, typically, he regarded the issue as lying between himself and the man who had "challenged" him, who had as "good as called me a liar." His frontier code would have been violated had he called for outside assistance.

"Yes sir," he said in tones as coldly angry as the drillmaster's.

Thereafter, though a long afternoon, Dwight mounted and dismounted at command. Pain stabbed through his injured knee, increasing with each maneuver until his vision darkened and his teeth clenched to keep back cries of agony. P.A. was at his side and in outraged whispers tried to reason with him. But Dwight was beyond reason. It was like the fight with Wes Merrifield. He'd never admit he was licked. When the drill was at last over, P.A. had to half carry his friend to the hospital—and one can imagine the drillmaster's emotional defeat as he saw the consequences of his afternoon's work. P.A. cursed the drillmaster, and Dwight for being a fool, and the drillmaster again with every step, and when they reached the hospital the doctor cursed too. The knee, red and swollen, was a mess.

It meant the end of Dwight's football career. It came very near meaning the end of his military career. Two and a half years later, in the final physical examinations, Dr. Keller had to stretch a point to let Dwight through.

No disappointment in his later life was bitterer than this. He loved football, its violent test of stamina and courage and rugged skill. But though bitterly disappointed, he was not embittered. He could take it, grinning ruefully. Again it was as though the accident were "like" the man, determined by the man's personal quality, for it confirmed in him still further the perspective and the vital strategy he had gained during his year of drift in Abilene. More than ever now he stood outside himself, watching himself play a game. With his dream of glory lost, he played the game rather carelessly for its own sake, determined to do respectably well but not caring at all for top honors. Probably the description of him written by P.A. for the 1915 *Howitzer* was more accurate, in its psychological implications, than P.A. suspected: ". . . poor Dwight merely consents to exist until graduation shall set him free. At one time he threatened to get interested in life and won his 'A' by being the most promising back in Eastern football—but the Tufts game broke his knee and the promise. . . ."

At the end of his plebe year he had been promoted to corporal but had contrived to be "busted" back to private a few weeks later. He continued to collect demerits: "late at reveille, late to supper formation, wearing improper uniform to drill, broom in roommate's alcove," and so on. As a yearling his academic standing showed a serious drop. From fifty-seventh in a class of 212 he had slipped to eighty-first in a class now shrunk to 177. By his own admission he fell far short of what West Point calls "a good cadet."

2

Nevertheless, he swaggered a bit when he came home, in the summer of 1913, for his thirty-day furlough. Home-coming made him aware of changes in himself, and the changes, he thought, were improvements. If West Point had failed to modify his essential quality, it had certainly given that quality a clearer definition, bolstering him with an external discipline. He could measure an increased firmness in his character by comparing it with what he now unconsciously termed a "civilian" slackness. He must have had that same flabbiness, that same lack of polish, two years before. . . .

He arrived at night. No one was at the station to meet him. He had told no one he was coming. He stood for a moment on the platform, consciously breathing the air of home, while the taillights of the train faded into the west. Then, bag in hand, he walked quickly across the courthouse square, past the blank walls of the creamery, and into a street which was like a black tunnel under arching elms. His footsteps rang on the wooden planks of a tiny bridge across a familiar ravine. A dog began to bark madly. Flip. The dog was at his feet, jumping joyously upon him, and the side door opened and his mother stood there in the streaming light, looking out. He sprang up the steps and gathered her in his arms.

It was all as he had hoped it would be during his occasional attacks of homesickness. David had severed all connection with the creamery and was now employed as superintendent of the gas plant, one of the first plants established by the rapidly growing Brown utility interests. Otherwise he remained the same quiet, reserved man he had always been. Mother Eisenhower remained the vivid, buoyant center of the family. Her joy at Dwight's return was almost painful for Dwight to see. He had to struggle to keep himself from an unmanly display of emotion. Even Earl and Milton seemed just about the same. They were bigger, of course, but they still looked up at him in round-eyed awe, just as they had done when he went away. He warmed himself in the glow of their admiration and of the admiration of other boys, and the girls, in the town.

He was, as Earl remembers it, the "town hero, and he acted the part." He "lost no opportunity to impress us with what he knew and had done, and occasionally he would put on his West Point uniform and parade through town, though I must admit he did this only a few times." The town, or that portion of it whose good opinion Dwight most valued, was certainly impressed. Wesley Merrifield was working that summer in a bakery. Looking out of the bakery windows one morning, he saw Dwight across the street in a sleek gray uniform. ("He looked like a million dollars.") Wes came across the street to greet him. Dwight turned and grinned delightedly as he shook hands, looking down at the boy who had been his friend ever since their famous fight. Wes had not gained much, if any, height since his high school days. They called him "Shorty" now, but he was stocky and strong. He might still be tough in a fight. Dwight said so.

"You remember that fight we had?" Dwight went on.

"Do I! I'll never forget it."

"Well, we called it a draw at the time. At least I did. But I had far the worst of it. I'm willing to admit now that you really licked me then."

Wes said he had thought so at the time.

"But what I want to know," said Dwight chaffingly, "is whether you have any ambitions now."

Wes looked Dwight up and down, taking in the broad shoulders, the thick chest, the weight advantage, the way Dwight stood on the balls of his feet with his elbows bent, as though he could bring those hands up fast if necessary.

"Ike," said Wes earnestly, "I'm the most unambitious man in town."

But others were not inclined to let Dwight's fighting reputation pass untested. There was a lad in town who needed taking down a bit. His name was Dirk Tyler. He was a Negro of magnificent physique who had "licked" all the local boys he had met in boxing matches in Sterl's basement. He had even fought professionally a few times in Kansas City. The trouble was, as the boys explained to Dwight, that Dirk had become a bully who went around with a chip on his shoulder, ready to give anyone who annoyed him a beating.

"You ought to take him, Ike," said Bud Huffman. "Otherwise he's going to get himself into trouble."

Dwight demurred. He wasn't anxious to meet a professional fighter, especially now that he had a trick knee which still required an elastic stocking.

But a short time later he went into a barbershop—and there was Dirk Tyler, working as a porter. Dirk was big; he looked tough all right, and Dwight in the barber's chair wasn't happy about it when the men in the shop began urging the two to put on the gloves. He'd have passed off the affair as a joke if it hadn't been for Dirk's attitude. That attitude was at best condescending, at worst contemptuous. Dirk let it be known in a loud voice that he was prepared to meet Ike "anywhere, any time." Sighing inwardly, Dwight agreed to a meeting.

"Soon's I get my hair cut," he said.

The barber hurried the job, while news of the impending fight spread through the business district. There was quite a crowd in the basement of Sterl's when Dwight and Dirk arrived. Dwight's spirits weren't lifted by the sight of Dirk stripped to the waist. The Negro was beautifully muscled and as he flexed his arms and danced around the room, warming up, he looked fully as dangerous as he intended to do. It would have to be a case of brain against brawn, Dwight decided as he pulled on the gloves. A referee was appointed, and the contestants agreed to fight in two-minute rounds, with a minute of rest in between. The spectators formed a squared ring. Time was called.

Dirk came out fast. His right hand, cocked, swung out in a huge clumsy arc which Dwight easily parried as he crashed his own right hand against the Negro's jaw. Dirk's head bounced back, and Dwight came in fast with a left and another right. The Negro's knees sagged. He didn't even raise his left hand against the final blow, a terrific right uppercut. He was stretched flat on the floor, sound asleep. The crowd cheered. Only then, after it was all over in a matter of seconds, did Dwight realize his own astonishment. Thirty-odd years later he told a reporter about it in Normandy.

"Everybody had talked about Dirk so much," he explained. "I went out determined to use every bit of skill to protect myself. And then to find that the boy didn't know the first thing about fighting! He telegraphed his punches from a mile away." With a shake of the head and a reminiscent grin he added: "Poor Dirk. Honestly, I've never been particularly proud of that scrap."

Others were proud. Dwight's local prestige soared higher than ever before. And poor Dirk had so much fun poked at him that Dwight finally had to intervene on his behalf, ordering the boys to "lay off." It was good for Dirk, though, the townspeople told one another. Dirk thereafter was a "nice guy" again.

A dream came true that month. Gladys Harding, prettier than ever, was still in town and Dwight, bolstered by his increased prestige, dared to ask her for a date. She was delighted to accept. He dated her again and again, grasping greedily at a dreamed-of happiness which must necessarily be brief. He talked a great deal about West Point, explaining it to himself as he explained it to her. He discovered in himself a feeling for the place he had not known he possessed. She listened with a genuine interest. She admired him tremendously, his sincerity, his rugged strength, his immense vitality. With no other boy had she had so much fun.

On several occasions Dwight arranged to have Earl bring to the back door of the Harding home a half-dozen bottles of Muehlbach beer. Poor Earl was again the exploited one. He bought the beer with money earned in the creamery, violating the Kansas liquor-prohibition law, and he was not even permitted to watch Dwight drink it. He had to cut across the Eisenhower alfalfa patch, down along the railroad, and up through the Harding back yard, there to be met by Dwight, who accepted the beer as his due and promptly dismissed his younger brother. One evening, however, Earl got back part of his own. Dwight was loudly lamenting the fact that he was "broke." He just "had to have a couple of bucks" to take his girl out. He had no compunction against asking Earl for a loan. Earl hardened his heart. He reminded Dwight that the latter already owed him a dollar and that the prospects for collection seemed slim. In desperation Dwight offered to put up his watch, the watch given him by his grandfather, as security. Against this security he borrowed two dollars and a half. Since this loan and the earlier one of a dollar were never repaid, Earl kept the watch. He still had it in the 1940s.

All too swiftly the summer days passed by. It seemed to Dwight that he had barely returned to the town when he had to leave again. Again there was the pain of farewell to the family, especially to Mother Eisenhower—though she did not weep this time before her sons. He actually hated to go. But as he boarded the eastward-bound train he held a hostage against the stern realities of "Hell on the Hudson." Gladys Harding had promised to come to West Point for June Week if she possibly could. Perhaps, too, she would meet Dwight in New York sometime during the winter. A talent for "expression" which she had displayed in college had yielded her a contract with a concert company, and she was to go East that fall on tour, doing pianologues and readings.

He hugged the promise to him as the miles roared under the wheels.

3

Fitting back into the West Point system required less of a spiritual wrench than he had expected. As he stood again on the tiny station platform, caught between the towering cliff and the mighty river, he could even feel that he belonged here. In a way he was almost as much at home here as he was in Abilene. He was eager to greet his friends. The occasional spasms of tense nervousness he had experienced two years before did not return as he climbed the long drive to the Plain. He knew what he could do.

His life continued, with little perceptible change, along the lines he had established as a plebe and third classman. In his second class year he found some compensation for his lost football glory by serving as cheerleader. He continued to add to his poker winnings and was assured that when he graduated, and all poker debts were paid in cash, he'd receive a tidy sum. Perhaps out of loyalty to his dream come true of the preceding summer, perhaps as a reaction against the romantic tendencies he had then displayed, he joined with two other friends in a professed indifference to girls and dances. The three friends made up a pool (on paper, of course, since no cash was permitted) to which each contributed ten dollars, the whole sum to go to the one who remained unmarried the longest.

In the fall of his first class year he assisted Lieutenant Selleck in coaching the Cullum Hall football squad. This activity was one of the few he took with any great seriousness. Once again he was the first to go out and the last to come in from the practice field every evening. The plebes looked up to him, worked hard for him. He had, he discovered, a happy faculty for getting men to work for him. Of four games that fall, the Cullum Hall team won three. The first game was a somewhat ignominious defeat at the hands of East Orange High School, 14–7, on October 10, but in the second game on October 21 Cullum restored its prestige by defeating Yonkers High School 27–7. On November 11 the Stevens scrub team was defeated 41–0. But the big game, a sort of plebe Army-Navy game, was the one on November 25 between Cullum and New York Military Academy. The entire corps turned out to watch this traditional contest, played on the Academy field. As the afternoon passed, with neither side scoring, Dwight paced nervously along the side lines. He was almost wild with joy when, in the last quarter, Cullum managed to score a field goal. The game ended 3–0 for Cullum.

As it turned out, the bright promise which had comforted him when he left Abilene was not completely fulfilled. He was in New York during the brief Christmas holiday, and he met Gladys there. They went dancing together and to the theater, and he was proud to introduce her to envious fellow cadets. But she was not able to come to June Week, either at the end of his third class year or for his graduation.

Meanwhile his over-all Academy record was somewhat improved. From eighty-first in a class of 177 he had climbed, by the end of his third class year, to sixty-fifth in a class of approximately 170. No doubt he would have gone higher had his conduct been less often a good-natured defiance of authority. He continued to collect demerits at a much higher than average rate. For 1914 the skin sheets record: "Talking in mess hall while battalion was at attention; using profanity at supper; improper expression at 2:33 P.M.; shoes under bed not shined; not wearing black tie at P.M. inspection," and so on. He was given an eight-hour walking slug, on one occasion, for "violation of orders with reference to dancing, having previously been admonished for same." He had, it seems, substituted an overly lively turkey trot for the recognized respectable dances. During his last five months before graduation he was slugged for being late to formations, for being absent from retreats and inspections, for "making no reasonable effort to have his room properly cleaned for A.M. inspection," and for numerous similar offenses. As a first classman he collected precisely one hundred demerits and stood one hundred and twenty-fifth in conduct among a class of 164 for that year. For his entire four years at the Point he stood ninety-fifth in conduct. (Omar Bradley, on the other hand, was one of the best-behaved cadets in the corps; he stood sixth in conduct for his four years.) In scholarship Dwight stood consistently at the very bottom of the upper third of his class. During his last year he was fifty-ninth in civil and military engineering, eighty-second in ordnance and science of gunnery, forty-fifth in law, seventy-second in Spanish (he hated languages), twenty-seventh in drill regulations and hippology, and fifty-seventh in practical military engineering. His graduation order was 61.

In the record as written there is certainly nothing to indicate the future commander. A typical judgment of him was voiced by an instructor in the department of tactics, the department responsible for corps discipline. "We saw in Eisenhower a not uncommon type," this officer said, "a man who would thoroughly enjoy his army life, giving both to duty and recreation their fair values [but] we did not see in him a man who would throw himself into his job so completely that nothing else would matter." He was damned with faint praise. He was still "average." There was still "nothing outstanding" about him.

But beyond his written record is the remembered one, held in the memories of those who knew him well, and from the latter a more accurate forecast might have been made. The Annapolis graduation in 1915 was held two weeks before West Point's June Week, and Swede Hazlett came up during his graduation leave to pay Dwight a visit. "It was no surprise to find him . . . generally liked and admired," Swede recalled. "Had he not indulged in so many extracurricular activities he could easily have led his class scholastically. Everyone was his friend—but with no loss in dignity or respect."

The last phrase is the key one. Dwight's popularity was immense, but more important than its quantity was its special quality. Some men are popular because they regard popularity as an instrument of power and work to achieve it. They employ a calculated flattery and make a practice of outward conformity with the mood and standards of the crowd. Dwight was popular simply because he was as he was. People liked him because he liked people. His conformity stemmed from the fact that the prevailing moods and standards were actually his own. His very lack of what others might call "ambition," his apparent disregard for personal advancement, caused his associates to trust him absolutely. He never flattered; he hated flattery, whether applied to himself or others. He practiced no forms of hypocrisy; his frank honesty was unquestionable. The rare fine thing he had was the capacity to bring out the *best* in other men. They wanted to please him simply because they valued so highly his good opinion of them. His total personal quality was a kind of catalytic agent stimulating effective co-operation among men who would otherwise have clashed with one another. No doubt it was this quality of his popularity which caused one perceptive instructor to say of him that he was "born to command."

P.A.'s deep affection for him is evident in the bantering lines published in the 1915 *Howitzer:*

This is Señor Dwight David Eisenhower, gentlemen . . . claims to have the best authority for the statement that he is the handsomest man in the Corps and is ready to back up his claim at any time. At any rate you'll have to give it to him that he's well developed abdominally—and more graceful in pushing it around than Charles Calvert Benedict. In common with most fat men, he is an enthusiastic and sonorous devotee of the King of Indoor Sports and roars homage to the shrine of Morpheus on every possible occasion. However, the memory of man runneth back to the time when the little Dwight was but a slender lad of some 'steen years, full of joy and energy and craving for life and movement and change.

'Twas then that the romantic appeal of West Point's glamor grabbed him by the scruff of the neck and dragged him to his doom. Three weeks of "Beast" gave him his fill of life and movement and . . . all change was locked up at the Cadet Store out of reach. . . . Now Ike must content himself with tea, tiddlywinks, and talk, at all of which he excels. Now lead us in a long, loud yell for—Dare Devil Dwight, the Dauntless Don.

Something of Dwight's own view of himself is revealed in the closing lines of his autobiography in the *Howitzer*, purporting to be a typical quotation from him: "Now, fellers, it's just like this. I've been asked to say a few words this evening about business. Now, me and Walter Camp, we think——" He wrote, too, a word portrait of Omar Bradley, but in a much different tone. "Brad's most important characteristic is 'getting there,' and if he keeps up the clip he's started some of us will someday be bragging that, 'Sure, General Bradley was a classmate of mine.' "

Throughout almost the whole of his cadet career he had worn a "clean sleeve." His rank as corporal was temporary indeed. His highest rank in the corps had been that of color sergeant. Behind his name in his autobiography he placed the initials A.B., meaning "Area Bird" (one assigned to walk punishment tours in the area), and B.A., meaning "Busted Aristocrat" (a non-commissioned officer reduced to the ranks).

But on a bronze plaque mounted on the wall of the gymnasium his name was emblazoned among those who had won their "A" in some major sport during cadet days. There were twenty names on that plaque, and ten of them would have "General" in front of them on the army rolls in 1944: Eisenhower, Bradley, Hubert R. Harmon, Leland S. Hobbs, Thomas B. Larkin, Vernon E. Prichard, Albert W. Waldron, Roscoe B. Woodruff, Walter W. Hess, and Reese W. Howell. Five of the twenty men would be colonels, among them Paul A. Hodgson.

For the fourth and last time he formed, on a bright June morning, a part of a living square. The square enclosed the statue of Colonel Thayer which stands in a clump of giant elms at the southwest corner of the Plain. In full-dress uniform the cadets stood at the Order Arms while the band marched up from the east, followed by the superintendent of the Academy, by the president of the Association of Graduates, and by an old man who strove valiantly to hold himself erect as he walked. Behind these three marched the alumni who had come to attend June Week festivities. The old man, the oldest alumnus present that day, took his stand at the foot of the statue, and the other alumni filled in the center of the hollow square. The cadet choir sang the "Alma Mater."

Then the secretary of the Association of Graduates read slowly the names of those graduates who had died since the preceding June Week. The chaplain prayed. The corps came to Present Arms while a bugler poured from the bell of his horn the sad, sweet strains of taps. The oldest living graduate came forward and laid at the feet of Sylvanus Thayer a memorial wreath. The West Point choir sang the West Point hymn to duty, honor, country, to a transcending tradition, to the endless procession of the living and the dead:

The Corps! The Corps! The Corps!
The Corps! Bareheaded salute it,
    With eyes up, thanking our God
That we of the Corps are treading
    Where they of the Corps have trod.

They are here in ghostly assemblage
    The men of the Corps long dead,
And our hearts are standing attention
    While we wait for their passing tread.

We sons of today, we salute you,
    You sons of an earlier day.
We follow close order, behind you,
    Where you have pointed the way;

The long gray line of us stretches.
    Through the years of a cent'ry told,
And the last man feels to his marrow
    The grip of your far-off hold.

Grip hands with us now, though we see thee not,
    Grip hands with us, strengthen hearts,
As the long line stiffens and straightens.
    With the thrill that your pressure imparts.

SOLDIER OF DEMOCRACY

Grip hands though it be from the shadows,
While we swear as you did of yore,
Or living or dying to honor
The Corps, and the Corps, and the Corps.

And it came to him again, that overwhelming sense of dedication, that sense of belonging to something which extended infinitely beyond the self. Duty. Honor. Country. Perhaps it defined too narrow a patriotism for the twentieth century, but he could hardly have been aware of that as he stood at stiff attention behind his upright rifle. The definition itself was beautiful. Whoever joined the long gray line could never wholly die. . . .

CHAPTER III

Of Love and War

". . . to be ready to sacrifice all for your country . . . you have undertaken a great responsibility. You may be called upon at any time to demonstrate your worth. . . . Upon your conduct may depend issues of vital moment to your country. . . . Unless you look upon yourselves as men who have actually, not only in words, pledged all that is in you for your country's safety, you have not imbibed the proper traditions and you cannot worthily hand them on. . . ."

LINDLEY M. GARRISON, the Secretary of War who would soon be succeeded by Newton D. Baker, was doing his duty at West Point. A certain period of time must be killed. He killed it. ". . . honorable, valorous . . . sacrifice . . . the nation to whose service the lives of you young men are consecrated . . . fair and just in your dealings with others . . . sacrifice . . . sacrifice." One expected to hear such things on Commencement Day. The listeners had a duty too. They must listen politely and applaud at the right times.

Blunt weapons, those words. They had lost their cutting edges at the clumsy hands of a thousand bored Men of Affairs, hacking to death a million ordinary moments. But these today were no ordinary moments. The words were sharpened by the living minutes into which they plunged, and as the minutes died one by one the speaker's voice took on an increasing note of urgency. June, this was. A June morning in 1915. Dwight Eisenhower and his classmates could reasonably have felt that "valiant death" and "honor" and "sacrifice" were terms forged only that morning, presented now to them all shining new. "You may be called upon at any time. . . ." It wasn't mere rhetoric but a statement of fact, and the fact applied not to a vaguely distant future but to an immediate tomorrow. The sun which had risen a few hours ago across the Hudson had, in those same hours, been setting behind a slate-gray sea where death lurked in scores of cigar-shaped forms. Barely a month ago the *Lusitania* had gone down beneath that sea. A generation of men was being slaughtered on Gallipoli, in the narrow strait of the Dardanelles, before Loos and Amiens and Rheims, north of the Carpathians in far-off Galicia, and on all the oceans of the world. Young men, they were, pouring out their youth in a tide of blood.

The tide was rising. It would drown forever the Europe of the nineteenth century. Its waves were washing higher and higher against the psychic shores of America.

Slowly but inexorably the foundations of Wilsonian idealism were being undermined. The unfinished structure of the New Freedom, that first true governmental expression of nineteenth-century liberalism in America, might soon come tumbling down around its builders, burying beneath its debris the promise which had shone so brightly in 1912. Was there a fatal flaw in that structure? Were the builders mistaken in their refusal to admit the reality of evil and to provide adequate safeguards against it? The good schoolmaster in the White House did not think so. Frantically he strove to shore up against lapping waves the breached walls of his "neutrality," while certain literary intellectuals, taking a backward look, began to recognize as prophecy the romantic defeatism of the Mauve Decade. *Fin de siècle,* they said to one another, nodding their agreement. Yes, this is the way a world ends. . . .

The initial cries of a world's death agony had been but faintly heard and little understood within West Point's insular walls. In a Serbian town of which Dwight had never heard an Austrian archduke of whom Dwight had never heard was shot to death. That had been a year ago. Nobody at West Point had paid much attention. To be sure the newspapers had spoken of another European crisis, but there had been so many crises, and nothing seemed to have come from any of them. The Austrian note to Serbia had been something of a surprise, but there were few who believed that this meant a general European war. Then came the mobilization of Russia, Austria, Germany, and France, while the British fleet put out to sea. These happenings aroused at the Point a purely technical interest. Was it possible for modern industrial states to mobilize, hold their armed forces in readiness for a period of time, and then demobilize again without a battle? The question was quickly answered in the negative. Mobilization, as conceived by Europe's military masters, was not a prelude to war but the actual initiation of it. There was no discontinuity between the gathering of forces and the launching of them into battle; the one involved the other. The declarations of war which came in such swift succession in early August were simply recognitions of a *fait accompli*, as superfluous as the other "scraps of paper" which statesmen had used to create an illusion of control over historic forces they could not or would not understand.

Dwight and P.A., during the summer encampment and through a golden autumn, had traced the pattern of war across the map of Europe. Lines of pins marked the tremendous wheel of the German right wing through Belgium and down, down against Paris. The pattern was familiar enough: grand strategy in the classic manner, according to the books. Dwight might have recognized in it the ancient *tulughma,* or "standard sweep," of Genghis Khan and his Mongol horde. But with the halting of the weakened German right on the Marne the war lost its familiar shape. The race to the sea, spewing behind it hundreds of miles of entrenchments, was something new in the world. "Battles are won by slaughter and maneuver," wrote Winston Churchill ten years later. "The greater the general, the more he contributes in maneuver, the less he demands in slaughter." By this standard there had been, through the winter and spring, no great generals on the Western Front. There was no maneuver, only slaughter on a vaster scale than anyone had seen before. What had happened? The answer was easily given, even by Dwight and his fellow cadets. What had happened was the machine gun. It altered everything. It gave the defense at the very least a three-to-one advantage over the offense. The failure of the military mind to take account of this fact, to devise an answer to it, was measured in windrows of dead between stationary lines. Here was an abundance of material for the education of a student-soldier. A future commander could look upon Europe from three thousand miles away as a laboratory demonstration of what not to do. Distance soaked up the sight and sound and smell of the mangled living and the rotting dead; it left for the interested cadet a residue of cold, significant facts.

How directly did those facts apply to himself? At first the answer to that question must have seemed to Dwight perfectly obvious.

The facts didn't apply personally to him at all. Everyone, including Teddy Roosevelt in the fall of 1914, seemed agreed that a policy of strict neutrality was the only correct one for the United States. If America was not involved, certainly Dwight would not be. He could turn his main attention to the coaching of the plebe football squad, and reserve for the facts of Europe about the same degree of interest he applied to the records of campaigns in his military history books. Even this degree of interest was lessened when the war of movement gave way to a bloody stalemate. The trouble with Mexico, where active soldiering was an immediate possibility, had much greater claim on the attention of cadets. The European war had become too boringly statistical. Its victor could be determined by a simple comparison of casualties with man-power resources. The Allies had more men than the Central Powers. The margin of their superiority in this respect was greater than the excesses of their casualties over those of the Central Powers. Therefore, the Allies would win the war.

But the sinking of the *Lusitania* and the almost simultaneous launching of the great German-Austrian offensive against the Russians had put a different complexion on our national relations to the European situation. Violent emotions engendered by the drowning of Americans on the high seas gave new point to predictions of dire consequences stemming from a German victory. Dwight's interest quickened as he heard the note of urgency in Lindley Garrison's voice. It was Europe that Garrison was thinking of when he spoke of "issues of vital moment to your country." Already Garrison was in violent disagreement with the President concerning the degree of preparedness necessary for America, and six months from now he would resign from the Cabinet as a consequence of that disagreement. "Unless you . . . have pledged all that is in you for your country's safety . . ." Perhaps those facts, three thousand miles away, had a direct personal application after all. (Winston Churchill, damned high and low for the failure on Gallipoli, had lost the Admiralty with the fall of the Asquith government. Adolf Hitler, one of the few members of the List Bavarian Regiment to survive 1914, had already won the Iron Cross.) It was another moment of high dedication when the speech ended and Dwight moved forward with the others, climbing the steps to the platform.

He was a West Point alumnus. He was commissioned a second lieutenant in the United States Army; an instrument of the state, ready for the testing. Homeward bound for his graduation leave a day or so later, he looked upon scenes grown familiar now through repetition, and the sense of urgency faded with the miles. Everything looked the same as it had four years before. The outward face of history through all of mid-America was still serene. The mud, the stink, the ruined cities, the seeds of death raining down the sky to flower in flame and smoke across Flanders fields—all of these were of a world too far away to be imagined.

After the baseball season in September of that year, Six Mac-Donell came home to Abilene. Dwight was there. The two continued the active friendship begun so long before. They watched the high school football team work out in the late afternoons; they played poker with Joner and the others in the Tip-Top; they went hunting through the open country around the town. The only change in Dwight that Six could see was a physical growth and a superficial polish that had been lacking four years before. Though there was nothing smug or conceited in Dwight, he was more sure of himself than he had formerly been. He had a future all mapped out for him and he happily accepted it. Six, regretting now that he had not gone on to college, wished that his own future were as certain and secure.

One evening Dwight, Six, and another young man, more drunk on the wine of youth than from the bootleg whisky one of them had bought, swaggered through the business district, bent on "taking the town"—all in harmless fun, of course. Their loud-talking exuberance aroused smiles from their friends, frowns from the more puritanical townspeople whom they encountered. By the time full darkness had come they were cheerfully uninhibited. They found themselves in front of Hal Wayte's café and went in.

The café occupied part of what had formerly been a large room, divided now by a wall of beaverboard. Next door, beyond the flimsy wall, was a real estate office. Wayte himself was a big man, a good-hearted fellow, but possessed of a fiery temper. He talked so "tough" that some of the boys in the town were a little afraid of him. Dwight and his companions were not. They sat in a corner of the café, next to the separating wall, and Dwight taught the other two some West Point songs. His voice, from all accounts, was particularly unsuited to singing. Joe Howe had remarked that fact many times; when Dwight lifted his voice in song his listeners pleaded with him to halt their torture. It seems unlikely that Wayte was particularly sensitive to music, but he did object to so much noise in his establishment, and he profanely told the boys so. Dwight continued singing, and Wayte came over to the table, roaring his displeasure. If the boys didn't quiet down he, tough Hal Wayte, would throw them all into the street.

Dwight, silenced for the moment, looked Wayte up and down.

"Yeah?" he drawled. "You and who else?"

"By God, I can do it all by myself," Hal shouted.

Dwight shook his head, grinning.

"Now, Hal," he said soothingly, "you wouldn't do that to your pals. I know you wouldn't."

And he lifted his right fist, pivoted in his chair, and drove the fist into the wall. Hal, openmouthed, stared. Dwight's fist had gone entirely through the wall and into the real estate office beyond.

"Well, I'll be god-damned," said Wayte at last, with a certain reverence.

But when Dwight tried to withdraw his arm he found that he couldn't do it. His forearm was tightly held by the shreds of board which had exploded outward with his driving fist. He tugged and tugged, while Wayte's astonishment gave way to loud laughter.

"I just don't know my own strength," said Dwight immodestly. "I didn't mean to do that." He looked up at Hal. "You sure can't throw me out of here until you get me loose," he went on.

Having permitted a suitable punishment time to elapse, Hal went into the kitchen, returned with a large knife, and with considerable effort managed to cut a hole in the wall large enough to enable Dwight to withdraw his arm.

"I got to give it to you, Ike," Hal said. "You're quite a man. Quite a man."

When Dwight's first army orders came he was somewhat surprised. He had expected to be sent to the Philippines and had gone so far as to purchase tropical uniforms in anticipation of that event. Instead he was ordered to report in mid-September to the 19th Infantry in Galveston. For the second time his life was directly involved in the main stream of American history. The nature of his first assignment was determined by the continuing trouble with Mexico, grown increasingly serious since Wilson seven months before had lifted the embargo on arms for Carranza, while maintaining the embargo on arms for Huerta. Huerta was forced to abdicate, but Carranza's regime rested on no solid popular support, and it was now being threatened by what property-conscious newspapers called "bandits." Further United States intervention in Mexico, which would mean real soldiering for Dwight, seemed no remote possibility. Mexico, or Europe, or both. . . .

He arrived in Galveston in the second week of September, only to find that his regiment had been forced out of its barracks by a flood and had moved west to San Antonio. He caught the next train west and reported at Fort Sam Houston, only a few miles from the Alamo, on the following morning.

2

Whatever misogynous attitudes he may have assumed at West Point were quickly lost in San Antonio. Romance—as quiet, as unpretentious, as genuine as the other main elements of his life— awaited him there.

He found life at the army post extremely pleasant and far easier than any he had known before. His reputation as a former football star and as an all-around good fellow had preceded him. His popularity among fellow officers was immediate. He formed several lifelong friendships, with Jim Byrom and Leonard Gerow, among others. Only a day or so after his arrival staff members of the Peacock Military Academy in San Antonio approached him to ask if he would coach the academy's football team that autumn. He accepted with enthusiasm. Each weekday afternoon found him absorbed in the sport he loved best, inspiring "his team" toward heights they had never scaled before.

On a Sunday evening in early October he was loafing in front of the bachelor officers' quarters on the post, waiting for suppertime. He was officer of the guard that day. A service revolver was slung at his hip; his uniform was freshly cleaned and pressed; his field boots had been newly polished by the orderly, Private Daniel S. Miller, who served him and several other shavetails. He was conscious of his spick-and-span appearance as he glanced toward the girls who, in crisp summer dresses, were sitting in canvas chairs on the lawn of the officers' club across the way. One of the girls, Mrs. Lulu Harris, whom he already knew well, called to him, asking him to come over. He responded with alacrity.

A few minutes later he found himself bowing over the hand of a girl he had never seen before, a slender girl in a white dress which set off to striking advantage her dark brown hair and violet eyes. She was, he was certain, the prettiest girl he had ever seen. Her features were delicately chiseled and remarkably expressive. She held her head proudly erect. Certain photographs taken that year reveal in her a striking similarity to the actress, Lillian Gish, soon to achieve fame in D. W. Griffith's *The Birth of a Nation*. His blue-eyed gaze upon her face was so intent, so obviously deeply interested, that she blushed a little as she acknowledged the introduction.

Her full name was Mamie Geneva Doud, Lulu explained to Dwight, but everyone called her Mamie.

They all had supper together—the Harrises, Mr. and Mrs. Doud (whom Dwight at once liked immensely), Mamie, and Dwight, who managed to make an excellent impression on everyone present. One imagines he was helped to do so by Lulu, who had arranged the meeting and who watched it through a matchmaker's eyes. Immediately after supper Dwight announced ruefully that he must go inspect the guard, and he asked Mamie, without much hope, if she'd walk post with him. Somewhat to her own surprise, she accepted. She had a date at seven o'clock, but she conveniently forgot it as she strolled with Dwight to the various posts and sat with him afterward on the steps of Brooke Hospital, exploring with him the grounds for a mutual understanding. Considering the great difference in their upbringing, those grounds were remarkably spacious. Both of them derived the greatest pleasure from human relationships; both of them liked to have crowds of people around. Their reactions to many things were similar. They seemed to have much the same standards for judging events and personalities. It was dusk when at last they returned to the club where Mamie's young man, feeling himself unfairly used, had been waiting for a long, long time. Dwight's mind was already made up. He had never felt this way toward any girl before, not even Gladys Harding. He intended to marry Mamie.

But if Dwight, in the flush of his success that first evening, regarded Mamie as an easy conquest, he was swiftly disillusioned. She liked him. He was "fun." But she had been by no means as profoundly impressed by him as he had been by her. Her family had been wintering in San Antonio since 1910, and there were many young men there who were "fun" and who found her extremely attractive. She was eighteen years old. It was exciting to have a multitude of dates with a multitude of different beaux. She adored her parents and sisters. She had no desire to marry—not for years and years—and she had sensed from the very first that no relationship between Dwight and herself could remain casual for long.

On the evening of the day following her first meeting with him she returned from an all-day fishing expedition at Medina Lake to discover that a "Mr. I-something" had been calling every fifteen minutes all afternoon. The Doud maid was annoyed. Even as she gave vent to her annoyance the phone rang again, and sure enough, it was that "same Mr. I." Very formally Dwight asked "Miss Doud" if she'd care to go dancing with him that evening. She was sorry, but she already had an engagement. The next evening, then? She had an engagement then too. Well, how about the "big night" at the Majestic that week? She almost laughed at him. Popular girls were dated up weeks ahead for those Majestic "big nights," and she was extremely popular. She told him that she wouldn't have a free "big night" for four weeks.

"All right, then," he said calmly, "how about four weeks from now?"

She was overwhelmed. She accepted the date and, feeling a trifle limp, rang off. Either he was the most amazingly self-confident young man she had ever met, or this was one of the great loves of the generation—or maybe both.

It was typical of Dwight's absolute democracy that he was in no way abashed by the difference, in economic and social status, between the Douds and the Eisenhowers. Neither he nor Mamie recognized that difference as a barrier between them. The difference, however, was very real.

Mamie was accustomed from birth to a life easy and luxurious beyond the comprehension of Dwight in his early childhood. Her paternal grandfather, Royal Houghton Doud, had made a fortune, first as partner in the firm of Foote, Doud, and Company, wholesale grocers in Rome, New York, and later as a pork packer in Rome and Chicago. Her maternal grandfather, Carl Carlson, had come from Sweden to Boone County, Iowa, in 1868, there to establish a prosperous mill. Her father, John Sheldon Doud, had greatly enhanced the family fortune by joining with his brother, Jim Doud, in an extremely successful packing-house venture in Boone, Iowa. Far back, beyond Royal, the Douds could trace their line without a break to one Henry Doude, who was born in Guilford, Surrey County, England, and who came to America in 1639 to become one of the founders of Guilford, Connecticut. Still farther back extended a tradition of English aristocracy, complete with manor houses and a Doude family crest. Small wonder that money and leisure were accepted by Mamie as a matter of course. The wonder is that so much ease of living had left her energetic, genuine, and unspoiled.

But then the Douds, as far back as records go, had always been an adventurous and capable race with a tremendous capacity for enjoying life. For example, old Royal Doud had joined in the Alaska gold rush in 1898, though he was then in his sixties and had long ago made his fortune. It was a high adventure which had cost him his life. He returned to Chicago to die in 1899. John Doud had thrice, as a boy, run away from home in search of adventure and had demonstrated on each of these occasions a sturdy self-reliance. He had worked as a day laborer on a Mississippi levee building gang, had later worked as a cook for that gang, had bummed his way through a good portion of Iowa, Indiana, Illinois, and Tennessee before settling down as a student at the University of Chicago, where four years later he took his degree. In 1894, with his marriage to Elivera Carlson, he had gained a wife whose adventurous temperament was similar to his own. Mamie told Dwight how her mother, in 1904, arose from a sickbed, where she was recovering from a severe attack of pneumonia, to attend the World's Fair in St. Louis—and almost died from a relapse. Two years later Mamie's father, in violation of that part of the American businessman's code which regards the making of money as an end in itself, had retired from active business. He was then thirty-six years old. He had moved his family to Colorado, first to Pueblo, then to Colorado Springs, and finally to Denver, where he built a large, unpretentious, but very comfortable house at 750 Lafayette.

Mamie was the second of four daughters. The eldest, Eleanor, had died almost three years before Mamie met Dwight. Eda Mae, four years younger than Mamie, and Mable Frances, aged eleven, were with the family in San Antonio in this fall of 1915. The family was an extremely happy one, with much the same sort of solidarity as the Eisenhowers displayed. Before many weeks had passed the persistent Dwight had made himself a welcome part of it.

As Mamie remembers it, this effortless integration with the family, this complete acceptance of the group life and loyalty, was the first important factor in Dwight's favor as he continued his courtship. He honestly enjoyed her father and mother. He liked going along when they all went driving, or fishing, or to the movies. He wasn't always trying to get Mamie off alone somewhere, away from her people. He seems to have found in the Doud house a second home, a continuation in somewhat different terms of his own family life— and no one felt a more intense need of a home and family life than he. It was one of the distinguishing marks of his character. The Douds loved him for it.

He is reported to have infected the family with his own enthusiasm for football that autumn. All of them attended the Peacock Military Academy's football games and found themselves cheering madly for "Ike's boys" as the latter won victory after victory over the stiffest opposition. By the time football season had ended Mamie's numerous beaux realized that Dwight had the inside track with her. Repeated rebuffs caused them to telephone less and less often. New Year's found him recognized in San Antonio's social circles as her "steady beau." It must have been at about this time that Mamie's parents pointed out to her certain facts about army life which might have some bearing on her decision with regard to Dwight. A second lieutenant's pay couldn't support her in the style to which she was accustomed, and the Douds had no intention of supporting her after her marriage (young people should learn to stand on their own feet); an army wife must be prepared to make a home under difficult conditions; she'd be shunted around the country from one army post to another, with no possibility of sinking roots into any local soil; she'd find that an army post is a world unto itself, different in ways obvious and subtle from the civilian world. But even as they listed these objections it was clear that they, who had been negatively critical of most of her other young men, were strongly in favor of Dwight's suit. Mamie admitted, with a reluctant farewell to her independence, that she herself favored it. She loved him. He had the strongest character, the quickest mind, the most charming manners, the sunniest temperament, and the greatest devotion of all the young men she had known. On St. Valentine's Day she could resist no longer. She accepted his West Point class ring.

They were married in Denver on July 1, 1916. In the music room of the Doud house at 750 Lafayette Street, a room bedecked with gladioli, Mamie in a white lace dress stood beside Dwight, who wore the immaculate white uniform he had bought in anticipation of a Philippines assignment. Dwight's trousers had a razor-edge crease, and Mamie recalls that he wouldn't sit down until after the ceremoney, for fear of losing the perfect press. The pastor of the near-by Presbyterian Church, of which the Douds were members, was on his summer holiday, so a visiting British minister, the Reverend Williamson, read the marriage service. Afterward Dwight melted candle wax and dipped into it Mamie's bridal bouquet of roses and lilies. He fondly believed that he could preserve the waxed flowers forever —but the hot wax merely shriveled the petals.

Dismayed, he turned to Mamie. She smiled and comforted him.

"I guess it was worth a try," he said wistfully. "It would have been swell if it'd worked."

On that very same day he received his promotion to the rank of first lieutenant.

On the afternoon of their wedding day they rode the Union Pacific eastward through the foothills, through the immense short-grass pastures, and on into the vast reaches of the High Plains of western Kansas. The July sun blazed down upon a land which shone like a burnished golden bowl beneath a brilliant sky. The train seemed to roar always at the very bottom of that bowl, climbing a gentle slope toward a rim of sky that was never reached, as though the sense of forward motion were an illusion.

The country itself seemed to be moving, flowing with a hot, dry wind. The ripe wheat leaned and lifted in waves as far as eye could see across a landscape of infinite distance, infinite solitude, infinite peace. The war belonged to another world, still too far away to be imagined, especially by two young people preoccupied with an intense personal happiness. (Five thousand miles in front of the locomotive, on this very day, the British had launched the Somme offensive. In the Somme, too, there were golden waves climbing a long slope, leaning into the wind, falling down upon the land like cut stalks of wheat. Only those waves were not wheat, but men. They spread upon the land a crimson stain.) Another world, too far away to be imagined; yet even the color pattern of this visible peace beyond the train windows, on Dwight's wedding day, had been shaped by the war. Two years ago much of that golden land had been green with a virgin buffalo sod. It was the war, reflected in a booming grain market, which had sent thousands of plows out into a soil that had never been turned before. Right now it looked as though the soil had happily accepted the plows. Twenty years passed before the land's rebellion became evident in suffocating clouds of dust which darkened half a continent and deposited on ships halfway to Spain a film of Kansas dirt. The golden bowl became the Dust Bowl, and the wheat piled up unsold in bins, walled off from millions of hungry mouths.

The sun went down. Dwight, staring out on a darkening scene, had good reason to find his happiness alloyed with an immediate apprehension. He must have been thinking not of future months but of tomorrow, when he and his bride would arrive at the Eisenhower home. What if Mamie and his family failed to like one another? Certainly that was possible. Her family, with its easy, graceful, moneyed life, was far different in many respects from his own. Mamie might find his family crude and ridiculously pious; his family might find Mamie frivolous and snobbish. There were so many grounds for mutual misunderstanding. True, Mamie had been delighted with the letter Dwight's father had written to her, in his beautifully flowing script, before the wedding. She had found the formal sincerity of the letter completely charming and had showed it to Dwight with pride. It was a hopeful sign.

As for Mamie, she was determined to employ all her tact, to *make* Dwight's people like her. She had no doubts about her liking Dwight's people. He had told her a great deal about his family, particularly about his mother, and she had liked all that she had heard. With regard to fundamentals, the two families, his and hers, must have much in common. Both of them placed the same high values on rugged self-reliance, on integrity, on kindliness. Nevertheless, she, too, was a trifle apprehensive as the hours of night came on and the train pulled out of the Hays station toward Ellsworth, Salina, Abilene.

It was four o'clock in the morning when Mamie first saw the Eisenhower house and barn silhouetted against a faintly dawn-washed sky. Inside, Dwight's father and mother awaited them. Ida's face was wreathed in smiles, heart-warming smiles, as she embraced Mamie and proclaimed that she who had had seven sons was proud and happy to welcome a daughter into the family. David's welcome, if more reserved, was equally heart-warming. Mamie, laughing and chatting gaily with her new parents, seemed to Dwight more captivating than ever. She turned to him and smiled, to let him know how much she liked them all. He swelled with pride. A few hours later Earl and Milton came downstairs, sleepy-eyed and self-conscious. Mamie's greeting of them was completely disarming.

Now at last, she said, she had some brothers. She had always wanted a brother. . . .

At a nine o'clock wedding breakfast, with corsages for Mamie and Ida and with the neighbors invited in to meet Dwight's bride, Mamie found need for all her social training. She was on exhibit, and everyone was suddenly stiff and formal. They were all so determined to do the right thing, to show this "rich" young girl that they knew what the right thing was. Mamie was a bit frightened. If she betrayed the slightest condescension, if she so much as hinted that she was amused by quaint customs and provincial manners, they'd all be horribly hurt—and they'd hate her. But of course their customs *weren't* quaint, and their manners were charming. She hid her nervousness so well that Dwight didn't even know about it until long afterward. She was so obviously genuine, so obviously eager to like them all and to have them all like her, that she soon melted their stiff formality into a spontaneous friendliness. Everyone, thereafter, had a marvelous time. For one thing, they were all immensely proud and fond of Dwight. It made her heart go out to them.

Dwight took her all over the Eisenhower acres and told her in detail how things had been when he was a boy. He pointed out the scenes of fights and accidents. There, next to the back porch, on one Fourth of July, Ed had placed a can of gunpowder packed tightly under a mound of dirt. He had attached a long fuse to it and watched the fuse burn down into the can. Nothing happened. "A fizzle," Ed had said disgustedly and had gone over to it. His face was directly above it when the explosion came. There'd been a houseful of company, Dwight remembered, and Ed had come in with his face blackened by powder and pitted with gravel. Lucky he wasn't blinded. Mother had had to pull out the gravel with a pair of tweezers. . . . And over there in the hayloft of the barn Earl had taught Milton to do flip-flops, diving from a rafter into the hay. Milton was having difficulty making the turn in the air, so Earl had told him to go up higher. Milton did. He went up about as high as he could go and dived straight down, headfirst. He lay very still in the hay. Earl had run screaming to the house and had brought Mother running back with him. Milton was just beginning to stir. He'd been stunned for a minute, and the wind had been knocked out of him. Lucky he didn't break his neck. . . . Once Dwight and Earl had painted the barn, Dwight on a tall ladder and Earl on a shorter one. Always Earl insisted on working directly below Dwight, where he caught all the slopped paint from Dwight's bucket. After a couple of weeks of this Earl's overalls were so stiff with paint that the legs wouldn't bend. . . . One evening Father had caught Earl and Milton snapping chickens off their roosts with a buggy whip and had whipped both of them. . . . There were dozens of such stories, and through them Mamie caught the spirit of the family, an impression of immense stir and vitality. Most of all she was impressed by the role Mother Eisenhower had played. What an amazing woman she was! How she'd managed at all, and kept her cheerful sanity, Mamie couldn't understand.

From Ida herself Mamie learned a great deal about Dwight and about the Eisenhower men in general. They were strong-willed men, her sons, and any woman who tried to mold them into a new pattern would have her work cut out for her. The best way to handle them was to do so as little as possible, and beyond that to employ persuasion, an appeal to their own ideals of conduct. A naked conflict of wills might be disastrous. With the Eisenhowers, the man of the family was the head of the family, always. That's the way the boys had been reared. Mamie smiled. She was, she said, old-fashioned enough to *want* the man to head the family. Her own job was to make a home for him, and she wanted that home to revolve about him. When it was necessary to "manage" him she'd do so with such subtlety that he'd never realize what was happening.

It was Ida's turn to smile. For, inevitably, Mamie broke her good resolutions. She did so almost at once, perhaps on the very day she put them into words. Like all Midwestern farm families, the Eisenhowers had their dinner at noon, and immediately after dinner one afternoon Dwight announced that he'd better go uptown and look up the "gang." Mamie said that was fine, because she and his mother still had a great deal to talk about. He grinned, kissed her, and sauntered out. Mamie watched him stroll up Chestnut Street, his blond hair gleaming in the sun. And that was the last she saw of him all afternoon. When suppertime came he still had not returned. They waited supper, Mamie's irritation swelling by the minute into a full-blown anger, tinctured with anxiety.

"What do you suppose can have happened to him?" she asked Ida.

"Nothing serious," Ida replied soothingly. "He's probably in a poker game with his friends down at the café."

Mamie was unsoothed. When at last they sat down to supper

without Dwight she was almost too furious to eat. The nerve of him, the callous selfishness, doing this to her on their honeymoon! It was desertion, unforgivable. He hadn't returned when darkness fell, and Mamie could stand it no longer. She looked up the number of the café in the telephone book and rang that number, tapping her foot impatiently while Dwight was called. He spoke before she had a chance to begin the speech she'd planned. He was sorry to be so late, but he never left a poker game while he was behind, if he could help it, and he was still behind. His suave tones put Mamie in the position of a nagging wife, and her fury rose to new heights.

"You come home this minute!" she commanded.

"Now, now, Mamie," he said, unmoved. "I've just explained. It's against my principles to quit when I'm licked. It won't be long——"

"If you don't come home this minute you needn't bother to come at all," she stormed, and banged the receiver into its hook.

He didn't come "that minute." He calmly resumed his game. When at last his footsteps were heard on the side porch it was two o'clock in the morning and the "gang" had contributed a comfortable sum of money to his pocket.

But whatever satisfaction he may have felt over his winnings was quickly dissipated in the storm which broke around him in the house, and when the storm at last subsided both he and Mamie had learned new things about each other and about the nature of the relationship into which they'd entered. Mamie realized what Ida meant when she spoke of the dangers of a conflict of wills, when one of those wills was Dwight's, and Dwight realized with some surprise that he'd hurt his bride deeply, that in effect he'd welshed on an obligation he owed to her. It was the first and from all accounts the worst quarrel they ever had. They emerged from it more deeply in love than before. She had spirit, this slender slip of a girl. He admitted ruefully and with pride that she was a worthy mate for a fighting man.

A day or so later they left Abilene. In view of the trouble boiling up along the Mexican border, the government had felt itself unable to spare the services of even a young lieutenant for more than ten days. (Pershing was leading an inglorious, futile chase through northern Mexico, searching for Pancho Villa, and National Guard troops were stationed all along the Mexican line.) Too quickly those ten days had passed by.

Back in San Antonio, Mamie did not begin housekeeping at once.

The newlyweds moved into Dwight's bachelor quarters at Fort Sam Houston, where in marked contrast to the spaciousness to which she was accustomed she found her life crowded into a living room, bedroom, and bath, all of them tiny. She didn't complain. She was as happy as a child with a new toy, and her husband was astonished by the efficiency of her management. She helped Dwight initiate, in these tiny quarters, the "Club Eisenhower" (though it was not christened that until long after, and was far more intimately friendly than any club), a tradition of genial hospitality which in dozens of different guises all the way from Paris to the Philippines would provide a happy life for both of them and play a major role in the shaping of Dwight's career. Officers of all ranks liked to drop in on the Eisenhowers. They always had a good time there.

Mamie made a point of learning all the curious ins and outs of social life on an army post in peacetime. She saw to it that calls were made and received in strict accordance with the rules. Even in that first year, despite limited resources, she did more than her share of entertaining. She created precisely the kind of home atmosphere most stimulating to her husband's finest traits.

She had, as she described it, found her own career—and its name was Ike.

3

Nineteen-sixteen. Americans, too, were now living in a double world. . . .

There was the immediate world of comfortable, tangible reality which Mamie could see outside her windows, a radiant peace under a Texas sun. The watered lawns on the post were a vivid green, and the flower beds were gay with color—until the days grew short and the open plains of the reservation took on a new beauty, all brown and red and gold. But beyond this lay the nightmare world whose monstrous shadows, flame-tinted, bloodstained, loomed higher and higher in the east. Was the trouble along the Mexican border one of those shadows, grown tangible as it fell across our continent? Some Americans said so, claiming that the Germans fomented that trouble to keep us occupied at home. . . .

The double world pressed most heavily upon the good schoolmaster in the White House. He had hoped to aid at the birth of that world Henry Adams had spoken of in 1907, "a world . . . sensitive and timid natures could regard without a shudder." Even

Adams, a despairing old man, had believed such a world was possible by "say 1938." Poor Adams's pessimism now appeared as the most irrational optimism in the blood-red light of the European civil war. Wilson was still "neutral"; he still refused to admit, through overt action, the reality of evil. He made no audible complaint that fall when his campaign managers, before the November election, chanted, "He kept us out of war." The chant may have gained votes for him, but it added to the enormity of his burdens as the old year died. With some bitterness he discovered that the men who had most loudly damned his idealism when he forced passage of the income tax and reduced tariff bill were greater idealists than he when it came to foreign relations. They charged that his eternal note writing was branding us as a nation of cowards. They wanted to go to war, or have the country go to war, to preserve their ideals—and Wilson, who may have suspected that "ideals" in their case meant "Allied loans," began to consider ways of gaining control over the forces which must otherwise crush him. If we *did* go to war, his would be the decisive voice at the peace conference. Yes, there was that to consider. He considered it all through the winter and early spring. . . .

Mamie, whose everyday life had a single focus, realized that nightmare world acutely only in times of loneliness. She realized it when Dwight, in charge of the military-police detail, walked the dangerous night streets of San Antonio's red-light district, or when he was sent for days at a time on detached service to Camp Wilson, where National Guard troops were patrolling the border. (Once a bullet mysteriously fired from a dark doorway whistled past him as he walked up Matamoros Street in San Antonio; once a Negro buck private from Chicago, roaring drunk in a tough little border town, emptied a revolver at him point-blank but with incredibly bad aim.) During these lonely times she thought of the two worlds in terms of Ike, wondering with an anxiety she couldn't deny what would be in store for him and for her if those two worlds, nightmare and real, should fuse. So many millions had gone into that nightmare world and died there, or come out horribly maimed. If we declared war Ike would be among the first to go. She was beginning to understand what it meant to be a soldier's wife in time of war.

By the time the old year died there were no "ifs" in Dwight's mind concerning our involvement in the war. The only questions were "when" and "how." It can hardly be said on the basis of available evidence that he had formed any general theories of war, but it is certain that he was studying the European war this year with a careful regard for particulars. The particulars were depressing enough to one who had made the profession of arms his own and who was naturally concerned with the honor of that profession. The massacre in the Somme churned dully on until it bogged down in the mud of November. Some eight hundred thousand Allied troops were sacrificed to gain a useless stretch of shell-ravaged earth twenty-four miles wide and only nine miles deep at the point of farthest penetration. The French, who had bled themselves white holding Verdun from February to June, began to bleed there again in an offensive action begun in November, though Verdun had, so far as Dwight could see, no particular strategic value. Dwight, from his study of military history, had reached agreement with those who asserted that basic strategic principles remain unchanged through time, but clearly this didn't mean that the particular tactical expressions of those principles remained unchanged. The latter were modified, or *should* be modified, in accordance with changes in weapons. This continuous flinging of frontal infantry assaults into the face of massed machine guns and artillery, a tactic which had failed time after time on an ever-increasing scale, was criminally stupid. It could be repeated only by commanders who, as Ernest Hemingway would write long afterward, "had that beautiful detachment and devotion to stern justice of men dealing in death without being in any danger of it." The French generals, "realists" all, said that the war would be won "by the side that can last fifteen minutes longer than the other." What a ghastly idea! Surely true generalship involved something more than a mass trading of lives or deaths!

New weapons called for new tactics—or for the invention of answering weapons. If mobility had been separated from fire power, and sacrificed to it, the thing to do was not to ignore the fact (Dwight never ignored facts) but to devise some means of recombining the two elements. Everyone agreed that the central problem, as yet unsolved in this war, was to re-create a fluid front, dissolving the stationary lines in a new war of movement. Very well. The means for doing so were at hand. They had been at hand since 1914.

It is impossible to say just how far along these lines Dwight's thinking had proceeded by the end of that year. He himself could not say. But it is certain that by the end of that year his attention had become fastened upon two weapons which would change the whole character of war: the airplane and the tank. If he didn't think of these weapons in terms of over-all command (he was only a lieutenant, after all), he certainly thought of them in terms of his own personal activity. Early in 1917 he began to consider requesting a transfer from the Infantry to the Air Corps. Flying fascinated him, just in itself, and its military possibilities seemed to him overwhelming. The future, he told Mamie, was forecast in the skies.

It was at this point that Mamie for the first time sought to influence directly his professional career. They had begun their married life on the tacit assumption that they had entirely different, if supplementary, jobs. In later years Mamie was to explain that "Ike runs the office and I run the home," that "Ike always leaves his problems at the office when he comes home and he never talks shop at home if he can avoid it." He abided strictly by those rules of silence imposed for purposes of military security. Mamie quickly discovered that she could learn more about what was going on at the post from the gossip of other officers' wives than she could from her husband. But on this occasion Dwight seems to have considered it only fair to talk matters over with his wife, and he found her unalterably opposed to the idea of a transfer.

"I won't have you going up in those flimsy crates," she said almost tearfully. "I simply won't. There are plenty of unmarried men for that. A man with a wife and—and a child——"

He looked at her quickly.

"What's that?" he demanded. "What did you say?"

"A wife and child," she said more calmly. "We're going to have a baby, Ike—in September or October, the doctor says. So you see——"

But she didn't have to argue any more. For the moment he had forgotten all about airplanes, and tanks, and war.

April 1917. The two worlds fused. The nightmare became real. . . .

On January 19 the German Government through official channels had urged Mexico to make war on the United States if the United States declared war on Germany. In return, the Germans promised to restore to Mexico the territories seized by the United States in the 1840s. On January 31 the German Government announced that she would thereafter sink on sight, without challenge, every vessel found in the Mediterranean or in the waters adjacent to Great Britain, whether the vessel be neutral or belligerent. On February 3 the German ambassador, Von Bernstorff, was handed his passports. Two weeks later the British intelligence service published the "Zimmerman Note," exposing Germany's machinations in Mexico. During February some two hundred ships were sunk by German U-boats, three fourths of them neutral, two of them American. Wilson asked Congress for authority to arm American merchant vessels, was voted that authority by an overwhelming majority of the House, and denied it by a filibuster of twelve senators, some of whom subscribed to the left-wing view that this was an "imperialist" war from which only evil could come to the common man, no matter who won. The filibuster also blocked passage of the army appropriation bill. After congressional adjournment Wilson promptly called for a special session to convene on April 2.

There was no doubt now about the temper of the country. The country wanted war. Wilson could hardly have prevented a declaration if he had tried to do so. Never, not even in the Europe of 1914, have a people disproved more completely the thesis that human nature is incurably selfish, that the masses of people are prompted primarily by motives of material self-interest. The average American did not seriously believe, despite all the propaganda to the contrary, that a victorious Germany would invade and conquer us. But his moral sense was outraged by tales of atrocities perpetrated as a deliberate policy of German terror, by the disregard for treaties guaranteeing Belgian neutrality, by the ruthlessness of unrestricted submarine warfare, and by the insufferable arrogance of the advocates of Pan-Germanism. To blot out a moral wrong, to create a world in which such wrong could not again occur, he was willing, even eager, to fight. Wilson spoke for the average American when, in his message to Congress on the evening of April 2, he proclaimed that the world "must be made safe for democracy," that "its peace must be planted upon the tested foundations of political liberty," that "we desire no conquest, no dominion . . . no indemnities for ourselves, no material compensation for the sacrifices we shall make." If certain powerful American interests had somewhat different aims, they perforce expressed them publicly in the same terms Wilson had used, terms of the highest idealism. The country as a whole had reached a pitch of sacrificial commitment which it was never in our time to reach again. The common man, with little sense of immediate national danger such as moved him in 1941, had nothing to gain from war save the preservation of those "principles" of which Wilson had so eloquently spoken, and the extension of them to other peoples. He had his comfort, his safety, and perhaps his life to lose.

. . . the right is more precious than peace, and we shall fight for the things which we have always carried nearest in our hearts—for democracy, for the right of those who submit to authority to have a voice in their own government, for the rights and liberties of small nations, for a universal dominion of right by such concert of free peoples as shall bring peace and safety to all nations. . . . The day has come when America is privileged to spend her blood and might for the principles that gave her birth and happiness and the peace which she has treasured. God helping her, she can do no other.

Dwight was in Leon Springs, thirty miles from San Antonio, when he read Wilson's speech in the morning newspaper, April 3. He had been assigned to the 57th Infantry, as regimental supply officer, only two days before. One imagines that his dominant feeling, like that of most professional soldiers, was one of relief. He'd seen the war coming for a long time, had watched with some exasperation the congressional efforts to prevent our adequately preparing for it, and must have been glad that now, at last, he and his fellow officers would be helped rather than hindered as they did what was necessary. By the time Wilson signed the declaration of war three days later, Dwight was almost literally buried in work. The 57th must be whipped into fighting shape in the shortest possible time.

Mamie had remained in San Antonio, moving into the home of her parents on McCullough Street. There were no accommodations for her at Leon Springs, and with the child coming she was in no condition for "roughing it." Thus, though she was with her parents again, she read the newspapers with an ache of loneliness for Ike. It was horrible to be separated from him now, wasting precious hours of what might be so little time. What if he were shipped overseas before the baby was born?

But then nobody seemed to have a private life in times like these; all private living was subordinate to a public duty defined by some "higher authority." All private conversation, even, seemed to be drowned out by a harsh public speech filled with commands to "work," "fight," "sacrifice," "buy Liberty Bonds." The days of spring no longer flowed gently toward summer, merging imperceptibly one with another in a pleasant murmur of green-growing life. The days marched now. They jerked along with the sharp discontinuity of soldiers' ranks from one screaming headline to another: THE PRESIDENT CALLS FOR WAR WITHOUT HATE. . . . WAR RESOLUTION PASSED BY CONGRESS. . . . WAR IS DECLARED! . . . HUGE ARMY BILL PASSED; PROVIDES FOR SOLDIER DRAFT. . . . BRITISH WAR MISSION ARRIVES IN WASHINGTON. . . . CONGRESS PASSES LARGEST FINANCE BILL IN WORLD HISTORY. . . . HUGE LOANS TO ALLIES—the days marching to what fearful climaxes, what bloody ends?

Mamie steeled herself under a burden much harder to bear than Dwight's, a burden of helpless waiting, of dull endurance. One day, when she was all alone in the Doud house, she could bear it no longer. It was a Saturday morning. Dwight had telephoned to inform her that once again he would not be able to get leave for the week end. Her longing to see him became desperate. She went to the garage back of the house, called over a next-door neighbor, and learned from him how to start and shift the gears of the Doud automobile. She had never driven before! The neighbor did his best to persuade her from her project, but she was adamant. On the following morning, very early, she backed the car out of the garage and headed for Leon Springs. Fortunately there was no traffic on the road, for she drove erratically, weaving from one side of the highway to the other, horribly frightened, through thirty dangerous miles. She arrived at the camp entrance without mishap, but if Dwight had not been warned of her coming and had not been waiting for her at the gates she might have been forced to drive the car until the gasoline was gone. He leaped on the running board and showed her how to stop. She hadn't known!

The days marched from April into May. The pace was swifter now. War missions from the Allied Powers were begging for American soldiers, millions of them, and as soon as possible. The Russian czar had abdicated. The Kerensky regime was insecure. Soon the Germans would be able to concentrate all their fighting forces on the Western Front. It looked as though the 57th might be overseas by midwinter, and Dwight, promoted to the permanent rank of captain on the fifteenth of that month, only hoped that he'd remain in Texas until after the baby was born. After that he was eager to go. May merged into June. Teddy Roosevelt was fuming in the public prints because Wilson had refused him an overseas divisional command. Pershing had been appointed commander of all American armies in Europe, to the hurt dismay of Leonard Wood and his Republican partisans. From France on June 6, Pershing cabled the War Department that one million American troops must be in France by the following May. To get those troops and their supplies across, liberty ships by the hundreds began sliding down the ways of scores of shipyards.

Dwight's commanding officers began listing on his record the first of a long series of "S's" for "Superior." The amount of work he got done, without loss of his genial good humor, was amazing. His talent for constructive leadership was evident in the trim efficiency of his men. Those men did not find him "easy"; he was a strict disciplinarian, but he made it clear to them that he regarded his position in strictly functional terms: he had one function to perform, they had another, and both functions were important. They worked hard for him because they liked and respected him. There was little lost motion in his outfit. Swiftly the summer was gone. Soon now, in just a few weeks perhaps, the 57th would be ready to go. Even sooner than that, in just a few days now, the baby would be born.

Orders came to him in mid-September. As he read them his spirits sank as low as it was possible for them to go. He would report on September 18 at Fort Oglethorpe, Georgia, there to serve as an instructor in the Officers' Training Camp. Gone was his chance of being with Mamie when the baby was born. Gone, too, was his chance of going overseas soon. Breaking the bad news to Mamie was one of the hardest chores he ever had to perform. But Mamie took the jolt like a front-line soldier. She wasn't the least bit afraid, she insisted, and Dwight mustn't be. Everything was going to be all right. . . . Nevertheless, Dwight lived in a hell of tense nervousness until the telegram came to him at Fort Oglethorpe on September 24. Everything *was* all right. Mamie had given birth to a son. They named him Doud Dwight.

4

There was irony in the fact that because Dwight did his assigned jobs too well he was cheated of what he considered a proper reward for good work. The place of a professional soldier in wartime was on the battlefield. Dwight felt that to be profoundly true, and he could not avoid a sense of guilt as he was shunted from one training

assignment to another while friends and classmates faced death—
and died, some of them—on the Marne and in the Champagne and
in the "quiet sector" of the Vosges. It wasn't his knee injury he had
suffered in football which kept him out of combat action—though
long afterward some journalists were to assume that it was. He was
kept out simply because he was too good at training men.

Colonel Douglas MacArthur was garnering fame and glory with
the Rainbow Division. Captain George S. Patton, Jr., was seeing the
war from two levels, as an aide to General Pershing and as a field
commander of a tank outfit. Dwight, on December 12, 1917, was
ordered to Fort Leavenworth to serve as instructor in the Army
Service Schools. On February 28, 1918, he was ordered to Camp
Meade, Maryland, where he spent some weeks organizing the 65th
Battalion Engineers. On March 24 he was ordered to Camp Colt,
Gettysburg, Pennsylvania.

He read the latter orders with mixed emotions. He was to command Camp Colt, a tank training center. It was a remarkably
responsible assignment for a young captain, an assignment which
would test to the utmost his abilities as a professional officer and as
a leader of men. He could even consider it a great opportunity, in
one sense, for the eyes of some very important people would be upon
him. But it also meant that an overseas assignment was even more
improbable than it had been before. For whatever disappointment
he may have felt at his failure to receive orders for France, there
were two compensations. One was that Mamie and their six-
month-old son, whom they'd nicknamed "Icky" (to his paternal
grandmother's probable horror), would be able to join Dwight at
Gettysburg, where they rented a small house. The other was that
Dwight, who had turned his professional attention to tanks after
he'd given up the idea of an Air Corps transfer, would now be
working full time with a weapon which, he was sure, would prove
a major factor in future wars if not in this one.

At Leavenworth, when tank outfits were still part of the Army
Engineers, he'd gone through a pioneer "tank school." He'd studied
avidly the use, or misuse, which had been made of tanks in the battles
of the Somme. Some twenty of the unwieldy monsters had been used
there. They'd achieved complete tactical surprise, had terrorized
German front-line troops, and had actually made a break-through,
though on a front too tiny to be decisive. At Cambrai, in November
1917, the possibilities of the tank had been even more thoroughly

demonstrated, if not realized. General Byng, by flinging scores of tanks into the battle, had gained a very real, if temporary, tactical victory *almost without loss!* Now if hundreds of tanks had been employed on dry ground that had not been torn to pieces by artillery fire, what could have kept them from going all the way to Berlin? Dwight was temperamentally about as far removed from the evangelistic type as one could imagine, but he could not avoid a certain irritation with those military authorities who refused to admit facts which proved their theories wrong. Dwight's respect for facts was one of his most outstanding traits. He could feel that at Camp Colt his work would be touched with a historical significance. He could enter upon it with the zest of a pioneer.

Nevertheless, his ardor was somewhat dampened when, upon his arrival at Gettysburg, he discovered that he was to train thousands of men for tank warfare without benefit of a single tank! The men were coming, picked men and eager. Their tents (no barracks had been built there) were spread in orderly array where Pickett had made his glorious charge in 1863. But of tanks there were none until, months later, a French Renault was shipped to them—to tantalize them, Dwight supposed. No one ever figured out precisely what happened to the tank-building program which was supposed to be under way at Dayton. All that was certain was that no tanks were forthcoming, that we had a Tank Corps without American tanks, until after the Armistice was signed.

One can imagine the gloom with which, at the outset, he regarded the task which had been set for him. An impossible task. There were not even ordinary facilities for taking care of the incoming men, and it was bitter cold in Gettysburg that March. Getting adequate food and shelter for his troops was the first job, and before he could come near to completing it the men themselves were coming in. Mamie in later years had a vivid recollection of her young husband pacing up and down, up and down in their tiny house, worried sick about those "poor hungry kids." He sent subordinates out on foraging expeditions, gathering loads of straw for use as bedding. Somehow he managed to get enough hot food. The men of his command, thank God, seemed to understand and to sympathize with him. He took them all into his confidence and explained just how it was, and morale, instead of sagging to the dangerously low point he had feared, seemed actually to be boosted by the hardships they were sharing together. He managed to imbue his command with that high quality of team spirit which had won football games for Abilene and Cullum Hall and Peacock in the past. It was not long before the elementary problems of supply were efficiently solved.

The big problem, the seemingly insoluble problem of training, still remained. The training would have to be theoretical. It would also have to be "practical," for if the men once sensed an antithesis between theory and practice the morale of Camp Colt was bound to sink to those depths Dwight feared. These men were volunteers, men who had passed special mental and physical qualifying examinations. They would be quick to sense any slackness in command. Dwight worked night and day and week ends. He built his organization around a training program which, from all accounts, was brilliantly conceived, since it enabled the "alumni" of Camp Colt to operate tanks effectively in battle after only a few weeks of training with real tanks in southern England. By midsummer Camp Colt was known as one of the "smartest" camps in the country—and Dwight had been promoted to the temporary rank of major.

His men at headquarters recognized in him a genius for organization. Claude J. Harris, a sergeant major at headquarters when Dwight arrived, remarked as the months passed those qualities which would later be published around the world. "Eisenhower," wrote Harris to Dr. Francis Trevelyan Miller in 1944, "was a strict disciplinarian . . . but most human, considerate. He possessed . . . the ability to place an estimate on a man and fit him into a position where he would 'click.' In the event his judgment (of a man) proved erroneous the man would be called in, his errors pointed out, and adjustments made to suit the situation. This principle built for him high admiration and loyalty from his officers . . . equaled by few commanding officers. . . . Seldom did one see a paper on his desk. Mail and papers for his attention were immediately attended to—his desk cleared. . . . He was always available to confer with his officers on either military or personal problems. . . . He . . . shied at publicity, preferring to remain in the background."[1] By autumn Dwight had some six thousand men under his command. He was not yet twenty-eight years old.

One anecdote, possibly apocryphal, persists from those days. A young lieutenant is supposed to have been so anxious to please Major Eisenhower that he praised to the skies all phases of the

[1]*Eisenhower, Man and Soldier,* by Francis Trevelyan Miller, John C. Winston, Philadelphia, 1944.

camp's administration. Dwight, working under strain and suspicious of insincerity, became increasingly irritated. One day his irritation broke through his restraint.

"For God's sake get out and find something wrong with the camp!" he roared. "It can't be as good as you say it is. Either you're not being frank, or you're as big a fool as I am."

In his rare moments of leisure he liked to wander over the battlefields, as he had done over the West Point hills, studying "on the spot" the maneuvers the Confederate and Union forces had made on those ghastly July days of 1863. Mamie claims he "knew every rock on that battlefield." On Sundays he used to take Mamie driving around Gettysburg, stopping every now and then to give her a lecture on how and where and why the regiments had stood and Longstreet had attacked and Pickett, for all the gallantry of his attack, had failed. Mamie, though her interest in ancient battles was limited, found Dwight's accounts fascinating. He filled them with so much vivid detail that old scenes lived again.

On October 14, his twenty-eighth birthday, Dwight was promoted to the temporary rank of lieutenant colonel. He might well have been satisfied with his position, now that the camp was going well and his work had received official recognition. He was happy with Mamie and Icky, his son of whom he was inordinately proud. But he wasn't satisfied. He continued to bombard his superiors with requests for overseas service. Men whom he had trained were living up to the Tank Corps' motto of "Treat 'Em Rough" as they opened holes for the Infantry in the Germans' Argonne forest lines. All along the front, from the channel ports to the Vosges, the enemy was in retreat, but Dwight, studying the official reports, was sure that a lot of fighting remained to be done. The high command talked of a "narrowing front" along which the Germans could increase their concentration of men and matériel. The final offensive, through which the Allies would crash into Germany itself, was being scheduled for the spring of 1919. Dwight knew that tanks were to play an unprecedented role in that final assault. They were to be employed by the hundreds, and according to Churchill in the British Ministry of Munitions, each of them would be equipped with means for making its own smoke. The iron monsters would advance and maneuver behind a screen of artificial fog. Technically these operations would be of vast interest. They would provide opportunities for tactical innovations, for individual initiative, of which Dwight longed to take advantage.

In early November the orders for which he had been praying came. Mamie, watching from the living-room window of their house, saw Dwight coming up the street with a jaunty swing, his lips pursed for the loud whistling which presaged all his announcements of impending moves. Inside the house he pulled out his orders and waved them dramatically before her eyes. He'd made it at last, he told her happily. He was practically on his way to France. Mamie forced a wan smile as she read the paper: "You will proceed to Camp Dix on November 18, 1918 . . . embarkation . . ." She was, she forced herself to say, glad for him.

Her heart ached. Dwight's orders were, for her, half of a double blow at her happiness. The other half was contained in letters and telegrams from the Douds in Denver. She told Dwight about it. Eda Mae, her seventeen-year-old sister whom she adored, was dangerously ill. Eda Mae's weak heart had been largely responsible for the family's wintering every year in San Antonio, away from high altitudes, and heart disease now threatened her life. At any moment the message might come. . . . There was only one thing to do, Dwight said. She and Icky must leave at once for Colorado. She wouldn't want to stay on here at Gettysburg anyway, after he'd gone. She should be with her people. And so next day she boarded a westbound train, with the year-old Icky in her arms, saying farewell to Ike, whom she'd not see, she knew, for a long, long time. It was for her a bitter day.

Thus she and Icky were in Chicago on November 11. Whistles shrieked and bells tolled above the crowds which stormed through the streets in a frenzy of joy. It was all over over there. The Armistice had been signed. But Mamie could not share in the crowd's joy. She could only feel a relief of tension, a deep gratitude that Ike, after all, need not go into that nightmare beyond the sea. Her grateful relief was underlaid with sorrow as she read the dreaded message, handed to her at the station in Chicago. Eda Mae was dead. She had died on November 9, seven weeks before her eighteenth birthday.

And Dwight, too, quite apart from his sorrow over Eda Mae, of whom he'd been very fond, could not respond to the Armistice with unalloyed joy. However wholeheartedly he joined in the celebration of a national victory, the Armistice was for him a personal disappointment. When he reported at Camp Dix on the eighteenth his sailing orders were, of course, canceled. He was suffering from the inevitable letdown in morale. Soldiering, here at the end of the war that was to end all wars, seemed a particularly futile occupation. Something of his feeling was expressed when a young officer who had been overseas complained to him that no promotions had been granted over there. "Well, you got overseas," Dwight growled. "That should be promotion enough." He wrote Mamie that for the time being she'd better stay in Denver. God only knew what the next assignment would be.

Perhaps the pain of his disappointment would have been somewhat alleviated had he known that ten years later he would be awarded the Distinguished Service Medal, in recognition of his work at Camp Colt. "While Commanding Officer of the Tank Corps Training Center," the citation read, "he displayed unusual zeal, foresight, and marked administrative ability in the organization, training, and preparation for overseas service of technical troops of the Tank Corps."

BOOK FOUR

The Years of Apprenticeship

CHAPTER I

Fox Connor Inspires a New Dedication

H<small>AD</small> Dwight Eisenhower developed an acute political consciousness, he might have watched the stream of history through the next
few months with an ironic eye. Irony seems to be a natural attitude
for a twentieth-century intelligence which combines, in a kind of
dynamic balance, the moral commitments and the pragmatic particularism of the American frontier. For a mind like Eisenhower's,
respectful of facts and insistent upon their existence independent of
the perceiving intellect and the egotistic will—for such a mind, irony
might have been an instrument for defining sharply and clearly a
middle ground between those landscapes of violence which extended
to the left and right, landscapes peopled with angry and often
cynical men who were only too willing to ignore facts in their
passionate pursuit of vague principle or narrow self-interest. He
might even have derived a wry amusement from the spectacle of two
willful men, remarkably similar in temperament, however different
in avowed purpose, wrecking on the rocks of their stubborn im-
periousness the great hope of the League of Nations.

Looking back, it is evident that Wilson had done much to wreck
the League even before he sailed for France on December 4 to write
the Covenant into the peace treaty. He had been too sure of his
vision and far too exclusive in his assertion of property rights in it.
He had made of it a party issue, calling upon the nation to vote only
for Democrats in the 1918 elections despite the support Republicans
had given, in a supposedly non-partisan spirit, to his war administration. Even after his party had suffered defeats in those elections,
which returned small majorities of Republicans to both houses of
Congress, he continued his highhanded tactics. His appointments
to the peace commission, which he headed personally, revealed no
effort to gain the support of the Senate. With his every move he
fastened more firmly upon himself that especially vicious hatred

] 183 [

which small men feel toward anyone who makes them realize their own smallness. With his every move he made more tragically evident the fact that his own stature as a man was not commensurate with the depth of his historic vision. At the very time that Wilson was receiving the acclaim of a messiah from the exploited masses of Europe, Teddy Roosevelt on his deathbed was plotting with Senator Lodge the strategy which would defeat the League. If their vision was narrower than his, their selfish pride and love of power were much the same as his. He came home in the summer of 1919, having appeased British and French imperialism in order to save the League, only to find the Senate opposition too strong for him. He broke himself against it. He was, thereafter, the sick conscience of the nation, helpless against the cold, precise cynicism of Senator Lodge.

The cynicism spread. It arose as a stench from the corpse of a murdered idealism, pervading every aspect of the national life. Americans were ashamed of themselves for having been the dupes (as they saw it) of Europe. They restored George Washington to his false position as prophet of a national isolation. They began to make a sharp distinction between "idealism" and "realism," branding the former as suckers' bait. Bathtub gin, speak-easies, gangsters, jazz, sex: titillation of the five senses became the chief goal of privileged living. A young man named Sinclair Lewis wrote a book which caught the prevailing mood of "revolt" and became the best-selling novel of the new decade. A certain obscure Senator Harding was playing poker with "the boys" in various back rooms and perhaps had already coined, out of his abysmal ignorance, a new word: "normalcy." A poet who had forsaken America for London was about to project upon the world a word-image of the growing despair. *Falling towers,* he wrote. *Jerusalem Athens Alexandria London. . . . Unreal.*

As for Dwight Eisenhower, his life in those years was a repetition, in different terms, of the slow, seemingly aimless drift he'd experienced in Abilene ten years before. He worked hard. He always worked hard. But he could perceive no clear goal toward which he worked. The fire of dedication which had been kindled in him during the war years had now, for the time being, gone out. Like his fellow Americans, he regarded another war in his lifetime as a possibility too remote for serious consideration. He confessed in later years that he had moments when he doubted the wisdom of his decision to make a career of the Army, when he wondered if Minnie Stewart had not been right when she asserted that there was "just no future" in the armed services. Had a suitable opening in civilian life presented itself, he might have resigned his commission. The Army itself seemed not to know what use to make of him. He remained at Camp Dix for a month, was transferred to Fort Benning, Georgia, on December 22, and "spent time" there literally through the early months of 1919. Mamie and Icky remained in Denver, in the house on Lafayette Street, through all that winter, and Dwight's longing for them added nothing to his happiness.

On March 15 he was ordered to Camp Meade, Maryland, and there his morale was somewhat improved. For one thing, Mamie and Icky were enabled to rejoin him; he had again the kind of home most conducive to his happy efficiency. For another, his work became more interesting. There were tanks at Camp Meade, lots of them: clumsy Britishers, French Renaults, and German Marks that had seen battle, as well as brand-new whippet tanks which, now that the Armistice was signed, began pouring out of the factory at Dayton. At first Dwight served as executive officer. Then he commanded a succession of heavy-tank battalions. If the military life had lost its seriousness of purpose, he could again look upon it as an interesting game to be played as well as he knew how. He could again regard his home, brightly cheerful and crowded with friends, as the center of his world. He began to indulge a passion for oriental rugs, starting a collection which would grow through the coming years.

Among the friends he made that year was a very erect, long-legged young man whose rather abrupt speech, interspersed with "tough" expressions, was delivered in a surprisingly high-pitched voice, and whose facial mannerisms (quite consciously employed) varied from an exuberant grin to a slit-eyed, taut-lipped sternness. He wore upon his shoulders the silver oak leaves of a lieutenant colonel. The tunic of his uniform was splashed with ribbons. His name was George S. Patton, Jr.

At thirty-three, Patton was already a legendary figure. Those pearl-handled .45 revolvers he carried on his hips, in violation of uniform regulations, were not idle ornaments. Everyone in the professional Army knew of that episode in Mexico, in 1916, when Patton was sent by Pershing to capture one of Pancho Villa's lieutenants, a man named Candelario Cervantes. Cervantes had holed up in a thick-walled adobe hut which had only one door and one tiny window. It looked as though taking him would involve a long siege. But Patton had gone in alone with his .45s and had come out, a minute later, with Cervantes's dead body slung over his shoulder. ("Yes, I had to kill a man down there," he'd say, in what was obviously intended as a deprecatory tone, whenever anyone referred to his Mexican exploit.) Only a few months ago, in September 1918, the 304th Tank Brigade which he commanded had been cut off by the Germans in the Argonne. Patton, instead of sending a subordinate back for help, had gone himself, alone, and had run into a German machine-gun nest on the way. He'd been badly wounded, but he'd knocked out the nest with hand grenades. Embroidering the legend, some of the men at Meade who had served with Patton in France claimed to have seen him riding into battle *sitting astride* a tank, as though it were a horse, and waving a sword! He was a professional hero. He gloried in the role.

The value which Patton attached to physical courage may have seemed to Dwight excessive. Dwight took that kind of courage for granted. And Patton's theory of command, expressed in the statement that soldiers fight for "glory" and because of "hero worship" for the commanding officer, may have seemed to Dwight to have a very limited validity. Certainly Patton's zest for killing, his apparent insensitivity to ordinary human values, outraged many people. But behind that façade of toughness lived a badly frightened little boy, a likable boy in many ways, who was driven to assume his poses by a fear of cowardice in himself and by the need, a deeply felt need, to be admired by his fellows. His egocentricity was the source of his insensitivity. A man always hates most violently in others the weaknesses he recognizes in himself, and when Patton's intimates realized that his blind hatred of cowardice was really a form of self-contempt, they could accept it sympathetically. No doubt Patton's upbringing as one of a wealthy family, with a tradition of Virginia aristocracy behind it, had had much to do with shaping his basic attitudes. Privilege seeks always to justify itself with assertions of personal superiority; aristocracy is a form of class egotism; and a "gentleman born" of the county fox-hunting variety defines prestige in terms of honor and glory as naturally as a banker defines it in terms of money. War, Patton might say, is a gentleman's profession. But since he lived according to his beliefs and was obviously willing to die for them, there was no doubting his value in battle situations which called primarily for courage and dash. Dwight recognized a real soldier when he saw one.

The two men had many common interests. Patton was an avid student of history, though he read it in a way somewhat different from Dwight's. For Dwight history was facts about people and events, filled with interesting lessons for a modern soldier. For Patton history seems to have been a romantic adventure story, filled with heroes on whom he might pattern himself. Like Dwight, Patton loved sports, particularly contact sports, and he'd won his "A" as an end on the football team at West Point. Like Dwight, Patton had a profound need for a home and family life. His wife, Beatrice Ayer of the American Woolen Mills family, was soon one of Mamie's closest friends. She was a gentle, cultured woman— superficially as different from her husband as one could imagine— but she understood her "Georgie" completely. She understood the passion for adventure because she shared it; she was a writer of adventure books. She made a home for that boyish and even kindly heart which beat beneath the flamboyant assumptions. Her husband was, she knew, a sentimental man. He wrote romantic poetry about war and romantic fiction about medieval knights. In later years he wrote a full-length novel set in the eleventh century with a plot compounded, in approximately equal parts, of blood and chivalry.

It became customary for Dwight and Patton to ride together every day. Two or three times each week they worked out map problems together, "never dreaming" (as Patton told a reporter in 1944) "that we'd ever actually use the information and experience we thus gained as commanders ourselves." They also, according to Patton, studied Clausewitz together and had long discussions of military theory. On one thing they were thoroughly agreed: armies of the future would be mechanized, mobility would return to warfare, and the tank would be a principal element. They discussed together the article Dwight prepared for the *Infantry Journal* sometime during the year. "The tank is in its infancy and the great strides already made in its mechanical improvement only point to the greater ones still to come," Dwight wrote. "The clumsy, awkward, snail-like pace of the old tanks must be forgotten, and in their place we must picture a speedy, reliable, and efficient engine of destruction." It required some imagination to do so. One day at Meade, Dwight and Patton managed to develop a speed of fourteen miles an hour in a Mark VIII, going downhill, but the engine was jolted off its bed!

In August of 1919 Dwight was sent as official observer on the first transcontinental truck-convoy expedition. He returned with hilarious tales of motor breakdowns in the desert and of practical jokes played on a gullible lieutenant who knew nothing of rattlesnakes and was desperately afraid of them. He had more serious things to say about the need for a new highway system in America if we were to make proper use of automobiles. That autumn he sought entrance in the Infantry School, which was generally considered a prerequisite for attendance at the Command and General Staff School at Leavenworth. The rules of the game he played demanded of a man that he go as far as he could, and only alumni of the Command School were eligible for high command. For some reason, however, Dwight's superior officer refused his service-school application. He consoled himself by attending the Infantry Tank School at Meade.

Sometime during the fall of 1919 Patton made, unwittingly, his greatest contribution to Dwight's education and future advancement. He introduced Dwight to Brigadier General Fox Connor, whom Patton had known overseas.

Connor, at this time, was in his mid-forties and had had an immense range of military experience since his graduation from West Point in 1898. Though his permanent rank was still that of colonel, he was on the Initial General Staff Corps Eligible List and was recognized as one of the outstanding officers in the Army. He knew the Army from both the field and staff points of view, had graduated from the Staff School and the Army War College, had served as a military observer of field artillery in the French Army in 1911 and 1912, and had served with the operations section of the General Staff of the American Expeditionary Forces in France during the World War. When he visited Meade he was Chief of Staff of the A.E.F. in Washington, having returned from France in September of 1919. He was a profound student of military science, a man of immense intellectual vitality, and, his vision sharpened by his years of contact with the realities behind the news, he read the signs of the time with more accuracy than most of his contemporaries. Already he had reached the conclusion that the war which had just ended was but the first act in the world tragedy. He seems to have expressed that conclusion during his first meeting with Dwight.

The attraction between the two men was immediate and mutual. Connor saw in Dwight no mere "good fellow" who would give "both duty and recreation their fair values." He saw a man whose capacity for leadership amounted to genius, a man capable of the most selfless dedication, a man who certainly should prepare for an important role in the approaching crisis. Perhaps he said something of the sort to Dwight that autumn. As for Dwight, his reactions to Connor were summed up in a statement he made to Patton and which he was to repeat again and again through the coming years: "He's a great man."

Christmas of 1920 was to be, according to plans they made weeks ahead of time, the happiest Christmas they had ever had together. Icky, who had celebrated his third birthday in September, was just old enough to be aware of holiday festivities. Dwight bought a Christmas tree and set it up in the living room. He and Mamie stuffed bureau drawers with presents, away from Icky's prying hands. One day Dwight bought home a shiny red "kiddie car" and hid it in a closet. Even Icky must have sensed some of the mood of excited anticipation which prevailed in the home.

On the post a huge Christmas tree was set up for the enlisted personnel, and the gifts for this tree must be purchased by Mamie and the other officers' wives. It was a big job. It required of Mamie an all-day shopping expedition to Baltimore a few days before the great day. She left Icky with his nurse. When she returned she was informed by the nurse that Icky wasn't feeling well. The nurse didn't think it was anything serious, and neither did the post doctor when he was called. There were no cases of contagious disease on the post at the time. Probably little Icky would be well again by Christmas Day.

But he wasn't. He lay in a feverish bed all through Christmas Day. Two days later his illness became alarming. His face flushed, his fever soared, and he was rushed to the post hospital where, too late, the doctor diagnosed the disease as scarlet fever. Remembering the horror of Milton's illness, Dwight was terribly frightened. Mamie, worn out by the excited preparations for the holidays, crushed with worry, became ill too. She wasn't able to come to the hospital to watch over Icky's bed. Dwight spent all his time there, alone, waiting through sleepless nights in a helpless agony he was never to forget. Icky's condition grew steadily worse. A specialist from Johns Hopkins was called in. He could only shake his head sadly and express uncertain hopes. There was really nothing to be done.

Early in the morning of January 2, 1921, Dwight stumbled from the hospital room, blind with grief. Doud Dwight Eisenhower, aged three years and three months, was dead. It was as though the end of the world had come, especially for Mamie, who, unlike her husband, had no work outside her home with which to mitigate her sorrow. Watching her, doing his best to sustain her, Dwight was afraid that the bright vitality which had been so abundantly hers was forever lost.

The journey to Denver, where they took Icky's body for burial, was the darkest pilgrimage they ever made.

2

Perceptive eyes could have seen little in the world at large with which to qualify a private grief. The nation as a whole seemed to have embarked on a dark pilgrimage as the months passed. By default of the collective intelligence, through a mood of sentimental cynicism which went by the name of "realism," America moved gracelessly toward fulfillment of Fox Connor's dire predictions. Lodge was a clever man. His parliamentary tactics thwarted what he himself admitted was the will of the majority. He gained this mean triumph over the sick man in the White House. Very soon that sick man moved out of the White House, replaced by the Harding "normalcy" and the Coolidge silence. Freedom for property seemed to have regained all its old ascendancy over freedom for men. Civil liberties were flouted again and again by a government which, in other important respects, refused to govern. The business of America was business—and the men of business, appalled by the spectacle of Lenin's Russia, saw red shadows in every corner of the land while prices crashed and unemployment mounted. Frantically they financed export balances to bolster foreign markets, stemming for the moment the ebb tide of industrial prosperity. The farm depression continued. Among the literary intellectuals, anti-democratic attitudes became fashionable. Mencken's sledge-hammer blows at the democratic ideal ("Anglo-Saxon herd," he said, "the booboisie of the Bible Belt") gained for him the reputation of a penetrating wit. Walter Lippmann, who was himself describing public opinion as a bundle of "stereotypes" devoid of logic, described Mencken as an essentially kindly American. The literary supplements announced books by Cabell and Hergesheimer and a score of forgotten exquisites, books curiously like the brightly colored baubles on Icky's tragic Christmas tree, all brittle surface enclosing nothing.

None of it touched Dwight Eisenhower's essential self. He neither accepted the new "emancipation" nor reacted against it. The frontier remained alive in him—and a professional soldier, being the instrument and not the author of policy, must not meddle with politics. He had never voted. Probably he never would. For relaxation he read, not the glorifiers of privileged cynicism or the purveyors of perfumed sex, but Western novels and pulp magazines by the score—a taste developed in boyhood which he was to retain all his life. His serious reading included military theorists and historians: Moltke and Clausewitz and Delbrück and the technical publications of the War Department. But if he remained unconscious of goals, his day-by-day education proceeded apace. The recognition of his keenly logical mind, his remarkably commodious memory, his talent for organization, was a steadily growing thing. He did not know it, but there were those in high places who had already tagged him for future advancement if and when the emergency came. Fox Connor at the headquarters of the General of the Armies mentioned Dwight to John J. Pershing. . . .

It was all future, of course, and vague enough, Dwight might have said. The present marked a retrogression. From his war rank of lieutenant colonel he reverted to his permanent rank of captain, in a shrinking army, on July 30, 1920. Three days later he was promoted to a majority. Looking ahead, he could tell himself that, with luck, he might someday be a "chicken" colonel. A good deal of luck would be needed, though. Seniority was virtually the sole determiner of rank, and he had that two- or three-year handicap of age. He shrugged and went ahead with the jobs at hand. In January 1921, he was graduated from the Tank School. He was in command of the 301st Tank Battalion.

By this time General Connor had been ordered to the Panama

Canal Zone as commander of the 20th Infantry Brigade at Camp Gaillard. Those were slack times in the Army. The junior officers seemed to want only sinecures. And Connor, driven by his conviction that another war was probable within twenty years, demanded an executive officer who'd see to it that directives were carried out, not haphazardly, but firmly and with attention to detail. Such a man must be a firm disciplinarian, but not a martinet. He must have poise and tact and good humor. These qualifications, so far as Connor could see, belonged to only one available man. In the fall of 1921 he wrote to Dwight Eisenhower and asked if the latter would be interested in a Panama assignment. Dwight was interested. Mamie, as always, was eager for adventurous voyages. The orders went through. On January 7, 1922, Dwight and Mamie left Camp Meade for Panama.

At Gaillard, a jungle post on the Canal, about halfway between the coasts, they lived in a house set on stilts driven into a steep slope, a house built by the French during their ill-fated attempt to complete the Canal decades before. It was surrounded on all sides by a veranda, one side of which faced the Culebra Cut. Here Mamie and Dwight used to sit with their friends during the evenings. Their friends, as always and despite the sorrow which still brooded in their hearts, were many. Once again the Eisenhower home was a favorite hangout for officers of all ranks, a center of good talk and good food and of some of the most astute bridge playing in the world. Dwight perfected an already amazingly good game while in Panama. Bridge suited his particular genius. Through it he could exercise his talent for logical analysis, his remarkable memory for detail, his ability to calculate chances. After the first card was played he seemed to know where each card was held.

The 20th Brigade was, in reality, not a brigade at all. It contained only one regiment, the 42nd Infantry; the other regiment was "inactive." Most of the junior officers were inclined to view General Connor as an extremely difficult person, a needlessly hard driver. Some of them soon viewed Dwight, despite his likability, in much the same light. As executive officer, Dwight supervised all administration and all the training program at Gaillard. General Connor explained in detail just what kind of outfit he wanted and then sat back to watch with a critical eye the way Dwight handled his assignment. It was something to watch. Dwight made few allowances for the languor of the climate. He saw to it that the camp grounds were restored from the slovenliness into which they had fallen. The lawns were closely trimmed; the drives and walks were bordered with white-painted rocks. He saw to it that all regulations were obeyed, that all of his commander's directives were complied with immediately and completely. Junior officers found his inspections painfully thorough. He seemed to know every detail of every man's job.

For instance, there was the time he heard some of the officers speak disparagingly of the Browning automatic rifle. Dwight, who knew the weapon thoroughly, contended that the critics didn't know what they were talking about. A day or so later he issued orders requiring every officer to fire the Browning for qualification, and to follow this with a combat problem or proficiency test. The results, as one of the officers recalled ruefully long afterward, "were terrible and bore out his initial contention that the officers knew little about the . . . rifle and cared less." Thereafter Dwight inaugurated a program of intensive training in the Browning. Every officer had qualified with it before Dwight was satisfied.

General Connor was more than pleased. His judgment was vindicated. More and more he came to regard Dwight as a protégé. He set himself the task of shaping the younger man's education, relighting the fires of dedication. The two had long talks together during which General Connor was at some pains to make clear the historico-military significance, as he saw it, of their present assignment. The United States, he pointed out, had come to regard the Panama Canal as a substitute for a two-ocean navy on the assumption (1) that we'd never have to face simultaneous attacks on the Atlantic and Pacific coasts, and (2) that through the Canal we'd be able to concentrate our one-ocean Navy in sufficient time to protect either coast against attack. Beneath these assumptions was the belief that the Canal itself was virtually invulnerable to the kind of attack which could close it. The World War and the Nine-Power Naval Pact, just signed in Washington, called for a critical examination of the basic belief and a revision of the assumptions. Defense of the Canal must now be thought of, not only in terms of land and sea, but also in terms of the air. Against the bombing plane of the future, the Canal was far from invulnerable. A few lucky hits on the locks, and the Canal would be closed. It was therefore of the hightest importance that defenses against air attack be planned, even though, in view of the passion for disarmament, those plans could not for the present be carried through. As for the Nine-Power Pact, it was, in General Connor's opinion, a dangerous mistake. The 5-5-3 ratio, now that Japan had the Marianas, left us far too weak to defend our interests in the Pacific, much less our interests in both the Atlantic and the Pacific in case Japan should have a European ally in a war against us. In another world war we'd have to count on the British Navy again—hardly the part of wisdom in the midst of international anarchy. What if Britain remained neutral?

Dwight's interest in Connor's arguments seems at first to have been wholly academic. A soldier must be flexible in his approach to his profession, of course. He must prepare, at least mentally, to meet all possible contingencies. But Dwight found it difficult to believe—really believe—that a second world war, of the kind Connor kept predicting, was in the making. He said so. It was as though he had waved a red flag in front of a bull. Connor's voice became harshly urgent as he marshaled his arguments.

The precise form of those arguments cannot, at this late date, be recalled. Evidently Connor's eyes were turned westward, toward Japan; the West Coast was seething at that time with angry talk about the "Yellow Menace." He may have envisaged an alliance between Japan and Russia, now that the Bolsheviks were in power, despite the traditional hostility between those two powers. Anything was possible in so chaotic a world. After all, we had joined in the attempt of the Allies to crush the Bolshevik revolution, had actually sent an expeditionary force into Siberia—a fact of some significance which hadn't penetrated the popular consciousness and which, somehow, would escape mention in most of the history books. Yes, almost any combination of powers was possible in the present fluid situation. The one certainty was that war, a second world war, was coming—and far sooner than anyone seemed to believe.

"How soon?" Dwight asked.

"Fifteen years, maybe," Connor said earnestly. "Twenty years. Surely within thirty years."

The argument was repeated again and again. Connor's deep sincerity, his evident belief that Dwight would be called upon to play a commander's role, was both flattering and (temporarily at least) convincing. It is impossible to say just how much of Connor's argument became a part of Dwight's permanent belief, but enough of it did to inspire him through the remaining years of his apprenticeship. If Connor was right the class of 1915 would certainly be called upon to supply general officers, and seniority would go by the board. Therefore, it behooved Dwight to work hard, to be ready. A national destiny just *might* depend on the soundness of his preparation. Not that he thought of it very often in such personal terms. He was simply inspired to do more than play the game, rather carelessly, for its own sake.

He made a workroom of a second-story porch in his house. He tacked up maps and arranged shelving for his books. Connor was at some pains to guide his protégé's reading. The general, as a result of his service with the French Army, had been strongly influenced by the French masters, and it was probably under Connor's influence that Dwight began to study, with far more seriousness than he had done at West Point, the campaigns of Napoleon. He read not only the memoirs of Napoleon but the commentaries on Napoleonic strategy by Jomini and, of course and again, Clausewitz. It is probably during this period that he read Ardant du Picq's *Battle Studies,* which had just been translated by Colonel John N. Greely and Major Robert C. Cotton. Almost certainly he read Foch's *The Principles of War* which had been published in 1921 in a translation by Hilaire Belloc. Always he compared theory with the events which the theory presumed to explain, finding often enough that the theory warped the facts. The trend of his own reasoning was always a posteriori, from the particular (which actually *is* "out there") to the general (whose "reality" he was inclined to doubt). He wanted facts. He stacked them up in his mind, neatly classified, ready for instant use, and he never had enough of them.

There was, however, one military writer whose theoretical work seems to have made a profound and lasting impression on him. Denis Hart Mahan, father of the great exponent of sea power, was a West Point alumnus who had taught at the Academy from 1832 to 1871. Though he had studied in Metz and been strongly influenced by Napoleon, Jomini, and Vauban, his approach to the problems of war was, in its salient features, peculiarly American. He eschewed the excessive systemics of the Germans, who placed so much emphasis on "laws," in favor of that kind of flexible pragmatism best suited to Dwight's own temperament. How could a commander really "plan" a battle, save in the most general way, when almost his every move must be a response to an opponent's move? In Mahan's belief, war was not so much a science as an art. He wrote in his *Outpost:*

How different is almost every military problem, except in the bare mechanism of tactics. In almost every case the data *on which a solution depends are lacking. . . . Too often the general has only conjectures to go on, and these based upon false premises . . . [for] what is true now, at the next moment may have no existence, or exist in the contrary sense. . . . These considerations explain why history produces . . . so few great generals.*

They might also breed in an honest commander a greater humility than is common among the generals of history; success must so often depend upon factors outside the commander's control. But even more important in shaping Dwight's own views must have been the following prophetic utterance:

Speed is one of the characteristics of strategic marches . . . [for] in this one quality lie all the advantages that a fortunate initiative may have procured. . . . By rapidity of movement we can, like the Romans, make war feed war. *. . . No great success can be hoped for in war in which rapid movements do not enter as an element. Even the very elements of Nature seem to array themselves against the slow and over-prudent general . . . in the presence of an enemy who, having lost his communications, is entirely disorganized and demoralized. . . . We have only to throw our forces into the midst of these broken-up fractions to determine them to fly. We may here attempt any blow; no movements can fail to turn out well except those which are too slow and methodical. . . .*[1]

It was as though Mahan were describing the battle for Poland in 1939, or the battle for France in 1944. Certainly, as Dwight noted in detail, Mahan was not forecasting the France of 1914–18. In Panama, Dwight read every bit of World War history he could find and had long discussions with General Connor about what he read. Connor, who from the vast store of his own experience presented Dwight with valuable information that had not found its way into print, was to testify years later that Dwight's "grasp of the lessons of the World War was superb."

It was during their discussions of the recent war that Dwight

[1]Quoted by Colonel R. Ernest Dupuy in *The Story of West Point,* published by the Infantry Journal, 1943.

heard for the first time of Major George Catlett Marshall, who had been a wartime colonel. Connor told Dwight with enthusiasm how Marshall, as G-3 (in charge of operations) of the First Army, had transferred 500,000 men and 2,700 guns from the Saint-Mihiel sector to the Argonne in two weeks with such secrecy that the Germans were not aware of the shift until the Argonne offensive began. A masterpiece of logistics, Pershing had said. Pershing would never forget it. . . .

"You and Marshall are a lot alike," Connor told Dwight seriously. "I've noticed time and again that you attack problems in the same way."

This was, Dwight soon discovered, Connor's highest praise. Whenever Dwight did something which especially pleased the general, Connor would say: "Eisenhower, you handled that just the way Marshall would have done."

The sorrow which had brooded in their hearts ever since Icky's death faded through the spring of 1922. Dwight and Mamie lived in a glow of anticipation. They were to have another child. Early in the summer Mamie sailed from Panama, and Dwight was soon soothing his natural anxiety with the letters she wrote to him from Denver. She was getting along fine, she wrote. No need to worry. On August 3 the wire came. A son had been born. In accordance with the agreement Dwight and Mamie had made before Mamie sailed, the son had been named John Sheldon Doud Eisenhower. "Mother and child are doing well."

Through three long months Dwight waited impatiently for Mamie's return. On an early November day he stood on the dock, gazing eagerly up the gangplank which leaned into the gray wall of a transport. Then he saw her. Mamie waved gaily to him with one arm while she carefully cradled in the other a tiny pink bundle. Dwight rushed to meet her, to look down for the first time upon the puckered red face of his son. At three months, Mamie said happily, John S. D. Eisenhower was a remarkable infant, and she detailed his separate brilliances. Dwight, looking down, was sure she was right. His pride was beautiful to see as he persuaded her to let him carry the baby, very carefully, to the waiting train. There he noticed with a new surge of joy that Mamie's eyes were shining again, just as they had when first he knew her. For both of them the memory of Icky was no longer a sharp pain, but a sadness which somehow sweetened their happiness. . . .

Several months later Dwight received an unexpected long-distance telephone call which delighted him. Mamie and her sister Frances, who was visiting them, heard him insisting that whoever had called must come out for the week end. It was Swede Hazlett, Dwight said when he'd hung up—Swede who had been largely responsible for his getting to West Point. The two men had kept up a desultory but continuous correspondence ever since the June Week of Dwight's graduation, which was the last time they'd seen each other. Swede was at the submarine base at Coco Solo. He'd be there for several weeks while the submarine he commanded was undergoing extensive repairs. A burned-out motor, Swede had said.

The following week end and several subsequent ones found Hazlett in the Eisenhower home. Mamie noticed that he and Dwight formed a two-man mutual-admiration society. Dwight was enormously proud of his friend, proud that Swede at so young an age had a vessel of his own. He was stimulated, as he had been in the old days, by Swede's swift mental processes. And Swede was not surprised to find his friend working and studying hard, though (as Swede explained long afterward) "this was particularly unusual at a torrid, isolated post where most officers spent their off hours trying to keep cool and amused." The two sat together until midnight and after in Dwight's second-story study porch, while Dwight explained the war plans for defense of the Panama Canal which he, at that time, was just completing. As Swede put it, Dwight made his explanations with the "enthusiasm of genius." But for all his study and intellectual vitality Dwight was "no studious recluse—he missed none of the fun, he never did." Even his intellectual interests were externalized.

The two went for long rides on horseback over the *bosque* trails, to Swede's probable discomfort since he, who had wanted to be a cavalryman, had not been astride a horse for years. Dwight pointed out the sites of proposed establishments called for in the war plans. In the evenings there were long sessions of poker. "This latter was bad news for me," Hazlett explained years later, "for Ike and his army friends set a much higher standard for the five-card game than did the Navy." Swede was almost sorry when his submarine was at last repaired.

On the day before he left he took Dwight aboard the submarine for a dive in Panama Bay. Dwight's obvious delight and interest was a heart-warming thing to see.

"I never had a passenger who was more avid for information," Hazlett recalled in 1944. "Whenever I was otherwise engaged he wandered through the ship, chatting informally with the crew— and they responded readily. I really believe that by the time he left the ship he knew almost as much about submarines as I did."

That night Dwight and Mamie and Frances and a crowd of friends gathered at the Union Club for a big farewell party for Swede—and on the following morning Swede sailed. He was not to see Dwight again for twelve years.

The climate, for which he had refused to make allowances, was beginning to tell on Dwight. He had lost weight. His energy was ebbing. Besides, the big planning job was completed. The months of 1924 were a long, rather boring drag through a monotonous routine. Occasionally Dwight felt a dull ache in his right side which the post doctor diagnosed, tentatively, as a mild but chronic appendicitis. The doctor said it wasn't anything to worry about, but something to watch. It might develop into an acute attack sometime. Nothing to worry about? Dwight never worried, but he was temperamentally opposed to taking uncalculated risks. That appendix might start "acting up" sometime when he was really busy, if Connor's predictions were fulfilled, and Dwight decided that he'd have it removed at the earliest convenient moment.

When at last the sailing orders came in September, Mamie and John, with the other officers' families, were sent on ahead. Dwight sailed in midmonth on a transport so crowded that he shared a stateroom with two junior officers: Captain (later Colonel) Rickard, who had served in Plans and Training at Gaillard, and Captain (later Colonel) James P. Murphy, who had served as adjutant of the 42nd. Both of these officers had had, in the course of their duties, daily and frequently unpleasant contacts with the executive officer. Murphy confessed in later years that as a junior officer he had considered himself a field soldier and had possessed a full quota of the field soldier's "critical attitude" toward staff officers. He and Rickard, partially because they were "covering up" for an inefficient superior officer, had "drawn a lot of heat" from Dwight. The injustice rankled. In addition, Dwight had repeatedly stressed, in a pointedly critical way, the advisability of junior officers' studying their profession far more seriously than most officers seemed to do. It is surely not unnatural that Rickard and Murphy should have conceived a measure of dislike for Dwight, a "resentment" (as Murphy later put it) of the Eisenhower passion for efficiency.

Indeed, there are several rather vague indications that Dwight, in Panama, had by no means perfected the technique of command which would later be so peculiarly his own. Several accounts have it that he "handled his job categorically, without kid gloves"; that he was impatient to the point of irritability with whatever seemed to him to be slipshod work; that he aroused antagonism among the kinds of men who, in later years, would be stimulated by him to do their best work. It may well be that as executive officer, always an onerous position, he was reflecting his commander's temperament rather than expressing his own. But even so there are few surviving anecdotes to indicate the frank, genial command system which, in the 1940s, would become world famous. Under the circumstances, it is unlikely that either Rickard or Murphy looked forward with much pleasure to six days of close confinement with the man who had, in the past, been so bluntly critical of them, and of whom they themselves had (to put it mildly) been "critical."

They were surprised. Murphy indicated long afterward that during the six-day journey northward he revised his estimate of Eisenhower. With the constraints of office removed, Dwight was his friendly, modest, charming self. The three played bridge incessantly for small stakes—sometimes with the dummy chair left vacant. It is reported that at Gaillard Dwight had occasionally betrayed impatience with Mrs. Murphy during bridge sessions at the Officers' Club, because she, though a good player, failed to concentrate on the game as Dwight would have liked. He betrayed no such impatience on the boat. Indeed, he had an exceedingly bad run of cards all during the trip and lost consistently—a fact which no doubt softened the junior officers' attitude toward him. He lost as gracefully as his play was brilliant; he grinned good-naturedly as he paid his losses. They added up to quite a tidy sum by the time the boat docked, and Rickard had won most of them.

3

The jungles of Panama were not more lush and hostile to a positive life than the mental climate of the country to which Dwight returned. During the almost three years of his absence, the country had been confirmed in the attitudes which, when he last saw it, were new and tentative. It had entered the "jazz age," a period of elaborate but superficial self-consciousness—and the man who had named the age had also named the casual "sophisticated" girls which the age produced. "Flappers," he had called them. He had written a book of short stories called *Flappers and Philosophers* in which the flappers came vividly alive while the philosophy revealed itself as a succession of bright, meaningless poses, negative in the extreme. The book, like the man himself, was symptomatic. In that country at that time, people could take their surface moods with the utmost seriousness—provided they were not obliged, like the mass of mankind, to earn all their incomes with hard work. It was as though they concentrated on surfaces because they were afraid to look beneath. The life of the time was shot through with a vague sense of guilt; it managed to transform a high tragic sense of realities into a low, petulant whine. To more perceptive souls it sometimes seemed that no absurdity, if presented in the proper trappings, could fail of acceptance by the newly "emancipated." Lothrop Stoddard, A.M., Ph.D. (Harvard), was writing treatises in scholarly jargon with titles like *The Rising Tide of Color against White World-Supremacy* and *The Revolt against Civilization: The Menace of the Under Man,* and a great many people took Dr. Stoddard very seriously indeed. Often enough, they were the same people who eulogized Benito Mussolini, when they returned from their European vacations that summer, because in Italy the trains now "ran on time."

Woodrow Wilson had for seven months been dead, and Senator Lodge had refused to attend the funeral. Harding had died, too, under somewhat mysterious circumstances, just before the Teapot Dome oil scandals were aired before a remarkably indifferent public. Silent Cal now occupied the White House, and there was little doubt that he'd win the election six weeks hence. He was no friend of Henry Cabot Lodge. At seventy-four Lodge was tasting the bitter fruit of his mean triumph. It appeared that no one loved him, not even those whose interests he had so faithfully served. The galleries had actually booed him at the Republican convention in Cleveland that summer, partially because he had opposed Coolidge on the Bonus Bill issue, partially because his own party was heartily sick of his snobbish arrogance. He was not placed on a single convention committee, not even the lowliest. He'd be dead within two months after Dwight's return. . . . And across the seas, in Red Russia, Lenin died that year, and Stalin assumed control, repudiating Trotskyism in his ruthless determination to make socialism succeed in One Country. In Germany, Hitler, confined in Landsberg Prison (it was more like a private club) after the failure of the Munich *Putsch*, was dictating to Rudolf Hess a book which he later called *Mein Kampf.* A world malaise, the leftists had said. They were still saying it.

Red Grange of the Illinois football team was running wild through the Big Ten that autumn, and it may well be this news was of more immediate interest to Dwight than most. Football was again, if briefly, a part of his job. He was sent to Baltimore, Maryland, where he served as recreation officer at headquarters of the Third Corps Area. It was a rather meaningless assignment, a stopgap, but he enjoyed it. He sponsored the sports program with enthusiasm. The next important step for him, he knew, was appointment to the Command and General Staff School at Fort Leavenworth, Kansas. Fox Connor, he knew, was trying to secure the appointment for him. It required a bit of doing. The fact that Dwight had not attended his service school was a serious obstacle. But almost the last words that Connor had said to him when the two had parted were that he, Connor, would use all his authority on Dwight's behalf. It behooved Dwight to study hard, to be ready for the appointment if and when it came. He put in a request for assignment to Fort Logan, Colorado, as recruiting officer—the nearest thing to a sinecure that the Army offered in those palmy days—and his request was granted. He obtained copies of problems which had been used at the Command School in earlier years. When he arrived in Colorado in mid-December, having stopped on the way for a visit with his mother and father in Abilene, he was fully prepared for an intensive study course. Every day that he was on duty at Fort Logan he worked out one Leavenworth problem.

It was a pleasant time. Fort Logan was practically a suburb of Denver, which meant that the Eisenhowers could spend a great deal of time with Mamie's family. The large house at 750 Lafayette, where Dwight and Mamie had been married, was as always a center of happy spontaneity. There was certainly nothing stodgy about Dwight's parents-in-law. Both of them remained exhilaratingly youthful, apparently untouched by the passing years. Father Doud was now called "poopa" and Mother Doud was "Miss Min," and there were elaborate stories to explain how those nicknames had happened to be applied. They were that kind of people. Through family rituals, through traditions consciously developed and maintained, they imparted a significant depth and a richness of texture to very simple events. One of their rituals was both beautiful and sad. Every Sunday morning before church they drove out to the cemetery and placed fresh flowers on the graves of Eleanor and Eda Mae, the two daughters who had died so tragically in their teens, and on the grave of little Icky. Whenever possible Dwight and Mamie accompanied them on these expeditions. When spring came the Douds and Eisenhowers often went picnicking and golfing together. Always the Douds made much over their grandson John, spoiling him thoroughly—or so Mamie sometimes complained.

A pleasant time, but Dwight became increasingly restless as the summer of 1925 came on. One day he went down to Fitzsimmons Hospital in Denver and had his appendix removed; Mamie didn't know about it until after the operation was performed and her husband was beginning his swift recovery on a hospital bed. He was as nearly ready for the Leavenworth grind as he would ever be and he wished that the appointment would come through, if it were coming at all. Then it came. First came a cryptic wire advising him to "make no move," to "be ready," signed by Fox Connor. A few days later the orders came. He was to report at Leavenworth on August 19. Mamie, accustomed now to making a home in short order under all kinds of conditions, prepared to move again. Perhaps she regarded the coming year with more apprehension than Dwight did. The Army set a killing pace, almost literally, at Leavenworth. Competition for a high graduation order number was so intense that many a candidate broke under the strain. (So many fine officers were ruined in this way that the Army, a year or so after Dwight's graduation, abolished the system of order numbers.) There had been cases of complete nervous collapse, even of suicide. . . . But when she looked at Dwight, taking in his calmly confident grin, she couldn't imagine him breaking under any amount of strain, much less committing suicide. He knew how to relax under the heaviest burdens.

Of the year which followed, virtually no anecdotes survive. John, who was three in September of that year, claims that he remembers his father "sweating over his books in a study at the top of the house" in Leavenworth. The Command School left neither time nor energy for a really personal life, and there was certainly nothing casual about Dwight's relations to his work there. The West Point instructor who had said that Dwight was not the kind to "throw himself into his job so completely that nothing else would matter" would have been surprised. Dwight was completely absorbed. As the months passed, an unbroken ordeal, he almost forgot that he had ever known a free-and-easy life. But by the time April came and the trees had leafed out again he was able once more to stand outside himself, take stock of himself. He was doing well. He knew that he'd graduate high. If he put on enough of a finishing spurt he might even graduate first.

He put on the final spurt. All through that spring he worked so hard that even his abundant energy was worn thin. He was surprised to find that it was difficult now to relax. His old resilience seemed to be gone; he could no longer snap back from a concentrated attention to a casual at ease as he had used to do. But all the while he was aware of triumph; triumph over the obstacles which had been placed before him, an even sweeter triumph over himself. It was good to have a measure of one's self, to realize the outermost limits of one's capacities for work, especially to know that those limits were wide enough to include almost any possible assignment. The days ran so swiftly now that they blurred together. Abruptly it was the end of May. The final tests were upon him, the crucial tests, but he faced them without fear. If any man beat him now, that man damned well deserved the victory. He, Dwight Eisenhower, had done his level best. He let down when the tests were done. He arranged with Leonard Gerow, who was a classmate in the Command School, for a big celebration in Kansas City with Dwight's brother Arthur. The mere fact that the two of them had completed the course was something to celebrate.

But when the final standings were posted a day or so later, there was even greater justification for a real party. Out of a hard-working class of approximately 275 men, including some of the best brains in the Army, Dwight David Eisenhower stood first! His name would be placed high on the General Staff Corps Eligible List. Fox Connor sent his heartiest congratulations.

It was a gay party.

They held it in the Muehlbach Hotel, and Arthur, who had already risen to a vice-president's chair in the Commerce Trust Company, had seen to it that there was a bountiful supply of what passed, in those bootlegging days, for "high-class" gin and whisky. Present were Major and Mrs. Gerow, Arthur, his wife, his sister-in-law, and her husband, and Dwight and Mamie. Dwight's none-too-tuneful voice boomed out in his favorite songs: "Abdul the Bulbul Ameer," "Casey Jones," and "Steamboat Bill." At eleven o'clock, when everyone was very gay, Arthur called the home of one of his associates in the bank, George Dillon. Dillon had just gone to bed, but the party sounded fine over the phone, so he dressed and came up. He was welcomed with cheers.

Dwight was by no means a heavy drinker. He had of course followed rigidly the regulations against liquor on the post. But even the Secretary of War could hardly have objected to an alcoholic evening for a man who had graduated first from one of the toughest military schools in the whole wide world.

CHAPTER II

An Interlude: Family Reunion

THE JUNE SKIES above Abilene were cloudless, and of a blue so rich and deep as to bring tears to peering eyes. The morning sun was just beginning to top the maple trees east of the house, pouring a golden warmth over the new brilliant green of the lawn. Red roses bloomed on the trellis, just as they had done fifteen years before when Dwight left home for West Point, and the earth between green rows of vegetables in the garden was again dark and rich. But the garden was much smaller now. The yard behind the house on South East Fourth Street was no longer worn bare by scuffling children's feet. The house itself, by contrast with the crowded memories it held, seemed silent and lonely.

Nevertheless, Ida Stover Eisenhower, slender and erect in her sixty-fourth year, was gloriously happy as she stood on the porch of her house, waiting for the morning mail to come. She agreed emphatically with the postman's assertion that it was a "fine morning" when he handed her that mail. Letters from Edgar and Earl and Dwight, she noticed. As she carried them into the house her eyes had all the brilliance which had fascinated young David Eisenhower forty years before. The topmost letter was addressed in Dwight's large bold scrawl. She read it eagerly. He had graduated "number one" from Leavenworth, he said, and if she didn't know exactly what significance that fact had, she could tell from the way Dwight spoke of it that it *was* important, something to be proud of. He was in Kansas City with Arthur. He'd come down to Abilene with Arthur on the following day. Earl's letter informed her in his tight small script, difficult to read, that he, too, would arrive tomorrow. Edgar's scrawl, much like Dwight's, said that he would arrive either that afternoon or tomorrow morning. Already Roy and Edna had told her they would be up from Junction City next day, and Milton had written from Washington to say that he'd arrive either that night or the next morning. Tomorrow, then, she told herself happily: by tomorrow night all the boys would be home. For the first time in almost twenty years the entire family would be together—and they'd stay together for three whole days! She telephoned David at the office of the United Power and Light Company, where he now had charge of the employees' benefit and savings program, to inform him that all their plans had been confirmed.

Because there would not be room for them in the house, none of the wives was coming except Edna, Roy's wife, who would help, as she always did, with the cooking and housework. Roy and Edna were the only two among the children who were really close, in spatial terms, to the old home. Roy—now a short (five feet six inches), plump, jolly man of thirty-three years (he'd be thirty-four in August)—had his own drugstore in Junction City, only twenty miles east of Abilene. Already he was known as a "civic father" of that community: a Republican stalwart in a Republican party stronghold, a Mason, an active Rotarian, one of the best golfers in the state, and so immensely popular that he might go far in politics if he ever chose to run for elective office (he never would). He had rather more than his full measure of the Eisenhower charm.

Roy had become interested in pharmacy even before he completed high school in 1911. He'd earned part of his way through high school by working at Northcraft's drugstore, Abilene's leading prescription druggists, and after graduating from high school he'd gone to a pharmacy school in Wichita to become a registered pharmacist. He'd worked in a drugstore in Ellsworth and had become part owner of that store in just a few years. It was in Ellsworth that he'd met Edna. She was Edna Shade, whose father owned a jewelry store in that town, and she was now the mother of three of Ida's most charming grandchildren: Patricia, Peggy, and Lloyd. Patricia, the eldest, was to make an outstanding record at Kansas University, where she was president of Kappa Kappa Gamma, her sorority. Peggy would make an equally outstanding record at Denver University. Lloyd, the youngest, was a year or so younger than John, Dwight's boy, and the 1940s would find him achieving a West Point appointment in emulation of his uncle Ike, whom he greatly admired, only to be disqualified because of a back injury received in high school football.

Yes, David and Ida saw a lot of Roy and his wife and children. Roy drove over with his family every week or so. Strangely enough,

Arthur, though he lived less than two hundred miles away, was in other respects the farthest from home of all the boys. Of course Arthur had been gone the longest—more than twenty years now—and he was extremely busy in the bank. As the eldest son he'd not been as much involved in the family solidarity as the younger boys had been. Then, too, he'd always been rather a "lone wolf" by temperament, shy and reserved like his father; he resembled his father in appearance too—had the same eyes, the same egg-shaped head. Dwight was perhaps the most devoted to his old home, and to his parents, of all the boys. He habitually thought of other people more than he did of himself. He always kept track of anniversaries, and when he journeyed to far countries he kept his eyes open for gifts which might please friends and relatives. From Panama he'd sent his mother a snow-white lace shawl, knee-length—one of the loveliest things Ida had ever seen. She'd be wearing it tomorrow when he came home. Not a year passed, except when he was out of the United States, in which Dwight failed to visit Abilene at least once, and on every trip he made some improvement in the Eisenhower homestead. One year he built a concrete foundation for a porch. Once he built a sidewalk. On another occasion he fashioned a rose arbor for the back yard. On still another occasion he gave the barn a new coat of paint. He was clever with his hands, Dwight was, and he liked to work with them. He had so much energy anyway that he couldn't bear to be idle for very long.

Ida smiled as she recalled what Dwight had said in his letter about giving Ed that long-postponed licking. To give Ed a licking had always been one of Dwight's major ambitions, and he was bound and determined that this time Ed wasn't going to get out of it. It wasn't just a joke—not from Dwight's point of view. He was serious. And it wouldn't be any joke for Ed, either, if Dwight's plans were carried through. After twelve years of law Ed was far better equipped to fight with words than with fists—and there was no doubt that he'd been pretty "mean" to Dwight when the two were boys. . . .

She didn't see Edgar very often any more. After graduating from Michigan in 1914 he'd gone out to the West Coast, to Tacoma, Washington, and that was a long, long way from Abilene. It was funny, the way Edgar had picked out Tacoma as a place to practice law. He'd pictured Tacoma as a Far Western pioneering community, center of the lumbering industry, and as a consequence of the old cow-town legends of his boyhood he'd always had a passion for pioneering, for "westering." He hadn't known a soul in Tacoma when he decided to go there. He'd simply gone through a legal directory in Ann Arbor and picked out the name of Charles Peterson, who had a Tacoma law firm. He'd written to Peterson, who had replied in a brief note to the effect that if Ed did come to Tacoma he, Peterson, would be glad to talk with him. It wasn't a particularly encouraging reply; Peterson hadn't even hinted that he might have a place for the young man. But Edgar had never lacked either courage or self-confidence, so westward he went—and he must have made a favorable impression on Peterson because the latter told him to make the law office his headquarters until the state bar examinations were held, a month after Edgar's arrival. After Edgar had passed the examinations, which he did easily, Peterson had given him a job at ten dollars a week, and within a year the young man was definitely on his way upward through the firm of Bates, Peer, and Peterson. His practice was mostly corporation law. He was making a lot of money—more money than was good for him, Ida sometimes thought.

(By the 1930s he'd have his own law firm—Eisenhower and Hunter—and he'd be making more money in one year than his father ever made in twenty. As the senior partner of Eisenhower, Hunter, and Ramsdell, he'd be one of the most prominent corporation lawyers on the West Coast by the time Dwight became a general.)

It was because of Edgar that Earl had gone to the University of Washington for his college degree. Earl and Milton had both graduated from high school in 1917, and both of them had spent that summer working in town: Milton for Mr. Harger on the newspaper, Earl as "engineer" in the Belle Springs Creamery. Milton had his plans all laid. He was going to Kansas University that fall, get into the Student Army Training Corps, and enroll in journalism. Earl wanted to become an electrical engineer, but he hadn't decided where to go to school, when Edgar wrote to him, extolling the beauties and virtues of Washington. Furthermore, Edgar explained, he'd like to pay back indirectly a debt he owed Dwight, by helping to finance Earl's college career. He recalled the arrangement he and Dwight had made, whereby the two were to help each other through college. Dwight had helped Edgar through that first year at Ann Arbor, but Edgar hadn't been able to do anything for

Dwight after the latter got his West Point appointment. Would Earl come out?

Earl would—and did. But he didn't enroll at the university that fall. Instead he took a job in the Todd shipyards in Tacoma, building liberty ships, and he stayed on this job until the fall of 1918, when he enrolled in the state university. Here he was in the S.A.T.C., just as Milton was at K.U. and Kansas State, until the war ended in November. They were still building liberty ships at the Todd yards—just why, nobody seemed to know—and after a few months Earl went back to Tacoma and into the yards again. It was a steel shipyard, and Earl felt he was learning something about engineering, and getting high pay while he did so. In October 1919, he'd gone back to the university, enrolled as an engineer for the third quarter, and he'd stayed there—working summers at various jobs—until he received his degree in electrical engineering in 1923. One summer, while he was still an undergraduate, he and a half dozen other fellows had made up a surveying crew, surveying a road through the mountains. He'd had a "swell time"; he'd written his mother a long letter about it.

Earl, like Edgar, was restless and adventurous—and those were restless times. Young men were finding it difficult to settle down to steady work after the tense excitement of the war. Earl had spent the summer after his graduation camping with a friend in the Canadian Rockies. In the fall he'd got a job as third assistant engineer on the U.S.S. *President Grant,* sailing for the Orient. From September until January of 1924 he'd toured the Pacific, visiting Japan, China, the Philippines. Sailing into Manila Bay, he'd seen Corregidor and Bataan. . . . In January he was back in Tacoma, working for one of Ed's clients who had an electrical shop. In the spring he and some classmates went back to the university for a visit, and the dean of the engineering school told him about an opening with the West Penn Power Company in Pennsylvania. Earl had taken the job, starting in at Connellsville, moving in succession to Uniontown, Charleroi, McKeesport, and back to Connellsville. It was from Connellsville that he was coming now for the family reunion. He was still unmarried.

Milton, the youngest, had been the one who, as a boy, had given the family the most concern. Not that he was in any sense a "bad" boy—he'd got into nothing like the mischievous trouble Dwight and Edgar had—but he'd been painfully sensitive all through his childhood years, sensitive to hurts and slights which Dwight or Edgar would have shrugged off indifferently or "paid back" in physical combat. It was as though the dreadful illness of his babyhood had stripped him of that tough protective layer which clothed the other boys, leaving his nerves all outside. He'd not been able to play football, as Earl had done. He'd been forced to earn his prestige in ways which Dwight and Edgar would have, at the same age, regarded with contempt. He'd gone in for musical and literary activities. He read constantly. He'd made almost straight E's on his report cards. He'd learned to fight, not with his fists, but with ideas—and Aunt Amanda, for one, considered some of his ideas downright subversive. Ida herself had found them disturbing, though she had never sought to coerce his thinking. About religion, for instance, Milton had strange views indeed. Sometimes it seemed to Aunt Amanda that he was almost an atheist, for he accepted nothing on faith; he questioned everything.

A lot of people outside the family had wondered how Milton would turn out, and some of them had expressed the opinion that he'd never amount to much. Charles M. Harger had not been among them. Ida was grateful for the kindly interest which Mr. Harger had taken in Milton, an interest which, she was convinced, had done more to help Milton along his chosen path than any other single thing. Mr. Harger seemed to understand Milton completely and to recognize in the boy certain latent abilities which, if properly employed, would take Milton far. Perhaps that was because Mr. Harger himself was an extremely sensitive person, sensitive to other people's opinions of him; he himself had been badly hurt by the rebuff the people of Abilene had given him when he ran for Congress (he'd carried all the rest of Dickinson County). Anyway, Mr. Harger had become a sort of second father to Milton. Not only had he trained Milton as a writer—and Mr. Harger was Abilene's dominant literary figure, a frequent contributor to the *Saturday Evening Post* and other magazines—he'd also helped the boy develop that talent for organization, for getting other people to work under him, which Milton shared with Dwight.

At Kansas State, where he'd gone after a semester at K.U., Milton had made an outstanding record, particularly in extracurricular activities. He'd been what they called a "big shot" on the campus. Important people, like Dr. William M. Jardine, the college president, had been impressed by him. Dr. Jardine had given him his first job, as instructor in the department of journalism at the college, after Milton had graduated in 1924—and Dr. Jardine had "fired" him a few months later so that he'd take a job as vice-consul for the United States in Edinburgh, Scotland. For almost two years Milton had been in Scotland. In the meantime, Dr. Jardine had become a national figure. President Coolidge had appointed him Secretary of Agriculture, and it was because Dr. Jardine wanted Milton as assistant to the secretary that Milton had returned from Scotland a month ago. At twenty-six Milton was already becoming prominent on the Washington scene, and Abilene was now proud to claim him as her own. (Two years later he'd be appointed Director of Information for the United States Department of Agriculture, at the astoundingly early age of twenty-eight—the youngest director in history—and within two years after that he'd have firmly established himself as one of the most brilliant administrators in the whole of the national government.)

Surely Ida might have been forgiven whatever pride she may have felt in the attainments of her sons, but it wasn't pride she felt this day. One consequence of her religion was that worldly greatness, in her sons or anyone else, failed wholly to impress her. What passed for greatness in the world—fame or money or power—seemed to her to have no necessary relation to the quality of the man who possessed it. Greatness was an accident, and any excessive devotion to it smacked of impiety. A few months later Secretary Jardine himself visited Abilene, accompanied by Milton and Milton's fiancée, Helen Eakin. Ida invited the secretary to dinner in the Eisenhower home as a matter of course, simply because he was Milton's friend. It never occurred to her that entertaining a cabinet minister in her home might give her claim to an enviable social prestige. She cared nothing for such things. But Goodness was of the man himself, a manifestation of God *in* man, and it was Goodness—compounded of all the solid virtues—which she and David had sought to inculcate by precept and example. She must have realized that in at least one respect the teaching was remarkably successful; it enabled her sons to resist manifold temptations to egotism, apparently without effort. One of her sons would be swept by such tides of power as had drowned the humanity of many another, yet he remained essentially unchanged.

No, it wasn't pride she felt this day. It was simple joy, counterpart of the grief she had suffered when the boys, one by one, left home.

AN INTERLUDE

The house had seemed so empty with the boys gone. She had never got used to the loneliness and the silence. She thrilled now to the realization that tomorrow the house would be full again, and as noisy as anyone could wish. The family, which had become almost an abstraction composed of common memories and felt allegiances, would again be a tangible, bustling, vital reality.

2

The memory of those three days in June 1926 became an important part of all their secret lives. For the sons, the values of childhood were reaffirmed. The solidarity of the family, in so far as it had been lost, was solidly re-established. In the family calendar thereafter events were always dated from this reunion, the only complete reunion they were ever to have. Roy would be dead before the next big family gathering was held.

They brought each other up to date on their various activities. Dwight told them about Panama and Leavenworth, and Ida put on the snow-white lace shawl which Dwight had sent from Panama City. Earl—the family called him "Red" because of his red, wavy hair—told them all about his Pacific adventures, about Japan and the Philippines. Milton told them of his experiences in Scotland and of what "official" life was like in high government circles. Arthur, Roy, and Edgar—with no far journeys to report—nevertheless had interesting experiences to recount. They spent a great deal of time reminiscing, recalling scene after scene from their boyhoods. One thing especially seems to have impressed them all, namely the *differences* in personality and career which distinguished them from one another. The remarkable cohesion of this family had certainly resulted in no standardized product. Other families produced doctors, or lawyers, or teachers. This family produced the widest possible variety of professional men: a lawyer, a journalist, a banker, a druggist, an engineer, and a soldier. The differences enhanced the interest of their associations with one another. In after years Dwight asserted that he'd never enjoyed another gathering as thoroughly as he enjoyed that one.

On the very first day Ida fed them fried mush and pudding meat. They whooped like children as the aroma spread through the house. At the table they bowed their heads over their plates, fidgeting as they used to do, while David, at the head of the table, offered prayer. Even after the prayer was done the talk which had been loud and constant heretofore did not start up again, because they were all too busy eating. Afterward Arthur asked his mother if she'd sell him a good big jar of pudding to take back to Kansas City, and David, the father, reminded by someone that he'd be sixty-three years old in just a few weeks, said with emphasis that he was "as good a man as he ever was and a better man than most of his sons." David offered to prove his assertion by "taking on" any one of them in a wrestling match. Dwight, grinning, promptly accepted the challenge.

After the meal had "settled" they all went out into the back yard. Dwight and his father stripped off their shirts, and Dwight proudly noticed that his father's sloping shoulders and deep chest were still, in appearance, those of a young man. Dwight well remembered how powerful physically his father had been in former years, but he remembered, too, that his father had had a severe illness a decade or so ago and had been working in an office ever since. Dwight was prepared to "let the old man down easy." He was almost thrown himself before he discovered, to his amazement, that he'd need all his strength and skill. For fifteen minutes the two grunted and strained before Dwight at last managed to pin his father to the ground. It was, certainly, a moral victory for David.

"All the same," panted Dwight as he wiped the sweat from his face, "don't think I'm not able to give you that beating, Ed, when we put on the gloves."

Ed said blandly that he was sure Dwight could do it, only Dwight had better rest up a bit first. Ed had been postponing that boxing match almost from the moment he and Dwight had met, and Dwight, looking at him now, could see why. Ed wore horn-rimmed spectacles, was losing his hair even faster than Dwight was, and was just a wee bit thick about the middle. He was probably twice as hard physically as most big-city lawyers, but he wasn't half hard enough to stay with Dwight. Well, turnabout was fair play. Dwight certainly hadn't been hard enough to stay with Ed in the old days. . . .

Roy suggested that they all spend the afternoon on the golf course at Abilene's country club. It was lucky that Roy was such an active fellow and walked off pounds of flesh on the golf course every week from April to November. Otherwise, instead of being pleasantly roly-poly, he'd have been really fat. Roy, the "runt" of the family, cheerfully admitted that he had to look up at all his brothers, but he asserted just as cheerfully that he could show any one of them how golf should be played. He did just that. The country-club crowd was treated to the sight of an Eisenhower sextet teeing off before the clubhouse. A couple of hours later, Arthur, Edgar, and Dwight came in with scores in the respectable eighties, but Roy had shot in the low seventies to win, according to plan.

Indeed, everything worked out pretty much according to plan during those three days with the exception of Dwight's fight with Ed. Somehow Ed, by employing all his lawyer's wiles, managed to dodge the fulfillment of one of Dwight's most cherished ambitions. . . .

One late afternoon all of the sons linked arms and walked in a sweeping line up Chestnut Street, across the railroad tracks, and through the business district. Ostensibly they were hunting for Henry Engle, the chief of police with whom they had had several minor brushes as boys, but in reality they were inspired by a cheerful exhibitionism. They wanted to flaunt the family's pride and strength in a good-natured challenge to the North Side. The challenge was impressive, but so joyous that the response to it was wholly friendly. Businessmen came out of stores and offices to greet them. Everyone on the street wanted to shake their hands. Their progress through the town became a kind of triumphal procession. It was marked by such an exuberant vitality, such a gay defiance of all hostile fate, that those who witnessed it never forgot it. Life *ought* to be lived this way, they might have said—completely, with nothing wasted. The scene became part of the Abilene legend. Decades later, when curious visitors asked about the Eisenhower family, local citizens recalled the Big Parade of 1926 and smiled as they told about it. Nobody seems to remember what happened to Henry Engle when the boys found him at last, but probably they merely took him to Joner Callahan's café and served him coffee, or a bottle of near-beer.

Jeffcoat, Abilene's leading photographer, was to take family pictures. He came to the house on South East Fourth Street with his huge plate camera in the morning. Ida took from the family album a photograph of the entire family made in 1902. Milton protested loudly when he saw it. Milton in that picture sat between his mother and father in the front row, wearing (he'd never forget them) long auburn curls, like a little girl. Ida laughed and told Jeffcoat that she wanted a picture of the family now, arranged just as it was in that earlier picture. So the photographer lined them up beside the bay window on the east side of the house, facing the sun, with Dwight in his uniform at the left and Roy at the right and Milton seated between Ida and David in the front row. Judging from the picture which resulted, no one was enjoying things much when the lens clicked. Then Jeffcoat took a picture of all the boys lined up in order of age behind the seated figures of David and Ida, with Arthur, the eldest, at the left. Dwight found a little box for Roy to stand on; he wouldn't let the "runt" disgrace the family this time, he said. When the lens clicked everyone was smiling pleasantly except Milton, who was caught with a rather insipid squint-eyed smirk on his face. They all went around to the front of the house and arranged themselves on the porch for what the photographer called an "informal" picture. For some reason Roy, Arthur, and Earl were frowning quite ferociously when Jeffcoat snapped this one, but Dwight, seated on the porch steps, his knee boots shining, faced the camera with a smile shy and strange. . . . Years later the Eisenhower boys, with mingled emotions, would find those pictures staring at them from scores of newspapers and magazines and books.

Even in that year of 1926 the family found itself "written up" in the newspapers of the region. Charles Harger had a story of the reunion in his paper, and exchange papers reprinted it far and wide. Milton, riding east on the train, shared a seat with Clif Stratton, a Kansas State graduate who was Washington correspondent for the Topeka *Daily Capital,* and Milton was so filled with the joys of the reunion that he told Clif all about it. Clif asked questions and jotted the answers into a notebook. Next day a long feature story about the reunion appeared in the *Capital.*

3

In the slow transitions of Dwight's personal life the family reunion marked the end of a phase. In one sense his life had come full circle. Mingling with his parents and brothers, he was reminded of the source and nature of his values. He saw himself again as one of many, deriving his individuality from his membership in the family. A philosophic biologist might have caught part of his feeling in the statement that the "Dwight" of his name was specific and formal, whereas the "Eisenhower" was generic and substantial. He was content with this view of himself. He wanted life to be a co-operative group endeavor rather than an anarchic conflict of individual assertions.

But he was not wholly content with the phase his life entered in this summer of 1926, though his awareness of the fact grew slowly through the years. With his graduation from the Command School his military career seemed to be arrested on a kind of plateau, a plateau on which there was considerable movement but no perceptible progress. Through the fat years of false prosperity Republicans and political liberals agreed on few things, but one of them was that the nation's armament establishment should be kept on a starvation diet. Armaments, said the Republicans, cost taxpayers money. Armaments, said the liberals, help cause wars. And one consequence of their conclusions was that Dwight, who had been a major for six years now, would still be a major after fourteen years had passed.

CHAPTER III

The Education of a Staff Officer: Paris and Washington

LOOKING BACKWARD through time, it is easy to see how effect proceeded from cause, how conclusions were inherent in premises, how beginnings in every case presupposed certain definite ends. Looking backward, it is easy to conclude as Mamie did that what men call "chance" is, in reality, a purposeful Fate, working out a predestined design. Considered apart from the flowing present, the past is static —and so neatly ordered. Every event has its assigned place in a perfectly logical pattern. *This* thing happened because *that* thing happened; the concavity of this occurrence was obviously designed to fit the convexity of that one. In Mamie's view, Ike had a "star" which guided him along a climbing road toward the eminence of supreme command. After that eminence was reached the road which led to it was obviously inevitable, part of Fate's vast highway system, and Ike could not have got off it if he had tried to do so. Indeed, he did try to do so at various times. Each time he was held to his appointed path, it seemed, by a controlling force outside him.

In December of 1926, while serving as executive officer for the 24th Infantry at Fort Benning, Georgia, he was asked if he'd be interested in an assignment to the American Battle Monuments Commission. The commission had been gathering material for a guide to the American battlefields in Europe. Now the time had come for someone to put all the material together in a. form that could be published through the United States Government Printing Office, and Major Eisenhower had been recommended (by Fox Connor, who was then Deputy Chief of Staff in Washington?) as a writer of clear, logical prose. Frankly, Dwight *wasn't* much interested in the assignment, which had the appearance of another routine stopgap job and had small relation to active soldiering, but he wasn't particularly enthusiastic about his present assignment either. With a shrug he informed the commission through channels that he'd be glad to do what he could for them. Back through channels his orders came. He reported to the commission in Washington, D.C., on January 15, 1927.

Thus, with no particular enthusiasm, he entered upon duties which were perhaps as important to his future advancement as his association with Fox Connor or his assignment to the Command School. The guidebook material, he found, was a confusion of intricate details with no organization whatsoever. There was a mass of descriptive material concerning the points of interest to be visited. There were pictures by the score. There were statistical data concerning America's participation in the war. There were scores of maps. Someone had prepared a detailed chronology of the war and written portions of a World War history. Altogether there was enough undigested material to fill several volumes—and what the commission wanted was a book of convenient size which the Government Printing Office could sell for seventy-five cents. Moreover, the commission wanted to issue the book next autumn, which meant that Dwight must complete his work in six months!

As he recognized the difficulties of his assignment his indifference vanished. He felt himself to be challenged. The basic problem was one of logical organization, quite as difficult of solution (so far as pure logic was concerned) as the much more momentous problems he faced later on. His method of attack was revealing. Obviously, a book of the contemplated size could not be a history of the war, an encyclopedia of the war, and a guide to its battlefields, with equal emphasis on all three. Some one purpose must be the dominant one, to which all others were subordinate. Which purpose? The very title of the book answered that question. The primary purpose was to provide a guide to the battlefields. But how could the book be an intelligent guide to historical sites unless history were included in it? Obviously it couldn't be. The problem then resolved itself into one of fusing history with geographical description, including only as much history and general information as would contribute to the usefulness of the book as guide.

As always when his mind was confronted with a confusion of variable factors, he was moved (1) to analyze the confusion into its "components" so that the factors themselves could be clearly realized; (2) to assign to some one factor the status of a constant or common denominator by which the variability of all other factors could be measured; and (3) to recombine the factors in a whole which had a clear outline and a central or dominant principle. It was a technique which denied validity to whatever fluid elements might be present in a problem; whatever could not be given a rigid definition was simply excluded from consideration. It therefore might not be successful if applied without qualification in situations where the prime factors, being connotative (as is so often the case in politics), are not fit subjects for a purely logical analysis. But it was a technique which led to great successes in Dwight's chosen field. In later years the constant by which he measured all other factors was the goal of military victory. Proposals in the fields of political action, or public relations, or administration were all defined in terms of military expedience and measured by a single question: If any one of these proposals were adopted, would it contribute to the victory of our arms? The result in the 1940s was a succession of remarkable strategical triumphs. In 1927 the result of the same basic technique was a guidebook on historical principles which is one of the best reference works on World War I that has ever been prepared.

Two facts made Dwight's work here of particular importance to his future. One was that by the time the job was done he probably had as much detailed knowledge of America's military role in the war—of the strategy, tactics, and logistics of the A.E.F.—as any man alive, not excluding the General of the Armies. The second fact was that his work was accomplished under the appraising eyes of that general, for Pershing was chairman of the Battle Monuments Commission. Ever afterward the general was one of Eisenhower's most enthusiastic sponsors. On August 15, 1927, Pershing wrote the following letter to Major General Robert H. Allen, Chief of Infantry, Washington, D.C.:

My dear General Allen:

The detail of Major Dwight D. Eisenhower, who has been assisting the American Battle Monuments Commission in preparing the guide book, expires today. I wish to take this occasion to express my appreciation of the splendid service which he has rendered since being with us.

In the discharge of his duties, which were most difficult, and which were rendered even more difficult by reason of the short time available for their completion, he has shown superior ability not only in visualizing his work as a whole but in executing its many details in an efficient and timely manner. What he has done was accom-

plished only by the exercise of unusual intelligence and constant devotion to duty.

> *With kindest regards, I am*
> *Sincerely yours,*
> *(Signed)* JOHN J. PERSHING

The book was printed in the fall, as scheduled. When it came off the press Dwight presented an inscribed copy to Milton, "whose many helpful suggestions contributed in no small measure to anything which may be considered creditable, appearing herein as a result of my efforts—with the esteem and affection of his brother." Here was the first instance of a fraternal collaboration which became increasingly fruitful as time went on. When the inscription was written Dwight was engrossed in his studies at the Army War College in Washington, which he had entered in September and from which he was graduated on June 30, 1928.

He, Mamie, and John were living at the Wyoming Apartments, on the corner of Columbia Road and Connecticut Avenue. Quite a clique of army people lived at the Wyoming, including Dwight's good friend Leonard Gerow whenever the latter had a Washington assignment. It was not one of the ultra-modern buildings which were springing up all over Washington in those years. On the contrary, it was the product of an earlier era and gave the impression of being much lived in. The apartments were made up of unusually large, comfortable, well-lighted rooms which pleased Mamie greatly. She had three bedrooms, a living room, a dining room, a large kitchen, and bath—plenty of space for the heavy, beautiful furniture which she had by this time acquired (partly with Dwight's subsistence allowance, partly with her own money) and for Dwight's collection of oriental carpets. Always she defied the Army to prevent her making a real home, however temporary an assignment might be. Within a week after they moved to a new place she managed to make that place look and feel as though the Eisenhowers had lived there for years. It was that way in Washington, and there the famous Eisenhower hospitality was again in operation. The apartment became the gathering place for hosts of people, each of whom was made to feel more than welcome. Mamie had a knack for that sort of thing. She could make an informal party "go" as few hostesses can, partly because she was sensitive to the needs of her guests, mostly because she had such a good time herself.

Among the most frequent visitors in the spring and summer of 1927 were Milton and his fiancée, Helen Eakin. Mamie and Dwight grew very fond of Helen, an extremely attractive, vivacious girl whose family background was in many ways similar to Mamie's own. Helen's father, L. R. Eakin, had owned the largest department store in Manhattan, Kansas, where Kansas State College is located; had been a director of a bank there, and had also "dabbled in oil and real estate" with such success that he had become one of the wealthiest men in the state. Helen was a member of Pi Beta Phi sorority while a student in the college, Milton was a member of Sigma Alpha Epsilon fraternity, and the two had first met at fraternity and sorority dances. The Eakins were close friends of the Jardines. It was partially for that reason that they had moved to Washington in the same year William Jardine became Secretary of Agriculture.

In the course of his duties as assistant to the secretary Milton made the acquaintance of Harry C. Butcher, who at that time was editor of *The Fertilizer Review,* a magazine published by the National Fertilizer Association. Butcher was a tall, strikingly handsome man of about Milton's age, with an almost incredible amount of breezy, personal charm. He had a talent for telling funny stories, a positive genius for public relations, and a charming wife named Ruth who was soon one of Helen's closest friends. The two young couples spent a great deal of time together. Inevitably they went together frequently to Dwight's apartment, which was always more fun than a night club, and as a result the Butchers were by the fall of 1927 intimate friends of Dwight's and Mamie's. It was a friendship which would be of some importance to history. . . .

Harry Butcher's charm was no product of easy circumstances. As a boy he had been as well acquainted with humble living and hard physical labor as Dwight had been, and he had been denied that quality of family life which had been so important to Dwight's development. He was born on a farm near Mount Vernon, Iowa, whence his ancestors had come in a covered wagon from Mount Vernon, Ohio, in the early 1850s. With the exception of a brief interlude spent in North Dakota, he was reared in Iowa until his twelfth year. After that, his father having died, he paid his way through high school with all manner of odd jobs, working through the summers on farms. During the summer after his graduation from high school he operated concessions at county and state agricultural fairs with such success that by the autumn of 1920 he had seventeen hundred dollars in the bank. He went to Ames, Iowa, and enrolled at Iowa State College for a course in electrical engineering.

Before long, however, he had changed his course from engineering to dairying because he felt he would be more "independent" in the dairy business—he might be able to buy a dairy and set up in business for himself. But when he took the course in agricultural journalism he changed his mind again. He switched to a combination course of agriculture and journalism and knew that he had found his vocation. He wrote articles for the *Iowa Homestead* while an undergraduate and covered the International Livestock Exposition in Chicago for that weekly farm magazine. One summer he worked his passage across the Atlantic, visiting England, Jersey, Guernsey, Belgium, the Percheron country of France, gathering material for a series of animal-husbandry articles published in the *Iowa Homestead, Successful Farming,* and other farm magazines.

But perhaps as important a factor in his college education as any other was his membership in a fraternity, Sigma Phi Epsilon, for this gave him a social life he needed more than most. He never forgot the first evening he was inside a fraternity house. As a freshman he knew nothing of the fraternity system; he had been invited to no fraternity parties during "rush week," and his invitation to the Sig Ep house a few days after his arrival in Ames had been an accidental occurrence. Some Sig Eps came to his rooming house to take his roommate to dinner, chatted a bit with Butcher, and finally asked him to come along too. He was astounded when a few days later they invited him to pledge, but he accepted the invitation and he never regretted it. The fraternity gave him a happy college home and an opportunity to acquire those social graces which, accentuating his natural charm, stood him in good stead in later years. Moreover, it was through the fraternity-sorority social life that he met Ruth Barton, the pretty daughter of a former mayor of Des Moines. By the spring of 1924, his senior year, the two were engaged to be married.

He began looking for a job which would enable him to support a wife. In April a Chicago publication asked him to come to that city, with travel expenses paid, to be interviewed for a thirty-five-dollar-a-week job. He did so, made a favorable impression at the interview, and was offered the job. But while he was in the city he went to the Gothic tower which Colonel McCormick had erected beside the Chicago River, to see Frank Ridgeway, the farm editor of the *Tribune*. He told Ridgeway that he was a student in agricultural journalism and that he "just wanted to chat." He did so with considerable effect. Ridgeway was delighted with him. Thirty-five dollars a week wasn't exactly high pay, Ridgeway pointed out, and there was a much better job open in Butcher's special field. The powerful Illinois Agricultural Association—the Farm Bureau organization for that state—was looking for a man to edit their weekly magazine, the *Agricultural Record*. Why didn't Butcher try for it?

Butcher did. Ridgeway called up the association for him, and within an hour Butcher was being interviewed for the editorial job. He gave the man who interviewed him his theory of writing for farmers—"do it as though you were chatting with the farmer beside a kerosene lamp in his home"—a theory taught him by the editors of the *Iowa Homestead*. The interviewer was deeply impressed and asked Butcher to appear at a meeting of the association's executive committee a few days later. The upshot was that Butcher, two months before his graduation, accepted an editorial job at a salary of thirty-six hundred dollars a year, the highest starting salary ever achieved by an Ames journalism graduate. He went to work at once, completing his college courses by correspondence, and returned to Ames in June to graduate with his class. On the evening of Commencement Day he and Ruth Barton were married in the home of the college chaplain.

He had come to Washington only a few months before he met Dwight. The move was inspired by a considerable advance in salary—the fertilizer association paid him five thousand dollars per annum—but he soon realized that the increase in pay was of small importance compared with the increase in opportunity which Washington offered. The national capital in those days was a happy hunting ground for any bright young journalist who knew Midwestern agriculture. The Department of Agriculture's information service was expanding. Farmer organizations were hiring editors and writers for their Washington bureaus. Network radio broadcasting was on the eve of its tremendous expansion and was looking for youthful talent which could help capture farm advertising accounts. Butcher found many doors to a profitable future opening before him, and one of them, the one he chose to enter later on, opened as a result of his association with Milton Eisenhower. In the spring and summer of 1927 Milton was living in the home of Sam Pickard, whom Jardine had brought to Washington from Kansas State College to head the newly established radio division of the department's information service. Pickard did not stay long in government service. He went into the Columbia Broadcasting System "on the ground floor" and, with Columbia's swift expansion, rose rapidly. He was impressed by young Butcher, who visited Milton often at the house; before many months had passed Butcher was hired to open the new Washington office of CBS at a salary which left him gasping.

From Dwight's point of view, the big event of the autumn of 1927 was Milton's marriage to Helen Eakin. The wedding took place on October 12, and Dwight was Milton's best man. The bachelor's supper for Milton was given in Dwight's apartment, from which Mamie and John had been excluded for the evening. Earl had come down from Pennsylvania to acquire what he insisted, next morning, was one of the great hang-overs of the century. Butcher was present, and Sam Pickard—among others. At the wedding itself Dwight was, for both Milton and Helen, a tower of strength. He wore his full-dress uniform, with scabbard and sword. Helen used the sword to cut, with a flourish, the great white cake at the wedding dinner. Dwight protected Helen's bag against would-be inserters of rice.

2

If Fate were controlling Dwight's footsteps, Mamie in the summer of 1928 was Fate's handmaiden. After his graduation from the Army War College he was presented with alternative choices. He could accept an assignment on the General Staff, which meant staying in Washington, or he could go back to the Battle Monuments Commission to prepare a revision of the guidebook, which meant going to Paris. He favored (not strongly) the former assignment. Mamie persuaded him to the latter. It was the second and last time that she influenced directly a professional decision. Here, she pointed out, was a rare opportunity to see Europe at no expense, to broaden John's childhood education, to study on the spot the World War terrain he had known heretofore only through maps, pictures, and printed descriptions. He protested feebly that he hadn't gone to West Point and made a career of the Army in order to write guidebooks for American tourists—but in the end, and without a great deal of argument, he yielded. If Mamie wanted the European experience, she should have it. Johnny would learn a great deal. And it *would* be interesting to study on the spot those battlefields he had missed seeing a decade before.

They sailed for France early in July. In Paris, Mamie found an attractive apartment on the Rue d'Auteuil, a few steps from the Pont Mirabeau, not far from the Bois de Boulogne. It was here that the phrase "Club Eisenhower" was coined. The Mirabeau Bridge became the "Pont Mamie," and the little square opposite the apartment became the "Place Eisenhower." All of these names were coined by George Hoekan, then a captain and later a brigadier general in the United States Army. Paris that summer was crowded with American tourists, and a good many of them, as well as army officers attached to the Monuments Commission, found their way to the Rue d'Auteuil. John, who had his sixth birthday in August of that year, began his schooling in September at MacJannette's near the Trocadero, a mile or so up the Seine.

It is certain that Dwight learned much that year which was of use to him at the climax of his career, but he himself would find it difficult to say precisely what it was that he learned. He visited every American battlefield from Ypres, where two American divisions fought beside the British, to the Argonne. John remembered always a visit he made to the Argonne sector with his father and mother, remembered his father's fascinating account of the break in the Hindenburg Line, remembered the picnic lunch they had in the tangled Argonne forest. Perhaps more important to Dwight than his studies of battle terrain and tactics was the study he made of French roads and railroads. It seemed to Mamie that before they left France Dwight knew every road in the country. He also learned something of the French Army, the French character, and French politics, though he was hampered in these studies by his ignorance of the language. He had taken French lessons while in Washington, but languages did not come easily for him, his time was limited, and he picked up only a smattering of words and phrases—not enough to enable him to converse easily with the French people. He carried away a blurred impression of French political life as an intense factional strife centering on slogans which, to him, had little meaning. Years later he was to regret deeply that his knowledge in this field was not more precise and profound.

It was only natural that the felt need to prepare himself should lose a good deal of its urgency that year. Never did Fox Connor's dire predictions seem less likely to be fulfilled. Dwight found it virtually impossible to believe that war would come again, in Europe at least, within his lifetime. Everywhere in France he saw solid evidence of a new prosperity, a greater prosperity than the country had ever known before. Economically that country which had suffered most in the Great War seemed to be completely recovered, now that Poincaré had "saved the franc" (at one tenth its former value). In the areas which had been devastated by war, some 2,700,000 people were now living. Of the millions of shell-blasted agricultural acres, virtually all were now restored to productive use. More than 800,000 houses had been built or rebuilt. Paris itself was the center of a vast apartment-house boom, and extensive projects were under way to beautify still further what was already the fairest city in the world. Industrially the country was advancing with amazing rapidity. There was a big new aluminum industry centered on the bauxite deposits in central departments. Of automobiles and glass, France was now the largest manufacturer in Europe. A prosperous people was not inclined toward war and had even, through Briand at Locarno in 1925, re-established friendly relations with the traditional archenemy, Germany. Indeed, the whole of the Western world was too prosperous to "want" or "need" war, for in a capitalist economy it is only when the consumption of goods fails through a maldistribution of income to match the production of goods that the drive toward war becomes real. In 1929 private enterprise seemed able to provide nearly full employment; there was no strong economic pressure for an expansion of government spending for armaments. Even Germany, a disarmed republic, expressed through her novels, paintings, and other art forms a strong pacifist-liberal sentiment. She was now a member of the League of Nations, and her good people laughed at the ranting Nazis who, after achieving some importance in 1923 and 1924, were now a steadily shrinking group which could be expected to disappear completely in a year or so.

It was a smiling America to which the Eisenhowers returned in September 1929. The people were assured by political and business leaders that the policy of reducing government expenditures and taxation, of leaving business free of governmental "interference" had enabled the country to solve completely, for the first time in history, the "problem of poverty." True, there were economists who considered security values to be vastly overinflated. The followers of John Maynard Keynes were pointing out that too high a proportion of the total national income (which amounted to one hundred billion dollars that year) was going to those who "saved" a good portion of their individual incomes; they asserted that there were not enough valid offsets for the twenty billions of dollars which annually sought "investment," and that consumption spending was lagging so far behind actual production of goods that an economic collapse was imminent. But these were lonely voices crying in a wilderness of bull-market speculation. When a month after the Eisenhowers' return the greatest financial panic in history swept Wall Street to herald two decades of unparalleled world catastrophe, President Hoover interpreted it as a "temporary" loss of confidence. There had been too much speculation in stocks, he said, but business remained "fundamentally sound." "Prosperity"—the phrase was to haunt him the rest of his life—"was just around the corner."

3

Again it was as though a purposeful Fate were working out, through him, a predestined design. During the years of deepening crisis Dwight Eisenhower's assignments were precisely those best calculated to further the kind of education he needed in the 1940s.

On November 8, 1929, he was made assistant executive in the office of the Assistant Secretary of War. Through the worst years of the depression he lived in Washington and experienced directly the process by which the capital became increasingly the nerve center of the nation—a distinction held by Wall Street during the fat years. His work was in that difficult administrative area where domestic politics, international diplomacy, economics, and military policy are forced together (not often harmoniously) within the framework of a total governmental program. Here at the very pinnacle of the Army's organization chart it was necessary to think in large terms, to view forests rather than trees. He accomplished the shift to an enlarged perspective without a perceptible wrench. Whether one were dealing with symbolic abstractions or concrete realities, with dozens of items or with millions, the logical processes remained the same. Of course when one dealt with men rather than with things or symbols, logic had to be informed by an intuitive human understanding, but that intuitive understanding was a gift he had had from early childhood; it applied quite as well to men in high positions as it did to those in more humble circumstances. In short, he was not surprised to find that he could function as easily in the rarefied atmosphere of high command as he could in lower echelons. It was simply a matter of doing a job, in both cases, with whatever elements were at hand. Later on there would be those who claimed that his lack of experience with small commands was, in terms of the job he had to do, not a lack at all but a positive asset. . . .

The National Defense Act of 1920 specifically charges the Assistant Secretary of War with the responsibility for mobilizing matériel and its production in case of war. Discharge of this responsibility involves the development of an industrial organization plan which can be made quickly effectual in an emergency. Dwight's first task was to aid in the development of such a plan. To this end he made an exhaustive study of Bernard Baruch's War Industries Board of 1917–18, became engrossed in surveys of America's industrial potential, and necessarily entered such related fields as administrative organization, priority and price controls, transportation systems, and (as one end product of all this) the mechanization of armies. He worked with industrialists on general plans for plant conversion and expansion. He made a considerable study of critical materials, of their source of supply, and of the possibility of securing substitutes for them in case supply sources should be cut off. Much of this work was summarized briefly in the annual report of the Chief of Staff for the fiscal year July 1, 1930, to June 30, 1931. There was a good deal of discussion of "M-day" in the public prints, much of it arguing that the War Department's proposals meant the total extinction of democracy on the day war was declared. Thereafter the industrial mobilization plan gathered dust in some filing cabinet, not to be referred to again until the Office of Production Management had badly bungled the plant-expansion program, particularly in steel and aluminum, during the early 1940s.

Eisenhower also played a part in founding the Army Industrial College where, according to the annual report of the Chief of Staff, "eminent industrialists annually deliver lectures on appropriate subjects and discuss present trends in the relationships of government to business." The college course was designed to give "the student an elementary understanding of the industrial processes in this country"—and Dwight completed it during his assignment to the assistant secretary's office. He himself gave several lectures there on various phases of industrial mobilization.

So far as Eisenhower's education was concerned, the social and economic context within which his work was done must have been as important as the work itself. It was strange to be planning for plant expansion—to be thinking in terms of material and manpower shortages—when all around you plants were shutting down, products went begging for non-existent buyers, and ten million men were unemployed. Strange, too, to be planning in terms of unlimited government expenditures during an administration whose principal answer to the depression was a *reduction* in government expenditures (as if reducing the amount of money in consumers' pockets would somehow help restore lost markets). Stranger still to be basing the whole of one's work on the assumption that the government had emergency powers which the government itself, at that particular moment, was denying it possessed. Yes, it was all a strange interlude during which the paradoxical gave way to the flatly self-contradictory—and the process was far from amusing.

No department of government suffered more severely from the so-called "economy act" than did the War Department. True, the Chief of Staff, General Douglas MacArthur (who had assumed this duty on November 21, 1930) seems to have been wholly in accord with the administration's economic theories, a fact which no doubt made it easier for him to bear the Army's grievous wounds. "In the face of the constantly growing Treasury deficit the need has grown acute for drastic reduction in government expenditures," he wrote in his report for the fiscal year ending June 30, 1932. "The need for retrenchment has become so great as to constitute a dominant factor in the shaping of national policy." Nevertheless, he devoted much of the remainder of his report that year to a strong argument in defense of the Army against further "retrenchment." It was an army whose regular strength had now shrunk to 118,000 men and which had barely missed further reduction through a proposal (accepted by the House but rejected in the Senate) to retire from service 2,000 of the 12,000 Regular officers. As MacArthur's report mentioned in passing, a major war was no longer a remote possibility. "The tense situation in the Far East, which, for some weeks during the past winter flamed into open hostilities, emphasized again the untrustworthiness of treaties as complete safeguards of international peace," wrote the Chief of

Staff. He referred to the event which, in later years, came to be regarded as the true beginning of World War II: Japan's seizure of Manchuria (Mukden was occupied on September 18, 1931) and the Sino-Japanese "trouble" in Shanghai to which the 31st Infantry had been dispatched on February 2, 1932.

MacArthur, too, made important contributions to Eisenhower's education. In many ways it must have been an education by contrasts. Never were two soldiers more unlike in temperament, in philosophy, in conscious techniques of command. MacArthur was fifty-two years old on January 26, 1932. He was the son of Lieutenant General Arthur MacArthur, had been reared in an atmosphere of luxury and high prestige, had graduated at the head of his class from West Point (where he made the highest marks any cadet had made in twenty-five years), and had made a brilliant record as commander of the 84th Infantry Brigade of the Rainbow Division in France, 1918. Like most men who fancy themselves as hardheaded "realists," he was extremely sentimental, capable of a purple rhetoric which less hardheaded individuals found painful to read. "It was seventeen years ago—those days have vanished tone and tint: they have gone glimmering through the dreams of things that were," he once said in a speech before the Rainbow Division. "Their memory is a land where flowers of wondrous beauty and varied colors spring, watered by tears and coaxed and caressed into fuller bloom by the smiles of yesterday. . . . The faint far whisper of forgotten songs no longer floats through the air. Youth . . . strength . . . aspirations . . . struggles . . . triumphs . . . despairs . . . wide winds sweeping . . . [et cetera, et cetera] . . . the still white crosses . . . And now we are met to remember." He ended that address with an elaboration of a quotation from Dionysius, the "ancient thinker," who had said: "It is a law of nature, common to all mankind which time shall neither annul nor destroy, that those who have greater strength and power shall rule over those who have less." A realist was one who realized that wars have always been and always will be, and that democracy (at least as most men understand it) is an impossible dream.

In the words of one of his most fervent admirers[1] he was "the youngest Chief of Staff our Army had ever known, the busiest, the handsomest . . . the most bedeviled by pettifogging critics. . . ."

[1]Frank C. Waldrop, editor of *MacArthur on War*, a collection of MacArthur's military writings published by John Lane The Bodley Head, London, 1943.

The word "pettifogging" is perhaps more revealing of MacArthur's personal attitudes than his eulogist realized. To Washington the new Chief of Staff had carried a reputation for battlefield gallantry, for intellectual brilliance, for aristocratic sentiments, for political ambition, and for personal arrogance. A great many politicians, aware of grass-roots sentiment, regarded him with distrust. It can hardly be denied that he did little to disarm his critics. On the contrary, though his reports were generally brilliant, he seemed to go out of his way in personal actions to arouse antagonism, and this in the very areas of public opinion where, as Chief of Staff, he most needed support. It was as though he were more concerned with the impression he personally made (particularly on the "better classes") than he was with achieving results.

For instance, Eisenhower must have learned a great deal from watching MacArthur's handling of the bonus-march incident in July of 1932. Here the Army came face to face with the unemployed in a manner which, to many observers, seemed a portent of democracy's collapse. Unemployed veterans of the Great War had poured into Washington by the thousands, had established a pitiful camp of shacks on Pennsylvania Avenue between Third and Fourth streets, and had announced through their spokesmen that they would stay in the encampment until the bonus was paid in full. The "Bonus Expeditionary Force" they called themselves, and though they were generally quiet and well behaved enough, their presence in the national capital was disturbing to say the least. It was even potentially dangerous, since President Hoover had no intention of acceding to their demands. On July 28 the President informed the Secretary of War, Patrick J. Hurley, that the civil government of the District of Columbia was "unable to maintain law and order in the District." Mr. Hurley at once sent an order to the Chief of Staff: "You will have United States troops proceed immediately to the scene of the disorder. . . . Surround the affected area and clear it without delay."

There was nothing in the order which required MacArthur to supervise the operation in person. Nevertheless, he chose to do so, going so far as to lead a "demonstration" down Pennsylvania Avenue. Even then it might have been possible to invest the episode with an atmosphere of duty firmly but regretfully performed; he made no efforts in this direction. In his own language, the Army was "composing" a "civilian riot,"[2] though spectators claimed there had been no disorder until the troops arrived. The country was treated to the spectacle (rare in America) of soldiers marching against poor, unarmed men, denying them the possibility of dignified retirement—soldiers led by a man who gave every appearance of enjoying his job. Fortunately no one was seriously injured; the bonus marchers had never been inclined toward violence. The directors of the Washington Board of Trade, representing thirty-eight hundred business and professional men of the city, were pleased. They wrote a letter to the Secretary of War saying so. But MacArthur thereafter was subject to the most violent political attacks, particularly from the left—and one must conclude that he had courted, deliberately, this worse-than-useless martyrdom. There were those who praised his courage in making himself "a target when he could so easily have stayed away,"[3] but the net result was a lessening of his effectiveness when he dealt with Congress, which is one of the most important functions of a Chief of Staff. One may be sure that Eisenhower, who habitually fixed his eyes on main objectives, would have handled the assignment quite differently.

One of Eisenhower's biographers[4] suggests that after the bonus-march 'furor MacArthur felt the need to strengthen his staff, especially in the field of public relations, and that it was for this reason that a request for Eisenhower's services was put through. However that may be, Eisenhower on February 20, 1933, was assigned to the office of the Chief of Staff. He was placed in an office next door to MacArthur's and had daily contact with his chief. He had much to do with preparing the report for that fiscal year.

If he had no active role in the mighty events of Franklin Roosevelt's historic "hundred days" in the spring of 1933, he was certainly in an excellent position for watching those events and learning from them. What he saw was a revolution, not of social classes or economic systems, but of American governmental theory and practice. Trends were abruptly reversed. The concept of "retrenchment" was replaced by the concept of "pump-priming" through federal expenditures. The concept of "relief" was replaced by the concept of "public works" to create jobs. A tacit opposition to

[2]Letter from Douglas MacArthur to Brigadier General Perry L. Miles.
[3]Frank C. Waldrop, op. cit.
[4]Alden Hatch in his *General Ike*, Henry Holt and Co., Inc., 1944.

labor unionism was replaced by the concept of "collective bargaining" guaranteed by law. Gone was the idea that a democratic government is necessarily *laissez faire*, the merest referee of private competitions, its function the negative one of "saving" and "preventing." To sophisticated observers it sometimes seemed that the new President, like the earlier Roosevelt, was "pure act," but at least he arrived on the scene at a time when the public was clamoring for action. Through word and deed the new administration proclaimed that the function of government is to govern and that it can operate positively, involving the direct participation of citizens, without losing its democratic character.

The "hundred days" placed new burdens on the Army. Dwight Eisenhower helped to tell about them as he worked on the annual report in June. "Time and again national leaders have likened existing conditions to those of war," the report stated. The government was engaged in a "powerful offensive against the forces of depression." As part of this offensive the Civilian Conservation Corps had been established in an act signed by the President on March 31, and the War Department had been assigned the task of assembling "approximately 300,000 men—more than were enlisted during the Spanish-American War—establishing them in a series of small camps in various and often isolated regions throughout the United States, and making therein adequate provision for health, welfare, and maintenance." As education, as a kind of dress rehearsal for wartime mobilization and recruiting, the assignment had been of particular value to the Army—and the report announced with justifiable pride that the assignment had been carried out with great efficiency, "in striking contrast to . . . the recruiting campaign carried on during the early months of America's participation in the World War." Members of the Officers' Reserve Corps had been called upon to supervise the mobilization and command the camps. They had "obtained valuable training in mobilization processes and leadership."

But the Army continued on a near-starvation budgetary diet. The emergency duties imposed upon it prevented its satisfactory discharge of its basic defense missions. The report went on to speak of a serious shortage of officers for assignment to the R.O.T.C., of shortages in matériel, of the effect of reduced appropriations on training efficiency and personnel, and (most interestingly of all from Eisenhower's point of view) of future trends in the organization, training, and equipment of the Army. With the writing of this latter section Eisenhower had much to do. He made a brief historical survey of the effect which changes in weapons have had on tactics and on the organization of armies. ". . . the only unchanging element in armies is man himself." He and his colleagues analyzed the probable future, in terms of organization and tactics, of the Infantry, the Cavalry, the Field Artillery, and the Air Corps. "For the hand-operated magazine rifle with which these [infantry] units are now armed, there will eventually be substituted semi-automatic shoulder weapons and very light machine guns. . . . The infantry will be enabled to minimize losses by a greater dispersion of its personnel in forward echelons." As for the Cavalry, "The time has . . . arrived when [this] arm must either replace or assist the horse as a means of transportation or else pass into the limbo of discarded military formations." Motorization and mechanization were forecast. Virtually the same thing was true of the Field Artillery. "Within recent years there has been developed an artillery carriage that makes possible the towing of field guns at high speed without damage to their delicate mechanisms." The Air Corps, in any war of the future, "will be called upon to carry a burden demanding efficiency, morale, and numbers." The War Department "has sacrificed much else that is required in a well-balanced defense program, with the result that no other arm or service of our Army is relatively so well prepared as the Air Corps.

"To sum up: the inevitable trend in warfare is toward greater speed of strategic maneuver through maximum utilization of relatively fast machines for transportation; increased fire-power on the battlefield through employment of weapons of much greater efficiency, with a resultant wider dispersion in tactical formations; more power in the attack through utilization of combat vehicles invulnerable to small-arms fire and capable of cross-country travel; growing dependency upon air forces for information, for assistance in defence of the coast line, for attacks against hostile ground troops, and for bombardment of sensitive points in the enemy's supply organization. All these things point to the probability that any major war of the reasonably approximate future will see a swing away from the tremendous and ponderous combat forces that have characterized campaigns of the past 75 years and that in their place will appear relatively mobile, highly trained, and very powerful, though somewhat smaller, formations. Control of such units in combat would be difficult, if not impossible, with old methods, but fortunately, alongside other technical developments, there have been comparable ones in signal communications to facilitate teamwork and co-ordinated action."

In 1935 the New Deal extended to the Army. MacArthur, whose tour of duty as Chief of Staff was to have ended in 1934, was required by Roosevelt to continue in that position for another year, and Eisenhower remained with him. The annual report for the fiscal year ending June 30, 1935, was markedly different in tone and content from those of preceding years. In the appropriation bill for 1936 Congress at last heeded the War Department's repeated assertion that a strength of 165,000 enlisted men for the Regular Army was the absolute minimum "consistent with safety." Recruiting of 46,250 additional men was begun on July 1, 1935. The Regular Army promotion system was revised to provide for a moderate acceleration in the officer promotion rate. The authorized number of cadets at West Point was increased from 1,374 to 1,960. Ten million dollars made available through the Public Works Administration made possible the partial motorization of both the Regular Army and the National Guard. PWA also provided $6,000,000 for procurement of new-type ammunition and $7,500,000 for procurement of airplanes. The 1936 appropriation bill increased the allotment for Air Corps purposes by almost 66 per cent over the allotment for 1935. Some $68,000,000 of PWA money was provided for construction of barracks, quarters, and other, facilities, and an additional $6,000,000 made possible "a partial rehabilitation of essential coast defenses." The Army had initiated a procurement program in modern tanks and combat cars and in the new semiautomatic rifle. They were small beginnings— but they *were* beginnings. MacArthur could look back with justifiable pride upon his accomplishments in the closing year of his tour as Chief of Staff.

Thus Eisenhower's education in the top levels of command continued apace. So far as his personal association with MacArthur was concerned, it continued to be an education by contrasts. There is no doubt that he learned much from MacArthur about the technical aspects of high command. So far as the purely technical was concerned, the two men were in substantial agreement; but it is clear from Eisenhower's subsequent operations that the two had widely divergent views as to the relation of a general to his armies.

In a very real sense the mechanization of armies made for a socialization of command, just as "total war" in general must produce a "planned economy" for every nation engaged in it. In the organization of war, as in the organization of other phases of modern economic life, individualism of the old type was yielding ground to the collectivizing forces inherent in an advancing technology. Eisenhower may well have concluded that the day of personalized supreme command—of Alexanders, Caesars, Hannibals, or even Napoleons—was virtually ended. The rise of the General Staff (the United States did not adopt the staff system until 1903, long after most other great powers had done so) bore testimony to this fact. Modern armies, like modern big industries, were much too vast and complex to be mastered by a single brain. Like big industries, modern armies required the planned co-operation of a multitude of specialized functions, each of which involved a highly trained personnel. This meant that modern armies, even those of Mussolini's dictatorship, were of necessity "more democratic" than those of earlier times; it meant that high command itself had become simply one specialized function of the Army, a co-ordinating and directing function which must of necessity be handled co-operatively through a large staff rather than by a single man. The supreme commander could most accurately regard himself as "chairman of the board," his operations similar in many ways to those of the typically modern administrator in government or business—though of course the capacity of command, to impose his will by force, would be present for use whenever necessary. A flamboyant, colorful personality, capable of dramatizing its every action, might still be regarded in some quarters as an asset to a general, but Eisenhower was quick to recognize dangers in it. In a position of supreme military power, such a personality was all too likely to become the source of serious falsifications and palpable injustices. In so far as it made for anachronistic command systems, it was certain to become a focal point for unrealistic attitudes, for sentimental attachments to outmoded forms, and for debilitating disgusts in the minds of less sentimental subordinates. Given the opportunity, it could even lead to the kind of anti-democratic political activity which Eisenhower had noticed in the French officer corps during his assignment in Paris.

Given the opportunity . . . The opportunity was, of course, wholly lacking in the Washington of 1930–35. Never had the Army had less political prestige. Never had the military idea presented fewer attractions to the popular mind. When Harry Woodring, the new Secretary of War, suggested that the CCC might be used for military-training purposes, he aroused a storm of opposition. Why should the youthful unemployed, the very men who owed the least to society, be given first call to defend that society in war? Such a procedure would certainly amount to peacetime conscription on the most unfair of all bases, the basis of economic class; it was an essentially fascist approach to the unemployment problem; it was a violation of the American spirit. Every step of the way, the Army had to fight for appropriations, until the Bureau of the Budget came to be regarded by some officers as a greater enemy of our national sovereignty than any foreign power. The psychological atmosphere within which professional soldiers had to work bred in some of them a species of persecution complex, a hatred of "politicians" which was not lessened by the fact that it had to be hidden.

Yet Eisenhower himself may be taken as proof that this psychological atmosphere, this instinctive distrust by a democracy of the authoritarianism of the military, was not wholly harmful to national defense. It might even be argued, from the long view, that the Army gained in certain important respects from the civilian hostility it had to face. For one thing, a tiny army is flexible in its relations to matériel. It can adapt the Garand rifle without scrapping millions of Springfields, or adopt a new airplane or tank type without fear of censure because hundreds of outmoded models had been purchased a couple of years before. But perhaps more important than this is the effect which civilian suspicion has on the quality of military command. In such an atmosphere the kind of reactionary military egotism which the Napoleonic legend bred in the French Army is not likely to develop. (In those years the French high command opposed De Gaulle's mechanization ideas on the ground that too much technology among the rank and file might breed political "radicalism.") Overweening political ambitions, such as animated the Prussian General Staff, are bound to be thwarted. In such an atmosphere there is no possibility of forgetting that a democracy's armed services are strictly that—servants and not masters of the people. The whole psychological context tends to elevate to command the soldier whose relations to power are realistically humble; who, in Milton Eisenhower's phrase, has "a civilian mind"; whose professional attitudes are scientific and whose devotion to duty is truly selfless. In the 1940s we found that we had a whole school of such generals: Marshall, Bradley, Hodges, Vandegrift—and Dwight Eisenhower.

4

In those years, despite the increasingly unsettled state of the world, elevation to high command was far from Dwight's thoughts. If he could only exchange his gold oak leaves for the silver ones of a lieutenant colonel he'd be satisfied. The possibility seemed remote. The great difficulty was the existence of the "hump"— the large group of officers commissioned during and immediately following the World War. Normally Dwight might have expected to become a lieutenant colonel at forty-six and a full colonel at fifty, but as things now stood he'd be lucky if he held a lieutenant-colonelcy on his fiftieth birthday—he who had held that temporary rank and commanded a whole camp when he was twenty-eight. The Navy's promotion system, combining the seniority method with a limited selective process in the higher grades, gave a good man a much better chance.

Dwight said so when he met Swede Hazlett again. Swede came to Washington in 1935 for a tour of duty with the Navy Department, and he found his old friend mildly dissatisfied with his "lack of prospects." Dwight's brothers, Arthur and Edgar and Milton, were climbing steadily, "getting somewhere," and here he was, stuck behind a desk, a staff officer who'd probably never obtain a field command because his superiors rated him as the "cerebral type," a major who'd probably still be doing chores for general officers when he reached retirement age. Swede, who had just been promoted to commander, was sympathetic. All the same, he pointed out, Dwight might jump clear above field grade, and in just a few months, if war broke out. The Army would expand so much faster than the Navy that it would pull away ahead of the latter in its promotions. Dwight shrugged.

During this period he again came very close to resigning his commission. His reputation as one of the most knowledgeable officers in the Army, capable of expressing himself in a clear, trenchant prose, had grown steadily ever since his assignment to the Monuments Commission. It had penetrated to the headquarters office of a chain of newspapers. That office sent a representative to talk with him. The chain, it seemed, wanted to hire a military editor, someone who could write and who could be properly classified as an "expert" on military organization and war. The salary would range somewhere between fifteen and twenty thousand dollars a year! Dwight restrained himself, with some difficulty, from snapping up the offer then and there—but after he'd thought about it and talked it over with Milton he decided to stay in the Army. Something held him to his course—his "star," Mamie would have said. More probably it was his recognition that strange dark forces were now loose in the world, that the great war which Fox Connor had forecast might emerge from those organized forces of angry men in Italy, Austria, Germany, and Japan. Hitler, after the death of Hindenburg in the summer of 1934, proclaimed the Third Reich. Mussolini had threatened war if the Nazis moved into Austria. It was no time for a professional soldier to leave the Army.

Aside from his mild dissatisfaction with his lack of promotion, his Washington life was a happy one. When they returned from Europe he and Mamie and John had moved again into the Wyoming Apartments. Gerow was in town. Patton was living in a large house on a hill overlooking Fort Myer; the Pattons and the Eisenhowers exchanged frequent visits. Harry Butcher, rising rapidly now toward a vice-presidency in the Columbia Broadcasting System, was, with Ruth, again almost a part of the Eisenhower family circle. Milton and Helen were now living in a large and beautiful home, a "show place" really with great sweeps of lawn and splendid gardens, in the fashionable suburb of Falls Church, which had been developed by Helen's father as a real estate project. (John, now in junior high school, loved the Falls Church house. "It's the only real home I've ever known," he'd say with the wistfulness of an army "brat" who had had no opportunity to attach himself to any locality.) There were dozens of other friends who liked to gather at the apartment to partake of the famous and stimulating Eisenhower hospitality. Whenever Dwight had extra work to do—and Mamie complained that he worked "too hard"; other officers, she pointed out, didn't work half as hard—he simply excused himself and went into a back room. The party went on.

Milton, as director of information for the Department of Agriculture, had survived the change in administrations. Indeed, the new Secretary of Agriculture, Henry A. Wallace, leaned more heavily upon him than former secretaries had done. A multitude of new agricultural agencies was being established—the Agricultural Adjustment Administration, the Soil Conservation Service, the Resettlement Administration—and older bureaus were being greatly expanded. Milton was called upon not only to expand his administrative role in the information field but (increasingly) to serve as a trouble shooter for the secretary and the President in the organization of new agencies and the reorganization of older ones. Like Dwight, he was in a position where he had to think in broad terms, taking into account not only the logical but the sometimes illogical human aspects of problems. The two men became fast friends. As boys, the differences in their ages had prevented their becoming well acquainted. In Washington they discovered that, for all their differences in interests and temperament, or perhaps because of those differences, they worked together wonderfully well as a team. Often Milton helped Dwight with the latter's writing assignments—mostly by reviewing what Dwight had written and making suggestions for revision, since Milton agreed with the War Department that Dwight was a remarkably competent writer.

They sharpened each other's wits in frequent arguments, particularly on the social and economic questions which were then foremost in everyone's mind. Though Dwight's political consciousness was by no means as far developed as Milton's, it had grown a good deal during his Washington years. In the language of the times, Milton viewed the world from a point "a little left of center." Dwight was "middle of the road." Hence their arguments fell often into the hoary pattern of idealism versus practicality, theory versus fact. The man who argues *for* change necessarily uses ideas as primary weapons; the facts, the elements of what *is*, are for him simply reflections of ideas he wishes to change. But the man who argues in favor of the status quo is inclined to substitute facts for ideas—and Milton was continuously amazed by the depth and breadth and detail of Dwight's factual information. Milton later confessed that he was often "embarrassed" in these arguments because "Ike knew so much" and pounced upon the slightest misstatement of fact, whether it invalidated Milton's argument or not.

One of these arguments, involving Earl and Edgar as well as

Milton and Dwight, achieved a permanent place in the Eisenhower family annals. Early in 1934 Edgar came to Washington as a representative of West Coast lumbering interests to help draw up a lumber code under the NRA. He had a fifty-dollar-a-day expense account. Immediately Dwight wrote to Earl, suggesting that the latter come down to Washington for a "reunion." In April of 1933 Earl had married a slender, dark-eyed girl named Kathryn (Kay) Snyder, daughter of the founder of the Connellsville, Pennsylvania, newspaper. He was eager to have Kay meet his brothers, and the two drove down through a blinding snowstorm which nearly stalled them a dozen times. The reunion, they agreed later, was more than worth all the hazards of the trip. The argument, which seems to have generated more heat than light, took place in Milton's house and centered on the New Deal. Edgar's assertive individualism was outraged by the Roosevelt "experiments"—and Dwight, for purposes of argument, sided with Edgar. Earl in those days was strongly pro-Roosevelt—so strongly so that Edgar charged him with being as "red" politically as he was of hair—and Milton backed him up. The argument lasted into the wee small hours.

Every autumn Dwight followed the fortunes of the Army football team with fanatical interest. On Saturday afternoons the crowd used to gather either at the Falls Church house or in Dwight's apartment to listen to radio reports of the games. Always Dwight had on hand a large diagram of the football field, on which he traced out in elaborate detail the individual plays.

His intimates of these years regarded him with more than affection. From his mother he had inherited a capacity for kindling enthusiasm in his associates; he himself found life so interesting. He was gentle, boyish, carefully regardful of other people, utterly simple in his personal tastes. Perhaps there was an element of surprise in the reactions of new acquaintances toward him; perhaps it was the surprise element which first bound them to him in delighted loyalty. Somehow one did not expect such gentle kindliness from a man so deep of chest and voice, so tough-minded, so obviously dangerous to an enemy. Never was a strong man less assertive in an egotistic way. He commanded respect, not by selfish force but through selfless example. He gave of himself without stint and without regard for recompense. He went to great lengths to please his friends. He never forgot an anniversary within the family, even in the busiest times. Always he sent flowers to Mamie on the birthday of Icky, their first-born son who had died. . . .

With John, his son, his relationship was beautiful to see. He had long talks with him, man to man, as the boy entered his teens, laying down a code of conduct which the boy followed without physical coercion. Remembering his own boyhood longing for sports equipment he could never buy, the father lavished on the boy gifts of baseball bats, masks, footballs, tennis rackets, and so on. He taught John the game of tennis, and in so doing taught a great deal more: about perseverance, self-control, the true nature of sportsmanship. ("I've seen Ike work at tennis hour after hour, knocking the ball against a wall, trying to learn a certain shot," Mamie once said. "Sometimes he got mad and butted his head against a tree, but he always went back to the tennis. He wouldn't give up until he'd learned.") In a curious way the boy, who was strongly drawn to his uncle Milton (whom he resembled in many ways), both loved and feared his father. Though Dwight never laid a hand on his son, the boy sensed tremendous force held in abeyance and knew that a conflict of wills would end in disaster for him. Sometimes, in the normal healthy fashion, he resented his father's domination, but there was no one else in the world whose good opinion he valued so highly.

It was all as Ida had told Mamie it would be, back in July 1916. The family was patriarchal, like those of the Eisenhower forebears. But the paternalism was as wise and kind as it was strong, stimulating rather than stifling to life, and Mamie, who willingly supported it, lived happily under it.

CHAPTER IV

On the Eve of Glory

THE "GOLDEN GLOW"[1] had become as tarnished brass, corroded in the acid of harsh realism. Gone was the mood of happy irresponsibility which had enabled the "intelligentsia" to poke fun at almost everything which common men took seriously. It was no longer considered "smart" to sneer at the democratic ideal, at social reformers, at humanitarianism. To those who had believed most strongly in the Harding-Coolidge-Hoover prosperity it sometimes seemed that the very foundations of order, not only in society but in mind, had fled. The high priests of that prosperity—bankers, brokers, great industrialists, chamber of commerce executives—were for the time being cast into the limbo of false prophets. When Roosevelt took the country off the gold standard and devalued the dollar without "wrecking the country" in so doing, it was almost as though the law of gravity had been repealed. Nothing was certain any more, absolutely nothing.

Looking across the seas, those who had been most attached to the old order could see little to comfort them. In the U.S.S.R. they saw one sixth of the total land surface of the globe—most of the "heartland" which Germany's mystic geopoliticians regarded with such longing—already embraced (or strangled, as some said) by socialism. If it was not the kind of democratic socialism which the American left wing had envisaged, it was at least a society that adhered ruthlessly to the two basic tenets of socialist economics: first, no individual could "own" capital goods; second, no individual could hire another and sell the product of that other's labor at a profit. There were those in America who shuddered when Roosevelt recognized officially that the U.S.S.R. existed. That, too, was a

[1]Phrase used by Charles A. and Mary R. Beard in *America in Midpassage*, Macmillan, 1939.

sign of the times: in the magic days of the "Golden Glow" one had denied existence to unpleasant things simply by *refusing* to recognize them. Through Litvinov in Geneva, the Russians were beginning to talk about "collective security" against "fascist aggression," but few Americans were inclined to listen with much sympathy. Those who did were "fellow travelers," dupes of the Communist party, objects of suspicious regard from right-thinking patriots.

Not even from the European enemies of socialism could the old guard draw comfort. Setting up a Western bulwark against Bolshevism was all well enough—and there were powerful Franco-Anglo-American interests which supported the move—but why did the "saviors of Western civilization" resort to pogroms and medieval torture chambers and a bestial anti-intellectualism which would have revolted an American gangster? Italian fascism had been bad enough, with its clubs and castor oil, but it appeared actually wholesome beside the dark horror which now spread across Germany. Mussolini's bombastic egotism, his wooings of the Italian people from balconies had had their humorous aspects; there was nothing humorous at all about Hitler. Free enterprise might still exist to some extent under Mussolini, though an American had difficulty recognizing it, but if there were freedom of any kind under the Nazis after the "blood purge," no honest observer could find it. Some of the German industrialists who had financed Hitler now realized (or so some reporters claimed) that they had made a ghastly error.

As for the Far East, it was best not to look in that direction at all, now that Japan was on the march and the British (though unhappy India was a land ripe for conquest) refused to join with us to stop her. The spectacle of the white man's burden in Asia was not an edifying one; an increasing number of perceptive Americans claimed to see in it the seeds of World War II. It was too bad that we had got involved in the Far East, committing ourselves to an aggressive foreign policy which we consistently refused to implement. Foreign policy? Viewed on a large scale, it was even doubtful if we *had* a foreign policy. We had refused to join the League of Nations. We had also, through the Smoot-Hawley tariff, done a good deal to create an economic environment which killed the League. And now, after rejecting any kind of collective security which might have made it safe to disarm, we persisted in our refusal to rearm. An intelligent soldier in those days could not look at the Philippines without shuddering. . . .

Of all the shibboleths of the expansive era, none was now regarded with more popular disfavor than the doctrine of Manifest Destiny, particularly as it related to the Philippines. The Philippine experiment was considered by many Americans to be a dismal failure. Even in the most golden days of the "Golden Glow" the Philippines had proved an embarrassment—and not only to a national morality which paid lip service to the "self-determination" of all peoples. Farmers and industrial workers were convinced that the Philippines were an economic liability. The former opposed the duty-free import of agricultural products in return for manufactured goods, and the latter opposed the immigration of Filipinos to compete with native-born labor on our West Coast. An immorality which was economically unprofitable must by all means be corrected. Congress determined to give the islands back to their people, going so far as to pass the independence bill over President Hoover's veto early in 1933. A comic spectacle followed. The Filipinos themselves, fearful of an expanding Japan, looked the gift horse straight in the mouth—and rejected it. Not until the United States took steps to guarantee Philippine independence against foreign aggression did the island legislators agree in 1934 to accept the status of sovereignty. After a ten-year period during which the United States must help them build their military defenses, the doubtful blessings of liberty would be theirs. From 1936–46 the Philippines were to have a commonwealth or transitional form of government, and that government was to be installed during 1935.

Thus was determined Dwight Eisenhower's next assignment, the next to the last chapter in his education for high command. Early in 1935 the Wyoming apartment and the Falls Church house were scenes of discussion as to whether or not Dwight should accept an offer tendered by General MacArthur. The general, upon mutual agreement of President-elect Manuel L. Quezon of the Philippine Commonwealth and President Roosevelt, had accepted the post of military adviser to the commonwealth. The appointment was to become effective upon the inauguration of the Quezon government and upon MacArthur's relief as Chief of Staff—and the general had asked Major Eisenhower to come along as assistant military adviser. It would be, for Eisenhower, a detached detail from the United

States Army. He would draw extra pay from the Philippine Government. The professional problem of planning and establishing the defenses of a new democratic nation was an interesting one. After some weeks of hesitation the offer was accepted.

Even before he left the United States he was engrossed in the development of a Philippine defense plan which, it was hoped, would be incorporated in a National Defense Act. It outlined a defense policy, a territorial and administrative organization, and a citizens' military-training program modeled on the Swiss system of compulsory military service. The contemplated defense system "reposes responsibility for ultimate defense, not in a costly professional force that could conceivably be made the instrument of autocracy, but in the people themselves, the final repository of power in a democracy," said the plan. A small regular force—930 officers and 10,000 enlisted men—was to serve as the core of defense around which in an emergency a reserve force would aggregate, composed of men between 21 and 50, each of whom had had at least five and a half months of military training. Fast, small, relatively inexpensive torpedo boats would be used for offshore patrol, constituting virtually the whole of the Philippine "navy." Of the Air Corps, "fast bombers with a reasonable radius of action will be the principal item of equipment." The Command and Staff System recommended for the Army was patterned "roughly . . . upon those obtaining in the world's principal military establishments."

In September 1935 Eisenhower sailed for Manila. He sailed alone. Mamie and John were not to come until the fall of 1936, after John had finished junior high school in Washington. Dwight, of course, hated the separation from his family, especially from his son who was just at the proper age for father-son comradeship; he was never wholly happy without a real home life. But in the Philippines he found professional compensations for his personal discomfort.

A few weeks after Eisenhower's arrival President Quezon submitted the defense plan to the National Assembly in the form of a National Defense Bill. Immediately the proposal became a center of controversy. It was attacked by many political liberals who thought that an appropriation of $8,000,000 per annum for military defense imposed far too heavy an economic burden on 14,-000,000 people whose per capita income was extremely low, who must make large governmental outlays for schools and roads, and who needed all the private capital resources they could lay hands on for the development of virtually untouched natural resources. MacArthur and Quezon defended the proposal in public speeches and press interviews, referring to the common defense as a "fundamental obligation of sovereign government," stressing the "economy" of the proposal in view of the "unsettled conditions" in China. The shadow of Imperial Japan lay heavy across the islands. The bill was passed. It went into effect on December 21, 1935, with the signature of the President.

Thereafter Eisenhower was tremendously busy. He was instrumental in founding a military academy, modeled after West Point, at the Philippine summer capital of Baguio. He had much to do with training, organizing, and equipping the First Reserve, composed of men between the ages of 21 and 31 inclusive; the plan called for training 40,000 of these men each year. He helped to devise the basic strategic and tactical plans for Philippine defense, plans based upon the doctrine that "a war of relentless attrition, of resistance from the water's edge to the farthermost retreat left available to a defending army, is the . . . purpose of any military unit that finds itself in the . . . situation that faces the Philippine military establishments." The strategy which MacArthur later employed for defense of the islands against Japan—including the retreat into Bataan—was worked out in detail during the period of Eisenhower's assignment. Caches for supplies which might enable defenders to hold out until help could arrive were located on the Bataan peninsula. The tactical training was designed primarily to achieve a "maximum speed" of concentration at any point where an attacking force might appear, to "hold the enemy under . . . the maximum volume of fire at every point where he is operating at a disadvantage, particularly at the moment he attempts to effect a lodgment on shore." The plan pointed out that the means by which tactical mobility is attained vary as widely as the characteristics of the terrain in which armies operate, and that to achieve it in a country of jungles and mountains, "obviously units should be relatively small, free of impedimenta that cannot be easily transported over difficult country, and trained to a minimum of dependence upon elaborate supply establishments and a maximum utilization of local resources for transportation and subsistence." Training must aim for the "conservation of ammunition, simplicity in supply, messing and camping arrangement, and development of the utmost endurance and hardihood among the soldiery of the command."

MacArthur and Eisenhower were convinced that after the defense plan had "attained fruition" the defensive situation in the Philippines would be strategically a favorable one. It was believed that the cost of reducing Philippine defenses after 1946 would be at least five hundred thousand casualties and five billions of dollars— far more than a conqueror could hope to gain from his conquest. As late as 1939, after Poland had fallen, MacArthur issued a public statement to the effect that a Philippine nation, after 1946, could defend herself successfully against an attack by Japan— though most of the statement was devoted to the argument that such a defense would almost certainly not be necessary. It seemed unlikely that Japan would attack because: (1) strategically, possession of the islands would "introduce an element of extraordinary weakness in the Japanese empire" by splitting that empire "militarily into two parts," and (2) the tactical difficulties of establishing an invasion bridgehead on a defended coast line were almost insurmountable. In view of later developments, the latter argument— which MacArthur derived partially from the Gallipoli operation during World War I—is of particular interest. The use of Gallipoli to support such an argument must have annoyed Winston Churchill, had he known about it. Churchill's assertion was that Gallipoli failed, not because of the inherent tactical difficulties of the operation, but because of the failure of high command to commit the weight of troops and matériel called for in the tactical plan. Eisenhower and MacArthur were themselves to prove time and again that invasion of heavily defended coasts is not only possible but, as executed under their commands, invariably successful. . . .

It was during the years in the Philippines that Eisenhower first gained, among those in high places, that reputation for "diplomacy" which later contributed so greatly to his advancement. Actually his dealings with the Filipinos were far removed from the devious indirection, the polite deception, the elaborately formal trickery which the word "diplomacy" has come to connote. He dealt with Filipinos as he dealt with all other men, on a basis of equality, sympathetic understanding, and unusual frankness. The Filipinos liked and trusted him because he liked and trusted them. He gave no slightest hint of the "white supremacy" prejudice which flawed the performances of many another American officer in Manila. Moreover, his understanding of the problems of Philippine statehood, even those having little relation to the military, was so profound that both Quezon and the American high commissioner, first Weldon Jones and later Paul McNutt, came more and more to rely on him.

Eisenhower's social attributes, particularly his talent for bridge and poker, stood him in good stead in his dealings with the President, who was an ardent bridge fan. Often Eisenhower spent the week ends on the President's yacht, the *Casiana,* where the men (the cruising parties were always strictly stag, save for the President's family) spent their time alternately between bridge games and bull sessions.

Eisenhower achieved a long-held ambition while he was on the islands. He learned to pilot a plane. Since he had to travel a good deal among widely scattered training cadres, and since the development of the Philippine Air Corps (including the laying out of air fields) was his "special baby," he could give Mamie excellent "official" reasons for breaking the promise he had made to her twenty years before. Besides, the new planes were a far cry from the baling-wire-and-canvas contraptions of 1917. Even so, his passion for flying came close, on two occasions, to costing his life.

The first occasion was in the autumn of 1936, soon after Mamie and John had arrived from the States. It had been decided that John should attend a school operated by Bishop Brent in the mountain city of Baguio. Captain William H. Lee, one of Eisenhower's good friends, offered to fly the boy and Dwight up from Manila in his light sports plane. The trip up was uneventful, but on the take-off for the trip back the plane was caught in a downdraft and came within a few inches of crashing into treetops along a mountain ridge.

The second occasion was when he took a plane up for his first solo flight. The plane was a two-seater trainer with dual controls, and when Eisenhower took it up a sandbag was strapped to the back seat to balance the machine. Somehow, as Eisenhower banked and looped at four thousand feet, the sandbag came loose and jammed down against the stick so that Eisenhower, prying back with all his might, barely managed to lift the nose enough to avoid a spin. His landing was steep and rough, but neither he nor the plane was injured. As soon as the sandbag was secured again, and really secured this time, Eisenhower went up again. He won a pilot's license in his forty-eighth year.

He was a "natural" in the air. Air Corps men told him so, and he believed them. He *felt* natural up there among the clouds, as though he were doing the thing he was best fitted to do. The wild, lonely freedom of the skies ("If you see something interesting you just drop down and look at it; then you soar up again—you can do anything you please") appealed to the individualism which had been nurtured in Abilene's cow-town tradition. John remembers how his father used to demonstrate flying at the dinner table, using a knife as a joy stick, and how his father tried to explain to Mamie what it was like up there. (Mamie, who had a slight heart murmur, was never allowed to fly.) His sensual pleasure in flying was reinforced by his professional interest in the air arm as one element of the "combat team" which, in those days, was just beginning to emerge as a military concept. He wanted to know what the airplane could do, both in tactical support of ground elements and in strategic bombing. Flying helped him to know.

The Eisenhowers lived in the Manila Hotel. They had a suite which looked out over Manila Bay toward Corregidor, across a harbor which was always teeming with activity. (All the great liners on the oriental run touched there; once the mighty German battleship, the *Scharnhorst,* was in the harbor.) Later, when the hotel added an air-conditioned wing, the Eisenhowers moved into it, into an apartment whose luxury, including a huge crystal chandelier, made Dwight feel uncomfortable. The apartment, of course, was a favorite gathering place for American officers and Filipino officials and members of the American high commissioner's office. In the summer of 1938 the Eisenhowers sailed for America for an extended leave. They visited Ida and David in Abilene. Dwight had long poker sessions with the "gang" in the basement of Joner Callahan's café, and he renewed his friendship with Bruce Hurd and Charlie Case. In Denver he amused himself by driving all over town in his mother-in-law's electric car, a museum piece with a maximum speed of less than fifteen miles an hour.

Early in the autumn of 1938 the Eisenhowers returned to the Philippines. Sometime during the following year Dwight and John toured the wild country of northern Luzon, enjoying a companionship more intimate than any they had known before. (John, going to school in Baguio, was separated from the family during most of

]251[

his Philippine years.) The boy told his father that he had definitely made up his mind to go to West Point. Dwight, though he claimed he was far from certain that a military career was the best one he himself could have chosen, was not able to hide his pleasure. It was good that the boy admired his father so much that he wished to emulate him. . . .

The climate in the Philippines was hard on Mamie. In the summer of 1939 she was thin and worn, suffering from stomach illness. Dwight knew that she must return to America. The work which he had come to do was now virtually completed. The Philippine defense system had been thoroughly planned, its foundations firmly laid. The training program was proceeding as satisfactorily as it could within the limitations of matériel. There were not enough torpedo boats, not enough motorized ground elements, far from enough planes, not enough of anything really—but Eisenhower had done all he could. He said so to MacArthur and Quezon. He had always regarded this as a temporary assignment. His real career was with the United States Army, from which he had been absent for four years.

The last days were both happy and sad. Quezon, Osmeña, and other top Filipino officials had begged him to stay, had even attempted to bribe him with all sorts of personal and professional inducements. Failing that, Quezon had attempted to "show his appreciation of all Ike has done for the Philippine nation" by giving Eisenhower a $100,000 annuity policy. Dwight, smiling, deeply moved, had refused. "But I want to see to it that Mamie is always provided for," said the President shrewdly. Still Dwight had shaken his head, saying as diplomatically as possible that taking care of Mamie was his job, and one he felt adequate to handle. In the end Quezon had awarded Eisenhower the Distinguished Service Cross of the Philippines, giving it to Mamie to pin on her husband's chest while Quezon stood by, grinning broadly, and the cameras clicked. . . . The President made a speech too. "Among all of Ike's outstanding qualities," he said, "the quality I regard most highly is this: whenever I asked Ike for an opinion I got an answer. It may not have been what I wanted to hear, it may have displeased me, but it was always a straightforward and honest answer."

There were parties, lots of parties. The last one was in the Eisenhower stateroom on the boat. Everyone came to see them off, even General and Mrs. MacArthur, who seldom took part in such gala farewells. Indeed, Mamie, feeling very proud, could remember only one other occasion on which the MacArthurs had come down to a boat to say good-by to an officer. The general and his wife stayed until the steward called the "all ashore," and they were standing on the pier waving when the boat pulled away.

2

The "Golden Glow"? It was history now, embalmed in scores of books, recognized as the emanation of a feverish world. In September 1939 that world went into convulsions—and Dwight Eisenhower, crouched beside his radio in the Manila Hotel, heard it happen. *Fox Connor,* he said to himself without surprise. *Fox Connor was right.* . . . It was then he had made his decision to go home as soon as possible.

He must also have engaged in some self-examination to determine whether he was ready for the role Fox Connor had predicted for him. At the moment his elevation to the grade of general officer seemed, certainly, a remote possibility, but it was by no means as remote as an outside observer might have believed it to be. Eisenhower knew that the long list of "Superiors" on his annual efficiency ratings, on file in Washington, placed him among the top dozen officers of all grades in the Army. He knew that the record he had made at Leavenworth placed him high on the Eligible List. Moreover, he was now only one step below the rank at which selection as well as seniority could operate to determine advancement, by the new promotion policy, even in a peacetime army. On July 30, 1936, he had at last been able to pin upon his shoulders the silver oak leaves of lieutenant colonel. If America were involved in the war he must be ready to assume tremendous weights of responsibility. The sense of dedication again flamed high in him. . . . America, he felt sure, *would* be involved, in Asia if not in Europe. Despite MacArthur's public statement a few weeks later—a statement probably dictated more by diplomacy than by conviction—there was hardly a military man in Manila who believed that America could avoid a clash with Japan. And had not Roosevelt himself said, in his Chicago speech of October 5, 1937, that if war came "let no one imagine that the United States will escape"?

The road to Armageddon had been clearly marked. Mukden, Shanghai, Peiping—the East Asia Co-Prosperity Sphere. Madrid,

Vienna, Munich—the New Order in Europe. One could not even say that this road was paved with good intentions. Good intentions there had been, certainly, but they had been frustrated again and again by what might be termed the great Liberal Fallacy: a failure to realize that evil is not just the absence of good but a powerful negative force against which good must define itself through struggle if it is to survive. The self-frustration of the political left had given the right wing free rein to pursue those policies which were culminating in the sweep of *Panzer* divisions across the Polish plain. Even now there were those in Britain and France and the United States who could regard that eastward sweep with satisfaction. The Nazi-Soviet non-aggression pact had jarred them (though not as much as it had jarred the political left), but they still believed that Hitler sooner or later would continue his drive all the way to the Urals and thus remove forever from the world the specter of communism. If Hitler did so, the diplomacy of the democracies—a diplomacy which had long since ceased to represent the majority of the people—would have achieved its crowning triumph.

But by the time the Eisenhowers sailed for America, in mid-December, the career diplomats were discovering that foreign affairs were no longer wholly in their charge. War, in the Clausewitz dictum which Eisenhower accepted, was "a continuation of politics by different means"—but the discontinuity in means was very sharp and clear. Generals replaced diplomats as the agents of foreign policy. Years later, on a bright morning in Normandy, Eisenhower himself, with a wry smile, told a reporter that a general's job is "to straighten out the mess that diplomats make, so the diplomats can do it all over again." When Hitler, after the swift conquest of Poland, made tentative peace proposals to England and France, the acceptance of those proposals was a political impossibility. Within the right wing itself an increasing number of people realized that Hitler threatened British and French sovereignty fully as much as he threatened Russian communism. Key officials in the foreign offices had at last got around to reading *Mein Kampf*. Chamberlain was on the wane; Winston Churchill was again a rising star.

Eisenhower watched events through eyes that were neither sharpened nor blurred by an ideology. Politics, in the ordinary sense of that word, was still not his job. Professionally he was concerned with means, not ends, and it was on the level of means that he saw

Poland as a continuation of Spain. Far more carefully than most of his colleagues, he had pondered the tactical lessons of Spain. What he saw in Poland was the application of those tactical lessons on a grand scale. During the latter half of the Spanish Civil War the Germans had for the first time made a practical application in modern terms of the idea of infiltration, using armored spearheads and aerial artillery. They had demonstrated that it was not necessary for armored columns to secure their flanks in the old style if those columns made full use of the speed of modern tanks. Having achieved a break-through, the armor fanned out behind enemy lines, cutting communications and crashing through command centers, creating such confusion that the enemy was virtually paralyzed. Meanwhile, the gap which armor had made was filled in and steadily widened by motorized infantry. A series of such breakthroughs, spaced a few miles apart, split the enemy into segments which were then rolled up into pockets of annihilation. The Germans had even carried out experiments in Spain to determine the minimum frontage of attack which could breach a line of trenches, concluding that a front of two thousand yards was sufficient to insure success. (At the same time the Germans made final tests of their political warfare methods. The United States and Britain placed an embargo on shipments to Spain. It was worth divisions of troops to the fascists.) The new pattern of war was made plain in Poland for all who had eyes to see. It had a name: blitzkrieg.

In its essence, of course, the "new" pattern was not really new. Eisenhower recognized as new only its implementation, the use of tanks and planes in a manner which he himself had in part forecast. What was it Denis Mahan had written? "Speed is one of the characteristics of strategic marches. . . . By rapidity of movement we can, like the Romans, *make war feed war.*" The reports which Eisenhower had helped MacArthur write had said much the same thing. The conclusion of the 1935 report, describing the conquests of Genghis Khan, might with small revision describe Hitler's Polish campaign. "He [Genghis Khan] insisted upon speed in action, a speed which by comparison with other forces of his day was almost unbelievable. . . . Over great distances his legions moved so rapidly and secretly as to astound his enemies and practically to paralyze their powers of resistance. . . . On the battlefield his troops maneuvered so swiftly and skillfully and struck with such devastating speed that times without number they defeated armies overwhelmingly superior to themselves in numbers." Speed was the essence of success. The American armies must be trained and equipped to achieve it.

In San Francisco the Eisenhowers took an apartment at the El Driscoe. Dwight was held over in San Francisco for several weeks, working on a command-post setup for the West Coast. Colonel Jim Byrom, of the 1914 class at West Point, who had been one of Eisenhower's good friends since the two had served together at Fort Sam Houston in 1915, was in town. He thought Eisenhower looked thin and tired and he said so. Dwight shook his head emphatically. He felt fine, he insisted; Mamie was the one who'd been sick. Of course the climate out there was bound to thin you down if you worked hard in it—and you had to work hard. There was so much to do and so little time. Byrom, who was to leave for the Philippines the following month, asked lots of questions. Yes, said Eisenhower flatly, the Japanese were getting ready to attack. Everyone in Manila thought so. There had been incidents; there'd be more of them during Byrom's tour. . . . The Philippines, after all, were like a spear aimed at the Japanese flank as the empire spread southwestward along the coast of China.

Byrom was willing to accept Eisenhower's judgment, but the country as a whole was not. It was like 1916, Eisenhower thought. The country refused to look facts in the face. Only it was worse this time because the danger was so much greater. What if the French Army turned out not to be the "best army in the world"? The French command, as Eisenhower noticed in Paris, was pretty hidebound, and it was facing an enemy who had demonstrated his ability to shape tactics to modern weapons. The Germans had thousands of planes, thousands of tanks, and if they used them through Holland and Belgium as they had used them in Poland the Schlieffen strategy might succeed this time, despite the Maginot Line. If it did succeed England might have to sue for peace unless we pitched in to help her—and God knows we needed the British Navy in the Atlantic. Japan was just waiting for an opportune moment to jump us. We needed our Navy in the Pacific. We weren't anywhere near ready, on land or sea or in the air, for the kind of war we'd have to fight. . . . Sometimes he lost his temper when his arguments aroused only bland, complacent smiles. (We could take the Japs in six months or less, people said. The Japs knew it. As for the French, everyone said that the Maginot Line was impregnable.) At Fort Ord, California, where he joined the 15th Infantry as executive officer in February 1940, people began to call him "Alarmist Ike."

The men of the 15th liked Eisenhower, however. By the time the regiment moved to Fort Lewis, Washington, in March, the new "exec" was immensely respected, immensely popular. He liked being with troops—he'd had far too little troop duty to suit him—and he knew how to handle men. His solution of the case of the feuding privates[2] caused the whole regiment to roar with laughter. He had ordered the two privates, who had hated each other for years, to wash a window, one on the outside and one on the inside. The two men had scowled at each other as they made vicious swipes across the pane until the grinning Eisenhower, standing by, laughed aloud. The laugh was infectious. The privates couldn't help grinning, first at him and then at each other. The feud was over. When the enlisted personnel complained about the manner in which charge accounts were handled at the Post Exchange the executive officer made a thorough investigation, decided the complaints were justified, and promptly remedied the situation. When a top sergeant, James Stack, found himself "in a spot" because his fiancée, a nurse at Tacoma General Hospital, had joined the Army as a lieutenant, Eisenhower fixed things up so that the two could be married without having trouble with the Army. One day when he was inspecting the kitchens the executive officer passed a huge pile of ground beef. He scooped up a handful, grabbed an onion, and continued his inspection, chewing alternate bites of raw meat and raw onion. The cook was awe-struck. "By God, *there's* a tough guy!" he said.

He *was* tough when he encountered laziness or inefficiency in his subordinates. On such occasions all trace of geniality vanished from his face. His deep voice came in precise, stinging phrases out of the corner of his mouth, and the stabbing gaze of his cold blue eyes seemed to cut right through a man. He was always fair, always humane, but he insisted upon strict discipline. There was nothing slack about his command.

Fort Lewis was only fifteen miles south of Tacoma, where the law firm of Eisenhower, Hunter, and Ramsdell was prospering mightily. Dwight and Edgar saw a lot of each other, and when they were together they had, as Mamie said, "a regular picnic." Edgar still

[2]*General Ike*, by Alden Hatch, Henry Holt and Co., Inc., New York, 1944.

liked to pose as the tough boy from the South Side, contemptuous of "sissy" refinements, loud in his opposition to the New Deal "experiments." His individualism was particularly rugged. He wanted no part of government controls. All the same he continued to shy away from that boxing match with Dwight continued to propose. He sought, with success, to divert his brother's energy into less belligerent competitions, such as golf.

Edgar grew enormously fond of John, who was now a junior in high school. The boy was a quiet, modest, clean-cut chap, with charming and rather old-fashioned manners. He said "sir" when he addressed his elders; he had none of the stridently self-assertive manner which characterized so many children of the "jazz age." Anyone could see that he had been well reared. Neither his father nor his mother had subscribed to the new-fangled notion that inhibitions were, per se, bad. They had insisted upon discipline, *self-*discipline, an obedience of standards understood and accepted. Discipline implied the inhibition of certain impulses, of course, but it also made for significant reserves of thought and energy; it made for a resilience of character.

John was by nature more introspective than Edgar or Dwight had been at the same age, and he was less of an athlete. He had grown very fast during his years in the Philippines, grown straight up without filling out much. He was a wee bit taller than his father, and very slender. In temperament he reminded Mamie more and more of his uncle Milton—and, like Milton, he was interested in journalism. If he ever wavered from the decision he had made to attend West Point it was because he thought sometimes that he'd like to make journalism his profession. He confessed shyly that he had tried to write some descriptions of his experiences in the Philippines, and he hoped someday to write an article based on those experiences which a magazine would buy. The boy was obviously intelligent. Edgar thought him brilliant.

One Sunday, when Dwight and Mamie and John were visiting in Edgar's home, Edgar laid a proposition before the boy. The law firm, Edgar said, was a prosperous one and he, Edgar, had built it up from nothing. In a way it was his monument, and he wanted very much to have the name Eisenhower continue with it after he was gone. His own son was neither interested in nor suited to the profession of law, but John, as anyone could see, would make a splendid lawyer. John grinned but said nothing.

"Well, here's the proposition," Edgar went on. "If you'll study law I'll pay your way through the university and take you into the firm as soon as you graduate. You'll make a lot of money, and the law is an honorable profession."

John looked at his father.

"You'd better think it over," Dwight said hastily. "It's a mighty generous offer."

John agreed. He thanked his uncle profusely. He was tremendously flattered. But he had already made up his mind what he wanted to do.

"Going to follow in the footsteps of your dad, eh?" Edgar asked, frankly disappointed.

"Yes sir," John said. "I decided while we were in the Philippines, and now that there's a war on and maybe we'll get in it I'm more sure than ever. I appreciate the offer more than I can say, but— I'm going to try for a West Point appointment next year."

"Well, the offer will still be open if you ever change your mind," Edgar said.

John didn't change his mind. Dwight's legal residence was still Abilene, Kansas, and John sought a Kansas appointment, writing in the fall of 1940 to his father's good friends: Charlie Case, Charlie Harger, and other prominent Abilene citizens. They in turn recommended him to Senator Capper. Dwight, meanwhile, wrote to Milton, asking the younger brother if he could "manage" John's campaign for an appointment, and Milton replied that he would gladly do so. John was then sent to the Falls Church house, where Milton and Helen took him in charge. Milton took the boy to Senator Capper's office, introduced him, and obtained the senator's consent to John's entering the competition. Then John entered Millard's, a West Point preparatory school in Washington, spending nearly every week end in the Falls Church house. It was there, after he'd taken the examination in competition with thirty-five other candidates, that he received a wire from Senator Capper informing him that he had come out first. He scored 92, the highest grade ever made by a Kansas contestant. He entered West Point in the summer of 1941.

Meanwhile, stupendous events rocked the world and were reflected in Dwight Eisenhower's professional career.

Through the fall and winter of the war's first year all remained quiet on the Western Front. "Sitzkrieg," the British called it. A "phony war," said Senator Borah. The Russians, facing the Nazi hordes east of Warsaw, grew increasingly nervous. Stalin sought to treat with Finland for the "rectification" of the border barely twenty miles north of Leningrad. When negotiations broke down he denounced the non-aggression pact and sent his troops onto Finnish soil. In mid-March the Mannerheim Line was broken. The Finns sued for peace. Russian terms were surprisingly mild, but Leningrad was no longer menaced so closely from the north.

April 9, 1940. . . . Germany invaded Denmark and Norway. A new word was added to the English language: "quisling." Within three weeks Norway was a Nazi conquest and the proud British Navy, lacking air cover, found itself unable even to attempt to cut communications between Germany and Norway under skies dark with Nazi planes. Daladier had already been replaced by Paul Reynaud as French Premier—and now the Chamberlain administration tottered.

May 10, 1940. . . . Germany invaded Holland and Belgium. Neville Chamberlain resigned as Prime Minister. The King of England asked Winston Churchill to form a new administration. King Leopold of Belgium, who had heretofore refused to permit British or French troops to enter his country (he was "neutral," he said), now begged for aid, and the British Army with some elements of the French moved north. Four days later Holland was crushed and the French defenses at Sedan and on the Meuse were broken. German armored divisions, eight or nine of them, cut around the right flank and into the rear of the armies of the northwest, separating them from the main bulk of the French armies.

The Maginot Line proved to be of great help—to the Nazis. It immobilized a million or so French troops. On May 28, without consulting his allies, King Leopold surrendered all of Belgium and an army of a half million men to the Nazis, exposing a thirty-mile flank on the British left. The British and French armies in the north were virtually surrounded. They cut their way through to Dunkirk and held there. Next day the evacuation of the British Expeditionary Force, and of the French who were also trapped, was begun.

"The Miracle of Dunkirk," people called it. It was an operation which Eisenhower watched with an intense professional interest and from which he learned a great deal. The Germans sowed magnetic mines in the channel; they employed U-boats and torpedo boats there; they committed an overwhelming numerical superiority of air power to attacks upon the beaches; and they hurled masses of armor, infantry, and artillery against the whole of the land perimeter of the beachhead, constantly narrowing it. Yet the British, using all available seacraft and concentrating their air power (including most of the fighter strength which had been assigned to the defense of London), managed to evacuate in one week 335,000 men. Here was a colossal military catastrophe which yet contained at its core a victory, with the promise of victories to come. The R.A.F. achieved a clear-cut decision over the German air forces, shooting down four planes for the loss of one of its own. Hurricanes and Spitfires, skillfully piloted, proved superior in quality to the best German types. The British seized and maintained control of the air over the narrow beach for three crucial days, and that control had been decisive of success in the evacuation. But suppose this had been not an evacuation, but an invasion bridgehead against which the enemy was mounting a massive counterattack? Did not this operation prove that the narrowest of footholds on a hostile shore might be maintained if the invader could protect it with an unbroken umbrella of air power? Eisenhower was to ponder these questions deeply in the coming months, when *Festung Europa* had become a reality. . . .

It became a reality very soon after Dunkirk. On June 4 Churchill spoke to the House of Commons. "The British Empire and the French Republic . . . will defend to the death their native soil," he said. ". . . we shall fight in France, we shall fight on the seas and oceans, we shall fight with growing confidence and growing strength in the air, we shall defend our Island whatever the cost may be, we shall fight on the beaches, we shall fight on the landing grounds, we shall fight in the fields and on the streets, we shall fight in the hills; we shall never surrender. . . ." Ten days later the Nazis had taken Paris and were driving rapidly through Champagne. On June 16 Reynaud resigned and Marshal Pétain formed a new government. On the following day Pétain sued for peace. All western Europe was a fascist conquest. Britain, virtually unarmed save for a growing air force, stood alone.

But not *quite* alone. Roosevelt, standing before the American Congress on May 16, had called for large-scale rearmament of the United States. "So-called impregnable fortifications no longer exist," he said, referring to the Maginot Line which had just been broken.

"A defense which allows an enemy to consolidate his approach without hindrance will lose. A defense which makes no effort to destroy the line of supplies and communications of the enemy will lose. An effective defense by its very nature requires the equipment to attack the aggressor on his route before he can establish strong bases within the territory of American vital interests." On June 10, the day of Mussolini's invasion of France, Roosevelt said: ". . . the hand that held the dagger has struck it into the back of its neighbor." Step by step, under the bitter fire of honest isolationists and their home-grown fascist allies, the President proceeded to educate his countrymen in the realities of the world situation. In August he made a secret deal with Great Britain whereby, in return for a ninety-nine-year lease on British bases in the Western Hemisphere, the United States transferred to the British Navy fifty over-age destroyers. In the tragic summer of an election year, while the R.A.F. and the *Luftwaffe* fought out the Battle of Britain, Roosevelt dared institute peacetime military conscription for the first time in American history, and he called out the National Guard for one year's active service. On December 17 he created one of the decisive weapons of war: lend-lease. Three months later the Lend-Lease Bill was passed by Congress. America was to become the Arsenal of Democracy.

Eisenhower, watching the new green troops pouring into the encampments, braced himself. An army of 172,000 was to be expanded into an army of 1,500,000. "This is it," he proclaimed to all who would listen. "We're already in the war," he said, asserting that we had now committed ourselves to a British victory, or rather to a Nazi-Fascist defeat, and that our commitment could not be fulfilled without our active military participation. Japan, he said to his friend Charlie Case when he visited in Abilene, was now more certain than ever to attack. Abilene's unmarried young men would do well to enlist in the Army without waiting for the draft, get all the training they could before the storm broke. A good man now was virtually certain to get a commission. Officer material was desperately sought. As for himself, he looked forward to a field command.

But although good field commanders were scarce enough, first-rate staff officers were even scarcer. Eisenhower could not escape the classification he had earned for himself. He was the "cerebral type." On November 20, 1940, he became Chief of Staff of the Third Division, which included the 15th Infantry, with headquarters at Fort Lewis. This was the famous Marne Division of World War I (George Catlett Marshall, appointed Chief of Staff for the War Department in 1939, had once commanded a brigade of the Third), and Eisenhower, as divisional staff chief, proceeded to make an outstanding record. Major General Charles F. Thompson, division commander, began listing more "S's" on the Eisenhower efficiency ratings.

Again his colleagues were amazed at the amount of work he got done without loss of his genial good humor. He seemed to thrive mentally and physically on fourteen-hour days, filled with knotty problems. In the periods of doubt and confusion which were all too frequent in those hectic times he was a reservoir of calm, confident strength on which other men, including his superior officers, could draw without stint. He understood war. He understood men. He had a detailed knowledge of the organization of citizen armies, bolstered by his long studies of history. He had intellectual brilliance without a single trace of intellectual arrogance. And combined with these sterling assets, he had a selfless devotion to duty which set him completely apart from those ambitious officers who, in the swiftly expanding Army, sought opportunities for personal advancement. Inevitably the advancements came to him, but they proceeded, not out of egotistic assertions, but out of jobs well done. In March of 1941 (the month during which Roosevelt ordered seizure of thirty Italian and German ships tied up in American ports, coldly rejecting Nazi-Fascist protests), Eisenhower was made Chief of Staff for the Ninth Army Corps at Fort Lewis. On the eleventh day of that month he achieved his chief personal ambition. He was promoted to the rank of full colonel (temporary).

No promotion he received afterward caused as much jubilation in the Eisenhower home as this one. Time and again the father had told his son that he never expected to be more than a colonel, that if he ever pinned "chickens" on his shoulders he'd have achieved all that he consciously aimed for. Mamie and John were thrilled. They had a celebration. When the men on the post, congratulating Dwight, said it wouldn't be long before he had a star on each shoulder, he was angry.

"Damn it, as soon as you get a promotion they start talking about another one," he complained to John. "Why can't they let a guy be happy with what he has? They take all the joy out of it."

A few days later he left for California where the Ninth Corps was engaged in intensive training. All that spring he worked nights and days and Sundays. The news from overseas continued bad. Studying it with a strategist's eye, Eisenhower shook his head grimly. There was no doubt about it. For all their gallantry and their real successes in the air and on the sea, the British were gradually losing the war. In April, Hungary was definitely in the Axis camp, and the Germans added Yugoslavia and Greece to their list of conquests. Aided by withdrawals of British troops which were sent to Greece, Rommel's armored columns were able to drive beyond by-passed Tobruk to the Egyptian frontier. In late May and early June, Crete was conquered. German troops were filtering into Syria, and Vichy France announced that it would "defend the country against the British without German aid." Obviously a gigantic pincers movement, designed to conquer the Middle East and feed its oil supplies into the Nazi war machine, was proceeding with considerable success.

Only those with ostrich minds could deny that the United States was now in the war, a "shooting" war. On April 29 Roosevelt announced that American patrols were ranging two thousand miles out into the Atlantic. On May 3 it was announced that the United States Navy would shadow Axis raiders in the Atlantic and report their positions by radio to the British. Two million tons of American shipping were pooled to aid Britain. In mid-May the *Normandie* was seized with all other French ships in United States harbors, and food shipments to Vichy France were halted. On May 27 Roosevelt declared a state of "unlimited emergency" for the United States. On June 9 an American cargo ship, the *Robin Moor,* was torpedoed by a Nazi U-boat. A week later all German consulates in the United States were ordered closed by the President. . . . But America seemed to be populated with ostrich minds. Even the communists, who had been the first to recognize fascism for what it was, who had struggled for a Popular Front against fascism, now denounced the war as "imperialist" and attacked the British almost as vehemently as they had attacked Hitler and Mussolini. The spectacle of the *Daily Worker* and the Chicago *Tribune* joining forces on so vital an issue created in the liberal view a vast confusion.

Then suddenly the confusion was ended. On June 22, on a fifteen-hundred-mile front reaching from Finland to the Black Sea, the Germans launched their attack on Russia. From Stalin's point of view, the Nazi-Soviet pact was merely a device to gain time; the

Soviets had read *Mein Kampf* and took it seriously. The incredible Hitlerian dream was the conquest of all the world, and Russia was the chief obstacle to such a conquest. At the core of fascist ideology was a hatred and fear of communist Russia. American communists proclaimed that the character of the war had now changed: it was no longer "imperialist," and Hitler had lost forever the strategic initiative. Soviet power would inevitably destroy fascism, they said. Most American military men and newspaper "experts" failed to share the communist optimism. Some of them, pointing toward Finland and quoting Lindbergh's strictures on the Soviet air force, expressed the opinion that the Soviets west of the Urals would be crushed by October.

In Washington that month the American high command was making plans for the biggest peacetime army maneuvers in American history. Preliminary maneuvers, involving 77,000 men of Lieutenant General Ben Lear's Second Army, were already under way in Tennessee. Lear was far from satisfied with them. The chain of command was woefully weak, he said. There was a notable "lack of proper defense against motorized columns, especially medium and light tanks," and he predicted "disastrous embarrassments and failures . . . during battle" unless the over-all quality of command were vastly improved. General Marshall, Chief of Staff, and Lieutenant General Lesley J. McNair, Chief of the newly created General Headquarters, agreed. They were designing the great Louisiana maneuvers, in which the Second Army would "fight" the Third Army, largely to train higher commands and staffs in handling large forces under simulated war conditions. The top command, to put it bluntly, was in search of general officer material and hoped to find it in Louisiana.

Thus the choice of a Chief of Staff for Lieutenant General Walter Kreuger, commander of the Third Army, was a matter of considerable importance. McNair consulted his Deputy Chief of Staff, Mark Wayne Clark, whom Marshall had brought to Washington in August of 1940, after the tall, slender officer had distinguished himself during amphibious maneuvers on the Pacific coast. Since then Clark had traveled some sixty thousand miles by air over the country—observing, giving advice, and reporting on the training program. He was among those who strove for "realism" in maneuvers, which he took very seriously indeed. He had seen in action every officer who could be considered eligible for the Kreuger assignment, and of them all his unhesitating choice was Eisenhower.

The orders went through. Reading them, Eisenhower must have known that he was being put to the test. If he passed that test—well, he'd probably be a staff officer, sitting behind a desk far from scenes of action, for the duration of the war. It wasn't an exciting prospect; he still longed for a field command. He reported at Third Army headquarters, Fort Sam Houston, Texas, in the last week of June.

3

For both of them, but for Mamie especially, it was a kind of home-coming. San Antonio had always been for her a second home. She loved the narrow streets of the business district, the slow, warm rhythms of the Southern life, the memories of old Spain which dwelt in the architecture and the atmosphere of the town. Fort Sam, long famed as the "Country Club of the Army," was lovelier than ever, with a fine new officers' club and a new theater. She was glad to be returning to the scene of so many happy memories, a place where she had many old friends, now that John had entered his plebe year at West Point. She missed John dreadfully.

They moved into a large house on the post, a house of big rooms and immensely tall ceilings—a far cry from the tiny bachelor's quarters where she and Dwight had begun their married life. She had lots of room for her furniture and the mementos of foreign lands which they had accumulated through the years. Within a week the house looked as though they had lived in it always and would remain there always, and the "Club Eisenhower" was again going full blast. Dwight, of course, was working tremendously hard. Often he had to excuse himself from the company gathered in the living room and go up to his study, or back to the office, to work at night. The big house and lawn meant a lot of work for Mamie. A colonel rated a striker. She posted a notice on barracks bulletin boards a day or so after she arrived, and as the days passed and the couple who had been working for her left she began to wish, a little desperately, that someone would volunteer soon. In the last week of July her wish was granted.

Among those who saw the notice was a certain Pfc. Michael J. McKeogh, a native of Corona, L. I., both of whose parents had come to the United States from Ireland. His father, who had died in 1935, had been a sergeant on the New York City police force.

Young Mickey at that time was a bellhop at the Plaza Hotel in New York—a stocky, black-haired, blue-eyed young man, wise beyond his years in the ways of the world. He had been at the Plaza seven years when his draft call came, and he had just completed fourteen weeks of intensive training when he saw the Eisenhower notice on the bulletin board. A striker's job was "right down his alley." He would be able to earn a little extra money helping the colonel's wife around the house. He volunteered.

As he puts it, he liked Eisenhower "straight off" because the colonel was "absolutely straight" and "you always knew exactly where you stood with him." There were, in the colonel, no irritating reticences, and there was certainly no trace of the master-servant attitude to irk Mickey's rugged Irish independence. As for Mamie, she was and is, in Mickey's phrase, "a very gracious lady." The admiration was mutual. It wasn't long before the Eisenhowers wondered how they had ever got along without Mickey. He seemed always to know what to do without being told. As the youngest in a family of six children—four brothers and a sister—he had developed much the same social attitudes, the same habits of extroversion, which Dwight himself had developed. His loyalty was absolute.

Mickey was the first of the Eisenhower "official family" which, a year or so later, had achieved international fame. The second member was added a few weeks later. His name was Ernest R. Lee, but everyone called him "Tex."

Lee was born and reared in San Antonio. He was a salesman by temperament and profession. For six years he was assistant manager of a Metropolitan Life Insurance Company agency in Chicago. From 1937 to 1940 he was sales manager of a Chevrolet agency in San Antonio. He began his military career in the Reserve Officers Training Corps in a San Antonio high school and enlisted in the Reserve Corps after graduation, attending C.M.T.C. camps during the summers, studying at nights during the winters, until he passed an examination which gave him a commission as second lieutenant in the Reserve Corps in 1932. He had entered active duty at Dodd Field, next door to Fort Sam, in August of 1940, had done personnel work in the adjutant's office, commanded troops as a first lieutenant, served as mess officer, and in December of 1940 had been assigned to headquarters of the Third Army at Fort Sam. In June of 1941 he had been ordered into the office of the Chief of Staff of the Third Army.

He was a tall man in his early forties, bespectacled, built much like Eisenhower's brother Edgar, with receding black hair above a high forehead which was markedly narrower than the cheeks below it. He had never married. Years of selling had developed a hearty, bluff manner which struck some people as being a trifle insincere, but this failed to hide from Eisenhower's sharp eyes a something shy and nice in him. He was profoundly humble in his attitudes toward himself, profoundly loyal in his friendships. It was as though in human relationships he had been unable to rely upon his own inner sense of fitness: what seemed right to him so often seemed wrong to others. His private intuitions must often have played him false. He had had to learn how to get along with people by rote, by objective study. Indeed, he himself tacitly confessed as much. Years later he told a reporter in Normandy that Eisenhower, answering the phone, never said, "This is General Eisenhower," but merely "This is Eisenhower." He believed this to be profoundly significant of character. He confessed that he himself, while selling cars, had once been called down by his boss because when answering the phone he had said, "This is Mr. Lee." A "right guy," the boss had said, always leaves off the "mister."

When the new Chief of Staff arrived Lee expected to be removed from his office assignment. Eisenhower, of course, would want to choose his own assistants. Lee didn't mind. For a long time he'd wanted to attend the Infantry School to prepare himself more thoroughly for the command of troops in the field. But one evening, as Lee was giving his colonel a ride home, the colonel asked him a lot of questions: What were his plans? What had he done in civilian life? And Lee, who had conceived an intense liking and admiration for Eisenhower, began to wonder if, after all, the new Chief of Staff would want him to stay. Nothing was said about the matter until some ten days later, when Lee was again giving his colonel a ride home. Eisenhower said he would like to have Lee stay on in the office if Lee wished to do so. A colonel, of course, is not permitted by regulations to have an aide, but he has an executive officer who performs virtually the same functions as an aide. It was the executive's assignment which Eisenhower now offered to Lee—and Lee quickly accepted.

Meanwhile, Kreuger, Eisenhower, and Eisenhower's deputy, Lieutenant Colonel Al Gruenther, were deep in strategical plans for the great maneuvers. In early August the Third Army, three hundred thousand strong, moved out into the pine country of eastern Texas and western Louisiana for the intensive preliminary training. The Second Army was to begin field maneuvers in Arkansas on August 18, continuing them until the end of the month. In mid-September, in a thirty-thousand-square-mile area centered on Camp Beauregard, General Lear's Second Army (the "Reds") and General Kreuger's Third (the "Blues") were to begin the "war." These were not to be controlled tactical exercises with predetermined outcomes, but "battles" whose decisions would depend, as the War Department put it, upon "the resourcefulness of individual commanders." The commanders were not to be given previous information on the size and equipment of the "enemy." G-2 (intelligence) was to work out its problems unaided—and "realism" was to apply particularly to the capture of prisoners under combat conditions, each prisoner to be searched, questioned, and sent to concentration camps in the rear. The result of each action was to be determined by umpires who, after hoisting "stop action" signals, would meet on neutral ground to decide which force had demonstrated the greater strength. Only the grand strategical pattern, within which each army was to work out its own strategy, was laid down by the Washington high command. Kreuger's numerically superior forces were assumed to have established a deep invasion bridgehead on the Gulf Coast and to be acting as a covering force for other troops being pushed north behind them. Third Army's strategic objective was to split the United States by an advance up the Mississippi River. Lear's troops were assumed to be the advance guard of a defending army whose strategic objective was to drive the invaders into the sea.

Kreuger and Eisenhower were far from pleased with the showing made by the Third Army in the preliminary maneuvers. Generally speaking, company and platoon leadership was inadequate, as is inevitably the case in hastily assembled citizen armies. On August 21 Kreuger issued a blistering criticism of the handling of troops. There was evident, he said, a "stupid disregard of the danger of air attacks." Troop convoys had clogged the roads so badly that his whole army might have been destroyed from the air. Proper camouflage and dispersal of parked vehicles were lacking. Kreuger himself had flown over the maneuver area in a small plane, warning his men through a megaphone. The critique's effect was evident as field maneuvers proceeded. Gradually, out of sweat and grime, under a sun which burned in sullen anger through a haze of dust, the battalions and the regiments and the divisions emerged as solid elements of an army, and not merely useful group classifications. The Army itself emerged as a *unit* of force, capable of responding with fair accuracy to the mind and will of a commander. Its total life and movement could measure, for an observer, the quality of its general officers. Here was an approach to the end of training. Here was the product of a long and arduous process, nearly ready now for fatal tests.

Eisenhower was conscious of the training process as he watched the troops deploy over the Louisiana countryside during the second week in September. This army was far from the peak of its efficiency, but it *was* an army. A year ago it had been just a crowd of young men. Eisenhower grinned, remembering the green youngsters who had poured into the encampments only a few months before, assertively civilian in their hatred of the military. As a first step, individual civilians had been transformed into individual soldiers, physically hardened, competent to move and survive in hostile country, competent to use weapons. Then, through endless drill, individual soldiers had been trained to act in units of a dozen or so, as squads. Squads had been built into platoons, platoons into companies, companies into regiments, all in units of three in the new triangular divisions—just as bricks are built into a wall with each brick first molded out of soft clay and then hardened in disciplining fires. But these bricks were of vital clay, each one a personality, a power in his own right. In the whole process of disciplined combination the individual man with his individual skills remained basic. These were no man's tools. The commander mastered them as soldiers only to serve them as citizens—or, rather, to help them serve themselves. A citizen's army. The best kind of army, Eisenhower was convinced from his reading of history. He watched it, and G.H.Q. watched it: critically, hopefully, sometimes a little fearfully, knowing how much the national destiny depended upon it.

(The United States had occupied Greenland and Iceland in July, and Vichy France had allowed Japan to occupy Indo-China which, said Pétain, was "menaced by British forces." The United States and Britain froze all Japanese credits and instituted—at long last—a trade blockade. In August, Roosevelt and Churchill met on the *Prince of Wales* in mid-ocean to frame the Atlantic Charter. That same month the Army of 1,500,000 men, so painfully built up, threatened to disintegrate under the agonized gaze of the men who had made it. By a margin of only one vote in the House, the Selective Service Extension Act squeaked through Congress—and certain isolationists promptly proclaimed that OHIO now had a special significance among draftees: it meant "Over The Hill In October." A Nazi U-boat attacked the United States destroyer *Greer* in the first week of September, and the United States fleet was ordered to "shoot at sight" any Axis raiders operating in American "defensive waters." In Russia, Leningrad was closely besieged and Kiev was about to fall. In Des Moines, Iowa, at a mass meeting sponsored by America First, Charles A. Lindbergh charged that the Jews and Roosevelt and the British were conspiring to drag an unwilling America into the holocaust. Germany had already won the war on the Continent, he said, and the part of wisdom for the British was to seek a negotiated peace.)

On September 13 all preparations for the great "Battle of Louisiana" were completed. Nearly 800 planes—army, navy, and marine—had arrived in the area and were fairly evenly divided between the two armies: 370 for Lear, 400 for Kreuger. The 502nd Parachute Battalion was also on hand, assigned to Kreuger's Blue army for the first phase of the maneuvers. There were to be two phases, it was announced. In the first phase Kreuger was to attack. In the second phase Lear was to attack. Co-ordination of ground and air forces was to be stressed, and two different systems of anti-aircraft were to be tested. Lear's army was to test the new radio warning system, while Kreuger was to rely on a "spotter" system within which 16,000 civilians would serve as lookouts. Though Kreuger's forces totaled 250,000 while Lear had only 150,000, the latter had an ace in the hole in the First Armored Corps, the only complete organization of tanks and armored vehicles in the nation. The Second Army, during this first phase, would have 300 tanks in each of two divisions, and 2,000 other armored vehicles. The Third Army would have several hundred tanks, assigned to it from G.H.Q., but would have no complete armored division. Zero hour was scheduled for midnight, September 14.

But a storm of hurricane proportions was blowing in from the Gulf. On the thirteenth it narrowly missed the massed troops of the Third Army bivouacked near Lake Charles, and military aircraft fled the area. Zero hour was postponed. At five-thirty in the morning of September 15 Kreuger launched his attack, despite lowering skies and intermittent downpours of rain, and within a few minutes airplanes had made contact with the ground forces of the two armies, which were at that time thirty to sixty miles apart. Fatal pre-dawn accidents brought home to the troops a realization that they were engaged in a serious business. Moving up along blacked-out roads, four Third Army soldiers were killed in traffic accidents. In a collision between two planes in mid-air later that morning, a young pilot was killed. . . . By nightfall ground forces of the two armies were in contact on a sixty-to-eighty-mile front.

Four days later the first phase ended in a decisive victory for Kreuger, and for almost the first time in his career Eisenhower found himself given newspaper credit for work he had done. Drew Pearson and Robert S. Allen reported in their syndicated column that it was "Colonel Eisenhower . . . who conceived and directed the strategy that routed the Second Army." Kreuger's Chief of Staff, they reported, "has a steel-trap mind plus unusual physical vigor [and] to him the military profession is a science and he began watching and studying the German Army five years ago." Back in Washington, Milton Eisenhower saw the column, proudly clipped it and pasted it in a scrapbook.

There was certainly no doubt as to which army displayed the superior strategy. The Second Army seemed not to know what use to make of the great preponderance of armored strength which had been assigned to it. On September 17 Hanson Baldwin reported to the New York *Times* that the Red tank divisions were "strangely quiescent." On September 18 those tank divisions managed to penetrate the Blue lines at two points, but the Blue strategists had prepared for them. Kreuger did not commit his reserves until the main tank efforts were spent. The holes in forward lines were then plugged and the salients nipped off at their bases. Meanwhile, the Third Army was making full use of the tactical formations assigned to it, including the paratroopers who landed behind Lear's lines on the morning of the seventeenth to destroy a bridge. In the center of the line Kreuger's Fifth Corps, pushing northward, made notable progress that day. By the afternoon of the nineteenth it was all over. The entire Red Second Army was forced back against the Red River in a retreat that was nearly a rout. "Had it been real war," Baldwin reported, "Lear's forces would have been annihilated." One entire regiment and a battalion of the Second had been captured, both flanks were bent back, and communications across the river were imperiled by bombers. Blue planes dominated the skies. Lear's armor had been immobilized by a midnight cavalry thrust which had captured the gasoline dump.

The second phase began on September 24, hampered again—as Eisenhower's operations were often to be—by bad weather. The fringes of a hurricane swept over the swamplands, across the open fields, as reconnaissance forces of both armies probed toward one another and made contact. Next day the battle was joined. Lear was attacking. Eisenhower, studying the reports as they came in, made swift, sure decisions; he seemed to know Lear's plans in detail from the moment of the first action. The Blues took the shock of attack, yielded here and there, pressed in against the flanks of salients, and counterattacked along the whole front next day. Again Lear's armor proved ineffective—to the fuming disgust of George S. Patton, now a major general in command of the Second Armored ("Hell on Wheels") Division. The Blues' Second Cavalry Division drove deep scallops into the Second Armored one afternoon, threatening to capture large numbers of Patton's beloved tanks. In reply he strove, with one bold stroke, to snatch victory from defeat.

Moving at night along blacked-out roads, Patton made a 380-mile encircling march from the vicinity of Jonesboro almost to Leesville. Several men were killed and injured in traffic accidents, but morning found the Second Armored on a ridge which dominated miles of country behind the Third Army's lines. Eisenhower stared, unbelieving, when the report came in; he asked for confirmation and received it immediately. Pin-pointing the Patton position on his large-scale map, he asserted promptly and profanely that Patton *couldn't* be there. It was a logistical impossibility. Where could Patton have got the gasoline for such a drive? Kreuger agreed. Both of them entered vigorous protests with the umpires. Patton replied toughly that his tanks were on the ridge, he'd "won the war" for the Second Army, and "what the hell are you going to do about it?" What the umpires did was rule out that night march and force Patton to retire. Later it was discovered that the "Green Hornet" (the nickname Second Armored troops had bestowed on their commander) had made arrangements ahead of time with filling stations along the way to have his vehicles "gassed up" whenever they pulled in—and had paid for the gasoline out of his own well-stuffed purse. The criticism heaped on him for risking lives in a peacetime maneuver angered him, but it did nothing to change his mind. Armored divisions simply had to learn to move swiftly at night under combat conditions, he asserted, and the only way they could learn was by doing it.

By the afternoon of September 27 the Blue Third Army had again scored a decisive victory. Kreuger and Eisenhower were naturally jubilant, though they agreed with the McNair critique which found many deficiencies in small unit leadership in both armies. The Washington observers and the "war correspondents" representing the nation's press had high praise for Third Army staff work. They praised the organization of Third Army supply under Lieutenant Colonel L. R. Lutes, Kreuger's G-4, and the excellent ground-air co-ordination which that army had achieved. It was also announced that the armored divisions would be reorganized on the new "triangular" design, with fewer light tanks and more mediums. Marshall and McNair both made a point of meeting and talking with Eisenhower. They talked about him, too, to each other. . . .

Two days later Eisenhower received his promotion to the rank of brigadier general (temporary). The promotion came as no surprise. An army's Chief of Staff rated a star, and his staff work had been notably successful. He was nowhere near as pleased and excited as he had been when he received his "chickens." But he confessed to a pleasurable thrill when, later at Fort Sam, the Third Division staged a big review in his honor. Mamie watched him proudly as he stood —a big, confident, outward-looking man—accepting in a spirit of friendship the salute of thousands.

4

The pressure of work did not slacken during the weeks following the maneuvers. Driving home the lessons learned in Louisiana was a fateful process, and it must be quickly completed. Anyone who followed events with Eisenhower's clear-eyed, literal-minded honesty knew that time had virtually run out. The hour of decision was at hand.

The principal focus of public attention shifted, during those weeks, from Europe to Asia, where Japan was reacting violently to the British-American boycott. On October 17 General Hideki Tojo, known to be strongly pro-German, was appointed Prime Minister of Japan, and the United States Government ordered all American shipping in the northern Pacific to return to port. All American bases in the Pacific were alerted. On October 24 Colonel Knox, the

Secretary of the Navy, said flatly that a clash with Japan was inevitable. On November 17 Kurusu, special Japanese envoy, began conversations with Cordell Hull in Washington, but the tension was only slightly relieved. Meanwhile, the United States had, in effect, declared a naval war against Germany in the Atlantic with the passage by a narrow congressional majority of the Neutrality Act Revision Bill. Hereafter American ships would be armed, would be protected by United States warships, and would carry lend-lease supplies directly to Allied ports. The situation with regard to the Middle East had improved, thank God. British and Free French troops, after bloody fighting, had won Syria from Vichy France. The Nazis appeared to have suffered a diplomatic defeat in Turkey. British and Russian troops had met in Iran. In North Africa the siege of the British garrison at Tobruk had been relieved. And on the Russian front the Germans had been held before Moscow, had even been forced into retreat from Rostov through Taganrog. . . .

The first Sunday in December was clear and warm in San Antonio. Eisenhower, though tired by a long succession of fourteen-hour workdays, arose as early as usual. To Mamie's protests he replied that there was some paper work on his desk which he wanted to take care of, in preparation for Christmas leave. Mamie could hardly object to that. She and Dwight had been looking forward for many weeks to spending Christmas with John at West Point.

Over his breakfast coffee he read the newspaper and listened to a radio newscast. The prospects for obtaining his two-week leave seemed somewhat brighter this morning. Judging from the news, Americans were to have a few weeks of grace before the storm broke. Some of the news commentators were saying that the storm might never break, that as long as conversations continued in Washington there was valid basis for hope. Knox was still being criticized for his "inevitable clash" statement; he had jeopardized the success of negotiations, it was said. Eisenhower shook his head. America stood firm on her demands that Japan withdraw completely from China, terms which the Japanese Government was in no position to accept. There were reports of heavy Japanese troop concentrations in Indo-China. Roosevelt had just dispatched an urgent personal note to the Emperor of Japan, pleading for a peaceful settlement of the Far Eastern crisis—obviously a last-minute appeal.

A brief postponement of hostilities seemed likely, Eisenhower thought, but only a postponement. The war was inevitable.

On his desk at the office the calendar said "Saturday, December 6." He flipped over the page—"Sunday, December 7"—and set to work. At noon he pushed back his chair and brushed his hand wearily across his eyes. Two other officers were at headquarters with him. To them he said that he was "dead tired" and "guessed he'd go home and take a nap." He asked the officers to call him if anything important came up, and left. At home he told Mamie that he didn't want to be "bothered by anyone wanting to play bridge." He wanted sleep, lots of it. In his room he flung himself down upon the bed and went at once into a deep sleep.

It was an element of his remarkable nervous control, this ability of his to alternate periods of the most concentrated labor with periods of complete relaxation. Mamie and John had frequently been amazed by it. Again and again he'd come home from hard days of work, his face drawn and tired.

"Well, God knows I've done the best I could today," he'd say, and shrug off the almost visible weight of his responsibilities.

In a matter of seconds after lying down he'd be sound asleep, and even a short nap (when it seemed to Mamie he needed to sleep the clock around) left him refreshed and alert. Sometimes, when the strain was unusually great, he took a Western pulp magazine to bed with him and read himself to sleep. It never took long. Waking him up was a different matter. In this respect he remained the "Little Ike" of Abilene who was so hard to rout out of bed on the mornings when he had the fire-making detail. Luckily the phone beside his bed in the San Antonio house had a loud ring. It awoke him instantly, after he'd slept away perhaps an hour of the Sunday afternoon.

Mamie heard him answer the phone: "Yes? . . . When? . . . I'll be right down." A moment later he emerged from the bedroom, buttoning on his blouse with its gleaming shoulder stars. He told Mamie that the Japanese were attacking Pearl Harbor, that she'd better switch on the radio, that he was going down to the office and didn't know when he'd return.

At headquarters the officers were gathering, a tense, grim group. "Well, boys," said Eisenhower calmly, "it's come."

He stood now on the threshold of his fame, a large man who, symbolically, did not seem large until one saw him in perspective, with other men. Save when he was tired, he looked fully ten years younger than his fifty-one years, erect, broad of chest and shoulder, hard physically, giving an impression of unusual mental and physical poise. He walked with a springy step, poised on the balls of his feet. His arms, slightly bent at the elbows, moved always in a controlled swing. He carried his hands like a boxer. He was almost completely bald now, with only thin strands of blond hair around and across the back of his skull. He had a wide, mobile mouth, with a flat, slightly overhanging upper lip. His eyes were bright blue; generally they were as soft and pleasant as a summer sky, but on occasion they could be as hard and cold as a glacier. The direct candor of his gaze was one of the two things most likely to impress a man meeting him for the first time. The other thing was his voice, and his manner of speech. He had a deep voice and used it with authority. He was remarkably articulate, with an unusually wide vocabulary range, and though he spoke with machine-gun rapidity he chose his words carefully and well.

His mental life was as well disciplined as his physical one, and it still retained at its core many of the attitudes of the American frontier. It remained a factual mind, pragmatic, externalized in its interests, but qualified by a profound regard for men as individuals and by ideal standards of conduct which were the heritage of his parents' Christian piety. His knowledge of his profession was profound. He habitually measured himself by historical standards, reinforcing his keen objective awareness of present situations with a studied awareness of how other men had met similar situations in the past. He was mentally equipped, as perhaps no other American general since Lee had been equipped, for the tasks which were about to be assigned to him. He knew that he was ready. His self-confidence was so immense and so objective that it went by the name of "modesty"; he felt no need to bolster it with grandiose pretensions. There need be no discontinuity between the private and public aspects of his life. Unlike many public figures, he was not afraid to show his real self before the world. . . .

Heretofore the history of the nation and the history of the man had run for the most part in parallel streams, the man reflecting in his life the events of history and being to some extent determined by them. Occasionally the two streams had bent toward each other, had even touched each other briefly and lightly. There had been no real interpenetration. But now the two streams were to flow together, intermingling so closely that even the personal traits of the man became items of history. It was to become a matter of historical importance that he was a man of simple personal tastes, that he had a rugged physical vitality, that he could draw upon a vast store of factual information in his own and related fields, that he reacted swiftly to changing situations, that he had an almost instinctive distrust of ideologies, that he knew how to relax under extreme pressures. And since he was to achieve his immense fame at the very point where the doctrine of "national isolation" was finally repudiated, where the history of the United States became continuous with the history of all the world, he emerged as more than a national figure. He became a world symbol, a remarkably valid symbol of democracy in arms.

BOOK FIVE

Portrait of a General
(*From Washington to Tunis*)

CHAPTER I

The Man and the Event

AT SEVEN O'CLOCK on Sunday morning, December 14, 1942, Brigadier General Dwight D. Eisenhower stepped off the express in the train shed of Washington's Union Station. Carrying a small duffel bag which Mickey McKeogh (now a corporal) had hurriedly packed for him in San Antonio two days before, he walked with his habitual springy step toward the gate. He moved with a throng of people, for the train had been jammed. Not even an upper berth had been available for him when he boarded the Texas Special at Dallas on the preceding Friday, and he'd have been forced to sit up all night if Bill Kittrell of the Lend-Lease Administration had not offered to share a compartment. . . .

The urgent call from Washington had come through to Fort Sam in the morning. Tex Lee had taken it. Eisenhower must proceed *immediately* to the capital for a highly important staff assignment. Hanging up, Lee had glanced at his watch. Nine o'clock. At that very moment the last train which could make suitable connections in Kansas City was pulling out of the San Antonio station. He gave Eisenhower the message, then called the airport. But it was a day of lowering clouds above San Antonio, and sheets of rain were being swept by a high wind all across the Mississippi Valley. Transport planes for the East were grounded. Lee, feeling that his hard-earned reputation as a crack facilitating officer was at stake, became almost desperate before he happened to encounter Lieutenant Ham Martin of the Army Air Forces. Martin was sure he could get through to the North with his C-45. The problem was solved.

All the same, Lee had been in no joyous mood as he said good-by to his boss. His affection for Eisenhower as a man and his admiration for Eisenhower as an officer were immense. He hated the thought of separation. Watching the C-45 roar down the runway, he had comforted himself with the promise Eisenhower had made to him.

] 281 [

"I haven't any idea what they're cooking up for me in Washington," Eisenhower had said, "but if there's a spot for you in my office I'll send for you. You've done a good job for me, Lee."

Through a decade of crisis the national capital had become increasingly a magnet of tremendous range and precise human selectivity. Now, in this week following Pearl Harbor, a dark week marked by the loss of Guam and by declarations of war on Fascist Italy and Nazi Germany, the magnet was operating at full strength twenty-four hours a day. It drew to itself, along the railroads and highways and sky lanes, this industrialist and that labor leader, this doctor and that agricultural expert, the engineer, the scientist, the inventor, the trained administrator, the soldier—all the key people who, co-ordinating their talents and efforts, must form the sensitive directing brain of a modern nation at war. There was drama in the mere contemplation of so enormous a co-operative enterprise. Eisenhower had caught glimpses of it through the windows of Kittrell's compartment as the train moved east and north and east again, across the rain-soaked fields of the great valley, past sprawling new-built chemical plants, through vast troop cantonments, and along factory-lined rivers which glittered at last in sunlight on Saturday morning. "Of this vast machine the fighting forces are only the cutting edge. . . ."[1]

There was no room for forgetting that, among the millions, no one man was indispensable. Certainly there was no danger of Eisenhower's forgetting it. Of all those who crowded with him toward the gate on Sunday morning, none had less assertive egotism, none was less inclined toward a smug self-importance. All the way East, as he watched the pattern of total war unroll itself outside the windows, he had thought of himself solely in terms of the job which awaited him in Washington. What would that job be? He had told Mamie that in all probability he'd be working on the problem of Philippine defense. He had not told her that the problem, in his opinion, was hopeless. He had no way of knowing how much damage had been done our Navy at Pearl Harbor—he'd find out about that in Washington—but from all appearances the Japanese would be dominating the Pacific for some time to come. The most that could be hoped for in the Philippines was a delaying action, with the defending forces converging and falling back into Bataan ac-

[1]From the conclusion of the annual report of the Chief of Staff for the fiscal year ending June 30, 1935.

cording to the plan already worked out. Well, then, after the Philippines—what? Europe? His was a programmatic mind, always casting ahead to determine the outlines of the future, to prepare itself for all possible contingencies. Already in that mind the basic strategical problem was clearly defined. We could conduct a war of maximum offensive intensity in only one of the two great theaters of operation; in the other we must content ourselves for the time being with a holding action. Then which theater should be primary, and which secondary? He thought he knew the answer to that question too. Europe, he told himself. In Europe we have effective allies.

Approaching the gate, he suddenly grinned delightedly and shifted his duffel bag to his left hand. Milton Eisenhower was waiting, watching the tides of men pour into the ringing concourse of the station. "Hi, Milton," Dwight said. "I see you got my wire." And the two brothers gripped hands.

Milton's car was parked far up the Union Station plaza. He had orders, he said, to bring Ike out to Falls Church for breakfast. Helen had promised to serve fried mush. And of course Dwight was to live with them while he was on the Washington assignment, at least until he knew whether that assignment was "permanent" or not. Dwight, grinning, accepted the invitations as the two walked out into the chill December dawn.

"Only I'll have to check in at the War Department first thing," Dwight said.

Milton nodded. "We can do that on the way out," he said as they climbed into the car.

The Capitol dome on the hill above the plaza was tipped with pale yellow light. The plaza itself still lay in the shadow of trees and houses far to the east where the sun was just beginning to rise. An endless stream of taxicabs poured in and out of the loading zones; streetcars were lined up in front of the station; the sidewalks were thronged with people, half of them in uniform. In the gray light most of the faces looked drawn and tense. Everyone was in a hurry. It was as though every man could see written, in those pale skies above the Capitol dome, gigantic words of warning: *The country is in grave danger!* The chill air seemed to crackle with electricity.

As Milton skillfully threaded his way through the traffic onto Constitution Avenue, he gave his brother a word picture of government life in wartime. Washington had the jitters, he said. All sorts of dark rumors were floating around concerning Pearl Harbor.

Some people in high places hinted that an invasion of our West Coast was imminent and that the Germans had secretly prepared a large fleet of long-range bombers for attacks on our Eastern cities. Luckily for the country, the President remained calm and confident. Whatever one might think of the President's policies in general, one had to admit that in a crisis he was magnificent. Dwight would appreciate that fact in the coming weeks, if he stayed on the General Staff. Dwight nodded, thinking of Marshall, remembering what Fox Connor had said about the man who was now Chief of Staff. Fox Connor had always held Marshall up as a shining example of what an officer ought to be. Marshall was a lot like Dwight Eisenhower, unpretentious, absolutely democratic in his attitudes, thoroughly competent professionally, and a great leader of men. The two would get along well together, Milton predicted.

The car drew to the curb before the old War Department building on Constitution Avenue. The overpowering Pentagon Building on the Potomac Flats, next to Fort Myer, was still under construction; the department was still spread through a score of buildings in Washington, but the Secretary of War and the Staff Chief held forth in the Constitution Avenue building—and that's where Dwight would have his office. He hopped out of the car and walked briskly into the building. Ten minutes later he returned. He'd have a few hours of leisure before plunging into his work, he said. . . .

His hours of leisure were few indeed as the weeks passed, and he was profoundly glad that he could spend them in Milton's home. He needed a place of warm human fellowship where he could completely relax and refresh himself in the narrow periods between sessions of work. A happy home life could do more than anything else to keep him on an even keel when he was working under pressure—and he *was* under pressure. Always he was out of the house by eight o'clock in the morning, and often he did not return until eleven o'clock at night. He worked through the holidays and the week ends with scarcely a break. Moreover, he was working in areas of supreme decision, where errors might have disastrous effects on millions of people. Milton and Helen and their two children helped him, as he would say, to "keep his feet on the ground."

He grew immensely fond of the two children. Milton, Jr., whom everyone called Buddie, was tall for his eleven years, in the sixth grade at school, and seemed to have a penchant for accidents—like Dwight and Edgar at the same age. He was always falling out of swings or from high places, generally with more damage to his mother's nerves than to his own body. Ruthie was four years old, a rather thin, remarkably serious little girl who adored her uncle Ike. Every morning before Dwight left the house he placed some shiny new pennies on his dresser for Ruth, and every night when he came home he tiptoed down the hallway for a good-night look at the sleeping children. Sometimes, when his work had kept him from visiting with them for several days, he woke the children up just to talk with them.

Helen was frequently amazed by the kindliness, the constant thoughtfulness of others, which her brother-in-law expressed. She had never known anyone more gentle and generous and sensitive in his relations with people. If he were ever irritable—and he must have been sometimes—he never showed it. How so busy a man could find the time or energy to do the kindly personal things he did, she never knew. At Christmas time, for instance, he managed somehow to make a carefully selected list of gifts for each member of the family. He couldn't get away to make the purchases in person, but he sent a junior officer out with the list and saw to it that the right things were bought and properly wrapped. He was as tickled as a boy when he saw how pleased everyone was with the things he had given. One night in January, Helen was giving a supper party in the Falls Church house. Dwight, of course, couldn't come to the party: he didn't get away from the office until almost midnight that night. But in the late afternoon a florist's delivery truck drove up to the house and the driver carried in a huge bouquet of flowers, "for Helen's table, from Ike."

His relationship with Milton in those months was fruitful of more than personal happiness. After sixteen years in Washington, Milton was remarkably wise in the ways of government. He had developed a talent for leadership, a strategy for handling people, which was very similar in its essential features to the command technique Dwight was soon to make world famous. Time and again, Milton had been employed by the Secretary of Agriculture, or directly by the White House, on administrative assignments far outside his special field of information. He had engineered the Mount Weather Agreement, which became a basic document defining the relations between state and federal agricultural agencies. In 1938 he had, at Henry Wallace's request, completely reorganized the Department of Agriculture, whose mushroom growth since 1932 had resulted in all manner of overlapping functions and internal conflicts. He had been made Land-Use Co-ordinator of the department in 1937 and still served in that capacity—a kind of super-administrator of the Soil Conservation Service, the Forest Service, the Farm Security Administration, the Agricultural Adjustment Administration, and all the other department agencies which carried out action programs affecting agricultural land. In the coming spring the White House would give him a new job, one which (as he told Dwight) he anticipated with no pleasure. He was to head the War Relocation Authority, whose big assignment would be the movement of Japanese-Americans from the West Coast to interior camps. Such a movement was no doubt a sensible insurance against fifth-column activity, but it was certain to involve injustices.

Thus when Dwight and Milton talked together they could achieve a genuine, mutually stimulating meeting of minds. They shared a common level of administrative experience, however different in detail their separate fields of experience might be. Both of them had become accustomed to dealing with large affairs and had acquired those subtle mental traits which distinguish successful large-scale administrators from those whose professional activity has been more narrowly circumscribed. Both of them thought easily in terms of vast action programs and policies involving millions of men, and they knew, as those who have had no high executive experience can never wholly know, the harsh, lonely nature of administrative responsibility in times of crisis. Somehow being with Milton, communicating with him effortlessly and completely, made it easier for Dwight to carry the increasingly heavy burdens which were being assigned to him.

2

He was working, through those first weeks, as Assistant Chief of the War Plans Division, headed by his good friend Brigadier General Leonard Gerow, with whom he had attended the Command and General Staff School. His first specific planning assignment was, as he had anticipated, the "Pacific problem"—and the Philippines portion of it was as hopeless as he had foreseen. We had on the islands nineteen thousand United States Army troops, twelve thousand Philippine Scouts, and approximately one hundred thousand hastily mobilized and only partially trained and equipped troops of the Philippine Army. These forces were virtually "blind" and defenseless against determined air attacks, since our lack of sufficient radar and our failure properly to disperse our planes had enabled the Japanese to destroy most of the planes on the ground in the first few days. MacArthur did what he had to do. His withdrawal into Bataan was masterly. Thereafter he fought for time, striving to delay the Japanese advance southward until Australia could be made secure—and Eisenhower did what little he could on the Washington level to facilitate the holding action. From early morning until late at night he was involved in the million details of logistics. He strove mightily to solve the problem of supplies for Bataan, a problem complicated by the fact that thousands of civilians had fled with the Army into the peninsula.

Usual methods of supply having been frustrated by Pearl Harbor and by the Japanese sea and air supremacy in the West Pacific, Eisenhower was forced to fall back upon devices as bizarre as they were untrustworthy. He was given a special fund, approximately ten million dollars granted to the Chief of Staff by Congress, to hire what he called "pirates" to run the blockade. Perhaps "pirates" was too harsh a term to apply to the small shipowners and crews whom Americans approached in Java, Timor, and New Guinea; they ran greater risks than money could ever pay for, but they did demand huge payments, and they refused to accept them in checks drawn against United States funds deposited in Melbourne banks. They wanted cash. Arrangements had to be made to fly bales of money halfway around the world—across Africa and the Middle East and India—for delivery in Java.

Neither the money nor the courage of its receivers was sufficient to purchase success. Of seven ships which sailed from Australia, only three arrived in Cebu, and all efforts to transship to Corregidor the supplies landed at Cebu were frustrated by the Japanese. At least fifteen of the blockade runners, totaling forty thousand tons, were sunk or captured by the Japanese. In desperation, several over-age destroyers were assigned to the blockade-running detail. None of them reached Bataan. Only submarines managed to get through, delivering medicines and critical munitions and evacuating key personnel. By mid-January Bataan's troops were on half rations; a further reduction was made in March, when it became necessary to slaughter horses and mules for food. Eisenhower was sick at heart as he read incoming reports of the gallant action but certain doom of an army he had done much to develop and which contained many personal friends.

By the end of January the Japanese held all of Indo-China and Malaya and had begun the siege of Singapore. Everyone knew that Singapore was doomed. The naval disaster at Pearl Harbor had been augmented by the sinking, off the Malayan coast, of H.M.S. *Prince of Wales* (on which the Atlantic Charter had been signed) and H.M.S. *Repulse,* two of Britain's mightiest battleships. The Japanese had taken the great oil center of Tarakan on the northeast coast of Borneo; Rabaul and Kavieng in the Bismarck Archipelago and Kieta on Bougainville Island in the Solomons had fallen, and strong Japanese forces had landed on New Guinea. From all the battle fronts of the world, save the Russian, the news was dark. In Russia the Nazi hordes had received their first check and were now being driven back in the first Soviet winter offensive, but even here there was little reason for optimism. The Russian advance was a far from decisive operation, and it was slow indeed compared to the earlier Nazi blitzkrieg. Hitler told his people to expect decisive operations in the spring, when the Nazis again attacked; all of Russia west of the Urals might be a Nazi conquest by next year at this time. In North Africa, British troops drove through Benghazi and Agadabia, only to be halted and sent into an abrupt reverse when Rommel launched a surprise attack on January 22. A week later Rommel captured Benghazi. In the Atlantic, U-boats were sinking our ships as fast as we could build them.

Yet Eisenhower—though his first task was to help plan the defense of the Aleutians, Hawaii, New Guinea, and Australia, and to allocate just enough troops and matériel to safeguard these essential bases—was not thinking primarily in defensive terms. This was a fact which made a great impression on the Chief of Staff. Marshall saw in his subordinate a man whose calm confidence in ultimate victory was derived from a remarkably accurate appraisal of the Allied military potential; from a clear conception of the proportionate emphasis to be placed on sea, air, and ground arms; and from a profound sense of global strategy. Even before the arrival in Washington of Winston Churchill and the British Chiefs of Staff, a little more than a week after Eisenhower's arrival, Eisenhower had expressed his conviction that Germany should have number-one priority as enemy. He used the arms of his office chair to demonstrate his view of the problem in its simplest form.

"Here's Europe," he said, pointing to the left arm. "Here our enemy is faced by three powers—Britain, Russia, and the United States. And here's the Far East"—pointing to the right arm—"where the United States faces Japan virtually alone. The logical thing to do is certainly not to weaken the European front by withdrawing one of the powers, namely ourselves, in order to strengthen the Far East, where the most we can hope for is a fifty-fifty break for some time to come. We must concentrate our forces in Europe, where a decisive operation is possible in the not-too-distant future."

Marshall and Roosevelt, and Winston Churchill of course, had reached the same conclusion. Marshall was already a man in quest of a commander for the European theater, and he already had his eye on the new Assistant Chief of War Plans. He saw with approval, as the weeks passed, that Eisenhower did not limit the application of logic to problems of small size, that he insisted that certain effects produce certain causes, always and everywhere. And Marshall knew that this refusal to quail before magnitude, this ability to think clearly through situations whose very vastness breeds in most minds a species of superstition, is one of the distinguishing marks of military genius. Such genius seems often to be not so much a matter of intelligence as it is of character. Three fourths of it is self-control.

It consists, for example, of the ability to add twenty-two and eleven quickly and accurately, though shells are falling close by and one's associates are tense with emotion and each unit of the thirty-three involves thousands of lives. It consists of being able to recognize a slight advantage of one alternative over the other, even when a mistaken choice between those alternatives could result in overwhelming catastrophe. "For," as Jules Romains once wrote,[2] "it seems that certain perfectly simple ideas which at times appear to be no more elaborate than those which dictate the behavior of a policeman directing traffic at a crowded street intersection, or of a fireman distributing water from his hose on the various centers of a conflagration, become extremely difficult to apply when they have to work with masses of armed men, in an atmosphere of tense collective emotion, and in an access of personal responsibility." Eisenhower had this quality of genius: he could keep his head when the people around him were losing theirs. Did he have other qualities as well? How would he work with the British?

Marshall had an opportunity to let Eisenhower answer this last

[2]In his novel *Verdun*, Volume 8 of Men of Good Will, Alfred A. Knopf, 1939.

question in action, when the Prime Minister and the British Staff Chiefs arrived in late December. It was to prove of immense advantage to Eisenhower, and hence of immense value to the Allied cause, that he was present at the birth of the United Nations. On January 2, 1942, twenty-six nations, headed by Britain and the United States, signed a Grand Alliance against the Axis, pledging themselves to a joint conduct of the war and a fight to the finish. The pledge was immediately implemented by the establishment of the Combined Chiefs of Staff acting under the direction of their respective governments. Here was an entirely new international structure, a pooling of naval and military forces under a single unified international staff—and Eisenhower was quick to recognize its historic significance. "Probably no other Allied action, in the field or otherwise, has exerted as powerful an effect on the conduct of the war as [this] prompt establishment of a prescribed procedure for achieving unity," said Marshall[3] later. Eisenhower agreed and made, thereafter, virtually a religion out of the principles of Allied co-operation. He saw the first fruits of this co-operation—a kind of forecast of the European command system—before the initial meeting of British and American military leaders ended on January 14. General Sir Archibald Wavell, commander in chief in India, was appointed supreme commander of all American, British, Dutch, and Australian forces in the Far Eastern theater. As Marshall put it, "The co-operative results obtained in this desperate emergency by the creation of a united command established a firm basis for future combined operations."[4]

At several of the meetings with Churchill and Roosevelt at the White House, and at nearly all of the initial meetings of the two staffs, Eisenhower was in attendance. He had private conversations with the President and the Prime Minister, both of whom made glowing reports on him to Marshall. The latter, greatly pleased, was almost certain that he had found his man. Later on, when the Combined Chiefs of Staff Committee began to meet regularly in the Public Health Service Building, Marshall saw to it that Eisenhower, though not officially a member of the committee, was frequently called in. It wasn't long before the British began to urge, as strongly as diplomacy permitted, that Eisenhower be sent to London. Marshall, listening and nodding, was shrewd enough to

[3]General Marshall's Second Biennial Report, July 1, 1941, to July 3, 1943.
[4]Ibid.

be noncommittal. It tickled him, and strengthened Eisenhower's hand, to have the British take credit for "discovering" the future commander.

Meanwhile, the War Department General Staff was going through a drastic reorganization. The newspapers called it Marshall's "revitalization" program, asserting that his "policy" was to rotate top general officers between staff and field assignments. Actually the Chief of Staff was studying and testing his men, deciding which men were most suitable for field and which for staff, building up the strongest possible top command. This, as he profoundly realized, was an entirely new kind of war, and its successful direction demanded a new kind of supreme command. It called for a unique combination of soldier-administrator-co-ordinator-diplomat—with a generous dash of native political talent —in every top compartment. It also called, in Marshall's own words, for a "fundamental reorientation of the conduct of the War Department and its methods of doing business."[5] When Eisenhower arrived in Washington a committee headed by Major General Josept T. McNarney of the Army Air Corps was putting the finishing touches on a plan to establish three great commands under the direct supervision of the Chief of Staff—the Army Air Forces, the Army Ground Forces, and the Services of Supply (later called the Army Service Forces). Eisenhower's assignment to W.P.D. was one of the "preliminary moves or readjustments"[6] to the application of the plan. In less than two months Marshall appointed new Assistant Chiefs of Staff for G-1 (personnel), G-2 (intelligence), and G-4 (supply). Brigadier General Harry L. Twaddle remained as G-3 (operations), but he had a new assistant in Brigadier General Harold R. Bull, just as Gerow had a new assistant in Eisenhower. It soon became evident to Eisenhower that he was slated to replace Gerow as Chief of W.P.D. He began, perforce, to think in the global terms of the W.P.D. job.

The basic strategical agreement had been made by Britain and the United States, and it had been officially and publicly announced. Germany was enemy number one; she must be crushed before the Japanese war could be conducted at full intensity. Eisenhower began to ask key people what was being done to implement this basic decision, and he discovered that virtually nothing—nothing

[5] Ibid. Conclusion.
[6] Ibid.

specific—was being done. We were gathering our forces. On January 6 Roosevelt had announced to Congress the huge production goals: 60,000 planes in 1942, 125,000 planes in 1943; 45,000 tanks in 1942, 75,000 tanks in 1943. We were to have an army of 7,500,000. Yes, we were gathering our forces, but we had as yet no clearly defined ideas as to how and where those forces were to be used. All that was clear was that we were going to hit our enemies "where they are" and not wait for them to come to us, and that masses of United States troops would (as Roosevelt had told Congress) soon be stationed in the British Isles. The rest was a kind of nebulous haze out of which the War Plans Division, the strategy arm of the General Staff, must bring form and substance.

Among those with whom Eisenhower talked was Joe McNarney. Referring perhaps to Dunkirk (certainly Dunkirk was involved in his thinking), Eisenhower expressed the opinion that a cross-channel operation—England to France or the Low Countries—was really feasible, given air supremacy. Control of the seas was assumed, though at that time the Battle of the Atlantic was going badly for us. McNarney said he was convinced such an operation was feasible and that without it Germany could not be defeated. General Touhey Spaatz, who was soon to go to London to direct the daylight bombing of Germany, expressed the same conviction. Many armchair strategists long ago had decided that we must make a frontal assault on Germany, opening in a few months that "second front" which the Russians were quite reasonably demanding—but when men like Eisenhower and Spaatz and McNarney expressed such opinions they must be prepared to assume full responsibility for them, backing them with other men's lives. These seemingly casual conversations in Washington early in 1942 were events of historic importance, for they marked the true beginning of the strategic plan for the final defeat of Hitler. Shortly thereafter Eisenhower had gathered around him a small group of men to work out, in a very tentative and general way, the basic plan for a cross-channel invasion.

On February 16—the day British and Japanese officers met in the Ford Motor Company plant in Singapore to arrange the surrender of that naval bastion—Eisenhower was named Assistant Chief of Staff, in charge of War Plans. Leonard Gerow, now a major general, was named commander of the Twenty-ninth Division. From now on planning for the cross-channel operation was an "official" part of Eisenhower's job. He took up the matter with Marshall, who made some suggestions and told him to go ahead. Thus as the weeks passed the development of an invasion plan, a basic pattern for applying the mightiest military force in history, became the central theme of Eisenhower's professional life, crowded as that life was with the defensive problems of the Far East. During this period he rarely consulted with Marshall concerning the details of the plan. Marshall picked his subordinates with great care and then insisted that they do their assigned jobs with a minimum of supervision. Not until the first general plan was completed, some thirty typewritten pages supplemented by maps and statistical tables, did Eisenhower present it to Marshall.

By this time the two men were fast friends. It was clear that if Eisenhower became the Pershing of this war there would be no possibility, between him and Marshall, of the animosity which had flawed relations in 1917–18 between Pershing and the then Chief of Staff, Tasker Bliss. Eisenhower and Marshall understood each other completely. Both were remarkably selfless in their devotion to duty, unpretentious in their public manner, wholly incapable of petty bickerings through egotistic "assertions of authority." In temperament and basic interests, even in physique, they were closely similar.

At sixty-one Marshall was still sandy-haired rather than gray and looked fully ten years younger than his age. He was erect and vigorous; in his physical movements he displayed much the same kind of poised resilience as Eisenhower displayed. The two men were of almost precisely the same height, just under six feet— though, like Eisenhower, Marshall was so well proportioned that he did not seem tall. They both had such immense physical courage that they took it for granted in themselves and other people. When Marshall was a freshman at the Virginia Military Institute in 1897 (he never attended West Point) he was run through with a bayonet wielded by a sophomore during a particularly vicious hazing. He came very close to death in the hospital, but he never reported the sophomore and it never occurred to him to leave V.M.I. (The experience convinced him, he told a reporter years later, that he was tough enough to be a soldier.) Like Eisenhower, he loved athletics, particularly football, and on the V.M.I. team he had starred at tackle—the same position in which Eisenhower had starred in high school. Like Eisenhower, he had a consuming interest in history. He had loved to hike over the old battlefields near the school, memorizing the positions occupied by both armies, just as Eisenhower had done at West Point and Gettysburg. As Staff Chief, he habitually illustrated his arguments with historical references, particularly to the Civil War campaigns of Stonewall Jackson, who once taught at V.M.I. and is the great legendary hero of that school.

Marshall's large, blue-walled, air-conditioned office became a kind of schoolroom in which Eisenhower learned many lessons useful to him in the final development of his own command technique. He learned, for instance, a great deal about the most effective fusion of military and political leadership on the level of supreme command. Marshall's dealings with congressmen were far different, in tone and result, from those of MacArthur. Marshall never condescended, never presumed to issue "orders" to civilians, and never impugned the motives of his opponents on specific issues. He made no grandiose public gestures calculated to inflame the prejudices or outrage the convictions of those who instinctively distrust the military. He counted on the truth—frankly stated, persuasively argued —to win its own points, and when he secured the agreement of a former opponent on an issue he never gloated over it. In his view, such a "victory" was never personal; it meant simply that his former opponent, like himself, now recognized an objective reality. Once or twice a week he held frank, genial press conferences during which he took reporters into his confidence, giving them what he called the "whole picture" and indicating which portions, for purposes of security, could not be published.

He had, so far as Eisenhower could see, no enemies. An atmosphere of friendly co-operation, remarkably free of even minor irritations, surrounded him. Yet he gained this co-operation without sacrificing one iota of his effective leadership; there was never any question among his subordinates as to who was the boss. He commanded respect, without ever insisting upon it, by his integrity, his profound knowledge of his job, and his obvious commitment to forces greater than himself and of which he personally was but an instrument. Eisenhower noted with approval how Marshall permitted his subordinates to operate freely within the limits of their abilities, limits which he measured with remarkable shrewdness.

For instance, as the brief Washington winter gave way to spring, the area within which Eisenhower was supposed to exercise his own initiative was steadily widened. On March 27 he was promoted to the rank of major general (temporary). On April 2, after the McNarney committee's reorganization plan had been put into effect, Eisenhower was named Assistant Chief of Staff in charge of the new Operations Division which replaced the War Plans Division. The new section was designed to break down the artificial barrier between planning and executing; it had the function of co-ordinating, within a single vast pattern of force, the various fronts of our global war, and it served as the link between the Army and the Joint Chiefs of Staff (the unified command of the United States Army and Navy) as well as between the Army and the Combined Chiefs of Staff of the Allied Nations. Hence the very fact that Eisenhower was working on a cross-channel invasion plan, with Marshall's approval, indicated that Marshall was personally committed to such a plan and intended to persuade our Allies to it.

When the first draft was presented to Marshall he took it home with him, studied it carefully, and then called in Eisenhower for lengthy discussions of it. He raised every possible objection to it, and Eisenhower answered as best he could. Obviously Marshall was testing not only the plan but the man who had framed it, exploring Eisenhower's concepts and studying his reaction patterns. It is significant of Eisenhower's strategical judgment that this very first plan called for establishing beachheads, not in the Pas de Calais area which was only twenty miles from Dover and could be covered by fighter planes of even limited range, but in Normandy. Cherbourg and Caen were to be the first objectives. It was characteristic of him that he did not let the limited range of the Spitfires of those days prevent his conceiving an operation in which long-range fighters in vast quantity must be used. Development of a plan, he insisted, must be guided by an accurate appraisal of the capabilities of matériel—but it is equally true that the development of matériel may be guided by a statement of needs in a plan. Even this first tentative plan gave a general idea of the number and kind of planes America would need, of the number and kind of landing craft, even of the number and specialized training of troops. The basic concept, Marshall decided, was sound. The plan, sketchy as it was, could provide a basis for discussions with Roosevelt and Churchill and the British military leaders.

Obtaining Roosevelt's blessing on the concept of a cross-channel operation was not difficult. The President, certainly, was animated by the "spirit of the offense." He knew that national morale, though heightened rather than lowered by the humiliating defeats in the Pacific, would be difficult to maintain during a long period of inaction. He was receiving urgent messages from Stalin, who anticipated possible disaster in European Russia during the coming summer unless a substantial portion of the almost three hundred Nazi divisions (4,500,000 men) on Russian soil was diverted to a second front. He urged decisive action as quickly as possible and he was willing to abide by Marshall's strategical judgment that the area of final decision lay between the English Channel and Berlin. Marshall then pointed out that success of the project was impossible without the wholehearted co-operation of the British. Mere lukewarm acquiescence would not be enough. The President agreed. He promptly arranged to have his personal representative, Harry Hopkins, fly to England with Marshall, there to achieve a "meeting of minds" on the basic strategical concept.

On April 8 Marshall and Hopkins arrived in London and went immediately into consultation with the Prime Minister and the top officers of the British Army and Navy. Here Marshall found the going somewhat heavier. The British agreed to the cross-channel operation "in principle," but most of them made a sharp distinction between "principle" and "practice." As one British general expressed it later, there were high British officers who spoke of the coast of France as though it were lined with huge concrete pillboxes, spaced ten yards apart, capable of laying down an absolutely solid wall of fire. Churchill himself was definitely opposed to a direct frontal assault from the west. He had his eye on North Africa and the "soft underbelly of Europe," influenced apparently by (1) his experience in World War I, and (2) the fact that a huge German rehearsal of invasion operations against England in 1941 had been frustrated by the British, who ingeniously spread oil slicks across the water and ignited them with incendiary bombs. During World War I, as every reader of *The World Crisis* knows, Churchill strove repeatedly to initiate grand offensive operations through the Balkans, thus substituting strategic maneuver for the massacre on the Western Front. He had a penchant, as one British officer put it, for "back-door strategy."

The agreement "in principle" was about all that Marshall could obtain in London, but upon his return he and Eisenhower continued to base their long-range planning on the assumption that an assault from the west would be the principal method of accomplishing Germany's defeat. Whatever we did along the Mediterranean, or elsewhere, could be only a preliminary to the western assault. Orders were issued for ever-increasing numbers of landing craft, for increased numbers of long-range fighter planes, for greater emphasis on amphibious operations in the troop-training program. On May 29, though the Battle of the Atlantic had worsened for the Allies and though Allied air supremacy in Europe was far from achieved, Marshall said flatly in a West Point commencement address that "American soldiers will land in France." It was as though he sought to mobilize public opinion, which in Britain as in the United States was clamoring ever more insistently for a second front, behind the invasion plan.

Second-front talk was especially rife that week. It had been stimulated by the announcement on May 26 that the chiefs of the United States Army and Navy Air Forces had arrived in London to prepare for a "joint offensive" against Hitler. It was considered especially significant that Lieutenant General Henry H. (Hap) Arnold, Chief of Army Air Forces, and Rear Admiral John H. Towers, Chief of the Navy Bureau of Aeronautics, were accompanied by Major General Dwight D. Eisenhower (a "tank expert," the newspapers said) and Major General Mark W. Clark, Chief of Staff of the newly set-up Army Ground Forces. This significance was pointed up in Washington where Roosevelt, in his press conference, emphasized that the air offensive against Germany was not the "exclusive topic" of the London conversations.

The plane in which Eisenhower had flown the Atlantic landed in Scotland on the evening of May 25. In a Glasgow railway station at nine-thirty that night he was met by Lieutenant General Sir Humfrey Gale of the British General Staff, in charge of administration at G.H.Q. Home Forces. He was one of the most senior of senior British officers. The two shared a railway compartment to London and got along famously. Gale, a jovial, pipe-smoking man of precisely Eisenhower's age (the two were born in the same month of the same year), reported later that he had never met a man whom he liked better on first acquaintance. He spoke of the American's sense of humor, his simplicity, his candor, his soundness of judgment. It is to be assumed that as the train roared southward through the night the two men discussed, if cursorily, the invasion plan—but they discussed other things as well. Gale found his companion remarkably well informed in a wide variety of fields.

The impact of Eisenhower on Gale was typical of the Eisenhower impact on all the British he met that week. They were all impressed by him, just as Marshall had hoped and expected they would be. He was, as the newspapers said, an "expert" in tanks, in logistics, in strategy. The whole pattern of mechanized warfare, from the beachhead to the last double encirclement, including the use of air power, seemed to be clear to him. But what made this professional competence so remarkably effective, in dealing with democratic allies, was his tremendous personal charm, reinforced as it was by absolute integrity of character. It was impossible not to like the man. It was equally impossible to mistake his meaning when he talked. His ability to persuade, moving men through their inner conviction, stemmed partially from his articulateness but even more from the impression he gave (like Marshall) of being the instrument of a larger, objective truth. If little perceptible progress was made toward final agreement on the cross-channel operation that week, the idea was certainly given increased vitality through Eisenhower's efforts. . . .

A chauffeur was assigned to serve him during his stay. She was a tall, slender, dark-haired Irish girl named Kay Summersby. Born in County Cork, reared by a succession of governesses and in a Catholic convent, she had come to London with her mother after the death of her father, an army officer, in 1932. A sensitive observer could sense in her, even on casual acquaintance, some of that moody lyricism, that almost passionate mysticism, which seems to be peculiarly Irish, but it had been tempered, hardened, by her experiences in the war. She had taken the air blitz against London in about as hard and dangerous a way as it could be taken. She had driven an ambulance through streets of fiery terror, witnessed horror piled on horror. . . . Since then, as a member of the Motor Transport Corps, she had served in a drivers' pool from which chauffeurs were assigned to officers. Some of the other drivers bragged to Kay, after the assignments had been made for the American party, that *they* had lieutenant generals to drive while she had only a major general. She smiled. "But he's such a *nice* major general," she said, and if he returned to England on a permanent assignment, as some people said he would, she hoped she could drive for him permanently. Meanwhile, after Eisenhower had left, she drove for General Spaatz, whom she liked immensely too.

On June 3 Eisenhower, Arnold, and Clark arrived in Washington. With them was Lord Louis Mountbatten, commander of the famed British Commandos, who had come for tactical discussions with the Americans and the Combined Chiefs of Staff. This was reported as "significant" by Washington correspondents who pointed out that Commandos had learned, through bloody experience, many valuable lessons concerning amphibious operations.

It was time, Eisenhower and Marshall agreed, to establish a European Theater of Operations for the American troops now arriving in North Ireland and southern England by the thousands. It was time, in other words, to appoint a theater commander. Rather casually Marshall asked his assistant for suggestions, and just as casually Eisenhower suggested, tentatively, Joe McNarney. McNarney's professional competence was high and it was recognized by his colleagues, but he had given little evidence of the special qualities required for an accurate expression on a theater level of the spirit of the Combined Chiefs of Staff. Marshall said, in that casual conversation, that Eisenhower might be the man, but the Chief of Operations merely grinned.

"I thought he was joking, to tell the truth," he said later.

He was operating freely now, in the manner which Marshall demanded, and without further consultation with his superior he proceeded to draw up a directive for the theater commander, whoever he might be. He worked hard on it, stressing the principles of Allied co-operation, defining general objectives, and when it was completed he brought it to Marshall's office. This was on June 15, 1942.

He laid the directive on Marshall's desk.

"For the commander of E.T.O.," he explained. "It's something so important that you'll want to study it yourself."

Marshall nodded, picked up the directive, glanced through it. Beyond him, through the closed windows, Eisenhower could see heat shimmering above pavements under a blazing sun, but in the air-conditioned office it was cool—cool and quiet.

"Does the directive suit you?" Marshall asked. "Are you satisfied with it?"

"Yes sir," Eisenhower said, "but you may have some suggestions
——"

"I'm glad it suits you," said Marshall, looking up, his gaze
stabbing-sharp, "because these are the orders you're going to operate under."

"Me?" asked Eisenhower, puzzled.

"You," said Marshall. "*You're* in command of the European
theater." Without giving his subordinate a chance to recover he
went on: "Whom would you like to take with you? When can you
leave?"

Eisenhower was, as he confessed, "flabbergasted." When he first
came to Washington his greatest hope was that he would be given
command of a division, but when he replaced Gerow in War Plans
he had resigned himself to remaining for the duration behind a
Washington desk. If he had felt, deep down, that he could handle
the European command better than anyone else he knew—excepting
Marshall—he had never in his wildest dreams believed that the assignment would be given him. He had had virtually no field experience, and no combat experience at all. A long minute passed before
he was able to speak, he who was normally so articulate.

"I'd like to take Mark Clark with me," he said finally.

"You can have him."

"And—I'd like to talk with Clark before I tell you when we can
leave."

He left the office in a daze. When he reached his own office he
dropped limply into his chair. The silence there must have seemed
enormous, almost ominous—like the dead quiet which precedes a
tornado. Perhaps he felt it to be, already, the substance of a
greater loneliness than he had ever known before, walling him off
from the human intimacies so natural to him, so necessary to his
happiness. Then he called Clark. It was Clark's turn to go into a
mental tailspin, but he finally told Eisenhower that he could leave
in a week. A few minutes later Eisenhower called Marshall.

"We'll leave on June 22," he said, "if that's all right with
you."

3

Only occasionally—when he was transferred from one post to
another, or when he received a promotion—did his professional

life make direct contact with his personal, home life. For the most part, in pursuance of the policy which he and Mamie had laid down at the beginning of their married life, the two streams of his living remained separate. Now they came together in a head-on collision which, it seemed to Mamie, must destroy his personal life completely.

She had come to Washington, with the furniture, in early February. It had looked then as though her husband would remain in the capital for the duration. They had moved into an apartment in the Wardman Park Hotel and had remained there until early April, when at Marshall's suggestion they had moved into a house on Officers' Row at Fort Myer. Marshall himself was living on the post. This was Mamie's fourth move in a year, but whenever anyone asked her why she didn't just store the furniture and rent a furnished place she always explained that "Ike loves to have our own things to live with—he wants a real home." He needed one now more than ever, a home he could relax in, and she struggled against great difficulties to give him one. Servants, outraged by the irregular hours which Eisenhower's work imposed on the household, came and left in a steady stream until Mamie, though she was hardly strong enough for it, was doing practically all the housework herself. Nevertheless, she achieved her objective. What little personal life remained to him, buried as it was in Washington under the vast burden of his professional duties, stayed just as it had always been—filled with happy, human intimacies.

Ruth and Harry Butcher, Milton and Helen visited quite often —whenever their separate duties permitted them to come together. Butcher, now vice-president of the Columbia Broadcasting System, had enlisted in the Naval Reserve long before Pearl Harbor and had been dividing his time since March of 1942 between the Navy Department and Columbia. In June he had taken a leave of absence from Columbia, becoming Lieutenant Commander Butcher, U.S. N.R.—a full-time naval officer. Other friends had dropped in, making the Eisenhower home their favorite hangout, just as they had used to do. Mamie could believe that after the first hectic days were over and the country had settled down to the business of war the pressure on Ike would be more evenly distributed and their life could resume a regular pattern.

Then the bombshell! On the evening of June 15, after dinner, he made his announcement as undramatically as Marshall had made it to him at the office—and Mamie was as jarred as Dwight had been. She stared as he said casually:

"Looks like I'm going to London next week. Not just a trip this time. I'm to be in command over there."

"In command of what?" she demanded.

"Of the whole shebang. We're setting up a European Theater of Operations for our troops. I'm to command it."

He made the announcement to Tex Lee in just as casual a fashion.

True to his promise, he had sent for Lee in February, when he became Chief of War Plans. For a while Lee worked in the great map-walled war room. Later, when Eisenhower was promoted and rated an aide, Lee was appointed, promoted to the rank of major. He became the general's facilitating officer: arranging whatever trips the general must make, setting up the office files, hiring secretaries, and handling the general's personal accounts. He was happy in the job; he thoroughly enjoyed being with Eisenhower. But he still had "a hankering," as he put it, to attend the Infantry School, and he mentioned this fact to his boss soon after the latter had returned from the first flying trip to England. Eisenhower asked how long the school would take. Three months, Tex had replied. "Well," said Eisenhower, "let's wait and see what happens."

What happened was something Lee had never expected, any more than Eisenhower had. The two were driving home together one evening when Eisenhower suddenly asked how Lee was "fixed" for "O.D.s." Both of them were wearing lightweight uniforms in deference to the Washington summer.

"I'm pretty well fixed," Tex said. "I need a blouse."

"So do I," said Eisenhower, "and we'd better get them right away because we're going to England next week, you and I. . . ."

On the following day he made a request which legalists in the War and Navy departments found disturbing. He asked that his good friend, Lieutenant Commander Harry C. Butcher, be assigned to him as a personal aide. A general with a naval aide! It was unprecedented. But then, as Eisenhower pointed out, the war itself was unprecedented in magnitude and in many of its tactical formations. For one thing, a closer co-ordination of ground and sea arms was required than had ever been necessary before—and what could better symbolize that co-ordination than a naval aide for the commander of E.T.O.? Privately, to his friends, Eisenhower gave the real reason for his request.

"I've got to have someone I can relax with," he said. "Someone I can trust absolutely. Someone who isn't subservient. Someone who'll talk back."

The request was granted. If there was no precedent for granting it, there was an equal lack of precedent for denying it. Butcher, grinning, promptly dubbed himself an "amphibian."

Mickey McKeogh, promoted to sergeant when Eisenhower became major general, was still the general's orderly, but unless he obtained written permission from his mother, said Eisenhower flatly, he would not be taken to England. Mickey promptly obtained the permission and was, thereafter, tremendously busy looking after personal details of the general's departure. He supervised the packing of the general's uniforms and other personal belongings. He promised Mamie that he would write to her every week or two, to keep her fully informed as to her husband's personal welfare. He made arrangements for keeping the general fully supplied with Western magazines, a task less easy than one might think, since Eisenhower devoured the contents of Westerns with amazing speed. For instance, he had to spend an afternoon in bed that week, after he'd taken all his immunizations (tetanus, typhoid, typhus, smallpox) in one jolt instead of spreading them out over the normal span of three weeks. He called for Westerns to read in bed, and Mickey brought a huge stack of them. Next morning the stack stood beside the general's bed, apparently undisturbed.

"Didn't he like the selections I made?" Mickey asked Mamie.

"Oh yes," Mamie said. "He's read every one of them. You can take them away."

John came down from West Point on a two-day pass that week end. He arrived shortly before Saturday noon and would have to leave Sunday afternoon. Father and son knew they would not see each other for a long, long time.

They had a long talk together about John's future—should John go into the Infantry or the Artillery? Would he want to stay in the Army after the war or go into journalism?—and about his present life on the dedicated Plain. He was a yearling now, had grown even taller during the last two years, without putting on much weight. He was slenderer than ever. Cheerfully he admitted that he was no athlete. He wasn't heavy enough for football, nor fast enough for either basketball or track. He hoped to make tennis his sport and was trying out for the West Point tennis team, but he had small chance of becoming a star. (As a matter of fact, he never made the team but was appointed manager of it in his last year.) Scholastically he was doing respectably well, but his record, as his father's had been, was far from brilliant. His deportment was perhaps a trifle better than his father's had been, though he got into his share of mischief. He was liked and respected by his fellow cadets. He had intelligence, courage, perseverance, integrity, and no pretensions whatsoever. He was to be more annoyed than pleased during the coming months, when the spotlight of publicity was focused on him simply because he was his father's son. He hated the thought of being ticketed through life, denied an individuality of his own, by a paternal fame.

Not that he took no pleasure in his father's success. He was immensely proud of him. His direct blue-eyed gaze showed that when the two shook hands in farewell Sunday afternoon. A quick, firm handclasp, a casual "good luck" and "good-by," and John had turned away. Eisenhower stood in the front door, watching his son go down the steps. On the sidewalk the boy paused, then swung around to face his father. He snapped to attention, saluted. Proudly the father returned the salute—and Mamie, watching, overcome by the poignancy of the moment, burst into tears. . . .

On the following day, Monday, June 22, Eisenhower boarded the plane for England. With him were Mickey and Tex Lee. Butcher was to follow in a couple of days. The party included Mark Wayne Clark, Colonel Lowell Rooks (later a major general), and Colonels Clarence Adcock and Claude B. Ferenbaugh (both of them were later brigadier generals). Mamie was not at the airport to see them leave. Eisenhower had asked her not to come, had requested instead that she stand beside the flagpole on the parade ground, before Officers' Row at Fort Myer. From the window of the Stratoliner he saw her, a tiny figure waving frantically. She was soon lost to his sight, as so much that was casual and easy in his life (all that depended upon his anonymity for its being) was now forever lost beneath the upward, eastward flight of his fame.

Perhaps as the plane turned north from the Potomac for the great northern sweep across the Atlantic he remembered his farewell to Marshall.

"General," he had said, "I haven't tried to thank you yet."

Marshall had simply looked at him very seriously for a long minute. So much depended on this man. Only events could prove whether the man possessed those special qualities which Marshall believed he had sensed in him, that unique combination of gifts which could effect an actual unification of Allied commands. Then Marshall had smiled and put out his hand.

"Don't try to thank me," he had said. "You go over and do a job, and we'll have cause to thank you."

Do the job! The immensity of it, the unprecedented difficulty of it may well have weighted Eisenhower's spirit as he looked down upon the lonely sea. In one sense that sea, a vast, formless waste scarcely defined by distant horizons, was an image of his job. Somehow he must give form and direction to forces as enormous as they were, at that moment, amorphous on the command level. If he failed in any essential of his job, those forces could so easily turn upon one another in self-frustration before a determined enemy. He must have thanked God that he had Marshall's example to guide him and Marshall's unqualified support to sustain him. But even with that example and that support he would have to invent a new technique of theater command and then employ it as skillfully as though he had been long drilled in it.

The all-important thing, without which nothing else could finally succeed, was the spirit of Allied co-operation. It existed now in a nebulous, tentative fashion. To solidify it, make it effective in practice, he'd have to become, in his own person, an actual embodiment of it. He must live it, breathe it. His every word, every gesture must foster it in others. He had learned long ago how to gauge accurately the impact of his personality on others; he had learned how to use his personality as a tool; but he realized now that this tool could not be adequate for the present enormous job unless it was absolutely genuine. There was no possibility for successfully faking, over the long pull, emotions he did not feel, attitudes he did not hold. He realized, too, that in the very moments when he participated most deeply and decisively in the living present he must stand outside himself and judge himself as impersonally as he judged any other actor on history's stage. He must strive always for the long view, for perspective on himself and on the events in which he took part. A certain aloofness was essential. In violation

] 305 [

of some of the deepest needs of his character, he would have to become something of a recluse.

To maintain this necessary aloofness without losing his sense of immediate realities, he had already planned very carefully his personal life in London. He must live simply, because any unnatural luxury would introduce an element of the unknown, a distracting influence which might flaw his judgment in moments of crisis. He must maintain close contact, as close and personal as possible, with the troops, not only because that contact would bolster their morale but because it would help his own, help him to keep his feet on the ground. For the same reason he would have frequent correspondence with his mother and his brothers and the friends of his boyhood; he wanted to maintain his sense of continuity with the boy who had grown up in Abilene and with the life he had known there. He had wanted Butcher with him because Butcher would help him create, in the lonely sea of his responsibilities, an island of warm human fellowship.

Even so, and no matter how he strove to mitigate it, his loneliness must be immense.

His mother was lonely too. Last night he had called her long distance, to tell her good-by. Her voice had sounded lonely, despite the great pleasure she had taken in his call. She had wanted to know when he was coming home. . . . Perhaps as the plane roared into the night beyond Newfoundland he thought of her again and remembered sadly how death had shut, with utter finality, one doorway to his past.

The message had come to him in the second week in March. His father, David Jacob Eisenhower, who had made the westward journey from Pennsylvania so long ago, was dead following a long illness. Dwight, with the pressure of work upon him, had not even been able to go home with Milton for the funeral. All he could do was ask his aides to leave him undisturbed for a while, and he had shut the office door and sat there at his desk for two hours, alone with his grief.

They missed David Eisenhower in Abilene. That quiet, sweet-tempered, modest man had become a far more influential person in the town than he himself had realized. The Abilene *Reflector-Chronicle* ran a long obituary, with his picture, describing him as "a prominent citizen," telling of his long, unpretentious service to the community and of the six distinguished sons he had helped to rear. In recent years, until illness forced his retirement, he had held a position of great trust in the United utilities company, serving as chairman for the employees' benefit and savings plan. His sons were surprised by the size of the estate he left. Somehow, through the years, he had managed to save enough money from his modest income to keep his widow comfortably for the rest of her life in that white frame house at 201 South East Fourth Street.

When Milton returned to Washington he told Dwight that Miss Naomi Engle, an old friend of the family, had offered to live with Mother Eisenhower and that the offer had been gladly accepted. Mother could not bear the thought of leaving the old home. Naomi, the sons agreed, was invaluable. She would do as much as anyone could to keep Mother happy.

"But I feel so lost now," the mother told a reporter later that summer, when her son's fame had brought a rush of copy-hungry journalists to Abilene. "With them all gone now, nothing seems real any more. They're all so far away. About all I have to look at is their pictures."

CHAPTER II

The Basic Pattern of Command

The news from the battle fronts was bad. Once again the Middle East, that great oil-rich land bridge to India, threatened on the other side by Japan, was the objective of a gigantic pincers movement. The strategic pattern of an Axis world victory was only too clear.

In Russia the northern arm of the pincers was about to press down toward the Caucasus and west toward Stalingrad, through Krasnodar, Mosdok, Novorossiisk. Timoshenko's attack on a one-hundred-mile front in late May, from Volchansk to Krasnograd, had failed in its tactical objective (Kharkov) and, for the most part, in its strategic objective (to prevent or seriously delay the Nazi attack on the southern front). On June 10 the Nazis launched an attack south of Kharkov which soon wiped out the gains Timoshenko had made there. On May 23 the Germans had taken Kerch in the Crimea, and on June 7 the siege of Sevastopol was begun. By the time Eisenhower arrived in England, on June 23, it was evident that Sevastopol—that thorn in the side of the Nazis' south Russian drive —was neutralized and must soon be destroyed.

Meanwhile, in North Africa the southern arm of the gigantic pincers was thrust forward. On June 6 the British under Ritchie launched a counterattack against Rommel in Libya, an attack which became a catastrophe on June 13 when it ran into a tank trap, implemented by the new German 88-millimeter guns, at Knightsbridge. On June 20 Tobruk fell with a loss of 30,000 troops. The battered Eighth Army staggered back through Bardia, Sidi Barrani, Matruh, all the way to El Alamein, barely forty-five miles from Alexandria. General Auchinleck replaced Ritchie, worked valiantly to strengthen and deepen the Alamein line, but the line remained dangerously thin and Auchinleck remained strangely unpopular, not only with the British public but also with his own

Eighth Army troops. Egypt, Suez, Arabia seemed ripe for Axis plucking.

To counter the impact of these dark events on the public mind, the Allied governments had recourse only to the achievements of British bombers over Germany and to a promise of future offensives. On June 25, the day Rommel's forces pushed across the Egyptian frontier, both the achievements and the promise were played up for all they were worth in the British and American press. It was announced that the R.A.F. had made another thousand-plane raid on Germany, with Bremen as the main objective—the "most concentrated raid in all history." More important, for morale-boosting purposes, was the promise implied in that day's War Department communiqué.

The communiqué's text was bare and dry enough:

1. European theater:
The War Department today announced the formal establishment of a European theater of operations for the United States forces. Maj. Gen. Dwight D. Eisenhower, formerly assistant chief of staff in charge of operations division, War Department General Staff, has been designated as commanding general, European theater, with headquarters in London, England.

Somewhat less dry, more specific in its promise, was the statement issued by General Eisenhower himself:

I have been assigned to command the European theater for the United States forces. The formal establishment of a European theater is a logical step in co-ordinating the efforts of Britain and the United States.

Six months ago the Prime Minister of Great Britain and the President of the United States heartened the peoples of the United Nations by moving swiftly to merge the military and economic strength of Britain and the United States in a common effort.

At that Washington conference they set a more effective pattern for unqualified partnership than has ever before been envisaged by allied nations in pursuit of a common purpose. Only recently they have met again to bring combined action into even closer co-ordination.

The presence here in the British Isles of American soldiers and pilots in rapidly increasing numbers is evidence that we are hewing to the line of that pattern.

On that same day Eisenhower held his first press conference in London, talking informally and off the record to a host of British and American reporters. They felt his friendliness, were impressed by his grin and manner of speech. They were, perhaps, a little disappointed by the content of his speech. He gave, as the New York *Times* reported, "an excellent demonstration of the art of being jovially outspoken without saying much of anything."

But from these sparse texts newspaper correspondents in both England and America drew the utmost of significant inference. It was pointed out that the American general had arrived "fresh from conferences with Prime Minister Churchill and President Roosevelt," who were meeting that week in Washington. Early creation of a unified command, to weld American, British, and Canadian forces into a co-ordinated fighting team, was prophesied. It was recalled that only three days ago Harry Hopkins had issued a statement predicting a "mighty offensive" against Hitler "with a second, third, and fourth front." Perhaps deliberately, in an effort to counteract the gloom emanating from the fighting fronts, the public was encouraged to expect decisive offensives in just a few weeks, brilliantly led by the new American commander who was variously described as a strategical and logistical "genius," a tactical "expert" in mechanized warfare, and one of the "finest administrative brains" in the Army.

Unfortunately for the success of such an effort, the people had grown distrustful of "official information." They suspected it to be designed all too often not to present the truth but to manipulate opinion. They were weary of military reputations which had been overinflated (like Gamelin's, Ritchie's, Auchinleck's, even Wavell's) only to be punctured by disastrous defeats. Hence they looked upon the newest untried hero with a somewhat jaundiced eye, prepared to hope for the best, equally prepared to discount heavily all optimistic appraisals of his abilities. They demanded facts about his past and present, not opinions of his future. Who was he? From what kind of people did he spring? What were his personal habits and characteristics? What events had led to his appointment?

Journalists strove mightily to satisfy the demand. They descended in droves upon Eisenhower's mother, upon his wife and son, upon his brothers, upon his personal friends. In Washington, Mamie, fearful of mistakes which might harm her husband, consulted Milton, who was now helping to organize the Office of War Information at President Roosevelt's request. Soon Milton was elected by circumstances as a kind of unofficial public-relations officer for the whole Eisenhower family. He laid down certain basic rules which, followed rigidly, contributed in no small way to the healthy growth of the Eisenhower reputation. Simplicity, frankness, absolute confidence in Ike—these were to be the keynotes of the family's "information policy." First, all members of the family would co-operate fully in any attempt to give the public an honest picture of the general's life; the public had a right to all pertinent information concerning the man who was to lead their sons and husbands and friends into bloody battle. Second, no member of the family would co-operate in an effort to capitalize on the general's fame; that fame was not a private possession of the family but a creature of the whole people which even the general himself held only in trust. Third, no member of the family would make any commitments in the general's name nor make the slightest claim to privileges which might derive from his position. Fourth, no member of the family would permit direct quotations of him or her on any save minor personal points, nor make any public expressions of opinion on controversial matters which might be construed as emanating from the general himself.

Back in Abilene, Charles M. Harger, at Milton's request, became a sort of facilitating officer for the journalists who poured into town. Against their zealous excesses he protected Mother Eisenhower as much as possible. Even so, she was soon wearied of interviews and photographs and wondered plaintively if all this were "really necessary to help Dwight." One day a reporter from Chicago, employing high-pressure methods with which Naomi Engle was unable to cope, went so far as to photograph a letter which was lying open on the dining-room table, a letter from the general to his mother. That same reporter obtained others of the general's personal letters to Abilene friends and published them in a two-page feature spread without bothering to obtain the general's permission —to his, and the family's, intense disgust. Newspapers and magazines carried countless stories, true and imagined, of the Eisenhower home life when Dwight was a boy, of Little Ike's boyhood fights, his pranks, his schoolwork, his prowess as an athlete, his dates with girls—stories which, however inaccurate in detail, gave in their total effect a fairly truthful picture.

Of Eisenhower's professional career it was more difficult to obtain "interesting copy." There was no drama, virtually no "human interest," a remarkable poverty of anecdotal material. No dramatic utterances, of the kind MacArthur was constantly making, could be attributed to him. He had performed no heroic deeds, had not so much as seen a battle, had scarcely commanded troops in the field. Indeed, journalists found it difficult even to point to specific accomplishments in the military field and say "Eisenhower did this or planned that." The whole of his professional life had been spent in subordinate positions, which meant that his superior officers had got public credit for his work—and most of that work had been of the paper kind, performed behind a desk. In the end journalists were forced to fall back upon the bare summary of assignments and promotions contained in the War Department's "official" biography and upon such generalizations as "Eisenhower is known as a soldier's soldier" or "Eisenhower's range of experience includes," and so on. Instead of the dashing, courageous, inspiring commander, they presented the relatively unglamorous scientist in war, the technical "expert."

Nevertheless, the public derived from these journalistic efforts a picture of a man who possessed many of the traditional qualifications of a Great American. He came from a humble home. He had worked with his hands. He had made his own way without benefit of special favors from the rich and powerful. He was devoted to his family. He retained his loyalty to the town and friends of his boyhood and lost no opportunity to express that loyalty. He made no claim to special brilliance, had never sought to overawe anyone. Yet those who should know asserted that he was a person of remarkable energy and talent who had demonstrated, in his profession, a definite superiority of intellect. Thus he seemed to satisfy the paradoxical demands which a democracy makes of its heroes: he was the ordinary man who is exceptional, the common man who, in moments of supreme importance, becomes great. In his public character he might become a mirror in which the common man saw himself reflected. His success, if he achieved it, could stir admiration untainted with malicious envy, since his triumph might be considered a triumph of the average. He could, if he succeeded, exemplify the belief which is one of the basic tenets of democracy— namely, that the leader and the follower can, and indeed essentially must be, the same person; that there is only a difference of function, involving no question of total superiority or inferiority, between those who command and those who obey.

2

If Eisenhower had no mental blueprint of the process by which democratic heroes are made, he certainly proceeded as though he had. His natural tastes, his conscious realization of the needs of his job combined to dictate movements which strengthened his popular appeal. With never a false step, he filled out in detail those portions of the public picture of himself which might be called "simple," "modest," "frank," "ordinary." He refused to ally himself, in the public mind, with the aristocratic class of the country to which he had come. He begged off from invitations to country homes, to ducal castles, to all manner of "high" social gatherings. Yet when his position required his presence at an official function he was entirely at ease, a charming table companion, revealing much the same kind of social talent as Benjamin Franklin had displayed in the salons of Paris a century and a half before. Correspondents reported that he was "the same with everyone," meaning that there was no hierarchy in his personal relationships; he looked at all men through level eyes and dealt with the King of England and G.I. Joe on a basis of equality.

On the other hand, he constantly identified himself with the common soldier. Probably America has never had a general who reviewed troops more effectively—and reviewing troops is one of the most important procedures of high command, as every military man knows. He rarely permitted correspondents to accompany him on his visits to cantonments; he spent relatively little time there with the ranking officers, but a considerable time making a careful inspection of the mess and living quarters. He disliked talking to troops when they were on parade, standing stiff at attention. His usual practice was to walk along the lines as the men were at ease, establishing personal relationships with soldiers picked at random. He talked with them, generally, about their jobs in civilian life. The fact that he himself, as a boy in Kansas, had worked with his hands at a wide variety of jobs made it easy for him to meet the average soldier on the soldier's own ground. After he had passed through the lines he had the troops gather around his jeep, on which a loud-speaker was mounted. He spoke to them without self-con-

] 313 [

sciousness, with obvious pleasure, telling a simple humorous story or two, stressing (always and emphatically) the importance of Allied co-operation, asserting that all he as a commander could do was map out general plans of battle and see to it that the men were properly supplied. *"You* are the ones who must and will win this war," was the gist of his message. No one listening to him could fail to be convinced that he took a very real personal interest in his men.

The simplicity of his personal tastes in living was soon famous. A special train was offered to him for his personal use. He refused it. Later that summer, when Major General John C. H. Lee was named commander of the Services of Supply for E.T.O., it was necessary for Lee to have such a train; he practically lived in it. Occasionally Eisenhower borrowed it for troop-inspection trips, but only because by doing so he saved time and relieved field commanders of the necessity of providing him with living accommodations.

When he arrived in London he and Butcher were assigned suite 408 in Claridge's, London's swankiest hotel. It was convenient to Grosvenor Square, heart of London's rapidly growing "Little America" and on which, at number 20, Eisenhower's office was located. (Correspondents dubbed the square "Eisenhower Platz.") But the hotel lobby seemed overly luxurious; the suite itself had gilded walls. Eisenhower visibly shuddered when he looked at them.

"I feel as though I were living in sin," he complained to Butcher, who was ordered to find "more suitable" accommodations.

Accordingly, in early July, the two moved into suite 312-14 in the Dorchester, across Park Lane from Hyde Park and only three short blocks from Grosvenor Square. The suite consisted of three rooms: a bedroom for Eisenhower, another for Butcher, and a living room. It was comfortable and unostentatious. Eisenhower had only two complaints concerning it. One was that the bathroom plumbing, characteristically "British," required that he take his morning shower sitting down in the bathtub, holding the hose nozzle over his head. The other was that, living in a hotel in the center of the West End, he felt both cramped and overly conspicuous. He wondered if it wouldn't be possible to find a week-end hide-out somewhere in the country near London, where he and Butcher could completely relax in privacy. Butcher thought so. He began to look around for a suitable place.

In August he discovered what seemed to him to be the ideal

house, and when he took Eisenhower out to see it the general was pleased too. It was called Telegraph Cottage, a modest, pleasant, seven-room house on the outskirts of the village of Kingston, Surrey. Though it was barely forty minutes by car from Grosvenor Square, it was so secluded that the proximity of a mighty city seemed impossible. Soon Eisenhower and Butcher were spending every week end there. They had the usual trouble with the headquarters supply people. These latter furnished the house with expensive sofa pillows and cut glass which Eisenhower promptly had removed. Behind the house was a pleasant little formal garden and a tiny wood through which the two men liked to stroll in the evenings. They were puzzled by the bomb craters which pockmarked a golf course beyond the wood. Why waste bombs there? Eisenhower asked. Butcher shook his head. Maybe crippled planes had simply unloaded there while turning back toward the Continent. Not until several weeks had passed did Butcher discover that he had ensconced the commanding general barely a quarter of a mile from an air-raid decoy station where, during bombing attacks, fires had been set to lure Nazi pilots into dropping their bomb loads harmlessly!

During that same month Eisenhower was presented with a short-legged, long-haired, pedigreed Scotty pup. In the office one morning he had asked Tex Lee if there was any regulation which forbade his having a pet. Tex Lee replied that, so far as he knew, there wasn't.

"Then I want a dog," the general said. "I want someone who can't ask questions about the war and can't repeat what I say if I say anything."

A few days later the Scotty came as a gift from Eisenhower's personal staff. The general, grinning, christened the pup Telek —the source of the name was a "military secret," he claimed—and saw to it that newspaper correspondents described the dog as a symbol of Anglo-American friendship.

By this time his "official family"—his personal aides, secretaries, chauffeurs, and house servants—was completed and widely publicized. Mickey McKeogh was quartered with other enlisted men in Green Street but spent his days at the Dorchester or at Telegraph Cottage, looking after "his" general. Kay Summersby's wish had been granted; she was one of the two drivers assigned to Eisenhower's personal headquarters. The other was Albert ("Lord")

Gilby, an elderly Englishman of great dignity. Colonel Thomas Jefferson Davis, who had been an aide to MacArthur when Eisenhower was in the Philippines, was now Eisenhower's adjutant general. Warrant Officer Walter Marshall was the general's stenographer, and a California girl, Mary Alice Jaqua, served as Butcher's secretary. These people, with Butcher and Tex Lee, really constituted a "family," cemented by a warm personal feeling for one another and by a filial loyalty to the family's "head." Stories about them, about their relations to the "boss," were part of the currency which purchased for the commander the good will of public and troops.

The fact that Mickey wrote letters regularly to the general's family was common knowledge. So was the story of the time Eisenhower went to Chequers, the official country residence of the Prime Minister, to spend the night, and discovered that Mickey had forgotten to pack pajamas. The general, as Butcher informed Mickey next day, had had to sleep in a suit of long silk underwear, the only garment in the house large enough for the general—and it was several sizes *too* large. The general, it was reported, never bawled out Mickey to his face. The merest hint of the general's displeasure was more than enough to prevent a repetition of mistakes, of which Mickey made very few in any case.

Eisenhower's dislike of excessive formality in his office was illustrated by the story of his mild tiff with Tex Lee soon after the Americans came to London—though Lee's name was tactfully omitted from the published accounts. Lee, as he himself explained it, was somewhat overawed by the boss's new eminence. He had been able to deal with the colonel of a year ago on a man-to-man basis. He had been able to keep his association with the brigadier general, even with the major general, on much the same basis. But when Eisenhower became a lieutenant general (he received his third star, temporary, on July 7) who consorted with kings and prime ministers, it was too much for Lee's sense of proportion. He took to holding doors open for the general and knocking on the private office door before entering. It got on Eisenhower's nerves. One morning he answered Lee's respectful tap with a loud roar.

"Damn it, Lee," he burst out, "come in without knocking! If you have something, bring it in. This is no boudoir!"

The same emphasis on directness, on simplicity, marked his relations with his staff. When a subordinate brought in a piece of bad paper work, whose excessive verbiage was designed to hide a paucity of clear logical thought, he did not, it was said, give way to explosive anger. He merely sighed and said sadly, "That's too complicated for a dumb bunny like me," or "I'm just too thickheaded to understand this damn thing. You'll have to make it simpler." The effect was equivalent to a reprimand, since Eisenhower's high mental quality was recognized throughout the Army, but it aroused no antagonism in the subordinate. The commander was reported to be "death" on long-winded reports flowing from his theater to Washington, or vice versa. He referred to them caustically as "trans-Atlantic essay contests." His own reports, like his speeches to the staff, were logically organized, clear in expression, relatively brief. General Staff officers in Washington said that in his last meeting with them Eisenhower covered the whole theater problem and the proposed solution with incisive brevity: "This is what it is. . . . This is what we're going to do. . . . This is what we need. . . . We're counting on you to see that we get it. Good-by."

His informality, his selfless devotion to duty, and his sunny disposition set the tone for the whole of his staff. Leonard Lyons, the New York columnist, overheard one day Eisenhower's end of a telephone conversation: "Hello. . . . Yes, this is Ike. . . . Oh, hello, Betty! How are you? . . . Lunch? Sure, Betty, I'll see you at one." Hanging up, Eisenhower had said to the correspondent, "Great fellow, Betty." Lyons showed his puzzlement, remarked a "fellow" called "Betty" seemed a contradiction in terms. Grinning, Eisenhower explained that ever since his Annapolis days Admiral Stark had gone by the nickname of "Betty," and that the admiral (who lived across the hall from Eisenhower in the Dorchester) and he often had lunch together. "We get a lot of things done that way." Obviously there was no jealousy here between Army and Navy!

In his dealings with the working press the general displayed a remarkable shrewdness, a shrewdness so great that it produced, in many a correspondent's mind, an impression of naïveté. His efforts here were helped immeasurably by Harry Butcher, who became in a very real if unofficial sense his personal public-relations counsel. Always Butcher was present at the press conferences, one of which was held in a small private dining room in the Dorchester. On this occasion a buffet luncheon and drinks were spread on a long table against the wall. The general flattered the correspondents and at the same time put them on their honor by referring to them as "quasi-members of my staff." He answered questions quickly and with disarming candor. When for some reason he could not answer he said: "Ask Butch. He knows all the answers." At that juncture Butcher generally told one of his stories, of which he had a vast and hilarious collection. The story, always apropos, invariably sent the crowd into a gale of laughter. "I keep Butch around just for laughs," the general would say. And the correspondents agreed that he would have been worth keeping around for that reason alone.

But of course Butcher, even in the field of public relations, performed other and more important functions. Correspondents, with good reason, regarded him as their friend. He understood their problems. Time and again he smoothed out for them what might otherwise have been difficult paths. For example, soon after Eisenhower's arrival correspondents complained bitterly that their dispatches were being held too long by military censors. Butcher heard the complaints, took them to Eisenhower. The trouble was, Butcher explained, that there were only two censors, who were expected to be on duty twenty-four hours at a stretch. The general heard the complaint late one afternoon. On the following morning four censors were at work.

"Correspondents with experience in Paris, London, and Washington from the outset of the war claim they have never seen such an absence of red tape," reported the Chicago *Daily News* gratefully.

Thus was filled out, confirmed in detail, the popular picture of a genial, modest, tolerant, kindly, hard-working man whom ordinary people could claim as "one of ours." It was a picture which— displayed in hundreds of news stories, magazine articles, and radio broadcasts, passed down through the ranks by word of mouth— soon set the dominant tone for the entire theater. It provided an atmosphere of tolerant good will, of fruitful compromise, of "happy efficiency." The troops were convinced that they had a friend in the top commander. The public was convinced that, whatever mistakes this man might make, he would not make them out of a desire for personal glory. . . .

Yet this public picture, pleasing though it be, was a far-from-complete portrait of a hero: he wore upon his modest brow no crown of laurel leaves. He remained unproved by triumphs. The efforts (if they were that) to bolster morale in June by encouraging the expectation of quick offensive action soon had a contrary effect. A species of irritable popular impatience sprang up from grounds which, sown with promises, remained barren of events. To keep these weeds of discontent down to a manageable size became, as the long summer passed, one of Eisenhower's major chores. He succeeded in it, but his own popular stature necessarily shrank somewhat through the autumn weeks of seeming inaction. By that time the very pleasantness of his published image had stirred, in some quarters, grave doubts concerning his professional abilities. Could so kindly, humane a man be tough enough to stand up against the Nazis? Those personal qualities he displayed, were they not, after all, the qualities of a "front man"—charming but militarily unimportant? The German marshals surrounded their professions with awesome mystery, as befitted high priests who dealt in life and death. By contrast, Eisenhower's frankness, his matter-of-fact approach to war seemed amateurish.

Did he quite appreciate the seriousness of the problems facing him? What steps, after all, had he taken toward a solution?

3

He had taken, and was taking, many steps—but most of them lay necessarily below the horizon of public view. Only those steps which had to do with Allied co-operation and with morale were taken before the eyes of the world. Even here it was easy to underestimate his accomplishment. What he did seemed so easily done.

. . .

It is true that the *will* toward Allied co-operation was present, but so were many obstacles to its achievement. Since part of Eisenhower's technique for dealing with these obstacles was to minimize them and focus public attention elsewhere, many people scarely realized that the obstacles existed. Certainly few people, then or later, realized the magnitude and importance of Eisenhower's psychological victories in that summer of 1942. Yet these victories were prerequisites to later victories in the field. The American commander was laying, with remarkable shrewdness and solidity, the foundations for joint operations.

The thousands of American soldiers pouring into the British countryside carried with them very dangerous possibilities. They received much higher pay than the British; they had snappier uniforms and the advantage of novelty when competing for the favors of English girls; their provincialism, which the British found particularly irritating, was expressed in a cocky swagger; worst of all, they had little understanding of what the war had meant to the English and hence were inclined to regard their national hosts as overly grim and overly sorry for themselves. Even the English climate, which the average American found discouraging indeed, could foster anti-British attitudes. So could the British passion for tradition, which most Americans described as "backwardness." Eisenhower had nightmare visions of bloody fights in pubs, of street riots, of all manner of frictions which might strike sparks into the massed tinder of Axis propaganda. He set about reducing the opportunities for friction, increasing the mutual understanding on which future success must rest.

To foster good will toward the British, he instituted a gigantic educational campaign which began operation on each soldier even before he had disembarked. Orientation lectures gave facts about the British war effort, emphasized the importance of Allied co-operation; it was made clear that any man who injured Allied solidarity was, whether he knew it or not, a Hitler agent. British agencies and the Red Cross were called in to help with the program. Sight-seeing tours for the Americans were routed through blitzed areas, to give the soldiers a clear idea of British sacrifice. The *Stars and Stripes,* a United States Army newspaper, conducted a continuous editorial campaign, stressing British gallantry and hospitality, the traditional bonds between the two countries, the aspects of British life and character most likely to appeal to an American. In September, with Eisenhower's public approval, the *Stars and Stripes* conducted a drive to raise funds, through American troop contributions, for the aid of war orphans in the British Isles. The latter project had, from Eisenhower's point of view, a double purpose: it fostered international good will, and it tended to reduce the possibilities for friction by draining surplus money from the pockets of American troops. Further aids to the "draining" process were the intensive bond-selling campaigns which he had instituted in every American unit.

But probably more effective than all these devices was the force of his personal example. In the warm glow of his friendliness, cold natures were thawed and icy dislikes melted away. He did as he had planned to do—he made himself the embodiment of Allied co-operation—and he could succeed in this, not because he was by nature immune to normal irritations (quite the contrary), but because he had a profound understanding of himself and of what "co-operation" means.

There is truth in the paradox that he made so superb a "co-operator" because he was, by nature, a fighter. The impression he gave of endless patience, of unfailingly calm good humor, was in reality a display of remarkable nervous control. Actually he had an unusually fast reaction time and was, as a consequence, more than normally irritable, more than normally impatient. Deep within him, the boy of Abilene, whose displays of anger had been a source of concern to his mother, was still alive. A man of strong emotions, he had, like Washington, learned with difficulty to curb an extremely hot temper. And this inner tension of his, this enforced self-control, increased his effectiveness in his present assignment. For one thing, it heightened his sensitivity to the reactions of those with whom he dealt. For another, it maintained in him, for all his frank friendliness, a certain reserve which prevented excessive familiarity on the part of those who worked under and beside him. Without seeming to do so, without his subordinates being conscious of it for the most part, he managed to keep a necessary social distance between himself and the men he must command. One of his secretaries once observed: "Somehow, even when he's in his most joking mood, you never forget that he's the big boss." And correspondents told one another that "he's a swell guy, democratic and all that, but you know all the time that he could get hard as hell if he wanted to." Most important of all, this inner tension had helped to develop and maintain in him that quality of selflessness remarked by everyone who dealt with him. He had been forced to know himself well in order to bring himself completely under control—and only by thinking of himself objectively, looking at himself "from the outside" so to speak, could he know himself well.

His actions revealed his profound understanding of what co-operation means. Obviously he made a sharp distinction between "co-operation" and "subordination" or between "co-operation" and what normally passes for "diplomacy." Co-operation, his actions said, is a two-way street, a give-and-take relationship between parties of equal standing who are in pursuit of a common purpose. It does not, indeed cannot, involve a denial of differences where differences in fact exist. Rather, it involves a frank facing of those differences with a determination to resolve them where necessary, or at least to prevent their causing friction.

For example, in his dealings with the British he never denied his Americanism. He stressed it. In conferences with British staff officers he often referred to his "home town of Abilene" and interspersed his arguments or analyses with liberal doses of American slang. "I told that s.o.b. to peddle his papers somewhere else," he said on one occasion. An informed person, in his language, was one who "knows the score." He described Lieutenant General Sir Humfrey Gale as a "big operator." The British liked it. One British reporter, impressed by Eisenhower's "breezy charm," said that his speech was "like that of an intelligent Oxford don combined with the facility of a Rotarian speaker." To preserve the alleged "purity" of American speech, he set up in his office a penalty box into which any American guilty of such Britishisms as "cheerio" or "I say, old chap," was required to drop an English penny. . . . But his insistence that the Americans in his command get along with the British was in deadly earnest. He made that clear in every conference, in every speech to his troops. The "slow boat" on which Americans who failed to get along were returned to the States was soon notorious.

One of those shipped on the "slow boat" was an American colonel, a procurement officer, who became involved in a heated controversy with his British counterpart. The American had harsh things to say about "that British son of a bitch." Eisenhower heard about it and called in the colonel.

"I've reviewed your argument and I think you were right," Eisenhower said. "The other man was wrong, and you might be excused for calling him a son of a bitch in the heat of an argument. But you called him a *British* son of a bitch! For that I'm sending you home."

When in mid-August a Washington correspondent charged that a rift between the R.A.F. and the United States Army Air Forces was preventing full-scale American participation in the air war against Germany, Eisenhower immediately called in the heads cf London news bureaus for a press conference. He "indignantly denied" that such a rift existed. "If there is one place where co-operation and collaboration are perfect, it is between the R.A.F. and the United States Air Forces," he asserted. All that was limiting American participation was a lack of men and planes, he said—a lack which was being speedily filled. He went further, in the first instance of a technique for dealing with such matters which later became standard for his theater.

"I am not asking you to take what I say," he said, "because I might be wrong and I might even lie to you, but I want you to go around and see for yourselves whether there is any friction between the R.A.F. and our Air Forces."

Some of the newsmen took him at his word. They "went around," and their stories supported with facts his assertions.

He made no secret of the fact that some British customs were not to his personal liking. One evening during dinner in a London club he lit a cigarette following the meat course, as is the American custom. A waiter promptly informed him that smoking was not permitted in the dining room, and when he found that this was the custom in all English clubs he good-naturedly declined all invitations to dine in them. Very soon after his arrival he told the British War Office that he didn't understand much of the system by which the British Army arrives at a decision. He didn't suppose he ever would. But he *did* expect to be informed of those decisions affecting his operations, just as soon as the system's mysterious processes were completed.

These frank recognitions of national differences in outlook and custom provided a solid bridge for understanding, whereas attempts to deny them would certainly have made for explosive inhibitions. Before the summer was ended he had become, if anything, more admired by the British than he was by his fellow Americans. He had so thoroughly prepared the grounds for Anglo-American co-operation in his theater, had so firmly established the procedures for cultivating those grounds, that no seeds of Axis propaganda could sprout there. He had his solid psychological base for joint military operations.

Field and staff morale by that time was higher by far than civilian morale. For one thing, Eisenhower personally was, as he himself once said to Churchill, "probably the most optimistic person in the world"—and his optimism set the tone for the whole of his command. At his very first staff conference he said flatly: "Defeatism and pessimism will not be tolerated at this headquarters! Any soldier or officer who cannot rise above the recognized obstacles and bitter prospects in store for us has no recourse but to ask for release. Those who don't will go home anyway!" For another thing, field and staff knew, as the general public could not, that action was imminent. Below the horizon of public view great decisions had been made, and steps to implement them were virtually completed.

4

Never was optimism more important to the success of an enterprise than it was during the crowded period which began, in E.T.O., on July 24, 1942. On that date Eisenhower assumed command of an operation in which, all things considered, the opportunities for success were no greater at the outset than the opportunities for failure. The balance between the two was, quite certainly, a moral one. A subtle shift of prevailing attitudes which lowered, ever so slightly, the efficiency of the preparations and the *élan* of the assault might measure the difference between victory and defeat. A strong, active faith was essential—and since faith had yet to be justified by works its chief source must be the new, untried commander in chief. He faced a situation in which optimism became synonymous with courage. He could hardly have imbued his subordinates with confidence and determination had he himself been unable to regard every imponderable as an asset.

When he arrived in England it was by no means settled that he would lead combined Allied forces into battle. It was not even settled what and when the battle was to be. Between June 25 and July 24 three principal factors had operated to determine his appointment to operational command: (1) his success as a theater administrator, (2) the statesmanlike qualities he had revealed in his relations with the British, and (3) the fact that he had a plan. During that same month two strategical patterns had been exhaustively reviewed and a choice made between them; in making the choice Eisenhower's voice had been among the most decisive.

He had five principal subordinates in his administration of E.T.O., many of whom outranked him in permanent grade. Major General Charles H. Bonesteel commanded in the far outpost of Iceland. Major General Russell P. Hartle commanded in Northern Ireland. Major General John C. H. Lee commanded the Services of Supply. Major General Carl Andrew Spaatz commanded the expanding Air Forces. Major General Mark Wayne Clark was Chief of the Ground Forces and served as Eisenhower's deputy commander. Eisenhower's administration placed only as much emphasis on "flow lines" and "descriptions of duties" as was necessary to insure efficient, virtually automatic handling of routine matters; for the rest, it was unusually flexible and left to each subordinate the maximum possible freedom of initiative. His own attention to small details was entirely of the "random sampling" sort. Subordinates knew that on his frequent inspection trips he was quick to see things which were wrong; they could never be sure that he, personally, would remain ignorant of the minor points of their jobs. But for the most part he left his own mind free to deal with large issues—and as he dealt with them he made of his administration a creative tool, molding the huge forces under him into a single tactical team. In every staff meeting, on every inspection trip, he stressed what he called "the value of integrated tactical power in war," asserting that there is no such thing as a separate "air war," or "ground war," or "sea war," or "logistic war."

"When you put sea, ground, and air together, the result you get is not the sum of their separate powers," he explained in a press conference years later. "You multiply their power rather than add."

All that summer, and afterward, he emphasized the need for co-ordination of arms as constantly as he emphasized co-operation between the Allies. He strove to make himself the personification of tactical co-ordination, just as he had made himself the embodiment of Allied co-operation. Butcher encouraged published stories of Eisenhower's "pioneering" in tanks, his choice of the foot-slogging Infantry as his service, his personal passion for flying, his close personal friendship with Admiral Harold R. Stark.

It was partially at Eisenhower's suggestion that the United States Air Forces struck their first blow in E.T.O. on July 4—Independence Day—though the symbolism of this gesture turned out to be a boomerang. Of the six fast A-20-A twin-motored bombers which joined the R.A.F. in a hedge-hopping daylight raid on a Nazi airfield in Holland, two were shot down and one returned home badly damaged. In terms of symbolism, only the gallantry of Captain Charles C. Kegelman, pilot of the damaged plane, had much value. Kegelman's plane had actually hit the ground when one engine was shot out. In an amazing display of skill and daring he had brought the plane up under control and had knocked out an anti-aircraft tower while going away. He received a D.S.C. from Eisenhower personally that evening, and the story of his action was spread across the front pages of all American newspapers. (On that day Eisenhower had attended an Independence Day function at the Embassy,

] 325 [

during which he had had to shake hands with twenty-six hundred people; he avoided all such affairs thereafter.)

He was everlastingly "paying tribute" to some one branch of the service—to the Air Forces when he spoke to the Infantry, to the Infantry when he spoke to the Air Forces, and to the Navy when he addressed the Army. His official relationship with the Navy in E.T.O. was ambiguous enough to have caused considerable friction, had he permitted unhealthy competitive attitudes to develop. The precise limits of his command over naval forces would have been difficult to define through day-by-day developments and could easily have become the subject of endless, disruptive argument. Eisenhower and Stark avoided the argument through their personal relationship with each other. Always Eisenhower treated the Navy as an equal partner in the enterprise, a partner of which he was genuinely proud. In October, when Nazi propaganda claimed that American troopships had been sunk in the Atlantic late in September, Eisenhower seized the occasion not only to deny the Nazi claim but to "pay tribute" to the two navies (Britain's and the United States') which "are daily according magnificent protection, a fact which every soldier in our Army clearly appreciates and gratefully acknowledges."

The evidences of these administrative techniques—the smooth efficiency of E.T.O. routines, the friendly atmosphere of American headquarters—were clearly perceived by the watchful Churchill through the early days of July. At least once a week Eisenhower conferred with the Prime Minister, often lunching at 10 Downing Street. If the two did not always see eye to eye on matters of strategy, they had a profound mutual respect which blossomed very soon into warm affection. It is certain that Churchill, who had lived through the bitter quarrels between the French and British high commands in World War I, quarrels which had to some extent been duplicated in the tragic months of 1940, was convinced that a unified Allied command, under some *one* general, was an absolute necessity. As the then Prime Minister, Lloyd George, had said in 1918, "It is not that one general is better than another, but that one general is better than two." Like Marshall, Churchill had studied Eisenhower carefully as a possible architect of unity.

Perhaps, if he recalled Lloyd George's words, Churchill recalled a certain General Nivelle of France who, in 1917, had so charmed Mr. George that the latter had promised to subordinate Haig and the British Expeditionary Force to him. The results in that case had been tragic enough to give Churchill pause. Like Eisenhower, Nivelle was, in Churchill's own words, "an officer whose modesty, whose personality, whose lucidity of expression, exercised an almost universal charm."[1] Like Eisenhower, Nivelle had been a comparatively junior officer whose advance had been of amazing rapidity until, after a local success before Verdun, he had been named commander in chief over the heads of all the best-known commanders of his country's forces. But there the similarity between the two men ended, as Churchill quickly realized if he made the comparison at all. Nivelle had been a man of One Idea, so passionately devoted to that idea as to be blinded to changing objective realities. Eisenhower's, on the contrary, was a mind of unusual flexibility, a chess player's mind which improvised swiftly and brilliantly on a basic strategic theme in answer to an opponent's moves. Nivelle had been a man of small diplomacy, who had provoked a needless quarrel with Haig even before joint operations could be launched. Eisenhower, on the contrary, had a rare genius for handling men of different nationalities.

These two Eisenhower distinctions—the high quality of his strategic thinking and his genius for co-operation—were much more clearly realized by the Prime Minister than they could have been by the general public, because Churchill was following closely the course of the strategic discussions between the Americans and the British through those July weeks. Twice each week Eisenhower was meeting with General Paget, Air Vice-Marshal Sholto Douglas, and Admiral Ramsay—of the British ground, air, and sea arms—for conversations on future operations. Eisenhower personally, of course, was committed to the cross-channel operation as the ultimate instrument of Nazi destruction, but on this operation no working agreement at this time could be reached. Each of the four commanders had his own staff and his own ideas as to when, where, and how the cross-channel attack should be launched. Paget and many another experienced soldier doubted that such an attack was feasible at all. Eisenhower argued that air power in overwhelming strength applied to a particular area could so immobilize the enemy, destroy his communications, and soften his defenses as to make possible "operations that would otherwise be and remain in the realm of the fan-

[1] Winston S. Churchill, *The World Crisis, 1911–1918,* abridged and revised edition, Macmillan, Ltd., London, 1943.

tastic."[2] He must have referred again to Dunkirk. He may have referred to El Alamein where, in the first days of July, air bombing on an unprecedented scale held up Rommel's offensive.

But—and here he revealed his great mental difference from Nivelle—Eisenhower could agree that the limited range of available fighter planes, the vast increase in the number of planes of all types which would be needed, the enormous numbers of landing craft which would be required, the necessity for a lengthy period of concentrated strategical bombing of the Continent to reduce Nazi industrial power and disrupt communications—that all of these factors militated against any early launching of a western assault. He was convinced that such an invasion could not be made until August of 1943, at the very earliest, and then only if every ounce of British and American effort (save that needed for the holding action in the Far East) were devoted to this one project. His commitment to the cross-channel operation did not blind him to the immediate needs of the situation. He could switch easily to an alternative proposal, which had been at the back of all their minds for many months—namely, the invasion of North Africa.[3] Here, certainly, was no One-Idea Man. Never was there a mind less inclined toward fanaticism, nor toward what Churchill called "professional formalism."

There were many cogent reasons, both military and political, why a major Allied action could not be delayed beyond 1942—and Eisenhower was aware of all of them.

(1) There was the morale factor, on the home front and among the troops. Morale could not be maintained at a high level through a long period of inaction, even if no other factors operated to lower it. Inaction, in itself, was psychologically debilitating.

(2) There was the necessity of implementing the global strategical decision in order to prevent a radical and disastrous revision of that decision. A substantial portion of American public opinion, particularly on the West Coast, persisted in regarding Japan as a greater enemy than Nazi Germany; they found unacceptable the argument that we were engaged, not in two separate wars, but in a global war with two great theaters; they listened sympathetically to the fulminations of the Australians, who were outraged by the decision to make the Pacific a secondary theater until Hitler was

[2]Press conference, Paris, June 15, 1945.
[3]It had been discussed during Churchill's visit to Washington in January 1942.

destroyed. People of this persuasion were, so far, in the minority, but a minority might grow into a majority through a long period of inaction—and if it did political pressure might force the Allies into a division of forces between the two great theaters which would leave us too weak to achieve a decision in either of them.

(3) There was the necessity for providing some kind of affirmative answer to the Russian demand for a second front. British diplomacy during the 1930s, obviously designed to use Hitler as a club against the Soviets, had aroused suspicions which could only be allayed in 1942 by positive military aid—particularly so since Churchill had virtually promised Stalin that a second front would be opened that year.

(4) There was the factor of German psychological warfare, which could be made immensely more effective through a period of inaction. All three of the above factors would provide abundant ammunition for the big guns of Nazi propaganda, aimed at splitting the Allied Nations and at dividing political and economic groupings within Britain and the United States. The latter division was already evident in public discussions of Russia's second-front demand.

(5) There was the urgent need of actual battle experience for our troops.

There were equally cogent reasons why a North African operation was indicated at that particular time. Viewed in the vast terms of global war, such an operation was only tactically offensive. Strategically it was defensive, designed primarily to prevent a flanking threat to our Atlantic communications, to remove the threat of Rommel's drive toward Suez, and to preserve in undiminished strength the war-born alliance between Russia and the western Allies. It is true that a North African operation failed to meet the principal specification of what Russia termed a second front: there was no certainty, indeed little probability, that it would divert a substantial number of German troops from the hard-pressed Russian line. But it would serve as a token payment on our obligations to the Russians and prove to them that the western Allies were capable of bold action. In addition, there was one positive gain in which the Russians would share directly. The securing of the Mediterranean would shorten by thousands of miles the shipping lanes over which supplies flowed from America to the Soviets and would therefore be equivalent to the capture of several hundred thousand tons of shipping, many millions of tons of matériel, by Soviet forces.

In Eisenhower's view, North Africa must be conceived not as a theater unrelated to E.T.O., but as an organic part of the strategy which had, as its climax, the cross-channel attack. In a very real sense it was part of the logistic phase of that cross-channel assault. Obviously the latter could be successful only if Allied supply lines across the Atlantic were safe, and they would be far from safe if the Nazis seized Dakar and operated it as a large-scale submarine base. Indeed, Dakar in German hands might make the Atlantic lines, on which our shipping losses already had mounted as high as 1,000,000 tons in a single month, virtually untenable. But in our hands North Africa could become a gigantic air base which would greatly enhance the power and scope of that strategic bombing of the Continent which must precede the western assault. With North Africa we might also, by posing a major threat from the south, force the Nazis into a dispersal of their western strength, thus softening the coastal defenses against which our cross-channel assault must be launched.

And what of the risks which must be balanced against these gains? In July the risks seemed much less great than they turned out, in fact, to be. Even so they seemed great enough. The chief imponderable was the French Army and Navy. Would the African French resist our landings? Eisenhower was encouraged to believe they would not. United States State Department officials believed they had, through clever fifth-column work, opened doors through which our armies might be welcomed. Assurances were made that the American policy of maintaining diplomatic relations with Vichy, whom most Americans rightly regarded as a fascist enemy, would now be vindicated.

Most of these assurances were at hand when General Marshall, Admiral King, and Harry Hopkins, accompanied by a party of army and navy officers, arrived in London from Washington on July 13. E. R. Stettinius, Jr., lend-lease administrator, had arrived two days before. Exhaustive and exhausting discussions of all phases of the North African operation followed, during which Churchill made it clear that the choice of Eisenhower as commander of such an operation would be acceptable to the British. The purely military discussions took place at a conference which was attended by more than seventy general officers—British, Dominion, and American—held at Largs, Scotland. There, on July 24, the final decision was taken. North Africa was to be invaded before the winter rains set in. Eisenhower was named to command.

CHAPTER III

The Lighting of "Torch"

Torch was the code name applied to the operation. Would it light the path to victory, or fires for our destruction? Many high officers must have asked themselves that question during the hectic weeks which followed, but (one may be sure) they asked it in the privacy of their own souls, since "defeatism and pessimism" were not to "be tolerated." Eisenhower himself, though he presented to his command a countenance serene and confident, confessed later to some very dark moments.

It would be impossible to overemphasize the complex difficulties which faced him. There was not enough of anything, least of all time. The whole operation must be mounted "on a shoestring" and launched within eleven weeks at the outside. Only by the most furious kind of work would British and American shipyards be able to turn out enough landing craft in time; some of the larger ships actually were not ready until just one week before the expedition got under way. The shortage in shipping must limit the initial assault force to little more than one hundred thousand men, which left no margin of safety for absorption of possible determined resistance by the French—a possibility the military had to take into account no matter how sanguine the State Department might be. Those men and supplies must be transported across thousands of miles of submarine-infested sea, and their movement must be so co-ordinated as to result in simultaneous tactical operations at the end of extended sea lines. Since some of the convoys must start from Northern Ireland, some from England, some from America's Atlantic seaboard, a veritable miracle of timing would be required. Finally, to the vast imponderable of French reaction must be added two others almost equally great—namely, the reaction of Franco's Spain, and the battle competence of the untried, only partially trained American troops. Eisenhower faced these difficulties, not with a single force, but with two forces of different national allegiances between which lay a thousand opportunities for friction. His government, and Britain's, had given him full authority to shape the two forces into a single one—but this was not the sort of thing one could do by edict. Genuine Allied unity must be *his* creature, almost a personal product, developed not over leisurely months but in crowded weeks, or even days, during which tempers would be frayed by weariness, by inevitable frustrations, by immense burdens of responsibility.

A few days after the Largs conference ended Eisenhower called a series of conferences of his own at Norfolk House out of which emerged a command arrangement unique in military history. He began by explaining very carefully the nature of the task confronting them, pointing out why that task demanded a unification of high command far greater than that achieved under Foch in the closing days of World War I. The Beauvais Agreement under which Foch operated in 1918 made a sharp distinction between the "strategic direction" of military operations and the "tactical employment" of military forces; Foch was "entrusted" with the former while the British, French, and American commanders in chief retained "full control" of the latter. Moreover, under the Beauvais Agreement each commander had the right of appeal to his government if, in his opinion, the safety of his army were compromised by any order received from Foch. Such an arrangement, which had greatly hampered the Allied command in 1918, would be fatal to effective command in 1942. Supplies and shipping must be pooled; the two armies and navies must use common bases; there was no margin either of time or resources within which differences between two linked staffs could be ironed out. Hence the staffs could not be merely linked; they must be welded together. A *single* command, a *single* staff, a *single* Allied army within which talents could be used and forces interchanged without regard to nationality—these were essential if success was to be achieved. As Major H. A. DeWeerd puts it, "Americans and Britons in alternating layers would have to be fused together like a plywood board."[1]

"This is an Allied battle," Eisenhower is reported to have said again and again. "I will clamp down on anyone who tries to start any trouble between the Americans and British under my command.

[1] H. A. DeWeerd, *Great Soldiers of World War II*, W. W. Norton and Co., New York, 1944.

There will be neither praise nor blame for the British as British or the Americans as Americans. We are in this together as Allies. We will fight it shoulder to shoulder. Men will be praised or blamed for what they do, not for their nationality."[2]

It is reported that when staff sections failed to agree Eisenhower had them virtually locked in an office together until they arrived at a satisfactory solution. He was himself a court of final decision to whom any subordinate had easy access and whom all parties could regard as truly Allied, neither British nor American but British-and-American. Since he was "the same with everyone" and "absolutely straight—you always know where you stand with him," he was a dependable measuring stick by which other men could gain perspective, measuring themselves and their achievements in terms of the total job to be done. His personality evoked an atmosphere in which pettiness withered away for lack of nourishment, in which to place differences of opinion on nationalistic grounds was recognized as an act of sabotage, and in which compromise was natural, decisive, creative. Eisenhower's brand of compromise in the military sphere, inspired by good will and characterized by candor, was always a positive force which achieved concrete results, never a merely negative "agreement" whereby "unpleasantness" was avoided by doing nothing. The fact that he maintained no artificial distances between himself and subordinates made for a prompt settlement of those differences which might have grown, with time, into conflicts. Thus it was always possible for strong personalities to express themselves freely and strongly. They were encouraged to do so. They need have no fear of releasing emotions so long inhibited as to be explosive. Operations could be geared to the capabilities of the highest and best rather than to the "lowest common denominator" of his staff. Even before those initial conferences were ended the men who must work so closely together knew one another well, were aware of individual eccentricities, individual tastes, individual reaction patterns, and they shared that affection for one another which almost always stems from a complete mutual understanding. There were certainly no lines of national cleavage into which an enemy who was a master of psychological warfare could drive his wedges. In view of the politico-military difficulties in which the North African enterprise was soon involved, this was indeed fortunate for the Allied cause.

[2]John MacVane, *Journey into War*, D. Appleton-Century and Co., New York, 1943.

Eisenhower saw to it that these bonds between his men were strengthened rather than weakened by the pressure of work during the following weeks. Almost every decision, arising from an initial disagreement, was reached through a process of logical persuasion which ended in a shared conviction. Rarely was a decision imposed from on high, as a dictatorial expression of the top commander's will; when a disagreement percolated to the top command Eisenhower himself employed persuasion. Thus the stronger the initial disagreement, the stronger the bond of final decision. The very emotions engendered in argument became a common fund of feeling on which mutual understanding could be based. True to his word, Eisenhower treated his men as individuals, not as citizens of different countries. British and American officers working on the same problems shared the same offices. It was impossible to say that "the British did this" and "the Americans did that," or "the British opposed this step while the Americans favored it." Later, in Algiers, visitors to headquarters were astounded when Eisenhower, asked if so-and-so were British or American, had to pause to consider the matter before he was able to answer correctly.

With a sure sense of historic values Eisenhower considered this unity the greatest, the most significant, of Allied victories. It was, he knew, the indispensable condition of a final favorable decision in the field. It was, he knew, the one victory which might stand in history as a truly constructive achievement, concerned in the building of a better world and not merely in the destruction of an evil one. He hoped that it would become one of the beacons which, across dark and turbulent waters, lighted a suffering humanity toward the shores of permanent peace.

For his Chief of Staff he chose an American with whom he had been closely associated, professionally, while on the General Staff in Washington. No choice of subordinates made in later months had greater historic importance than this one. None revealed more clearly his ability to judge men—to find the real man who is so often hidden behind a mask of public manner.

There were few points of obvious similarity between Eisenhower and Brigadier General Walter Bedell Smith, but one of them was that Smith, like Eisenhower, was a native of the Midwest. Another was that his rise had been unusually rapid since 1939. When Hitler launched his invasion of Poland, Smith had held his majority for barely eight months. He became a member of the General Staff Corps in April 1940, serving first as assistant secretary and later as secretary of the War Department General Staff. He was promoted to lieutenant colonel in May 1941, to full colonel in August of that same year, and to brigadier general on February 2, 1942. Only the day before he achieved the rank of general officer he was appointed secretary of the United States Joint Chiefs of Staff. He was serving in this capacity and as United States secretary of the Combined Chiefs of Staff when Eisenhower, as Chief of War Plans, first got to know him well.

He was almost exactly five years younger than Eisenhower (he was born in Indianapolis, Indiana, on October 5, 1895) and had behind him perhaps a greater range of professional experience than Eisenhower had had. Though not a West Point graduate (he attended Rensselaer Polytechnic Institute), he had made the Army his career ever since he enlisted in it as a private in 1917. On November of that year, after attending Officer Candidate School, he was commissioned a second lieutenant in the 39th Infantry, Fourth Division, and he served with this unit in France until wounded. After his recovery he returned to the United States to serve in the War Department Bureau of Military Intelligence. He was a first lieutenant when the war ended, and he remained one for eleven years. Between the wars he served at various military posts throughout the country, on the Mexican border, and in the Philippines. As a captain, a rank he achieved in 1929, he was graduated from the advanced course of the Infantry School in 1932, from the Command and General Staff School in 1935, and from the War College in 1937. He served two tours as instructor and one as secretary of the Infantry School.

Unlike Eisenhower, he presented to the world the aspect of a hard-bitten professional officer, the kind of soldier whose presence makes a civilian uncommonly aware of his civilian status. He often described himself in what he obviously considered unflattering terms as the "Prussian type of officer." Certainly he gave that impression to those meeting him for the first time. He did not meet people easily, or in such a way as to put them at their ease. He had a stern face: his slightly protruding front teeth gave his mouth a rather sardonic appearance when the face was in normal repose, and he seldom smiled. On casual acquaintance he seemed abrupt, unbending, humorless. He had moments of irritable impatience during which he sometimes used his rank unjustly as a weapon against annoying subordinates. Junior officers were inclined to regard him with a fearful respect rather than with affection. Yet Eisenhower quickly knew that under the hard crust of his professional manner Smith was a sensitive, witty, even a charming personality with wide intellectual interests, and that the hard crust itself was at least partially a defense of Smith's essential shyness. Among his few intimates "Beedle" Smith was as far from the "stern Prussian type" as one could imagine, revealing a shrewd humor, a genuine modesty, a kindliness, which were somehow all the more attractive because they were so unexpected.

Nearly all of his personal traits, some of which would certainly have been liabilities in a supreme commander, would be assets in a Chief of Staff—and he was to become, in Eisenhower's own words, "one of the great Staff Chiefs of history, worthy of rank with Gneisenau." His loyalty, his devotion to duty, his modesty were absolute. He could express himself easily and well, both in speech and in writing. When called upon he presented his views with complete frankness and without regard for their popularity or lack of it. He was by nature as solitary as Eisenhower was gregarious, perhaps as inclined toward pessimism as Eisenhower was toward optimism, and his desire for personal privacy—almost passionate at times—bred naturally that self-effacement before the public eye which is part of a Staff Chief's stock in trade. He had an instinctive distrust of appearances; his intellect tended naturally toward a probing critical analysis. In purely military matters he and Eisenhower thought, as Eisenhower himself often said, "exactly alike." Thus his mind could serve as an extension of the commander's, and his temperament could serve as a balance for those personal traits in Eisenhower which, if wholly unchecked in their expression, might sometimes throw the commander off an even keel.

Actually Smith had been operating as Eisenhower's Chief of Staff ever since the latter came to England, though the public announcement was not made until early September, when Smith arrived in London. On the day Marshall gave Eisenhower the E.T.O. assignment the latter asked Smith to serve as Chief of Staff, and Smith accepted. As Smith explained it later, he and Eisenhower were walking along a Washington street together when the offer was made, and when Smith reached his office he was rather sorry he had accepted because he found on his desk an order giving him command of a division. Like most soldiers, he much preferred a field command to staff work. He stayed with Eisenhower then and turned down later offers of a field command because he admired Eisenhower enormously as man and as soldier.

All through August he'd been working in Washington on final plans for North Africa. By the time he arrived in London those plans were virtually completed.

2

Three task forces were to be employed. They were known as the Western, the Center, and the Eastern.

The Western Task Force, composed entirely of Americans under the command of Major General George S. Patton, would sail directly from America and make a series of landings on a two-hundred-mile stretch of the west coast of French Morocco. As far back as March, Patton had begun specialized training of American troops in desert warfare. At that time some eight thousand officers and men drawn from units of the First Armored Corps and including units of the Second and Third armies were gathered in a desert training area, 180 miles long and 90 miles wide, in the American Southwest. Under Patton's command in the Morocco landings would be the 3rd Infantry and 2nd Armored divisions, the major part of the 9th Infantry Division, with supporting ground and air services. In charge of assembling the convoys at sea and commanding them until landing points were reached was Rear Admiral H. K. Hewitt.

The Center Task Force, composed of American troops stationed in the British Isles, commanded by Major General Lloyd Fredenhall and escorted by the British Navy, would land in the vicinity of Oran. Under Fredenhall's command would be the 1st Infantry Division and one half of the 1st Armored Division, reinforced by corps troops. The Eastern Task Force, composed of both American and British troops, would sail from the British Isles and land at Algiers. This force, commanded by Lieutenant General Kenneth A. N. Anderson of the British Army, consisted of British Commando and Infantry units and of two United States regimental combat teams, one from the 34th and one from the 9th Infantry divisions, with a Ranger battalion. Major General Charles W. Ryder of the American Army was to direct the first landing, and General Anderson was to take over after the American troops were ashore. This force, too, was to be covered by the British Navy.

It was planned that the Western and Center task forces, after securing Port Lyautey, Casablanca, and Oran, would effect a juncture in the vicinity of Fez, thus giving us control of the single rail line running from Casablanca through Fez and Oudja to Oran. In addition, the Center Task Force was to drive eastward for a juncture with the Eastern Task Force landing at Algiers. A fifteen-hundred-mile flight was to be taken by the American Troop Carrier Command, carrying United States parachute troops, to facilitate the capture of the airfields near Oran. Once these fields were secured, fighter planes would be poured in from Gibraltar. All three task forces were to strike simultaneously, timing their operations as closely as possible to a coincidence with the long-awaited offensive of the British Eighth Army. Reorganized under General Bernard L. Montgomery and adequately equipped for the first time with modern weapons, the Eighth Army stood poised at El Alamein.

Originally it had been planned to make initial landings to the east of Algiers—at Bône, Philippeville, possibly even at Tunis itself. Lack of shipping, of landing boats and aircraft carriers, made it impossible to attempt these landings unless we abandoned the idea of landings on the western coast of Morocco. The latter proposal, that of renouncing the western landings in order to commit our total force inside the Mediterranean (the area of decision), was made and very carefully considered. Regretfully it was rejected because of the questionable attitude of Franco Spain. The possibility that Spain, with Spanish Morocco, might collaborate with the Axis to seal off the Strait of Gibraltar after our troops and shipping had been funneled through posed an awful hazard which we were unprepared to accept. It had also been planned originally to launch the invasion in early October, to give us more time for land operations before the winter rains set in. The alternative was a postponement until November, when more shipping would be available, and Eisenhower decided in favor of it. Anything less than the maximum possible force for our initial landings would pose, in Eisenhower's view, unjustifiable risks.

Even without such risks the conception was bold in the extreme. Eight hundred miles of coast line and a half million square miles of hinterland—held by French troops who, in the initial stages, would outnumber the landing forces—were to be penetrated by an

Allied army of only 107,000 men whose overland communications, following any swift advance, must be extremely tenuous, and whose nearest home bases lay more than a thousand miles across dangerous seas. Save for a few carrier-borne planes and a few long-range transports and heavy bombers, all the combined air forces must be routed through the single restricted field at Gibraltar. This field could be put out of action by aerial bombardment in less than an hour, leaving our troops without air cover. Enemy aerial action might interrupt the single rail line from Casablanca to Oran during the early crucial days of build-up, leaving forward units inadequately supplied. And all of these hazards had to be accepted in the full knowledge that a major failure at that particular time could have catastrophic consequences. A serious shipping loss might be fatal to commitments scattered from the Aleutians to Australia. Even more dangerous would be the psychological impact of a major defeat crowning a virtually unbroken series of Allied defeats all around the world.

3

These known, calculable risks, which were certainly great enough, were being augmented all through that summer by others: unknown, incalculable, and, for the most part, unnecessary. The Beauvais Agreement of 1918 had demonstrated that any sharp distinction on the command level between the "strategic direction" and the "tactical employment" of military forces is artificial and dangerous. The North African operation of 1942 was to demonstrate that, under modern conditions, any sharp separation of "political warfare" and "military warfare" on the command level is equally artificial and perhaps even more dangerous. Here was an operation in which political and military warfare must be, at the point of application, inextricably mingled. Yet in the planning stages they were so poorly co-ordinated as to be virtually separate. The event proved that while Eisenhower was directing with remarkable competence the intricate, detailed military planning, the chances for his final success were being seriously compromised by one of the most inept attempts at *Realpolitik* in all history. It was an attempt over which he had, and was to continue to have, no effective control.

Future historians must record with some amazement the manner in which the two great democracies had permitted their foreign offices to become separated from the people. In America those branches of the executive dealing with domestic affairs were forced to conduct their operations in the full light of day. Their policies were subject to constant public review and effective criticism; their direct responsibility to the people was demonstrated when their appropriations bills were presented to Congress. The State Department's diplomatic corps, on the other hand, shrouded its operations in the utmost secrecy and had long since ceased to express the majority opinion of the country it presumed to represent in the vital field of international relations. The diplomats seemed to believe that their machinations were much too subtle, too complex for ordinary men to understand. And the ordinary man was inclined to believe that the "striped-pants boys," with their constant substitution of devious intrigue for straightforward honesty, were much too "smart" to be intelligent.

For instance, the State Department's policy toward Franco Spain had, since the beginning of the Spanish Civil War, been bitterly opposed by the vast majority of Americans. Public-opinion polls had revealed again and again the extent of this opposition. Yet the State Department continued its "appeasement" policy; Franco's prestige was bolstered by full diplomatic recognition, despite his openly avowed loyalty to the Axis, and his crumbling economy was bolstered by continued shipments of American goods. The sole justification for these unpopular acts was that they maintained Spanish "neutrality." Actually, as the North African operation proves, this was no justification at all. Eisenhower and his colleagues had already been forced to recognize that Spain's "neutrality" was in reality a myth. If it had been real we could have taken Tunis almost literally for nothing by concentrating all our landing forces inside the Mediterranean. The "race for Tunis," which we were to lose by the narrowest of margins, would in that case have been unnecessary.

The same pattern of "appeasement," justified on the same dubious grounds, was being followed with regard to Vichy France. At first the aged Marshal Pétain, whose authoritarian political philosophy had been notorious ever since World War I, was represented to the American people as a brave, if pitiful, figure, doing his best for the Republic under almost impossible conditions. Later, when the marshal's own words and actions had proved beyond any reasonable doubt that he was pro-fascist, our continued full diplomatic recognition of his regime was justified on the grounds that it was "neutralizing" the French fleet at Toulon and providing us with a "listening post" whereby we could keep track of fascist intrigues and maintain contact with the French underground, both in Africa and France itself. To the argument that we might best keep track of the fascists and maintain contact with the underground through General de Gaulle and his Free French, the State Department turned a deaf ear. It preferred to make its own contacts, through Vichy, and continue its snubbing of De Gaulle.

However self-contradictory such a policy might seem to be on the surface, it had, we were assured, a deep inner logic whose conclusions would be of immense value to the Allies. What was this "inner logic"? North Africa was to reveal it as nothing more than an old, old argument—namely, that "the ends justify the means." It is an argument whose advocates (for some strange reason) are called "realists" and whose consequences throughout history have been uniformly disastrous. Time and again history has shown that ends and means are no more discontinuous in politics than they are in physics and cannot be made so, however clever the attempt. Time and again the practitioners of *Realpolitik* have foundered on the simple fact that certain causes *always* and *inevitably* produce certain effects. It is only during the considerable time which may elapse between initial causes and final effects that the "realists"—Napoleon, Metternich, Bismarck, Hitler, et al.—have even an illusion of "success." In the case of Vichy France and North Africa the interval between our sowing of error and our reaping of error's bitter fruit was brief indeed.

The chosen instrument of State Department policy in North Africa was Robert Daniel Murphy, American chargé d'affaires in Algiers. Though unknown to the general public in this summer of 1942, he was a veteran of some twenty-five years in the diplomatic corps—a smiling, affable, youthful-appearing man of forty-eight with an extremely likable personality. Born of an Irish Catholic family in Milwaukee, Wisconsin, he had attended George Washington University, had studied law and been admitted to the bar in the District of Columbia, and had obtained his first government employment as a clerk in the Post Office Department in 1916. In the following year he had entered upon his diplomatic career as a clerk in the American Legation at Berne, Switzerland. He had been counselor of the American Embassy in Paris when France fell and had been assigned to Vichy in the same capacity when the Pétain regime was established. According to a magazine article published with

State Department approval, "When the problem of preventing the Germans from occupying French North Africa and gaining control of vital naval and air bases in that territory arose, Murphy was sent there to try diplomatically to combat the pressure which the Nazis were asserting."[3] He was credited with working out an economic agreement whereby the United States would give French Africa (which meant *Vichy* Africa) non-military supplies in return for "assurances that the bases would be kept out of German hands"[4]— an agreement, in other words, whereby tangible American goods were exchanged for highly intangible "promises" given by men of doubtful honor. In the summer of 1942 he was operating out of Algiers under a directive from the State and War departments "to win over as many of the French military and political leaders as he could to ensure there would be little or no resistance when the Allied landing occurred."[5]

Unfortunately for the Allied cause, Murphy's acquaintance among the French seems to have been limited to reactionary political and business leaders, and he seems personally to have shared the State Department's unreasonable aversion to General de Gaulle and the Free French. There *was* an effective French resistance movement, as later events proved, but since it was wholly De Gaullist, Murphy made no effort to obtain its assistance. Instead he and S. Pinkney Tuck, chargé d'affaires in Vichy, entered into secret negotiations with one Jacques Lemaigre-Dubreuil whom they later represented to the American public as a "leader of the French underground." Who, in fact, was Lemaigre-Dubreuil?

According to the Free French, he was among the most notorious of French collaborators with the Germans, one of those big businessmen whose passion for personal profit is unqualified by patriotic ideals or humane considerations. Before the war he had been head of the Taxpayers' League, one of the most powerful of those reactionary pressure groups which contributed so much to the impotence of the French Republic. He had been publicly accused of involvement in the fascist march on the Chamber of Deputies in 1934 and of helping to finance the Cagoulard (a kind of French Ku Klux Klan) attempt to overthrow the Republic in 1937—

[3]Kingsbury Smith, "Unrevealed Facts about Robert Murphy," *American Mercury*, November 1944.
[4]Ibid.
[5]Ibid.

though neither charge was ever legally proved. He was a member of the largest vegetable-oil company in France, Huiles Lesieur, and a regent of the Bank of France, a position he continued to hold after the German occupation of Paris. (The Free French claimed that through his regency of the Bank of France he operated as an agent of the Banque Worms through which the French economy was enslaved by the Third Reich.) It is clear that the Nazis considered him thoroughly "trustworthy," for they not only permitted him freedom of movement throughout France and North Africa—though he lived in the occupied zone—but permitted him to reopen the Dunkirk plant of his company shortly after the fall of France. He made frequent business trips to North Africa to supervise the raising and shipping of the peanuts which were a main source of his company's oil. This freedom of movement, far from arousing suspicions that Lemaigre-Dubreuil might be something less than absolutely loyal to the principles for which the Allies were fighting, was viewed by State Department officials as a great advantage to the Allies. The military was assured that Lemaigre-Dubreuil only *seemed* to be collaborating with the Germans in order to facilitate his "underground" activities. The chief proof of this latter allegation seems to have been that Lemaigre-Dubreuil, a gentleman of rich means and polished manner, said so himself!

One thing is clear. Lemaigre-Dubreuil and his colleagues were bitterly opposed to De Gaulle and the Free French. It was a prejudice which Murphy and Murphy's superiors shared, if from different motives. The evidence seems to indicate that Lemaigre-Dubreuil and his fellows had become fearful that the Germans, after all, might lose the war. In view of their known records it behooved them to gain as much support as possible from the politically naïve Americans so as to save not only their profits, but their lives—both of which would be endangered if the Free French assumed control of a liberated France. They assured Murphy that De Gaulle would never be accepted by the French Army and that he had only a tiny following among French civilians. Murphy was only too inclined to believe them: perhaps he was ignorant of the facts concerning the underground; perhaps, though he was a self-styled "liberal," he was fearful of the leftists who, as always, were among the leaders of the anti-fascist forces. Accordingly a rather complicated conspiracy was hatched which had, not one purpose, but two—and these two were by no means wholly consistent with each other. The way was to be

] 343 [

paved for an easy Allied invasion *and* De Gaulle was to be kept out of North Africa. Thus the Allies were deprived of the only French support which was really trustworthy, and Eisenhower's immense assignment was needlessly complicated by political problems which were unexpected and which he was ill equipped to solve. He hadn't the time, the political education, nor (in the last analysis) the authority to solve them. Even if his political authority had been more than nominal he would have been greatly handicapped by the fact that his chief political adviser was to be Robert Murphy himself, the man who had helped to engineer the conspiracy and who therefore had a personal stake in defending it.

But if De Gaulle was to be kept out, who should be the leader of the French African Army and the chief of French African civil affairs? According to Waverly Root, the first approach made by Lemaigre-Dubreuil's group was to Edouard Herriot, the leader of the Radical Socialist party and a former French premier.[6] Herriot, sincerely anti-German and therefore an opponent of the Vichy government, is said to have refused the offer on nineteen separate occasions. Perhaps too many strings were tied to the offer: Herriot would not have been likely to wish to supplant De Gaulle, nor would he be likely to grant immunity to the Lemaigre-Dubreuil group from the punishment they probably deserved. Weygand was then approached. He not only refused the offer but promptly informed Pétain of his conversations with the conspirators. The choice then fell upon General Henri Giraud, who had recently escaped (with rather mysterious ease) from the German fortress of Königstein, where he had been confined since his capture in 1940. Lemaigre-Dubreuil assured Murphy that Giraud, whose hatred of the Germans was notorious, had enormous prestige among North African troops and civilians. At the general's orders the French would almost certainly aid rather than resist us. It was even possible that the French fleet would sail to join us. As always, Lemaigre-Dubreuil's word was enough to convince Murphy. Through Lemaigre-Dubreuil the American got in touch with Giraud.[7]

Thus entered upon history's stage, to strut briefly and ingloriously,

[6]Waverly Root, *The Secret History of the War,* Volume II, Charles Scribner's Sons, New York, 1945.

[7]According to "The Backstage Story of Our African Adventure," by Demaree Bess, published in the *Saturday Evening Post,* July 3, 10, and 17, 1945, Murphy began negotiations with Giraud *before* the final decision to invade North Africa had been reached.

a human anachronism straight out of the eighteenth century. Giraud was sixty-three years old, more than six feet tall, and physically vigorous despite a limp which remained from a World War I wound. His mustached face was a frozen mask whenever he faced a camera, and the stiffly wooden figure he then presented was an accurate portrayal of his inner quality. He was honest and courageous. He was also bigoted and willfully stupid. He seems to have lacked almost completely the faculty for self-criticism and the sense of humor which accompanies that faculty. His egotism was as immense as his sense of realities was small. Whenever he spoke of himself in formal meetings he used the third person: "Giraud cannot accept less," or "Giraud favors landings in the south of France." It was clear that he regarded his opinions as dicta from on high, which ordinary mortals should not presume to question. Moreover, he had an ideology which was at least as strongly anti-British and anti-republican as it was anti-German. When first approached by Murphy he had just completed a seventeen-thousand-word analysis of the causes of French defeat in which he repeated, point by point, the standard fascist doctrine: he blamed the "declining birth rate," a "negation" of things "spiritual," too much luxury among working people, the forty-hour work week, above all a lack of "authority" and "order." He also asserted that France would do well to profit from Germany's example: "Sincere Frenchmen who have been in Germany as prisoners of war can bear witness to its prosperity and to its physical and moral health. Admittedly the Germans do not perhaps have liberty, but there is certainly neither disorder nor anarchy. Everywhere it is work, the only fortune for a people which wishes to live and live happily." On May 7, three weeks after his escape from Königstein, he had written a letter to Marshal Pétain in which he said: "I am in complete agreement with you. I give you my word of honor as an officer that I shall do nothing which can, in any sense, disturb your relationship with the German Government, or interfere with the task you have put into the hands of Admiral Darlan and Premier Pierre Laval to carry out, under your high authority."

From the first even Murphy found Giraud extremely "difficult." The general made impossible demands, and his strategic concepts were fantastically out of line with realities. He stipulated that he be named commander in chief of the entire operation, that he name the time and place of the landings, and that simultaneous assaults be made on North Africa, western France, and southern France, with diversionary strokes in other parts of Europe! In the words of one officer, Giraud had always been "the sort of French general who sends his men into battle with a rousing *'Allez, mes enfants!'* and a cheerful disregard for logistics";[8] his overpublicized reputation for military "genius" was largely derived from the facility with which he managed to be captured, and to escape from capture, by the enemy. Faced with these demands, what did Murphy do? He seems to have countered them with typical diplomatic double talk. At any rate (as Eisenhower later discovered to his chagrin at a time when he was overburdened with other anxieties), Giraud thought his demands had been met: he believed that *he* had been named commander in chief.

To understand clearly the compromising situation in which Eisenhower was being placed, one must realize that through all these months of *opéra bouffe* intrigue Robert Murphy was, of course, reporting directly to his superiors in the State Department. He did not go *through* Eisenhower to reach Washington; indeed, the general who was soon to be saddled publicly with full responsibility for North African developments seems to have been ill informed as to what was taking place. At that time, and later, the line of *real* (as distinct from *nominal*) authority ran from Murphy through Secretary of State Cordell Hull to the President—and in the President's office, playing a very active role in the whole affair, was Roosevelt's chief diplomatic adviser, Admiral Leahy, ex-ambassador to Vichy and a frequent apologist for the Pétain regime. It was in Washington that all the important North African policy determinations were made. The British Government had little, and Eisenhower virtually nothing at all, to do with them. This fact must be kept always in mind, for later on we shall find the Secretary of State asserting repeatedly that the State Department was *not* responsible for North African developments, that these developments were of a War Department policy determined on the ground by the commanding general, Dwight D. Eisenhower. This piece of sophistry did nothing to protect the State Department from bitter popular criticism, but it was to come close to costing the Allies the services of a very great general.

As a matter of fact, Eisenhower's only direct intervention in Murphy's intrigues that summer seems to have been an effort to

[8]Waverly Root, op. cit.

prevent their violating military security. The army command apparently regarded Lemaigre-Dubreuil and his colleagues through eyes less trusting than Robert Murphy's. The command knew that in a military operation mounted with so small a margin of safety, strategic surprise was absolutely essential to success; secrecy was a decisive weapon. Accordingly Murphy received through channels an order *not* to reveal to any of his French collaborators the date and places of the landings. The disclosures were not to be made until four days before the invasion occurred. As Marshall later explained it in his second biennial report, "This of course made it extremely difficult, in cases impossible, for these French officials to take all the steps necessary to facilitate our landings [but] the consequences of disclosure of our purpose to the enemy . . . involved too great a peril to justify earlier notification." Certainly this concern for security seems more than justified. Would it have been if the State Department had chosen to collaborate with the Free French, men who had proved in action at the risk of life and property their loyalty to the Allied cause?

Why was the State Department so opposed to De Gaulle? It is a question for future historians to answer. On the face of it, the opposition appears fantastic and none of the reasons so far adduced by commentators seems adequate to account for it. Granted that certain elements in the State Department actively favored the kind of Catholic-flavored fascism which Franco and (to some extent) Mussolini espoused. Granted that career diplomats tend to be aristocratic in outlook and to place excessive values on fine clothes, rich houses, and polished manners. Granted all this, it still seems impossible that the State Department as late as 1942 should have failed to realize that its policy was sure to fail and that the failure (which could cost thousands of American lives) would be sure to strengthen the very forces which the State Department opposed.

All that is certain is that when Eisenhower and De Gaulle shook hands at a Bastille Day ceremony in London, July 14, it had already been determined that the two military leaders were to be estranged from each other. The Allied military unity which Eisenhower so brilliantly achieved was not to include, for a long time, the Free French—and the total cost to America, in terms of world prestige, has not yet been counted. De Gaulle himself was a "difficult" person—humorless, relatively inexperienced in politics, overly sensitive to personal slights, and not wholly free of the egotism which

Saint-Cyr seems to inculcate in French professional officers. But he *was* the leader of the only French who, in the long run, were worth much to our side, and the treatment being accorded him that summer was hardly calculated to improve his disposition. Later on Eisenhower would have to work with De Gaulle. He would find the problem of doing so immensely complicated by the rankling memory of State Department injuries.

4

There was only time enough to hold one set of master exercises early that fall on the coast of Scotland. Eisenhower came up from London to view them. What he saw was not encouraging. Ground-air co-ordination was faulty; tactical units were grossly mishandled; individual soldiers seemed not to know how to handle themselves. Obviously these young Americans were far from adequately trained, and Eisenhower had horrible visions of what might happen to them on a hostile shore. The bloody memory of the Dieppe raid on August 19 was still fresh in the minds of all—and Casablanca might all too easily become another Dieppe. If only there were time to hold a second master exercise! As it was, individual units would barely have time to correct their individual glaring errors.

"But then you never learn anything from a perfect exercise," Eisenhower consoled himself to Butcher as the two returned to London. "You only learn from bad ones—and this one was surely bad enough to scare the boys into trying harder."

The worry about military security grew steadily more intense. Secrecy had been risked again and again in confused intrigues whose tangible results might well have seemed, to Eisenhower's logical mind, slender indeed. There were still no guarantees that the French would not resist. The French fleet at Toulon, so often used as a veiled threat by Vichy to gain concessions from the State Department, remained an imponderable. Even the French general who had been selected to rally French troops to the Allies remained an imponderable; ensconced in his sister's house near Lyons, Giraud was completely out of touch with the North African situation. Eisenhower had no accurate information as to the disposition of French troops and no clear arrangements for concerting his action with that of those Frenchmen who were (he hoped) collaborating with us. To get the information and make the arrangements he sent his deputy, Mark Wayne Clark, to North Africa in late October.

The story of Clark's daring trip has often been told, how he and his party flew to Gibraltar, boarded a submarine there, and landed via a rubber boat at Cherchel, near Algiers, after signal lights had been flashed from the beach. He spent hectic, hazardous hours in Algiers. Through one nerve-racking period he hid in the basement of a house whose rooms, above his head, were being searched by French militia. It was a glamorous performance and, unlike much of the "glamour" which had preceded it in Algiers, it yielded definite results. Against all the disadvantages of the arrangement with Giraud, a single great advantage must be balanced at this point: General René Maste, Chief of Staff in Algeria, was a Giraud man. From him Clark got the military information he needed; through him arrangements were made for a concert of action during the landings at Algiers. By the time Clark boarded the rubber boat for return to the submarine he could congratulate himself on having carried through to considerable success his hazardous assignment.

On October 24 the ships of the Western Task Force assembled at sea off the Atlantic coast of America and, under the command of Rear Admiral Hewitt, sailed for Casablanca. On that same day, with more tanks and artillery than the British Eighth Army had ever seen before and with the way paved by tremendous R.A.F. assaults under Air Marshal Tedder's direction, General Bernard Montgomery launched his offensive against the Germans on a forty-mile front from El Alamein to the Qattara Depression. On the following day the Eastern and Center task forces sailed from the British Isles. The commitment was made.

As the convoys plowed slowly through autumn seas there was little Eisenhower in London could do except ready the proclamations to be made to the French on D-Day, handle a multitude of last-minute details, and make a few feeble gestures toward preserving security. He saw to it that several small troop units were fitted out with arctic clothing and equipment. The word got around that Mickey McKeogh was obtaining heavy woolen underwear and fur-lined gloves for the general. Promptly the rumor spread that an invasion of Norway was impending. On October 29 newspaper stories filed in Washington reported that Eisenhower had been called home for "important consultations": he'd be in the United

States "within a week," according to "reliable informants who asked that they not be identified in any way." The stories were cleared through the Office of Censorship and featured on front pages from coast to coast. On the following day Eisenhower was reported to have been seen eating lunch in a London hotel and to have slept in the hotel that night. Headquarters in London refused comment on the story of the general's return. On October 31 President Roosevelt chided the newspapers for publishing a story "revealing the movements of a commanding officer."

Minds already troubled by security worries could hardly have been soothed by news reports coming out of North Africa and Vichy that week. Admiral Jean François Darlan, supreme commander of the French Army and Navy and second only to Laval as a Vichy political leader, was completing a tour of French West Africa and Morocco. On October 30 he returned to Vichy and presented to the Laval cabinet his report on North African defenses. "Circumstances give very special importance" to the tour, said the Vichy communiqué ominously. On that same day Vichy's Propaganda Minister said, in a speech at Nice: "She [France] must, above all, defend her empire and even aim at a triumphant counterattack." He made bitter references to British and "De Gaullist" conquests of Madagascar, Syria, Martinique, the Lake Chad region of Africa—and no reference at all to French Indo-China, which had been seized by Japan. Had there been a leak? It was true that, according to Vichy accounts, Darlan had paid special attention to the defenses of Dakar. That might indicate successful camouflage by the Allies; we had sent planes over Dakar repeatedly, presumably to take reconnaissance photographs in preparation for invasion, and German planes had undoubtedly sighted Allied warships plowing southward on courses which might take them to Dakar. This hope was sustained by Allied intelligence reports indicating that women and children were being evacuated from Dakar. . . . But the very fact that Darlan had chosen to go to North Africa at that particular time was disturbing, to say the least. The French journalist, Pertinax, writing in the New York *Times* on October 30, said that, according to diplomatic reports, Darlan might soon succeed Laval as head of the Vichy government and had made his African tour in order "to ingratiate himself with the Germans."

"Don't worry about things you can't help," Eisenhower had said often to Mamie. "Worry about those you can." He must have repeated the maxim often that week. In the period between commitments to an issue and the decision of that issue, all a commander can do is hope for the best. "God knows I've done the best I could. . . ."

Outwardly he remained calm. He was unusually quiet, Mickey noticed; he didn't want to talk much, just sat silently in the living room at Telegraph Cottage that week end. But he was as pleasant and thoughtful of others as usual. A person not intimately acquainted with him would never have known from his manner that he was under extreme pressure.

Back in London on Monday he was comforted by reports from El Alamein. The 2nd New Zealand Division, with elements of the the 50th and 51st divisions, had broken through the last Axis line at Kidney Ridge on Sunday, November 1. On Monday the Eighth Army's tremendous victory was sealed in a great tank battle at El Aqqaqir. The commanding Nazi general, Ritter von Thoma (Rommel had gone to Berlin a month before to be feted as a hero), not only lost the bulk of his armor but was himself captured. Pounded continuously by Tedder's air forces, the Germans were in full retreat. For the first time the Allies had achieved in battle a perfect air-ground co-ordination.

On Wednesday an innocent-looking cable went from Algiers to the South of France. It was passed without question by the Vichy censors. It said: JACQUES WILL ARRIVE ON THE EIGHTH. At last our French collaborators were informed of our landing date. General Giraud is reported to have been walking in the garden of his sister's house when a French army captain came to him with the message. He stared in amazement and chagrin. "It's too soon," he muttered. "Too soon." He stood silent for a moment. Then he shrugged. "When do we start?" he asked.

From London that day Eisenhower dispatched to General Marshall the following message:

I cannot leave the United Kingdom without expressing to you once more, and to all your assistants in the War Department, my lasting appreciation for the perfect assistance and support you have provided us. If you deem it appropriate, and a convenient occasion will occur, I should like you to pay my respects to the President and

the Secretary of War and say to them that all of us are determined
to make this operation a real success.

In the evening he left London by plane to open, at Gibraltar,
his post of command.

For weeks advanced groups of British and Americans had been
preparing for his coming. Deep in the bowels of the mighty Rock,
under fourteen hundred feet of limestone, they had prepared forty
air-conditioned offices and installed signal facilities. To reach these
headquarters one had to pass through a dripping tunnel, three
fourths of a mile long. Eisenhower walked through it on the
morning of his arrival. After that he invariably trotted the whole
length. It was his only chance to exercise, he explained, and besides, it was chilly in the tunnel.

With Eisenhower's arrival several time-honored Gibraltar traditions were shattered. In the first place, he was in command of the
Rock, the first "foreigner" in two centuries to control the fort.
"Never in my wildest dreams in my West Point days did I think that
I—an American general—would ever command the British fortress
of Gibraltar," he confessed in awe-struck tones to newsmen. Actually, of course, the British Lieutenant General F. N. Mason
MacFarlane remained in charge, but he was responsible to Eisenhower during Eisenhower's stay. Another precedent was shattered
when British Wrens, counterparts of the American Waves, were
brought in to decipher messages; women had never been permitted
in the fortress before. The famous Eisenhower informality, which
seemed to increase rather than decrease efficiency, set a new tone
for the Rock. It was abetted by the British Admiral Sir Andrew
Browne Cunningham, commander of the Mediterranean fleet, who
kept himself warm in the chill offices by wearing a white turtle-
neck sweater. He looked like an American football player of the
1890s as he popped in and out of Eisenhower's office.

Between Eisenhower and Cunningham there developed at once
one of the warmest and closest of Eisenhower's numerous personal
friendships. Cunningham, a stocky man with a remarkably direct
gaze, had the bluff, hearty manner traditionally attributed to an
"old salt," and his salty humor, masked by gruffness, was soothing
to taut nerves. His hatred of red tape was as great as Eisenhower's;
he saw eye to eye with the American on military matters. Like

most top British naval and air commanders, Cunningham was frequently and frankly critical of what he termed the "timidity" of certain ground generals. In Eisenhower he saw a man whose offensive boldness, whose willingness to accept carefully calculated risks in order to achieve clear-cut decisions, matched his own. In the trying days ahead he was to prove a tower of stength, supporting his American friend again and again in bold decisions which many members of the staff opposed.

CHAPTER IV

The Conquest of North Africa

AFTER THE VICTORY IN EUROPE Eisenhower confessed that the most trying hours of the entire war for him were those separating sunset on November 7 from dawn on November 8, 1942. Never before in modern history had so many men gone down to the sea in ships, preparatory to landing on hostile shores. Never before in history had so much shipping, a million tons of it, been committed to a single enterprise. There were ships of all shapes and sizes: great twenty-five-thousand-ton liners, stubby channel steamers, sliverlike destroyers, battle cruisers, carriers, merchantmen from Poland, South Africa, New Zealand, the Dutch East Indies—hundreds of ships whose continued existence would spell the difference between victory and defeat on scores of far-flung battle lines. Eisenhower well knew that he was hazarding, in this venture, not only lives of those men who closed now on the shores of Africa, but also the lives of thousands in theaters halfway round the world.

In so far as possible the convoys heading into the Mediterranean had been funneled through the strait under cover of darkness. Even so, the Bay of Gibraltar had been jammed with shipping, and airplanes were massed wing tip to wing tip beside the runway of Gibraltar's airfield. The enemy—German or Vichy French—could not fail to knew that a large movement was under way. From the roof tops of Algeciras and La Línea, on "neutral" Spanish soil above the bay, German observers watched bay and narrows twenty-four hours a day through powerful glasses. From now on the only opportunity for surprise inside the Mediterranean lay in the multitude of contingencies which the enemy command must take into account, and in the possibility that the enemy was deceived as to the size of the movement. The enemy command must consider the possibility of landings on Sicily, Sardinia, Corsica, at a score of points scattered over hundreds of miles of African coast; assuming

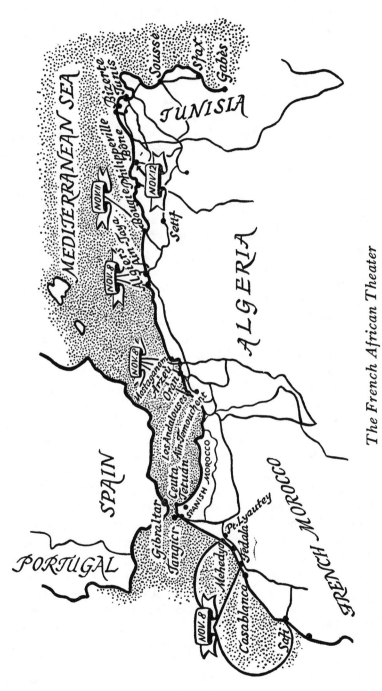

The French African Theater

he was deceived as to the size of the movement, he must consider the possibility that the Allies were making another and larger effort to reinforce the British garrison on Malta. There was the additional remote possibility that the whole Mediterranean movement might be a feint to divert attention from the west coast.

By comparison the contingencies Eisenhower had to take into account at that point were fewer in number but more crucial in their consequences. His final plan, like all his operational plans, was beautifully flexible. Back in the British Isles scores of thousands of troops were moving into concentration points. If the French fleet joined us, if the French Army welcomed us into Africa and fought with us against the Axis, those troops in the British Isles would sail directly against Sicily and Sardinia. We would seize control of the entire Mediterranean before the enemy knew what was happening. If our African landings were bitterly opposed, those troops in the British Isles would be used to reinforce our landing parties. The Center and Eastern task forces were to sail on past Oran and Algiers in broad daylight, on toward Malta, then circle back in the night and head straight for the beaches. If the ruse were successful, the Luftwaffe would be concentrated swiftly in Sardinia, Sicily, and southern Italy, prepared to attack our convoys in the narrow seas between Tunisia and Sicily, and we would have dominance of the skies over Algiers and Oran for the first crucial days. Only if everything went wrong—if the French and Italian fleets came out against us, if U-boat packs were concentrated in the Mediterranean, if the Luftwaffe were concentrated to cover our landing points, if the French offered the bitterest resistance—only then would the Allies face overwhelming catastrophe.

But of course everything *could* go wrong. Off the west coast of Africa, Eisenhower knew, the weather was bad; Hewitt must guide his ships in through crashing breakers up and down the coast from Casablanca, his captains performing miracles of seamanship if serious losses were to be avoided. From inside the Mediterranean, radio reception was unexpectedly bad; reports came through in a garbled state or not at all. Through the long dark hours Eisenhower must simply wait, not knowing. What he *did* know was far from comforting. As the climax to all his anxieties, presenting complications wholly unexpected, came the gentleman who was supposed to be our ace in the hole, General Henri Honoré Giraud.

The French general had been taken from the French coast by

submarine. One of his numerous stipulations was that an American, *not* a British, submarine be used to ferry him; all along he had opposed the inclusion of British forces in the operation. As it happened, there was no American submarine available in the Mediterranean, so an American, Captain Jerauld Wright of Washington, D.C., was given temporary command of the British submarine *Seraph*, in the expectation that this would satisfy Giraud's peculiar logic. Wright, who had gone with Clark to Algiers two weeks before, entered the French harbor submerged, surfacing a thousand yards offshore. Giraud came out from shore in a rowboat, fell into the sea while transferring to the submarine, and was rescued by members of Wright's crew. The submarine then submerged and proceeded to a rendezvous point, where Giraud was transferred to a seaplane. The plane landed in the Bay of Gibraltar a few minutes after four o'clock on the afternoon of November 7.

The Frenchman was taken at once to headquarters, where Eisenhower and Clark awaited him. His first words left the Americans gasping.

"General Giraud has arrived," said General Giraud, his tone and posture indicating his firm conviction that this was one of the great moments of history. "General Giraud is ready to assume command of the operation."

It was hardly a great moment, but it must certainly stand among history's strangest. Deep in the limestone cave—barely twenty-five miles from Cape Trafalgar, whose bitter memory still lived to deny us the French fleet—two traditions came face to face; two vital strategies proceeded to define themselves through opposition. It was one of those moments in which the deepest inner qualities of men are revealed, a moment profoundly symbolic in so far as those inner qualities represent national ideals. On one side of the desk sat the Frenchman, bred in the tradition of Napoleon, his will as sharp and hard and inflexible as a knife, his mind narrowly legalistic in all its formulations but soaked through and through with the mysticism of *"la gloire."* On the other side sat the American from Kansas, bred in the tradition of the Western frontier, his will subordinate to objective needs and flexible in its response to them, his mental energy focused always on the job to be done "out there." Giraud was inclined to confuse personal egotism and national patriotism, believing that to gain power and glory for himself was to gain power and glory for France. Eisenhower never employed "power" and "glory" as concepts at all. Gazing across at Giraud, trying to "size up" a creature strange to him, he was thinking only of how this man might be used, how he might be persuaded to help us or at least prevented from injuring us. If he felt a stir of anger at having been put in so compromised a position, he quickly fought it down.

The situation was further complicated by the language barrier. Eisenhower's knowledge of French was rudimentary, and Giraud spoke no English. Clark had to serve as interpreter. Slowly and as gently as possible Eisenhower explained the situation. He was sorry. There had been a dreadful mistake. The operation was already under way, and the landing forces were exclusively British and American. It would be impossible for any Frenchman at this late date to assume effective command, especially one who was unacquainted with both troops and matériel, unacquainted with the operational plan, unacquainted even with the English language. He was sure the general would understand. . . . He watched the Frenchman's face as Clark translated, watched the face flush with anger and injured pride. The Frenchman's eyes narrowed and his voice was harsh when he spoke.

"Giraud cannot accept less," he said.

He produced a letter signed by Robert Murphy which, he claimed, promised him the command. On the strength of it he had risked his reputation, even his life. Eisenhower was limited in his information concerning the personalities with whom Murphy had intrigued, and he was wholly misinformed as to Giraud's strength with the French African military and civilian population. Hence the situation seemed to him much more delicate than, in fact, it was. He hoped that Giraud had the power to halt, by edict, whatever resistance the French chose to make—the power, in other words, to save lives. He believed, too, that the Allies were under some obligation to Giraud; the Frenchman, as he himself claimed, had run risks on the basis of what now appeared to be false promises. Eisenhower was therefore prepared, on his own responsibility, to make concessions.

Employing all his tact and persuasion, he argued patiently into the night hours while the hands of the wall clock moved inexorably toward H hour, one o'clock on the morning of November 8. Slowly the Frenchman retreated from his original position, fighting a stubborn rear-guard action all the way. His final demands were two in number: (1) he must be recognized immediately after the landings as the chief of both military and civil affairs for all of North Africa; (2) the Americans (he chose to ignore the British) must help him recruit and equip a French army for use in an invasion later on of the South of France. Wearily Eisenhower acceded to both demands. He is reported to have listed on his memo pad at that point his seven principal worries.[1] Numbers four and five were: "No Frenchman seems able to help us," and "Giraud is difficult to deal with."

While this comedy of errors was being played out deep in the fortress Rock, an astonished General de Gaulle, in London, was being informed for the first time of the impending landings. Until now the leader of the Free French—whose followers had fought for the Allies in Syria, Madagascar, Lake Chad, Martinique, and off Dakar; who was clearly the only valid symbol of a fighting France—had been kept in complete ignorance of the North African expedition. State Department officials had referred to the ill-fated Dakar expedition as evidence that Free Frenchmen could not keep secrets; Vichy, they pointed out, had been tipped off concerning the Dakar effort; we could not afford to risk security of the present operation by admitting Free Frenchmen into our councils. (Just why this argument did not apply with even greater force to our dealings with Giraud, Lemaigre-Dubreuil, et al., has never been satisfactorily explained.) The British Foreign Office, apparently with some reluctance, had concurred in the State Department decision. It was now the unhappy task of Foreign Secretary Anthony Eden, on this evening of November 7, to tell the touchy French leader that once again he had been snubbed and sidetracked. One imagines that Eden approached his task with some trepidation and performed it with all the diplomatic tact he possessed. De Gaulle was hurt, naturally, but he quickly rallied. Next day he made a radio broadcast from London, acclaiming Giraud's action in taking over the leadership of the African French, urging all patriotic Frenchmen to support Giraud.

Shortly before dawn on November 8 fragmentary reports began to come in from the beaches. By noon Eisenhower, in Gibraltar, had a fairly complete operational picture. Low-flying Allied planes at dawn had showered the landing areas with leaflets, according to plan—leaflets signed by Eisenhower urging the French to help

[1]Waverly Root, *The Secret History of the War*, Volume II, Charles Scribner's Sons, New York, 1945.

us. Continuous radio broadcasts had been made in Eisenhower's name: "Frenchmen of North Africa, the forces which I have the honor of commanding come to you as friends to make war against your enemies. . . . I have given formal orders that no offensive action be undertaken against you on condition that you . . . take the same attitude. To avoid any possible misunderstanding, make the following signals: Fly the French tricolor and the American flag, by day, one above the other . . . or two tricolors, one above the other. By night turn on a searchlight and direct it vertically toward the sky. We come, I repeat, as friends, not as enemies. We shall not be the first to fire. . . ." The French had replied with fire. At Casablanca, at Oran, the fire was heavy. Among the Allied ships the signals flashed: "Play ball!"—and the battle was joined.

On the west coast resistance at two of our landing points—at Fedala and at Safi—had been light. At Safi there had been practically no fighting at all; we were already pushing northward toward Casablanca, one hundred and fifty miles away. There had been some fighting at Fedala, only ten miles north of Casablanca, but it was clear that by the end of the day the forces landing there would be marching on the city. Thus the great naval base was, by noon, bracketed. At Casablanca itself, commanded by Governor General Charles Noguès, resistance was determined. Forts and warships, including the *Jean Bart* with her fifteen-inch guns in Casablanca's harbor, were exchanging shells with Allied naval units offshore. At Mehedya and Port Lyautey—the northernmost landings on the west coast—resistance was heavy, but even here we had, by noon, secured our beachheads.

It looked as though we would have no trouble establishing cordial relations with the Sultan of Morocco, but the reaction of Franco Spain was still uncertain. General Orgaz, high commissioner of Spanish Morocco, would have to be closely watched, a procedure which would necessarily immobilize a portion of our troops.

East of Spanish Morocco all three of our landings in the Oran area were contested. At Arzeu—in the town, along the beaches, and in the fields—there was heavy sniper fire even after stiff resistance in the dock area had been broken. By nine o'clock it was clear that the French had had time to concentrate at Saint-Cloud, halfway between Arzeu and Oran. Next day, after heavy fighting, General Terry Allen was to by-pass Saint-Cloud. The 1st Infantry Division was doing well. The infantry coming in from Les Andalouses was not moving at all. Pinned down on the ridge of Djebel Mourdjadjo,[2] it nevertheless played an important part in the whole operation by containing enemy forces which would otherwise have slowed the other advances along the roads. The ambitious paratroop attack which was supposed to take Tafaraoui Airfield, key air base for all western Algeria, failed completely—mistakes were made from which we could learn a great deal—but success beyond our expectations had been achieved in the bombing attacks on hangars at La Senia and on coastal batteries, in the air defense against submarines, and in fighter-plane coverage of our landings. General Oliver's tanks, which were to crush the last resistance in Oran itself two days later, were rolling ashore. . . . Here, too—east and west of Oran—our beachheads were all firmly secured by noon. Eisenhower could see with proper pride that ground-air-sea co-ordination had been, for the most part, amazingly good.

From Algiers came the best news of all. Here, it seemed, Murphy's fifth-column work had produced tangible results. From a short-wave radio transmitter which had been secretly installed in the house of a young Algerian doctor garbled reports came through to Gibraltar from Murphy and his fellow conspirators shortly after H hour.

At first all was confusion. Finally it developed that some four hundred poorly armed young Frenchmen, under the leadership of Henri d'Astier de la Vigerie (whose brother in London was one of De Gaulle's chief subordinates) and a young priest, Father Cordier, had occupied the central and branch police stations in the city shortly after midnight. They had also seized the Algiers radio station and the main post office, where telephone and telegraph facilities were located. Against repeated attacks by pro-Vichy militia, these young Frenchmen held all the key points through the early morning hours, waiting with increasing desperation for the entrance into the city of American troops. Meanwhile, at Blida, some twenty-five miles southwest of Algiers, General Montsabert with a tiny force was holding the principal airfield. He had a guard of honor drawn up to receive General Giraud, who, according to the original plan, was to arrive shortly after H hour. The guard of honor was dismissed when Giraud had failed to arrive by seven o'clock.

[2]David Rame's *The Road to Tunis*, Macmillan, New York, 1944, contains an excellent account of the Oran action.

Major General Charles W. Ryder, commanding the American landings, had no inkling of what was happening inside the city. Accordingly he was grouping his forces, preparatory to launching an attack next day, when one of the French conspirators, Pierre Alexandre, arrived to inform him of the true situation. Ryder thereupon sent his forces into Algiers at ten o'clock in the morning. Shortly after noon all firing ceased. Algiers was ours, and at practically no cost in British and American lives—though several young Frenchmen had been killed or wounded.

Before this picture was anywhere near complete in Eisenhower's mind he was informed of a surprising development. Admiral Jean François Darlan was in Algiers; the supreme commander of the French fleet was our prisoner! Though this fact opened up new possibilities, it probably did not seem at first to be of great importance. It was good for prestige purposes to have in our hands one of the three most important Vichyites; he would strengthen our bargaining power, but that was all. Later that day armistice terms for Algiers came through. They had been "approved" by Darlan, Eisenhower noticed, but that certainly did not indicate that Darlan was collaborating with us; rather it indicated that he was a defeated enemy. Since the terms amounted to unconditional surrender of the city (this first armistice had no application elsewhere), Eisenhower promptly approved them. He still recognized Giraud as the leader of the African French; in his mind Giraud remained the man whose orders would be most likely to halt the bloodshed at Casablanca and Oran. He had made commitments to Giraud in good faith and he was not one who makes commitments lightly.

A few hours later Mark Clark and Giraud left Gibraltar by plane for Algiers, Clark to act as Eisenhower's deputy in an attempt to clear the confused political picture. Next morning in London spokesmen for the Free French said that, while there had so far been no direct contact between Giraud and De Gaulle, the question as to how the two could best serve together would be "rapidly settled." At almost the same hour Eisenhower issued in Gibraltar his Giraud proclamation:

General Henri Giraud has arrived in Algiers from France. It can be expected that his presence there will bring about a cessation of scattered resistance, which is tragic between soldiers who have the same enemy. General Giraud has assumed the leadership of

*the French movement to prevent Axis aggression in North Africa
and will organize the French North African Army again to take
up the fight side by side with the forces of the United Nations for
the defeat of Germany and Italy and the liberation of France and
her Empire. The Allied Commander in Chief has agreed to support General Giraud in this theater with the strong forces under
his command. The Government of the United States has pledged
itself to assist in providing arms and equipment for this new
French Army.*

Eisenhower's sincere expectations were very quickly disappointed.
Far from being welcomed into Algiers as a hero, Giraud had to go
into hiding for a time to avoid arrest by pro-Vichy police—and this
at the very moment newspapermen in Gibraltar were filing officially inspired stories about Giraud's "tremendous reputation" in
North Africa, where "French troops love him as a great general."
He arrived in Algiers after the fighting had ceased, and his appeals
had no effect whatever on the fighting in Oran and Casablanca,
fighting which continued severe. Obviously all our political and
military leaders, including Eisenhower, had been completely misinformed concerning Giraud. The French general had no power
over the Army, a professional army whose members were concerned
more with pay and pensions than with principles, and who demanded a legal succession of authority whereby pay and pensions
would be guaranteed. Nor did the general have any important
following among French civilians. Politically and militarily,
Giraud—whom Eisenhower had promised full armed support in
the name of the United States—was a nonentity. The only weight
he had in the present scale of circumstances was the weight of the
commitments Eisenhower had made to him, and he used this
weight to initiate, at once, a political tug of war with Darlan.
Viewed from Gibraltar, that tug of war was confusing in the extreme. Only gradually, over a period of several days, did the outlines of the situation become clear to the top Allied commander, and
even then he had no solid base of information on which to rest his
political decisions.

In striking contrast to the political confusion was the swiftness
and clarity with which Eisenhower defined the military situation
early on November 9. His reaction to that situation was prompt,
bold, sound. It was clear that the Allies had effected a strategical

surprise. There was no question as to the final outcome of the fighting in Oran and Casablanca—there was only a question of time—and Algiers, the landing point nearest the area of decision, was already ours. Accordingly Eisenhower began to pave the way for a full and rapid exploitation of our initial success. Arrangements were made for re-embarkation from Algiers of elements of the British First Army, with a few American units. These troops, on receipt of the "Go" signal from Gibraltar, were to sail for Bougie, one hundred miles east of Algiers. Arrangements were also made to land at Bône, barely one hundred miles from Tunis itself, with two companies of British parachute troops aided by Commandos coming up by sea. Mobile units at Algiers, and even at Oran where resistance was weakening, were told off for an overland march against Tunisia. From Washington, President Roosevelt dispatched a message to Sidi Mocef Pasha, Bey of Tunis, asking for free passage of American troops through his country.

The anxieties which weighted Eisenhower were not evident to newspaper correspondents who met with him that evening for a press conference. The commander, they wrote, was "smiling and affable." He claimed that he was "well satisfied with progress" thus far. "The only thing I was disappointed in was the resistance of the French Navy, particularly the coast batteries," he said mildly. "We don't want to fight the French and they are opposing us, holding up the job and expending effort which might well be used against the common enemy, Germany." He heaped praise on the brilliant operations of the British Navy under Admiral Cunningham's command, and he spoke of a new American trench mortar which had reduced an Oran strong point "almost at once."

It looked as though the maximum possibilities of the highly flexible operational plan might be realized. Before the eyes of Eisenhower's mind there dangled now, tantalizingly, the fruits of an enormous victory. Almost, those fruits were within his grasp: Bizerte, Tunis, Sousse, Sfax—all of Tunisia and all for virtually nothing. Rommel would be denied his only dependable ports of supply, and the entire Afrika Korps—which had for so long held arrogant sway over North Africa—would be hopelessly trapped between Eisenhower's forces and Montgomery's advancing Eighth Army. The way would be open for the immediate attack against Sicily, an attack already partially mounted in the British Isles. The enemy would be completely off balance; there was even a remote possibility that Italy might be knocked out of the war in a matter of weeks. These fruits could be snatched only through exercise of the utmost offensive boldness, and Eisenhower was prepared to exercise it. He was *not* prepared to sacrifice that minimum of prudence without which boldness becomes foolhardy, a mere gamble of uncalculated risks. To move on Tunis while fighting continued in the rear areas would be foolhardy. Even with the rear areas secured, our supply lines would be stretched almost to the breaking point.

On the morning of November 10 Eisenhower dispatched a message to Patton at Casablanca: "Algiers has been ours for two days. Oran defenses are crumbling rapidly with naval shore batteries surrendering. Only tough nut is in your hands. Crack it open quickly." Patton was confident that he could do so. But the critical point, so far as an immediate launching of the dash for Tunis was concerned, was Oran. The troops on the west coast were too far away to participate in that dash. Besides, they would be needed, even after the fall of Casablanca, to guard our rear against a possible hostile movement through Spanish Morocco. Accordingly it was to Fredenhall, commanding at Oran, that Eisenhower sent his most urgent order. "Clean it up today," he said. Fredenhall replied at one o'clock with the announcement that Oran had surrendered.

The moment had come. Eisenhower—informed that resistance at Casablanca was near an end, informed that Darlan was about to sign armistice terms for all of North Africa—threw the switch that afternoon. Our offensive machine began to move eastward in high gear. We were to occupy Bougie on November 11 and Bône on November 12 while our ground units thrust toward the Tunisian border against no opposition whatever. The race was on.

The moment of bold decisions, confidently made, is always an exhilarating one. It is during the period between a commitment and its outcome that a commander's spirits are likely to be depressed. On military grounds Eisenhower's footing was sure, and when he met newspaper correspondents on that evening of November 10 his spirits were high. The military picture was bright indeed. There would be an early end to all French resistance, he prophesied confidently. Our troops had performed splendidly at Oran, where there had been "considerable fighting." The tank action which broke into the city at noon had been decisive. . . . One of the correspondents asked, somewhat diffidently, about the exact status of

Admiral Darlan. Eisenhower brushed the question aside. Political developments, he said, had "no place at present in the important military developments."

2

Politics, which seemed of minor importance that day in Gibraltar, dominated the scene in Algiers. The whole of a continent, the Nazis' best ground-gaining general, hundreds of thousands of the Nazis' best troops—these were the enormous prizes of a race so close that hours, even minutes, counted; yet in Algiers, Frenchmen wasted those hours in a wrangling of unbelievable pettiness. Obviously we were dealing with the wrong Frenchmen. Chief among them was the suave, tricky opportunist, Admiral Darlan.

Precisely why Darlan happened to be in Algiers on the crucial night of November 7–8 is a question which has not yet been satisfactorily answered. The official version has it that he had come to visit his son, who lay ill of infantile paralysis in an Algiers villa, but since the admiral had left Algeria only a few days before, and his son's condition had grown no worse in the meantime, the "explanation" leaves a good deal to be explained. Robert Murphy himself suspects that Pétain had told Darlan of Murphy's conversations with Weygand, and that Darlan had come again to Algiers "intending to look into the situation."[3] Suffice it now to say that Darlan's unexpected presence compromised still further Eisenhower's already badly compromised position, since it rendered false the promises Eisenhower was making that same night to General Giraud. Mark Clark discovered this fact, to his chagrin, when he sought to effect a North African armistice on the morning of November 10.

As to the main events, all the numerous accounts of what happened in Algiers on the crucial night are in agreement; it is only in the interpretation of those events that they differ so radically. At seven o'clock on the evening of November 7, Murphy, D'Astier de la Vigerie, and several other conspirators were gathered in the doctor's house, where the secret short-wave radio had been established. At nine o'clock it was evident that Vichy officials had grown suspicious; a few minutes later the chief of the political police arrived

[3]Kingsbury Smith, "Unrevealed Facts about Robert Murphy," the *American Mercury*, November, 1944.

at the house to make a personal investigation and was promptly arrested by D'Astier de la Vigerie's men. At midnight the young Frenchmen working with us seized the Algerian key points and surrounded with armed guards the homes of leading officials, including the villa of Vice-Admiral Raymond Fénard, where Darlan was staying, and the home of General Alphonse Juin, Vichy commander of Algerian troops. Juin was the senior local French official, in the absence of Governor General Yves Chatel. Forty-five minutes later Murphy arrived at the home of General Juin. "So well had the secret of Allied plans been kept that the French general was asleep upstairs in his bedroom when Murphy arrived," says Kingsbury Smith in his semiofficial account.[4] The general came down in his pajamas. To Murphy's announcement of imminent landings with "half a million men," Juin replied with heated protests against the "invasion" of French territory. Murphy claimed that the Allies were *not* invading, but came by invitation. Whose invitation? Why, General Giraud's! One imagines that Juin found this answer far from satisfactory, since Giraud was without authority to issue such an invitation and was not even in North Africa at the time. Murphy then asked Juin to order his troops not to oppose our landings, and Juin promptly passed the buck—to Admiral Darlan.

"Is he here?" Murphy exclaimed, completely surprised.

"He has arrived unexpectedly to see his son," Juin went on. "He is my superior. He is commander in chief of all French forces. He can immediately countermand any orders I issue. If he does so, the commands will respect his orders, not mine."[5]

Obviously Darlan could not have countermanded anybody's orders if he had been immediately arrested and held incommunicado—but this "undiplomatic" possibility seems not to have occurred to Murphy. Instead he agreed with Juin that Darlan must be called over immediately.

Summoned by phone and followed by the armed guard which had been thrown around Fénard's house, Darlan arrived at General Juin's half an hour later. With him were Fénard and Rear Admiral Battet, the latter a Darlan protégé who had become head of the Navy Department in Darlan's Vichy office. All accounts agree that the admiral received Murphy's announcement with an explosion

[4]Ibid.
[5]Ibid.

of anger. His face "turned purple with rage," according to the Smith account.

"I knew the British were stupid," he cried, "but I did not think you Americans would be so stupid!"

The stupidity, in Darlan's view, consisted of launching an invasion with forces too small to succeed, thus forcing the Germans to occupy all of France and North Africa.

Murphy countered this with his usual "diplomacy." According to his own story, he reminded Darlan of a statement made to Admiral Leahy at Vichy in July 1941. At that time Darlan is supposed to have told the American ambassador, "If and when the Americans have half a million men to invade France, come to me." Well, said Murphy, we now had nearly half a million men, they were about to land in North Africa, and "we have come to you." He "appealed to Darlan's patriotism"[6]—which, in view of Darlan's known record, was certainly a doubtful quantity. He "emphasized that America and Britain were taking the first step in the liberation of France"—a liberation which, if it restored a French Republic, would almost certainly cost Darlan his life. He begged the admiral to order the French forces not to resist. There followed what Demaree Bess describes as a "protracted and somewhat heated discussion."[7] Darlan at first refused Murphy's request categorically. Then, as the hopelessness of his personal position became evident to him, he attempted to pass the buck to Marshal Pétain. He had "taken a solemn oath to the marshal." Surely Murphy, as a man of honor, would not ask anyone to violate a "solemn oath"?

The American's "diplomacy" continued unperturbed.

"If Marshal Pétain knew what was going on," said Murphy, "you know he would instruct you to offer no resistance."[8]

Darlan, of course, knew no such thing, and he "paced the floor for fifteen minutes" while "beads of perspiration rolled off his forehead." He must ask Marshal Pétain what to do, he said finally. He could not on his own responsibility issue the orders Murphy requested. Murphy kindly placed at the admiral's disposal the communication facilities which our friends had seized. According to some accounts, he didn't even bother to read the message which

[6]Kingsbury Smith, "Unrevealed Facts about Robert Murphy," the *American Mercury*, November, 1944.

[7]Demaree Bess, "The Backstage Story of Our African Adventure," the *Saturday Evening Post*, July 3, 10, and 17, 1943.

[8]Kingsbury Smith, op. cit.

Darlan sent. In any case, the message elicited no reply from the marshal, and Darlan remained "helpless" to issue the non-resistance orders.

The whole scene must appear ludicrous to minds untrained in the peculiar logic of "diplomacy." We had elected to engage in *Realpolitik*. Why, then, did we not do so at the very moment when it would have been most likely to save lives? Our troops were landing; our friends held all the communication facilities in Algiers; the leading French officials were in our hands. Murphy might have issued whatever orders he pleased in Darlan's name, or in Juin's, or "in the name of the Chief of State, Marshal Pétain." What was to stop him? Nothing, apparently, save his incredible ineptitude.

According to Murphy's own story, Darlan did not sign the armistice for Algiers until late in the morning of November 8, *"after ascertaining the strength of our landing."*[9] Several days prior to the invasion the French General Montsabert (who seized and held the Blida airfield for us) had deliberately ordered several divisions of Vichy troops into the desert for "maneuvers," hundreds of miles from Algiers. Thus there were few Vichy troops in the city to oppose us. By midmorning, with Allied armor rolling through the streets, it was obvious to Darlan that the city was, in fact, ours. Only then did he sign the cease-fire order. We may be certain that if the Germans had succeeded in driving us out of North Africa later on, Darlan would have claimed that he signed the order because his forces were defeated and further bloodshed was useless. He flatly refused to sign an armistice for all North Africa when pressed to do so by General Ryder on November 9. By this time Pétain had issued his notorious answer to President Roosevelt's note: "France and her honor are at stake. We are attacked; we shall defend ourselves; this is the order I am giving."

This, then, was the situation at ten o'clock on the morning of November 10, when General Clark opened his conference with Darlan and other French officials in Algiers. Clark, with Murphy beside him, asked for an immediate armistice covering all North Africa. Darlan said that he had sent a message to Vichy, asking for instructions, but had received no reply and was therefore unable to act. Clark, somewhat heatedly, said that we were not negotiating with Vichy but with the North African French and that he was prepared to deal with any French official who could issue a cease-fire

[9]Kingsbury Smith, op. cit.

order and make it stick. Darlan insisted that such an order could be issued only "in the name of the marshal," whereupon Clark said pointedly that Giraud was willing to issue the order on his own responsibility. Darlan smiled. Giraud, he said blandly, might issue whatever orders he pleased; they would not be obeyed.

But as the conference proceeded the events of battle forced Darlan to retreat from his position, just as they had done two days before when the tanks entered Algiers. The Allies now held Algiers; they would soon hold Oran; a final offensive was being mounted against Casablanca. If Darlan were to switch to the winning side with any profit to himself, he must do so very soon. One can almost see the wheels go round in the admiral's shrewd, selfish little brain. He had been wrong when he implied that the Americans were not as stupid as the English. These Americans were of an incredible naïveté! Under the present circumstances he, Darlan, had no power; none whatever. If he had issued on Monday the orders Ryder and Murphy demanded, Noguès at Casablanca would certainly have ignored them, pending the receipt of confirmation from Pétain. Noguès's oath, like his own, was *not* to France but to the marshal's person as "Chief of State," and the marshal had now ordered resistance. It seemed impossible that the Americans should not recognize so obvious a fact, but apparently they did not. Very well, then. For Darlan it became a matter of timing—of very nice timing. If he issued a cease-fire order which was not obeyed it would be evident, even to these Americans, that he had no power. But if he issued such an order just *before* the fighting ceased, or before the information of surrender reached Algiers, these Americans would certainly leap to the conclusion that he, Darlan, had *stopped* the fighting. In that case who knows what concession he might not gain from them?

Fortunately he knew Noguès—knew him well. Noguès, like himself, was a man of sense who sought always to be on the winning side. He would never resist to the bitter end. Already it must be clear to him that, so far as resistance was concerned, the point of diminishing returns had been reached. Soon, very soon, Noguès must accept an armistice. Very well. He, Darlan, would allow himself to be convinced that it was his duty, as a Frenchman, to throw in with the United Nations. . . . It must have been at about this point that Clark issued his ultimatum, containing flat alternatives: either sign the armistice immediately or be arrested and deprived of all means of communication. Darlan was sad. The poor old marshal, he decided, was no longer a free agent but was operating under compulsion by the Germans. Darlan, therefore, would obey the "spirit" of Pétain whose "body" was so tragically enslaved. He would sign the armistice "in the name of the marshal." He did so, after some haggling over terms.

Kingsbury Smith and other apologists for Robert Murphy claim that there was, in reality, no "deal" with Darlan. Smith asserts that we never *agreed* to keep Darlan in power in return for his aid to us, though he can hardly deny that we *did* keep him in power in return for what our officials interpreted as his "aid." "Darlan signed an armistice agreement presented to him by the American high command," writes Smith. "That agreement has never been made public. It can now be revealed, however, that it gave General Eisenhower absolute control of all French African territories. In its all-embracing terms it was as complete as the unconditional surrender imposed on a defeated and conquered nation"[10]—which, of course, is precisely what Vichy North Africa was. This effort to shift all responsibility for political developments onto Eisenhower's overburdened shoulders is only too typical of the State Department's defensive strategy. So, too, is the sophistry which denies the existence of a "deal" simply because its terms are not explicitly stated in some formal document. The *fact* of the "deal," so costly to Allied prestige, is implicit in every main political event which followed from it.

There was, first, the order to cease resistance. That order contained four main provisions: (1) "Engagements having been fulfilled and bloody battle becoming useless, the order is given to all the land, sea, and air forces in North Africa to cease the fight against the forces of America and her allies as from the receipt of this order and to return to their barracks and observe strictest neutrality"; (2) the French commanders were ordered to "put themselves in liaison with the local American commanders on the subject of the terms for the suspension of hostilities"; (3) it was announced that Darlan had assumed authority over French North Africa "in the name of the marshal" and that "the present senior officers retain their commands, and the political and administrative organizations remain in force. No change is to be made without a

[10]Kingsbury Smith, op. cit.

fresh order from Algiers"; (4) all prisoners were to be exchanged.[11] Point 3 of this order is, of course, the key to our policy, determined in Washington and London. In so many words it stated that all Vichy institutions, all Vichy officials, and all Vichy laws were for the time being to remain in force. By "surrendering unconditionally" a "defeated and conquered nation" had certainly gained for itself some remarkably lenient terms. Significant, too, is the phrase "America and her allies" in point 1. The admiral, whose great-grandfather had been killed by Nelson's guns off Trafalgar, simply could not bring himself to admit the partnership of the British in the African enterprise. Only with extreme reluctance had he consented to the word "allies," without which a few fanatic Vichyites might conceivably have continued to resist the British.

This order has been justified officially on the sole grounds of military expediency. How effective was it, actually, as a savior of lives and time?

When it was issued Oran had already surrendered. The only place where fighting continued was Casablanca, where the French were, militarily, in an utterly hopeless position. The two American columns driving from north and south had met outside the city and were preparing to move in following a heavy naval bombardment. Outside the harbor United States warships were in line, waiting for the signal which would submit the city to an unmerciful shelling. In the harbor only one of the batteries of the *Jean Bart* remained unsilenced. And above the city Allied planes held complete dominance of the skies. As G. Ward Price remarks, "it was fortunate that the end came when it did,"[12] since the shells which United States warships were preparing to hurl on the port "would have caused tremendous havoc of life and property."[13] In other words, Darlan's order—assuming that it had any effect at all on events in Casablanca—operated more to save French than American lives.

But did Darlan's order, in fact, cause resistance at Casablanca to cease? There is no positive evidence that it did, and a good deal of evidence that it did not. Among the latter is an interview with General Noguès himself, reported by William Stoneman of the Chicago *Daily News* under the date of February 9, 1943. In that

[11]Waverly Root, op. cit.
[12]G. Ward Price, *Giraud and the African Scene,* Macmillan, New York, 1944.
[13]Ibid.

interview Noguès makes no reference whatever to the Darlan order as a factor in his determination to surrender. "At the moment of the American landing there was no other course than to put up a resistance," Noguès told Stoneman. "When it became evident that further resistance was impossible I sent an emissáry to Vichy by plane to say that we had defended our honor and that now we wanted to assist in defeating the Germans. On Monday [November 9] I called Wuledth, the German representative, and asked him whether in his opinion we had any possibility of resisting successfully. He replied that we had fought well but that our position was hopeless. 'Now you can see,' I told him, 'what you have done by taking our weapons away. It is entirely your fault.'"

It would appear from that that the military situation and a Nazi official's opinion were what determined the surrender, which was decided upon some thirty-six hours before the Darlan order was received. The official surrender was at seven o'clock Wednesday morning, November 11. Waverly Root suggests that Noguès continued the hopeless fight through one and a half days, at the expense of American and French lives, so that if the Germans at last won the war Noguès's position would remain "safe." All this time the pro-Allied French General Bethouart, who had attempted to facilitate the American entrance into Casablanca, was imprisoned in a Casablanca cell, charged with treason, his life or death depending on whether the Americans won or lost their battle. It certainly looks as though Noguès, brave warrior that he was, was playing it "safe." What the Darlan order did do was secure Noguès's position with the Allies. Far from treating the defeated general as a prisoner of war, the Americans, in accordance with the decision to accept the French as allies, retained him as governor general of Morocco while he, in turn, kept all the Vichy fascist laws in force— with our arms. Most of Morocco's political prisoners (men who believed enough in our professed principles to fight for them against tremendous odds) were still in concentration camps as late as February 1943—and Vichy's concentration camps were fully as horrible as their German models.

If there is doubt about the effect produced by the Darlan order in Casablanca, there is none at all about the effect in Vichy. Pétain sent a radiogram firing Darlan and ordering him to turn all his authority over to Noguès, who on this afternoon of November 10 was still resisting. Darlan, still playing both ends against the middle in as cowardly a piece of opportunism as history records, brought the message to Clark.

"In view of this, I shall have to revoke my order," he said, having decided apparently that the marshal's "spirit" was free again.

This was too much for Clark. He said flatly that Darlan would not be permitted to revoke the order.

"Then you must arrest me," Darlan said.

Clark did so, placing guards again around Fénard's villa, where Darlan was staying.

At this point Giraud, who had been sidetracked while Darlan issued the cease-fire order, entered the picture again with the demand that the Americans now fulfill the promises Eisenhower had made to him. He demanded that he, Giraud, be named chief of North African civil affairs and commander in chief of the French Army. Since Eisenhower's proclamation of Giraud's arrival in Algiers had already, in effect, named Giraud to these high positions, the general certainly had a strong legal case. Clark, however, felt himself unable to do as Giraud wished. In terms of the information he possessed, and in view of Murphy's political advice, Clark's action was natural and reasonable. He wanted to wait until the effect of Darlan's order was made clear, and he managed to persuade Giraud to this course of action. When the news of Casablanca's capitulation came through, Clark at once interpreted it as evidence of Darlan's power over the French forces.

On that same morning, November 11, Nazi troops began to move into unoccupied France. Pétain (who continued his loud screams against "Anglo-American aggression," who continued to order French African troops to resist to the utmost) offered no resistance at all—not even a token resistance—to the invading Germans. He merely sent a note to Hitler in which he protested "solemnly against these decisions which are incompatible with the armistice agreement." (According to news dispatches of that date, he did not even write a note but made his protest "orally" and, the Nazis claimed, merely "as a matter of form.") Darlan, in Algiers, was now able to reverse himself again. The marshal had become a "prisoner" of the Germans. It was up to him, Darlan, to carry on in North Africa as the marshal, in his secret heart (he certainly kept the secret well), would wish him to do. Accordingly Darlan was suddenly no longer a prisoner of war but again the chief French authority for all North Africa. Clark began to dicker with him in the hope of obtaining two things: (1) the French fleet at Toulon, and (2) the full co-operation of French forces in Tunisia.

Later that day, in Gibraltar, Eisenhower himself broadcast an appeal to the French fleet, asking that it "join with the United Nations in the fight for freedom" by sailing for Gibraltar. Darlan, in Algiers, did not broadcast to the fleet until several hours later. First he raised all kinds of objections—until Clark's patience gave way. "I see no visible indication of any desire on your part to aid the Allies," said the American angrily. Darlan immediately retreated. He realized only too well that he was helpless without American support. He broadcast his "appeal." As a London correspondent for the New York *Times* noted on November 12, Darlan's broadcast did *not* order the warships to sail but merely "suggested" that they do so, or "at least flee the German menace." Against their long-standing orders to scuttle the fleet rather than permit it to fall into any foreign hands—orders either issued or confirmed by Darlan himself—the naval officers at Toulon could now balance a mere "request" from this same Darlan who, in their view, was a captive of the Allies. At the same time Hitler was offering his usual "solemn assurances" that his troops would not occupy Toulon. Naturally the French naval officers chose to leave their ships in the harbor. Sixteen days later, when Hitler's forces moved into Toulon, the fleet was scuttled, save for four submarines (three of which reached North Africa) and some fifteen small units which the Germans managed to seize intact. It may be argued that Darlan did not have the "authority" to order the fleet to sail. Perhaps he did not. Perhaps the fleet would have ignored his orders had he issued them, since hatred of the British was one of the fleet's dominant motives. All the same, Darlan *claimed* to have authority and was gaining concessions from the Allies on the basis of that claim. Was he not taking over supreme authority in the name of the poor old marshal, now, alas, a prisoner of the Germans?

The admiral's orders to French commanders in Tunisia were similarly ineffective. The orders were issued, under pressure from Clark, simultaneously with the "request" to the fleet; they demanded that French forces in Tunisia join with the Allies in resisting the Germans. Vichy, at the same time, was ordering those commanders *not* to resist the Germans who, on November 11, were pouring troops into Tunisia by transport plane. Darlan's orders were revoked by a "subordinate" during the night of November 11–12 and had to be reissued on the morning of the twelfth, when Clark discovered the attempted double-deal—a fact which might well have caused the Tunisian French to doubt the validity of those orders. In any case, Darlan's orders were ignored. Vichy's were obeyed.

In summary, then, what had we gained thus far from our dealings with Darlan? Algiers? Certainly not, for Algiers was, in fact, ours before Darlan issued the cease-fire order. Oran? That, too, was ours before Darlan's signature to a North African armistice was effective. Casablanca? If Darlan had anything to do with the surrender there, Noguès, the commander on the spot, failed to acknowledge it. The French fleet at Toulon? It remained at Toulon. The co-operation of French forces in Tunisia, which was the area of decision? No, for these forces refused to join us and they permitted the Germans to come in without firing a shot. The future co-operation of French forces in Morocco and Algeria? Surely it seems clear, in retrospect, that this co-operation was not contingent upon the maintenance in power of Admiral Darlan. As John MacVane, who was in Algiers at the time, says in his book *Journey into War,* "whomever the Americans and British wanted to name as boss of North Africa would have the support of the majority of North Africans—whether he were De Gaulle or an insignificant member of the Blida town council."

Eisenhower himself was informed that the French Army was so legalistic in its outlook—so concerned with pay and pension rights —that it demanded a "legitimate succession of authority" whereby those rights would be guaranteed. Granted that this is true, what evidence is there that the Army regarded Darlan's usurpation of power as a "legitimate succession of authority"? After all, Darlan had been flatly repudiated by Marshal Pétain, who was the only "legal" French authority; moreover, the admiral's orders and "requests" had been wholly ineffective in those areas where French commanders retained any freedom of decision. If pay and pensions were what determined the French Army decision, the Army must surely decide that the Allies were now in a better position to guarantee these things than was Vichy. At least if French soldiers threw in with us at that point their pay would continue and they would remain free. If they refused to join us their pay would stop and they would probably be locked in war-prisoner stockades.

But this is to view matters in retrospect, judging them in the light of facts which were only grudgingly revealed over a period of several months. Those facts were not available at the time to Eisenhower. In Gibraltar he must make a series of snap judgments on the basis of limited and often erroneous information, in an atmosphere of crisis, knowing well that mistakes must be paid for in other men's lives. His primary assignment was not to determine political policies but to win battles; if he had both political and military decisions to make at the moment it was only because the former were subservient to the latter. He was determined to keep them so. Whatever political decisions he made must, he insisted, be regarded as *military* expedients of a temporary nature—and in making them he naturally relied heavily on his government's chief political representative, Robert Murphy. Then, too, the basic political pattern had been determined long before he assumed command of the operation. It only remained for him to "acquiesce," to "confirm," and to take the blame. He must harvest fields which had been sown with error and, in harvesting them, assume public responsibility for the poor quality of the crop.

His overwhelming concern at the moment was to protect the right flank and the rear of those forces he had sent racing toward Tunis. To do so he needed, at the very least, positive assurances of French neutrality. The margin of success might well be provided by full French co-operation. Anxiously scanning the dispatches from Clark and Murphy, he was informed that Giraud was powerless to effect the needed co-operation. He was informed that Darlan *could* effect it. The latter information was, he believed, confirmed by the fact that Darlan's order had been "obeyed" at Casablanca. It was still too early to tell what the French fleet at Toulon would do. Darlan, if he were named French authority, might yet persuade the Toulon officers to throw in with the Allies. The same thing was true with regard to Dakar and French West Africa. In Dakar Harbor were the battleship *Richelieu*, the submarine tender *Jules Verne*, three 7,600-ton cruisers, three destroyers, and a dozen submarines. If Darlan's orders had been (as Eisenhower believed) effective with Noguès, they might be equally effective with Pierre Boisson, the governor general of West Africa. Apparently Darlan had been in-effective in Tunisia, but this might indicate merely that the Tunisian French were in a hopeless position; the Germans, certainly, were pouring in reinforcements at a tremendous rate. This latter fact, the speed of the German build-up, conditioned all of Eisenhower's thinking. It increased his impatient disgust with the wrangling in Algiers. He replied to a message in which Clark detailed his difficulties:

Valuable moments have been wasted trying to bring the Frenchmen together. What do these men want? Are they not content with leadership in a great movement to raise France from bondage or do they desire to disappear into disgraceful obscurity by allowing France to suffer without lifting a hand to save her? . . . Will these men confess that we have a greater love for America than they for France? They have an opportunity to achieve immortality in the hearts of their countrymen by uniting with the common aim of fighting for their country's liberation. They must not abandon France in her moment of despair by engaging in selfish fighting— fighting that can only result in their own destruction.

Clark read this message to the assembled French who, by this time, included Noguès from Casablanca. Clark then presented Eisenhower's ultimatum: the French leaders must, within twenty-four hours, accept an arrangement satisfactory to the Americans or they would all (with the exception of Giraud) be arrested. As it always is with opportunists, an ultimatum, backed by force, was effective. Well within the allotted time the French agreed to accept Darlan as supreme political authority, with Noguès and Yves Chatel remaining as governors general of Morocco and Algeria, respectively. Giraud, continuously snubbed by Darlan and the others during these meetings, was named to command the French military forces—but only as a result of American pressure. Even so Darlan persuaded the Americans to delay announcing Giraud's appointment for several days. He hinted that an immediate announcement might cause disaffection in the Army; many officers, said Darlan, persisted unfortunately in regarding Giraud as a "traitor." Eisenhower promptly approved these arrangements. He had, on the basis of the information he possessed, no alternative. He had previously radioed Washington, stating the case for the appointment of Darlan and asking for instructions; he had been informed that he was free to make whatever political arrangements seemed to him necessary for successful prosecution of the war.

On Friday, November 13, Yves Chatel, governor general of Algeria, announced to a somewhat astonished world the Darlan appointment. Speaking over the Algiers radio, Chatel read Darlan's first proclamation:

"Inhabitants of North Africa! The marshal appointed General Noguès as his delegate in North Africa on November 10, 1942, before the entry of German troops into the unoccupied zone of France. He did this believing that I was deprived of my liberty. General Noguès arrived yesterday, on November 12, in Algiers. In full possession of my liberty, and in full agreement with him, I resumed the responsibility for French interests in Africa. I have the approval of the American authorities, with whom I intend to guarantee the defense of North Africa. Every governor or resident has to remain in his place, and is to take care of the administration of his territory according to the laws in force, as in the past. Frenchmen and Moslems, I rely on your complete discipline. Everybody at his post. Long live the marshal! Long live France!"

Simultaneously, Clark, speaking as Eisenhower's deputy, was making the announcement to assembled correspondents in Algiers. Clark's manner was one of confident poise, but his choice of words —dictated perhaps by the expressions on some of the correspondents' faces—betrayed his unease. Certainly the general was not bubbling over with enthusiasm for the admiral. "We are being realistic," Clark said (the inevitable "justification" for decisions which have no moral base). "We cannot afford to risk our bases and lines of communication over a political squabble. . . . All of you must understand that Admiral Darlan was the one man in power here who controlled the land, sea, and air forces. . . . Whatever you may think of him, he was the only man who could issue the proper order to bring all factions together. He was the only man the armed forces would obey, and I had to play along with him."

3

Thus was revealed to the world that political "line" which formed so discordant an accompaniment to military events in North Africa—a "line" originated and sustained by the official hostility to the Free French. Thus was established a political precedent dangerous in the extreme to the Allied cause. The story has been told here in some detail because it is necessary to an understanding of Eisenhower's personal role. Despite various official efforts to falsify the picture, it is clear that the Allied commander's political role was almost wholly passive and that it continued so to the end of the African adventure. Subsequent political developments need therefore be treated here in only the broadest outline.

The immediate reaction to the Darlan "deal," among Allied citizens well grounded in the realities of French politics, was one of bewilderment and suspicion, tempered by a willingness to "wait and see." True, Raymond Daniell, London correspondent for the New York *Times,* summarized the unofficial British reaction as one of "disgust," but there were many who were willing to accept the explanation that the arrangement was a military necessity. Perhaps the French journalist Pertinax summed up the informed reaction with accuracy in his column of November 14 in the New York *Times.* The Americans, he reported, were apparently keeping Giraud "in reserve, feeling that Darlan can render the greatest service." Darlan, Pertinax was confident, was to be employed as a "temporary makeshift"—but he warned that Darlan was a "supreme intriguer" who "does not want to be a makeshift." It was obvious that Pertinax regarded any dealings with such a man as a mistake, but he was inclined to believe that the mistake would be swiftly corrected. "All odds are that he [Darlan] will disappear from the scene when it has become plain that he cannot serve any justifiable purpose. But, even on that assumption, the present state of affairs is truly bewildering."

Bewilderment and suspicion were not decreased by President Roosevelt's explanatory statement of November 17. It was a statement which placed responsibility for the situation squarely on Eisenhower's shoulders. "I have accepted General Eisenhower's political arrangements made for the time being in northern and western Africa," said the President. "I thoroughly understand and approve the feeling in the United States and Great Britain and among all the other United Nations that, in view of the history of the past two years, no permanent arrangement should be made with Admiral Darlan. People in the United Nations likewise would never understand the recognition of a reconstituting of the Vichy government in France or in any French territory. . . . The present arrangement in North and West Africa is only a temporary expedient, justified solely by the stress of battle." Implied in this statement was the kind of self-contradiction which Socrates discovered, two thousand years ago, in the sophist argument—namely, that *if* the argument were true it must, for that very reason, be false. The contradiction was not lost upon careful observers at the time. Waverly Root sums it up as follows: ". . . if it were true that Darlan possessed the power which . . . was the justification for the deal with him; and if it were also true, as the President said, that his past record was one which made him a man not to be dealt with on a permanent basis, then it would seem to have been very unwise to give him public warning in this fashion that he was to be pushed aside later. And if he were so impotent that there was no risk involved in thus warning him that his best interests lay in thwarting those of the United Nations, then the whole argument for using him at all fell flat."[14] At any rate, as the weeks passed, revealing Darlan ever more solidly entrenched in power, the announcement of the admiral's "temporary" status came to be regarded as a deliberate attempt to mislead the public, especially so since the Vichy laws (including the anti-Semitic decrees) and the Vichy concentration camps were maintained in North Africa without appreciable change.

The chorus of public criticism swelled steadily, and much of it was focused—especially in Britain—upon Eisenhower. In London the Free French General Georges Catroux (who, incidentally, outranked Giraud in the Army of the Republic) held a press conference. "The agreement with Admiral Darlan was concluded on military grounds," he said, "and, speaking on military grounds, I say that Darlan is dangerous. Hitler might make an attack on Gibraltar. Think where the Allied force would be left then, the enemy coming from both sides, and Darlan in the middle! If I were fighting in Tunisia I should not like to feel that I had Admiral Darlan in my rear." As if to give point to Catroux's argument, Franco of Spain on the following day (December 8) made a speech in which he placed himself unequivocally on the Nazi-Fascist side. The choice, he said, "is between communism or fascism" for Europe— and he chose the latter; if Hitler attacked through Spain it was clear that the Franco forces would offer no opposition. The suspicions of the Free French, meanwhile, gave way to anger. A secret radio station operated by the underground in France made nine separate broadcasts to England, on November 27, 28, and 29, urging the Allies not to endorse Darlan. De Gaulle began demanding an "immediate clarification" of Darlan's status. Wendell Willkie

[14]Waverly Root, op. cit.

demanded the same thing. "I make no defense of expediency, military, political, temporary, or otherwise," said Willkie in a Toronto speech. "For I believe that the moral losses of expediency always far outweigh the temporary gains." In an article published in the London *Evening Standard* on December 7 Willkie bitterly assailed the "international censorship" which, he said, had prevented his discussing the Darlan arrangement and which was "being used to cover up official mistakes."

Correspondents in North Africa were making the same complaint, pointing out with ever-increasing exasperation that the best radio station in West Africa, the Morocco Radio at Rabat, was being permitted to send out thinly veiled Vichy propaganda which must, necessarily, be the chief source of on-the-spot political news from Africa for millions in America and Britain. On December 7 Washington correspondents filed stories to the effect that Darlan "retains sufficient influence" to hold up broadcasts to Europe by the Office of War Information. Harold Callendar of the New York *Times* said flatly that the Rabat station was "not available to O.W.I." because Darlan declined to make it available. The admiral opposed the type of broadcast O.W.I. wished to make to France, and O.W.I. refused to make the type of broadcast which Darlan wanted, according to Callendar. The truth of the matter is that neither Allied headquarters nor (apparently) Darlan knew what was going out over the Rabat station. Milton Eisenhower, now associate director of the O.W.I., arrived in North Africa on December 7 to help implement the psychological-warfare program. One of his assignments was to clarify the radio situation, and he was the first to bring detailed information as to the nature of the Rabat broadcasts. He discussed the matter with Murphy, who sent him to Rigault, the director of information for the Darlan government. Rigault stalled, in typical Vichy fashion. Milton then took up the matter directly with his brother, who directed him to Darlan. As soon as the admiral heard Milton's story he picked up his phone and ordered Noguès to permit Americans to take control of the station, the change to occur at midnight that night (the phone call was made at five o'clock in the afternoon). On December 21 Washington correspondents announced that Rabat was now broadcasting O.W.I. material.

In vain did Washington officialdom seek to justify its policies by pointing to the acquisition of Dakar and the adherence of Pierre

Boisson to the Allied standard in early December. Dakar alone would justify the Darlan deal, asserted the War Department—but others were quick to point out that Boisson's position in any case had been hopeless. Darlan or no Darlan, Boisson had no real alternative to surrender. To the south of him, in French Equatorial Africa, and to the east of him, in the Lake Chad region, were the Free French. To the north of him, in Morocco and Algeria, were the Anglo-American forces. Whether he surrendered or not, there was no possibility of his doing serious harm to the Allies, though from his capitulation the Allies did gain some naval units. From Moscow came the report that Russian public opinion was unanimous that Darlan was no true friend of Allied interests. Not even from the defenders of the Darlan arrangement in the United States could Washington officialdom derive much comfort. Chief among them were Senator Vandenberg, who had not yet retrieved his national reputation from the slough of pre-Pearl Harbor isolationism, and Representative Hamilton Fish, whose opinions were forever discredited by his long record of protofascism.

Again and again officials sought to remove the heat of hostility from themselves by focusing it on Eisenhower. Secretary Hull's conversations with two Free French representatives in Washington, as reported by Arthur Krock in the New York *Times* on December 9, were typical. Because the Free French persisted in regarding our recognition of Vichy France as an organic element of the pattern which now included Darlan, Hull began by defending the State Department's Vichy policy which, he asserted, made it possible for American agents to "move freely . . . and gauge with accuracy what elements of assistance to the United Nations could be relied on in North Africa." At the time of the invasion, Hull went on, our forces were perilously exposed and Eisenhower did "what has proved to have been the most effective thing in the protection and advance of the Army to its objectives"; that was not the moment to "stop fighting and ask the names and addresses of those French who offered to aid us and showed they could do so." As a result of the Darlan arrangement, said Hull, the "military timetable was two months ahead of schedule" and "the lives of 18,000 American soldiers, probably much more before the chapter is ended," had been saved.[15] In short, it was all Eisenhower's doing—but he, by some

---

[15]The Allied casualties for the entire campaign—killed, wounded, captured, and missing—totaled 18,738.

strange coincidence, had done precisely what the State Department wanted him to do. The Free French, needless to say, were not satisfied with Hull's explanation.

On December 17 the Distinguished Service Medal was awarded to Robert Murphy, with Eisenhower personally officiating at the ceremony. As he pinned the decoration on Murphy's lapel the general remarked, "You certainly deserve it." The citation, which aroused acid comments in both Britain and the United States, referred to Murphy's "distinguished service to the United States" and to his "outstanding qualities of leadership and sound judgment." Thereafter, whenever Murphy's removal was demanded (and it was demanded even by such sober commentators as Walter Lippmann), the State Department invariably referred to Murphy's D. S.M. as evidence that he had done an excellent job in a dangerous and difficult assignment.

Political censorship continued to mangle the stories filed by correspondents in North Africa, a procedure symptomatic of the total Allied attempt to "sit on the lid." Beneath that lid the pressure of outraged public opinion, denied a safety-valve outlet, increased to dangerous proportions until violence, the inevitable answer to repression, flared on December 24.

A twenty-two-year-old student named Bonnier de la Chapelle was waiting in the anteroom of Darlan's office that day, armed with a .22 revolver—hardly the kind of weapon which would have been chosen by a professional assassin. When the admiral entered the anteroom the student arose and fired two shots at close range. Darlan died forty-five minutes later. The student made no real effort to escape, had no accomplices, and was tried on the following day by a French military court. No record of the trial proceedings was made public; the very identity of the assassin was kept secret for weeks while fantastic rumors were circulated of "royalist" plots, and "fascist" plots, and (most persistently) "De Gaullist" plots. On the morning of December 26, barely thirty-six hours after his deed was done, Bonnier de la Chapelle died before a firing squad. This haste and secrecy aroused, quite naturally, grave suspicions. Certainly the speed with which justice was meted out to this lonely boy stands in marked contrast to the excessive formalism and delay of later war-criminal trials.

It might have been expected that the removal of Darlan would encourage the Allies to correct the more glaring of their political errors in North Africa, but this did not happen. Actually the situation for a time was worsened. The immediate official reaction in Washington was one of extreme anger, as though a great champion of democracy had fallen, martyred, beneath a fascist gun. President Roosevelt said that the "cowardly assassination" was "murder in the first degree," and Secretary Hull said that the assassination was an "odious and cowardly act"—though cowardice, under the circumstances, seems a peculiar charge. The Free French, on the other hand, pointed out simultaneously that the event made possible the union of all Frenchmen—the entrance, in other words, of the Free French into the North African government. But most De Gaullists were frankly angered when they learned of Roosevelt's "murder in the first degree" statement; the chief radio station of French Equatorial Africa spoke for them when it broadcast that "Darlan's actions have finally caught up with him" and that "never has assassination been more similar to a punishment from heaven." Thus was the breach between the Free French and Allied officialdom widened. Later on Bonnier de la Chapelle was to be honored as one of the war heroes of a liberated France, and his act was termed, not "assassination," but "execution."

Giraud was immediately chosen unanimously by the Imperial Council "to exercise the functions of high commissioner of North Africa," while retaining his position as commander in chief of the French Army. This choice was promptly approved by Eisenhower, who reported himself "highly pleased" with the selection and who, certainly, was relieved to find that his Gibraltar promise to the Frenchman was at last fulfilled. There is no doubt that Giraud, alike in his personal character and his public acts, was a distinct improvement over the slippery Darlan. He was no opportunist. If he had considerably less political talent than the situation demanded, he was at least honest and straightforward in his dealings. He made no effort to hide his sincere anti-Republican bias, but he was as determined as Eisenhower himself to subordinate political questions to military interests. This latter determination was indeed so great that, in the absence of Robert Murphy and the State Department, a relatively quick agreement with De Gaulle might have been reached. As it was, Giraud's reactionary political views were used as a weapon against De Gaulle, and the machinations of the State Department served to exaggerate rather than minimize the differences which separated the two leaders.

Certainly Giraud's initial acts, made with the full approval of American officialdom, were not calculated to allay the suspicions of sincere democrats. A few days after he took office he arrested a number of Frenchmen, including several who had actively aided the Allied landings, claiming that he had discovered a plot to assassinate him and Robert Murphy. There has been no published evidence that such a plot actually existed, and the men themselves were later released (though some of them had by that time been imprisoned for months) without trial. Even after the announced "relaxation" of political censorship on January 27 correspondents were not permitted to report the names and records of the arrested men. Thus it was made possible for "responsible" American authorities to deny that, among the imprisoned, were some of the truest friends of the Allies. At one point, "responsible" authorities denied that they had ever heard of Pierre Alexandre, Father Cordier, and Henri d'Astier de la Vigerie, all of whom (as we have seen) performed invaluable services to the Allies on November 7–8 in Algiers and all of whom were imprisoned by Giraud in January.

Hard on the heels of this unfortunate occurrence came an even greater outrage of democratic opinion. The notoriously pro-fascist Yves Chatel was dismissed from his post as governor general of Algeria—in itself a good thing—but he was replaced by the even more notorious Marcel Peyrouton, the former Vichy Minister of the Interior who was held directly responsible for the torture and murder of thousands of anti-Axis Frenchmen in the concentration camps which he installed in unoccupied France. Giraud wanted a trained administrator who had had North African experience. Peyrouton had served twice as governor general of Tunisia and had been high commissioner and resident general of Morocco. Moreover, he was a personal enemy of Laval—a fact which the State Department repeatedly emphasized in its official statements, as though being an enemy of Laval were the same thing as being an enemy of fascist principles. These qualifications, urged by Giraud and no doubt ably argued by Robert Murphy, may have seemed convincing to Eisenhower, preoccupied as he was with enormous problems of supply and army reorganization. Later he admitted (privately) that he had not so much as heard of Peyrouton until then; he approved the appointment (after having taken up the matter through channels with the President of the United States) on the theory that if Giraud were to be political chief he must be permitted to choose his own men. And the storm broke—a storm of such fury that it threatened for a brief time to force Eisenhower's removal.

If this were a "liberalization" of the North African government, the liberals of Britain and America wanted none of it. On January 19, the day Peyrouton's appointment was announced, Clement R. Attlee, Deputy Prime Minister, found it necessary to defend Eisenhower in the House of Commons. Attlee said that His Majesty's government had implicit faith in Eisenhower's "military leadership" and that "politically" Britain and the United States had a "single objective, which is to promote the union of all Frenchmen against the Axis for the liberation of France." It was only natural, he claimed, that the United States and Britain should see French affairs "in a somewhat different light" because "after all we were nearer the crisis in 1940" than was the United States. As for the Free French, they were placed in such a position that compromise with Giraud involved a compromise of fundamental principle and was, therefore, impossible. On January 20, a spokesman for the Free French said, "We cannot imagine anything less indicative of a cleanup than the sudden appointment of one of the first and most brutal of the Vichy leaders." That afternoon the House of Commons forced Anthony Eden to parry a barrage of questions concerning "dirty politics" in North Africa. Eden was forced to admit that the "situation [is] unsatisfactory" with regard to "anti-Jew and other fascist laws" but that the French, meaning the Free French, "are well aware of our views." He concluded lamely with the pious hope that "necessary steps will be taken as soon as circumstances permit" —a statement which seemed to indicate a divergence of views between the British Foreign Office and the American State Department. It was later discovered that Winston Churchill himself had sent repeated messages to Eisenhower approving the latter's political arrangements in North Africa and pledging his wholehearted support, and that a secret session of the House of Commons had voted (in December) a *unanimous* approval of the Darlan "deal" as a "temporary military expedient." The appearance that the British Government was reluctantly following the lead of the United States in this matter seems to have been deliberately created in order to soothe De Gaulle. There is, however, no question but what De Gaulle had more friends among British policy makers than he had among the American.

On the following day the London weekly *Tribune,* edited by

Aneurin Bevan, Independent Laborite member of Commons, made a direct, personal, and bitter attack on both Eisenhower and Murphy. Bevan called his attack an "all-out blitz" against the two Americans, charging that "prospective military action is hampered because a complete Vichy regime in North Africa, staffed as it is with Axis sympathizers, is in a position . . . to sabotage the Allied war effort." The situation, said Bevan, had become a "matter of urgent political expediency which can no longer be solved by arbitrary actions of the general on the spot." Attacks of almost equal bitterness were made in certain sections of the American press and by liberal American politicians. Thus did *Realpolitik* jeopardize Eisenhower's position. Thus did moves justified on grounds of "military expedience" threaten military catastrophe, for there is no doubt that the removal of Eisenhower at that juncture would have constituted a military disaster of the first magnitude.

Eisenhower's personal role in this long comedy (or tragedy) of errors was, as we have seen, not one of his own choosing. It was assigned to him. Washington officialdom seemed determined to make of him the fool of the play, the scapegoat of errors, the whipping boy of public opinion. That officialdom failed in these efforts is a measure of the general's strength of character, his talent for public relations, and his military ability. He was simply not cut out by nature for the part of fool; his innate dignity made the role of scapegoat impossible for him. Whatever he lost in prestige through political ineptitudes he more than gained back by personal example and military prowess. The very fact that he made no effort to dodge his personal responsibility for events over which he had, in fact, no control counted in his favor among the men most intimately associated with him; he commanded such immense personal loyalty among his subordinates that there was no possibility of disastrous splits on political issues. Moreover, news correspondents, inspired by personal affection and admiration for the general, saw to it that truth pierced the official smoke screen. They exerted themselves to give the public an accurate view of a man who bore his immense burdens with grace and good humor and whose personal commitment to democracy was beyond all question. They managed, in the end, to absolve him of nearly all guilt in the public mind.

Of the abundant evidences of his innocence, contained in newspaper dispatches, one alone will here suffice. After long negotiations through the early months of 1943 it was decided that the groundwork had at last been laid for an agreement between De Gaulle and Giraud. Accordingly the announcement was made that De Gaulle would soon come to Algiers for personal consultation with Giraud. But on April 5, after De Gaulle in London had literally packed his bags for the trip, he received a letter bearing Eisenhower's signature asking him to postpone the journey, "for military reasons." The timing of this letter was extremely embarrassing to De Gaulle. He expressed "disappointment" and asserted that a prolonged delay would involve a "serious disadvantage" to all concerned. His subordinates were angered; they claimed that the opposition to De Gaulle was "making a last-ditch stand." Two days later, in Algiers, Eisenhower expressed "surprise" concerning published reports that he had urged a postponement of the trip. His public-relations officer said that "since the communiqué [the Free French statement] was issued in London he [Eisenhower] has no doubt that a full statement of circumstances will be made." In London, De Gaulle expressed "surprise" at Eisenhower's "surprise." In Washington, Secretary of War Stimson, in a press conference, strove to clear up the confusion by saying that Eisenhower's expression of "surprise" was, no doubt, occasioned by the failure of "this French political group" (a rather insulting reference to the Free French) to appreciate "the impracticability" of a visit to North Africa "at the height of a battle." Correspondents, unsatisfied and unfooled, needled Stimson until he admitted that "another possible cause" of the general's surprise was that he, Eisenhower, was not at his headquarters but at the front when the message to De Gaulle was "sent in his name." Harold Callendar, summing up the matter in a dispatch to the New York *Times* on April 9, wrote: "All these clues to the mystery seemed to fit in with the statement today by persons in close touch with the affair that the suggestion to put off General de Gaulle's visit came originally from the British and that General Eisenhower, as is the case of certain oft-criticized appointments, merely acquiesced in a political decision." It seems evident that Eisenhower had not so much as seen the letter which was "sent in his name."

Despite Giraud's early colossal blunders, the fact remained that his attitude toward De Gaulle and the Free French was much less intransigent than Darlan's had been. For one thing, Giraud's life and liberty did not depend upon keeping De Gaulle from political leadership as Darlan's had done. De Gaulle, for his part, felt no such personal animosity toward Giraud as he had felt toward Darlan. At the Casablanca conference in late January he shook hands with Giraud, before the seated figures of Churchill and Roosevelt, while the cameras clicked. The handshake was rather perfunctory; the two men remained far apart in political philosophy and actively opposed for a long time as regards the government of North Africa. Nevertheless, it *did* symbolize a measure of progress when one considers that under no circumstances would De Gaulle have permitted himself to be photographed shaking hands with Admiral Darlan.

From this slender beginning progress was made, slowly, painfully, toward a solution of the political problem, a solution which was not merely expedient and which might serve as a foundation for a reconstituted French Republic. It was progress through struggle. On one side stood the enemies of French Republicanism, backed by the major forces of American officialdom, passively supported by the British Foreign Office. On the other side stood popular opinion, ever more articulate, ever more solidly organized as news correspondents managed to get out the story, piece by piece. In the end popular opinion won out. The British in late December sent Harold Macmillan to serve as their diplomatic representative in Algiers, and he seems in the following months to have exerted a moderating influence. A memorandum addressed to Giraud by De Gaulle's French National Committee in London on February 23 served, in the late spring, as a basis for the establishment of a Joint Central Executive Committee, presided over alternately by Giraud and De Gaulle. Peyrouton and other notorious Vichyites were removed from office. Vichy legislation was repealed, the laws of the Republic were restored, civil liberties were guaranteed, and a public declaration was issued to the effect that the future French government must be determined through free elections by the French people.

In July, weeks after the fall of Tunis, De Gaulle was firmly established as political head of the interim French government, with Giraud serving as commander in chief of the Army. By that time it was abundantly clear that De Gaulle was supported by the overwhelming majority of Frenchmen, that Giraud had virtually no following at all, and that the withdrawal of the American forces from French territory must make Giraud's position wholly untenable. The net result of State Department machinations had been the creation of a dozen De Gaullists where one existed before, and an official visit to the United States that summer did nothing toward raising Giraud's prestige at home. Shortly thereafter this strange figure faded from the scene, never to be heard from again.

It remains to appraise these political matters, so far as possible, in terms of Eisenhower's personal development. His was, as we have seen, a remarkably "unpolitical" education, from a Kansas village through West Point into the Army. It is true that he had read a great deal of history, but he had concentrated on military history, and his attention had been confined primarily to events and personalities. He himself asserted that when he studied the war campaigns of the past he paid special attention to the personalities and reactions of the commanders—"for war is a human drama," and the human element is relatively constant while weapons and tactics undergo ceaseless change. His study was to help him immeasurably as a general. By knowing where various commanders of the past had made their mistakes, he was enabled to avoid similar mistakes himself. But it seems evident that he had relatively little conception of history as trend or process, of the ideological history which leads, for example, from the German romantics through Nietzsche and Spengler to Hitler, or from Marx through Lenin to Stalin's Russia. Consequently he was perhaps too inclined to underrate the importance of principles, of ideologies, as determining forces in history.

As a matter of fact, he once said in private conversation that he distrusted abstractions and ideological generalizations, believing that they tend to make the mind inflexible and to obscure its view of external realities. Certainly a general, who is required by his profession to think primarily in terms of physical forces and their distribution, might find an ideology in his professional field (a "theory of war," for instance) a doubtful asset. Gamelin in 1940, for example, provided a tragic object-lesson of a general who was so much a slave to theory as to be blind to modern practice. On the other hand, an ideology somewhat more rigid than Eisenhower's seems to have been, or at least an understanding of prevailing ideologies, would seem to be a necessary guide in a realm where ideas rather than guns, philosophies rather than regiments, are the dominant factors. North African politics was, in large part, such a realm. Here physical facts, just by themselves, gave a deceptively permanent appearance to what was in reality a fluid situation. Perhaps, without generalizing too far, one might say that here the frontier pragmatism which has so largely determined the character of modern American education revealed, through Eisenhower, certain basic weaknesses.

He played, as we have seen, a passive role—but perhaps his role would have been less passive, perhaps he would have been less inclined to "acquiesce" without a struggle to arrangements of doubtful wisdom, had his mind been conditioned to regard consistency rather than immediate expedience as the test of value and of truth. A mind which had submitted to a severe classical discipline might have regarded much more critically than Eisenhower seems to have done the precepts of that *Basic Field Manual, Military Government* which, with Robert Murphy's advice, was to constitute his chief guide through the intricacies of French politics. The manual, prepared in 1940 by the judge advocate general and later supplemented, was issued by the War Department to all American commanders. As a political guide for democratic forces invading fascist lands it was worse than useless; it was downright dangerous. It contained the seeds of tragic mistakes in such statements as the following: ". . . so far as reliance may be placed on them to do their work loyally and efficiently, subject to the direction and supervision of the military government, the executive and judicial officers and employees of the occupied country . . . should be retained in their respective offices and employments and be held responsible for the proper discharge of their duties. . . . The personnel of the military government should, so far as possible, deal with the inhabitants through the officers and employees of their own government. . . . The existing laws, customs, and institutions of the occupied country have been created by its people and are probably those best suited to them. They and the officers and employees of their government are familiar with them, and any changes will impose additional burdens on the military government." It is only too easy for pragmatical minds to sacrifice ends to means, to forget that the actions of the moment are what determine, step by step, the direction of total movement or (which is the same thing) the ultimate goal.

But this "passivity" of Eisenhower's—and it is difficult to see how, under the circumstances, he could have been anything *but* passive— is certainly the full measure of his culpability. He paid for it many times over. The religious tradition, which was his family heritage; his early family training; his personal temperament—all these combined to insure his profound commitment to democratic beliefs. Hence he was particularly sensitive to and defenseless against any

] 392 [

criticism which fastened upon him a moral opprobrium. When his brother Milton arrived in Algiers in December, bringing the first detailed information concerning popular reactions to the Darlan deal, the general was deeply hurt. The hurt remained. As late as the summer of 1944 he said repeatedly in private conversation: "The liberals crucified me in North Africa. All this talk about my 'betraying the common people'—it's absurd. I'm a comman man myself, more so than most of these people who are always talking about the 'proletariat.' I've worked with my hands at about every kind of job there is. The liberals didn't try to understand that I had to protect my communications, that by securing French co-operation we almost got Tunis for nothing. They didn't try to realize that you can't do everything at once, that the world moves forward in little steps. No, they just crucified me." But by that time, and as a result of his hurt, he had learned a great deal about political tactics in the area under his military jurisdiction. He made, in France, virtually none of the mistakes which had been made in North Africa. . . .

4

It is a relief to turn from the confusion of politics to the field in which Eisenhower was actually, and not merely nominally, the dominant figure. In the military field there was a remarkable clarity of analysis, brilliance of conception, and boldness of execution. Here every act was consistent with ultimate aims and contributed to them.

By November 18, 1942—the day on which Eisenhower moved his headquarters from Gibraltar to Algiers—Allied forces were already well inside Tunisia. They were makeshift forces, composed of units of all sizes hastily organized without regard to nationality (though they were predominantly British) and thrust eastward so rapidly that they had already outrun any adequate air support. On November 15 American parachute troops had been dropped near Tebessa, at Youks les Bains, barely twenty-five miles west of the Tunisian frontier, to capture the airfield and gasoline stores. On the following day British parachute troops had been dropped at Souk el-Arba, only seventy-odd miles from Tunis itself, there to co-operate with French army units which had declared their willingness to fight under General Giraud and were organizing to oppose the enemy. Meanwhile, the British troops landing at Bône continued their eastward advance and on the eighteenth repulsed a German attack mounted with thirty Mark IV tanks and approximately four hundred infantry at Djebel Abiod. Eleven of the German tanks were destroyed. On each of the following six days enemy columns made probing attacks against the extended and very thinly held Allied front.

From Algiers, Bougie, Philippeville, Bône, the British First Army under General Anderson was poured piecemeal into Africa. On the evening of the twenty-fourth that army began a general advance, though its communications were far from completely organized. One column advanced along the coast toward Mateur. To the right of it, another column (of British parachute troops and infantry, mingled with a few French troops) aimed for Medjez-el-Bab, gateway to the Tunisian plain. Across the latter column's line of march, a mixed American and British armored column, called "Blade Force," was thrust northeastward from Souk el-Arba. On the twenty-fifth "Blade Force" reached a point midway between Mateur and Tebourba after considerable fighting, and on the following day American light tanks hit the enemy airfield at Djedeida, destroying forty Axis planes on the ground. Tebourba and Medjez-el-Bab were occupied while far to the south the United States parachute troops dropped at Youks les Bains, co-operating with French army units, drove all the way to Gafsa and Faid Pass, protecting the right flank of the First Army, which would otherwise have been dangerously exposed. This was the high tide of the Allied advance. On November 30 the northernmost column made an attack on a hill north of Jefna, which dominated the road to Mateur, and was repulsed with heavy losses. There followed several days of confused fighting during which the Allies were forced out of Tebourba but managed to hold the vital points of Faid and Medjez-el-Bab.

By this time it was clear that the Axis had reacted as strongly as possible to the Allied advance and would continue to do so. By air and by sea enemy forces poured into Tunisia at the rate of one thousand men a day, despite heavy losses inflicted by Cunningham's Mediterranean fleet and by the Allied air forces. By early December upward of twenty thousand first-class troops, with considerable armor and having the advantage of short interior lines of communication, opposed what was little more than an Allied screening force. German troops had a firm grip on Gabès, Sfax, Tunis, and Bizerte. By Christmas, Eisenhower knew that the chance for gaining Tunis at once and at little cost was gone.

His troops operated under tremendous handicaps which were beyond his power to overcome. The enemy had permanent bases in Sicily and Sardinia, one hundred miles from Tunis; the Allies had hurriedly improvised bases of which the nearest, Algiers, was four hundred miles from Tunis. The Axis had numerous all-weather airfields immediately behind the front; the Allies had only one really good airfield near the front, the one at Souk el-Arba. The Axis had a network of wide highways and railroads, with excellent rolling stock for the latter, through which to feed supplies and reinforcements; the Allies had a single railroad from Algiers, with rolling stock that was both over-age and insufficient, while the roads were often little more than mountain trails which became rivers of mud during the rainy season. Lastly, the tactical loading of Allied convoys—determined by the possibility of prolonged Vichy troop resistance—denied the possibility of any swift reinforcement of the Allied Tunisian front. At both Oran and Algiers assault parties with their transport had been the first to land, followed by administrative and anti-aircraft personnel, then by transport for the entire army, and finally (some days later) by the main body of combatant troops. It was impossible to make any quick radical changes in the disembarkation order.

But for Eisenhower's disappointment in the loss of his "race," there were very real compensations. Several unhappy incidents had demonstrated beyond all doubt that the American troops under his command were far from ready for any such hazardous enterprise as a frontal assault against *Festung Europa*, even had they possessed the numbers and matériel which might have made such a project seem feasible. At Oran ground-air co-ordination had been better than expected, but even there American fighter-plane pilots had twice in two days strafed American vehicles. A more disastrous recognition failure had occurred near Medjez-el-Bab on the morning of November 25, when C Company of the 701st Tank Destroyer Battalion (American) was virtually destroyed as a fighting unit through strafing attacks by American P-38s—and this at the most critical point of a critical battle. Nor were these failures of ground-air co-ordination the only tactical failures. The Americans, for all their courage and dash, lacked tactical efficiency. They could gain it only through battle experience. And Eisenhower, taking the long view, could see that the experience gained through months of hard fighting in Tunisia might be worth more to the Allies, in the end and in terms of lives and time, than would the taking of Tunis by Christmas. Beset as he was by political troubles in Algiers, uncertain how far the French could be trusted to guard his tenuous communications, he resigned himself to limited Tunisian objectives, for the time being, without serious qualms.

From the command point of view, the campaign had become by January an Allied holding action. With limited forces the Allies must contain an Axis bridgehead which threatened continually to expand. Medjez-el-Bab especially must be held at all costs, for it was the jump-off spot for any drive into the plain. From the east Rommel's Afrika Korps was streaming toward Tunis, pursued—but not too closely, with typical Montgomery caution—by the British Eighth Army. People in Britain and the United States hooted derisively when Berlin propagandists broadcast that the Germans were "continuing their westward advance" through Tobruk, Benghazi, El Agheila—but from Eisenhower's standpoint that is precisely what the Germans were doing. The American must prepare for renewed and dangerous pressures against his slender front once the Afrika Korps had retired behind the Mareth Line—and it looked as though that might be soon. It looked as though Tripolitania might be abandoned without a fight. Give him any appreciable margin of superiority in men, tanks, planes, and the Desert Fox might break completely out of the Tunisian encirclement. With his amazing mobility he might then threaten the whole African enterprise. It was up to Eisenhower to see to it that Rommel never obtained that margin of superiority. For a long time the top Allied command must fight a quartermaster's war, a war which would be won by the army that brought up most rapidly its supplies and reinforcements and which spread over its forward units a superiority of air power.

Hence there was little glamour in the job Eisenhower now had to do. It was largely an administrative job—incredibly intricate and detailed—in which the triumphs would remain anonymous while the defeats, if he sustained them, would be trumpeted to the world. Harbors must be cleared of sunken ships. Dock facilities must be swiftly repaired and expanded. Rail lines must be prepared to carry increasingly heavy traffic. Old roads must be improved and new ones constructed. Measures must be taken to protect sea lines against submarine attack and rear areas against a possible Axis thrust through Spanish Morocco. French troops must be equipped with modern weapons and transport. Above all, the civilian population must be provided with the necessities of life while the French African economy was started on the road to recovery. By the latter part of January ten thousand tons of food a month were being landed in French African ports. Eisenhower must have thanked God that his past experience had not been exclusively or narrowly military, especially that he had worked in the field of industrial mobilization. It is small wonder that he was inclined to adopt a laissez-faire attitude toward political developments, leaving his "expert," Robert Murphy, a virtually free hand.

Among his minor anxieties was an unfortunate confusion of authority between civilian-controlled psychological-warfare agencies and the military-censorship units of his own staff. The confusion was delaying and even preventing an adequate news coverage of the African campaign. The actual censoring was done by military censors, but representatives of the State Department, the British Foreign Office, and O.W.I. all had much to say about what could be, and what could not be, passed. Beedle Smith, the Chief of Staff, who was inclined to regard newsmen as evils of doubtful necessity, felt that the Army should have exclusive control of psychological warfare and he would have shed no tears if the obstreperous journalists had all packed up and gone home. But Eisenhower, who may sometimes have shared Smith's feeling, took a larger view. He was much relieved when his brother Milton arrived to help straighten out the matter, with the result that both censorship and psychological warfare were centralized in one section headed by a brigadier general.

During his three-week stay in Algiers in December, Milton lived in his brother's villa which, with another villa occupied by Admiral Cunningham, stood in an enclosure on the ridge above Algiers. The villas were built in the Moorish style, with large luxurious rooms downstairs, but small rooms, in insufficient numbers, upstairs. Butcher, Mark Clark, and Mickey McKeogh lived with the general. Both villas, Butcher explained gaily to Milton, were mounted on a "floating landscape"; the enclosure was "sliding downhill" at the rate of a few inches a year, a speed which was accelerated during air raids. This was perhaps fortunate for the Allied cause, said Butcher, grinning, because it meant that Ike must wind up the campaign as quickly as possible to avoid riding his villa down into the sea. On the night of their arrival, Butcher went on, the general's dinner had been cooked in the large fireplace in the downstairs

salon because both gas and electricity had just been bombed out by
Nazi aircraft. The balcony upstairs, commanding a beautiful view
of Algiers Harbor, was dubbed "the bridge of my ship" by the irre-
pressible naval aide. He loved to stand up there during air raids with
Williams, the colored servant, who was dubbed the "bosun's mate."
"Williams," Butcher would say, "my glasses"—and through the
binoculars he would watch the fantastic spectacle of diving planes,
flak, tracers, and exploding bombs. As it had always done, Butcher's
extravagant nonsense, which masked a solid core of efficiency,
brought smiles to the general's weary countenance, relaxing tensions
which sometimes seemed almost unbearable. Telek, the Scotty puppy
who shared the villa, also contributed in inimitable Scotty fashion to
the general's morale.

Milton was more pleased than surprised to find his brother taking
his anxieties in stride. Never had the amazing resilience of his character, trained from earliest childhood in the Kansas family, displayed
itself to better advantage. He was so completely the master of himself that even the unprecedented, unexpected, and unjust burdens
imposed on him failed to arouse the slightest perceptible resentment. He continued to direct all his attention *outward*.

At Algiers he put in very long workdays. He arose at seven o'clock
each morning. A few minutes later he was busy with dispatches
accumulated overnight which called for his immediate personal
attention. As he breakfasted he made the decisions which the messages demanded. Often he had staff officers in for breakfast, beginning thus early the round of conferences which, shortly after eight
o'clock, were continued in his office at headquarters. Headquarters
was in the St. George Hotel which stood above the city, not far
from the villas. Eisenhower's personal office had, somewhat unfortunately, three doors; his aides found it difficult to guard them. Eisenhower himself dubbed his office "Grand Central Station" because
people were always running in and out. Here, between conferences,
he dictated his dispatches and orders, generally pacing up and down
as he did so. Once, while dictating a "top secret" dispatch, he
flung open the door of his office and walked out into the hall, calling
the concluding sentences of the dispatch back over his shoulder
—an instance in which his restless physical energy proved to be
rather embarrassing, since a newspaperwoman waiting in the anteroom heard every word and had to be sworn to secrecy. His stenographers were awe-struck by the rapidity and precision of his dicta-

tion. Ofter they had to take dictation at the rate of 150 to 200 words a minute, and he seemed always to say exactly what he meant. Seldom did he find it necessary to revise what he had dictated.

He lunched in the main dining room at one o'clock, often continuing a conference as he ate. After lunch came more conferences —he talked to perhaps fifty different people a day—and more dictation. Constantly, with few moments of relaxation, he was receiving information, making decisions. He and his assistants could hardly have borne such burdens had he and Butcher not made a kind of game of work. Office jokes and legends smoothed the path of routine. Eisenhower even managed to tincture with humor his rare spasms of irritability. Once, when Tex Lee and Butcher had, as Lee put it, "messed things up more than usual," Eisenhower muttered rather bitterly that "one of the chief problems of a general officer is the care and feeding of an aide." On another occasion, when things were going wrong, his loud bellow penetrated the closed door into the anteroom where Butcher and Lee were working. "Send me," he roared, "one of my so-called aides!" He rarely left the office before seven o'clock in the evening. Often it was later, and always he brought officers home to dine with him, so that dinner became more a business than a social event. It lasted, generally, until ten o'clock. By midnight he was in bed, where in tense periods he read himself to sleep with the pulp Western magazines which Ruth Butcher and Mamie sent him by the bale. Sometimes, but not often, he was awakened during the night by urgent telephone messages; he strove to keep such calls at a minimum, not because he prized excessively his personal comfort, but because without sufficient sleep he could not keep the healthy nerves, the swift reaction time, which were essential to effective command. By keeping thus a reserve store of strength he could sustain long bursts of sleepless energy when situations demanded them. In Africa, as in London, he avoided formal social functions. On two occasions he had formal dinners with Pierre Boisson, the French commander of West Africa, but even these were largely business functions, for they were involved with the surrender of Dakar.

From this routine his frequent visits to the field provided a welcome and necessary variation. He kept in close touch with the physical realities, the passionate action, of which the words pouring into headquarters were merely symbols. In the field he wore what he, borrowing the phrase from Churchill, called his "goop suit." It consisted of overall-type trousers which came up nearly to his armpits and the bottoms of which were buttoned around his shoes, plus a heavy battle jacket. Instead of a military cap he often wore a knitted helmet during the winter months. He ate ordinary field rations, C or K, consisting of hard biscuits, chocolate, coffee, canned vegetables, and beef stew. He was always in such a hurry on long rides that he never stopped to heat the stew or make coffee. His immense physical energy was a source of awe, and exhaustion, among those who accompanied him. Often he covered two hundred miles a day by jeep over bad roads —and jeeps, as anyone who has ridden them can tell you, have virtually no springs. On one trip he left Algiers by plane at three o'clock in the morning, had commanders meet him at various airfields along the way, transferred to a command car for further inspections, and kept going until midnight. He snatched three hours of sleep before starting out again. By noon he was back in Algiers, where he continued conferences until evening, had the usual number of officers out for dinner, and was busy with maps and reports until eleven o'clock. Next morning he was in his office at the usual time, apparently none the worse for wear.

His advanced command posts moved with the course of the campaign. The first one was located at Constantine. The second was at Youks les Bains—and there were several subsequent ones. During the Sicilian campaign a command post was located at Amilcar, immediately outside Carthage. Said Butcher later: "We could spit upon the ancient ruins, and frequently did."

But if Eisenhower spat upon ancient fallen walls, it was certainly no sign of contempt for the past. He was frankly fascinated by the visible history which spread itself across his theater—the broken temples and aqueducts, the desolate hulks of once-mighty cities, the ancient rock-slabbed military roads through deserts which once had blossomed as the "granary of Rome"—and he often bemoaned the fact that he had no time to explore the antiquities which lay on every side. (After Wild Bill Hickok, Hannibal had been the foremost hero of his adolescence.) There were abundant reminders of the continuity of the present with the past. They helped to give him a detached, passionless view of his immediate problems, a historical perspective on his own operations. During plane and car rides into the field he often regaled his companions with lengthy and erudite dissertations on Roman and Carthaginian campaigns. He grinned deprecatingly when, later on, correspondents dubbed him "Eisenhower Africanus," but he could not fail to recognize a valid, if slight, analogy between his position and that of the Roman Scipio. He, too, was commanding in a Punic war which could end only with the complete destruction of one of the antagonists. . . .

"Ike's job," said an old Abilene friend in the spring of 1944, "is mostly that of a diplomat."

This friend was reflecting what must by now be recognized as a popular misconception, gleaned from newspaper reports. It is a curious fact that during the African campaign and for a long time afterward the British and American publics were given an erroneous picture of Eisenhower's function as a commander, and that the errors of the picture had their source in the very efficiency of his command. Time and again he was pictured by correspondents as "primarily a fixer," "more a politician than a soldier" (hardly a compliment in view of the political bungling), or, in his own words, a mere "chairman of a board." Correspondents were inclined to assume, perhaps unconsciously, that Eisenhower's "personal charm" was doing substitute duty for "military genius." Many of them failed to realize that he could hardly have functioned successfully even as "chairman" had he been unable to meet the strong personalities under him, and exert his leadership of them, on their own professional ground. Correspondents liked and admired him. They strove to present the facts about him. They did all they could to defend him against political attacks. But what he did in the miltary sphere seemed so easily, almost casually, done that it was easily underrated.

Actually the African campaign revealed in him a rare fusion of personal charm and military genius; he employed both as tools of his job. It is true that the spirit of intelligent, effective compromise which permeated his command stemmed partially from his instinct or temperament. To this extent it was a kind of unconscious effusion. But it was even more a creature of his conscious will. The most careful and intimate observers soon realized that it sprang from a conscious *control* of the will, a dynamic control by which the will's tension was varied all the way from an unyielding tautness to complete relaxation, depending upon the needs of a given situation. In the military-administration sphere, which absorbed nine tenths of his energies, the objective needs and the proper responses to them were determined by an extremely sharp, well-informed, analytical intelligence. He picked his staff with great care and leaned heavily upon it—he delegated authority "beautifully," in the words of General Smith—but the staff was always *his* and at all critical points he dominated it absolutely. He listened to advice; he made his own decisions. On several crucial occasions his decisions ran counter to the advice of a majority of his staff, with fortunate results.

Nor was his command "easy" or "soft" in its relations to the field. On the contrary, there were frequent complaints concerning his "ruthless breaking" of men for inefficiency. His standard answer was that "you can't have rotten timber in a strong structure"—and why should he send a man home at his present rank to serve as a problem for the War Department? If a man had proved himself incompetent to hold the rank, his keeping it was dangerous to the war effort and particularly to the men whom he might command. On the other hand, Eisenhower cautioned subordinate commanders against breaking an officer without thoroughly studying the man concerned and attempting to find a place in which that man's special attributes would be of value. His favorite metaphor in this connection was a tree: should we cut down the tree or transplant it? A tree which grows poorly in one soil may do splendidly in another. . . . Tactical commanders were left free to make tactical decisions, but they knew that a critical tactical intelligence was constantly watching them. During his frequent visits to the field (where he became immensely popular with the troops; they all called him "Ike" with sincere and respectful affection), his advice frequently clarified for field officers situations of doubt. On the rare occasions when he intervened directly in tactical operations, reversing the decisions of tactical commanders, he was invariably proved right by the event.

But even those who sometimes complained about his "ruthlessness" in removing field officers knew Eisenhower as a humane, generous, kindly man. He was as far from the "blood and guts" type of commander as one could imagine, and the troops knew it. Conditioning every phase of his command system was a feeling of genuine humility and gratitude toward the men in the front lines, a fact frequently remarked by the favorite G.I. war correspondent,

Ernie Pyle. Eisenhower knew now that he hated war as bitterly as any man in a foxhole. He knew, too, that the men in the foxholes were, en masse, infinitely more important than he. Deep within him there was even a kind of spiritual unease because he lived in relative comfort far behind the lines while men whom he liked and admired were dying at the front. It wasn't a sense of guilt. He knew that his function was essential and that it would be stupid for him to take needless chances. But he had an acute realization that those men fought and died by his orders and that a mistake on his part could kill them uselessly. There are generals who can make a sharp distinction between themselves as men and themselves as commanders. As generals they are simply the top compartments of a vast organization chart, impersonal vessels of authority; they can dispose of whatever feeling of personal responsibility for casualties which they as men might have by assigning it to the impersonal organization. Not so with Eisenhower. He had a very personal feeling for his men, and the casualty lists made him ache. His feeling was communicated directly to the troops during his inspections. They sensed it in his orders of the day. The latter were always free of those grandiose sentimentalities which so often measure an unbridgeable psychological gulf between a supreme commander and the grimy, weary, frightened man in the line.

All these attributes of his command were abundantly demonstrated during the early months of 1943. After the loss of the race for Tunis, Eisenhower was involved immediately in problems of staff and field reorganization. At the Casablanca conference in January three basic decisions were made: first, the ultimate goal of the European war was clearly defined as the "unconditional surrender" of the fascist powers; second, the strategic pattern by which that goal was to be achieved was confirmed; and, third, a unified command was created to absorb the forces advancing on Tunis from the west and the British Eighth Army advancing from the east. (Tripoli fell on January 23.) It appears that there was some difference of opinion concerning the second of these three decisions. Churchill spoke still of the "soft underbelly of Europe" and kept his eye on what looked to him like an "open door" into the Balkans through Yugoslavia—a stratagem which Eisenhower opposed. But there was no difference of opinion as to who should command the final phase in North Africa and the subsequent campaigns against Sicily and Italy. Already it was evident that more Americans than British would be involved in the approaching campaigns; it was equally evident, to Roosevelt and Churchill as well as to Marshall, that Eisenhower in a purely military way had done all that had been expected, and more, and that he had displayed superlative qualities in the creation and leadership of coalition forces. Accordingly Eisenhower was named to command.

The choice of a deputy commander in chief to direct the ground forces was, for Eisenhower, an easy one. General Sir Harold R. L. G. Alexander, under whose leadership Montgomery had made his grand march from El Alamein, had been the "last man off the beach at Dunkirk," had directed the last stages of the ill-fated Burma campaign, and was recognized as one of the two or three top British ground commanders. Not the least of his attributes was his ability to handle the highly individualistic Montgomery of whom Eisenhower must now make a "team-play" man. As commander of the 18th Army Group, which Eisenhower now established, Alexander had under him the British First Army headed by General Anderson and including the bulk of the French forces under General Koeltz, the British Eighth Army under Montgomery, the American Second Corps under General Fredenhall, and some Saharan forces of the French. On the field level, thereafter, Allied forces were to operate as integral national units. Eisenhower realized that by doing so the field forces would be more effective, fighting with their own equipment under commands they were used to; he realized, too, that public opinion in both America and Britain demanded such an arrangement. When he announced in a press conference on February 15 that the Americans had been regrouped, that they would now fight in units "at least as large as a division," he compared his decision to that of Pershing in World War I. In March 1918, Pershing had responded to a dangerous German offensive by permitting American units to be scattered among the British and French "wherever needed." Later he had insisted upon an integral American army. The decision, then as now, said Eisenhower, was "simple common sense."

The choice of a deputy commander in chief to direct the air forces was equally simple. Eisenhower had first met Air Chief Marshal Sir Arthur Tedder in Algiers in December. The two men had liked each other at once. Tedder was a small man physically, as unpretentious as Eisenhower, and even more retiring than the American (he slumped down in the back seat of his car so that he wouldn't have to return salutes)—but he was a lion in courage. As a flier in World War I he had been mentioned several times in dispatches, and in World War II he, like Cunningham, was critical of what he termed the "timidity" of too many ground commanders. "They'd shudder at the casualties we take in the air," he said, "and on the sea too. Cunningham has sent cruisers in when he knew they had only a fifty-fifty chance of coming through. You have to do it in war. You save lives, and time, in the end by doing it." Yet his feeling for his men was much like Eisenhower's. His men loved him. They told friendly stories about him and the pipe which was almost constantly in his mouth, a pipe whose puffs punctuated his sometimes acidly humorous speech.

He was recognized as perhaps the greatest air tactician the war had produced, but he was far from being a narrow air specialist. His appraisals of over-all strategy and of personalities were remarkably shrewd. He gave Eisenhower useful tips on how to handle the peculiar Montgomery temperament. Asked for his opinion of Rommel, he said flatly that Rommel was *not* a great general; the German was a fine leader and ground gainer, but his tactical judgment was frequently faulty and he was impatient of logistics; he was always outrunning his communications. Asked, finally, to serve as Eisenhower's military adviser, Tedder smiled and shook his head. "No advice without responsibility," he said—and Eisenhower saw at once the justice of that position. The two men agreed that some one command should control the air arm for the entire theater. At Casablanca, Eisenhower insisted that Tedder assume the command. Under Tedder were Air Marshal Sir Arthur Coningham and Major General Carl A. Spaatz, who were charged with the tactical execution of Tedder's strategic plans, employing the forces of the British Middle Eastern Air Command and the United States Army Twelfth and Ninth Air Forces.

Admiral of the Fleet Sir Andrew Cunningham continued as commander of British and American naval forces in Northwest African waters, but his command was extended to include "all cognate operations in the Mediterranean." Vice-Admiral H. K. Hewitt of the American Navy served as Cunningham's deputy. Thus Eisenhower's three principal deputies were Cunningham on the sea, Tedder in the air, and Alexander on the ground.

Changes were also made in Eisenhower's personal staff. Beedle Smith, whose staff work had been outstandingly good all through the initial stages of the African campaign, remained as Chief of Staff. His deputy was Major General J. F. M. (Jock) Whiteley, known as one of the best staff officers in the British Army. Serving as a kind of super-co-ordinator of all staff sections, especially of G-1 (personnel) and G-4 (supply), was Chief Administrative Officer Lieutenant General Sir Humfrey Gale. An American, Brigadier General Benjamin W. Sawbridge, headed G-1, with British Brigadier Victor Westropp as his deputy. For the highly important post of G-2 (intelligence) Eisenhower counted himself fortunate to obtain Brigadier Kenneth W. D. Strong, who probably knew more about the inner workings of the Nazi military mind than any other man on the Allied side. Strong had spent four years inside Germany, first during the Rhineland occupation in the 1920s and secondly from 1936 to 1938, when he witnessed what he called "the most humiliating event in British history" at Munich. His receding chin and horn-rimmed spectacles caused him to be called affectionately "the ugliest man in the British Army," but he was better known, at forty-three, as one of the Bright Young Men of that army. Strong's deputy was the American Colonel Thomas E. Roderick. Heading G-3 (operations), which devises battle plans and maintains direct contact with combat units, was the American Brigadier General Lowell Rooks, whose deputy was the British Brigadier C. S. Sugden. Heading G-4 which must win a logistic triumph against almost insurmountable odds before a combat victory could be obtained, was Brigadier General Clarence Adcock of the United States Army. Brigadier R. R. Lewis of the British Army was Adcock's deputy.

Thus, while forces in the field operated as integral national units, the top command remained an amalgamation of British and Americans who worked together and messed together without regard for differing national allegiances. (Brigadier Sugden, who messed with twelve Americans, used to complain regularly that he was "picking up all their bloody American habits.") To weld the new elements of his command into a single smooth-working team, Eisenhower employed the conference method which he had developed with so high a degree of success in London; the top men knew one another so intimately, were so thoroughly conversant with one another's eccentricities of mind and speech, that there was little possibility of their misunderstanding one another. Headquarters, concerned now with the Sicilian and Italian campaigns as well as with the Tunisian, grew swiftly to what seemed, to outside observers, a fantastic size. Attached to it were eleven hundred officers and fifteen thousand enlisted men, scattered through thousands of offices in hundreds of Algiers buildings. The signal center handled one thousand code messages a day. "Why, it's a hyperthyroid War Department!" exclaimed one American officer, newly arrived from Washington's enormous Pentagon Building. Yet once one became familiar with its inner working, this vast and sprawling organization revealed itself as an amazingly flexible, unified instrument of command, dominated by Eisenhower's personality. Never before in history had staff work of such intricacy been performed with such great efficiency. There were some military failures in North Africa, but they were not traceable to faulty staff work.

For several weeks Eisenhower was outranked by many of the men under his command. The War Department corrected this situation on February 11 by promoting him to the rank of full general (temporary). A radio broadcast from Washington, closely followed by a cablegram from Mamie, gave Eisenhower the first news of his promotion. The official notice came on the morning of February 12, just as an enterprising French jeweler arrived at headquarters with twelve handmade silver stars to sell. . . . Later that day Eisenhower left Algiers for the front, taking Telek with him.

Bad luck seemed to dog his steps in the field. On December 24, during his last visit to forward units, he had seen his forces bogged down in seas of mud under cold, ceaseless rain. At General Anderson's headquarters outside Souk el Khemis that evening he had received the news of Darlan's assassination. He would never forget the ride back to Algiers in a jeep (no aircraft could take off from the rain-soaked field at Souk el-Arba) through a seemingly endless night and day. Trapped in the mud-spattered jeep, watching the rain slant down from leaden skies on Christmas Day, his mind had been helpless prey for the most intense anxieties. It had looked to him then as though everything might be lost, for he well knew that a serious civil war in his rear, abetted by a fascist thrust through Spain, could force the entire African expedition over the brink of destruction. . . . And now, in February, he was to witness in person the American "bloody nose" at Kasserine.

Though Tripoli had been occupied by Montgomery on January

23, eight sunken ships blocked the entrance to that harbor, and all dock installations had been so badly damaged by Allied air attacks and German demolitions as to be virtually useless for a time. This meant that the Eighth Army, coming up against the strongly fortified Mareth Line, had stretched its communications almost to the breaking point. The nearest supply port was the extremely limited one at Benghazi, hundreds of miles to the east. Even without the Mareth Line, a pause in Montgomery's offensive would have been inevitable. Accordingly, Rommel had left two Italian corps, two German light divisions, and the 15th Panzer Division to guard the line and its right flank while he moved northward with the 21st Panzer and Centauro divisions. At Sfax he was reinforced by elements of the 10th Panzer Division sent down from northeastern Tunisia by Colonel General Juergen von Arnim. His great concern at that moment was that the American Second Corps, under Fredenhall, might smash down from the hills into the Sfax plain, thus splitting the Axis Tunisian forces. He decided to prevent such an occurrence by launching an attack of his own.

The Allies knew that an attack was being prepared, but their intelligence reports indicated that the main force would strike down through Pichon Pass against Sbeitla. When Eisenhower arrived at Fredenhall's headquarters at Tebessa he was somewhat alarmed to find the field commander placing an excessive trust in those intelligence reports. Fredenhall had dispersed his armored strength. Combat Command B, consisting of the 1st Armored Division with strong artillery and infantry contingents, was disposed to guard against a Sbeitla attack while two smaller combat teams were placed near Sidi-bou-Zid, far to the south, there to watch Faid Pass. This dispersal, said Eisenhower, was dangerous; it denied flexibility to the American forces. In one of his rare direct interventions in tactical operations he ordered the 1st Armored and the 1st and 34th Infantry divisions to be concentrated as quickly as possible in the valley between Sbeitla and Sidi-bou-Zid, where they would be in a position to shift swiftly either north or south in answer to Rommel's moves. But before execution of these orders was completed Rommel had struck.

On February 13 Eisenhower left Tebessa and went up through Kasserine Pass into the mountains above Sbeitla, where he inspected Combat Command B. Then he rode down through Sbeitla to Sidi-bou-Zid, into the mouth of Faid Pass, where he inspected

Combat Command A and Combat Command C. He was at Brigadier General Paul Robinett's headquarters at Sidi-bou-Zid on the morning of February 14, when the 21st Panzer Division burst through Faid Pass, preceded by diving Stukas. Sherman tanks rushed out to join unequal battle with Mark IVs and with the terrible new Mark VI Tigers of the 19th Panzer, which followed the 21st through the pass. Against the tough skin of the Tigers, the shells of Sherman 75s burst harmlessly. Combat Command A, Eisenhower could see, was in danger of being wiped out. Reluctantly, with a sense of humiliation, he fled Sidi-bou-Zid. An hour and a half later Sidi-bou-Zid was in German hands.

The long drive back to Tebessa was as fraught with anxiety as had been the drive on Christmas Day toward Algiers, and it was much more dangerous. The jeep had to thread its way between truck and armored convoys all afternoon, then crawl perilously over narrow mountain roads which twisted in hairpin turns around the cliffs in the night. Eisenhower and the sergeant who had been assigned to drive him took turns at the wheel. Just before dawn on the fifteenth, with the sergeant at the wheel and Eisenhower asleep, the jeep went entirely off the road and crashed into a ditch. It was typical of the general that, though his back was badly bruised, his first anxious words were, "Are you all right, Sergeant?" The sergeant was, and he upbraided himself bitterly for his "carelessness."

"That's all right," said Eisenhower. "If I'd been at the wheel, probably the same thing would have happened."

At Tebessa, reviewing the front-line dispatches with a crestfallen Fredenhall, Eisenhower was able to take stock of the situation. The Americans had already sustained a tactical defeat, certainly. Many of the fresh-faced lads who had cheered him two days ago now lay dead; the 1st Armored Division had been almost consumed in the furnace of battle at Sidi-bou-Zid (this division was restored to fighting efficiency in a few weeks, however). It was a bitter loss, but it could not have serious strategic consequences unless Rommel managed to thrust beyond the Kasserine Gap in much greater strength than seemed possible. If Rommel got through to Tebessa and Thala communications for the entire Tunisian front would be seriously threatened; Anderson, in the north, would be forced to withdraw in order to protect an exposed right flank. And if Rommel recovered enough Allied tanks to replace his own losses, giving him reasonable security for a battle with Montgomery, his capture of Tebessa might be only the first step in an appalling catastrophe for Allied arms. But this was to take the worst possible view of things, and Eisenhower refused to accept it. Working with Fredenhall and Alexander, he issued swift orders. Combat Command B was to be concentrated near Tebessa. Anderson was to rush down a British armored brigade from his First Army in the north. Artillery from the American 9th Division was to guard Thala and the vital road which swept northward across First Army communications. Kasserine Pass was to be mined and, to be ready for the worst if it happened, preparations were made to blow up the great supply dumps at Tebessa.

That afternoon at Fredenhall's headquarters the correspondents who gathered for a press conference with Eisenhower caught no hint of the general's worries. He was as breezy, as informal, as casually confident as ever. He announced the regrouping of the American forces in units "at least as large as a division." He had been up front and seen some action. He had talked to a lot of G.I.s. He had had more time this trip than he had had on his last one. . . .

Back at his headquarters in Algiers, Eisenhower found dispatches which told of further American withdrawals. On the afternoon of the fifteenth an armored column which Rommel had sent southward from Faid had occupied Gafsa without a fight. On that same afternoon an American counterattack, mounted with medium tanks, had thrown the advanced guard of the Germans back six miles, to the vicinity of Sidi-bou-Zid. But on the following day Rommel renewed his attack in force too great for the Americans to withstand. By the eighteenth the Germans had taken Sbeitla, Kasserine, and Feriana. By the twenty-first they had swept up the hastily sown mine fields and pushed on through Kasserine Pass. Beyond the pass two heavily armored columns were formed, one driving due north against Thala, the other driving northwest toward Tebessa. In the war room at headquarters Eisenhower and Smith stood before the wall maps while the new positions were pin-pointed. The most optimistic eyes could discern, in those rows of pins, the outlines of possible disaster.

"This," said Eisenhower, "is the pay-off. We ought to be able to hold them with the artillery. Even a Mark VI can't stand up under a 155-millimeter shell."

Smith nodded. He was still studying the map when Giraud burst in. The Frenchman's nerves were unstrung. He waved his hands in tragic gestures as he spoke.

"We've lost Tunis!" he said. "The First Army must withdraw at once."

He spoke in French, but his meaning was clear to Eisenhower. The top commander remained perfectly calm. He spoke soothingly.

"We haven't lost anything, really," he said. "Look at the map. Look at the terrain. Even if we weren't able to oppose Rommel with any stronger forces than have faced him so far, he hasn't enough stuff to follow through. He'll get stopped short of Thala and Tebessa. He'll lose a lot of armor and he won't even have gained any time."

All the same, it was a serious tactical reverse, and Eisenhower unhesitantly shouldered full responsibility for it. ("A commander must have broad shoulders," he once explained. "Any general who gets into the bad habit of blaming subordinates when things go wrong soon works himself into such a position that he can no longer exercise effective command.") That day he sent a radio message to General Marshall: "Our present tactical difficulties resulted from my attempt to do possibly too much, coupled with the deterioration of resistance in the central mountainous area which began about January 17. That deterioration has absorbed the bulk of the United States 1st and 34th divisions . . . but you would have been impressed could you have seen the magnificent display everywhere by the American enlisted men. . . . The troops that come out of this campaign are going to be battle-wise and tactically efficient." Four days later Secretary Stimson, in Washington, told his press conference of another Eisenhower message. "All complacency on their [the troops'] part has been dropped," the message said. "They are thoroughly mad and ready to fight." If Eisenhower strove, through these messages, to mitigate the effects of defeat on the home front, he did so by telling the simple truth. Fatally handicapped by tactical command errors, their armor uselessly sacrificed in piecemeal fashion, the American troops had nevertheless exacted from the arrogant Afrika Korps a heavy price for every key point. And in the space of a few bloody days those green troops had been transformed into grim, battle-hardened veterans.

As Eisenhower had predicted, Rommel never reached either

Thala or Tebessa. He came uncomfortably close. On February 22, at noon, his tanks reached a point only four miles from Thala, but they were met there by the new forty-two-ton British Churchill tanks sent down from the First Army and by an intense fire from concentrated American artillery. By nightfall the offensive punch was gone from the 21st Panzer Division. When Eisenhower came down from Algiers on the following day to meet Alexander on the battlefield and watch the American counterattack he found the landscape south of Thala littered with the scorched hulks of Mark IVs and Mark VIs. Meanwhile, to the south, a two-pronged attack against Tebessa had been met, stopped, and rolled back toward Kasserine Pass by American tanks, infantry, and anti-tank guns. On February 23, aided by the mightiest air assaults yet launched in the Tunisian theater, a smashing counterattack knocked Rommel's Thala arm back fourteen miles—all the way to Kasserine Pass. On the morning of the twenty-fifth, after an all-night artillery barrage, the Americans retook the pass without opposition. Thereafter it was Rommel who was in trouble. Harried by Allied tanks, pounded by fighters and bombers, he fled across the Faid plain sowing mine fields behind him while Von Arnim, in the north, strove to relieve the pressure by launching an attack toward Béja on the British First Army front. The attack failed. The Americans were in Sbeitla on March 2. Two days later they had recaptured Sidi-bou-Zid and were within three miles of Faid Pass.

With the Allied position "restored" and the mistakes of battle thoroughly digested, Eisenhower decided upon a change of commanders for the Second Corps. The decision was typical of his ability, demonstrated again and again, to judge a commander in terms of the job to be done. Fredenhall was an infantry general who had little flair for tank warfare. In Casablanca, chafing at his enforced inaction (though he served a useful strategic purpose by continuously "bluffing" the Spanish command north of him), was Georgie Patton, the American Army's great specialist in tanks. Mark Clark was sent to Casablanca to relieve Patton, there to continue "bluffing" the Spaniards. Patton, in the first week of March, replaced Fredenhall.

Meanwhile, on February 24, Major General Omar N. Bradley had arrived in North Africa. Eisenhower, his mind's eye gazing as always several months into the future, began grooming his old West Point friend at once to take over the Second Corps for the final phase in Tunisia. He would need Patton to command the Americans in the Sicilian campaign, which, according to plans, was to be the kind of blitzkrieg for which Patton's special talents were particularly suited.

"You're my special representative for the next several days," said Eisenhower to Bradley on the twenty-fourth. "Go around the central sector and see things and report to me what I would see and decide if I had time to make the tour."

Bradley was on this assignment for ten days, and his concise reports enabled Eisenhower to judge the quality of his old friend's military thinking. Bradley was a careful observer, a sound strategist and tactician, a good judge of men, as selfless in his devotion to duty as Eisenhower himself. If he had any military defects, they were the defects of his virtues: he was, perhaps, as Patton once complained in a fit of friendly annoyance, "too damned sound"; his "soundness," reinforced by a deep personal concern for his men, might prevent his exploiting to the maximum a break-through situation. If this was a defect, Patton, certainly, was the man to correct it, and when Patton went into the line Bradley went along as deputy corps commander. Together they prepared an attack toward Gafsa and a juncture with Montgomery's Eighth Army and launched it with remarkable initial success in the third week of March. The Americans took Gafsa on March 17, after a swift forty-two-mile thrust. They were in the tactically important town of El Guettar on the following day. On March 23 they captured Maknassy.

Meanwhile, through a battle plan brilliantly conceived and beautifully executed, Montgomery with his Eighth Army was forcing the south gate into Tunisia. In a radio message to General Marshall on March 11 Eisenhower—with his battle of supply now won—had said: "Once we have the Eighth Army through that bottleneck [the Mareth Line], this campaign is going to assume rapidly a very definitive form with constant pressure and drive kept up against the enemy throughout that region." But Mareth *was* a bottleneck, difficult to force. The strongly fortified line reached across a corridor barely ten miles in width. Its left flank was secured by the Gulf of Gabès, its right flank by the rugged Matmata range of hills. Beyond the hills lay a waste of drifting sand which the enemy believed was impassable by any force large enough to turn the line. Yet it was across this "impassable waste" that the

2nd New Zealand Division with a United Kingdom light armored brigade, reinforced by the 1st United Kingdom Armored Division, made a one-hundred-mile sweep in five days, while a two-division frontal assault, which was forced back, together with persistent aerial bombardment of the coastal area, convinced the enemy that Montgomery's main effort would be straight up the coastal road to Gabès. On March 26 Montgomery's famous "left hook" was delivered with complete tactical surprise and devastating effect upon the enemy at El Hamma, forty miles behind the Mareth Line. The most concentrated and sustained aerial assault ever made in North Africa up to that time accompanied the El Hamma attack. On the twenty-eighth El Hamma was in Allied hands and the Italian General Messe, who had replaced Rommel, was beating a hasty retreat, having sustained heavy losses in armor and men. On March twenty-ninth Montgomery's forces were in Gabès. On April 5 the enemy defense line at Wadi Akarit was broken and Montgomery was moving swiftly against Sfax along roads "that had known Hannibal's elephants, St. Augustine's sandals, and Roger de Norman's armored horse." On April 7 a patrol from the United States 9th Division met a patrol from the Eighth Army forty miles southeast of Gafsa and only twenty miles from the sea.

During these days of crucial action Eisenhower spent much time in the field. In the last week of March he and Beedle Smith conferred with Montgomery in the latter's field headquarters. (Something of the spirit of Eisenhower's command is evident in an incident that began during the conference with Montgomery, a conference which won for the American the complete loyalty of the dramatic British commander. Smith promised Montgomery a Flying Fortress "like Ike's" in return for the early capture of Sfax. On April 10 Montgomery sent a message to Eisenhower: "I have taken Sfax. Please send one Flying Fortress with American crew, per agreement." Eisenhower did so.) On that trip Eisenhower also met with Alexander, Patton, and the French commanders. Back in Algiers on April 3, he told a press conference that the most impressive lesson which the front now gave was of the value of Allied unity. British, Americans, and French, he said, "are inspired by the common purpose of crushing the enemy and are working in complete harmony" as a team. A few days later he was in the field again for one of his most extended tours, during which he was several times under fire. He and his party spent hours threading their way through mine fields to inspect gun emplacements, mortar positions, and advanced airfields; the latter were being constructed in great numbers and at amazing speed (some of them in little more than a single day) behind the advancing lines. In the British First Army sector he examined closely several Mark VI tanks, noting the gun length and armor thickness and watching a maneuverability test of one Tiger which had been captured intact. Again he conferred with Generals Spaatz, Alexander, Patton, Allen, and again he returned to Algiers (on the fifteenth) to praise the "spirit of co-operation" which not only unified the forces of the different nations but also made for a close tactical and strategic co-ordination of the different arms: land, sea, and air.

All through February and March, Eisenhower had submitted himself, a willing pupil, to Tedder's tutelage in the employment of air power. Butcher was fond of recalling, in later years, how Tedder and Eisenhower sat on the porch of the latter's Algiers villa night after night, Eisenhower asking questions and Tedder answering them until the American was himself an authority on air power. "I picked his brains," said Eisenhower, grinning, later on. "I taught Ike a lot," said Tedder with a shy smile, sucking on his pipe. Teacher and pupil could be well satisfied with the classic demonstrations of air-ground co-ordination which were now to wreak havoc on German and Italian forces.

5

Within three weeks General Messe had lost approximately thirty thousand prisoners and fifteen thousand killed and wounded. He had lost all his supply dumps in southern Tunisia, the bulk of his armor, much of his motor transport, and a number of airfields. His air forces were disastrously reduced. The Allies now had more than air superiority over Tunisia. They had air supremacy and at any given point they could obtain a virtually absolute dominance.

Nevertheless, Von Arnim, who now assumed supreme command of the Axis "African Army Group," was ordered to hold out as long as possible, in order to delay Allied operations against the European Continent—and he had good reason to believe that he could conduct a prolonged defense. Though the Axis Tunisian bridgehead had now shrunk to an area thirty miles wide, centered on Tunis and Bizerte, behind a front 110 miles long, it was manned by 250,000 troops (fully as many as Eisenhower could supply), including some of the very best German and Italian units. These troops were well supplied from existing stock piles, and they continued to receive a trickle of reinforcements by sea, despite the

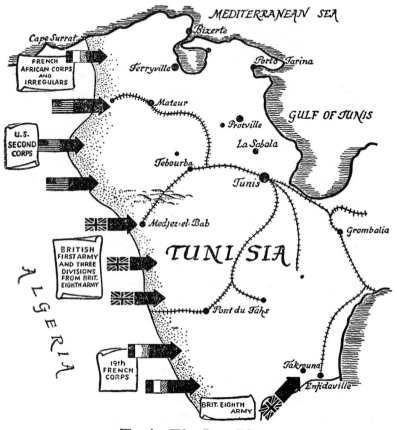

Tunis: The Last Phase

serious shipping losses inflicted through Allied air-force and Royal Navy operations. Moreover, Von Arnim had previously prepared defenses running from Enfidaville west to Pont du Fahs, then north in a snaking line along the hills to the coast. Behind these defenses his short and excellent interior communications enabled him to reinforce a threatened position more easily than the Allies could mass for an attack.

In view of these facts, the achievement of a swift Allied victory

]416[

clearly involved the achievement of surprise, and to achieve surprise it was necessary for the Allies to make a maximum exploitation of two valuable instruments: first, the mastery of the air which enabled us to see while the enemy remained blind; second, the tremendous reputation of the British Eighth Army. In his original battle plan Alexander made the utmost use of Allied air power—but he was limited in his exploitation of the enemy's "blindness" and of the Eighth Army's reputation by his grave doubts concerning the tactical efficiency of the American troops. On the record, and taking a strictly military view of the matter, Alexander's doubts were abundantly justified. At Kasserine, in February, the American tactical leadership had been faulty, with near-disastrous results. At Foudouk Pass, in the second week of April, American troops who were to clear away German artillery units on a hill guarding a mine field arrived too late at the jump-off point, with the result that infantry could not remove the mines. Because of this American failure a force of British tanks had had to be deliberately sacrificed to clear the field—and Alexander would have been less than human if that bitter memory had not weighed heavily with him. It was all very well, on paper, to feint with the Eighth Army, causing the Germans to concentrate in the south, and then swing the main offensive punch in the north. But who was to swing that punch? The Americans?

Precisely, said Eisenhower. The Americans—*and* the British, *and* the French. He frankly admitted that, had he been in Alexander's position, he would have been as reluctant as Alexander was to have the Americans play an active role in the final offensive. But he was not in Alexander's position. He was supreme commander, and as such he had to look beyond the immediate battle, take into consideration such factors as public opinion at home and the future role of American forces. He pointed out to Alexander that Britain was nearing the end of her man-power reserves, that American man power must be counted upon increasingly in the future, and that therefore the Americans must gain confidence in themselves through successful battle experience. The very fact that they had sustained a "bloody nose" made it imperative for them to engage now in a successful assault. Moreover, he, Eisenhower, was prepared to stake his professional reputation on the fighting qualities of those American troops; they were, he was convinced, eager to correct the impression they had made during the Kasserine reverse. This being so, the advantage of tactical surprise gained by having the major attack launched by the left wing rather than the right might be quickly decisive. But more important than all these, and the chief reason for his interference, was the effect which a failure to use the Americans as a decisive unit might have on public opinion in the United States. We could not afford to risk a popular outcry which might damage future Allied co-operation.

It is a tribute to Alexander's breadth of view, as well as to Eisenhower's powers of persuasion, that the British commander agreed wholeheartedly with Eisenhower's conclusion, once the reasons for it were explained. It is a tribute to Alexander's military capacities and to the amazingly high quality of Allied staff work that he was able to implement effectively the modification of his plan. A miracle of logistics was demanded. The entire American Second Corps, consisting of the United States 1st Armored Division and the United States 1st, 9th, and 34th Infantry divisions, must be moved two hundred miles from southern Tunisia to its new positions in the north, cutting straight across the communications of the British First Army, which occupied Medjez-el-Bab and the central sector. Heavy streams of traffic must cross one another at right angles. Under Omar Bradley's command (Patton had been relieved shortly after El Guettar and sent west to activate the American Seventh Army for the invasion of Sicily) the Second Corps made this movement between the thirteenth and nineteenth of April without a hitch. The appearance of the Americans in the north came as a complete surprise to the German command.

Meanwhile, Tedder and his deputies were demonstrating the strategic uses of air power. Allied air forces had studied for a long time the time schedules of enemy air-transport activities across the Sicilian straits. On April 5—at a moment when there was a maximum concentration of transport planes on the Tunisian and Sicilian fields and when the enemy was in the greatest need of his air-transport service—the Allied air forces struck devastating blows which were continued for fourteen days. More than 150 planes were destroyed on the ground, and 50 were destroyed in the air. In all, 147 large transport planes and 31 vessels were either destroyed or badly damaged. In the words of General Marshall: "The suddenness of this complete and violent rupture of Axis communications with their Tunisian forces undoubtedly came as a surprise, upset their plans for delaying actions and the defense of the Cape Bon

Peninsula, and precipitated the collapse of the German and Italian forces."[16]

Events now moved to a swift conclusion of the campaign. On the evening of April 19 the British Eighth Army attacked toward Enfidaville and secured the town on the following morning. As Alexander and Eisenhower had anticipated, the bulk of the German and Italian armor was concentrated in the south, and Montgomery's attack convinced Von Arnim that the main assault would come from that direction. Simultaneously, in the north, the American Second Corps attacked swiftly and with immediate success, catching the enemy off balance and clearing the way for an armored thrust through the Sedjenane and Tine valleys toward Bizerte. Along the northern coast French Goums paced the American attack with a ten-mile thrust eastward from Cape Serrat. On the night of April 20–21 the enemy had launched an attack against Medjez-el-Bab and Bou Arada, on the central sector, in order to delay the First Army attack, but the attack failed. The First Army launched its assault on April 22. On May 3 the American 1st Armored Division broke through all the way to Mateur, only twenty miles from Bizerte. Eisenhower, on May 5, reported to Marshall: "Tomorrow morning we start the big drive which we hope and believe will see us in Tunis in a day or so. I believe we can clear up the Bizerte angle very quickly, but the Bon Peninsula may be a difficult matter."

On May 7 Tedder laid down his famous "air carpet" in front of the British First Army. It was an awesome demonstration of what air power can do in tactical support of ground operations. Waves of bombers, with tremendous fighter escorts, bombed and strafed for hours an area only four miles by a thousand yards in size, so that when ground units advanced in that area they were unopposed. The thrust into Tunis that day was so swift that German officers were drinking coffee in Tunis restaurants, wholly unaware of danger, at the very moment British armor was moving into the outskirts of the city. On that same day the American Second Corps, fully justifying Eisenhower's faith in it, thrust into Bizerte. Six days later, completely demoralized by the power and speed of the Allied offensive, the Germans and Italians who had backed into the Cape Bon Peninsula surrendered unconditionally. Von Arnim himself was among the captives.

[16]General Marshall's Second Biennial Report, July 1, 1941, to June 30, 1943.

Thus ended the first and, all things considered, the most difficult of Eisenhower's campaigns. Hampered by political difficulties beyond his control, by logistical problems of unprecedented magnitude, and by the inexperience of his American troops, he had wrested a continent from the hands of a powerful foe who was determined to hold it at all costs. More than 340,000 of the enemy had been killed, wounded, or captured. The prisoner bag between May 5 and May 13 alone totaled 252,000, including fifteen German and seven Italian generals. A total of 1,696 enemy aircraft had been destroyed, and 633 had been captured intact on the ground, as compared with a loss of 657 Allied planes. Ninety-five enemy ships had been sunk by air attack, 47 by submarines, 42 by surface forces. The will to fight of the Italian people had been dealt a blow from which it never recovered. Hundreds of thousands of the enemy's best troops had fought for Africa, and of these only 638 men had managed to escape. . . .

It was eleven o'clock at night when the news of the final breakthrough came to Eisenhower and Smith. Eisenhower was at Smith's house in Algiers. As Smith said later, it was all anticlimactic, for Eisenhower had predicted early in April that Tunis would fall before May 15, and Smith had agreed. The two men were tired and had just drunk a scotch and soda (something they rarely did during a campaign) when the phone call came. Smith, who was to leave on the following day for Washington, whose plane was ready at the airfield, took the call and relayed the news to his chief.

"Well," said Eisenhower, "I guess you'd better get ready to leave tomorrow, Beedle. The Sicily plans are complete. I'll look for you back pretty soon."

"I'm all ready to go," Smith said.

There was a moment's pause. Then Eisenhower said:

"Well, I'm pretty tired. I'd better go home and get some sleep."

BOOK SIX

Portrait of a General
(*From Tunis to Berlin*)

CHAPTER I

The Road to Rome

JUNE 1943 saw a pause in the violent convulsions of World War II. The warring nations, their front-line strength spent in mighty offensives during the preceding months, were gathering their energies for renewed struggle. On the Pacific front, Attu in the north and Guadalcanal in the south had been secured by the Allies, and preparations were being made for the assault on New Georgia, to be launched on July 5. In China, Japanese forces, having overextended themselves in a May offensive, had been virtually cleared from the rice bowl. In Russia the siege of Leningrad had been lifted and the epic stand and counterattack at Stalingrad had robbed the Nazis of the gains they had made in the south, at great cost, during the summer of 1942. The Russians, awaiting a renewal of the Nazi offensive, continued to demand a "true second front." In Britain and America the conquest of North Africa had produced a wave of optimism so great that it was reflected in lowered production figures. The two great publics engaged in endless speculations as to where the next Allied blow would fall.

To prevent such speculations among war-wise correspondents in North Africa—speculations which might endanger the security of the Sicilian operation—Eisenhower and Beedle Smith took a unique step. They called in the correspondents, put them on their honor, and told them precisely what, where, and when the next operation was to be. The move was a carefully calculated risk, and it resulted immediately in a drop in liquor consumption among the newsmen, many of whom were permanently cured of the temptation to write "think pieces" concerning future military events. (They came to Eisenhower afterward with an urgent plea: "Don't *ever* do that to us again!") In the first week of June, General Marshall and Prime Minister Churchill arrived at Eisenhower's headquarters, fresh from strategy conferences with the Combined Chiefs of Staff in

Washington. They reviewed the massive preparations for Sicily, witnessed the secret rehearsals of the invasion forces, and gave Eisenhower renewed assurances that he had their unqualified support during the trials which lay ahead of him.

One may be sure that Eisenhower received these assurances gratefully. It is true that he could look toward Sicily with far more confidence than he had been able to muster in the days preceding "Torch." He had more confidence in himself, he had now (he was convinced) the best staff in the world, he had first-rate field commanders, and he had battle-hardened troops. Moreover, this operation need not be mounted on a shoestring. The 15th Army Group, which was to make the invasion under the command of General Sir Harold Alexander, was composed of three crack infantry divisions of the British Eighth Army, under Montgomery; three infantry divisions, the 82nd Airborne Division, and the 2nd Armored Division in the American Seventh Army, under Patton; and an infantry division and armored brigade of the Canadian Army, under Major General Guy Simons. To land, cover, and supply these troops, an armada of nearly three thousand ships—the largest ever seen up to that time—was to be employed. To prepare the way for the assault and support it tactically, approximately fifty thousand air sorties were to be flown by the Northwest African Air Force, the R.A.F. based on Malta, and the Middle East Air Command. The Allied navies held, and should easily keep, control of the sea approaches.

Nevertheless, the Sicilian campaign, which was to seem relatively easy in retrospect, presented, in anticipation, very serious difficulties. In the first place, no amphibious operation on so vast a scale had ever before been attempted, and the opportunities for disastrous miscalculation were almost limitless; the staff work must be precise and intricate beyond anything heretofore attempted. In the second place, it seemed certain that the enemy would make desperate efforts to hold Sicily for as long as possible, perhaps going so far as to sacrifice deliberately the island garrison in order to gain time in which to strengthen defenses on the Continent. For Sicily was the key, both physically and psychologically, to Italy. Without it, the Nazis could not hope to hold Sardinia and Corsica, nor was it likely that they could hold the Italian people in a war which, from the first, had been unpopular with them.

It was estimated that the Axis had, in Sicily, between 200,000 and

300,000 men. Nominally under the command of the Italian General Alfredo Guzzoni, these troops were actually controlled by the German General Hans Hube. Among the German forces were the reconstituted 15th Panzer and Hermann Goering divisions, the 29th Motorized Infantry Division, parts of the 19th Panzer Division, and the 1st Parachute Division. Three Italian infantry divisions and three Italian coast-defense divisions were also on the island. These forces had what amounted to solid land communications with the rear, since the Strait of Messina across which supplies could flow from the toe of Italy is only two to five miles in width. The rugged terrain of much of the island's 9,936 square miles was well suited to defensive operations, while a large portion of the coast line was ill suited to amphibious assault.

The Allied problem was further complicated by the presence of the fortified island of Pantelleria, Mussolini's Gibraltar of the Mediterranean, midway between the Bon Peninsula and the northwest coastal plain of Sicily. No one knew how many planes were hidden in Pantelleria's underground hangars, ready to rise and pounce on Allied shipping at a critical moment. No one could know, for sure, how many airfields, in addition to the one visible one, were masked by clever camouflage. But the Allied staff knew that Pantelleria's strategic location athwart the shortest sea route from Tunisia to Sicily must, so long as the tiny island remained in enemy hands, make the achievement of tactical surprise in the Sicilian operation more difficult than it would otherwise be. They knew, too, that the island port was a nest for E-boats and submarines which preyed on shipping in the Sicilian straits.

It was decided to take Pantelleria as a preliminary to Sicily. The decision was Eisenhower's. Those who considered the commander in chief a mere "front man" would have been surprised had they attended the staff session at which the Pantelleria decision was reached.

The question presented to Eisenhower and his staff was this: Were the hazards of permitting the island to remain in enemy hands sufficiently great to justify the cost of seizing it? The answer to this question turned, of course, upon the answer to a subsequent one: How great would the cost of seizure be? Upon the latter question there was great difference of opinion. The majority of the staff was convinced that the cost of reducing the island would be enormous. Those holding this view—and they included the British general who would command the landing—pointed to the precipitous coast line which bounded the island's thirty-two square miles and to the mountains, rising nearly three thousand feet, which formed the interior surface. They pointed out that the only possible landing point was the port itself on the northern tip of the island, and this port was ringed with strong fortifications. Unless the forts were first reduced by air or sea bombardment, a landing would be suicidal. The staff majority did not believe that the fortifications could be reduced by air. Eisenhower turned to Air Marshal Sir Arthur Coningham and the American Major General James H. Doolittle.

"How long do you think it will take to reduce the island from the air?" he asked.

"Two weeks," said Coningham promptly.

And Eisenhower, firmly supported by Admiral Cunningham, gave the order.

There followed an awesome demonstration of what air power, aided by close sea blockade, can do to the most "impregnable" of island fortresses. In the first eleven days of June more than seven million pounds of bombs fell on Pantelleria. On the single climactic day of June 11—while Eisenhower and Admiral Cunningham watched from aboard the British cruiser *Aurora*—more bombs were loosed on this small target than had been dropped in the entire month of April that year on Tunisia, Sicily, Sardinia, and the Italian mainland. The air traffic was so heavy that pilots had to circle warily to avoid collisions. Thirty-seven Axis planes were shot down. Shortly before noon, three quarters of an hour before British landing parties went ashore, Pantelleria surrendered. With it fell the other strait islands of Lampedusa (which had also been heavily bombed), Linosa, and Lampione.

Immediately the air preparation for Sicily was stepped up. The pattern of bombings revealed clearly enough that Sicily was to be the next objective, followed by the Italian toe, but Eisenhower strove for tactical surprise by concentrating air attention on the western coastal plain, an obvious area for amphibious assault since the beaches there were wide and sloping. Other heavy bomb loads were delivered on Sardinia and far up the Italian mainland, to raise as many doubts as possible in Axis minds. Meanwhile, Pantelleria and Lampedusa were swiftly transformed into Allied fighter bases.

During this period Eisenhower—in ceremonies which he recognized as necessary but to which he attached no personal importance whatever—received two decorations. The first was the French Grand Cross of the Legion of Honor, presented to him, with a kiss on each cheek, by General Giraud. The second was the Knights Grand Cross of the Order of the Bath, presented to him by the King of England, who was making a tour of North Africa.

In charge of arrangements for the King's tour was a man who was to be of considerable importance to Eisenhower's personal life during the remaining months of war. Lieutenant Colonel James Frederic Gault of the Scots Guards was a man of some forty years (he had been too young to serve in World War I), of slightly above average height, slender, balding, rather thin-faced, with a mouth—probably the most distinctive feature of his face—that appeared to be narrower than most. He had a habit of pursing his lips in a highly expressive way when he talked, and he spoke in the crisp accents of the British upper class. His basic attitudes were in harmony with his manner of speech. He had a rather terrific sense of what's "done" and what isn't, sustained by the typical aristocratic sense of one's responsibilities as a member of the ruling class. Later on these attitudes were to arouse some resentment in Mickey McKeogh, whom Gault—all unwittingly: it didn't occur to him to do otherwise—treated as a servant. It was quite easy to trace, through even a casual acquaintance with him, his family and educational background: a feudal family as close-knit as Eisenhower's, though on a far different social plane; Eton; Trinity College, Cambridge; the Guards' Club in Brook Street, London. He was, withal, a charming person, widely read, with a very sound and quick intelligence, friendly and pleasant and extremely likable.

He had had a rough time in the early part of the war. For some eighteen months he had served in the Middle East, where the ceaseless dust of desert warfare had affected his lungs. When he began to cough blood he was shipped out. For a time he had been attached to the staff of Jock Whiteley, who recommended him highly as an aide to Eisenhower. As a guide through the intricacies of British custom, Gault would be invaluable; as a companion during leisure hours, he would be charming; in his conduct of whatever assignments were given him, he would be thoroughly dependable and immensely tactful. Accordingly Eisenhower requested that Gault be assigned to his staff as British military assistant—the

British equivalent of the position occupied by Butcher and Lee. Gault received this assignment on June 26, immediately after the conclusion of the King's tour. On the following day he arrived in Malta to set up, in a tunnel, Eisenhower's advanced command post for the Sicilian operation.

On July 8—D minus two—Eisenhower flew to the fabulous island of Malta. At the airfield to meet him, a gesture which touched him greatly, were Cunningham, Alexander, and Tedder. They all drove immediately through the bomb-ruined town of Valletta to the summer palace of the governor—the town palace had been destroyed in one of the thirty-three hundred air raids which Malta had endured—where they were greeted by the governor himself, Field Marshal Lord Gort. The palace, built in 1586 and named for Cardinal Verdala, a Grand Marshal of the Knights of Malta, was to serve as Eisenhower's living quarters during his Malta stay. With him there would be General Whiteley, Butcher, and Gault, who was a personal friend of the governor. (Gault's elder brother, who had been killed on the Somme during World War I, had served in Gort's old regiment, the Grenadier Guards.) The Verdala palace had stone walls so thick that they were proof against anything but a direct bomb hit; underneath were dungeons which, according to John Gunther, were believed by the servants to be haunted; there was a huge spiral marble staircase leading to the floor on which Eisenhower was ensconced in a magnificent room with ceilings thirty feet high. Lord Gort, showing the room, hoped that the commander in chief would "be comfortable." Eisenhower grinned.

"I think it'll do," he said. "I'll have room enough."

But his office, deep in a tunnel, was far from comfortable. It was a cubbyhole, damp and so bitter cold that he had to work in an overcoat until an oil stove was brought in, though the temperature outside hovered near a hundred degrees.

With the completion of the Sicilian plans and the making of final commitments, his active role in the military operation was almost ended. Active command passed now to Alexander, Montgomery, Patton, and the other tactical leaders—but of course his responsibility for all that might happen grew greater rather than less as, step by step, the operational plans were implemented. Under the burden of his responsibility he had, for the time being, rather more free time than he liked. He busied himself with problems of press and radio "coverage." Unlike many generals, he regarded these problems as serious ones. He recognized a clear obligation to keep the people at home as fully informed of the impending events as military security would permit. ("In the last analysis," he once told correspondents, "public opinion wins wars.") With Butcher's assistance he had worked out a "pool" arrangement whereby one British and one American correspondent would be assigned to his personal headquarters to represent the combined press and radio of both countries. Whatever dispatches these two correspondents filed were to be available to every newspaper and radio station in Great Britain and America. For the opening days of Sicily, John Gunther was to be the American representative and E. J. Gilling the British one.

At eleven-thirty on the following morning—D minus one—Eisenhower held a press conference. Gunther, who gave an excellent account of it in his book *D-Day*, says that "all [the] talk was on press matters." Eisenhower went deep into the details of censorship and press communications, impressing the journalists with his sympathetic understanding of their problems and with the practical value of his suggestions. The conference lasted more than an hour. Later that afternoon Eisenhower saw Gilling and Gunther again. He wanted their dispatches to stress "Anglo-American co-operation" and the "close co-ordination" of all arms. "Unity" was the watchword. He wanted no personal publicity whatever, no mention of himself at all unless a reference to the commander in chief was essential to the story. In the latter case, mention should also be made of the other top officers of the Allied command. He had long ago established the rule that all news dispatches filed from his headquarters must bear the date line "Allied Headquarters," never "General Eisenhower's Headquarters."

As this talk proceeded the convoys were already on their way from North Africa. They plowed through uneasy seas. The wind was rising. Along the Malta beaches, breakers were rolling in, and in his tunnel office close to Eisenhower's, Alexander was admitting that the weather worried him a bit. He and Eisenhower discussed the matter after the newsmen had left. They walked out of the tunnel together, stood together in the sun-baked yard watching the dust clouds define, in sweeps and eddies, the speed and direction of the wind. The skies were clear.

"Usually the wind dies down at sunset," said Alexander hopefully.

Eisenhower nodded, watching the skies through the weather-wise eyes of a plainsman.

"It does, when it's clear like this," he said, thrusting his hand into his pocket to finger his three lucky coins—a British, an American, a French.

He believed in his own luck. Any general has to, if he is to bear up under the strain, he used to say. But that evening, as the wind, instead of dying, rose to forty miles an hour, his nerves were drawn taut as piano wires. If this kept up seasick men would land on hostile shores. It might not be possible to land on schedule the heavy equipment—the armor and transport—without which those men could not move inland. In the hope of gaining tactical surprise, relatively difficult beaches had been chosen for the landings in preference to the coastal plain in the northwest—but the advantage of surprise, assuming that he gained it, might be more than over-balanced by the hazards which the weather now posed. The slaughter on the beaches could be horrible. Even worse would be the predicament of the men in Major General Matthew Ridgway's 82nd Airborne Division if they came down in a gale. With their faces blackened, those men stood now beside their transport planes on Africa's airfields, waiting tensely for the take-off. So long as they remained in Africa it was still possible to halt the operation, postpone the landings. . . .

A message came from General Marshall, who had been told of the weather conditions. "Is it on or off?" the message asked. A reply was demanded in four hours, but by the time the message arrived Eisenhower had barely twenty minutes in which to make his decision. It was, for the commander in chief, a moment of utter loneliness. He went outside. The dust-laden wind blasted his cheeks as he gazed up into the sky. It was still clear. There would be a moonlight on those tossing seas. Carefully, with enforced calm, he calculated the risks. If he called it off now there would be abundant opportunities for isolated catastrophes. The message might not get through in time to halt some of the landings, and the troops who made them would be massacred. The chance for tactical surprise would be lost; the entire timetable, carefully designed to keep the Axis off balance, would be disarranged. He judged the wind again, his jaw muscles tightening. Abruptly he turned on his heel and went back into his tunnel office. At his desk he dictated in a calm, steady voice.

"It's on," he said. "A high wind, but I think we'll have good news for you tomorrow."

That night, under the moonlight, he stood alone on a wind-swept point of Malta beach and watched the planes roar overhead. He fingered his lucky coins. He prayed.

2

Early on the morning of D-Day, after an almost sleepless night, Eisenhower was in the war room, waiting for the pattern of success or failure to spread itself across the huge maps. The first fragmentary reports came from the British Eighth Army, which had landed on the southeastern coast against feeble opposition. Even seasick Eighth Army veterans had more stomach for the fight than the doubly betrayed and heartsick Italians. The latter, reported Montgomery, were surrendering by the hundreds, and all beachheads were firmly secured. The Canadians were safely ashore, too, on the Pachino Peninsula. But as the sun rose high in the sky and the wind, providentially, died down, there was no news at all from Patton. Eisenhower could console himself, however, with his knowledge of Patton's character. Georgie always wanted to make *big* impressions: he would wait until he had *big* news to report.

The big news came at last, shortly before noon. Everywhere, and despite seasickness, the assault parties had got ashore with unexpectedly light losses. The 1st, 3rd, and 45th Infantry divisions were pushing inland, capturing hundreds of Italian troops. Naval and tactical air-force units had covered the landings beautifully. The 2nd Armored was going in with its tanks. By nightfall it was clear that tactical surprise had been achieved, that the major Axis forces were concentrated in the north, and that all beachheads were sufficiently secure to permit the landing of the matériel needed for a swift exploitation of the initial successes. There had been no major counterattacks. A special flight of Liberators had, only a short time before H hour, bombed out the San Domenico Hotel at Taormina, which was, according to Allied intelligence, the Axis military headquarters. Apparently this feat had for several crucial hours paralyzed the nerve center of the entire island-defense organization.

Eisenhower's immense relief was evident in the broad smiles which wreathed his countenance.

"By golly, we've done it again!" he told Gunther and Gilling. "It seems impossible, but we surprised them again!"

Next day came news of a different sort. The first serious Axis counterattack was launched by the 4th Italian Division, supported by approximately a hundred German tanks, against the American beachhead at Gela. The attack scored quick initial gains and was savagely pressed until the Americans, having suffered heavy losses, stood at one point only one half mile from the sea. Disaster threatened until the cruisers *Boise* and *Savannah* moved close in and crushed the Axis armor with amazingly accurate gunfire. The Italians and what was left of the German armor beat a hasty retreat. This heartening example of tactical co-ordination was balanced, in Eisenhower's mind, by another tragic failure of co-ordination between ground and air arms. Reinforcements for the 82nd Airborne Division had come over the American-held beaches shortly after a heavy Nazi air raid. Jittery anti-aircraft gunners had at once put up a curtain of fire. Before that curtain was dropped twenty-three C-47 transport planes had been shot down, carrying to destruction 410 young American lives. Eisenhower gave immediate orders for a revamping of the entire recognition system; he blamed himself bitterly for not having done so before. In general, the airborne assaults had not been as successful as had been hoped for, not as disastrous as had been feared. Only one group managed to seize its objectives, but these were so important that they justified the whole airborne effort. All the airborne units had, within a few days, linked up with ground units.

In the early morning of July 12—D plus two—Eisenhower was himself off the coast of Sicily in a British destroyer. With him were Gault, Butcher, and the two assigned correspondents. He breakfasted with Patton and Admiral Hewitt aboard Patton's command ship, the *Monrovia*. (Bradley, commanding the Second Corps under Patton, had already established his headquarters ashore.) Eisenhower told Hewitt of the wholehearted praise which Cunningham had given the American Navy. "They had the worse of the weather on the west coast," Cunningham had said, "and the way they handled the landing craft in those big waves was magnificent." Hewitt and his men had repeated their Casablanca performance. Eisenhower was grateful. After breakfast Eisenhower and his party boarded the destroyer again and cruised southeastward toward the Pachino Peninsula. At one point German coastal batteries opened fire. The shells missed by several hundred yards. The destroyer replied. Eisenhower stayed on deck watching the action until he saw that his presence was making the ship's officers nervous. Then he yielded to a request that he take cover. "It seems I'm the bird in the gilded cage," he is reported to have said.[1]

On a beach in the Canadian sector, near the southeastern tip of Sicily, Eisenhower went ashore. He had come to make one of those gestures whose psychological impact helped to achieve Allied unity. This was the first action in which the Canadians had joined as part of what Eisenhower called "the Allied team," and he wanted personally to welcome them. There were no Canadians on the beach— they had all moved inland—so Eisenhower borrowed a jeep and went inland himself, despite warnings that there were still snipers about. At last he found a junior Canadian officer, Captain J. E. Moore of Vancouver. Eisenhower put out his hand.

"Through you, Captain," said the commander in chief, "I welcome Canada to the Allied command."

On July 13—D plus three—British troops made new landings far up the east side of the island, near Catania. Syracuse and Augusta were already in Allied hands. On the western coast, Pozzallo, Gela, and Licata had fallen, and Patton's men were pressing close to Porto Empedocle. Other Seventh Army units were pressing eastward toward the center of the island, covering the British left flank. Allied control of the air was virtually unchallenged. Six thousand Italian troops had been captured.

Eisenhower was in high spirits that day as he stepped from his plane at a Tunis airfield. He went at once to the headquarters which had been set up for him in a splendid white modern house with brilliant mosaic floors. He acceded readily to the request of newsmen for a conference. He told the assembled correspondents that enemy resistance was "negligible," that Allied casualties were "far lighter than expected," and that "a decision should be reached in about two weeks, if our present good luck continues."[2] He was, perhaps, overly optimistic, though it was later believed that the decision to abandon Sicily was actually taken at a conference between Hitler

[1]John Gunther in *D-Day*, Harper and Brothers, New York, 1943.
[2]Richard Tregaskis, *Invasion Diary*, Random House, New York, 1944.

and Mussolini at Verona on July 19. Certainly his estimate of Axis resistance was much lower than that of Alexander, who, in a press conference on August 20, expressed surprise at the rapidity with which Sicily had been conquered. "If you had asked me how long the campaign . . . would take, I would have said, 'Anything up to three months,' " he said.[3]

The original plan had contemplated a ninety-day campaign. That Sicily fell instead in thirty-eight days was due chiefly to the slashing, driving tactics of George Patton. The deep inner tensions of that strange character—the endless war within him between the most callous ruthlessness and the softest sentiments, between the love of Glory and the fear of Fear—caused him to drive his men to the limits of endurance, and himself beyond them. His theory of war, as he himself said, was simple: "Go like hell!" yet he demonstrated a tactical shrewdness which Tedder later referred to, admiringly, as "a certain low cunning." He gave Omar Bradley vivid battle lessons in the value of offensive boldness during fluid situations. Sacrificing his reconnaissance units in the most ruthless fashion, sending his armor forward with little regard for flank security, insisting always on *attack! attack!* he finally achieved his objectives at less cost in lives and time than more cautious tactics would have involved. "Remember that we as attackers have the initiative," he had written in his order of the day for June 10. "We must retain this tremendous advantage by always attacking rapidly, ruthlessly, viciously, without rest. However tired and hungry you may be, the enemy will be more tired, more hungry. . . . God is with us. We shall win." Twice he ordered Bradley forward when the Second Corps commander, concerned for his exhausted men, had paused. . . .

By D plus six the Seventh Army had virtually completed the assignment given it in the original battle plan. It had been expected that Patton would draw off enemy troops from in front of Montgomery so that the latter could drive straight up the east coast through Catania to Messina, whose occupation meant the conquest of the island. But the Eighth Army encountered stiff opposition outside Catania, and Montgomery, whose tactical concepts were far different from Patton's, paused until he could obtain the artillery preparation which, facing a determined enemy, he always demanded. Nothing was halting Patton save an exasperating phase

[3]Tregaskis, op. cit.

line. Sitting on the running board of a car, he rewrote the battle orders, then flew with them to headquarters to get them confirmed. He happened to encounter Eisenhower immediately after landing, and the two men went together to Alexander's office. If Patton had expected opposition to his new plan he was surprised. With Eisenhower's concurrence Alexander immediately canceled the older orders, issued new ones. Patton returned to Sicily.

From Enna—a communications hub in the heart of the island—the Seventh Army turned northwest and drove straight for Palermo,

The Battle for Sicily

the island's capital, which fell on July 22. Enemy troops remaining in the northwestern tip of the island (they were mostly Italian) were hopelessly cut off. Eight days later, when Eisenhower made a flying trip to Palermo and Syracuse, the 3rd Infantry and 2nd Armored divisions were driving eastward through the mountains in a race for Messina while the Eighth Army, having taken Catania after bitter fighting, was pinned down on the slopes of Mount Etna by the best German troops in Sicily. Patton stories were now as common as "Monty" ones. Among them was one concerning a British colonel with the Eighth Army who, pin-pointing the Seventh's positions on a map, said with mingled awe and exasperation:

"That bloody Patton! He has us surrounded!" This was precisely the kind of story which Eisenhower liked least to hear. By fostering dangerous rivalries between Americans and British, it tended to destroy the concept of Allied *unity* which had been so carefully developed. After the fall of Messina (captured by the American 3rd Division on August 17) and the completion of the campaign Eisenhower told a press conference, with careful emphasis: "I can only say this. Today the Seventh Army is worthy to fight alongside the Eighth. I can offer no higher praise."

In the words of the famous American military historian, Major H. A. DeWeerd, "The Allied campaign in Sicily . . . should be regarded as one conducted against an opponent already committed to a general withdrawal, who was attempting to gain time by utilizing terrain favorable for the defense."[4] Despite the unexpected swiftness of Patton's drive and the virtuosity with which he changed the direction of his flying columns, the German forces in Sicily managed to conduct an orderly withdrawal, screening their retreat with Italian sacrifice troops. Anti-aircraft guns were massed on both sides of the Strait of Messina to protect the ferries which, day and night, moved German troops and equipment from Sicily to Italy. Nevertheless, the Allied triumph—considered from the purely military point of view—was a great one. In six brief weeks 135,000 Axis troops had been captured and 32,000 killed and wounded at a cost of 25,000 Allied casualties. Valuable air bases, complete control of the western Mediterranean, considerable Italian matériel, and a springboard for possible attacks on the Balkans, Sardinia, and Italy had been gained. It was certainly, as DeWeerd says, an "organizational triumph" of the first magnitude.

But the man who had contributed so greatly to that triumph now robbed Eisenhower of much of the pleasure he might have taken in it. Only a few days before the campaign ended General Patton visited an evacuation hospital at Sant' Agata di Militello. His emotional balance, always precarious, was disturbed by strain of the intense campaign; it was completely upset by the sight of so many of his desperately wounded "boys." Always Patton had been the kind of officer who curses his men, drives them mercilessly, praises them extravagantly when they please him, and weeps over their

[4]H. A. DeWeerd, *Great Soldiers of World War II,* W. W. Norton and Co., New York, 1944.

wounds. When in a ward of badly wounded men he came upon a young soldier sitting on a cot, head in hands, he spoke kindly.

"What is the matter with you?" he asked.

The soldier looked up in a dazed fashion.

"I don't know," he said. "I guess it's my nerves. I don't seem to be able to stand the shelling."

Battle neurosis! In Patton's vocabulary it was a euphemism for "sheer cowardice" and it could be "cured" by a "shock," a "sudden stimulation of the individual's sense of shame." That, at any rate, was the rationalization he later made of his action, and he certainly never stopped to consider the difference between applying the "shock" at the front, when the neurosis is just coming on, and applying it at a base hospital after the neurosis is "set." Those who were with him, including the colonel who commanded the hospital and a chief nurse, claim that Patton's face turned purple with rage. It seems evident that he saw in the dazed man an image of that fear which lay deep in himself. He cursed the boy, called him "yellow," and struck him twice across the face with the gloves he was carrying in his hand. The nurse sprang forward to intervene but was restrained by a doctor. The ward was in an uproar. Patton went on through the hospital, shouting expressions of sympathy for the wounded and of contempt for the "coward."

A report of the incident came to Eisenhower (not through "official channels," which were of course controlled by Patton) from the hospital commandant. It was confirmed a few days later by two correspondents, Merrill Mueller of the National Broadcasting Company and Demaree Bess of the *Saturday Evening Post.* They had prepared what amounted to an affidavit signed by fourteen eye-witnesses. They presented it to Eisenhower in person in Algiers and expressed the opinion that the story could not be "killed"—too many people knew about it—and that Patton would not be able to hold active command again, at least not in the near future. The soldier whom Patton had struck had been a Regular Army man with an honorable record. He had been sent to the hospital against his will and now felt himself to be forever disgraced. "Please don't tell my wife!" he had cried again and again. . . . Inevitably an angry resentment was spreading through the Army.

Eisenhower, conducting an immediate investigation of his own, arrived at a somewhat different conclusion. He was heartsick. For two nights he had scarcely slept at all. He agreed that Patton's conduct had been disgraceful and inexcusable. On the other hand, he was informed that the damage done to Patton's command effectiveness might not be irreparable: time heals many wounds. He was further informed, by his chief press adviser, General McClure, that the story *could* be kept under cover: relatively few people knew about it, and all reports concerning it were being kept in Eisenhower's personal secret file. He needed Patton desperately, he explained, not for an active command in the immediate future, but to provide "cover" for impending operations. The Patton prestige among the Germans was now so great that they followed his movements closely; .those personal movements might therefore be almost as effective for deceiving the enemy as large-scale feint operations. Moreover, Patton's command record in Tunisia and Sicily had been brilliant; few, if any, Allied generals had displayed an equivalent talent for swift offensive movements. It would be a great pity to lose that talent if there were any possibility of saving it.

Eisenhower went on to explain, with complete frankness, the action he had taken with regard to Patton. He had sent the latter a blistering reprimand by letter and had ordered him to apologize in person to the man whom he had insulted. He was to do this in front of as many of those who had witnessed the original action as could be gathered together. Patton had also been ordered to visit the various staff headquarters under his command, apologize to the assembled officers, and have them convey his apology to the troops. These orders were now being carried out. Patton's apologies, Eisenhower was informed, were abject and were effectively quelling the resentment among his troops.[5] Eisenhower had given orders that no censorship be imposed on stories of the incident, but he personally hoped that Bess, Mueller, and the other correspondents would impose a voluntary censorship.

Faced with such a request from their chief news source, a man whom they all admired, the sixty-odd newsmen in Algiers did, of course, as Eisenhower wished. Not a word concerning the incident was filed. Indeed, at least one of the correspondents[6] came to the conclusion that Eisenhower's pragmatic handling of the episode was

---

[5]As a matter of fact, according to several witnesses, Patton's apologies were more in the nature of a defense: "Some people think I did wrong, but I'm a general who likes to win battles," and so on. He *was*, however, popular with the troops.

[6]Quentin Reynolds.

"Solomon-like" in its wisdom. In his report to General Marshall, Eisenhower concluded: "Summing the matter up: it is true that General Patton was guilty of reprehensible conduct. Following exhaustive investigation I decided that the corrective action, as described, was suitable and adequate. Eventually it has been reported to me many times that, in every recent public appearance of Patton before any group composed of his own soldiers, he is greeted by thunderous applause."

But eventually and inevitably the story *did* break. Drew Pearson broadcast it on his radio program in late November, and Eisenhower (who was attending the Cairo conference that week) was immediately subjected to severe criticism for denying to the public news to which the public was entitled. Correspondents rushed to his aid, explaining that the "censorship" had been purely "voluntary," but this defense was rendered ineffective by the actions of Beedle Smith, who resented the press criticism and sought to protect Patton. Eisenhower, aware that his Chief of Staff's great weakness lay in the field of public relations, had warned Smith repeatedly against attempting to "deceive the press." "Tell them nothing sometimes," Eisenhower had said, "but *never* deliberately mislead them." Despite this warning, Smith, in his official release concerning the Patton incident, stated that Patton had *not* been reprimanded. Technically, in terms of official army jargon, the statement was true, but it *was* deliberately misleading. On the following day, when the Chief of Staff was confronted with incontrovertible evidence of the facts, he tried to defend himself by saying that he had no "official" information concerning the affair. He asked Merrill Mueller to give the entire story to the assembled correspondents, and Mueller did so. Then Smith made his specious distinction between an "official" and "unofficial" reprimand. Press criticism, of course, became more savage. By the time Eisenhower returned from Cairo the Staff Chief was writhing in self-disgust, firmly convinced that he had made one of the great mistakes of his life. In Eisenhower's office he reviewed the press summaries and blamed himself bitterly.

"I certainly messed it up," he summarized, and awaited the severe rebuke he expected and believed he deserved.

But Eisenhower simply looked at him for a long minute, taking in his subordinate's woebegone expression. Perhaps the commander in chief felt, deep down, that he himself had been mistaken, not in his retention of Patton (he remained convinced of the wisdom of that decision), but in discouraging the immediate publication of all the facts. Then he grinned.

"Oh well, Beedle," he said, "I'll allow you one mistake a year."

3

If the Sicilian campaign was an organizational triumph of the first magnitude, it was a still greater psychological triumph. Cleverly exploited by Allied psychological warfare, the conquest of Sicily sealed the fate of Italian fascism and of the imitation Caesar who had created it. . . .

Never in all history have a people been more flagrantly misled and misrepresented than were the Italian people by Benito Mussolini. Hitler represented, however distortedly, a national ideal. His great strength lay in that fact. It was possible to trace his roots deep into the dark soil of German culture and find his grotesque pattern in a long succession of ruthless warrior heroes extending back to the days of Rome. Millions of his people saw themselves reflected in him. His leadership supplied certain deeply felt needs: for System, for Authority, for a Power "beyond good and evil." But Mussolini was a creature without antecedents. In every sense of the word he was an impostor. His fascism, seeking to emulate a Rome that had been dead for fifteen hundred years, was wholly synthetic and imposed. Far from expressing a national ideal, the corporate state —with its emphasis on discipline and imperialism and the subservience of the individual—violated a strong liberal tradition extending back to the Renaissance. Its bleak northern sternness outraged a quality of warm spontaneity which had always been characteristically Italian. Its grandiose military pretensions were absurd for so impoverished a nation and so unmilitaristic a populace.

Such an imposture could survive only so long as it need not be taken too seriously. It seems probable that Mussolini himself did not take it with complete seriousness. He quite consciously played the role of the Great Man, and his balcony ravings had always seemed like something out of an Italian opera: picturesque, sometimes moving, but never quite real. His great misfortune was to have arise, across his northern border, a warped, powerful figure who was in deadly earnest and who soon forced upon a reluctant Italy the necessity to be deadly earnest too. When that happened the imposing façade of fascism began to crack and heave. The spirit of rebellion, fostered by Allied propaganda, rose steadily against government corruption, against the enforced poverty of the common people, against the increasing arrogance of the Germans and the open contempt they now expressed toward their partners in crime, against a war in which Italian troops had been ruthlessly sacrificed to cover German withdrawals and in which a vast African empire had been lost. Disgrace in Albania; the loss of Italian Somaliland, Ethiopia, Libya; the swift crushing of "impregnable" island fortresses; the invasion of Sicily—these were the major items of an unbroken series of catastrophes. The decisive climax came on July 19, 1943, with the bombing of Rome.

The Allied high command had engaged in much soul-searching before deciding that the Eternal City, which Fascists and Nazis had transformed into a prime military target, must be attacked from the air. Allied propaganda broadcasts had warned repeatedly that such a bombing might be necessary. The bombs of July 19 were preceded by leaflets addressed to the citizens of Rome: ". . . the fascist government . . . will pretend that we are trying to destroy those cultural monuments which are the glory not only of Rome but the civilized world. . . . We leave it to your intelligence to decide whether it is likely that we should waste our efforts on targets whose destruction is useless for our purposes. . . . We repeat that we shall be aiming at military objectives." Then the bombs. The raid was made in daylight. The pilots were carefully briefed. All bombs fell in the target areas save one stray, which damaged San Lorenzo. Nevertheless, the expected Vatican protest was widely echoed by leading Catholics in all countries. . . . Six days later, on July 25, Mussolini was deposed and placed under arrest.

Marshal Pietro Badoglio, who was certainly no friend of democracy, was named Prime Minister. He had been a member of the Fascist party since 1936, had led Italian forces against the Ethiopians and Republican Spain. It is true that he had opposed many of Mussolini's policies, but he had done so on grounds of expedience rather than principle. The reactionary forces which now elevated him to the premiership were the same forces which, in earlier days, had supported Mussolini. Nevertheless, it was evident from this shift in façade that the Italian rulers were seeking a way out of the war, and Eisenhower sought to ease their search. The Allied commander at once ordered all bombings of Italian mainland cities to cease temporarily, and he began broadcasting appeals for a surrender. At the same time he began preparations for an airborne assault which, with the aid of the Italians, might capture Rome and thus paralyze the entire communications system in southern Italy.

The impending negotiations were rendered difficult by the presence of the Germans, who kept a firm control of communications facilities and a watchful eye on the movements of Italian officials. Not until the second week in August did Badoglio manage to slip two envoys secretly out of the country. That week Signor Franco Montellari and General Giuseppe Castellano arrived at the British Embassy in Madrid, frightened of the Gestapo but fully accredited to discuss armistice terms. A meeting was arranged in Lisbon on August 13, at which Eisenhower was represented by Beedle Smith and Brigadier General Kenneth Strong, Chief of G-2 (intelligence). The Allied terms were simple—unconditional surrender—and the Italians were prepared to accept them. The discussion turned chiefly upon the manner and timing of the surrender, for it was hoped that the Italian collapse could be employed in such a way as to force a German evacuation of all Italy south of the Po River line, with the possible entrapment of the Nazi troops below Rome. The two Italians then left for Rome to obtain the approval of surrender arrangements from Badoglio and the King.

Meanwhile, Eisenhower, with Gault, had flown to Quebec, Canada, to attend sessions of the conference there among President Roosevelt, Prime Minister Churchill, and the Combined Chiefs of Staff. The joint statement issued by the two heads of government at the conclusion of that conference, August 24, said: "It may . . . be stated that the military discussions of the Chiefs of Staff turned very largely upon the war against Japan and the bringing of effective aid to China." Actually one of the most important items of business at that meeting was a final decision on the place and approximate time of the western assault against Germany. The general outlines of the invasion plan—on which hundreds of officers had been working for many months and which now filled four massive volumes—conformed with those in the tentative plan Eisenhower had submitted to Marshall in 1942. The first landings were to be made on the Cotentin Peninsula, with additional landings up and down the coast if the response of the enemy to the initial assault made them feasible. The time was to be during the early months of 1944. But while these crucial decisions were being made one may be sure that the heads of government and Eisenhower himself were keeping in close touch with Italian developments. These latter proceeded swiftly as the Badoglio government sought to retain its precarious position atop a rising wave of popular discontent and against an incoming tide of Germans.

When Eisenhower returned to his theater he had to make swiftly a number of very close and difficult decisions. By August 29 plans were complete for the maximum exploitation of the military situation which might prevail following the surrender of Italy. These plans included an immediate amphibious assault against Salerno to cut off all the lower part of Italy, capture Naples, and secure the huge air base and communications hub at Foggia. Simultaneously the 82nd Airborne Division was to land in the vicinity of Rome, take the city, blow bridges, and otherwise disrupt German communications. The British Eighth Army was to assault across the Strait of Messina at Reggio Calabria. The toe of Italy was already being subjected to heavy artillery fire. It was expected that the Eighth Army's initial moves would encounter little, if any, resistance from the Italians. The Salerno operation, on the other hand, appeared risky in the extreme and it was, from the outset, opposed by a majority of Eisenhower's staff.

No one can deny that this majority could support its conclusions with powerful arguments. For successful cross-water invasions, two things are absolutely essential: control of the sea and supremacy in the air over the beaches. The Italian fleet, still an imponderable when the operation was first discussed, might conceivably deny us the former at a critical moment. The limited range of Spitfire fighter planes—which from Sicilian beaches could operate over Salerno for a maximum of twenty-two minutes!—might enable the enemy, operating from bases only a few miles from the beach, to deny us the latter. Moreover, once the Reggio landings were made, the achievement of surprise at Salerno would be virtually impossible. The Germans, as Eisenhower himself was fond of saying, could read a map as accurately as the Allies (often they did so with greater accuracy) and they were fully informed concerning our fighter range. They must certainly fix their attention on Salerno as soon as our commitment was made at Reggio; they would undoubtedly reinforce there as powerfully and rapidly as possible.

But how quickly and powerfully could they reinforce? If they were surprised by the Italian armistice, they *might* not have their forces disposed in such a way as to make possible a swift concentration at the critical point. Certainly they could not do so if, with Italian aid, we made a successful airborne assault on Rome. To summarize: the military equation, as originally presented, was so filled with variables as to be insoluble—but Eisenhower saw that, through the careful timing of Italian political developments, some of those variables might be transformed into constants, enough of them at least to make the military risks calculable. We could gain the Italian fleet: that must be a certain consequence of the Italian surrender, for Eisenhower would tolerate no repetition of the tactics the French had employed at Toulon. We might, by deceiving the Germans as to the imminence of the armistice, delay the enemy build-up at Salerno. We might, with the very maximum of luck, seize Rome itself and with it all of lower Italy at very little cost.

Thus the problem which now faced Eisenhower and his approach to it were similar in many respects to those of the opening phase in North Africa. There was one important difference. This time Eisenhower could not be held responsible for political developments which were out of his control and which must be quite as unpopular in Britain and America as the Darlan "deal" had been.

The decision to recognize Badoglio as head of the Italian state might be justified on grounds of "military expedience," but the public knew that political leaders, and not Eisenhower, had made it. Moreover, this decision was no hasty improvisation. Presumably it was exhaustively reviewed at the Quebec conference—and when, later on, the Badoglio government received diplomatic recognition from the Soviet Union it appeared that Stalin had concurred in the arrangement. Eisenhower's sole political function in Italy was to exploit a given situation to achieve military ends.

The Italian armistice was signed in an olive grove near Catania, Sicily, on September 3, 1943. Castellano signed for Italy and Beedle Smith for the Allies. Eisenhower did not sign himself because Badoglio had not done so. The armistice was not, however, to take effect until announced in simultaneous radio broadcasts by the Allied commander and Badoglio. It was left to Eisenhower to determine the most opportune moment for that announcement. Meanwhile, on September 3—the day of the armistice signing—the Allied commander made what he always afterward insisted was one of the boldest of his military gambles. He ordered the Eighth Army, under Montgomery, across the Strait of Messina.

In Eisenhower's view, the Reggio commitment was of a piece with the Salerno one, for without Salerno the progress up Italy from the toe would be a costly operation which could achieve no quick decisive result. The Italians put up no more resistance than had been expected. They fired a few rounds, then surrendered and told their captors that the Germans, three days before, had "retired into the hills." In the following days the Eighth Army pushed ahead against light opposition while the prisoner bag swelled to thousands. But it was on the projected airborne operation, and the assault by Lieutenant General Mark Clark's Fifth Army at Salerno, that Eisenhower's main attention was now focused. D-Day for these operations had been set for September 9, and the margin of their safety appeared from Ken Strong's intelligence reports to be dwindling steadily.

On September 7 Eisenhower dispatched Brigadier General Maxwell Taylor and Colonel William T. Gardiner to Rome to obtain precise information concerning the disposition of German troops in the Rome area and the amount of aid the airborne units might expect to receive from the Italians. It was, for the two Americans, a hazardous trip, and the information it yielded was disheartening. Formerly there had been three thousand Germans in the south and eight thousand in the north of Rome, but since the fall of Mussolini these forces had been greatly expanded. There were now forty-eight thousand German troops in the Rome area, equipped with hundreds of heavy and light tanks and with much artillery. They had supplies for a long campaign. The Italians had four divisions in the Rome area, but they had been deprived of all their gasoline and much of the ammunition by the suspicious Germans. General Carboni, chief of the Italian army corps defending Rome, claimed that he had facilities for only a few hours of fighting. It was soon clear to the two Americans that the Italian Government, from Badoglio on down, was frightened of the Germans and was attempting to stall off the Allies. Badoglio claimed that Salerno was "too far south" to be effective—though he was not supposed to know of that impending operation. He was convinced that the airborne troops would be slaughtered uselessly if they landed in Rome as planned. He could not guarantee the use of Italian airfields. And finally, as the climax to all this, he declared that it was now "impossible" for him to announce the armistice in a broadcast following Eisenhower's on the evening of September 8 because if he did so the Germans would immediately occupy Rome and restore the fascist government. "I would be shot," said the marshal. He was willing to send Eisenhower a message pointing out the impossibility of an armistice declaration at that time. Taylor sent a message, too, asserting that, in view of the Italians' "change of attitude," the airborne operation must be canceled.

Though these messages were filed early in the morning of September 8 they did not arrive at Eisenhower's headquarters until late that afternoon (due to transmission difficulties), just as the 82nd Airborne Division was about to board its planes. Immediately Eisenhower canceled the entire Rome operation. There were those at headquarters who felt that Salerno should also be canceled. The Germans, according to intelligence reports, had been pouring troops into the Salerno area for the last forty-eight hours. If the Italians now reneged on their surrender agreement, the Fifth Army would face overwhelming odds. It seemed clear that Badoglio was attempting to double-cross us. . . . But Eisenhower refused to heed these counsels. His blue-eyed gaze was bleak and there was no hint of a smile on his grim lips as he thought of those ships which crowded, at this very moment, toward the shores of Italy. Then he dictated his reply to Badoglio. He, Eisenhower, was going to make the scheduled broadcast no matter what Badoglio chose to do. The marshal, if he then failed to carry out the terms of his agreement, would find himself in a position worse than "impossible." He would be unable to seek sanctuary behind the Allied lines, and the Germans would certainly arrest him. The Allies' carefully fostered reputation for truth-telling in official pronouncements was, at that point, bearing valuable fruit: there was no doubt that the world, including the Nazis, would believe that Eisenhower spoke the truth.

At six-thirty on the evening of September 8, Eisenhower spoke into the microphone:

"This is General Dwight D. Eisenhower, commander in chief of the Allied forces. The Italian Government has surrendered its armed forces unconditionally. As Allied commander in chief I have granted a military armistice, the terms of which have been approved by the governments of the United States, Great Britain, and the Union of Soviet Socialist Republics. . . . Hostilities between the armed forces of the United Nations and those of Italy terminate at once. All Italians who now act to help eject the German aggressor from Italian soil will have the assistance and support of the United Nations."

There followed an hour and a half of waiting, during which the hapless Badoglio strove to make up his mind. For most of Eisenhower's staff this was a period of intense strain. For Eisenhower himself it was not. As he explained it later, he knew all the time that Badoglio *would* broadcast. The logic of the situation demanded it. The marshal did so at approximately eight o'clock, ordering all Italians to cease hostilities against Anglo-American forces and to "oppose attacks from any other quarter." He and the little King then fled southward from Rome in a black limousine, arriving at Taranto at about the same time as the British Fifth Corps made its landings there on the morning of September 9.

Three days later, on September 11, the bulk of the Italian fleet surrendered to the Allies at Malta.

It was well that the Allied commander had a supreme faith in logic, for that faith defended him against useless worries. Having calculated with extreme care all the chances and having arrived at what seemed to him the inevitable conclusion of a sequence of events, he dismissed the matter from his mind and concentrated on problems yet unsolved. Had he let Badoglio's procrastination worry him on the evening of September 8, he might easily have broken under the strain of anxieties too great for even his iron nerves to bear. The Germans were fully alert at Salerno. From the hills of that beautiful section of Italian coast they could pour a devastating cross fire upon the landing craft and the beaches. Behind those hills the terrain was well suited for defensive operations. The margin of Allied superiority in the air was far too small for safety. Though Eisenhower had discounted the possibility of an attack by the Italian fleet, he had to admit that a faint possibility of it yet remained. In the first crucial days Allied troops, most of whom had never before been under fire, would be called upon for exertions and endurance which might well have snapped the fighting wills of veterans. If those troops failed to endure, if their courage broke under the heavy casualties they were certain to suffer, Allied arms would suffer their greatest catastrophe since Dunkirk. Indeed, Salerno—with its consequences on the British to the south—might be in some respects worse than Dunkirk. This time there might not be an army left to take off the beaches.

Eisenhower's choice of a commander for this operation had been carefully made. Tall, youthful, scholarly Mark Clark was a precisionist who calculated carefully the limits of the possible and strove to operate precisely at those limits. In what must be, in terms of over-all strategy, a holding operation designed to pin down as many German troops as possible in Italy while we launched the cross-channel assault, Clark could be counted upon to maintain a constant pressure without sacrificing his troops in grandiose offensives. Patton, after the first crucial days, would have been likely to attempt too much with too little. This was a job for a careful, patient man, and Clark, for all his occasional surface irritability, was temperamentally suited to it.

Only a few hours after the surrender announcement Beedle Smith spoke to assembled newsmen in Algiers. "We are trying one of the biggest bluffs in history," he said frankly. But Eisenhower, who held a press conference, too, took a somewhat different line. A grim determination was evident in his words—an awareness of the enormous stakes in what must be a bloody struggle, and a hope that, after all, the maximum possibilities (the pinching off of all of southern Italy in a quick move) might be achieved. "We're playing in the big leagues now," he said. "You can't hit a home run by bunting. You have to step up there and take your cut at the ball. The time has come to discontinue nibbling at islands and hit the Germans where it hurts. I don't believe in fighting battles to chase someone out of somewhere. Our object is to trap and smash them." He spoke confidently. The correspondents, as always before a big operation, were impressed by his calmness. . . .

So certain had the Germans been of the exact landing area that they had moved their defenses down almost to the water's edge. Trees and brush and all other obstacles had been cleared so that the beach and its approaches could be covered by interlocking zones of fire. Almost from the moment the first wave of landing craft started for the beaches, at three-thirty in the morning of September 9, the flares came down and the guns behind the hills roared a fatal defiance. Higgens boats and ducks were hit. Men died horribly. The screams of many wounded were silenced by the dark waters which drowned them. The survivors came on, poured out upon a strip of sand so crisscrossed with machine-gun and mortar fire that no man, it seemed, could live upon it. But men did live. They pushed on. The second and third waves came in behind them. They took their casualties and pushed on. With the dawn came the Messerschmitts, roaring in low over the hills through inevitable gaps in an Allied air cover that was operating at extreme range. Still the Americans and the British came on, forcing the first defenders back into the hills, widening the beachhead bit by bit, until in the afternoon it was possible to begin landing the heavy equipment. The Allies were on the beaches. They would stay.

And they did stay. For seven bitter days it seemed impossible that

On the Road to Rome

they could take it, withstand the endless counterattacks and then attack themselves. The Germans did not think it possible. When a few German tanks actually broke through all the way to the beach the Ministry of Propaganda in Berlin announced the complete destruction of the Fifth Army. Back at headquarters Eisenhower held a staff conference which was far different in tone from those of calmer times. He called for opinions, listened to them carefully as he always did—but this time he did not maintain the illusion that this was a mere board meeting of which he happened to be chairman. He com-

]449[

manded. The beachhead could be saved only if the turn-around of the ships bringing supplies and reinforcements was shortened, only if air cover was increased, only if Montgomery's rate of advance was vastly accelerated. Far from trapping the Germans, the Fifth Army was itself entrapped with its back to the sea, and Montgomery's troops must now assume the role of a relief force. The commander in chief issued swift orders, and their urgency was communicated to all the lower echelons. On September 10, seven days after the Reggio landings, Montgomery stood at Pizzo, having moved forty-five miles against feeble resistance. In the following seven days he covered more than twice that distance against stiffening resistance, until on September 17 his advanced units made contact with patrols of the Fifth Army a few miles southeast of Salerno. The beachhead was saved.

Two days later Eisenhower visited the Salerno front. He communicated to his troops his immense pride in their achievement. It was, certainly, one of the magnificent achievements of the war, an epic of courage and endurance which will long stand as a monument to a generation of men who had so often been dubbed "soft" and "weak" by their elders. To scale those hills and the mountains beyond them through intense fire was, on the face of it, impossible. Yet relatively inexperienced troops had done and were doing it. It was the most difficult kind of positional warfare. It was, as Eisenhower said, a "G.I. and Tommy" war. Hill by hill, mountain by mountain, in an endless ordeal which had no soft spots in it, the troops must fight their way across and up the peninsula, employing all their tactical skill, all their endurance, all their courage. Looking at the terrain, Eisenhower shook his head and deprecated the role of a strategic commander. "This," he said grimly, "is not the place for masterminding." He returned to headquarters, filled with enthusiasm for the quality of the men he was (and he meant it) "privileged to command." During the following months he spent as much time as possible on the Italian front. He established a series of command posts there and conducted scores of inspections. "According to the textbooks, a commander should meet and talk with his troops in order to inspire them," he would say in his talks to the troops. "For my part, I draw my inspiration from you." The troops cheered madly when he appeared.

Thus began the bitter twenty-month campaign for Italy. Foggia fell on September 27, justifying the enormous Salerno gamble. Naples fell on October 1. There followed the bloody breach of the Volturno line; the crossing of the Sangro; the capture of Termoli, Venafro, Isernia; the long stalemate at Cassino. The road to Rome and beyond was almost incredibly hard, but by pressing up it with dogged, unremitting determination, the Fifth and Eighth armies under Alexander's superb leadership accomplished their strategic assignment. They made of Italy another "Spanish ulcer" which ate deeply into Hitler's military strength. They held constantly on their front hundreds of thousands of the best Nazi troops (including such crack outfits as the 1st Parachute Division, the 15th Panzers, the 90th Panzer Grenadiers) which, had they been deployed in France, would have delayed for many months the western assault. They also made direct contributions to that assault by obtaining air bases from which bombers could operate in a great arc against Bulgaria, Greece, Rumania, Hungary, Austria, Germany, and southern France, and by providing a springboard for an amphibious assault against the South of France.

4

It was on the western assault that Eisenhower's attention was now concentrated. Early in November he was much occupied with arrangements for the conference which was to open, on the twenty-first of that month, in Cairo. The principals of this historic meeting were President Roosevelt, Prime Minister Churchill, and Generalissimo Chiang Kai-shek. Each of them would be accompanied by a large staff of military and political advisers. With Roosevelt—whom Eisenhower was to meet at Oran on the nineteenth—would be Harry Hopkins, General Marshall, Admiral King, General Harold H. Arnold, and Admiral William D. Leahy, among others. Eisenhower was responsible for the transportation, comfort, and safety of these V.I.P.s (the R.A.F. abbreviation for Very Important People') during their stay in his theater and he personally reviewed the preparations for their arrival. When the long flight from Oran to Cairo was completed without mishap he was frankly relieved.

Eisenhower of course took an active and important part in the strategy discussions with the British and American representatives of the Combined Staffs. The cross-channel plan was now so definite and detailed that decisions could be reached concerning the troop units to be employed, the specialized training to be given them, the items of special equipment to be supplied and in what quantity.

One may be sure that through all these discussions Eisenhower emphasized two prime needs: for Allied unity and for flexibility.

The lessons of North Africa, Sicily, and Italy were clear. Only through an actual amalgamation of staffs on the level of supreme command could the necessary unity be achieved, and only if the supreme commander had a maximum freedom to choose between alternatives, to shape his strategy in swift response to an opponent's moves, could he have assurance of victory. There must be provision for feints and diversions, even for an abrupt cancellation of an operation already launched from distant overseas bases if a changed situation demanded it.

Then came—for Eisenhower certainly, and perhaps for the world —the climax of the conference. It was on the last day of the meeting, November 2. A folded slip of paper was handed him. He opened it and read brief scrawled notes initialed F.D.R. and G.C.M. Then he looked out of the window, experiencing a surge of emotion similar to that which had welled up in him in response to another Marshall communication, back in the Washington of 1942, in a world that now seemed ages past. A Supreme Headquarters of the Allied Expeditionary Forces was to be established in London. Churchill, Roosevelt, and the Combined Staffs were unanimous in their choice of Eisenhower for supreme commander. . . .

It cannot be said that the decision came to Eisenhower as a complete surprise. He had known that the choice must lie between himself and Marshall, and that Marshall, much as he might have liked to assume the command, would never do so from motives of purely personal ambition. Marshall would have had to be convinced that only by relinquishing his present post as a global strategist and taking this new one could he best serve the Allied cause. Such a conviction, in view of the records Marshall and Eisenhower had made, could have no logical base. All the same, Eisenhower could not fail at such a moment to look back, with a kind of wonder, over the long journey he had made: from a Kansas village, from a family "on the wrong side of the tracks" in that village, to a position of such supreme power and responsibility that the mere contemplation of it might well have made him tremble. But he didn't tremble. The moment of wonder passed quickly, and his mind was focused again on the needs of his "new job." So gradual had been his ascent, so logically had one step led to the next one, that even this last immense stride represented only a "bigger job" which he was confident he could handle, as he had handled former ones, through the constant exercise of "simple common sense." It seems never to have occurred to him that "common sense," in the positions he occupied and under the pressures which were upon him, was so uncommon as to amount to genius.

Typically, his initial nervous response to the new challenge was one not of increased tension but of relaxation. From Cairo the President and Prime Minister, with their staffs, were to proceed to Teheran for the epochal and long-awaited meeting with Josef Stalin. Following that meeting in early December, Roosevelt was to meet Eisenhower at Carthage for a two-day conference, after which he was to visit Malta, there to present a citation to that heroic island whose steadfast stand under a rain of bombs had contributed so greatly to our Mediterranean victory. Gault had left Cairo for Malta before the conference had ended to arrange the details of the President's ceremonial visit. (It was over breakfast coffee in Malta one morning that week that Beedle Smith asked Gault if he would like to "go to London with Ike.") Eisenhower, meanwhile, took a two-day sight-seeing trip through the Lower Nile Valley, visiting the Sphinx and the Pyramids, and a one-day trip by plane to Jerusalem, where his guide was a certain Father Pasquale. With him he took Tex Lee, Butcher, and Mickey McKeogh, all three of whom were astounded by the detailed knowledge of biblical history which "the boss" displayed.

"I practically had to memorize the Bible when I was a kid," the general explained.

During the meeting at Carthage, Roosevelt told Eisenhower that Stalin had expressed particular pleasure concerning the choice of a supreme commander and was satisfied with the approximate time set for the invasion. The President also conferred upon Eisenhower the Legion of Merit, in recognition of the work the general had done while a member of the General Staff in Washington. (Eisenhower had received an Oak Leaf Cluster for his D.S.M. in September, in recognition of his success in Africa and Sicily.) Said the citation in part: "He played a major part in placing in effect the United States Army's plans for war. . . . He served with distinction during the most critical period in the history of the United States. . . . He rendered invaluable service by organizing the European Theater, establishing an effective supply system and training and preparing for battle the large American Ground and Air Forces which have since played such an important part in active operations from the United Kingdom, in Africa, and in Italy. His outstanding contributions to the Allied cause and to the successes now being realized by the Armed Forces of the United States are deserving of the highest praise and reflect great credit upon himself and the military service."

It was on Christmas Eve, 1943, while Eisenhower was touring the Fifth Army front in Italy, that the official announcement of his appointment to supreme command was made. Two days later he sent his farewell message to the Allied forces in Italy and North Africa.

"Soon I leave this theater to assume other duties assigned me by the Allied governments," he said. "I take my leave of you with feelings of personal regret that are equaled only by my pride in your brilliant accomplishments of the year just passed. All together you comprise a mighty machine which, under your new commander, will continue a completely unified instrument of war to make further inroads into the enemy's defenses and assist in bringing about his final collapse. Until we meet again in the heart of the enemy's Continental stronghold, I send Godspeed and good luck to each of you along with the assurance of my lasting gratitude and admiration."

For twenty days following his farewell to the troops Eisenhower's movements were a "top military secret." With Butcher, Lee, and Mickey he flew to America.

It was long after midnight when the plane landed. Mamie and Ruth Butcher, who lived in apartments across the hall from each other in Washington's Wardman Park Hotel, were in a fever of excitement, which had mounted steadily ever since the secret notification that their husbands were coming. Then a muffled laugh in the hallway, a knock on the door—and Ike and Butch were home! With them were two Scotty puppies, offspring of Telek, one for Butcher's daughter and one for Milton's children. . . .

Eisenhower had needed this respite from the pressures of command even more than he had realized. It helped him to keep his life all of a piece, with no sharp discontinuities between his past and his present, or between his personal and professional attitudes. It was good to know that Mamie had not changed, that she was as gaily animated as ever. It was heart-warming to see John, now in his last year at West Point, ramrod straight in cadet gray, as slender as ever but very fit. John was wholly unspoiled, if a trifle awed, by his father's fame. As a matter of fact, that fame, from the son's point of view, was more enemy than friend. It embarrassed him to be photographed and interviewed and fawned upon simply because he happened to be the son of a Great Man; it even stirred in him, for all his pride in his father, certain obscure resentments. He was inclined to defend himself by puncturing some of the legends about his father's constant "affability": "Sure, he's good-natured at home as long as everything goes his way, but if someone musses up the paper, for instance, before he's had a chance to read it he has a fit. Mother makes the house revolve about him, and he just sits back and lets it revolve. With me he's been plenty strict, though he's let up a little in recent years."

The meeting with John took place on January 4, 1944, in General Marshall's private railway car, loaned to the Eisenhowers for this trip and parked now under the granite cliff which sustains the West Point Plain. For nine happy hours John, Mamie, and Dwight were together, and the general was once again wholly submerged in the husband and father. The old argument was reviewed: should John go into the Infantry or the Artillery? The boy still hadn't made up his mind, and whenever he argued in favor of one his father pointed out advantages in the other. (A few weeks later John chose the Infantry.) Five of John's cadet friends were invited to dine on juicy steaks in the car that night, and it amused Dwight to break down their stiff reserve so completely that before the evening was done the cadets were offering advice on the conduct of the war. That evening Dwight and Mamie returned to Washington, and on the following day they went to White Sulphur Springs, where General Marshall had lent them his house for two restful days. Save for a visit which the general made to the army hospital there, he and his wife were alone together.

On January 7, having been delayed by bad weather, the general flew to Fort Riley, Kansas. (Mamie, who was not permitted to fly because of a heart murmur, could not accompany him.) From the airfield there he was driven in a curtained army car to the near-by town of Manhattan, home of Kansas State College. Last spring Milton had written to his brother in Algiers saying that he was relinquishing his O.W.I. post in order to accept an offer of the presidency of Kansas State, tendered him by the Kansas Board of Regents. He wondered if he was doing the right thing in leaving a war job in wartime. The general thought so. "A large part of the kind of peace achieved after this war rests on the principles laid down in American schools," he replied. Milton had taken over his duties as college president in September 1943. He and Helen, with their two children, Buddie and Ruth, now lived in a large limestone house surrounded by trees on the college campus. It was a secluded spot, and for that reason it had been selected as a gathering place for the Eisenhower clan. In the white frame house in Abilene, which Dwight longed to see, it would have been impossible to maintain the necessary secrecy.

The gathering was far from complete. Jolly, roly-poly Roy had died with tragic suddenness in 1942, only a few weeks after his father's death—the "first break," said Edgar, who took it very hard, in the "ring of boys." Edgar and Earl lived so far away that it had been impossible, in the limited time available, to arrange for their coming. But Arthur, with his wife Louise, had come from Kansas City, and the Douds had come from Denver. Mrs. Eakin, Helen's mother, was there. And—most important of all—Mother Eisenhower, with Naomi Engle, had been driven over from Abilene.

"Why, it's Dwight!" she cried, laughing rather tearfully as she embraced her soldier son.

They had warned him that he would find her changed. She was very old now, almost eighty-two, and since her husband's death ("they're all gone now") she had lost much of that zest for living which had been so abundantly hers. "Nothing seems real any more," she used to say. It was as though a curtain had dropped down between her mind and present realities. She lived mostly in the past. But now, with Dwight and the others, the curtain for a time was lifted and she was her former self, bright and quick and laughing. Dwight noticed little change in her and was inclined to think his brothers had been mistaken. She delighted in the pleasure which Milton's children, Ruthie especially, took in their uncle Ike's gift of Telek II. She thought that Dwight was "just the same" as he had always been.

But he wasn't just the same. Others noticed subtle changes in him. He had, they said, "grown." His mental perspectives were now immensely broad, and even in his moments of casual spontaneity he gave an impression of perfect self-control. Though he seemed as frankly friendly as ever, he never let himself go "all out." Those who knew him best sensed a quality of withdrawnness, as though he were keeping a good deal of himself in reserve for emergency uses. They spoke of his "serenity." Milton himself was amazed by his brother's calm confidence. Even among his intimates, when he need not keep up appearances, Dwight gave no slightest sign of apprehension in the face of his unprecedented assignment. He did not believe that the victory would be easy. He knew that it was certain. Rather rashly, he was to make a public statement in which he flatly predicted the victorious end of the European war in 1944—"if everyone does his part." Said one of his old friends, who met him in Washington just before he flew back to England, "Looking at Ike now, you can't help but feel a little sorry for his enemies."

He boarded the plane on January 12. Mamie's farewell cry rang in his ears:

"Don't come back until it's over, Ike. I couldn't bear to lose you again."

CHAPTER II

SHAEF and the Great Design

THE PLAN was the product of no one mind. Since the dark days following Dunkirk, when Britain stood alone and virtually unarmed against the Axis fury, anonymous men had been plotting the Return to the Continent. Churchill had assigned a small group of British officers to this specific task even before Alexander was off the Dunkirk beach in 1940. That group had grown to hundreds, finally thousands, of British and Americans, and even they represented but a tiny fraction of the total number who contributed directly to the final great design. What had begun as a gesture of defiance against hostile Fate and continued as an academic exercise through months of bitter defeat had become, by the autumn of 1943, a project of such vast bulk and concrete detail that it overwhelmed even the arguments of the man who had fathered the enterprise and who now sought to disown his offspring: Winston Churchill himself. The over-all naval plan alone, a terse summary of the part the navies were to play in the invasion, ran to more than eight hundred type-written pages. A complete set of navy orders, including the necessary maps, weighed three hundred pounds. Equally bulky were the air plans, the ground plans, and—most intricate of all—the logistical plans. All of these were fused into a single unified stratagem for crushing Germany, a stratagem which SHAEF[1] was now to implement. The whole planning project was a *co-operative* enterprise of enormous scope and complexity. To attempt an outline of its trials and vicissitudes, in terms of a single man, is to court grave errors of fact, grave injustices to individuals.

Nevertheless, it can hardly be denied that in the immense background for invasion the British Lieutenant General Frederick E. Morgan, C.B., was a central figure. For a long time the proposed cross-channel operation was tagged with his name—the "Morgan

[1]Supreme Headquarters, Allied Expeditionary Forces.

Plan"—and this despite the fact that he did not become officially associated with it until after the Casablanca conference, by which time (as we have seen) much of the spadework for the operation had been completed. From the first, however, Morgan had been among the moving spirits, and it is questionable whether the seeds Eisenhower had planted in his tentative cross-channel plan of 1942 would have been permitted to flower in the immense victories of 1944 and 1945 if Morgan had been absent from the scene. During the period when the vast majority of his British colleagues pooh-poohed the possibility of a successful assault against the French coast Morgan remained convinced, and argued convincingly, that such an assault not only could but *must* be made.

He was a man in his fifties, with great physical vigor and a tangy, humorous speech. He had close-cropped white hair and a small sandy mustache, also closely cropped. He smiled a great deal, showing white even teeth. His gray eyes were very clear and *aware.* His speech was so "Americanized" that it puzzled the American correspondents who later interviewed him. He explained that though he was born in Kent he had spent most of his thirty years in the Army on assignments outside of England. He had served with Canadians, spent nearly twenty years in India, and had had "much dealings with Yankees."

"Then, too," he said, "one speaks a certain number of languages. A neutral accent is a natural consequence."

His rise since 1940 had been unusually rapid. He had been a colonel, commanding troops in the field, when France fell. Three months later he was made a brigadier and assigned to defend the Wash against the German invasion which at that time seemed inevitable and imminent. In the spring of 1941 he was promoted to major general and assigned to defend Devon and Cornwall against invasion. Nominally a division commander, he had at that juncture some 150,000 men under his command, including Home Guards. "That was a delightful assignment," he was fond of recalling, "defending some scores of miles of the most beautiful coast in the world. The fact that it was for the most part a vertical coast simplified my problem. I am proud to say," he would add, his eyes twinkling, "that not a single German landed in Devon or Cornwall during the period of my command." His main attention, during all this time, seems to have been focused on the "return to France." His profound personal commitment to a cross-channel assault became known

] 459 [

throughout the higher levels of command in the British Army. It was a commitment much less common among the high officers in England than it was among their counterparts in America.

He first came into Eisenhower's orbit in July 1942, during the planning of "Torch." His admiration for the American was tremendous, and he was immensely pleased to find the latter as convinced of the feasibility and need of a western assault as was Morgan himself. At the Largs conference, where "Torch" was born, Morgan had been among the proponents of the cross-channel plan, opposing his views to those of such top-ranking British officers as General Paget. He had, of course, concurred in the decision to invade North Africa, but, like Eisenhower, he always insisted that this operation was a preliminary to the western assault. One of the doubtful items of "Torch," as we have seen, was the attitude of Franco Spain, and Morgan was assigned the task of planning, and carrying through if necessary, the occupation of Spanish Morocco in case Spain became an active belligerent. By February of 1943 it was evident that "Backbone," the code name for the Spanish Moroccan plan, would never become a real operation, and Morgan, as he put it, was allowed to "stand down" and return to England. There, as a consequence of the Casablanca decisions, he was assigned to give "cohesion and impulse" to the cross-channel invasion planning. At that time it was tacitly assumed that the invasion commander would be British, and Morgan was to be his Chief of Staff.

Thereafter, save for a brief interlude during which he was involved with plans for a possible invasion of Sardinia, Morgan's exclusive concern was with the invasion of France. He was told to acquire a staff composed of both British and Americans. He had little trouble making his British staff selections, for he had served two years in the War Office before the outbreak of the war and had become intimately acquainted with army personnel. To help him choose American representatives and co-ordinate the over-all planning, the American Major General Ray W. Barker was assigned to him. The staff chosen, the "Morgan Plan"—and the selling program aimed at those in high places who doubted its efficacy—began rapidly to assume their final shape. One great initial objection to the plan, namely the limited range of Spitfire fighter planes, was being overcome by the new long-range fighter types pouring now off the American assembly lines. The enormous logistical problems were squarely faced and solved, one by one.

There is a very real sense in which the logistical phase of the plan won the battle for France many months before the invasion was actually launched. It was assumed by the Germans—and by the Allies, too, at first—that initial invasion operations must be aimed at securing a port of sufficient size for a rapid build-up of supplies and men. This, it was believed, placed severe limits on the possibility of tactical surprise. The ports of the Netherlands and Belgium had special flood defenses which made them extremely hazardous, if not impossible, for successful landings. Calais, Boulogne, Dieppe, Le Havre, Cherbourg, Brest, Lorient, Saint-Nazaire—these, it was believed, were the sum total of available targets for a cross-channel assault. Each of them had been strongly fortified by the Germans during four years of occupation; the seizure of any one of them would, it appeared, be an extremely costly operation; and no one of them, by itself, would be sufficient to supply a rapidly expanding bridgehead.

"Very well," said an American naval officer at the close of one of the staff sessions, "if we can't capture ports, we must make them and take them with us."

Though this suggestion seemed, at first, fantastic, there were many precedents for it. British scientists had long ago carried out experiments in the making of "sheltered water" (apparently as a result of a Churchill request) for use in the Far East. A device called a "lielow" had been constructed, first of rubber, then of steel. It had not worked well. In the meantime, Russian scientists had worked out a method of using air bubbles blown up from the sea bottom to create a breakwater. This had worked out well in theory, but in practice it required such an enormous expenditure of power as to be unfeasible. The time-honored device of sinking ships to create a breakwater was then fallen back upon in the plan, until the American naval officer's suggestion began, in May of 1943, to bear fruit. At that time concrete caissons, which not only created sheltered water but could serve as floating docks, were developed and arrangements were made for manufacturing them in sections (and with the utmost secrecy), then towing them across the Channel for assembly, in a remarkably short time, to make huge artificial harbors on the French coast. Partially as a result of this device, and despite storms which severely damaged the installations, it was possible in the first 109 days to land 17,000,000 ship-tons of supplies (twice the tonnage delivered to Pershing in nineteen months of World War I), 500,000 vehicles, and 2,000,000 men—though apparently the Allies had, during that time, only one good usable port. Half of these men were landed in the first three weeks, before Cherbourg was captured.

A device equally bizarre, and equally effective, was developed for the delivery of gasoline from England to the fighting fronts. As a result of a suggestion made by Lord Louis Mountbatten when he was Chief of Combined Operations, vast quantities of limber four-inch pipe, which could be coiled and unwound like a rubber hose, were manufactured. Laid under the English Channel and hooked up to pipe laid rapidly across the surface of the ground on the Continent, behind the advancing armies, continuous pipe lines hundreds of miles long were created. Supplementing the tanker deliveries, these lines enormously accelerated the gasoline supply. The first four of them were laid from the Isle of Wight to Cherbourg, and they were tapped in Normandy in August, only a little more than two months after D-Day. Eventually twenty pipe lines were pumping high-test gasoline under the Channel, delivering it to Cherbourg, Paris, Boulogne, Antwerp, Eindhoven, Egerich, and Frankfurt at the rate of one million gallons a day.

These logistical devices and others (such as the creation of a complete military railroad system which could be transported across the Channel and assembled in an amazingly short time, and the use of one-way "Red Ball Express" highways for top-priority motor convoys across France) were to disrupt completely the German defensive strategy. Utter disbelief in the ability of the Allies to build up so rapidly caused the German high command to make last-ditch stands instead of the orderly withdrawals which alone could have saved hundreds of thousands of troops. First-class units, badly needed for the later defense of Germany, were left behind to garrison French port cities which the Nazis were convinced the Allies *must* capture in order to supply their armies. The logistical phase of the plan gave Eisenhower his greatest instrument for achieving surprise, and he exploited it to the maximum. By the time of the Quebec conference Morgan's chief concern was to secure adoption, by the heads of government, of the virtually completed plan. Despite Casablanca—despite the commitment of Marshall, Eisenhower, and other top military and naval commanders to the western assault—there were many in high places who remained doubtful. Churchill was fearful that this frontal assault against Fortress Europe, like the frontal assaults of World War I, would drown the Allies in a blood bath. He well knew that Britain could not survive another Pyrrhic victory such as she had won in 1914–18. It was only natural that he, who had witnessed the abundant command stupidities on the old Western Front, should find it difficult to shift from defensive to offensive attitudes. The former were the proper response to the weapon development of World War I, but the latter were the inevitable response to modern tanks, planes, and radio communications.

Morgan had wanted to go himself to Washington, immediately preceding the Quebec meeting, to review the plan, "sell it" to the Combined Chiefs of Staff. He was refused permission. He then went to the United States theater commander in England, Lieutenant General Jacob Devers, and obtained permission to send Barker and two other American members of Morgan's staff to Washington. These three men accomplished their assigned mission. Meanwhile, a British brigadier, who was a member of Morgan's staff and a "lovely salesman" for the plan, crossed the Atlantic with Churchill on the way to Quebec. Time and again Morgan had called on the brigadier to "do his stuff" when opposition to the plan developed, and the brigadier's "stuff" was always so convincing that it crushed the opposition, or converted it. Churchill was converted. Lying back in his bed smoking his cigars, the Prime Minister listened to the brigadier, raised every objection he could think of, and had every objection answered. At Quebec, as we have seen, the plan won final approval.

Following Quebec, Morgan had three assignments. First, he was to conduct feint operations aimed at Calais to synchronize with the Italian invasion. Second, he was to get everything ready for the true invasion. Third, he was to plan for immediate operations in Europe in case Germany collapsed suddenly before the time scheduled for invasion. Fortunately, he could regard the Calais feint as a dress rehearsal of the "real thing," since otherwise the problem of allocating supplies, time, and men among the three projects would have been insoluble.

D-Day for the Calais feint was September 9, 1943. During the preceding week five thousand sorties were flown by aircraft of Fighter Command, and heavy-bomber raids were made on nine communications centers and nine airfields in France. On the night of September 8–9 heavy bombers made concentrated attacks on airfields, gun emplacements, coastal defenses, and other military objectives in the Boulogne area. On D-Day itself heavy bombers raided nine airfields while fighter planes flew fifteen hundred sorties. Masses of troops had been moved into Kent and adjacent areas, loaded into boats with full invasion equipment, and sent down through the Strait of Dover, within ten miles of the French coast. Three hundred warships of all kinds accompanied them. To the surprise of the Allied command, the Germans made no response whatsoever to this challenge, not a single air, submarine, or sea-surface attack. Nevertheless, the operation, as a "dry run" of the invasion, was invaluable. Lessons were learned concerning the assembling and loading of troops and matériel which made the real invasion much smoother and more efficient than it would otherwise have been. More important than this, the feint helped Eisenhower to achieve a far greater measure of tactical surprise when the big D-Day came than had been believed possible. The Germans believed that the invasion would be made in the Pas de Calais area, where robot-bomb installations were being made.

In the following month Morgan was sent to America for what he afterward referred to as "five incredible weeks" with the United States General Staff and the Combined Chiefs of Staff. "You've no idea what stiffs we British seem when viewed from the Pentagon Building," he once told a group of American correspondents. He attended all the meetings of the Combined Staffs and the United States General Staff meeting in Marshall's office every morning. If he had had any doubts concerning the outcome of the invasion, the American visit would have dispelled them. The "simply stupendous" American production effort "had to be seen to be believed," he claimed. One day he was called to the White House for a private one-hour talk with President Roosevelt. Morgan thought he had been called over to explain the plan and answer questions concerning it, but when he arrived Roosevelt began telling him of the great advantages to be gained by invading through Yugoslavia. Morgan suspected that the President had just had a long letter from Churchill. Finally the President asked Morgan what he wanted from America, and Morgan replied promptly that he wanted two things —a huge American army, and Marshall as supreme commander. Roosevelt replied that Morgan, certainly, would have the army, but he didn't know about Marshall. The Chief of Staff came as close to being the "indispensable man" as anyone in Washington. . . .

Later Morgan was inclined to wonder, with a laugh, if America were not a bit *too* impressive for normal British nerves. He returned to England in early December and had to go at once into a hospital. He spent Christmas there. When he was released Eisenhower had been appointed supreme commander.

2

On January 17, at his old headquarters at 20 Grosvenor Square, London, Eisenhower held his first press conference since assuming his duties as supreme commander. It was "off the record."

He explained once again his view of the function of war correspondents. "You people have a job in war just as much as I have," he said, "and we ought to be on the same side of the fence." He wanted the newsmen to have free access to his headquarters; he was willing to regard those who were properly accredited as "quasi-staff officers"; he believed that the public should be honestly informed concerning "the character of the work being done here," so that the public could support that work or "get another team or commander." Censorship would be applied solely for military security, and never, under any circumstances, would a censor be permitted to delete criticisms of the supreme commander. "I will not tolerate in my theater an atmosphere of antagonism between myself and the newspaper people," he asserted. "I take it you are just as anxious to win this war and get it done, so we can all go fishing, as I am." He mentioned that "on his way here" he had visited both President Roosevelt and Prime Minister Churchill. "I was particularly delighted to have the chance to visit both," he went on. "I am an Allied commander, and the keynote to my headquarters and any operation conducted under my command will be that they are Allied. The British-versus-American question . . . does not occur in my headquarters. . . . I get a directive from the Combined Chiefs of Staff and it is carried out with what I have with a grand team of fighters, both American and British, in the best way we know how, and with the questions solved on a military basis. Nothing else." He referred to the Italian campaign which, according to many critics, had "bogged down." "It seems that some of our critics expect all war to be conducted in great marvelous strategic strokes with advances by the hundreds of miles, and they forget that there are times when the dirty business of war just comes down for a while to the business of slugging. . . .

War inevitably is a series of, you might say, low points in great strategic gains while you build up to make a determined thrust somewhere, and during those low points what you can do is keep on top of the other fellow in morale and keep hitting him, slugging him, advancing some, and dominating him in the field of morale, which is the most important in war. . . ." The Allied soldiers in Italy, he asserted, needed "no apology from me, or anyone else." As for his personal position: "In coming into this theater to take up the duties given me by the Combined Chiefs of Staff, I think it would be almost a discourtesy if I failed to mention what has been done here in advance of my coming. The grand work of the naval forces . . . The grand work done by the Air Forces . . . The grand work of the base people, and the fine Infantry in training and getting ready out on the cold moors and countryside in the mud and rain . . . getting themselves toughened and ready for any job that lies ahead. I would like to mention it now, because I don't want to appear as a person that just comes in and says, 'I am starting now.' That is not the case at all. There has been a grand job done, and now there is a special job starting, and I happened to be picked to fill it. That is all there is to that."

Soon the nerve center of SHAEF was established at Wide Wing, in a village just outside London, forty minutes by bus from Grosvenor Square. Rows of one-story gray concrete buildings huddled there under green mounds of camouflage netting. From here the communications network spread out to every unit of Eisenhower's vast command. His personal office was in a sprawling, unimpressive building one hundred yards or so from the high brick wall which shut off Wide Wing from a village lane. Unlike his office in Algiers, this one could be reached only by passing through the anteroom where Butcher, Gault, and Lee had their desks. The office itself was twenty feet square, with a fireplace in an inside wall faced by two brown leather easy chairs. The general's large walnut desk was set in a corner, where the light from two windows bathed its top. Behind it was a flag stand bearing flags of all the United Nations. On the desk were three phones, one of them a green-colored "scrambler" for confidential conversations. Across the room, in the corner at the general's left, was a door opening into his private surface air-raid shelter.

His "official family" had gained some new faces since he last served in London. In January 1943 the first Wacs (then called

Waacs) had arrived in North Africa. Among them was Sergeant Margaret Chick, a girl in her early twenties, whose home was in Toledo, Ohio, but who had gone to high school in Uniontown, Pennsylvania—General Marshall's home town, as she was fond of pointing out. She remembered well her first meeting with Eisenhower. Butcher had called her into the anteroom, then had opened the door into the general's office. "In there?" she had asked, frightened. "Sure," said Butcher. "Come on in. He won't bite you." He didn't. He laughed and put her at her ease at once. She managed to take the dictation satisfactorily, and she had remained as one of the general's two stenographers.

His personal secretary was now Wac Captain Mattie Pinette, who came from Maine and had been, before the war, a secretary in the Civil Aeronautics Authority. She, too, had arrived in Algiers with the first contingent of Wacs and had been assigned to the public-relations officer, General McClure, serving with him through the final phase of North Africa and through the Sicilian and Italian campaigns. She came into Eisenhower's office when he was appointed supreme commander. She was a woman of great energy and strong opinions (she was a good Maine Republican, an economic individualist of the most rugged sort), and she loved an argument. Indeed, she was so argumentative that she occasionally annoyed Butcher and Gault. But her office work was above reproach. She was extremely intelligent and hard-working; she could take and transcribe dictation with remarkable speed and accuracy, and she understood the "boss" rather more profoundly than did many of his high-ranking subordinates. She found him not an "easy boss." On the contrary, he was exacting; he was sometimes impatient, and he hated inefficiency; but he never lost his temper with a subordinate and he was "fun" to work for.

Captain Pinette was particularly impressed by two Eisenhower attributes: his phenomenal memory, and the rapid precision of his speech. He always spoke, she noticed gratefully, in complete sentences. At his first press conference after he became supreme commander the motion-picture people asked him to make a statement for the newsreels. Eisenhower went off into a corner of the room, dictated a three-hundred-word statement almost as rapidly as he could speak, and had Captain Pinette transcribe it immediately. When she brought it in he was with the newsmen, sitting at his desk. He glanced swiftly through the statement, laid it aside, and said he was ready. He didn't read the statement when the cameras began to grind. He looked directly into the lens and talked. But Captain Pinette, following his words in her carbon copy, was amazed to find that he gave the entire three-hundred-word statement verbatim, save for two minor alterations which, incidentally, were improvements. Once, when poetry was being discussed during a leisure hour, Captain Pinette heard Eisenhower quote almost the whole of Gray's *Elegy* to support his argument that it was the "most perfect poem ever written." On another occasion Eisenhower used an uncommon biblical quotation in some public statement. Butcher questioned the quotation's accuracy, but when he looked it up he found that Eisenhower was exactly right.

Another very important addition to the "family" was Wac Corporal Pearlie Hargrave of Pillager, Minnesota. She served as Eisenhower's second driver and also helped with office work. Almost from the moment he first saw her in North Africa, Mickey McKeogh had been in love with Pearlie. The two were now engaged to be married, "after the war. . . ." But the war was to outlast their patience by several months. In the chapel of the Great Palace at Versailles—where kings of France once took their marriage vows —Pearlie and Mickey were married on December 16, 1944. The one-time hotel bellhop had for his wedding guest the supreme commander of the mightiest expeditionary force in history. The bride was given in marriage by Tex Lee; she had been given permission to be out of uniform for the occasion, and she wore a gown and veil designed by a leading Paris fashion house. Beedle Smith and many other high-ranking officers of the staff were in attendance. After the ceremony the supreme commander gave a reception for the couple. Millions reading the story in the newspapers felt an obscure thrill of pride in the American democracy which made such things possible. . . .

Kay Summersby remained as Eisenhower's first driver, but she had new duties now. She had suffered, in North Africa, a bitter personal tragedy—an American officer with whom she was in love was killed—and in order to keep her from brooding during the long periods which sometimes separated her driving assignments, Butcher had arranged for her to help Eisenhower with his personal correspondence. The general received an average of forty personal letters a day from strangers—far more than he could possibly find time to answer in person. Yet he felt an obligation to answer them promptly, for all save 5 per cent of them were what he called "genuine" (the others were from crackpots and publicity seekers). Kay proved to be extremely skillful in framing replies for Eisenhower's signature. She used the distinctive Eisenhower idiom. She expressed his sentiments. Her judgment was sound, her tact unfailing. The general read each letter carefully before signing it—he insisted that the signature must be his own—but he rarely had to send it back for revision.

The pilot of the general's planes was Major Larry Hansen of the United States Army Air Corps. He hailed from Cleveland, Ohio, was twenty-six years old, and had become part of the Eisenhower entourage in December 1942. Before that time he had been a bomber pilot on submarine patrol off the American Atlantic coast and had flown several operational flights over the Continent from England. He piloted two planes for the general: a modified two-motored Mitchell which cruised at an indicated air speed of 250 miles an hour and could carry four passengers in addition to the crew, and a modified B-17 (Flying Fortress) which cruised at an indicated air speed of 180 miles an hour and could carry eight passengers in addition to the crew. The B-17 was equipped with bunks, an electric range, and a frigidaire. The crews—all under Hansen's command—consisted of Captain H. C. Nixon of Macon, Georgia, navigator; Lieutenant R. F. Underwood, Mount Tom, Massachusetts, co-pilot; Technical Sergeant Everett J. Behrens, a farm boy from Nebraska, radio operator; Master Sergeant A. J. Windham of Panama City, Florida, engineer; and two ground-crew men, Master Sergeant V. J. Romagosa of Savannah, Georgia, and Staff Sergeant R. E. Wood of Louisville, Kentucky.

Larry was a tall young man, handsome in the blond Scandinavian fashion, with thin cheeks, a direct gaze, and strong white teeth which showed in frequent smiles. He kept himself in training, like an athlete, for his assignment. He felt very keenly his immense responsibility for the supreme commander's safety. But he bore his responsibility with easy grace, with some of the same casual charm as that Butcher displayed, and he was very popular with "family" and staff. He and the general were fast friends. Often the general took over the controls during a flight (before his civilian pilot license had lapsed he had piled up some 350 flying hours) and he loved to talk about flying. It was intelligent talk, too, Larry was proud to say. Eisenhower knew every plane type and what each one could do.

The tone of the "family" remained as it had always been—relaxed, friendly, efficient. Eisenhower's personal life continued along the lines laid down when he first came to England. He was reestablished in Telegraph Cottage with Butcher and Mickey. He lived very quietly, rarely appearing at a public function of any kind. After he had his "invasion team" organized he drove it with a light rein, watching its members closely, of course, and guiding it whenever alternative choices were presented, but leaving his subordinates the maximum possible freedom of initiative. As a result it was possible for him to spend fully one third of his time in the field visiting troops. Between January and June he visited thirty divisions, British and American. He insisted, as he had always done, that no parades or formal inspections be arranged for him. Commanding officers were ordered to continue their regular training schedules when he arrived. Gault, who accompanied the general on these trips, was pleased to find the supreme commander as effective with British Tommies as he was with the American G.I.s. With the British, Eisenhower liked to use his Mae West story to put the soldiers at their ease: "A British soldier was seen blowing up his Mae West in the morning. Someone asked him what he was doing. 'Blowing it up,' the soldier replied. 'This is the only bloody air support I'll get this day. . . .' Well, men, I can tell you that *you* are not in the position of that soldier. You'll *have* air support in overwhelming strength." With both British and Americans he often used his story about two privates who had just seen a four-star general ride by in a big car. "Boy, that's the one job I'd like in the Army," one soldier said. "Oh, I don't know," said the other. "There're disadvantages. For one thing, you'd never be able to look forward to a promotion." These simple stories, and the strong, friendly talk which followed, never failed to put him *en rapport* with his audience.

"I could really make quite a speech on my opinion of . . . the people who have been given me," he had said in his press conference of January 17. "I am an intense admirer of all of them. . . . I am delighted. . . . I am highly pleased." For the most part they were men who had served with him either in England or through the North African, Sicilian, and Italian operations.

General Sir Bernard L. Montgomery commanded the British Ground Forces and was scheduled for top operational command during the opening phase in Normandy. Lieutenant General Omar Bradley was commander of the American Ground Forces. Lieutenant General George S. Patton, still under a cloud of public disapproval as a result of the soldier-slapping incident, was in England (though his assignment was secret), being groomed to lead an army, heavy with armor, for exploitation of the expected Normandy break-through. Admiral Sir Andrew Cunningham was now First Sea Lord in the British Admiralty, and sixty-one-year-old Admiral Sir Bertram H. Ramsay had been named commander of the combined naval forces under the supreme commander. (It was Ramsay who had commanded the amazing operation "Dynamo" which took the armies off the beach at Dunkirk in 1940.) Admiral Harold R. Stark commanded United States Navy forces in the theater. Air Chief Marshal Sir Trafford Leigh-Mallory commanded the combined air forces. Lieutenant General Carl A. (Touhey) Spaatz was in command of all United States Air Forces and under him, commanding the mighty United States Eighth Air Force, was Major General James Doolittle. On Eisenhower's immediate staff, Lieutenant General Walter B. Smith remained, of course, as Staff Chief. Lieutenant General Sir Humfrey Gale served as Smith's deputy and as chief administrative officer for SHAEF. Major General Ray Barker was G-1 (personnel); Major General Kenneth Strong was G-2 (intelligence); Major General J. F. M. (Jock) Whiteley was G-3 (operations); Major General Robert W. Crawford was G-4 (supply); and British Lieutenant General A. E. Grasett headed the newly created and highly important G-5 (civil affairs), which had the responsibility for keeping economic and political order among civilians behind the battle fronts. General Morgan was an anonymous member of the staff. It would be difficult to overestimate his importance during these months of final preparation.

With these men the command system which Eisenhower had initiated in 1942 and tested in the fires of North Africa and Sicily and Italy was brought to its perfection in SHAEF. This unique and highly significant historic structure was the greatest of our "secret weapons"; it was the one which most surprised and dismayed our enemies. But it was more than that. There are lessons here for the student of history, as Eisenhower himself realized. For a limited time and for a special job, the logical absurdities, the bellicose arrogance of national sovereignty were laid aside. The result was a structure which might well serve as one conceptual bridge from warring national states to that true world organization which *must* obtain if civilization is to survive. More than any other man's, SHAEF was Eisenhower's creature—fashioned by his logical appraisal of objective needs, embued with his personality, sustained by his selfless integrity—and he often thought of it as a guide to peace. In a press conference in Normandy on August 15, 1944, he praised (as he always did) the "splendid spirit of co-operation which had existed among Allied commanders." These strong personalities had worked well together, he said, not once failing to do their utmost for the success of operations which some of them may have opposed at the outset.

"It proves," he asserted, "that people can work together if they are animated by a selfless desire to achieve a common purpose—in this case to win the war. Perhaps it gives a pattern for future co-operation to keep the peace. . . . But I have nothing to do with that," he added hastily, in a jocular vein and off the record. "They use fellows like me to correct the mistakes of diplomats."

These men *were* strong personalities all, and they *did* truly function as an Allied "team." Among them was only one major figure who, now and again, gave slight evidences of not being wholly happy in his role of team-play man.

Montgomery was occasionally the focal point, if not the true source, of minor frictions among the staff, of perhaps more serious frictions among the troops and publics of the two great Allies. It was not wholly Montgomery's fault. At the time of El Alamein the British were badly in need of a hero, and the Ministry of Information seems to have seized upon Montgomery rather desperately. Officially inspired publicity portrayed the general at several times life size as one of the three or four greatest captains of all time: magnificent in his leadership, brilliant in his conceptions, immensely bold in his execution. His personal idiosyncrasies made good "copy." The public, for a time, was entranced by a soldier whose favorite reading was the Bible, whose tastes were so ascetic that he permitted no smoking in his presence, whose face (under the inevitable black beret) seemed to mirror the juxtaposition in his character of medieval monk and swooping, hawklike killer. Even his excessive use of the first person singular in his public statements was widely regarded for a time as an eccentricity of genius. Unfortunately Montgomery's temperament was peculiarly ill suited to bearing such immense "glory" with a proper humility, and his military prowess, though great, by no means measured up to the dimensions which had been publicly prescribed for it. He was a magnificent leader in many respects. Certainly the *élan* of the Eighth Army was his creature, and it was one of the great things in the war. His tactical conceptions were generally brilliant. But military boldness was one quality he lacked; he was cautious to the point of timidity; and this fact, which contrasted so sharply with the public's picture of Monty, presented problems which Eisenhower had to solve with the greatest tact. The supreme commander had to steer a nice course between the *appearance* of Monty and the *reality* of General Montgomery. Any move which could be interpreted as a "slap" at Monty was certain to arouse a storm of British press criticism: On the other hand, permitting General Montgomery to receive public credit for other men's work and decisions aroused resentments, no less among British than American commanders. It is a tribute to Eisenhower's abilities as a "human engineer" that he kept these irritations down to manageable size.

The plan was now divided into two phases. The first phase, which was given the code name "Bolero," was the stock-piling of material and the training of men, the endlessly complicated arrangements for shifting huge forces of armed men rapidly from England to the Continent. The second phase was the invasion itself, the battle for France, and to it was assigned the code name "Overlord." Inevitably "Bolero" was a period of mounting tension and continuous readjustment as the staff responded to unexpected developments in supply, and to the information concerning the enemy which poured in through G-2. Air-force pilots, making suicide runs within a few feet of the ground on Normandy's beaches, garnered photographs showing five main types of bombs and underwater obstacles. The new types had to be met by new clearing devices. Information concerning the enemy's pillboxes and troop dispositions called for changes in Allied tactical plans. Everything was in flux, and the streams of change had to be closely co-ordinated. But the co-ordinating pattern into which all the changes were fitted was the basic plan, which was itself changed only slightly in the direction of expansion as more troops and supplies became available than had been originally contemplated.

General Morgan had originally planned for a three-division American landing, with a fourth division standing offshore. Eisenhower, Montgomery, and Bradley all insisted upon an expansion to five American divisions. The final plan called for landings on three segments of the Normandy coast. The British Second Army was to land opposite Bayeux and Caen. The American Fifth Corps, commanded by Eisenhower's good friend Major General Leonard Gerow, was to land between the mouth of the Vire River and the village of Sainte-Honorine-des-Pertes, at the eastern base of the Cotentin Peninsula. This beach was marked on the operational maps as "Omaha." The American Seventh Corps, under Major General J. Lawton Collins, was to land halfway up the east side of the Cotentin Peninsula, directly opposite the town of Sainte-Mère-Eglise, on a beach shown on the maps as "Utah." All three beaches were of hard sand and gravel, gently sloping, providing a shelf up which tanks, guns, and transport could roll rapidly.

It was Bradley who had insisted upon the Utah landings. He claimed that the Germans would inevitably respond to the initial assault by reinforcing Cherbourg as rapidly as possible. We needed Cherbourg badly, we had to have it if we were to build up for any quick break-through, and we could only obtain it quickly by flanking the Cherbourg communications and then driving into the city before the Germans had time to reinforce. Later Bradley claimed that without Utah it "might have taken us four months to get Cherbourg." Morgan and Leigh-Mallory both opposed the Utah idea on the grounds that it involved a dangerous dispersal of forces. Morgan was finally convinced by Bradley's arguments, but Leigh-Mallory remained flatly opposed clear up to the end of the conference in which this particular matter was threshed out. Montgomery remained silent, listening closely. Finally Leigh-Mallory said that he would agree to Utah only if Bradley went on record as taking full responsibility for it.

"I'll be glad to take full responsibility," said Bradley quietly.

But Montgomery, ever jealous of his own prerogatives and obviously convinced that Bradley was right, intervened.

"That won't be necessary," Montgomery said. "*I'll* take the responsibility."

Eisenhower grinned and approved.

Later, when Eisenhower had made his decision to invade during the week beginning June 2 and ending June 10, he personally decided that the initial assault should be made not in the dark at high tide, but at dawn some four hours before the tide reached its

]474[

flood. It was a move which contributed greatly to tactical surprise and which undoubtedly saved many lives and landing craft. In the daylight the beach obstacles which the Germans had sown in the expectation that the assault *would* come at high tide were clearly visible. It was possible for the skippers of landing craft to avoid them. On June 6 sunrise came at 5:47 A.M., high tide was at 10:33 A.M., and the initial landings were made between 6 and 8:25 A.M.

By April, England was so weighted with invasion material that, according to one barrage-balloon girl worker, the island would have sunk beneath the sea if the balloons had been cut loose. More ammunition was stacked along the English country lanes than had been expended in the whole of World War I. Huge parks of tanks, trucks, bulldozers, ducks, jeeps, self-propelled guns were spread behind the hedges. Airfields were jammed with planes parked wing tip to wing tip beside the runways. The embarkation ports, according to Nazi radio reports based on reconnaissance flights, were "bristling—positively crammed to the bursting point—with all manner of invasion equipment." More than four thousand ships, not counting small craft—by far the largest armada ever assembled —would ferry the men and equipment across. Protecting the convoys and covering the landing would be the task of a dozen battleships, scores of cruisers and destroyers, literally hundreds of gunboats, corvettes, destroyer escorts, and other fire-support craft.

On March 29 this enormous yet remarkably sensitive machine began to move into low gear. Troops began moving into staging areas from whence they would move, by intermediate steps, to the embarkation ports and, at last, into the loading zones.[2] Nearly two thousand troop trains were to run to coastal ports. A huge illuminated wall map in a SHAEF control room showed the exact location and progress of every convoy along the roads. Meanwhile, civilians were evacuated from large sections of coast and from great areas within the island. Here, in detailed rehearsals of the impending operation, troops trained with live ammunition. In the neighborhoods of Barnstaple and Ilfracombe and Dartmouth endless landing rehearsals were conducted. Nazi coast defenses, in-

[2]Allan A. Michie's article, "The Great Decision," in the *Reader's Digest,* August 1944, is a vivid and accurate account of Eisenhower's D-Day decision. It was based on Captain Harry Butcher's diary. The present author is indebted to the Michie account, recommended to him by Butcher and supplemented by personal interviews with Gault, Butcher, and General Eisenhower.

cluding all known types of beach obstacles, were duplicated and overcome.

In late April SHAEF established a forward command post in a wood near Portsmouth. Here Eisenhower lived in what he called his "circus wagon," a single-room caravan mounted on the chassis of a two-and-one-half-ton truck which could be easily hauled from place to place. Here the drama of Eisenhower's D-Day decision was enacted.

3

All was in readiness. For eight weeks Allied air power had been making preparatory attacks, knocking out eighty-two strategic railway centers and blasting so many of the rail and road bridges leading into the Cotentin Peninsula that the Germans were forced to make long detours over bad roads as they supplied and reinforced their Cherbourg defenses. The final ship loadings for the first assault, begun in the last week of May, were completed. Down the Bristol Channel huge convoys were already moving. At Plymouth, Torquay, Portland, Weymouth, Portsmouth, and a dozen tiny south coast ports, the ships were gathered, were moving out in ones and twos, hugging the English coast, ready to swing into huge convoys at rendezvous points. All that human foresight could discern in this mighty enterprise had been taken into account in the plan. Every factor that human ingenuity could control was prepared for. There remained one factor which was beyond human control, a factor difficult to predict with precision, yet a factor of such overwhelming importance that it conditioned all the others and could determine, by itself, the margin of success or failure. That factor was the weather.

Beginning in March, Eisenhower and Morgan had a weather expert attend a staff conference every Monday morning for a "dry run" of the invasion decision. Eisenhower, turning to the weather expert, would say, "I want to move on Wednesday. What kind of weather will I have?" The expert would make his predictions, exhaustively reviewing the factors to be considered in arriving at them, emphatically refusing to make predictions with any claim to accuracy beyond the first forty-eight hours. Eisenhower then asked the other commanders individually how the weather, as predicted, would influence their operations. Air, ground, and sea presented their views, and Eisenhower concluded by making a "dummy" decision, either to move or not to move. On the following Monday, Eisenhower had the expert review his prediction of the preceding week, telling where he had been right, where wrong, and why, in so far as possible. This expert's forecasts were of course carefully checked against others arrived at independently. A weather prediction was then made for the coming week, followed by another "dummy" discussion and decision. Thus by May the command knew just how the weather expert thought, what he meant when he said certain things, and how the weather would influence the coordination of arms and the problem of supply. The expert, for his part, knew what weather elements were most important to invasion operations.

June 5 was to be D-Day. On Friday, June 2, Prime Minister Churchill and Field Marshal Smuts, affected by the mounting tension, toured the coast to watch loading operations. That afternoon they visited Eisenhower at the Portsmouth camp, and Churchill added to Eisenhower's worries by insisting that he be permitted to "go along" with the assault forces on D-Day. At first Eisenhower thought that "Prime" (he always addressed Churchill as "Prime" or "sir," while Churchill always called him "Ike") was joking. When he discovered that Churchill was serious the supreme commander said flatly that Churchill would not be permitted to "go along." There was too much risk. If anything happened to the Prime Minister the resultant disorder in Britain might endanger the whole operation. But Churchill, that strange compound of genius and puckish irresponsibility, had looked forward too long to this great day to be easily dissuaded. Not until a phone call came from Buckingham Palace, where the King had learned of Churchill's purpose in visiting Eisenhower, did the Prime Minister yield. He yielded to His Majesty's command. Under no circumstances, said the King, was the First Minister to consider going to France on D-Day. . . .

On the following day, Saturday, June 3, Eisenhower was faced with more serious problems. By some strange fluke there was developing what the weather expert called a "typical December depression"—and in early June! It meant high winds and rough seas and low-riding clouds, which would make the landings difficult and air support impossible during the next forty-eight hours. That evening Eisenhower, Montgomery, Tedder, Ramsay, and Leigh-Mallory gathered at Southwick Park, a large country house in a wooded private park six miles from Portsmouth, for a conference which was not a "dry run" but the "real thing." The weather would definitely be bad on June 5. It might be better on June 6, it might be worse. The weather maps, with the lines of that "December depression" drawn upon it, looked far from hopeful. The long-range forecast—which, the weather expert insisted, was always tentative—was not good. It was decided to postpone a final decision until four-thirty the following morning, June 4, and the commanders went to their quarters for a few hours of sleep. Eisenhower, to the amazement of his aides, slept soundly.

In the predawn darkness of Sunday, June 4, the weather expert, his forecasts checked against others arrived at independently, confirmed his predictions of the night before. The conference was gloomy. The commanders watched Eisenhower after they had given their opinions, watched his eyes grow glacial cold and his jaw muscles tighten as he weighed the factors. He decided upon a twenty-four-hour postponement, "at least." D-Day, more tentative now than ever, was set for Tuesday, June 6.

Eisenhower spent the day anxiously scanning the weather reports which arrived almost hourly, gazing often at the fateful skies. That evening Churchill, Smuts, and De Gaulle all visited Eisenhower and sat with him for an hour, discussing the great decision which Eisenhower alone must make. At nine o'clock, after the three experts had left, Eisenhower held another staff meeting. This time three weather experts, who had arrived at their forecasts independently, were called in singly. Their forecasts confirmed one another, and they added up to a predicted improvement in the weather during the next forty-eight hours. Beyond that, the long-range forecast (always a "guess," the experts insisted) was decidedly unfavorable. In other words, a postponement now might mean an indefinite postponement. . . . It was tentatively decided to move on June 6. The final decision was reserved for a conference to be held at four-thirty Monday morning, June 5.

At four o'clock on the following morning, after a few hours of fitful sleep, Eisenhower was back at Southwick Park. There, around the conference table, he, Tedder, and Beedle Smith met Montgomery, Ramsay, and Leigh-Mallory with their Chiefs of Staff. The weather men were called in. Again their forecasts tallied. Tuesday would be windy but not stormy, with a reasonably high ceiling.

Skies would probably clear at noon, and the wind should die down in the afternoon. The "guesswork" long-range forecast remained unchanged; a "December depression" was moving in. Eisenhower then reviewed aloud the factors which must be considered and called for opinions. Ramsay and Leigh-Mallory were the ones whose operations were most dependent upon the weather. If they could move Montgomery and Bradley could. Leigh-Mallory indicated that he was willing to take what they all recognized as a gamble. Ramsay said, "If the 'Air' thinks he can do it, the Navy certainly can." There was silence. All looked toward Eisenhower, who was plunged now into one of those moments of terrible solitude which, again and again in recent years, had measured his inner resources. His subordinate commanders were good men, strong men, but the supreme responsibility was not theirs. It was his. He alone must make the decision.

There was nothing dramatic in the way he made it. He didn't think in terms of "history" or "destiny," nor did there arise in him any of that grandiose self-consciousness which characterizes the decisive moments of a Napoleon or a Hitler. He simply weighed rapidly in that remarkably logical mind of his the factors of the situation. The troops were all set; they'd never get that fine edge twice. A promise made to Stalin (we'd promised him a second front by the end of May) was already in default by several days. Public opinion in America and Britain clamored for action. Failure to move now might mean an indefinite postponement and consequent danger of a "leak" which would destroy the possibility of surprise. With luck, beachheads *could* be established firmly enough in one day to hold, and the weather experts admitted that the weather might be better beyond the forty-eight-hour period than forecasts indicated. Success now might mean a quick decision in Europe.

Adding them up that way, the risks of delay outweighed the risks of immediate action—even though, as it turned out, we had the worst weather in forty years in Normandy.

"All right," Eisenhower said, "we move. . . ."

The subordinate commanders hurried from the room to issue the necessary orders. The supreme commander was the last to leave. "He was walking heavily," writes Allan Michie, "and those who saw him remarked later that each of the eight stars on his shoulders seemed to weigh a ton. . . ."[3]

4

Empty time stretched before him, a seemingly endless succession of minutes whose anxieties were particularly heavy because they could not be squarely met by decisive action. He had immense confidence in his men and in himself, he was convinced that all would go well, but confidence and conviction were not adequate substitutes for accomplished facts. For all his optimism, he had learned to dread this period of waiting which separated a major commitment from its known consequences. A dark sense of helplessness, even uselessness, always descended upon him. He had learned, too, to fill the minutes with activity, meaningless activity perhaps, but capable of killing the time which might otherwise kill his spirit.

The activity with which he filled that long Monday of D minus one was, however, far from meaningless. He visited the troops who must measure—with their courage and skill and sacrifice—the efficacy of the plan. In the morning he visited an embarkation port where British soldiers were loading into LCIs. In the afternoon he visited the airfields where units of the 82nd and 101st Airborne divisions (American) were lined up beside their planes. He was gambling with the lives of these superbly trained troops. He knew it. They knew it. Many on his own staff had strongly opposed the move, and at least one of them had asserted that to land these men behind the Atlantic Wall, in view of the doubtful weather, would be "murder." He had calculated the risks carefully. If the beachheads did not hold, these troops, certainly, could not be evacuated. On the other hand, Eisenhower had pointed out that the beachheads would be much less likely to hold if the airborne landings were not made. "Never risk men in operations that cannot achieve a decisive result," was one of his battle mottoes, and its reverse implications were clear enough: to achieve great decisions, great risks, if necessary, are justified—and this, above all others, was to be a decisive operation. Yes, he was sure his decision was the right one. Nevertheless, no anxiety of D minus one weighed more heavily upon him than the doubtful fate of these splendid men.

Murder! The word rang in his ears as his Cadillac drove up to

[3]Allan A. Michie, op. cit.

airfield after airfield and he dismounted to move among the men. Only with extreme reluctance had he permitted the four correspondents who were assigned to his personal headquarters to accompany him on this, the most dramatic and heartfelt of his inspections. He ordered them to keep at a distance. He wanted nothing to interfere with his direct, personal relationship with these young Americans on whom so much depended and who were now, very many of them, so soon to die. They stood at ease. Many of them had already colored their faces with cocoa and linseed oil, and one of them, as the general passed, was licking the mixture from his lips.

"Does it taste good?" Eisenhower asked.

"Damn good," said the boy, laughing.

Where are you from? What did you do in civilian life? How many bushels of wheat do you raise per acre on your Dakota farm? Is there anyone here from Kansas? He was delighted when at last he found a paratrooper from Kansas. . . . It was evening when he drove up to the last airfield. There, as he watched the men climb into their planes, a spasm of emotion broke through his iron self-control. He swallowed heavily and his eyes blinked rapidly. He raised his hand and shouted, "Good luck!" He climbed to the roof of a headquarters building to watch the planes roar down the sky, southward toward the coast of France, and he raised his hand again and waved and said softly, "Good luck and Godspeed."

Next morning the first D-Day phone call which came to Eisenhower's personal headquarters concerned the airborne landings. It was from Leigh-Mallory at seven o'clock, and Butcher took the call. Then he went across to the general's caravan, where Eisenhower, unable to sleep despite the exhausting hours of the preceding day, was propped up in bed reading a Western magazine. The paratroop and glider landings had been "unbelievably successful," and the first assault waves had reached the beaches. There had been one bad moment, shortly after dawn, when a signal had come through from Omaha saying that the first assault wave had been "drowned." Two minutes later a correction had come through. The word was not "drowned" but *"grounded."*

"Am I glad!" said Eisenhower gratefully.

At breakfast he was more cheerful than he had been for days. Admiral Ramsay had reported that the naval operations had achieved surprise, had succeeded with far fewer losses than had been expected. A decoy convoy sent north through the Channel on the evening of June 5 had been heavily attacked by German coastal guns in the Pas de Calais area, but the true invasion convoys had sailed through the night unmolested. Signals from the beaches indicated that, though some of the landings were being bloodily contested, particularly on Omaha, others were encountering surprisingly light resistance. It was nothing like as bad as D-Day for Salerno, nor as nerve-racking for headquarters as D-Day in North Africa, said Eisenhower to Butcher.

A short time later he made his invasion broadcast to all the subject peoples on the Continent:

"People of western Europe! A landing was made this morning on the coast of France by troops of the Allied Expeditionary Force. This landing is part of the concerted United Nations' plan for the liberation of Europe, made in conjunction with our great Russian allies.

"I have this message for all of you. Although the initial assault may not have been made in your own country, the hour of your liberation is approaching. All patriots, men and women, young and old, have a part to play in the achievement of final victory. . . . The day will come when I shall need your united strength. Until that day I call on you for discipline and restraint.

"Citizens of France! I am proud to have again under my command the gallant forces of France. . . . Follow the instructions of your leaders. A premature uprising of all Frenchmen may prevent your being of maximum help to your country in the critical hour. . . .

"As supreme commander of the Allied Expeditionary Force, there is imposed on me the duty and responsibility of taking all measures necessary for the prosecution of the war. Prompt and willing obedience to the orders that I shall issue is essential. Effective civil administration of France must be provided by Frenchmen. . . . Those who have made common cause with the enemy will be removed. As France is liberated from her oppressors, you yourselves will choose your representatives and the government under which you wish to live. . . .

"This landing is but the opening phase of the campaign in western Europe. Great battles lie ahead. I call upon all who love free-

*dom to stand with us. Keep your faith stanch! Our arms are reso-
lute. Together we shall achieve victory!"*

Then the long hours of waiting again, reading the fragmentary
messages which reflected the chaos of the beaches, smoking an endless chain of cigarettes, wondering if the enemy counterattack
would come before the heavy stuff was ashore and organized,
watching anxiously the rack of clouds through which, now and
again, the sun broke through. What had happened to the German
air? The Luftwaffe had made scarcely an appearance. . . . He
had the habit of scribbling notes to himself on a memo pad during
these periods of uncertainty, as though listing his worries gave him
partial relief from them. One of his scribbled notes that day was a
masterpiece of understatement.

"Now," he wrote, "I'd like a few reports."

In America, John Eisenhower, having completed the speeded-
up three-year course at West Point, was graduating that day. The
coincidence resulted in an embarrassing amount of attention from
reporters and photographers. At the West Point hotel, Mamie, who
had come to witness her son's great day, was awakened by a phone
call from a New York *Post* reporter.

"The invasion?" she cried. "What about the invasion? Why
hasn't someone told me?"

CHAPTER III

The Road to Berlin

WITH the launching of the western assault, the curtain was raised on the last act of the European tragedy. Everywhere the German monster, abandoned by one after another of her active or passive allies, was on the defensive. Under the relentless pressures of her foes, her bloodied tentacles were being forced back mile after reluctant mile toward that "sacred soil" which Hitler had sworn could never be invaded. In the south the British Eighth and American Fifth armies had occupied Rome two days before the cross-channel operation was launched. They pushed slowly forward now behind massive heavy-bomber attacks, along the roads to the industrial Po Valley. The Balkans, whose possession had for so long been contested by Tito and his Yugoslav partisans, were now vulnerable to a flanking attack across the Adriatic. In the east, Soviet forces, stronger than ever before, stood well across the borders of Poland and Rumania, had just crushed the besieged German garrison at Sevastopol, and were striking north in a determined move to knock Finland out of the war. Only Hitler's repeated promises of new and terrible secret weapons kept alive in the Germans a slender faith in ultimate victory.

It was in this context that Eisenhower viewed the picture which, after many anxious hours, was pieced together from the beachhead reports. The picture, on the whole, was more favorable than had been expected. The enormous casualties which many pessimists had predicted for invasion day had not occurred. By the end of D plus one it appeared that we were on the Continent to stay, that Rommel had missed his chance to drive us back into the sea while the beaches were still disorganized. The airborne divisions had accomplished their missions—they had disrupted enemy communications, seized air strips, held other strategic points until a link-up with ground forces was made—but their casualties had been sickeningly high. Several parachute units had been wiped out completely. It made Eisenhower ache to think how many of those boys he had talked to, who had been so intensely alive a few hours ago, were now dead.

At the two British beaches in front of Caen and Bayeux (they were called "Sword" and "Juno" on the maps) the Germans had been, apparently, caught off guard. Bayeux, so swiftly taken that it was virtually undamaged, was ours by the end of the first day, and some British units actually entered Caen that day, though they had been withdrawn later in the face of a determined German counterattack. The Caen area, as the plan had anticipated, swiftly became the German anchor point. A break-through of the Orne River line by the British Second Army could drive a wedge between the German Seventh Army in Normandy and the German Fifteenth Army which held the coast from Normandy to the Belgian border, and it would menace the Pas de Calais area where German robot-bomb installations were being rushed to completion, despite almost incessant Allied air attacks. It was in the Caen area, therefore, that the Germans concentrated the bulk of their Normandy armor, and it was the Caen area, which must become the hinge for a swing south and east by the Americans on the right flank after Cherbourg had been captured.

At Utah, too, a large measure of surprise had been achieved. The fighting there was bloody, but after the first few hours there seemed little question that Utah would hold. The American Seventh Corps was quickly in Sainte-Mère-Eglise. At Omaha the story was different. Here, for many bitter, bloody hours, the issue was in doubt. From the moment the ships and landing craft came within range of the heavy guns on the cliffs at Pointe de Hoe, Americans began to die. Before the sun was well up behind the gray clouds the shore was lined with burning craft, with blazing tanks and trucks and ducks. Many tanks and bulldozers were hit by gunfire as they sought to roll down the ramps, and their·tangled wreckage denied use of the ramps to other units of "heavy stuff." The first assault wave of troops was met by a concentrated fire which checked it at the water's edge. The second, third, and fourth waves were similarly checked. Huddled against the sea wall and in holes scooped out of the sand, the survivors were pinned down all day by mortar and machine-gun fire and by 88-millimeter shells lobbed over the coastal bluffs by tanks of the 21st Panzer Division, hidden now in blossoming apple orchards as once they had hidden in the olive groves of Sicily and Italy. Nevertheless, men and supplies poured ashore, taking their heavy casualties and coming on until, by nightfall, it was possible to push a little way—a very little way—inland. Behind them a heavy surf, gradually diminishing, rolled hundreds of dead bodies up onto the shelf of sand and gravel. "American troops did absolutely magnificently . . . hanging on by their eyelids," said Montgomery to the press, stressing (as Eisenhower always urged his commanders to do) the *Allied* nature of the operation. Omaha, too, appeared to be secured. The "impregnable" Atlantic Wall had been breached.

On Wednesday, June 7—D plus one—Eisenhower went across the Channel to see things for himself. With Butcher and Gault and Admiral Ramsay, he boarded H.M.S. *Apollo,* a fast mine layer, which anchored a few hours later off Omaha. The weather was still bad. A heavy surf still pounded the beaches, increasing the difficulty of landing supplies and reinforcements, but the sun which now and then peeped through the overcast shone down on long snaky lines of men and tanks and trucks, moving up and over the bluffs, moving in. Beyond them, ahead of them, shells were crashing. Eisenhower did not go ashore—to do so would have worried his field commanders needlessly—but he held conferences on board ship with Bradley, Montgomery, and United States Rear Admiral Alan Kirk. Montgomery, wearing a fleece-lined jacket and corduroy trousers and the inevitable black beret, was in high spirits. "Our soldiers" were "in tremendous form . . . full of beans," he asserted, and they had "already taken the measure of the enemy." From Omaha the *Apollo* sailed eastward, pausing before Juno and Sword. Here, late in the afternoon, the mine layer went aground. Eisenhower returned to England that evening on a destroyer. Next morning the supreme commander gave his appraisal of the first fifty-four hours of Overlord: "My complete confidence in the ability of the Allied armies, navies, and air forces to do all they are asked to do has been completely justified."

But the top command well knew that on that day, and for all that week, the beachhead was vulnerable to a counterattack which, if launched with the full forces which the Germans were known to have available, might prove fatal. On the second day patrols from Omaha made contact with patrols from Utah, but it was not until the capture of Carentan on June 12—D plus six—that the two

American beach operations were firmly welded into one. (On the preceding day Eisenhower had set foot on the soil of France for the first time since 1929. With him came distinguished visitors from Washington: General Marshall, Admiral King, and Generals Arnold and Kuter of the United States Army Air Forces.) That same week end an American drive through Trévières to Sully cemented a juncture with the British Second Army. The Allied foothold in France now covered an area thirty miles long and from six to twelve miles wide, a slender foothold whose communications were menaced by the storms ("the worst weather in forty years") of the predicted "December depression." For several days relatively little tonnage came ashore, and Allied air supremacy was nullified. Why, then, did not the Germans counterattack in major force? Perhaps a Nazi military spokesman, in a surprisingly frank broadcast monitored by Allied listening posts, gave the reason. "If we could be sure that the beachhead would remain the only one, we could liquidate it when it pleased us," he said. "However, we are counting upon the establishment of more Allied beachheads where also we are holding reserves in readiness."

Whatever the reason, Rommel's strategy was wholly defensive, and in this he was aided by the peculiarities of Normandy terrain. It was a country in which our superiority in armor and motor transport was of little use. By damming the bridges across the fast-flowing Vire River and by plugging smaller streams and culverts, it was possible for Rommel to flood an area the size of Rhode Island west and south of Carentan. Through this flooded country American troops must wade, in water sometimes waist and even neck high, under heavy fire and without tank support. Even on dry ground, beyond the flooded territory, advances must be slow and costly, for each of the ancient Normandy hedgerows (first planted, according to legend, by the Romans) was a tank trap and a natural fort that could be taken only by frontal assault. They surrounded small, irregularly shaped fields which were, in many cases, less than one hundred yards in width. The hedges grew on double earthen dykes three or four feet high whose walls were cohered to the toughness of stone by weather and ancient roots. Between the dykes were deep trenches in which a handful of Germans with a few machine guns could dispute the advance of a regiment.

Nevertheless, the right wing continued to extend itself. On June 18 advance units of the Seventh Corps reached the Atlantic in the vicinity of Barneville, sealing off the Cherbourg tip of the Cotentin Peninsula. Swiftly the corridor was widened to an average of seven miles. Engineers moved in to lay down landing strips, often under heavy shell fire, so that close tactical support of ground units could be provided by the fighter planes whose operations continued to be hampered by bad weather. The cost was great. In the first ten days the Americans lost 3,283 dead, 12,600 wounded, and 7,959 missing.

Within twenty-four hours after reaching the sea Bradley's forces had begun their northward drive toward Cherbourg. We needed Cherbourg badly. Behind the front the supply situation had been greatly complicated by the storms which had wrecked one artificial harbor and severely damaged the other; by the debris of wrecked ships, trucks, tanks, and bulldozers which cluttered the beaches and delayed unloading; by the enemy shell fire and night air bombardment which, in the first few days, had raked the whole of the narrow beachhead and caused such confusion in the location of supply dumps that no one could say with certainty what supplies were where. Without Cherbourg or Le Havre (and it was obvious that the British, halted before Caen, would be denied Le Havre for a long time to come) we could stay on the Continent, but we could not exploit to the full our superiority in men and matériel. A strong enemy garrison, which carried out remarkably complete demolitions of harbor installations, remained in Cherbourg. It fought with the utmost stubbornness for nine days. On the ninth day—June 27— a thousand bombers poured death upon the defenders. Then came a brief but intense artillery barrage. Then came the infantry, the men of the 4th, 9th, and 79th Infantry divisions. They took Cherbourg. They captured 40,000 prisoners.

Every warehouse, every pier, every crane had been destroyed. The breakwater had been blasted; large ships had been sunk across the harbor mouth and in the anchorages; the water and shore were thickly sown with mines and ingenious booby traps. Yet within forty-eight hours after Cherbourg's capture the first cargo ship entered the harbor, and within six weeks that harbor was handling more tonnage than it had ever done in peacetime. By August the tonnage was more than double the harbor's peacetime load. . . .

Though he was full of praise for the achievements thus far of Bradley's men, Eisenhower was quick to point out the British and Canadian contribution to Cherbourg's fall. In the Caen area, on the left flank of what was no longer a beachhead but a real front, four German armored divisions were concentrated. Had they been able to launch a co-ordinated drive northwestward toward Sword, Juno, and Omaha, these divisions would certainly have forced a diversion of American troops from the Cherbourg offensive. They were not able to launch such a drive because Montgomery kept them continuously off balance with his probing attacks, one of which, on the very day Cherbourg fell, drove the enemy back two miles in the vicinity of Tilly-sur-Seulles. Montgomery was fighting the kind of battle for which he was eminently best suited, containing the enemy, conserving his troops and armor, building up a vast superiority of matériel, waiting for the moment when he could strike with absolute certainty of success.

With the capture of Cherbourg, Eisenhower made his first major change in the operational plan. It had been originally intended to make a second French landing on the Brittany Peninsula between Nantes and Saint-Nazaire, aimed at securing additional ports— notably Brest—through which to pour men and matériel into the Continent. It was a move which the Germans themselves, aware of the fifty-odd Allied divisions which yet remained in the British Isles, expected. "Let us not forget that there is more than one invasion army assembled in the British Isles," said General Kurt Dittmar, the German military commentator, that week. "Our strategy has to take its bearing from this fact." This dispersal of enemy forces, derived from the enemy's firm conviction that the Allies *must* obtain ports, determined Eisenhower's adherence to the "principle of concentration" in Normandy. He canceled the Brittany landing. All available strength was poured into the Cotentin Peninsula in the expectation of obtaining a speedy break-through and a transformation of the battle into a blitzkrieg. "In view of the complicated character of modern war and the detailed planning needed to meet supply schedules, the pressure on a commander not to change previously agreed upon plans is terrific," writes Major H. A. DeWeerd. "Eisenhower's willingness to cancel the second landing showed a real flexibility of mind and a willingness to accept major risks."[1]

The vindication of this Eisenhower decision was by no means immediate. Though Bradley's troops were soon reinforced by the Eighth and Nineteenth Corps, and though he had a heavy concentration of armor and an abundance of other matériel, he could for

[1]Major H. A. DeWeerd, "General Eisenhower," in the *American Mercury*, July 1945.

many weeks make little progress against the nearly three hundred thousand Germans who now infested the hedgerows south of him. The enemy had had ample time to dig in, to develop strong points, to lay out interlocking zones of fire across hemmed-in fields. Bradley, as humane a man as ever engaged in the ugly business of war, chose to sacrifice time in order to save lives. His tanks were of slight use to him. Charging a hedgerow, a tank was tilted almost on end, and into its lightly armored belly the enemy poured a fatal fire. Wrecked, burned-out hulks marked advances which were now measured in yards rather than miles. And Bradley declined to oppose machine guns with the breasts of gallant men in the style of World War I. He refused to order mass infantry assaults which could not fail to cost three of his men's lives for every one exacted from the enemy. Suppose you took a hedgerow by storm. The enemy had only to fall back to the next one, with light casualties. And suppose you took that one, leaving rows of your dead behind you. There was always another hedgerow just ahead, and then another and another in a seemingly endless succession. In each of them the enemy would be waiting, only slightly hurt by the charges which had cost you grievous losses.

The phase lines which, before D-Day, had been drawn on maps to mark the positions to be occupied on D plus twenty-five, D plus thirty, and so on, now bore no relation to the battle situation in Normandy. Montgomery, who had asserted that he would take not only Caen but Falaise on D-Day, was still immobilized before Caen. In the American sector the maps recorded little perceptible progress. The Allies were so far behind the original timetable that there were those who wondered if, in canceling the Brittany landing, the supreme commander had not made a mistake. From war correspondents who pointed to the enormous stock piles of matériel behind the almost stationary lines, from members of Eisenhower's own staff, came complaints concerning "command timidity" in Normandy. Eisenhower and Beedle Smith, aware of the problems of terrain, listened and watched and waited. Eisenhower might well have said that Normandy's hedgerow country, like Italy's mountains, was "no place for master-minding in the grand strategical manner." It was a place for "slugging the enemy, advancing some, and dominating him in the field of morale." This, too, was a G.I., not a general's, war—and G.I. ingenuity had perhaps as much to do with winning this phase of it as did generalship.

THE ROAD TO BERLIN

Technical Sergeant J. R. May of Dallas, Texas, improvised from the metal of a G.I. spoon and from other bits of aluminum a device for timing hand grenades so that they would burst directly over an enemy hedgerow. It increased the lethal power of the advancing infantry in that harsh country. Sergeant Curtis G. Culin of Cranford, New Jersey, a tank man, solved the problem of keeping a tank's nose down as it charged a hedge. From the steel obstacles which the Germans had left on the beaches to halt tanks, Culin fashioned a kind of fork. He welded it to the front of his tank, level with the ground, and tried it out behind the lines. It worked. The steel tines bit into the dyke, kept the tank's nose from lifting, so that when Culin "gave it the gun" the tank went straight on through. Culin's commanding officer watched a demonstration, was excited by it, and passed the word of its success up through channels with remarkable swiftness. On the following day Bradley himself watched a demonstration. Immediately he ordered ordnance mechanics to manufacture, with utmost secrecy, some five hundred forks similar to Culin's. Not until the five hundred forks (Culin called them "rhinos") were on the tanks did they go into battle for the first time. The Germans were surprised. The advance through the hedgerows assumed a faster pace. . . .

Meanwhile, Eisenhower in England plucked the last bitter fruits of his government's Vichy and North African politics. Once again, at a moment when his military anxieties were most intense, he was forced to deal with the intricacies of French politics. Once again, driven by forces beyond his control, he had to regard as an opponent the man who at that point should have been his warmest ally: General Charles de Gaulle.

The tall, humorless, fifty-three-year-old French leader had come a long way as a political force since the last days of the African campaign. Out of the old Free French movement had evolved what he and his followers now called the Provisional Government of France, with headquarters in Algiers. Its ruling body was the French Committee of National Liberation, whose composition had been carefully designed by De Gaulle to represent all shades of French political opinion, from rightist to communist. The committee was advised by a Consultative Assembly, most of whose one hundred members had actually come, by the escape route, from occupied France. The Assembly had no legislative power, but De Gaulle in many cases considered its advice tantamount to a legal decree. Though he dominated this government, the general was by no means its dictator. On several occasions his wishes were overruled by the committee majority. But he was now far more than the Great Symbol of resistance he had become on June 18, 1940, with his famous broadcast over the BBC: "France has lost a battle [but] France has not lost the war." He was now the Great Leader in fact, the spearhead and, to a large extent, the organizer of resistant elements within occupied France. With every rebuff from Allied officialdom his political strength with the French people had grown. With every one of his stubborn assertions of "French national sovereignty," assertions which so frequently irritated the other Allies, he had gained new French adherents.

He had come a long way, too, in terms of his personal education, since those days in the early 1930s when he was writing his most famous book, *The Army of the Future*. In those days he had subscribed to the "leadership principle" almost as fervently as Der Führer himself. There was more than a taint of fascist ideology in those passages of his book which dealt with "powerful" men who are "destined to leave their impress rather than to receive one" and who "alone stand up" during the "tragic hours when the storm sweeps away conventions and customs." His contempt for democracy had seemed evident when he spoke of the man "made for great deeds" whose "faculties, shaped for heroic feats, despise the pliability, the intrigues, and the parade through which most brilliant careers are achieved in peacetime." His commitment to the mysticism of *"la gloire"* was only too obvious in one of the most quoted of his rhetorical flourishes: "For Glory gives herself only to those who have always dreamed of her." Since then De Gaulle had discovered that the true enemies of his advanced military ideas were not the French political leftists, but the very rightists among whom he may at one time have numbered himself. He had discovered that such men as Pétain (whom once he had idolized) were not Heroes but only selfish egotists whose pretensions to Greatness masked an essential inferiority. And in his own lonely heroic struggle for the French Fourth Republic, De Gaulle had found that his support came not from the Best People, the elite whom he had so fervently praised (and who now hated him), but from the People, the common men whom he himself had once despised. In view of this experience he could not have failed to revise some of the fundamental tenets of his philosophy.

But the revision, in this summer of 1944, was far from complete. He was a personality in transition, a mind in flux, curiously divided between inconsistent ideals, and he was extremely difficult to deal with because he *was* so divided. In some respects he reminded one of Woodrow Wilson, truly great in his moments of supreme dedication to his historic mission, incredibly trivial in some of his personal reactions to real or imagined slights. He had not learned to endure the inevitable snubs and rebuffs with grace or good humor (if there was a trace of humor in his bleak personality he hid it well). He had not freed himself of that egotistic sensitivity which elevates superficial feelings to the level of universal Principle. He had, moreover, to contend with wrongs and irritations which might well have aroused a flaming anger in a man of much greater self-control.

There was no question that he represented the only possible provisional French government. Yet on the eve of the invasion, when the establishment of a stable government in the liberated areas of France was a prime Allied military concern, he had gained from a reluctant United States only a strictly limited recognition, couched often in insulting terms. He had gained scarcely more from Great Britain, though the British were less free with their insults. He was more fully recognized by the Soviet Union, but even here the attitude of Roosevelt denied him the complete recognition he demanded and, indeed, had to have if he was to guide France toward the Fourth Republic. When De Gaulle arrived in London by plane from Algiers on the Sunday before D-Day, he was in a particularly intransigent mood, determined to fight for his just ends without thought of compromise, and equally determined (or so it seemed) to fly into a rage at the slightest crossing of his will. He was somewhat mollified by the reception committee which awaited him at the airfield. It included Prime Minister Churchill, Foreign Secretary Anthony Eden, and Eisenhower's Chief of Staff, Beedle Smith. He became actually friendly when Smith handed him a copy of Eisenhower's proposed D-Day proclamation and asked him to suggest whatever changes he thought advisable. But on the following morning, after he had worked all night on his revisions of the proclamation (he practically rewrote it), he met with another rebuff. He was told that no changes were now possible, that the recordings had been made, the leaflets printed. He was told that he should prepare a proclamation of his own, to be broadcast following Eisenhower's. Deeply hurt, his nerves frayed by weariness, De Gaulle's self-control gave way. Angrily he cried, "I cannot follow Eisenhower," and strode out of the office, leaving consternation in his wake.

No one knew whether De Gaulle meant that he could not follow Eisenhower in a radio broadcast or that he could not follow him in principle. Eisenhower knew, as well as did Churchill, that if the French heard no word from De Gaulle on D-Day the problem of maintaining order behind the fighting front would be greatly complicated. According to some reports, the British Cabinet spent all of the afternoon and evening of D minus one discussing the matter. At midnight, just an hour or two before the airborne landings were made, it was discovered that De Gaulle, in his Connaught Hotel apartment, was at work on a proclamation. He broadcast next day, hours after Eisenhower had done so, pledging his support to the Allied cause but making it clear that he claimed for his government the exclusive sovereignty in France. He continued to raise objections, and the fact that they were well grounded did nothing to soothe the nerves of the Allied high command during a period of enormous tension. He objected to the printing of invasion money without consultation with his government, claiming that it was a clear violation of French sovereignty. He objected to the Allied plan of having the interim government of France handled by the Allied military command. He demanded that he be permitted to visit France to organize the civil administration under his government—a demand which, according to unconfirmed reports from correspondents, was flatly refused.

Thus Eisenhower faced again, as he had done in the Rock of Gibraltar in an earlier period of intense anxiety, an irate French general who must be handled with utmost tact if the needed co-operation was to be obtained. Moreover, Eisenhower was in no position to make the kind of commitments which the French leader demanded. He could only strive—publicly, at any rate—for an agreement "on military levels," and this agreement, by his own announcement, he obtained. He seems to have convinced De Gaulle of his personal sincerity, his overwhelming concern for Allied unity, his willingness to go as far as his authority would permit toward a true solution of the political problem. So far as his own G-5 (civil affairs) policy was concerned, it could be summed up in one sentence: "Let Frenchmen govern Frenchmen." He was certainly going to do all in his power to avoid a repetition of the political confusion which had so plagued him in North Africa. . . . And in all of this De Gaulle seems to have seen a green light. At least he was encouraged, perhaps unwittingly, to present the Allied command with a *fait accompli*.

On Tuesday, June 13, General de Gaulle boarded the French destroyer *Combattante* and sailed across a stormy Channel to his native land. One can imagine his emotions as he set foot again on the soil he had been forced to flee four bitter years ago. After a brief ceremonial visit to Montgomery's headquarters he rode a jeep into Bayeux, where he was madly cheered by the crowd. He spoke briefly in the park: "We will fight by the side of the Allies. . . . Our victory will be a victory of a free people. . . ." He drove through other villages and towns. In Isigny the cheers were deafening. He had come to Isigny, he said, because Isigny had suffered most in the battle that was necessary for the liberation of France. That afternoon he boarded the destroyer again and sailed for England, but he left behind two representatives of his government, François Coulet and Colonel Pierre de Chevigné. M. Coulet was appointed regional commissioner, and Colonel de Chevigné was ordered to recruit and train a French fighting force for Normandy.

It was a neat coup, and Eisenhower—though he could easily have claimed, and with some justification, that his own authority had been flouted—wisely accepted it. He continued to measure political matters in his theater by the yardstick of military expedience. He had, with regard to France, much more political information than he had had with regard to North Africa. It was clear to him that the French people were willing, even eager, to accept De Gaulle's government as their own until such time as free elections could be held. It was equally clear that any move toward withdrawing De Gaulle's men from Normandy would precipitate "incidents" which might be dangerous to Allied arms. If he had, at that point, grave and legitimate doubts concerning De Gaulle's capacities as a leader, he had none at all concerning what he as supreme commander should do. He thanked De Gaulle for his "co-operation" and promptly ordered Lieutenant General Grasett, his G-5, to administer Normandy's civil affairs, in so far as possible, through De Gaulle's representatives. At the same time he reiterated, to Grasett and De Gaulle, a basic policy laid down long before: there must be no indiscriminate "blood bath" in the liberated areas; the French should be allowed to settle their own differences, but they must do so in such ways as would not interfere with conduct of the military campaign.

The situation was fairly jammed with explosive possibilities. The fact that there was no "blood bath," no such orgy of passionate revenge as had been feared, indeed no serious disorder of any kind, is evidence of Eisenhower's great capacities as an administrator. The immensity and complexity of the problems he handled through his G-5 have been little realized by the public at large. Aside from the political question (though involved in it) were the problems of food, of preventing inflation, of handling refugees—any one of which, if unsolved, must have unfortunate and perhaps disastrous effects on the military campaign. In Normandy there was an immediate surplus of such perishable food as butter, created by the sudden cutting off of the Paris market. (Preparations for feeding Paris, when the city was liberated, were already being made.) These Normandy surpluses were disposed of through army purchases. In other respects the troops were prevented from buying in competition with the French by having all save 5 per cent of their pay impounded, placed to their credit back home. Through a program which had been carefully organized and which operated with great efficiency, masses of refugees were moved by military transport to dispersal camps, where they were housed and fed and given medical care until they could be moved into areas of economic productivity. By handling these problems in Normandy through or with the co-operation of the French themselves Eisenhower developed a trained native-born personnel who could operate efficiently with increasing independence as larger areas of France were liberated. He was able thus to prevent large-scale diversions from military purposes of his military personnel and supplies.

2

The first flush of exhilaration, occasioned by the breaching of the long-feared Atlantic Wall, had passed by the first of July. As Cherbourg's fall was succeeded by long weeks of almost stationary warfare before Caen and among the Normandy hedgerows the road to Berlin seemed to lengthen day by day. The first scattered criticisms of "command timidity" in France were echoed and re-echoed until a widespread irritable impatience developed, not only among the publics of Great Britain and America but among military men who were only too well aware how far the operation was falling behind its time schedule. The suspicion that Eisenhower might have made a major mistake in canceling the Brittany landings hardened, in many military minds, to a conviction. We now had more than a million men in Normandy and were landing more every day. Through air transport alone we were delivering close to five hundred tons of top priority supplies to the air strips of liberated France. Ships and landing craft unloaded across the invasion beaches approximately one hundred thousand tons a day, and this was augmented by the increasingly large tonnage landed through Cherbourg. Obviously the Allied superiority in men and matériel was immense. Obviously the "principle of concentration" was now translated into objective fact. Why, then, was our progress so slow?

The question was given increased urgency by the robot bombs which began to rain on London and southern England on June 15. Launched from platforms in the Pas de Calais area and in Belgium, these aimless, jet-propelled missiles carried a ton of high explosives in their noses, enough to blow down a block of workingmen's houses in the south of London. If they were far less effective as a purely military weapon than Goebbels's propaganda claimed, they were far more effective as terror weapons than Allied officials would admit. There was a quality of ghostly horror in the very fact that the bombs, which looked and sounded like planes in the sky, were pilotless. They came across the sky at any hour of the day or night, with an awesome roar, trailing fire, until the motor cut out and the bomb dived or glided into a target selected by blind chance. Since they exploded on contact, without digging a crater, the blast effect of the bombs was tremendous. London was soon a city almost without windows, and the hospitals were filled with casualties caused by flying glass.

At Wide Wing, Eisenhower issued orders that all personnel take cover, either in the surface air-raid shelters there or in slit trenches, whenever the "imminent danger" warning was broadcast over the SHAEF loudspeakers from the observation towers where watchers were posted. ("Flying bomb approaching, take cover!" the loudspeakers would proclaim. Butcher called this the "intimate danger" alert, and he had various ingenious but unprintable names for the bombs themselves.) Eisenhower himself took cover in the private surface shelter which opened off his office, complaining irritably that it was a "damned nuisance." He, Butcher, and Mickey now slept at night in the shelters prepared for them at Telegraph Cottage. But it was more than irritation which Eisenhower felt when on Sunday, June 18, a robot scored a direct hit on the Guards' Chapel. The bomb dived at eleven o'clock that morning, when the chapel was crowded with people attending church services. Some 480 were killed, including several of the supreme commander's friends and associates. Eisenhower immediately called his office to find out whether Gault, who frequently attended the chapel, had done so that morning. He found to his immense relief that Gault had spent the morning in the office.

(The personal concern which Eisenhower always felt for the welfare of his associates was illustrated by another incident in which Gault was involved. On April 1 that year Gault had taken his first leave in more than two years and had gone to Devonshire with his wife Peggy. There, on April 9, Easter Sunday morning, he and Peggy went riding. It was clear, level country, but somehow Gault's pony crossed its legs and fell, smashing Gault's shoulder and collarbone. Gault was driven at once to the American 2nd General Hospital at Oxford, was X-rayed and put to bed. On the following Sunday, unannounced and alone, Eisenhower was driven up by Kay Summersby. He had come for the sole purpose of visiting his British military assistant. Gault and Peggy were deeply moved.)

It was soon discovered that anti-aircraft fire was ineffective against the robots. It simply diverted their flight, was as likely to increase as reduce the damage they caused, and it added to the danger of blast the danger of falling shrapnel. On clear days fighter planes could shoot down a certain percentage of the robots (though the latter's speed so closely approximated that of the fighters that the operation was difficult), but on foggy or rainy days there was virtually no anti-robot defense. It became evident to the harassed people of southern England that the only way to stop the robots was to capture their launching platforms—and by early July the Pas de Calais area and Belgium seemed farther from Normandy than Berlin had seemed in early June. The question was asked with ever-increasing impatience: why did not the Allied armies move?

THE ROAD TO BERLIN

The Russians were moving. In White Russia a tremendous Soviet offensive captured in six days five major Nazi strongholds: Vitebsk, Orsha, Mogilev, Bobruisk, and Zhlobin. Some Soviet thrusts gained twenty to twenty-four miles a day, and German casualties (according to Soviet reports) totaled 183,000 the first week. In the second week Polotsk, Borisov, and Slutsk fell. A gigantic pincers closed down behind Minsk. Then Minsk fell, trapping an estimated 150,000 Germans. Vilna, Riga, Königsberg, Brest Litovsk were threatened. In Great Britain and America delighted amazement at the Soviet successes was permeated with a vague sense of guilt because the western Allies were, seemingly, doing so little. The Soviets in Poland now stood barely 500 miles from Berlin. The western Allies, at Caen and on the Italian front, were 640 miles from Berlin.

On June 24 Eisenhower had flown to Normandy with Tex Lee, Tedder, and Second Lieutenant John Eisenhower, whom Marshall (knowing how important family intimacy was to the supreme commander's morale) had ordered across the Atlantic for an "inspection trip" immediately after the West Point commencement. On July 1 Eisenhower had flown again to France, meeting Bradley at air strip A-1 near Omaha Beach. He had spent that night at Bradley's headquarters in Isigny and on the following day had toured the sector held by the British 21st Army Group on the left flank. He had also visited the Fifth Corps, commanded by Gerow, and had met his aunt Amanda's grandson, Sergeant G. C. Etherington, during a visit to the American 2nd Infantry Division. The American 1st, 29th, and 30th Infantry divisions and the 2nd and 3rd Armored divisions were all visited that day. On July 3 he visited the Eighth Corps whose headquarters were shelled only a short time after he left. From a German flak tower he viewed the hedgerow country to the south, toward Saint-Lô. . . .

Thus from personal inspection as well as through dispatches the supreme commander was fully cognizant of the difficulties which faced Montgomery and Bradley. The weather continued abominable, nullifying for days on end the Allied air superiority. Bradley had, as he put it, to fight his way "beyond the marshes" to a line running through Saint-Lô and Coutances before there was any possibility of a break-through, and he could achieve one then only if the weather cleared enough to permit full use of his air power. As for the British on the left flank, they remained halted by the bulk of the Nazi armor and, perhaps, by the conservative temperament of Montgomery. It was on his old friend Bradley that the supreme commander now began applying pressure for a speed-up of the operation. The American drive which was scheduled to begin before La Haye-du-Puits on the night of July 3 must, Eisenhower insisted, be pressed relentlessly until the battle for Normandy became the battle for France. That should be possible. Bradley's tactical plans for the break-through were soundly conceived, and there was excellent tank country to the south and east. Georgie Patton—complaining bitterly at his enforced inaction (he had offered Eisenhower one thousand dollars a week for every week he was in the line before July 1)—was waiting. . . .

It was agreed that Bradley's First Army, now grown to the unwieldy size of seventeen divisions, should remain intact until after the break-through. A completely unified command on the right wing would be necessary to "unscramble the divisions" swiftly during the confusion which must inevitably accompany a breakthrough. But as soon as the "unscrambling" process was completed the First Army was to be transformed into the 12th Army Group, with Bradley in command, and the group was to be divided between the American First Army, with Courtney Hodges in command, and the American Third Army (the armor-heavy army), with Patton in command. It was further agreed, at Eisenhower's insistence, that no announcement should be made of Patton's command—or, indeed, of the entire command change—until after the Third Army had accomplished a large part of its assigned mission. Eisenhower well knew that he was taking a considerable personal risk in giving Patton a command at all. The American public had neither forgotten nor forgiven the soldier-slapping incident, and in May the hapless Patton had heaped more coals of fire upon his head by making a singularly inept speech at Bristol, England. Patton had been told that his speech (to a very small group) would be "off the record," whereupon, with his love for the spectacular, he had proceeded to make a number of flamboyant statements to the effect that the "destiny" of Britain and the United States was to "rule the world." Next day, spread across the front pages of newspapers in Britain and the United States, the statements aroused not only a storm of popular criticism but a considerable anger in Eisenhower, who had ordered Patton not to make speeches and not to issue statements to the press. Patton, aware that he had jeopardized his promised command, strove nervously to mend matters by telling reporters that he had meant to include Russia among the "world-ruling" powers—a statement which, of course, did nothing to improve the situation. Thus the decision to adhere to the original command plans, determined though it was by Eisenhower's knowledge of Patton's superb fighting qualities, required of the supreme commander a considerable hardihood. If issued before Patton had won a battle, any announcement that he had been given a command would provoke such an outcry that the entire command arrangement would be threatened. On the other hand, if things went wrong, if the Third Army failed to make its planned swing, Eisenhower would be even more severely criticized for having delayed the announcement. The latter fact, however, did not worry him. He had every confidence in Patton's ability to move. He had no other commander whose talents for swift offensive warfare were anywhere near as great.

On the night of July 3, advancing through a heavy rain, American infantrymen surprised the German strong points on the hills above La Haye-du-Puits. Next day they were fighting in the town itself, a road junction of considerable strategic importance. Meanwhile, in the British Second Army sector at the other end of the front, Lieutenant General Sir Miles Christopher Dempsey's men managed to encircle Caen on three sides, cutting highways and railroads north and southwest of the city. On that day, as the fighting rose to new pitches of violence, Eisenhower visited the American 79th and 90th Infantry divisions and was, for a brief time and by accident, actually behind a pocket of Germans. In the afternoon he boarded a Mustang fighter plane from which wireless equipment had been removed in order to make room for two men. Piloted by General Quesada of the United States Army Air Corps, the supreme commander swept back and forth across the flaming front, watching the pattern of action spread out below him. On the ground again, he grinned like a truant schoolboy.

"Marshall," he said gleefully, "would raise hell if he knew about this."

On the following day he returned to England. From Wide Wing and Portsmouth he watched the Allied war machine move ponderously forward, advancing in alternative heaves and halts like a locomotive striving to start a heavy train on a slippery track. La Haye-du-Puits was captured after three days of bitter house-to-house and street-to-street fighting. At the other end of the line, in the Caen sector, Montgomery launched a drive (announced as a "break-through" operation) which ground forward, not very far, for five days before coming to a halt. A week later, after the greatest artillery barrage and air bombardment he had ever employed, Montgomery launched a second drive which, after the first day, was reported to have "shattered German defenses in the Caen area so that British armored formations and mobile troops streamed onto the flat open country" east of the Orne and southeast of Caen, there to clash with "elite German armored divisions." Actually the clash never occurred. For almost the first time since El Alamein, Montgomery's tanks were in front of his infantry, but after five miles, facing a heavy mortar and 88-millimeter fire, he halted his armor. To correspondents on the spot it looked as though Montgomery's brilliant tactical conception (he had sucked part of the German armor out of position with a feint toward Evrecy, southwest of Caen, before launching the real drive east of Caen) had again been frustrated by "conservativism." Some of the correspondents praised "Monty's economy of casualties." In the second week of July an American offensive was launched southward from the Bayeux–Carentan road toward the communications hub of Saint-Lô, the point which Bradley had selected for the break-through. The Vire River was crossed on July 13, and more than fifty villages were captured. There followed bitter, almost stationary fighting at La Meauffe (the G.I.s pronounced it "Murphy"), five miles north of Saint-Lô, and before Saint-Lô itself. By July 19 the Americans held Saint-Lô, though the town was under heavy German artillery and mortar fire. The weather remained vile. Bradley was praying for a succession of clear days in which a Tedder-like "carpet of bombs" could be laid for the final push out the hedge-row country.

On July 22, a day of rain-swept gloom, Eisenhower flew to France, conferred again with Bradley and Montgomery, and, one suspects, maintained his pressure for a big, swift push on the right flank. The Americans were now on the line which Bradley had selected for the final breakout. The initiation of the big drive, after careful study of weather forecasts, was set for July 25. The day dawned clear; the ground was hard and dry. Eisenhower flew again to France to watch, with Bradley, the crucial operation. . . .

It opened with one of the greatest aerial preparations in history.

On the Saint-Lô–Périers road and beyond, in an area two thousand yards wide and nine thousand yards in depth, the carpet of bombs was laid at the rate of ten bombs per acre. Some three thousand planes were employed. The day was marred by another tragic failure of air-ground co-ordination. The smoke line indicating the bombing area drifted backward with the wind until Flying Fortresses were raining bombs (for a brief time) on American forward units; many were killed, including Lieutenant General Lesley McNair, Chief of the United States Army Ground Forces, who was in France on a secret assignment. But it was otherwise a day of magnificent achievement. Out of the woods swept the tanks, hundreds of them, halting here and there to permit infantry to wipe out strong points, speeding forward elsewhere at speeds as high as thirty miles per hour, by-passing points of determined resistance. Eisenhower returned to England that night highly pleased.

It was a blitzkrieg as brilliantly conducted as any of the Nazi or Soviet thrusts. Beyond Coutances and Saint-Lô the armor raced toward the sea, encircling pockets of stunned Germans, destroying the best part of six German divisions, thrusting so rapidly through Villedieu to Avranches, from Coutances to Granville, that the enemy had no time to mine the roads. At Avranches the Third Army was born. Officially George Patton went at last into the line at noon on August 1. On the night before Bradley had talked to him.

"Georgie, you used to play end on the Army football team," said Bradley in his slow Missouri drawl. "Well, your job will be to catch a forward pass and make an end run. You'll be taking over troops which are on the move, and you're to keep them moving. You'll wheel 'em down through Brittany, down to the Loire. . . . It's the kind of war you like. You'll be pretty much on your own. Just so you keep moving in accordance with the general strategical plan."

And Patton moved. In one of the greatest offensive actions of all time he thrust flying armored columns through Brittany, taking Rennes on August 3, mopping up the entire peninsula—save for Saint-Malo, Brest, Lorient, and Saint-Nazaire, which Eisenhower had ordered by-passed—in little more than a week. All four ports were closely besieged, and Saint-Malo, the least of them, soon fell. One flying column drove down to the Loire, through Nantes and Angers toward Tours. Another thrust eastward from Rennes through Laval. A thunderous, continuous air assault (one thousand, two thousand, three thousand planes) massacred with rockets, cannon, and machine guns the German troops and armor and transport which streamed in disordered flight along the roads. Prisoners were taken by the tens of thousands. The Germans, knocked off

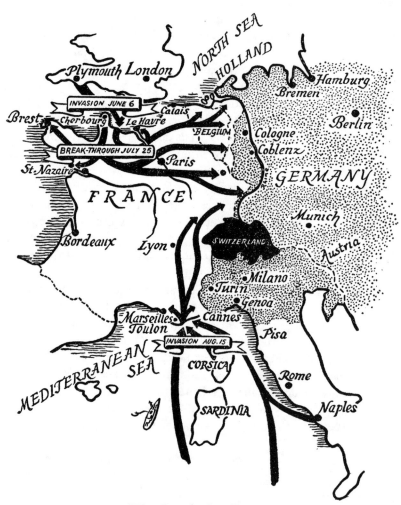

The Battle for France

balance by the swift power of our armored punch, were given no opportunity to organize a defense.

It was at this point that Bradley was called upon to make one of the big decisions of his great career. The German command, in a desperate effort to retrieve the situation by splitting the Allied armies in two, withdrew much of its armor from the Caen sector and sent it westward toward Avranches. The enemy drive made initial gains which worried the cautious Montgomery. His normal reaction would have been to halt Patton's eastward thrust and send Third Army units north to flank the German drive; he suggested this to Bradley, who by this time was operating on virtually the same level of command as Montgomery himself. Bradley stood firm. He believed he could contain the Germans below Avranches without diverting Patton and he said so.

"But are you sure?" asked Montgomery insistently.

Bradley, of course, was not "absolutely sure." There are, after all, few certainties in war. But he *was* sure, on the basis of available information, that the strategic loss of halting Patton's drive outweighed the risks of a German break-through to the sea. Boldly, knowing full well the bitter penalty he must pay if his calculations proved wrong, he ordered Patton toward Le Mans on the very day the German drive was at its peak. The event was extremely fortunate; undoubtedly it cut many bloody weeks from the battle for France. The German drive, successfully contained, cost the enemy much needed armor and gained nothing of importance, while Patton's armor thrust eastward fifty-five miles in thirty-six hours to take Le Mans at very little cost. Thus the trap was set which, Eisenhower hoped, would destroy completely the German Seventh Army as well as those units of the German Fifteenth Army which Field Marshal Gunther von Kluge had foolishly sent across the Seine in an effort to stem what he should have known was an overwhelming tide.

Eisenhower himself was now established in France. To all intents and purposes he had assumed operational command of the expanding battle. Leaving most of SHAEF in London and the Portsmouth camp, he had, on August 7, moved his personal headquarters to a tent camp centered in an apple orchard midway between Bayeux and Saint-Lô—a site selected by Gault on a visit made to France for that purpose on July 30. The camp was small, consisting of perhaps a dozen tents hidden in the hedgerows which bounded the tiny fields adjacent to the orchard, and of the general's "circus wagon" and office tent, and the living tents of his immediate "family," located under the apple trees of the orchard itself. Here, on August 13, he issued one of the most memorable of his orders of the day. He called upon his troops to seize one of the great opportunities of the war, to "let no German escape." "We can make this week a momentous one in the history of this war—a brilliant and fruitful week for us, a fateful one for the ambitions of the Nazi tyrants," he wrote.

He was referring to Patton's armored thrust due north from Le Mans which, by meeting a Canadian drive coming down through Falaise, would encircle an estimated twenty German divisions. Elements of those divisions had already escaped toward the Seine, and other elements, in Eisenhower's own words, would "no doubt escape," but it looked that day as though the bulk of the German strength below the Seine could be completely destroyed. Patton swiftly achieved his assigned objective. He stood near Argentan. But the British and Canadian drive from the north achieved no such speed. Through a ten-mile gap in the encirclement, while Patton fumed, elements of the German divisions fled north and east. They were mercilessly pounded from the air; their casualties were heavy, yet a considerable number of them managed to reach and cross the Seine. The Allies would meet them again, inside Germany. Before the gap was finally closed, far less than the estimated twenty divisions remained in the trap, and Montgomery was the target of angry criticism, from British and Americans alike, for what seemed to them another evidence of "command timidity." No such criticism was voiced by Eisenhower. If the fruits of victory were not as great as he had hoped they would be, the victory was none the less real. With the invasion of the South of France by Major General Alexander M. Patch's American Seventh Army the battle for France was virtually won. . . .

But Eisenhower was quick to point out that the war was by no means over. On August 15, the day of the Seventh Army landings in the south, he called into his tent office the four correspondents, representing the combined press and radio of the Allied world, who were assigned to his personal headquarters. He spoke with his usual machine-gun rapidity. First he outlined the command arrangements within the 12th Army Group, releasing at long last the names of Courtney Hodges and George S. Patton. (The Patton news made headlines on both sides of the Atlantic; Eisenhower's judgment in retaining this general, despite the pressure on him to do otherwise, was everywhere acclaimed; and the United States Congress, which had long held up Patton's promotion to the permanent rank of major general, hastily confirmed the appointment.) He then proceeded to make a "clarification" of the misunderstanding which, he feared, might proceed from his order of the day.

"This week sees the climax of one phase of the operational plan we have been following since D-Day," he said. "It is certain that the German forces which have been rolled up to and concentrated in the Falaise pocket are being given a sound beating. This is a major tactical victory [but] in the campaigns lying ahead, numbers of such victories must be won. There are still lots of soldiers between us and the Rhine."

Questions about the probable length of the war led him to say emphatically that anyone who attempted to measure that length in weeks was "crazy." He pointed out that the Allies faced an enemy who had created "probably the most effective instrument of mass repression in history, the Gestapo," and that the Nazis well knew that they had no choice but to fight on to the bitter end. Hence "the ordinary rules of war, by which the soldiers quit once they become convinced that they cannot win, don't hold in this case." Hitler "can give his troops the choice of dying facing the enemy or being shot down from the rear by machine guns in the hands of their own comrades."

Eisenhower then strove indirectly to mitigate the criticism of Montgomery's "failure to move" in the Caen area, criticism which he did not deign to mention but which he certainly regarded as ill advised.

"A glance at the map," he said, "will show you how important the Caen area has been in this campaign. It has been the pivot, the hinge of our swinging door. It was, as you know, recognized as such in our original conception of the operation. The Germans were forced to hold Caen, if possible, because if we broke through beyond Falaise, into that perfect tank country, the Germans would have had to retreat at once beyond the Seine. Almost all their *Panzers* were concentrated near Caen until static defenses could be put in. That's why the British and Canadian advance has not been as spectacular as the American swing on the right wing. Every foot of ground before Caen has been as important to the Germans as many times that amount of ground on the American front."

His final words were those which had become world famous through his constant repetition of them—and he apologized to the correspondents for repeating them yet again. He expressed once more his own conception of the nature of Allied command. He didn't like to think of the British and American armies, with the French units scattered among them, as distinct entities, but rather as left and right wings of the same army, an Allied army. He praised again the "spirit of co-operation" which enabled French, British, and American commanders to rise in selfless devotion above the narrow barriers of nationalism. The event, he indicated, might have far more than martial significance. . . .

Of all the brutal conquests of the Nazis, none caused more dismay among civilized peoples than the fall of Paris in 1940. The great City of Light, whose rays had for so many centuries stimulated the cultural life of the Western world, was more than a national capital. It was the great center and symbol of all that the fascist barbarians most hated: spontaneous *joie de vivre,* cultural individualism, love of beauty, intellectual vitality, contempt for Philistinism. When Paris fell it was as though a beacon tower had gone down, plunging the whole world into that sex-ridden nightmare which the monster of reaction had created and over which he held sway for a time. To free Paris of the monster became the dream of many thousands of brave men.

Georgie Patton had shared that dream. In the second week of August 1944 he had it in his power to make the dream come true. Paris was his for the taking. His Third Army stood in the outskirts of the city and had only to move in from the west and south to cover itself and its commander with new glory. The Germans, Patton was informed, had only one combat battalion in the whole of the capital. Nothing stood in the way—nothing save a phase line and the unalterable will of Eisenhower and Bradley. Patton protested bitterly to Bradley during the week which ended on August 19 and was answered with patient, matter-of-fact arguments which at last convinced him.

There were many reasons why Eisenhower, at that moment, did not want Paris in Allied hands. Chief among them was the fact that Paris would have to be fed and otherwise supplied. Thousands of trucks badly needed to supply the offensive drives toward the Rhine would necessarily be diverted from military uses. Moreover, Paris as a tactical objective (and it was now only that) was already partially achieved. The Allies had cut nearly all the network of highways and railroads which spread to the south, west, and northwest of the city. The military usefulness of the city to the enemy was so far gone that he had already withdrawn most of his garrison. The wire communications center within the city itself, the airfields which ringed the capital, the storehouses of German arms which might remain there—these had some tactical importance, but their importance was overshadowed by the strategic possibilities which lay behind and beyond Paris, possibilities which added up to nothing less than the total destruction of all German forces this side of the Rhine. The road to Berlin seemed open if only we could keep moving at our present pace, and the limitations on our movement were logistical. To all these reasons, Eisenhower, from the immense perspective of supreme command, added a final one. He had elected to treat De Gaulle as head of the interim French government. If De Gaulle was to fulfill this function, if he was to maintain order behind the lines, his personal prestige and the prestige of his movement must be enhanced at every opportunity. Therefore, De Gaulle and the French fighting units of whom he was leader should have the glory of liberating Paris. . . . But the time of liberation, in Eisenhower's schedule, should be the first week of September at the earliest. The supreme commander argued the case persuasively, if with doubtful effect, in his talks with De Gaulle. Surely, he said, the people of Paris could endure their sufferings for a few weeks more if, by doing so, they helped shorten the war by months.

But here again he was faced with forces beyond his control. Inside Paris the French Forces of the Interior, under General Joseph-Pierre Koenig, were already fighting. Early in the third week of August, De Gaulle, perhaps desiring to present Eisenhower with another *fait accompli,* proclaimed that Paris was, in fact, liberated. SHAEF issued an immediate denial of the De Gaulle statement, pointing out that Allied reconnaissance planes flying over the city that day had been fired upon and that heavy fighting continued in the streets. The SHAEF denial gave rise to a considerable criticism of Eisenhower in portions of the British press. Was this, the press asked, another "official attempt to discredit De Gaulle"? Eisenhower remained calm, if somewhat disgusted. Obviously the timing of the "liberation" was no longer in his hands, and a lesser man, yielding to a natural irritation with the French, might have sent American armor roaring into the city. Instead, Eisenhower sent Brigadier General, Jacques-Philippe Leclerc's Second French

Armored Division into Paris on August 23. Two days later these troops were reinforced by other French units and by American units who, pouring through the Porte d'Orléans and the Châtillon Gate, soon fought to the center of the city. At six o'clock that evening, in the baggagemaster's office of the Montparnasse railroad station, General Dietrich von Choltitz, commander of the German Paris garrison, surrendered unconditionally. The City of Light, only slightly damaged by small-arms fire, was again free. . . .

Paris, Eisenhower realized, would provide the first great test of De Gaulle's capacities as an administrator. Young men, many of them yet in their teens, roamed the street of the capital with F.F.I. bands on their arms and tommy guns in their hands. Could De Gaulle control these men? Would he be able to restore order to his hungry capital after the first mad celebration of liberty had died down? Certainly he could not do so without full Allied support, and Eisenhower was determined to give it to him. General Grasett was told to put into immediate effect the G-5 plans for feeding Paris, and Eisenhower himself, after discussing the matter with Bradley at the latter's field headquarters near Chartres on the evening of August 26, decided to visit Paris the following morning. A visit from the supreme commander might strengthen De Gaulle's hand.

At approximately nine o'clock on the morning of Sunday, August 27, Eisenhower, his car driven by Kay Summersby and with Gault beside him, entered Paris through the Porte d'Orléans. He was met by his old friend Leonard Gerow, who had commanded the American corps sent into the capital two days before and who now took him to the French War Office for the ceremonial visit with De Gaulle. The French Presidential Guard was drawn up at the entrance of the building. Guards, standing at present arms, flanked every step of the long winding stairway which Eisenhower climbed toward De Gaulle's office. The magnificence of the guards' uniforms, the stiff formality of the occasion made the supreme commander uncomfortable, but he faced the tall French leader with a proper dignity. He made his formal statement, immediately passed for publication: "I have come to pay tribute of the Allied forces to the indomitable spirit of Paris." There followed a twenty-minute private session with De Gaulle.

The French leader appeared nervous, ill at ease, and not too sure of what was going on in the streets. He asked Eisenhower, first of all, for fifteen thousand uniforms. He wanted to incorporate the F.F.I. in the regular army at once to prevent the violence which must otherwise proceed from those roving bands of armed men who, at that moment, were almost wholly undisciplined. He also asked for food, and Eisenhower was glad to tell him that food was on its way, that some twenty-six hundred trucks had been assigned to the food-hauling job. After leaving De Gaulle, Eisenhower paid a visit to Brigadier General Koenig's headquarters at Number 6, Boulevard des Invalides. Here, too, a guard of honor was drawn up, and Eisenhower, who had specifically asked that no formal attention be paid to his visit, was so annoyed that he almost refused to leave the car. He finally did so, spent a few minutes with Koenig, and then drove down the Avenue de la Grande Armée to the Place de l'Etoile, where under the Arc de Triomphe he paid his respects to the tomb of the Unknown Soldier. The news of his coming had spread swiftly through streets thronged with celebrants. Soon the Place de l'Etoile was jammed with madly cheering people who cried his name: "Eisenhower, Eisenhower!" and pressed against the car. It was his first experience of a great popular ovation. He grinned and waved.

But his mind was troubled. Was he making a mistake by adhering, in Paris, to his policy of having Frenchmen govern Frenchmen? Certainly there were explosive possibilities within the city. The "blood bath" which had thus far been prevented in the liberated areas might here so easily occur. Any murder could be justified on the grounds that the victim was a "collaborationist," and any civilian, by donning an arm band, could become a "member" of the F.F.I. . . . He flew back that evening to the air strip nearest his command post, motored from there to the apple orchard, and at nine o'clock called over the four correspondents who had "covered" his visit to Paris. He reversed the usual procedure that night; he interviewed the press. What was going on in the streets of Paris? What were people saying? What did they want? What was their attitude toward De Gaulle? Were they fearful of violence? What opinions did the correspondents themselves have concerning the situation? He listened carefully to the correspondents' replies and found that their observations checked with his own. Paris was hungry. That was the dominant fact. Food was therefore a primary essential to the preservation of order. But even with Paris fed, there was no clear assurance that De Gaulle would be able to establish a stable government. The correspondents had sensed that Paris was like a rudderless ship on stormy seas. There was no strong hand at the helm. The correspondents, like Eisenhower himself, were uneasy. . . .

The supreme commander smiled wryly.

"You fellows raised hell with me when I used existing authority to maintain order in North Africa," he pointed out. "This time I'm following a hands-off policy. I'm playing along with the people the liberals support—and they now appeal to me to defend them against the excesses of their own group."

His smile faded and he spoke more slowly, as though he were thinking aloud.

"But so long as the situation does not interfere with military operations I'm going to keep hands off," he said. "After all, this is De Gaulle's first experience with this sort of thing. He's in a tough spot. He doesn't quite know yet what he should do or what he can do. But I think, if we let him alone, he'll grow up to the job. I hope so."

And the event proved the wisdom of his decision. Paris was fed, though at the cost of that margin of military superiority which might have carried the Allies, in a continuous thrust, across the Rhine. The hand of De Gaulle was steadily strengthened. The foundations of the Fourth French Republic were firmly laid. . . .

On the following morning, a day of chill, rainy gloom, one of the correspondents had a private interview with Eisenhower in the office tent. The correspondent had had several such interviews in recent weeks. This time the supreme commander spoke again of the situation in Paris, compared it with the problems he had faced in North Africa. He defended his North African policy with considerable vehemence, asserting that the French Africans at that time would not have accepted De Gaulle. He, Eisenhower, had had to deal with "available" material, and it was the settled policy of the British and American governments to treat the French as full allies. "You can't drastically reform everything at once, though the extremists always want you to," he said. The world, he repeated, moves forward in little steps. "If you strive to gain everything at once, without compromise, you end up with nothing. . . ." And the correspondent, though he was unable to agree that the basic political decisions in North Africa were wise, found himself impressed once again by the bigness, the essential goodness, of the man who faced him. Such a man, whatever his superficial errors, could not, if left free, go seriously wrong. He was a kindly man, so selfless as to disarm the most cynical. He was an intelligent man, possessing such swiftness of logic and such wealth of information as to make argument with him a hazardous though pleasurable enterprise. And he was an honest man, so committed to the fundamental tenets of Christianity and democracy that no amount of temptation could betray him into paths of authoritarianism. The correspondent was grateful for him and for the providence which had thrust him into supreme command.

As if to give point to the correspondent's thoughts, the telephone rang just as the interview was ending. Eisenhower picked up the instrument. It was Beedle Smith calling from England, and after some discussion of military matters Eisenhower mentioned his visit to Paris.

"By the way, Beedle," he said, "there were some British trucks moving in, and they had stickers pasted on their windshields—a British flag and below it the words, '*Vivres pour Paris.*' That's right, '*Vivres pour Paris*' and the British flag. Now don't make an issue of it, Beedle, but you might tell them over there that I think the trucks we send in, if they have stickers on them at all, should have stickers with the flags of *all* the Allies and then, maybe, '*Vivres pour Paris.*' It's an Allied show, you know. . . ."

3

With characteristic boldness Eisenhower exploited to the maximum the victory his armies had won below the Seine. As he sent the 12th and 21st Army groups north and west in a vast wheeling movement he was again presented with alternative choices. Should he pause to clear the Channel ports, in each of which the enemy had left strong garrisons, or should he plunge on in an effort, seriously hampered by logistics, to turn the West Wall in the north? Prudence might well have counseled the former choice. Cherbourg, with Marseilles and Toulon (soon opened by the American Seventh Army), lay hundreds of miles behind the fighting lines. The Red Ball express highways were opened on August 25 to rush supplies at the rate of six thousand tons a day from the Saint-Lô area to Soissons and, later, Rheims, but the reserves of matériel which had been accumulated before the Normandy break-through were now dangerously small. There was a shortage of trucks, tires, and spare parts. The shortage of gasoline and 155-millimeter shells was so acute that transport planes were being used to fly them from the ports to the front or directly across the Channel from England. Antwerp, where the Germans stood stubbornly against British and Canadian units, was as desperately needed at that moment as Cherbourg had been in the early stages of the Normandy fighting. . . . But a supreme decision might be reached quickly by flanking the West Wall beyond the Ruhr, and Eisenhower—as he had done in his race for Tunis, in his commitments at Reggio and Salerno, in his cancellation of the Brittany landings and his pressure for the Saint-Lô breakthrough—aimed for a supreme decision. He chose to by-pass Le Havre, Boulogne, Calais, Antwerp.

The strategic assignments of the British and Americans were now reversed. Montgomery's 21st Army Group on the left wing was assigned the task of flanking the West Wall. Bradley's 12th Army Group, which soon included Patch's Seventh Army (Patch's troops quickly drove through Maqui-held country to the Vosges Mountains), held the center and right wing and was assigned the task of maintaining maximum pressure against strong fortifications in difficult terrain. The German monster was now fatally wounded. The signs of his approaching collapse (the attempt on Hitler's life on July 18; the collapse in the Balkans, where Rumania had made a sudden switch to the Allied side; the approximately half million men he had lost in the west since D-Day) seemed unmistakable. But there were also signs, clearly read by the Allied high command, that the monster's death struggles might be long and bloody. Beyond the Seine the German Fifteenth Army, with battered remnants of the German Seventh, executed a masterful withdrawal, sowing land mines behind them by the hundreds of thousands. If the Germans could hold on the river lines of the Maas, the Waal, and the Lek in Holland until the defenses of northwestern Germany were organized, they could, in view of the logistical handicap on Allied operations, prevent any such "swinging door" drive as Eisenhower contemplated. Accordingly the Allied command decided to leap the river barriers with airborne troops.

In late September the attention of the Allied world was focused on three Dutch towns: Eindhoven, some twenty miles south of the Maas; Nijmegen, where a five-span mile-and-a-half-long bridge crossed the Waal; and Arnhem, on the Lek. In the vicinity of all three towns Allied parachutists were dropped well in front of Lieutenant General Dempsey's British Second Army. At first events moved according to Allied plan. The airborne units at Eindhoven accomplished their missions and were quickly reached by the British Second Army. At Nijmegen, American paratroopers found it impossible to seize the southern end of the bridge. Boldly, under heavy fire and with heavy casualties, they crossed the Waal in rubber boats, while British artillery shelled the old fort of Belvedere. The northern end of the bridge was seized, the infantry seized the slopes behind Fort Belvedere, and within twenty-four hours the first Allied tank rolled over the bridge toward Arnhem, only ten miles away. But at Arnhem eight thousand British airborne troops were fighting in what the lone correspondent dropped with them called "this patch of hell." They were hemmed in on all sides by a wall of fire (heavy artillery, mortars, machine guns) and, as the weather turned bad, they soon suffered from a lack of air-dropped supplies. Meanwhile, Dempsey's slender salient above the Waal was itself in imminent danger of encirclement. The Germans, fully aware of the enormous stakes for which this battle was being fought, stormed forward in desperate counterattacks mounted with all the tank strength they could muster. Dempsey's salient was flanked, almost cut off, and his own tanks were halted. For nine bitter days the men of Arnhem (the British 1st Airborne Division) fought on against hopeless odds, waiting first for relief and finally for rescue, stubbornly refusing all offers of surrender. On the ninth day units of the British Second Army managed to reach the south bank of the Lek. The 1st Airborne Division, climaxing an epic of courage and sacrifice and endurance unsurpassed in the war, broke through the German encirclement, fought to the north bank of the Lek, and was ferried in rubber boats across the river. Of the eight thousand men who had landed at Arnhem, two thousand survived, of whom many were badly wounded.

Thus, in glorious failure, ended the bold gamble to win the war in one swift stroke. There supervened what appeared, to the over-optimistic publics of Britain and America, a dreary epilogue to the brilliant drama of France. The Allied war machine, like an uncoiled spring, was held almost stationary by the Siegfried Line, while in the communications zone a vast but anonymous logistical battle was fought. Eisenhower, who had moved his personal headquarters to Granville on August 31 and to Versailles a week later, directed again an unglamorous "quartermaster's war." Gradually, and at a considerable cost, the needed ports were cleared: Brest, Boulogne, Calais, and, at last in November, Antwerp. Again and again the miracle of harbor repair which had been accomplished at Cherbourg was repeated in the Channel ports. At Antwerp, for example, the first supply ships entered the harbor on November 26. Within two weeks supplies were pouring in at that port at the rate of thirty thousand tons a day, and this pace was continued despite the rain of V-bombs (jet-propelled robots and the new rocket V-2s) which soon fell on the city. Rail and road communications were restored, new stock piles of matériel were built up, one thousand guns were moved in, fresh troops were landed and shaped into new armies, new command arrangements were made. And while all this was being done a continuous pressure was maintained against the West Wall, grinding slowly forward into the "sacred soil" of the Reich. Aachen had already fallen to Hodges's United States First Army, and Cologne was only twenty-five miles away. . . .

In December, as the rain and snow of winter closed down, Eisenhower had six armies in three army groups facing the Germans on a 450-mile front stretching from Venlo in the north to Belfort in the south. Montgomery's 21st Army Group, composed of Lieutenant General H. D. G. Crerar's Canadian First Army and Dempsey's British Second, stood before Venlo and Roermond west of the Ruhr and maintained a constant pressure against the Arnhem "hinge." Crowded into the line between Aachen and Geilenkirchen was a new American army, Lieutenant General William H. Simpson's Ninth, which, with Hodges's First Army (predominately infantry) and Patton's armor-heavy Third, composed Bradley's 12th Army Group. South of Bradley, from in front of Strasbourg to the Swiss border, stood Lieutenant General Jacob Devers's 6th Army Group, composed of Patch's United States Seventh Army and General Jean de Lattre de Tassigny's French First Army. The disposition of these forces was a carefully calculated compromise between offensive and defensive needs. Spread evenly over the whole front, Eisenhower's strength would undoubtedly have been great enough to contain, with relative ease, any offensive thrust the Germans might have made. But in that case Eisenhower would not have had a superiority of strength in any one sector great enough to mount a decisive offensive of his own. He therefore chose to concentrate at decisive points—before the Cologne Plain and the Ruhr, before the Saar industrial basin, and before Strasbourg and in the Belfort Gap—

leaving only two divisions to hold a wide sector in front of the unprofitable Ardennes Forest country. One of these divisions had been heavily engaged in the Hürtgen Forest, near Aachen, for many weeks and had been sent to the quiet Ardennes sector to recuperate. The other was a wholly new division sent into the line for the first time. Eisenhower well knew that a German break-through in the Ardennes was possible—the Germans had driven through that country in the blitzkrieg of 1940—but he believed that the German salient thus formed would be vulnerable to decisive flanking action from the north and south. He counted upon his G-2 to protect him against tactical surprise, though he knew the handicaps which winter fogs, long nights, and heavily forested terrain placed upon intelligence.

His awareness of the risks to which his dispositions exposed him could not fail to be enhanced by his knowledge that, facing him across the line, was the most able of the enemy's commanders: Field Marshal Karl Gerd von Rundstedt. This wily strategist, scion of an ancient *Junker* family, schooled from early boyhood in the arts of war, had demonstrated repeatedly his ability to do much with little and to restore situations which, in their initial stages, appeared catastrophic for his armies. In early December it became evident that Rundstedt was preparing a last desperate gamble, that he was determined to seek a decision west of the Rhine. In this he was to some extent encouraged, and deliberately (or so it appeared) by Eisenhower himself: the Allied air forces in their raids on military objectives left intact the bridges across the Rhine over which Rundstedt's reinforcements and supplies could flow. The Allied strategical pattern for the Battle of Germany was, in many essentials, a duplication of the pattern for the Battle of France. In a slugging match the hard crust of German defenses west of the Rhine was to be shattered; beyond the Rhine, as it had done beyond the Saint-Lô–Coutances line in Normandy, the battle was to become a blitzkrieg. Within this pattern, whatever increased the rate of attrition of German forces west of the Rhine speeded the day of Allied break-through—and a German drive into the Ardennes, safely contained by the Allies, would fit neatly into Allied plans. In the second week of December, Hodges's First Army held twenty-seven miles of the west bank of the Roer (the largest river barrier before the Rhine), and Patton's Third Army, its offensive of a month slowed almost to a halt, kept much of the Saar under intense artillery fire; while in the north, where the enemy had opened the Waal River dykes to flood the country before Arnhem, the British and Canadian troops which had cleared Antwerp were now in line. At any one of these three points the mounting pressure might assume break-through proportions. . . . But Rundstedt, too, had plans, very clever plans in that they sought to turn the Allied strategy to his own advantage.

Of the three factors which might be manipulated to gain surprise —the factors of Time, Place, and Strength—only two remained under Rundstedt's control. The probable place and strategic aims of any major German attack were known to the Allied command. So was the fact that an attack was being prepared. But Time and Strength remained imponderables. Behind a screen of fog in the daytime, under the black curtains of cloudy nights, cleverly exploiting the deceptive possibilities of hilly and wooded terrain, Rundstedt massed with the utmost secrecy his supplies and men. Twenty-four divisions, heavy with armor, to be supported by the last but still impressive strength of the Luftwaffe, were moved behind a sixty-mile front reaching from the Hürtgen Forest to Trier. Thus Rundstedt obtained a better than ten-to-one superiority in strength at key points of this sector. He established his personal headquarters at Coblenz. He was ready. While the attention of the Allied command, uninformed by G-2, was centered on the impending drive across the Roer, Rundstedt struck. . . .

Friday, December 15, was a day of steady, dreary rain in the valley of the Moselle. Aside from light and scattered artillery fire, the sector was quiet. American troops were huddled in their waterproofs, marking time, cursing the weather which kept aircraft grounded and postponed the day of final decision. Soon a thick fog moved in to blanket the valley and Allied patrols were blinded. Night came swiftly. It was still pitch dark when, at six-thirty on the following day, Saturday, December 16, a thunderous artillery barrage fell without warning on American front-line positions. It grew steadily more intense as the gloomy morning wore on. At nine o'clock enemy patrols were reported advancing. By noon it was only too evident that this was no minor action but a major offensive whose scope and strength were wholly unexpected. The German troops, their minds soaked in the propaganda which had recently been focused on them by their high command, fought with the savage conviction that their action would snatch victory from the jaws of defeat, that they would be in the Channel ports, perhaps even in Paris, by Christmas. Rundstedt's order of the day rang in their ears: "Your great hour has struck. Strong attacking armies are advancing today against the Anglo-Americans. I do not need to say more to you. You all feel it. Everything is at stake. You bear the holy duty to achieve the superhuman for our Fatherland and our Führer." Brutal action flamed along the whole of a sixty-mile front. Spearheaded by the new seventy-five-ton King Tiger tanks, sustained by speeding truckloads of German infantry, the attack broke completely through the two hapless American divisions, slashing regiments to pieces, encircling whole companies and even battalions, capturing supply dumps and disrupting the communications which hold a front together. One division was driven back thirty miles and, when it stood at last to organize a defense, found that only six hundred of its men remained. Some of the others had managed to escape to other divisions, but thousands had been killed or captured.

Bradley had been at Eisenhower's headquarters when news of the offensive came through. He remained calm, unruffled. Eisenhower, however, as he later confessed, was "a little worried." While the group commander hastily boarded his plane and flew to the front the supreme commander ordered two armored divisions against the left and right flanks of the enlarging enemy salient. One armored division came down from the Ninth Army in the north, the other from the Third Army in the south. Every effort of command was thereafter exerted to canalize the German drive into what was quickly named the "Ardennes Bulge," preventing those strokes to the north and south which might cut communications behind the Roer River and Saar fronts. All available reserves of the Central Army Group were used to strengthen the northern and southern flanks. A forty-eight-hour "stop" on operational news stories was imposed by censorship to prevent possible leaks of valuable information to the enemy. Anxiously Allied commanders watched the sensitive points along the northern flank of the Bulge—Monschau, Malmédy, Stavelot—while they strove to shore up defenses in advance of the German tide. That tide, all through Saturday and Sunday, flowed west, lapping to the north in continuous probing attacks which sought a weak spot for a break-through, seeking to outrun the defense wall which the Allies were hastily building. At Monschau service troops joined a single combat battalion of the 2nd Division to hold that vital hinge until the whole division could swing into line. The 1st Division was rushed from a rest camp into the line west of the 2nd Division, blocking the northward probe of a Nazi armored division. The 82nd Airborne Division linked up with the 1st at Stavelot. On Sunday night the 7th Armored Division was rushed to Saint-Vith, an important road hub, there to make a desperate improvised "hedgehog" defense for six days while the tide of Germans pressed against and around it. To Bastogne, where the Liége–Arlon highway meets six other roads, the 101st Airborne Division was rushed in trucks to join with parts of the Ninth and Tenth Armored divisions (from Patton's army) in one of the great epics of the war. Bastogne was quickly cut off and surrounded while the German monster, though slowed, roared on.

Monday, December 18, was the crucial day. On the afternoon of that day Rundstedt suddenly shifted the direction of his main effort from west to north, and his design was at last made frighteningly clear. He was aiming, first, for Liége, where the largest supply dumps behind the Allied front were located. With the gasoline, trucks, and tires he captured there he might go all the way to Antwerp, splitting the Allied forces. The troops in the north would be cut off and the way would be opened for a crushing offensive southward toward Paris. The maximum objective was nothing less than the trapping on the Continent of the whole Allied war machine! General Hodges's headquarters were at Spa, a Belgian resort town halfway between Monschau and Liége. On the morning of the eighteenth he ordered his headquarters staff to remove all documents and move north, while he remained with only his ranking officers and the service troops attached to headquarters. All that day, with desperate haste, trucks were rushed into the threatened area, loaded with gasoline (one dump contained three million gallons in five-gallon cans), and rushed northward. And all that day service troops in the area, men who had received only limited combat training or none at all, were mobilized and sent to the thinly held front. Farther south, in response to an urgent call from Eisenhower, service troops under Brigadier General Eddie Plank and Brigadier General Charles O. Thrasher were ordered to the front by Lieutenant General John C. H. Lee, Chief of the Services of Supply. They were clerks, press censors, bakers, truck drivers, cobblers, laundry operators, quartermaster and ordnance men—they were almost anything but trained fighting troops. They had no artillery and, in any case, would not have known how to use it. They had no tanks. They had only rifles,

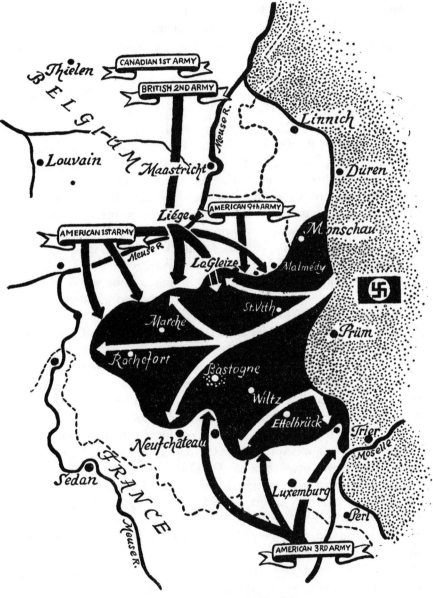

The Battle of the Bulge

pistols, carbines, a few machine guns, a few anti-aircraft pieces—and a magnificent courage. They stood in the line with the weary, battered infantry, stood without flinching against the most savage Nazi onslaughts, and they denied to Rundstedt the vital city of Liége. By the fourth day of the Battle of the Bulge it was as clear to Rundstedt as it was to Eisenhower that the desperate Nazi gamble had failed. From that point on Rundstedt fought his battle, not to gain the victory he knew to be impossible, but to stave off the defeat he knew to be inevitable. . . .

On that day, Tuesday, December 19, direct communications were severed between Bradley's 12th Army Group headquarters and that portion of the group north of the Bulge (it consisted of all the Ninth Army and most of the First). Eisenhower, capitalizing on the Allied unity he had so carefully fostered, immediately transferred all American troops north of the Bulge to Montgomery's command, and Monty, in his own words, proceeded to "tidy things up a bit." Meanwhile, Patton was ordered to attack toward Bastogne, where Brigadier General A. C. McAuliffe's men, hemmed in on all sides and outnumbered nearly four to one, fought stubbornly on with no thought of surrender despite the bad weather which denied them air-dropped supplies for several days. (To a German demand that he surrender or be annihilated, McAuliffe made a typically American reply: "Nuts!") Other Patton columns drove against the German flank in Luxemburg. Thus Eisenhower's offensive deployment, so bitterly criticized at that time in the press, enabled him to apply swift and effective pressure against the base and flanks of the German salient. He had matters well under control.

But on the maps, and in the eyes of the uninformed public, the Allied situation appeared to worsen steadily for many days. Rundstedt turned westward again. As Saint-Vith fell and Bastogne's position appeared increasingly desperate, the Germans threw everything they had into a thrust toward the Meuse. V-1s and V-2s fell in droves far behind the lines. German soldiers wearing American uniforms and riding American jeeps spread confusion behind the lines. Panicky correspondents reported that Eisenhower's forces had suffered "the worst disaster ever to befall American arms," while others, comparatively optimistic, pointed out gloomily that Rundstedt had lengthened the front by some 225 miles, had immensely complicated the Allied logistical problem, and had delayed any decisive Allied offensive by at least four to six months. In this context Eisenhower's order of the day, issued December 22, sounded suspiciously like whistling in the dark.

"The enemy is making his supreme effort," said the supreme commander to his troops. "He is fighting savagely to take back all that you have won and is using every treacherous trick to deceive and kill. He is gambling everything, but already in this battle your gallantry has done much to foil his plans. In the face of your proven bravery and fortitude, he will completely fail. But we cannot be content with his mere repulse. By rushing out from his fixed defenses the enemy may give us the chance to turn his greatest gamble into his worst defeat. So I call upon every man of all the Allies to rise to new heights of courage, of resolution, and of effort. Let everyone hold before him a single thought to destroy the enemy on the ground, in the air, everywhere—destroy him. United in this determination and with unshakable faith in the cause for which we fight, we will, with God's help, go forward to our greatest victory!"

The supreme commander was *not* "whistling in the dark." He meant precisely what he said. And in a very real sense the Battle of the Bulge *was* transformed into an Allied victory. As in the case of the Kasserine reverse in Africa and the attempted German breakthrough to Avranches in Normandy, the enemy achieved no strategic results through his Ardennes thrust. The losses he inflicted on the extended Allied lines—losses quickly replaced—were overbalanced by the irreplaceable losses suffered by his own forces. In the last days of December and the opening days of January the Allied air forces were released from the bondage imposed by bad weather. Heavy and medium bombers dumped almost thirty-five thousand tons of high explosives on Rundstedt's supply centers, blasted the hangars and runways of his airfields, poured ruin upon his rail and road communications. Strafing attacks destroyed hundreds of tanks, thousands of motor vehicles. The Luftwaffe's carefully hoarded strength was broken in an unprecedented series of air battles during which more than one thousand German planes were destroyed against a loss of three hundred of our own. The heroic stand of the Bastogne garrison and of the ill-fated garrison at Saint-Vith so slowed Rundstedt's advance that even his farthest-flung spearhead gained no profitable ground. Moreover, the barren country it occupied was quickly relinquished. On Christmas Day, when his tanks were halted at a point three miles from the Meuse and fifty miles west of the original front, Rundstedt prepared a hasty retreat. On the following day United States Sherman tanks of the 4th Armored Division broke through the German lines to Bastogne, and on December 27 the weary garrison, which had destroyed 148 German tanks and killed thousands of enemy troops, was relieved. Thereafter the action was, for the Germans, another "masterful withdrawal." Aided by a blizzard which soon grounded the Allied planes, Rundstedt's forces narrowly escaped from the trap sprung by a triple drive—from the north, west, and south—by the American First Army, the British Second, and the American Third. Soon the Bulge was reduced to a shallow bowl, and by January 31, 1945, even the bowl had been smashed. . . .

"Weren't you frightened by the Rundstedt attack?" someone asked the supreme commander.

"Well, not at the time," replied Eisenhower thoughtfully. Then he grinned. "But I was scared stiff three weeks later when I got around to reading the newspaper accounts."

The newspapers, British and American alike, were not kind to Eisenhower during those first three weeks. He was severely criticized for an alleged "failure to delegate authority," for the failure of his G-2 (though his G-2 made a remarkably quick recovery, identifying seventeen of the attacking enemy divisions in the first two days), and for the manner in which his troops were deployed. The first-named criticism was patently absurd to anyone acquainted with Eisenhower's system of command, and the latter ones failed to take account of two factors: first, that battles cannot be won without risks unless one side has an overwhelming superiority of strength (we had no such strength at that time); and, second, that the enemy has generals, too, who sometimes are so unkind as to do the unexpected thing. To the charge that the battle was won, in spite of bad generalship, by the courage and devotion of outnumbered troops, Eisenhower might reasonably have replied that the courage and devotion of those troops were among the factors he considered when he made his deployments. In any case, with a few exceptions, the violence of the criticism was in direct proportion to the distance of the critic from the front lines—and it was more revealing of the basic dualism in human nature than it was of the objective realities on the Western Front. Human beings think and feel naturally in terms of opposites. Ideas are judged by assigning them a position on a scale ranging from positive to negative, and the emotions demand with equal fervor a god and a devil. When the war went well the glory was assigned to a hero, and when it went ill the blame was assigned to a scapegoat. Eisenhower, who cared little for laurel crowns, could bear with equanimity a temporary crown of thorns. His chief concern was to preserve Allied unity, which was subjected in those weeks to perhaps the greatest strains of the war.

But if the criticism which was focused on Eisenhower had little factual content, the forms it assumed derived from what, in retrospect, appears to have been a mistaken public-relations policy. There is a very real sense in which the criticism he harvested in Germany, as the year ended, sprang from seeds sown in Normandy during the preceding July. From the best of motives the supreme commander had allowed the public to obtain a false view of the command structure during the battle for France, and when command appearances were at last brought in line with realities the event coincided with a deterioration of Allied military fortunes. The critics, quite naturally, mistook the coincidence for a casual relationship and derived from that mistake some quite absurd conclusions. In this matter, as in his approach to French African politics and to the public-relations aspects of the soldier-slapping incident, Eisenhower was perhaps too exclusively pragmatic, too willing to sacrifice the long view to short-term gains. It was a mistake he rarely made, and then only in fields where the factors are fluid and the problems require, for their solution, more of intuition than of logic. . . . The entire episode is of minor importance in terms of total command. But it is not without interest, nor perhaps without significance, in terms of Eisenhower's personal portrait.

For the initial landings in Normandy it had, of course, been necessary to have a single operational commander. Montgomery was that commander. Indeed, Eisenhower, in view of the immense popular prestige which Montgomery at that time possessed, and in view of the necessities of Anglo-American co-operation, could hardly have made any other choice—and there is no evidence that he wished to do so. But after the first few weeks of build-up, the operation, as we have seen, was so vast that the over-all operational command passed, in actual fact, to the supreme commander. Butcher, during this period, began urging Eisenhower to make public announcement that he was taking over the operational command. The supreme commander, fearful of unfortunate repercussions in the British press, felt that the time was not yet ripe for such an announcement. Nevertheless, Butcher, whose talent for public relations was unsurpassed, repeated his urgings with such insistence that he was, for a time (and in his own words), "in Ike's doghouse." He was left behind at Wide Wing one week while Eisenhower went down to the Portsmouth camp.[2]

By the last of July, Omar Bradley and Montgomery had for weeks been operating on virtually the same level of command, Bradley in command of the right wing and Montgomery of the left wing of the Allied forces. With the formation of the 12th Army Group, to balance Montgomery's 21st Army Group, this command relationship was still further confirmed. As we have seen, it was Bradley who evolved the tactical plan for the break-through at Saint-Lô, and it was Bradley who, on August 1, "passed the ball" to Patton and Hodges while Montgomery and the British maintained their pressure against the bulk of the German armor before Caen. The usual procedure was for Bradley to inform Montgomery of his plans, whereupon Montgomery would issue an order telling him to go ahead with them. But the British press, quite naturally, didn't play the story that way. A substantial portion of that press portrayed the whole of the French operation as "Monty's Show." Several stories specifically gave him all credit for the tactics at Saint-Lô, and a typical British headline referred to the American Third Army drive as a movement of "Monty's Right Wing." As everyone knows, Montgomery himself was by no means averse to favorable publicity, and he made no moves toward correcting the misconception in the public mind.

On August 7 Eisenhower moved his personal headquarters to Normandy in order to maintain close personal contact with field commanders. That would seem to have been a logical moment for announcing the realities of the command situation. Why did the supreme commander refuse to do so?

There were two principal reasons. One was that Patton was still under a cloud of public disapproval, had not yet completed his amazing "end run," and was, moreover, in need of further disciplining. ("It won't do Georgie a bit of harm to operate a while longer without publicity," is the way one of SHAEF's generals put it.) The other and more important reason was that Allied strategy was

---

[2]This event, if unfortunate in other respects, was fortunate for the author of this book, who, during the general's absence from London, was enabled to spend much time with Butcher and even to sleep one night in the general's bed at the then highly secret Telegraph Cottage.

just beginning to pay big dividends. Hence an abrupt announcement that Eisenhower was now operational commander in France would inevitably have been interpreted by the British as an effort to deprive Montgomery of the glory which was his due. By mid-August the situation was further complicated by the feeling in certain quarters that Montgomery was acting too literally in accordance with his motto of "no risks." As has been said, the German armor which counterattacked toward Avranches was withdrawn from the Caen sector, and the feeling was that Montgomery should then have been able to move with much greater rapidity than he did to effect a juncture with Patton and thus complete encirclement of the Germans in the Caen-Falaise-Argentan "pocket." Perhaps this criticism did not take into account the static defenses which the Germans installed before they withdrew their armor from Caen, but the criticism was there and it had to be reckoned with.

It is significant that this criticism, among Eisenhower's subordinates, was in no case based on nationalistic grounds. Among military men in a position to know the facts, Montgomery was never criticized as a *British* general, but simply as a general—and, if anything, the British were more caustic in their comments than the Americans. Obviously things could not be allowed to go on indefinitely as they were: the effectiveness of command would be impaired. Even Bradley—who was not only incapable of dramatic pretension, but quietly contemptuous of it in others—was human enough to resent another man's getting public credit for things he himself had done. The problem which Eisenhower faced, therefore, was in large part one of timing, and in it were involved not only British and American public opinion but the private feelings and future co-operation of top field commanders. He awaited the opportune time, trusting himself to recognize it when it came. In the meantime he strove to mitigate the undercover criticism of the "rusty hinge" at Caen, notably in the press conference of August 15 which has already been described.

But two days after this press conference was held an Associated Press dispatch filed in London by Wes Gallagher made a premature exposure of the real command situation. It had precisely the effect which Eisenhower had feared (how it managed to clear censorship was a mystery), and the correspondents who were attached to the supreme commander's personal headquarters will never forget Eisenhower's anger on that occasion. He had a warm and lengthy session with Lieutenant Colonel Thor Smith, the public-relations officer at his personal camp, and relented only when he was firmly convinced that neither Smith nor the four correspondents had had anything to do with the release. On the following day, when he and the correspondents were at Bradley's headquarters near Saint James, he let the correspondents know in no uncertain terms that dire things would have happened to them had any of them "pulled such a stunt."

For the next few days SHAEF was the target of bitter criticism in the British press. Editorials decried this "unwarranted slap" at Montgomery. An immediate denial by SHAEF that Eisenhower had officially assumed any new command or that any criticism of Montgomery had been made or was intended smoothed matters somewhat —but the timing was now out of Eisenhower's hands. The Eisenhower personality, his ability to command respect and affection in a face-to-face meeting, was at this juncture an invaluable asset which the supreme commander used quite consciously. On September 1, after Paris had been liberated, he held in London one of his largest press conferences. He discussed, with disarming candor, the command situation. He praised Montgomery's contribution to the liberation of France and paid tribute to him as one of the greatest captains of the age. He pointed out that operations had now expanded far beyond the beachhead phase in which a single commander could exercise effective control, that all of western Europe was now involved, and that he himself, therefore, was not assuming a command formerly held by someone else but was simply continuing as supreme commander. Headlines a few hours later proclaimed the conference a huge success. The British promoted Montgomery to the rank of field marshal (creating a minor furor among the Americans, because it meant that technically Montgomery outranked Eisenhower). The Americans countered a few months later by promoting Eisenhower to five-star rank, making him General of the Army. The crisis in public relations appeared past.

But in view of subsequent events this was only an appearance. As the Battle of France was succeeded by a bitter slugging match on the German border, the failure of the Allied war machine to continue its swift movement was ascribed by many "experts" to the "change in command arrangements" which had allegedly occurred on September 1. Rundstedt's drive into the Ardennes Bulge brought criticism to a focus. The focus was Eisenhower. L. S. B. Shapiro, Sir

Douglas Brownrigg, and A. J. Cummings—to choose three journalists at random—all claimed that Eisenhower couldn't possibly serve
effectively as both administrator and strategist and that his function
as supreme commander should be solely administrative. Just how the
top command could be so neatly divided into "administration" and
"strategy" they did not say. Sir Douglas Brownrigg, in his newspaper
article, hinted gently that perhaps Montgomery should "come back
into the picture" as chief strategist. A. J. Cummings, in the London
News-Chronicle, was more definite. He quoted "many people's
opinion" that Montgomery should be made Eisenhower's acting
deputy and chief planner. Eisenhower's time, according to these
"many people," was too much occupied with "routine administrative" and non-military matters to leave him sufficient leisure in
which to "think in terms of strategy." Obviously Cummings's own
opinion was that Eisenhower, being no great shakes as a strategist,
should limit himself to the "routine" matters and let Montgomery—
who was "an exceptional soldier, the very man to match against
Von Rundstedt"—handle the fighting. He went even further, claiming that the reason this wasn't done was that "neither Eisenhower's
generals nor the Washington War Department nor the American
public would acquiesce in the appointment of Montgomery to a vital
position on the supreme staff."

There were "many people" who regarded the Cummings piece as
fifth-column talk, in so far as it attempted to drive a wedge between
the British and American members of SHAEF. Its implications were
of course wholly false. There were more British than American
officers in the top positions at SHAEF—the excellent G-2, at that
time so bitterly criticized, happened to be British—and if SHAEF's
members would not "acquiesce" in the appointment of Montgomery
as top operational commander it might well have been because they,
British and Americans alike, had doubts about his ability to handle
such an assignment. In the very week that Cummings's piece was
released Eisenhower's command was giving an impressive demonstration, under extreme pressure, of Allied unity. Montgomery's own
account of the battle, given in a press conference at his headquarters
in the second week of January, emphasized "Allied teamwork" as
the decisive factor. He managed to convey the impression that without Monty the Allied "team" would have been in a bad way—as
indeed it might have been—but it seems evident that he was trying
hard, in that hour of crisis, to become a team-play man.

"When Rundstedt put in his hard blow and parted the American Army, it was automatic that the battle area must be untidy," he said. "Therefore, the first thing I did was busy myself in getting the battle area tidy—getting it sorted out. I got reserves into the right place and got balanced—and you know what happened. . . . It looked to me as if Rundstedt was trying to do a big left hook to the River Meuse. There was not much there—there was damn little there—so I collected here and there, pulled in divisions and formed an army corps under that very fine American General Collins.[3] It took a knock. I said, 'Dear me, this can't go on. It's being swallowed up in the battle.' I managed to form the corps again. Once more pressure was such that it began to disappear in a defensive battle. I said, 'Come, come,' and formed it again, and it was put in offensively by General Hodges after we had consulted together, and that is his present job."

He praised the "good fighting qualities of the American soldier. I take my hat off to . . . such men. . . . I salute the brave fighting men of America—I never want to fight alongside better soldiers. . . . I have tried to feel that I am almost an American soldier myself." He said with emphasis: "It is teamwork that pulls you through. . . . Let us rally round the captain of the team and so help to win the match. . . . Let me tell you that the captain of our team is General Eisenhower. I am absolutely devoted to Ike. . . . It grieves me when I see uncomplimentary articles about him in the British press. . . . He needs our fullest support. . . . And so I would ask all of you . . . to stop that sort of thing. . . . Ike is a very great friend of mine. My own airplane was damaged the other day. I cried to Ike, 'Can you lend me another plane?' He sent me his own at once—wonderful."

Eisenhower adhered rigidly to his policy that no censorship be imposed on criticism of him. He took no apparent notice of that criticism, counting on his past record and future performance to preserve the prestige necessary to supreme command. After communications had been restored between Bradley's headquarters and the American troops in the north, those troops were returned to the 12th Army Group. The Allied command team, more firmly welded together than ever before by the crisis through which it had passed, prepared with confidence its last victorious campaign. . . .

[3]Major General J. Lawton Collins.

4

Four to six months, the gloomy critics had said. It would be early summer before the western Allies could launch a major offensive. The Germans would have time to organize new defenses in depth, to perfect new secret weapons, to make of their country a rock whose crushing would require a year of blood and toil. Through February and early March the gloom-mongers cried out against an alleged inferiority of Allied military equipment, an inferiority which reflected the shortcomings of Allied military leadership. . . . And during this period the Allied war machine reached a peak of efficiency unequaled by any other army in history.

In mid-February, with an attack by the Canadian First Army near Kleve, Eisenhower's forces launched an offensive which, gathering speed as it went, never halted until the body of the German monster lay hacked into bloody pieces on the "sacred soil" of the Reich. The attack in the far north was soon followed by operations of the American Ninth and First armies which cleared the west bank of the Rhine as far south as Cologne. The American Third Army, attacking in the Eiffel sector, prevented the German reinforcement of Cologne, which fell on March 6. On the following day an American First Army patrol, spearheading a southward drive, reached the west bank of the Rhine opposite the town of Remagen. There the patrol found the Ludendorff Bridge across the Rhine still intact, though explosive charges had been set to destroy it. The intrepid Americans pushed onto the bridge, yanked out the explosive charges, and beckoned the First Army to follow them into the heart of Germany. Meanwhile, the Third Army plunged through the hilly country beyond the Siegfried Line, two of its armored columns advancing fifty-five miles in four days to reach the Rhine and Moselle rivers. A juncture with the First Army was effected. Fifty thousand enemy troops were killed or wounded, and 84,000 were captured in this operation, which cost the Americans less than 26,000 casualties. Units of the Third Army cut southward across the Moselle River and eastward from the vicinity of Trier, movements which were co-ordinated with those of the American Seventh Army which attacked from the south against the Siegfried Line. In nine days the west bank of the Rhine from Coblenz to the Karlsruhe area was cleared.

Said the official War Department review issued on March 29: "General Eisenhower's entire campaign, in three phases, for the west bank of the Rhine cost the Germans 230,000 men who were taken prisoners by Allied forces and 100,000 or more killed and wounded. The campaigns of the Ardennes (which had cost the enemy 220,000 casualties and vast quantities of tanks, guns, and transport) and of the west bank of the Rhine thus weakened the enemy by depriving him of a total of about 550,000 men."

And now the enemy made the final payments for his futile Ardennes gamble. His plans for a prolonged and organized retreat to "redoubt" regions in the heart of Germany and in the Bavarian Alps were everywhere frustrated by his own weakness and by the swiftness of Allied movements. All that Eisenhower and his men had learned of war, in four victorious campaigns, was brought to bear in an amazing demonstration of arms co-ordination, of supply organization, of strategic boldness and tactical brilliance. It was a demonstration unique in military history. The Nazi campaigns of 1939 and 1940—conducted against armies poorly equipped and led, armies already half destroyed by treachery before the first shot was fired—were completely eclipsed by a series of perfectly executed double envelopments which slashed to bits a still stubborn and skillful foe. *Without pause* (in itself an amazing achievement) the Allied forces leaped the Rhine and roared on, at speeds of twenty-five to fifty miles a day, along the network of super-highways which Hitler had conveniently spread across the German landscape. Within a week there were five rapidly expanding bridgeheads across the great water barrier. Units of the Third Army, achieving complete tactical surprise, crossed the Rhine south of Mainz without the loss of a single man. At the same time the British Second Army and the American Ninth Army made crossings from the area of Rees to points just north of the built-up area of the Ruhr. North of Wesel a virtually complete Allied airborne army was landed from thirty-one hundred transports and gliders, with remarkably small losses of planes and men despite intense anti-aircraft fire. These troops quickly seized all their objectives and linked up with the advancing ground troops.

Soon nine Allied armies were beyond the Rhine, plunging their spearheads deep into the writhing body of the Reich.

"The Germans as a military force on the Western Front are a whipped army," Eisenhower announced to the Allied peoples. To the Germans he said: "The German Government has ceased to exercise effective control over wide areas. The German high command has lost effective control over many units, large and small, of the German forces." He called upon the *Wehrmacht* to surrender and prevent useless bloodshed. But he made no pause in his own military operations, knowing well that the absence of a unified enemy control made it well-nigh impossible for the Wehrmacht to surrender in other than piecemeal fashion. Fanatic Nazis continued to make last-ditch stands, inflicting heavy casualties on the advancing forces, but the only real limitations on Allied movements were now logistical, and those limits were made amazingly wide by the continuing miracle of Allied supply. Spurred by the conviction that the end was now in sight, aroused to cold fury by the bestial atrocities which their advances daily revealed, the Allied troops now fought with an even greater dash and daring than they had displayed in the earlier campaigns. No assignment was too difficult for them, no sacrifice too great. In the largest double envelopment in history the Ruhr was encircled and crushed into a bloody pocket from which, at last, more than three hundred thousand German prisoners were taken. The Canadian First Army pushed east and north toward Emden and Wilhelmshaven. The British Second Army drove toward Bremen, Hamburg, Kiel. The American Ninth and First armies roared eastward across the heart of Germany until they stood on the Elbe River, there to await a meeting with the westward-driving Russian forces. The American Third Army drove into Czechoslovakia while the American Seventh pushed down the Danube River Valley toward Austria. The bag of prisoners taken by the western Allies since Normandy D-Day was swelled to well over two million men. . . .

For all these movements the way was prepared by the Allied air forces. Having smashed the Luftwaffe, Allied planes dominated the German skies, spearheaded the long advances, and gave close tactical support in the areas of Nazi resistance. Everywhere the advancing troops saw evidences of air-force destruction—in wrecked enemy communications, smashed factories, and ruined and desolate cities. In late March heavy bombers and fighters based in Italy added massive weight to the sky attack on the Reich, making their first attack on Berlin. The Italian-based forces also attacked enemy transportation and other military targets in Austria, Yugoslavia, Hungary, and Czechoslovakia in direct aid of Russian ground forces.

Meanwhile, from the south, southeast, and east, irresistible pressures were being applied to the enemy by the American Fifth and British Eighth armies in Italy and by the Russian forces which drove relentlessly through Austria, Czechoslovakia, and eastern Germany. Bratislava, third largest city in Czechoslovakia, fell to the Russians on April 4. Victory guns boomed in Moscow for the capture of Vienna on April 13. Bologna fell to the British and Americans on April 21, and the stage was at last set for the last act in the industrial Po Valley of Italy. On that same day the Russians drove into Berlin from the east. Desperately the Nazi propagandists strove to sow dissension between the Soviets and the western Allies—desperately and with utter failure. On April 27, with whoops of joy and spontaneous demonstrations of mutual admiration, Russian and American troops met on the Elbe. Omar Bradley issued an order of the day: ". . . American troops of the 12th Army Group joined forces with Soviet elements of Marshal Konev's 1st Ukrainian Army Group. These armies have come down from the ruins of Stalingrad and Sevastopol, across the scorched cities of the Ukraine. In two years they have smashed fourteen hundred miles through the German Army to drive the enemy from Russia and pursue him to the Elbe. . . ." Three days later, Berlin, where the fanatic Nazis took to the sewers for their last bloody stand, was entirely in Russian hands. The Nazi radio in Hamburg announced that Hitler was dead, that Grand Admiral Karl Doenitz had succeeded him as Führer of the Reich.

The fighting war was finished. On May 2, in the palace of the Bourbon kings at Caserta, twenty miles from Naples, enemy envoys signed the instrument of unconditional surrender for all German and Italian fascist troops in northern Italy and western Austria. On May 3 British forces took Hamburg. On May 4 negotiations between Marshal Montgomery and Admiral Doenitz, involving the surrender of all enemy forces in Holland, northwest Germany, and Denmark, were concluded, and on the following morning the actual surrender was made. On that same morning the First and Nineteenth German armies surrendered to the Allied 6th Army Group in the south. With the exception of remnants of the German Seventh Army, all opposition to Eisenhower's forces was now removed. . . .

The spectacle presented by those last weeks appalled mankind. To the victors, to Eisenhower himself, the face of war had never seemed more hideous than it did in the hours of greatest triumph. The character of war, and of those who had willed this war, was stripped of all which might hide its depravity from the eyes of the world. Not since the fall of Carthage had a great Western power been so completely destroyed in war, and never in all history had such foul corruption been exposed, naked, to the horrified gaze of decent men. The least ideological of people, the typical American G.I., saw at last what fascism meant in terms of torture and murder and organized human filth.

In the prison camps at Bad Orb and Limburg, United States soldiers who had been captured in the Battle of the Bulge barely four months before were found reduced by starvation to spidery skeletons, their eyes burning dully in almost fleshless skulls. The Germans "explained" that Allied air attacks had prevented food shipments. The liberating troops, who remembered the murder of 130 captured Americans by Germans in Belgium on the third day of the Bulge, pointed bitterly to the well-fed Germans in adjacent towns. As American troops neared the concentration camp at Erla, SS guards herded 295 political prisoners into a barracks 40 feet by 120 feet in size and set fire to the building with acetate. The one hundred-odd flaming men who managed to dash screaming from the building were shot or clubbed to death by the SS. The 295 burned corpses were found, unburied, by the Americans. At Belsen the concentration camp was a six-mile-square barbed-wire enclosure into which some 60,000 men, women, and children were packed and slowly starved. SS guards, men and women alike, watched unmoved while 17,000 of the prisoners died of starvation in the single month preceding liberation. Survivors had cut out the hearts, livers, and kidneys of scores of corpses and had eaten them in order to keep themselves alive. British Tommies liberated Belsen. At the point of guns they forced the captured SS men and women to bury in huge common graves the thousands of stinking corpses. At Buchenwald the concentration camp contained 21,000 emaciated men and women, approximately half of the normal contingent (the other half had been moved into the interior to provide further sadistic pleasure for the SS). There were hooks in the walls at Buchenwald, and from them living men had been hung by the neck, their toes just touching the floor, to prolong the agony of their strangulation. There were two ovens in which 150 to 200 corpses (sometimes the still forms were not yet quite dead) had been daily consumed. There were pillories on the parade ground where men had been tied down and flogged until they fainted or died. On the day the Americans arrived 200 of the prisoners died of starvation and disease. . . .

Eisenhower, shocked to the depths of his being, used his high position to insure a full knowledge, among the people at home, of the horrors he had witnessed. He saw to it that the brutal scenes were photographed and that the photographs were displayed in the press and in motion-picture theaters. He invited congressional committees and top-ranking American newspaper publishers to come and see for themselves and to talk and write about what they saw. He was coldly determined that these evidences of Nazi depravity should not be dismissed, in the smug manner in which earlier Nazi atrocities had been dismissed, as mere "phony propaganda." He was equally determined that, in so far as it was in his power to prevent it, the perpetrators of these crimes against humanity should not go unpunished. But deeper than his hatred of these evils and broader than his desire to punish evildoers was his realization of the need to create, out of that shadowy future beyond the victory, a new world in which common men could live in peace and freedom and in which all institutions were grounded in a profound commitment to human dignity.

In those last days of European war he pondered deeply the role which he himself must play in the years which lay ahead. In former days, whenever anyone had asked about his personal plans for after the war, he had always replied that he couldn't think that far ahead. When pressed further he had said that what he would really like to do was travel around the world and see all the far places he had not yet visited. "Only," he would add with a deprecating laugh, "I can't see what good that would do anyone." The statement was significant of a changed attitude toward himself. Only with extreme reluctance had he admitted to himself that he was now a world figure; he had hoped to return, at the war's end, to the casual, intimate private life he had known before the war began. He now knew that this was, to a large extent, impossible. People were already publishing books about him. Milton, back in Kansas, had four huge scrapbooks filled with magazine and newspaper stories describing not only his military character but his personal mannerisms: how he lived at camp, what he ate for breakfast, what he read for relaxation. Never again could his life be wholly his own.

] 536 [

Never again could he move about the world with the inconspicuous freedom of ordinary men. Millions of eyes would be watching his actions, and millions of ears would listen to what he said. His personal example could have tremendous influence for good or evil. It was a situation which called for a new and higher dedication. . . .

The last scene was in a plain red brick building which, before the war, had housed a trade school at Rheims, France. Here Eisenhower had established an advanced headquarters. And here, on the afternoon of May 6, a German delegation arrived to sign the instrument of unconditional surrender.

The delegation was composed of Colonel General Alfred Jodl, recently appointed Chief of Staff of the disintegrating German Army; General Admiral Hans Georg von Friedeburg, commander of the impotent German Navy; and Major General Wilhelm Oxenius, Jodl's aide. Beedle Smith, acting for Eisenhower, received them and served as chairman of their meeting with Russian, British, and French officers. All afternoon and evening victors and vanquished discussed technical details involved in the surrender: the manner in which surrender instructions were to be transmitted to scattered and communicationless German forces, the specified points at which German arms were to be relinquished, the demobilization of German troops. At last, at two twenty-five on the morning of May 7, the discussions were completed. Correspondents were assembled in the map-walled war room. A few minutes later eleven high Allied officers—Russian, British, American, French—entered the room and remained standing at their assigned chairs until the three Germans entered. Jodl and his companions went at once to the three unoccupied chairs and sat down. The others sat down. After a few words by General Smith the surrender document was placed before Jodl. The German was handed a pen and told to sign. He did so. Then Smith and General François Sevez of the French Army signed on behalf of the supreme commander of the Allied Expeditionary Forces. General Ivan Susloparoff signed for the Russian high command. It was 2:41 A.M. The ceremony had taken four minutes. After five years and eight months of war a ruined Europe was at peace.

Jodl asked for permission to speak. Smith granted it with a curt nod. Jodl stood up, very stiff and straight.

"With this signature the German people and the German forces are, for better or worse, delivered into the victors' hands," he said in a voice hoarse with emotion. "In this war, which has lasted more than five years, both have achieved and suffered more than perhaps any other people in the world. In this hour I can only express the hope that the victors will treat them with generosity."

If he expected his words to arouse sympathy among those who heard them, he was disappointed. The Russians and western Allies were only too well aware of what the Germans had "achieved" and of what others had suffered in the war which Jodl and his ilk had willed. Jodl saw only cold contempt in the faces of the victors. He turned and left the room. He and his companions were then conducted, for the first time, to the office of the supreme commander.

It was no friendly visit. Sternly Eisenhower asked two questions. Did the Germans fully understand the terms they had signed? *"Ja,"* said Colonel General Jodl. Would the Germans carry out those terms? *"Ja,"* said Colonel General Jodl. That was all. Eisenhower arose and dismissed from his sight the representatives of a state which, cruelly arrogant in victory and viciously treacherous in battle, now whimpered in utter defeat. It was over. He spoke to the correspondents. The unconditional surrender formula announced at Casablanca had been faithfully carried out, he said. Germany had surrendered unconditionally. . . .

Perhaps he mentally reviewed the myriad chances, the awful hazards, the thousand harsh and lonely decisions through which he had led the way to victory. But probably he did not. He allowed himself to be photographed holding aloft, in the sign of the V which had been shaped in days of darkest peril, the pens with which the instrument of complete victory had been signed. He was smiling, but even in that joyous moment his smile was tired. It was late, and the way had been long and hard. He needed sleep.

By Way of Conclusion

SPEAKING *in very general terms, there would seem to be two responses to the exercise of great power. One involves a vast egotism, the other a profound humility. One involves, necessarily, an enormous amount of lying pretension, of conscious or unconscious hypocrisy; the other calls for the most clear-sighted, literal-minded honesty.*

The man of power may seek to identify himself with that power. He may say, "I am Destiny," or "I am the State," or even (as Alexander did) "I am God." He may boast (as many dark characters in this book have done) that he is a Nietzschean superman or a Spenglerian Caesar "beyond Good and Evil," and that the men he commands exist only to implement his will. Thus he develops a complete disregard for the lives of other men, throwing away whole armies without, apparently, a slightest twinge of conscience—as Napoleon did in Egypt, in Spain, in Russia. Almost certainly he ends by convincing himself that the masses move, and history moves, in obedience to his "supreme" will. If the historical situation permits it, he spreads around himself a rigid system of authority, displays ostentatiously a vast personal "glory," and employs a huge propaganda machine to foster the myth of his own mysterious "greatness" and to hide the colossal blunders of which he (being the kind of man he is) always manages to make a great many. From the point of view of sober men the final significant fact about such conquering "heroes" is that they use their power to so little permanent effect. Their empires crumble, their "glory" vanishes—though unfortunately it remains embalmed in "official histories" to tempt future egotistical fools along paths of destruction—and if any good is accomplished under their regimes it is usually in spite of them and at an excessive cost. Their response to power seems quite adolescent and all too common in history; their "glory" is of that gaudy, terrifying sort which appeals strongly only to children and savages.

SOLDIER OF DEMOCRACY

The other response to power, the humble and realistic one, is much rarer—perhaps because those who could exercise great power sensibly have too much sense to seek it. The classic American example is, undoubtedly, Abraham Lincoln. History tells us that he had a certain amount of personal ambition, but it was so feeble that it quite probably would never have led him to high office had it not been constantly prodded into action by an overly ambitious wife. And once his high office was achieved, the storm which .broke about him literally forced vast power upon him. He didn't seek it; he derived small pleasure and a great deal of personal suffering from it; and he certainly never, for a single moment, identified himself with it. He seems to have been well aware that his power was real only in so far as he expressed the aspirations of the people, and that even this real power was closely hedged about by the limits of the possible; to do violence to the limits was to invite disaster to the country he loved and to himself. He seems to have known well that deep paradoxical truth (revealed again and again in this book) that one can guide the stream of history only by yielding to it, which is perhaps another aspect of that profound moral judgment of Jesus: "To save your life you must lose it." Hence much that Abraham Lincoln did and a great deal of his essential quality remain as permanent contributions to the spirit and form of the American democracy.

It is in that spirit and within that form that Dwight Eisenhower has made his career. He has wielded vast power. Millions of men have moved into vital danger by his orders. To a large extent he has been the instrument by which the destinies of nations are decided. And his response to power has certainly been Lincolnian in its simplicity, its realism, its selfless devotion to duty, its utter personal humility. Lacking Lincoln's lyrical personality, lacking the moody depths which have made the Great Emancipator so inspiring to the tragic artist, Eisenhower has nevertheless become perhaps the most perfect embodiment in our time of America's national ideal. The fact that, in the process of becoming a great national figure, he has become an international hero signifies the universal validity of what is best and highest in the American dream. It signifies that the American dream of human liberty, of true democracy, is not exclusively American but is shared by the great masses of ordinary, decent citizens of all countries. In Eisenhower's character and in the spirit which imbued his command (it reached its highest pitch in SHAEF) can be found common denominators to which the aspirations of nearly all men of good will can be reduced. Here, surely, are lessons for all mankind, written large in letters of fire and blood. They are lessons whose very simplicity and ancient recognition seem to have denied their acceptance by modern Western man, committed as modern man is to the novel and complex. They are lessons in the nature of positive compromise, in the virtue of tolerance, in the necessity of a unifying world principle, and, most important of all, in the proper relations of Freedom to Authority and of the individual to the social life.

In the autumn of 1944 a correspondent who had been assigned for several weeks to Eisenhower's personal camp returned to London. He was asked by a friend to give an informal talk about the supreme commander before a group of O.W.I. employees in the American Embassy. He was a fairly typical product of his American generation, this correspondent, and perhaps for that reason his response to the "problem of Eisenhower"—for Eisenhower was, to him, a "problem"—may have some significance. As he glanced over his notes to prepare his mind for his little speech the correspondent was struck by the fact that he had held two distinct and contradictory attitudes toward the supreme commander.

"It is almost impossible to write a biography of any depth, any significant density, when its subject is a man who has no interior life," said one of the notes, written, apparently, in a moment of despair. "Eisenhower . . . is a man whose whole mental life is involved in external *strategy. If he cares about* meanings, *even historical ones, I am not aware of it. . . . Yet he is caught up in historic circumstances. In writing about him one is impelled to carry meanings to him. . . ." Another note said: "Meaning, significance, is not rooted in him; it only* adheres *to him. His significance is all external, imposed. He drifts with a destiny he probably does not understand, and he does nothing (practically) to determine it." Still another note said: "He is in a heroic position without himself being a hero. None of that moody grandeur, depth, et cetera, which inspire men to be better than themselves. One can't imagine him leading a great historic movement. No* creative *will. There is no beyondness in him."*

] 541 [

In addition to these was a series of transitional notes through which, apparently, the correspondent's mind had worked its way from a negative to a positive attitude toward his subject. "Don't try so hard to understand him," said one of them, "or you'll falsify the portrait by forcing its subject into preconceived molds. Be passive. Passivity need not be negative. You have to accept before you can criticize and reject. Let him work on you. Stick to facts, as he does." Said another transitional note: "Eisenhower is a mirror of democracy. Use Sidney Hook's neat distinction between 'eventful' and 'event-making' men. Ike mirrors events, colors them with his personality, but never (in the deep sense) causes them. . . . But that's absurd. To color such mighty events as these is in itself a creative act. Moreover, SHAEF is perhaps the greatest fact of this war, and SHAEF is certainly Ike's creature. It didn't exist before him and it couldn't have existed without him. History may yet write Eisenhower's special qualities down as determining forces in the world stream. Must avoid the intellectual fallacy—belief that if a thing is simple it is without significance, or if obvious without truth."

The final notes were all affirmative in tone. They followed thousands of words in which facts about Eisenhower's command, his decisions at crucial points, were set down, and the admiration they expressed was wholehearted. "Do not his vital attitudes," said one of the notes, "constitute a psychological base for world-wide co-operation? Tolerance, gradualism, et cetera. Are not these attitudes possible to all mankind? Cannot they become commonly operative, part of a world-wide common mind?" Another note proclaimed that "in a world of such vast destructive forces, a world of such close-knit interdependencies, egotism is more than a mistake—it's a crime. That's one thing one learns from Eisenhower." A third note said that "history is a by-product of ordinary workaday effort, and you have to stand a long way back from Eisenhower to realize what an immense and truly creative job he's done in a situation where, one would have thought, only vast killing and destruction were possible." It was on that note that the correspondent, at last, based his little talk. And as he talked, studding his speech with facts about what the supreme commander had said and done, he caught from his listeners a glow of enthusiasm for his subject which never afterward left him. . . .

BY WAY OF CONCLUSION

ii

As Eisenhower had foreseen, millions of eyes were fixed upon him, and millions of ears listened to what he said. On June 10, 1945, he received, from Marshal Georgi K. Zhukov, Russia's highest award, the jeweled Order of Victory. At a luncheon at his headquarters at Frankfurt on the Main that day he said: "All of us who are right-thinking want the common man of all nations to have the opportunities that we fought to preserve for them." In London on June 12 he received one of the greatest triumphs ever accorded any man, and by far the greatest ever accorded by that ancient capital to one who was not an Englishman. Millions cheered him madly as he rode in an open carriage, with Tedder beside him, through the streets. At the Guildhall he was granted the freedom of the city.

"Humility must always be the portion of any man who receives acclaim earned in the blood of his followers and the sacrifices of his friends," he said in a speech which one London paper printed side by side with the Gettysburg Address. "This feeling of humility cannot erase, of course, my great pride in being tendered the freedom of London. I am not a native of this land. I come from the very heart of America. In the superficial aspects by which we ordinarily recognize family relationships, the town where I was born and the one where I was reared are far separated from this great city. Abilene, Kansas, and Denison, Texas, would together equal in size possibly one five hundredth of a part of great London. . . . Yet kinship among nations is not determined in such measurements as proximity of size and age. Rather we should turn to those inner things—call them what you will—I mean those intangibles that are the real treasures free men possess. To preserve his freedom of worship, his equality before the law, his liberty to speak and act as he sees fit, subject only to provisions that he trespass not upon similar rights of others—a Londoner will fight. So will a citizen of Abilene. . . . To my mind it is clear that when two peoples will face the tragedies of war to defend the same spiritual values, the same treasured rights, then in the deepest sense those two are truly related. So even as I proclaim my undying Americanism I am bold enough and exceedingly proud to claim the basis of kinship to you of London."

SOLDIER OF DEMOCRACY

In Paris on June 14, following a parade during which he was cheered by more than a million Parisians, he was made a "Fellow of the Liberation" by General de Gaulle, who presented him with a Bronze Medal in an elaborate ceremony under the Arc de Triomphe, before the tomb of the Unknown Soldier. In almost his only public appearance since his retirement from public life Giraud was present at the ceremony, on the tactful invitation of De Gaulle. In response to a toast from De Gaulle the supreme commander said: "There have been differences—you and I have had some. But let us bring our troubles to each other frankly and face them together. . . . General de Gaulle, I propose to you a toast of friendship—let's be friends."

Four days later he arrived in America. Even before the wheels of his huge transport plane touched the American earth his triumphal procession across his native land was begun. At the Atlantic coast line on the morning of June 18 his plane was met by more than thirty fighters and bombers which, flying in formation, escorted him to the national airdrome across the Potomac from Washington. At precisely 11:11 A.M., Eastern War Time, his plane braked to a stop on the runway. Mamie and General Marshall rushed to meet him as the door of his plane opened. It was, for Mamie, a joyous double reunion, for behind the supreme commander stood the tall, slender figure of Lieutenant John Eisenhower, who, through the battle for Germany, had served as an aide to General Bradley. Tenderly the supreme commander embraced his wife, and his first words were, "It's been a long time, darling." He shook hands with Marshall, who said, "General, I'm glad to see you." Scores of photographers focused their lenses upon him, and the air vibrated to the roar of thirty thousand voices, chanting, "Ike, Ike, Ike!" Again the sea of faces, spreading on either side of the streets he rode, and again his response to the cheers—on behalf of the three million Americans who had fought under him—with heart-warming grins and swooping waves of his hands.

At twelve twenty-five he arrived at the Capitol. He appeared before a joint session of Congress and was greeted with cheers and loud applause from the nation's lawmakers. He said:

"My imagination cannot picture a more dramatic moment than this in the life of an American. I stand here in the presence of the elected federal lawmakers of our great Republic, the very core of our American

political life and a symbol of those things that we call the American heritage. To preserve that heritage, more than three million of our citizens, at your behest, resolutely faced every terror the ruthless Nazi could devise. I am summoned before you as the representative—the commander—of those three million American men and women to whom you desire to pay America's tribute for military victory. In humble realization that they who earned your commendation should properly be here to receive it, I am nevertheless proud and honored to serve as your agent in conveying it to them. . . . I have seen the American proved on battlegrounds of Africa and Europe over which armies have been fighting for two thousand years of recorded history. None of those battlefields has seen a more worthy soldier than the trained American. . . .

"When America entered the war arena the arrogant Nazi machine was at the zenith of its power. In 1940 it had overrun practically the whole of western Europe, while a year later, in the east, it had hammered the great Red Army far back into the reaches of its own territory. The Allies met this challenge with vision, determination, and a full comprehension of the enormity of the task ahead. America brought forth her effort from every conceivable source. New techniques of war were developed. Of these the most outstanding was the completely coordinated use of ground, air, and sea forces. To his dismay the German found that, far from having achieved perfection in the combined employment of all types of destructive power, his skills and methods were daily outmoded and surpassed by the Allies. . . . The battle front and the home front, together we have found the victory! But even the banners of victory cannot hide from our sight the sacrifices in which victory has been bought. The hard task of a commander is to send men into battle knowing some of them—often many—must be killed or wounded in order that necessary missions may be achieved. It is a soul-killing task; my sorrow is not only for the fine young lives lost or broken, but it is equally for the parents, the wives, and the friends who have been bereaved. . . . The blackness of their grief can be relieved only by the faith that all this shall not happen again! Because I feel this so deeply I hope you will let me attempt to express a thought that I believe is today embedded deep in the hearts of all fighting men. It is this: the soldier knows how grim and dark was the outlook for the

Allies in 1941 and 1942. He is fully aware of the magnificent way the United Nations responded to this threat. To his mind, the problems of peace can be no more difficult than the one you had to solve more than three years ago, and which, in one battle area, has now been brought to a successful conclusion. He knows that in war the threat of separate annihilation tends to hold allies together; he hopes we can find peace a nobler incentive to produce the same unity. . . . He passionately believes that . . . the problems of peace can and must be met."

He paid tribute to his late commander in chief who, on the very eve of victory, had become a fatal casualty of the war. Perhaps, as Eisenhower spoke, he recalled the manner in which the news of Roosevelt's death had come to him. On April 12, with Bradley and Patton, Eisenhower had inspected the horrible concentration camp at Ohrdruf, Germany. He had also visited the treasure cache of gold and looted art which Patton's men had discovered in an abandoned salt mine. Altogether, he and his companions had traveled many hundreds of miles that day, by plane and by jeep, and they returned to Patton's headquarters—a house formerly occupied by the German commandant—physically wearied by the miles they had covered, spiritually sickened by the things they had seen. It was midnight when at last they went to bed. Bradley and Eisenhower were assigned two upstairs bedrooms, while Patton went out to his caravan parked near by. Patton's watch had stopped and he switched on his radio to get the correct time. A BBC announcer was summarizing the news. The President of the United States had died! Patton hurried back to the house and awoke Bradley. The two went together to Eisenhower's room to break the news. The supreme commander would never forget the stunned grief of that moment, the sense of enormous personal loss. Whatever his faults, the President's buoyant personality had been through twelve years of unparalleled crisis one of the positive assets of the whole Western world. It was as though a great mountain from which one had been accustomed to taking his bearings had suddenly crumbled into dust.

"Because no word of mine could add anything to your appreciation of the man who, until his tragic death, led America in war, I will say nothing other than that from his strength and indomitable spirit I drew constant support and confidence in the solution of my own problems," said Eisenhower to the Congress of the United States.

BY WAY OF CONCLUSION

On the following morning (at precisely 10:17½ A.M., according to the New York Times*), Eisenhower stepped out of his plane at La Guardia Field, New York City. Four million men, women, and children cheered him as he rode through thirty-seven miles of New York's streets. At City Hall, Mayor La Guardia presented to him, on behalf of the city, a Gold Medal and conferred upon him the honorary citizenship of New York City. Eisenhower said:*

"As my first act as a citizen of the city of New York I want to issue to the mayor a word of warning. New York simply cannot do this to a Kansas farmer boy and keep its reputation for sophistication. . . . There is [one] thing, Mr. Mayor, that impressed me very much as you and I rode down through the cheering throngs this morning: first, the reason for the cheering—it was not because one individual, one American, came back from war; it is rejoicing that a nasty job is done—one nasty job is finished. . . . How much better it would have been had there been no cause for rejoicing, had there been no war.

"At one stretch in our trip this morning the mayor told me there were 450,000 school children. I looked at them carefully. I suppose they averaged twelve years old. Can the parents and the relatives of those children look ten years ahead and be satisfied with anything less than your best to keep them away from the horrors of the battlefield? It has got to be done. It is not enough that we devise every kind of international machinery to keep the peace. We must also be strong ourselves. Weakness cannot co-operate with anything. Only strength can co-operate. If we are going to live the years of peace to which this weary world is entitled and which we passionately want for our children, then we must be strong and we must be ready to co-operate, and in the spirit of true tolerance and forbearance."

At the Waldorf-Astoria, at the dinner given in his honor that night, the supreme commander said:

"As I see it, peace is an absolute necessity to this world. Civilization itself, in the face of another catastrophe . . . would tremble, possibly decay and be destroyed. . . . I believe that we should let no specious argument of any kind deter us from exploring every direction in which peace can be maintained. I believe we should be strong, but we should be tolerant. We should be ready to defend our rights, but we should be considerate and recognize the rights of the other man. This business of *preserving the peace is a practical thing, but practicality and idealism are not necessarily mutually antagonistic. We can be idealistic and we can be practical along with it."*

Three days later, on June 21, he came back into his home country. Shortly after noon his plane landed at the Municipal Air Terminal in Kansas City. His son John and Mickey McKeogh, with forty-two Midwestern veterans of the European war, accompanied him. Awaiting him were Mamie, who had come out by train; his eighty-three-year-old mother; and his four brothers, Arthur, Edgar, Earl, and Milton. Awaiting him, too, were hundreds of thousands of cheering people lining the three-mile parade route which led to Liberty Memorial Hill. Here, standing beneath the great memorial shaft, he spoke.

"This country here, this section, has been called the heart of isolationism," he said. "I do not believe it. No intelligent man can be an isolationist, and there is no higher level of education anywhere in the world than in the Midwest. . . . [The] very force of circumstances is going to make you take an increasingly important part in world affairs. The world today needs two things: moral leadership and food. The United States with its great strength and its prosperity is forced, even if unwillingly, into a position of leadership. Missouri, through its great son, President Truman, has become a factor in world leadership—call it enlightened statesmanship—that will be of the most tremendous importance to the whole world. His background is here; he is one of you; he will carry to his task the qualities of this great Midwest section. I believe he could carry no better equipment.

"Food. Here is the great production area of the world. Great sections are starving. My associates and I have just left starving areas. . . . In spite of floods, in spite of drought, every handicap that can be imagined, this country must produce food. Without it, there will be no peace. At best there will be an uneasy cessation of hostilities. We cannot stand that. We must have peace and, among other things, that means we must have food. The eyes of the world, therefore, are going to turn more and more to the great Midwest of America with Kansas City at its heart."

BY WAY OF CONCLUSION

A special train bore him along the Union Pacific tracks into Kansas that evening. Avidly he gazed out upon familiar scenes in those few moments when he was not signing his name for autograph collectors, or greeting relatives and friends and Important People, or appearing on the observation platform—at Lawrence, Topeka, and Manhattan—to acknowledge the cheers of great crowds. At Topeka he stepped from the train for a moment to shake hands with admirers, and when he turned back to climb the car steps he slipped and fell heavily. His knee was badly bruised, but no sign of pain was on his face as, grinning, he waved to the throng from the moving train.

He was a little worried about his mother. The day had placed a great strain on Ida Elizabeth. At the Liberty Memorial, under the hot June sun, she had begun to feel faint and ill. She was now lying down—she'd be all right soon, she insisted—and her sons arranged among themselves a stratagem for carrying her from the train in Abilene without attracting attention. It was decided that Dwight should leave the train first, from one of the forward cars, and draw the crowd to him. Then the other sons would carry their mother from the rear of the train. . . . The stratagem was perhaps too successful. It was dark when the train arrived, and the thousands of Abilene citizens who had been waiting for hours surged forward in an uncontrollable mass when the supreme commander at last appeared. They pressed so closely against him that he turned pale. . . .

But he laughed happily when Joner Callahan, whose soft-drink place had for decades been the favorite hangout of Ike's old gang, presented to him the symbolic keys to his home town. One entire floor of Abilene's Lamar Hotel had been reserved for the Eisenhowers, of whom seventy-five had gathered for the largest of all their family reunions, and here at last, with the family he so dearly loved, Dwight Eisenhower could feel that he was home.

Abilene, whose normal population is five thousand, was packed with more than twenty thousand people on Friday, June 22. The streets, under the harvest sun, were gay with bunting, and the two-mile parade route was lined eight deep with spectators long before parade time. For weeks—in garages and barns and machine shops—Dickinson County citizens had been preparing the scores of floats for the great parade. Those floats depicted the history of Abilene, the life of the Eisenhower family and of the general, and, at the end, the present agricultural prosperity of Dickinson County. One float, which gave the general immense pleasure, was driven by Joner Callahan and carried ten members of the Abilene High School football team on which Little Ike had played. Edgar (Big Ike) rode that float, with Six MacDonell, Bud Huffman, Earl Briney, and Orrin Snider, the coach. The general's only twinge of unhappiness that day was that his mother could not join in the festivities. She had recovered from her illness, but she was still very tired. The doctor had ordered her to rest.

At ten o'clock that morning the parade began. Shortly thereafter, in a characteristic gesture, the general halted his car and motioned into the seat beside him Sergeant Walter T. Sapp, an Abilene farm boy who had fought in the European theater and who had come home on the general's special train. Sapp hung back, but the general was insistent. The sergeant then occupied the seat beside the supreme commander which had been intended for Mother Eisenhower. All along the parade route the general waved and cried his greetings to old friends and neighbors. At the city park—it had been newly named Eisenhower Park—he mounted the speakers' stand. There, speaking without notes, struggling to keep his emotions under control before the multitude, he acknowledged the introduction by Charles M. Harger and the cheers of the largest crowd Abilene had ever known.

"Because no man is really a man who has left out of himself all of the boy, I want to speak first of the dreams of a barefoot boy," he said. "Frequently they are to be a streetcar conductor; or he sees himself as the town policeman; above all, he may reach the position of locomotive engineer, but always in his dreams is that day when finally he comes home, comes home to a welcome from his home town. Because today that dream of forty-five years or more ago has been realized beyond the wildest stretches of my own imagination, I come here first to thank you, to say that the proudest thing I can claim is that I am from Abilene.

"The first and most important part of the celebration today, from my own viewpoint, was this: I was not set apart, I was merely another

BY WAY OF CONCLUSION

'Abilenite' putting on a celebration for something other than just one individual, an expression of our rejoicing that one nasty job is done in Europe; that in one section of the world no longer will we have the fear of losing our sons, our relatives, and our friends; that in that theater, at least, we no longer have to pour out our wealth in order to sustain our fighting armies.

"That is the real thing we are celebrating today. . . . The parade itself was so unique in conception that to everyone who had a part in planning it, developing it, or an actual participating part on the street, I want to extend . . . my very great thanks. . . . I cannot believe that there would be anything better for all the cities of the United States today than to see that parade.

"In that parade a whole epoch passed before our eyes. Its beginnings were coincidental with the coming of my own father and mother to this section, in the days of the independent farm and the horse and buggy, where each family was almost self-sustaining; certainly the community was self-sustaining. We grew our corn and we grew our meat and we grew our own vegetables and we didn't have much connection with the outside world. As you noticed, at the end of that parade you saw the most modern types of machinery. No longer was it necessary for farmers to join up with neighbors to get in the crops, to carry out the roundup, to get the house built. We have become mechanized. No longer are we here independent of the rest of the world. . . . Our part is most important. There is nothing so important in the world today as food, in a material way. Food is needed all over Europe and must be sent to preserve the peace. In that way you see immediately your connection with the problems of Europe. . . . In a more definite way, since I am now a citizen of New York City, that city is part of you—one of your larger suburbs. . . .

"Through this world it has been my fortune, or misfortune, to wander at considerable distances. Never has this town been outside my heart and memory. Here are some of my oldest and dearest friends. Here are men who helped me start my own career and helped my son start his. Here are people that are lifelong friends of my mother and my late father—the two really great individuals of the Eisenhower family. They raised six boys and they made sure that each had an upbringing at home and an education that equipped him to gain a respectable place in his

own profession. My brothers and I, with our families, are the products of the loving care, the labor and work of my father and mother—just another average Abilene family. . . ."

He spoke of the three million soldiers whom it had been his "great honor" to command. He urged the community to "accept each of those [Dickinson County] men back to your heart, as you have me." He paused, searching for his concluding words.

"And now," he said, "on the part of myself and my wife, my brothers and all their families, I want to say thanks to Kansas, to Dickinson County, and to Abilene for a reception that so far exceeds anything any of us could imagine."

His voice broke. He went on falteringly:

"All of us are practically choked with emotion. Good luck, and God bless every one of you."

The applause, the cheers rose like thunder, sweeping against him and through him. It rolled in long waves of sound across the miles of ripened wheat beyond the town. Dwight Eisenhower swallowed heavily. Then, with an effort, he grinned and waved.

Acknowledgments

A GREAT MANY BUSY PEOPLE have made contributions to this book. To all of them the author wishes here to express his deep personal gratitude and his hope that what he has done with the material they gave him will not disappoint or displease them. However it may be for other writers, the present author finds the actual writing of a book to be dull, grinding toil, broken here and there by hours of the most acute agony. The only pleasures he has derived from the present work have been in his visits with the people who gave him his basic materials. Without exception, they have been patient, generous, and stimulating. It is a key to the general's character that his family and friends and associates are all strong and vital personalities with whom conversation is a genuine joy.

The author's first thanks are, of course, due General Eisenhower himself, who, though by no means anxious to have a biography written about him, gave freely of his few hours of relaxation in England and Normandy. It goes without saying that the author's views of the general and of the events in which he took part are not necessarily the general's own. Indeed, as is indicated in the book, the two views are occasionally in opposition. The author's great concern has been to present the truth as he sees it, fairly and objectively, and his great hope is that in striving to do so he has not falsified his portrait.

In Abilene, Kansas, the author obtained valuable information from Mrs. Ida Elizabeth Eisenhower, the general's mother; Miss Naomi Engle, Mother Eisenhower's companion and nurse for many years; Mr. G. M. (Bud) Huffman, Abilene postman; Mr. Charles Case, Abilene merchant; Mr. Charles M. Harger, publisher of the Abilene *Reflector-Chronicle;* Mr. Paul Royer, Dickinson County attorney; Mr. Phil Heath, Abilene postmaster; Mr. Orrin Snider, Dickinson County farmer; Mr. Roy G. Shearer, assistant postmaster of Abilene; Mr. Joner Callahan, proprietor of the soft-drink parlor which is the general's favorite Abilene hangout; Mr. Bert Dyer, Dickinson County fruit

ACKNOWLEDGMENTS

farmer; Mrs. Beulah Brechbill, a cousin of the general; and Mr. and Mrs. C. O. Musser, the general's Uncle Chris and Aunt Amanda, who, in their home on a farm near Abilene, not only gave the author his most valuable information on the early Eisenhower life in Pennsylvania and Kansas but also introduced him to the pleasures of pudding meat. Officials of the Abilene public schools kindly permitted the author to go through the reports of Dwight Eisenhower's scholarship and through the files of the high school yearbook, the *Helianthus.*

Among the boyhood friends of the general from whom the author obtained material were Mr. John (Six) MacDonell, shop superintendent of the Salina (Kansas) *Journal;* Mr. E. E. Hazlett, Jr., Commander, United States Navy (Ret.), acting head of the department of English, History, and Government of the United States Naval Academy, Annapolis, Maryland; Mr. J. W. Howe, former Abilene newspaperman who now lives in Emporia, Kansas; and Mr. Wesley Merrifield, superintendent of grounds and buildings at St. John Military Academy, Delafield, Wisconsin. Colonel James P. Murphy, of the United States Army, contributed information concerning the general's life in Panama.

Special thanks are due the general's brothers, with each of whom the author had long and fruitful interviews. They are Mr. Arthur Eisenhower, vice-president of the Commerce Trust Company, Kansas City, Missouri; Mr. Edgar Eisenhower, senior partner of the law firm of Eisenhower, Hunter, and Ramsdell, Tacoma, Washington; Mr. Earl Eisenhower, engineer with the West Penn Power Company, Charleroi, Pennsylvania; and Dr. Milton S. Eisenhower, president of Kansas State College of Agriculture and Applied Science, Manhattan, Kansas. Mrs. Kay Eisenhower, Earl's wife, and Mrs. Helen Eisenhower, Milton's wife, have also been extremely helpful.

In Europe the author had interviews with Air Marshal Sir Arthur Tedder, deputy commander of Supreme Headquarters of the Allied Expeditionary Forces; General Walter B. (Beedle) Smith, Chief of Staff at SHAEF; Lieutenant General Sir Humfrey Gale, chief administrative officer at SHAEF; Major General J. F. M. (Jock) Whiteley, in charge of Operations at SHAEF; Major General Kenneth W. D. Strong, in charge of Intelligence at SHAEF; Lieutenant General A. E. Grasett, in charge of Civil Affairs at SHAEF; Lieutenant General Frederick E. Morgan, whose position at SHAEF, though untitled, was, as the book indicates, of great importance; Lieutenant General Omar Bradley, commander of the 12th Army Group; and Lieutenant General George S. Patton, commander of the United States Third Army. For

ACKNOWLEDGMENTS

facilitating his visits with these men, the author wishes to thank Lieutenant Colonel Thor Smith, public-relations officer at General Eisenhower's personal headquarters, and Major Burrows Matthews, who was Colonel Smith's assistant.

General Eisenhower's two American aides, Captain Harry C. Butcher, U.S.N.R., and Colonel Ernest R. (Tex) Lee, and the British military assistant, Colonel James Frederic Gault, were of special help in filling in details of the general's personal life during the period of his overseas command. Through them the author was introduced to and had private talks with all of the Eisenhower "official family," including Sergeant M. J. (Mickey) McKeogh, the general's orderly; Sergeant Margaret Chick, Wac stenographer; Captain Mattie Pinette, Wac, the general's secretary during the Normandy campaign; Lt. Kay Summersby, Wac, formerly chauffeur and now personal secretary; and Major Larry Hansen, pilot of the general's planes. The four news correspondents assigned to the general's camp also made, unwittingly and perhaps unwillingly (two of them were writing books of their own), valuable contributions to the author's materials. They were Mr. Howard Cowan of the Associated Press; Mr. Marshall Yarrow of Reuter's; Mr. Robert Barr of the British Broadcasting Corporation; and Mr. Merrill Mueller of the National Broadcasting Company.

Major portions of the manuscript were read by Dr. and Mrs. Milton Eisenhower, Mrs. Dwight D. Eisenhower, Captain Butcher, and by the Review Branch of the Bureau of Public Relations of the War Department. A small portion of it was read by General Eisenhower one afternoon in Normandy. As the book itself makes clear, a great deal of information was gathered from Mrs. Dwight Eisenhower and Lieutenant John S. D. Eisenhower, the general's son. It must be emphasized that, in their reviews of the manuscript, none of these people acted as censor. For the most part they confined their comments to factual inaccuracies, all of which, it is hoped, have been corrected. Here and there they indicated disagreement with the author's interpretations. Sometimes these indications caused the author to change his interpretations and sometimes they did not. In other words, the author assumes full responsibility for all errors of fact and interpretation which may be found within this book.

K. S. D.

Index

Abilene, Kansas, 2, 18, 20, 23–25, 27, 31, 34, 38, 43–45, 48, 50, 70, 71, 73–78, 81–82, 88, 91, 94, 144, 206, 215, 251, 312, 456, 543, 549–51; newspapers, 86, 109, 110, 306–7
Abilene High School, 81–82, 97–98, 106, 114–16, 133
Adcock, Brig. Gen. Clarence, 304, 406
Afrika Korps, 364, 396, 411
Agheila, El, 396
Alamein, El, 308, 328, 338, 349, 351, 404, 472, 502
Aleutians, 288, 339
Alexander, Sir Harold, 404, 410, 414, 417, 419, 424, 428, 429, 430, 434, 435, 451, 458
Alexandre, Pierre, 362, 386
Algiers, 334, 337, 338, 341, 349, 356, 357, 361–70, 374, 376, 378, 383, 389, 393–95, 466, 467, 491, 493.
Allen, Maj. Gen. Robert H., 220
Allen, Gen. Terry, 360, 415
American Battle Monuments Commission, 218–21, 225–26, 239–40
Anderson, Lt. Gen. Kenneth A. N., 337, 394, 404, 407, 409
Antwerp, 462, 514, 516, 518, 520
Aqqaqir, El, 351
Ardennes, 517, 523, 532
Ardennes Bulge. *See* Battle of the Bulge.
ARMY:
American: First, 500, 516, 517, 522, 524, 531, 533; Second, 337; Third, 337, 500, 501, 503, 505, 508, 516, 517, 519, 524, 526, 531, 532, 533; Fifth, 446, 449, 450, 451, 534; Seventh, 418, 424, 433, 434, 435, 436, 506, 513, 514, 516, 531, 533; Ninth, 516, 519, 522, 531, 532, 533
Air Corps, 469; Air Forces, 322, 323, 325, 487; Eighth, 471
Airborne divisions: 82nd, 424, 432, 443, 446, 480, 520; 101st, 480, 520

American Corps: Second, 404, 408, 412, 418, 419, 432; Fifth, 474, 499; Seventh, 474, 485, 487; Eighth, 489, 499
American divisions: 3rd, 274; 9th, 410; 29th, 292; Cavalry, 273
Armored Corps: First, 271, 337
Armored divisions: 1st, 337, 408, 409, 418, 419; 2nd, 273, 337, 424, 431, 499; 3rd, 499; 4th, 524; 7th, 520; 9th, 520; 10th, 520
Army groups: 6th, 516, 534; 12th, 500, 506, 513, 514, 516, 522, 526, 530, 534; 15th, 424; 18th, 404
Tanks: 701st Destroyer Battalion (C Company), 395; 301st Tank Battalion, 191; 304th Tank Brigade, 186
Army Industrial College, 229–30
Army of the Future (De Gaulle), 492
Army War College, 221, 225
Arnhem, 514, 515, 516, 518
Arnold, Lt. Gen. Henry H. (Hap), 297, 299, 451, 487
Atlantic Charter, 270, 288
Atlantic Wall, 480, 496
Attlee, Clement R., 387
Auchinleck, Gen. Sir Claude, 308, 310
Australia, 287, 288, 328, 339
Austria, 533, 534
Avranches, 503, 505, 523, 527
Axis, 264, 308, 320, 323, 356, 415, 424, 431, 436, 458

"Backstage Story of Our African Adventure, The" (D. Bess), 344, 368
Bad Orb prison camp, 535
Badoglio, Marshal Pietro, 441, 442, 443, 444, 445, 446, 447
Baguio, 248, 250, 251
Balkans, 403, 436, 484, 514
Barker, Maj. Gen. Ray W., 460, 463, 471
Bastogne, 520, 522, 523, 524
Bataan, 248, 282, 287
Battet, Rear Admiral, 367
Bayeux, 474, 485, 495, 502, 505

INDEX

Beard, Charles A. and Mary R., 244
Beauvais Agreement of 1918, 332, 339
Behrens, Tech. Sgt. Everett J., 469
Belgium, 171, 256, 260, 461, 485, 497, 498, 535
Belsen concentration camp, 535
Belvedere, Fort, 515
Benghazi, 288, 396, 408
Berlin, 496, 498, 499, 509, 533, 534
Bess, Demaree, 344, 368, 437, 438
Bethouart, General, 373
Bevan, Aneurin, 388
Bizerte, 364, 394, 415, 419
Blida, 361, 369, 376
Bliss, Gen. Tasker H., 293
Blitzkrieg, 255, 503
Boisson, Pierre, 377, 382–83, 399
"Bolero" (code name), 473
Bône, 338, 364, 365, 393, 394
Bonesteel, Maj. Gen. Charles H., 324
Bonnier de la Chapelle, Fernand, 384–85
Bonus-march incident, 202, 232–33
Borah, Senator William E., 260
Bougie, 364, 365, 394
Boulogne, 461, 462, 464, 514, 516
Bradley, Lt. Gen. Omar, 134, 146, 148, 239, 412, 413, 418, 432, 434, 471, 474, 479, 486, 488, 489, 490, 499, 500, 502, 503, 504, 505, 508, 510, 516, 519, 526, 530, 534, 544, 546
Bratislava, 534
Bremen, 309, 533
Brest, 461, 489, 503, 516
Briney, Earl, 96, 550
Bristol Channel, 476
Bristow, Joseph L., 108–9, 110, 111–13, 117
Brittany, 489, 497, 503
Brownrigg, Sir Douglas, 529
Buchenwald concentration camp, 535
Bulge, Battle of the, 519, 522, 523, 524, 528, 535; map, 521
Bull, Brig. Gen. Harold R., 291
Bureau of the Budget, 238
Butcher, Capt. Harry C., 222, 223, 224, 225, 240, 301–4, 314, 315, 316, 317, 318, 325, 348, 397, 398, 399, 400, 415, 428, 429, 432, 453, 454, 466, 467, 468, 469, 470, 475, 481, 486, 497, 498, 525–26
Butcher, Ruth Barton (Mrs. Harry C.), 222, 223, 224, 240, 301, 399, 454
Byrom, Col. Jim, 157, 256

Caen, 295, 474, 485, 488, 490, 496, 499, 501, 502, 505, 507, 526, 527
Caen-Falaise-Argentan pocket, 527
Cairo, 439, 451, 453

Calais, 461, 463, 514, 516
Callahan, Joner, 117, 155, 215, 251, 549, 550
Canadians, 431, 433, 506, 516, 531, 533
Cape Bon Peninsula, 418–19, 425
Cape Serrat, 419
Carboni, General, 445
Carentan, 486, 487, 502
Carthage, 453, 535
Casablanca, 290, 338, 339, 349, 356, 360, 362, 363, 364, 365, 370, 372, 373, 376, 377, 378, 403, 405, 412, 459, 460, 462, 538
Case, Charlie, 110, 251, 259, 262
Castellano, Gen. Giuseppe, 442, 444
Catania, 433, 434, 435, 444
Catroux, Gen. Georges, 381
Center Task Force, 337, 338, 349, 356
Chamberlain, Neville, 254, 260
Chatel, Gov. Gen. Yves, 367, 378, 379, 386
Cherbourg, 295, 461, 462, 474, 476, 485, 496, 497, 514, 516; capture of, 488–89, 513
Chiang Kai-shek, Generalissimo, 451
Chicago *Daily News*, 318, 372
Chicago *Tribune*, 264
Chick, Wac Sgt. Margaret, 467
Choltitz, Gen. Dietrich von, 510
Church of the Brethren in Christ, 11, 12–13, 17
Churchill, Winston, 153, 154, 178, 249, 254, 260, 261, 270, 288, 289, 290, 295, 296, 309, 310, 316, 323, 326, 327, 328, 329, 330, 387, 390, 400, 403, 404, 423, 442, 451, 452, 453, 458, 461, 462, 463, 464, 465, 477, 478, 493, 494
Clark, Maj. Gen. Mark Wayne, 265, 297, 299, 300, 304, 324, 349, 357, 358, 362, 366, 369, 370, 374, 375, 376, 377, 379, 397, 412, 445, 447, 448
"Club Eisenhower," 167, 226, 266
Coblenz, 518, 531
Collins, Maj. Gen. J. Lawton, 474, 530
Cologne, 516, 531
Combat Command A, 409; Command B, 408, 410; Command C, 409
Combined Chiefs of Staff, 3, 290, 295, 299; in Cairo, 451, 452; in Quebec, 442; in Washington, 423–24, 463, 464, 465, 466
Command and General Staff School, 188, 202–5
Coningham, Air Marshal Sir Arthur, 405, 426
Connor, Brig. Gen. Fox, 188–89, 190, 191, 192, 193, 194, 195, 196, 202,

INDEX

Marshall, Warrant Officer Walter, 316
Martin, Lt. Ham, 281
Maste, Gen. René, 349
Mateur, 394, 419
Matmata range, 413
Matruh, 308
May, Tech. Sgt., J. R., 491
Mediterranean, 2, 297, 329, 338, 340, 354, 356, 453
Medjez-el-Bab, 394–96, 418, 419
Mehedya, 360
Mennonite sects, 11, 12, 32, 40
Merrifield, Wesley, 76–78, 89, 139, 141–42
Messe, General, 414, 415
Messina, 425, 434, 435, 436, 443, 444
Meuse, 260, 522, 523, 530
Mexican troubles, 154, 156–57, 166, 167, 170–71
Michie, Allan A., 475, 479–80
Middle East, 264, 275, 308, 424
Miles, Brig. Gen. Perry L., 233
Mills, Col. Albert L., 129
Minsk, 499
Monschau, 519, 520
Montellari, Franco, 442
Montgomery, Gen. Sir Bernard L., 338, 349, 364, 396, 404, 407, 408, 410, 413, 414, 419, 424, 428, 431, 434, 444, 450, 470, 472–73, 474, 477, 478, 479, 486, 489, 490, 495, 499, 500, 502, 505, 506, 507, 522, 525, 526, 527, 528, 529–30, 534
Montsabert, General, 361, 369
Moore, Capt. J. E., 433
Morgan, Lt. Gen. Frederick E., 458, 459, 460, 462, 463, 464–65, 471, 473, 474, 476
Morocco, 337, 338, 350, 360, 373, 376, 378, 382, 383, 386, 460,
Moselle, 518, 531
Mountbatten, Lord Louis, 299, 462
Mueller, Merrill, 437, 438, 439
Mukden, 231, 253
Murphy, Col. James P., 199–200
Murphy, Robert, 341–47, 358, 361, 366, 367, 369, 370, 371, 374, 377, 382, 384, 385, 386, 392, 397
Musser, Chris O., 29, 30, 31, 35, 37, 43, 49
Musser, Hannah Amanda Eisenhower (Mrs. Chris O.), 8, 9, 10, 18, 22, 27–30, 31, 35, 43, 49, 54, 211, 499
Mussolini, Benito, 201, 237, 245, 262, 264, 347, 434, 440, 441, 445

Nantes, 489, 503
National Defense Act (1920), 229

National Guard, 166, 236, 262
Neutrality, 154, 168
New Deal, 236, 258
New Guinea, 288
New York Post, 483
New York Times, 136, 272, 310, 375, 380, 382, 383, 389
New Zealand 2nd Division, 351, 414
Nijmegen, 514, 515
Nine-Power Naval Pact, 193, 194
Nivelle, General, 326, 327, 328
Nixon, Capt. H. C., 469
Noguès, Gen. Charles, 360, 370, 372, 373, 376, 377, 378, 379, 382
Norman, Ruby, 102, 106, 114, 115, 117
Normandy, 295, 462, 471–74, 485, 487, 489, 490, 495, 496, 497, 498, 500, 514, 517, 525
North Africa, 423, 424, 444, 452, 460, 467, 470, 471, 491, 495, 512; conquest, 296, 354–420, 523; basic pattern of command, 308–53; map, 355
Norway, 260, 349

Office of Censorship, 350
Office of Production Management, 229
Office of War Information, 310, 382, 397, 455
Ohrdruf concentration camp, 546
Oliver, General, 361
"Omaha" (code name), 474, 481, 482, 485, 486, 489, 499
Oran, 337, 338, 339, 356, 360, 362, 363, 364, 365, 370, 372, 376, 395, 451
Orgaz, General, 360
Orne River, 485, 502
Outpost (D. H. Mahan), 196
"Overlord" (code name), 473, 486
Oxenius, Maj. Gen. Wilhelm, 537

Pachino Peninsula, 431, 433
Pacific, 286, 328, 423
Paget, General, 327, 460
Pantelleria, 425, 426
Parent, Judge, 114
Paris, 261, 462, 508–13, 519, 520
Pas de Calais, 295, 464, 482, 485, 497, 498
Patch, Maj. Gen. Alexander M., 506
Patton, Maj. Gen. George S., Jr., 175, 185–88, 240, 273, 337, 365, 412–15, 418, 424, 428, 431, 432, 434, 435, 436–37, 438, 439, 448, 471, 500, 503, 505, 506, 508, 522, 526, 527, 546
Peace, commission, 183; conference, 168; treaty, 183